NEW PERSPECTIVES ON

COMPUTER CONCEPTS

Comprehensive

by June Jamrich Parsons and Dan Oja

6th EDITION

Includes an interactive BookOnCD that contains the entire contents of the textbook with figures that come to life as videos, software tours, and animations. Plus labs, computer-scored practice tests, and more!

THOMSON
COURSE TECHNOLOGY

25 Thomson Place
Boston, MA 02210

Australia • Canada • Denmark • Japan • Mexico • New Zealand • Philippines • Puerto Rico • Singapore • South Africa • Spain • United Kingdom • United States

MANAGING EDITOR
Rachel Crapser

SENIOR PRODUCT MANAGER
Kathy Finnegan

TECHNOLOGY PRODUCT MANAGER
Amanda Shelton

PRODUCT MANAGER
Karen Stevens

ASSOCIATE PRODUCT MANAGER
Brianna Germain

EDITORIAL ASSISTANT
Emilie Perreault

MARKETING MANAGER
Rachel Valente

DEVELOPMENTAL EDITOR
Kathy Finnegan

PRODUCTION EDITOR
Debbie Masi

TEXT DESIGN AND COMPOSITION
MediaTechnics Corporation

PREPRESS PRODUCTION
GEX Publishing Services

MEDIA DEVELOPERS
Donna Schuch, Fatima Lockhart, Keefe Crowley, Tensi Parsons

PHOTO AND VIDEO RESEARCHER
Abby Reip

PHOTOGRAPHERS
Greg Manis, Joe Bush

ILLUSTRATOR
Eric Murphy

NARRATORS
Chris Robbert and Michele Martinez

BOOKONCD DEVELOPMENT
MediaTechnics Corporation

New Perspectives on Computer Concepts, 6th Edition is published by Course Technology.

Printed in the United States of America.

1 2 3 4 5 6 7 8 9 10 BM 06 05 04 03 02

ISBN : 0-619-10005-2

For more information, contact:
Course Technology,
25 Thomson Place, Boston,
Massachusetts, 02210
www.course.com

CONTENTS AT A GLANCE

TABLE OF CONTENTS

PREFACE

FROM THE AUTHORS

Technology seems to be moving forward at an increasingly rapid pace. To help you and your students stay in step with the march of technology, we've worked industriously to bring you *New Perspectives on Computer Concepts 6th Edition*—our first edition on an annual cycle. With this annual edition, we've retained the same organization for Chapters 1 through 10, and updated their content to reflect current developments.

We are happy to report extensive additions to Chapter 11: Computer Programming, which now includes substantial material about visual development environments, such as .NET, object-oriented programming in Java, and Prolog programming. We've also added a chapter, Beyond Desktop Computing, designed to expand students' understanding of high-performance and enterprise computing systems. We're certain that your students will enjoy this chapter's new Grid Computing lab, which uses SETI@home as the primary hands-on example.

A year ago, we completed an extensive revision of this text, designed to meet the needs of today's students who typically have more practical experience with computers than their counterparts of 10 years ago. The goal of the 5th Edition was to take students beyond basic computer literacy and provide them with information that a college-educated person would be expected to know about computers. That goal remains in place for the 6th Edition. We hope that you and your students enjoy the learning experience provided by our text-based and technology-based materials.

ACKNOWLEDGMENTS

Every edition of this text requires extraordinary effort by a dedicated and creative team. The content of every page is subjected to the scrutiny of professional educators, such as Beverly Amer, Ken Baldauf, Mary Caldwell, Becky Curtin, Ed Mott, Catherine Perlich, Martha J. Tilmann, and Mary Zayac. Student reviewers and testers, such as Kitty Edwards and Heather House, help us target our readers. Technical reviewers, such as Jeff Harrow, Barbra D. Letts, John Lucas, Ramachandran Bharath, and Karl Mulder, hold our feet to the fire when it comes to accuracy. We get additional help from professionals all over the world and are grateful to a number of Webmasters who have responded to our requests for additional information on topics of their specialties.

The book would not exist—and certainly would not arrive on schedule—were it not for the efforts of our media, editorial, and production teams. We thank Rachel Crapser and Kathy Finnegan for their tireless work on the entire New Perspectives series; Barbra D. Letts and Stephanie Low for their invaluable contributions to research and writing; Debbie Masi for managing production; Fatima Lockhart, Donna Schuch, Tensi Parsons, Keefe Crowley, Greg Manis, Joe Bush, and Eric Murphy for creating videos, screentours, interactive tests, photos, illustrations, and animations; Jean Insinga for her work on the Instuctor's Manual; Chris Robbert for his clear narrations; Sue Oja, Debora Elam, Deana Martinson, Karen Kangas, Jaclyn Kangas, and Kevin Lappi for checking and double-checking the alpha and beta CDs; Stacy Moran for making sure that every comma is in the right place; Keefe Crowley for designing and maintaining our Web site; Kathy Finnegan for her insightful developmental edit; Janet Lavine, Jennifer Hambly, and Abby Scholz for designing the frontmatter and chapter openers; and Abby Reip for photo research. We want to thank you all!

—June Parsons and Dan Oja

> *I am very impressed with this book. It is exceptionally well done and has clearly succeeded in talking TO, rather than AT readers. The integration of multimedia, "corrected" exercises, and live Web content exceeds anything I've previously seen in this genre.* —*Jeffrey R. Harrow, www.TheHarrowGroup.com*

THE STUDENT EXPERIENCE

STUDENT

CONNECT

Get customized notes from your instructor with the Instructor Annotations and Web Syllabus features, accessible directly from the BookOnCD. You can make sure your studies are on track by reading the extra notes and having a direct connection to the latest course syllabus.

READ

The comprehensive coverage of this textbook goes beyond basic computer literacy. Each chapter is divided into manageable sections, so you'll be able to plan your study time. And, with each section's QuickCheck questions, you'll be able to gauge when you're ready to learn more!

INTERACT

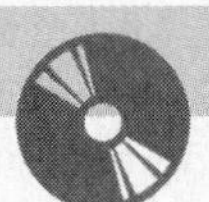

For those of you who want to go beyond the written word, the BookOnCD provides a structured environment to enhance your learning experience. Interact with the animations, experience simulated versions of software with the screentours, and watch videos of common tasks to make the experience come to life.

ENGAGE

And for those of you who want to "kick the tires" on the concepts you're learning, the labs present concepts through the use of step-by-step, interactive tutorials available on the BookOnCD. Each lab concludes with QuickCheck questions to help you evaluate your understanding of the material in the lab.

EXPLORE

Keep up with the latest trends and technologies. The InfoWebLinks allow you to get up-to-date information on important topics. While using the BookOnCD, you can click links to access www.infoweblinks.com—a collection of regularly updated Web pages that are directly related to what you're learning.

INVESTIGATE

Learn more than just how a computer works. The TechTalk sections present challenging technical topics in an easy-to-understand way. The Issues sections not only expose societal and sometimes controversial topics related to computing, they also give you the opportunity to express your opinions.

CHECK

When you're done with a chapter, you'll want to know "what you know" (before your next exam). Extensive end-of-chapter assignments and activities allow you to assess your progress using interactive summaries, key terms, situation questions, practice tests, study tips, and projects.

COMMUNICATE

Stay in touch. The WebTrack feature allows you to keep your instructor in the loop on your progress. With just a few mouse clicks, you can send the results of the interactive summaries, situation questions, practice tests, and lab QuickCheck questions directly to your instructor.

THE INSTRUCTOR EXPERIENCE

PLAN

Use the Web Syllabus feature to prepare and post a course syllabus. Your students can access the syllabus directly from the BookOnCD, allowing you to give them the most up-to-date course information quickly and easily.

CUSTOMIZE

With the Instructor Annotations feature, you can deliver additional educational content directly to your students—just when they need it! From the BookOnCD, students simply click a special Annotation button to link to a relevant video, audio clip, diagram, or note that you supply.

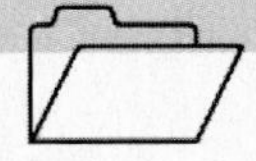

ORGANIZE

The variety of Instructor Supplements—including the Instructor's Manual and ExamView testing software—makes it easy for you to organize and enhance your teaching experience (see page xviii for more details).

PRESENT

Course Presenter, a CD-ROM-based presentation tool, gives you the choice of ready-made or custom presentations for use in class to complement your lectures.

CHALLENGE

Encourage your students to "go beyond" the topics at hand. Each chapter includes a TechTalk section that goes into greater detail and presents more challenging content. You can choose to assign these sections or skip them, depending on your students' progress and your specific goals for the course.

REINFORCE

The labs are highly interactive tutorials that your students can complete using the BookOnCD. Use the labs to reinforce material presented in the chapters and to give your students hands-on practice with important concepts and skills.

ASSESS

The end-of-chapter assignments and activities help you to evaluate your students' mastery of material:

- *Interactive Summaries* require students to fill in key terms and concepts.
- *Interactive Key Terms* work like electronic flashcards to help students remember important terms.
- *Interactive Situation Questions* help students apply their knowledge to realistic troubleshooting situations.
- *Interactive Practice Tests* generate computer-scored tests from a bank of over 100 questions per chapter.
- *Study Tips* provide activities students can complete for review or as pre-exam preparation.
- *Projects* encourage students to research and explore issues and technologies.

TRACK

WebTrack is an online delivery and reporting system that allows students to send you the results of the interactive assessment activities. You can download these results at your convenience and incorporate them into various reports.

INSTRUCTOR

LABS

Each lab offered in New Perspectives on Computer Concepts, 6th Edition is a highly interactive tutorial that presents important computer concepts through the use of concrete step-by-step examples. A lab is divided into sections. Each section has its own set of objectives and QuickCheck questions. Lab Assignments are printed in the text on the corresponding lab page.

CHAPTER 1:

Operating a Personal Computer

- startup
- sleep mode
- screen savers
- keyboarding
- reset procedures
- shutting down

Making a Dial-Up Connection

- how to connect cables
- subscribing to an ISP
- installing ISP software
- creating manual connections
- disconnecting

Browsing and Searching

- using the URL box, site list, history list, and navigation buttons
- creating bookmarks
- changing your home page
- using search engines

Using E-Mail

- working with Web-based e-mail
- composing a message
- replying to a message
- printing and deleting mail
- using the address book
- working with attachments

CHAPTER 2:

Working with Binary Numbers

- comparing binary and decimal number systems
- counting in binary
- manual conversions
- using Windows Calculator

Benchmarking

- computer performance factors
- using benchmark software
- interpreting and comparing benchmark results

CHAPTER 3:

Using the Windows Interface

- common elements of Windows software
- using ToolTips
- menu conventions
- working with dialog boxes and toolbars
- screenshots

Installing and Uninstalling Software

- installing software from a distribution CD
- installing downloaded software
- upgrades
- uninstalling software applications

CHAPTER 4:

Working with Windows Explorer

- expanding and collapsing the directory structure
- locating files
- renaming and deleting files and folders
- creating a folder
- working with groups of files

Backing Up Your Computer

- creating a backup job
- different types of backups
- backing up the Registry
- working with compressed backups
- restoring an entire disk
- restoring a single file

CHAPTER 5:

Tracking Packets

- using Ping
- using Traceroute
- interpreting an Internet Traffic Report
- pinpointing problems with your Internet connection

Securing Your Connection

- checking the security of your Internet connection
- using NetStat to check your computer's open ports
- using an online utility to get a hacker's view of your computer
- disabling file and print sharing
- protecting your computer with personal firewall software

CHAPTER 6:

Working with Cookies

- how Web servers use cookies
- why cookies might pose a threat to your privacy
- viewing and deleting cookies
- blocking cookies
- P3P compact privacy policies

Browser Security Settings
- adjusting security settings in Internet Explorer
- using security zones
- understanding signed and unsigned ActiveX controls
- understanding Java applets and permission levels

CHAPTER 7:
Working with Bitmap Graphics
- capturing an image from the Web
- eliminating red eye
- manipulating brightness, contrast, and sharpness
- cropping versus resizing; reducing file size
- palettes and dithering
- preparing a graphic for use as an e-mail attachment

Video Editing
- using video editing software
- arranging clips on the timeline
- adding transitions
- adding sounds
- specifying a codec and other video attributes
- creating a streaming video for Web distribution

CHAPTER 8:
Online Job Hunting
- registering with an online job bank
- converting your resume to ASCII format for posting online
- searching for a job online
- configuring a search agent
- finding information on salaries, employers, and places to live

CHAPTER 9:
Working with DFDs
- the purpose of DFDs in the system development life cycle
- how to read a leveled set of DFDs
- the meaning of each DFD symbol
- the differences between Gane/Sarson DFD notation and Yourdon/Coad DFD notation
- how to label data flows, entities, data stores, and processes
- how to create a Context DFD
- how to "explode" a DFD to show additional levels of detail
- why "black holes" and "miracles" indicate DFD errors

CHAPTER 10:
Working with Database Software
- how to use tables and forms to view data
- creating a table
- entering and editing data
- why relationships between tables are so important
- sorting data
- creating an index
- searching for data
- setting filters and creating queries
- creating and modifying reports

CHAPTER 11:
Using a Visual Development Environment
- working with a form design grid
- selecting controls, such as buttons, menus, and dialog boxes, for the graphical user interface of a program
- how a visual development environment displays control properties
- setting properties that modify the appearance and operation of a control
- events that can affect a control
- adding code that specifies how a control responds to events
- adding a component to the Visual Basic toolbox
- saving and test a program
- compiling a program and running the executable version

CHAPTER 12:
Grid Computing
- the basic elements of a grid computing system and the purpose of grid client software
- downloading and installing grid client software
- the methods used by grid client software to become active during idle CPU cycles
- what happens on a client computer during a typical processing session
- viewing the results produced by the SETI@home screensaver
- the role of server-side computers for managing a grid; how server-side computers integrate the results uploaded by grid clients
- recognizing the security threats to grid clients, and taking steps to safeguard your computer
- how to determine whether or not a grid project is legitimate

SUPPLEMENTS

BLACKBOARD AND WEBCT CONTENT

We offer a full range of content for use with BlackBoard and WebCT to simplify the use of New Perspectives in distance education settings.

MYCOURSE 2.0

MyCourse 2.0 is a powerful online course management and content delivery system. MyCourse 2.0 is maintained and hosted by Thomson, ensuring an online learning environment that is completely secure and delivers superior performance. With MyCourse 2.0, instructors can manage and customize courses with ease.

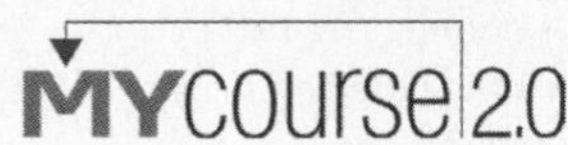

EXAMVIEW: OUR POWERFUL TESTING SOFTWARE PACKAGE

With ExamView, instructors can generate printed tests, create LAN-based tests, or test over the Internet.

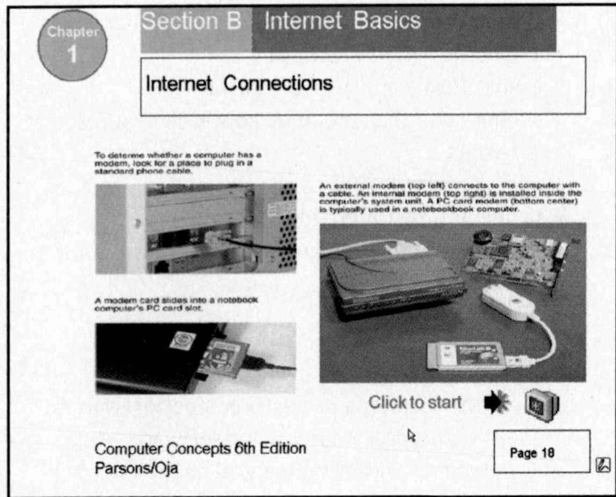

COURSE PRESENTER: READY-MADE OR CUSTOM-MADE PRESENTATIONS

Course Presenter is a CD-ROM-based presentation tool that provides instructors with a wealth of resources for use in the classroom, replacing traditional overhead transparencies with computer-generated presentations. Course Presenter includes a structured presentation along with videos, animations, labs, and more for each chapter of the textbook.

INSTRUCTOR'S MANUAL: HELP IS ONLY A FEW KEYSTROKES AWAY

This enhanced Instructor's Manual offers an outline for each chapter; suggestions for instruction on the chapter content, including how to effectively use and integrate the InfoWebLinks, the CD content, and the labs; answers to the end-of-chapter activities; and numerous teaching tips.

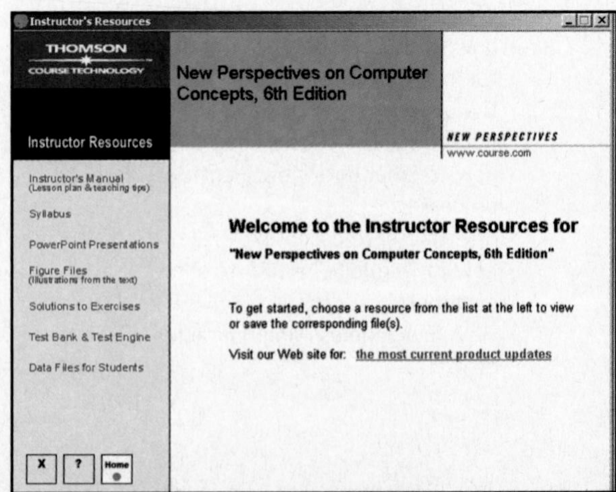

USING THE BookOnCD

Bring the concepts you've been reading about to life with the BookOnCD that accompanies the *New Perspectives on Computer Concepts, 6th Edition*. It's a snap to start the BookOnCD and use it on your computer.

The BookOnCD works on most computers that run Windows. The easiest way to find out if the BookOnCD works on your computer is to try it! Just follow the steps below to start the CD. If it works, you're all set. Otherwise, refer to the system requirements listed inside the front cover of this book, or contact your local technical support person.

STARTING THE BookOnCD

The BookOnCD is easy to use. Follow these simple steps to get started:

1. Make sure your computer is turned on.

2. Press the button on your computer's CD-ROM drive to open the drawer-like "tray," as shown in the photo below.

3. Place the BookOnCD into the tray with the label facing up.

4. Press the button on the CD-ROM drive to close the tray, then proceed with Step 5 on the next page.

FIGURE 1
To use the BookOnCD, your computer must have a CD-ROM drive. If you have any questions about its operation, check with your local technical support person.

5. Wait about 15 seconds. During this time, the light on your CD-ROM drive should flicker. Soon you should see a screen that displays the Computer Concepts menu. The first time you use the BookOnCD, your computer will check for several necessary Windows components. Any missing components will be installed automatically. When this process is complete, you might be prompted to reboot your computer, and then you can use any of the options on the Computer Concepts menu.

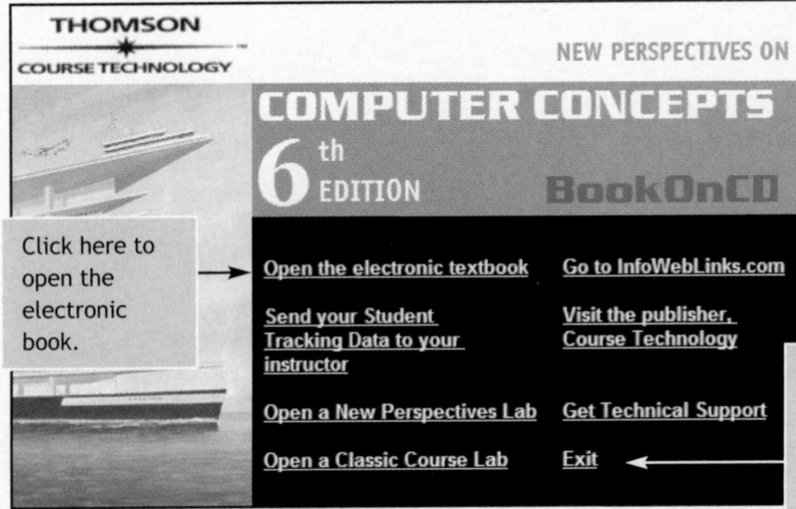

Click here to open the electronic book.

Click here when you're done to exit the program; then you can remove the BookOnCD from the CD-ROM drive.

FIGURE 2
The Computer Concepts menu should appear on your computer screen after you insert the CD.

FIGURE 3
Manual Start: Follow the instructions in this figure only if the Computer Concepts menu did not appear automatically in Step 5.

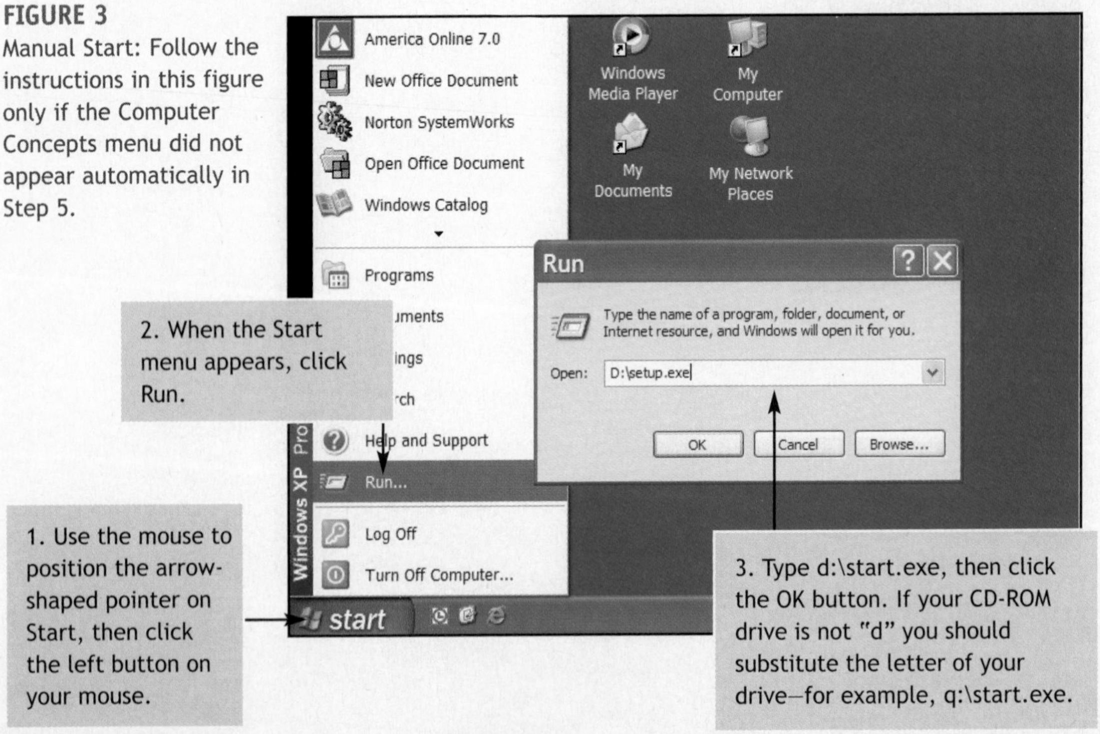

America Online 7.0
New Office Document
Norton SystemWorks
Open Office Document
Windows Catalog
Programs
Help and Support
Run...
Log Off
Turn Off Computer...
start
Windows XP Pro
Windows Media Player
My Computer
My Documents
My Network Places
Run
Type the name of a program, folder, document, or Internet resource, and Windows will open it for you.
Open: D:\setup.exe
OK Cancel Browse...

1. Use the mouse to position the arrow-shaped pointer on Start, then click the left button on your mouse.

2. When the Start menu appears, click Run.

3. Type d:\start.exe, then click the OK button. If your CD-ROM drive is not "d" you should substitute the letter of your drive—for example, q:\start.exe.

NAVIGATING THE BookOnCD

A menu bar, which stretches across the top of each page, provides all the options you need to move through and use the BookOnCD. Figure 4 describes each of these options.

FIGURE 4

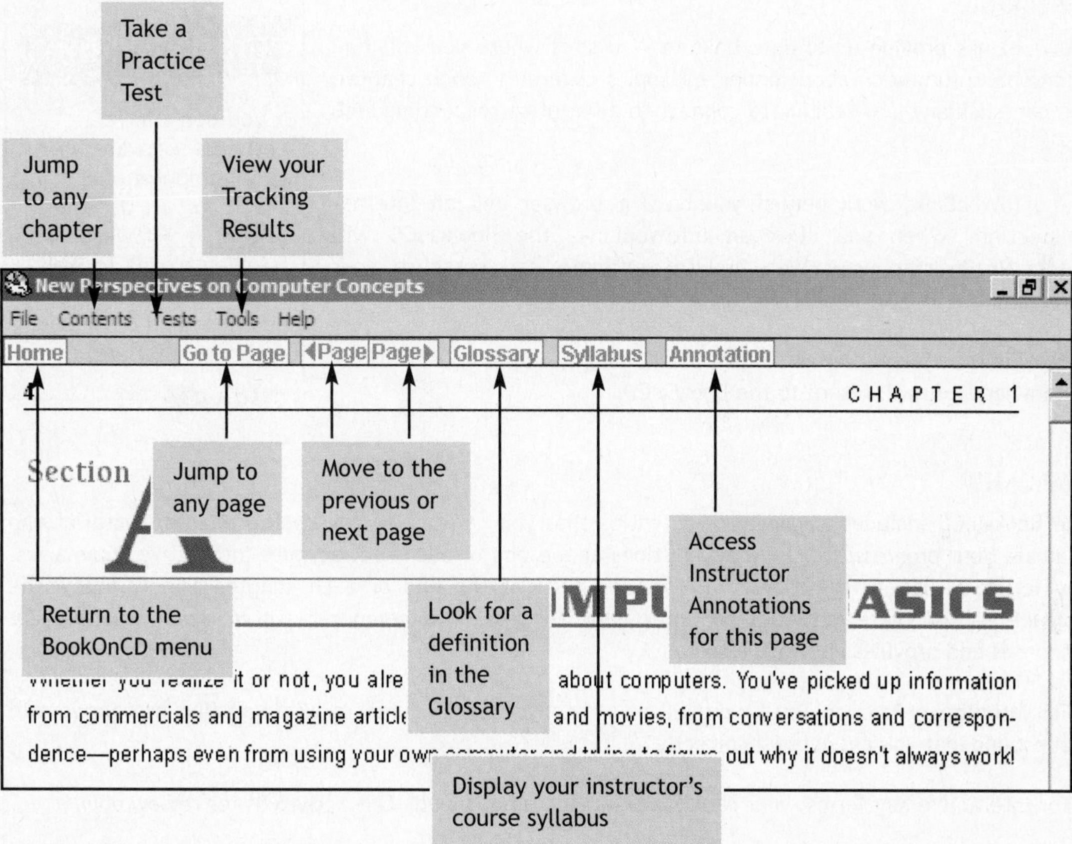

INTERACTING

Many of the figures contain links such as **click to start**. You can click these links to see video clips, watch animated conceptual diagrams, and tour popular software packages.

Note: If your computer is equipped for sound, you should hear audio during the videos and screentours. If you don't, check the volume control on your computer by clicking the speaker icon in the lower-right corner of your screen.

COMMUNICATING

Your instructor can communicate with you by using the Annotation feature. An Annotation button appears on your screen only if your instructor has provided a note for a page, and you are using a Tracking Disk. When you send Tracking Disk data to your instructor, the Annotation links are downloaded to your Tracking Disk.

EXPLORING

InfoWebLinks provide up-to-date links to Web sites where you will find additional information about important topics covered in each chapter. You can click any InfoWebLink to connect to a list of corresponding Web sites.

The InfoWebLinks work only if you have a browser and an Internet connection. When you click an InfoWebLink, the BookOnCD will automatically start your Web browser software and establish your connection.

When finished exploring an InfoWebLink, simply close your browser window and you will return to the BookOnCD.

If you don't have antivirus software for your computer, you should get it. Use the Antivirus Software InfoWeb to link to Web sites where you can purchase and download antivirus software.

EVALUATING

The BookOnCD includes a variety of activities that you can use to review the chapter material and evaluate your progress: QuickCheck questions at the end of each section, plus Interactive Summaries, Key Terms, Situations Questions, and Practice Tests at the end of each chapter. Simply follow the instructions for these activities to enter your answers. The computer automatically checks your responses and provides you with a score.

- For Interactive Practice Tests, you will also receive a study guide to help you find the answers to questions that you answered incorrectly.

- For Interactive Key Terms, your results are not scored or saved. This activity is for review only.

TRACKING

A Tracking Disk tracks your progress by saving your responses to the "What Do You Think?" questions on the Issues pages, as well as your scores on the labs, QuickChecks, and Interactive Summaries, Situation Questions, and Practice Tests. Follow these steps to create and work with a Tracking Disk:

1. The first time you want to save a score, click the Create button and insert a blank, formatted floppy disk. You only need to create a Tracking Disk one time.

2. When you complete an activity, such as a QuickCheck, a message is displayed asking if you want to save your score. Click the OK button, and then insert your Tracking Disk as instructed.

3. To view or print a summary report of all your scores, click the Tools menu on the Welcome screen.

NEED HELP?

Text Size: If the text appears small on your screen, your monitor is probably set at a high resolution. The type will appear larger if you reduce the resolution by completing the following steps:

1. Open the Control Panel (available from the Start menu).
2. Double-click the Display icon (or choose the Display option), and then click the Settings tab.
3. Move the Screen Area slider to 800 x 600 or 640 x 480. (This setting is optional; you can view the BookOnCD at most standard resolutions.)

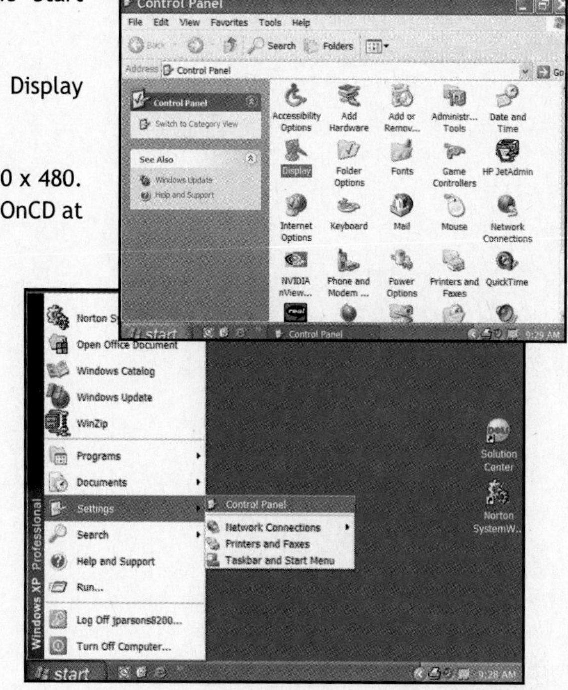

Text Quality: If the text on your screen looks jumbled, your computer might be set to use Windows large fonts instead of standard fonts. Complete the following steps to change to standard fonts:

1. Open the Control Panel (available from the Start menu).
2. Double-click the Display icon (or choose the Display option), and then click the Appearance tab.
3. Click the Scheme list arrow, and then click Windows Standard.

Annotations: If you do not see the Annotation button on your screen, and your instructor has indicated that annotations have been provided, first use your Tracking Disk to send any results—the results from a QuickCheck, for example—to your instructor. If you still do not see annotations, check with your instructor.

Technical Support: For answers to technical questions, click the Get Technical Support link on the Computer Concepts BookOnCD menu or go to www.infoweblinks.com/np6/troubleshooting. Additional technical information is provided in the Readme.doc file on your BookOnCD.

NEW PERSPECTIVES ON

COMPUTER CONCEPTS

by June Jamrich Parsons and Dan Oja

6TH EDITION

1 COMPUTER, INTERNET, AND NETWORK BASICS

CONTENTS

InfoWebLinks

The InfoWebLinks, located in the margins of this chapter, show the way to a variety of Web sites that contain additional information and updates to the chapter topics. Your computer needs an Internet connection to access these links. You can connect to the Web links for this chapter by:

- clicking the InfoWeb links in the margins
- clicking this underlined link
- starting your browser and entering the URL ***www.infoweblinks.com/np6/chapter1.htm***

TIP

When using the **BookOnCD**, the  symbols are "clickable."

CHAPTER PREVIEW

1

The Net Generation has been the first to grow up in a world where "mouse" means a computer input device as well as a pesky white rodent. "Gen-N" is not, however, the only generation taking advantage of computer, network, and Internet technology. Members of the Great Generation that fought in World War II tote digital cameras on their annual pilgrimages to Florida. Grandparents and grandchildren exchange e-mail messages. Baby boomers mull over the latest technology innovation and its probable effects on their investment portfolios. Gen-Xers and Net-geners merrily trade music files on the Internet. Chapter 1 provides an overview of the technologies that have a major effect on people, regardless of their membership in one generation or another.

Section A begins by defining the basic characteristics of a computer system, and then provides a quick overview of data, information, and files. It concludes with an introduction to application software, operating systems, and platform compatibility. Section B introduces the Internet, a communications technology that's the "magic" behind e-mail, video conferencing, instant messaging, and e-commerce. Section C focuses on the Web—that seemingly bottomless ocean of information populated by "dot coms," connected by links, and accessed with a browser. Section D focuses on e-mail—how it works and how you use it. You'll get some tips on e-mail "netiquette," including the scoop on those flamboyant little symbols called "smileys."

When you complete this chapter you should be able to:

- Define the term "computer" and identify the components of a personal computer system
- Compare the computing capabilities of the following computer categories: personal computers, handheld computers, workstations, videogame consoles, mainframe computers, supercomputers, and servers
- Explain how an operating system affects compatibility between computer platforms, such as PCs and Macs
- Describe how data moves from point A to point B on the Internet, and list some of the most popular Internet resources
- Evaluate various ways that you can connect a computer to the Internet and select an ISP
- Describe how Web servers, URLs, HTML, HTTP, and browsers contribute to the Internet resource known as the Web
- Demonstrate that you can use a search engine to locate information on the Web
- List the features that you would expect to find in a typical e-mail software package
- Explain how an e-mail system works, and the difference between POP mail and Web-based mail

TIP Click  to access the Web for a complete list of learning objectives for Chapter 1.

Section A: COMPUTER BASICS

Whether you realize it or not, you already know a lot about computers. You've picked up information from commercials and magazine articles, from books and movies, from conversations and correspondence—perhaps even from using your own computer and trying to figure out why it doesn't always work!

Section A of this chapter provides an overview that's designed to help you start organizing what you know about computers, provide you with a basic understanding of how computers work, and get you up to speed with a basic computer vocabulary.

A COMPUTER IS...

How old is the word "computer"? The word "computer" has been part of the English language since 1646, but if you look in a dictionary printed before 1940, you might be surprised to find a computer defined as a *person* who performs calculations! Prior to 1940, machines that were designed to perform calculations were referred to as calculators and tabulators, not computers. The modern definition and use of the term "computer" emerged in the 1940s, when the first electronic computing devices were developed.

When using the BookOnCD, click any boldface term to see its definition. You can also use the Glossary button at the top of each page to locate a definition for any term that was introduced in an earlier chapter.

What is a computer? Most people can formulate a mental picture of a computer, but computers do so many things and come in such a variety of shapes and sizes that it might seem difficult to distill their common characteristics into an all-purpose definition. At its core, a **computer** is a device that accepts input, processes data, stores data, and produces output, all according to a series of stored instructions.

Computer **input** is whatever is typed, submitted, or transmitted to a computer system. Input can be supplied by a person, by the environment, or by another computer. Examples of the kinds of input that a computer can accept include the words and symbols in a document, numbers for a calculation, pictures, temperatures from a thermostat, audio signals from a microphone, and instructions from a computer program. An input device, such as a keyboard or mouse, gathers input and transforms it into a series of electronic signals for the computer to store and manipulate.

In the context of computing, **data** refers to the symbols that represent facts, objects, and ideas. Computers manipulate data in many ways, and we call this manipulation **processing**. The series of instructions that tell a computer how to carry out processing tasks is referred to as a **computer program**, or simply a "program." These programs form the **software** that sets up a computer to do a specific task. Some of the ways that a computer can process data include performing calculations, sorting lists of words or numbers, modifying documents and pictures, and drawing graphs. In a computer, most processing takes place in a component called the **central processing unit** (CPU), which is sometimes described as the "brain" of the computer.

A computer stores data so that it will be available for processing. Most computers have more than one location for storing data, depending on how the data is being used. **Memory** is an area of a computer that *temporarily* holds data that is waiting to be processed, stored, or output. **Storage** is the area where data can be left on a *permanent* basis when it is not immediately needed for processing.

Output is the result produced by a computer. Some examples of computer output include reports, documents, music, graphs, and pictures. An output device displays, prints, or transmits the results of processing. Figure 1-1 helps you visualize the input, processing, storage, and output activities of a computer.

FIGURE 1-1

A computer can be defined by its ability to accept input, process data, store data, and produce output, all according to a set of instructions from a computer program.

Computers produce output on devices such as screens and printers.

A computer accepts input from an input device, such as a keyboard, mouse, scanner, or digital camera.

Data is processed in the CPU according to a set of instructions that was loaded into the computer's memory.

A computer uses disks and CDs to permanently store data.

What's so significant about a computer's ability to store instructions? Take a moment to think about the way that you use a simple hand-held calculator to balance your checkbook each month. You're forced to do the calculations in stages. And although you can store the data from one stage and use it in the next stage, you cannot store the sequence of formulas—the program—required to balance your checkbook. Every month, therefore, you have to perform a similar set of calculations. The process would be much simpler if your calculator remembered the set of calculations that you needed to perform, and simply asked you for this month's checkbook entries.

Early "computers" were really no more than calculating devices, designed to carry out a specific mathematical task. To use one of these devices for a different task, it was necessary to rewire its circuits—a task best left to an engineer. In a modern computer, the idea of a **stored program** means that a series of instructions for a computing task can be loaded into a computer's memory. These instructions can easily be replaced by a different set of instructions when it is time for the computer to perform a different task.

The stored program concept allows you to use your computer for one task, such as word processing, and then easily switch to a different type of computing task, such as editing a photo or sending an e-mail message. It is the single most important characteristic that distinguishes a computer from other simpler and less versatile devices, such as calculators and pocket-sized electronic dictionaries.

COMPUTER CATEGORIES

Why is it useful to categorize computers? Computers are versatile machines, which are able to perform a truly amazing assortment of tasks, but some types of computers are better suited to certain tasks than other types of computers. Categorizing computers is a way of grouping them according to criteria such as usage, cost, size, and capability. Knowing how a computer has been categorized provides an indication of its best potential use.

During the 1940s and 1950s, very few computers existed, and there was really no need to categorize them. Because the main circuitry was usually housed in a closet-sized metal frame, computer techies called these computers "mainframes." The term soon became synonymous with a category of large, expensive computers that were sold to big corporations and government agencies.

FIGURE 1-2

Personal computers are available in desktop and notebook configurations.

A desktop computer fits on a desk and runs on power from an electrical wall outlet. The main unit can be housed in either a vertical case (like the one shown) or a horizontal case.

A notebook computer is small and lightweight, giving it the advantage of portability. It can run on power supplied by an electrical outlet, or it can run on battery power.

In 1968, the term **minicomputer** was used to describe a second computer category. These computers were smaller, less expensive, and less powerful than mainframes, but were, nevertheless, able to provide adequate computing power for small businesses. In 1971, the first microcomputer appeared. A **microcomputer** could be clearly differentiated from computers in the other categories because its CPU consisted of a single "chip" called a **microprocessor**.

At one time, then, it was possible to define three distinct categories of computers: mainframes, minicomputers, and microcomputers. Technology has advanced rapidly since then. Today, just about every computer—no matter how large or small—uses one or more microprocessors as its CPU. Therefore, the use of a microprocessor is no longer a distinction between microcomputers and other computer categories. Furthermore, the term "minicomputer" has fallen into disuse. To reflect today's computer technology, the following categories might be more appropriate: personal computers, handheld computers, workstations, videogame consoles, mainframes, supercomputers, and servers.

What is a personal computer? A **personal computer** is a type of microcomputer designed to meet the computing needs of an individual. It typically provides access to a wide variety of computing applications, such as word processing, photo editing, e-mail, and Internet access. Personal computers are available as **desktop computers** or **notebook computers** (also called "laptop computers"), as illustrated in Figure 1-2. Basic personal computer prices start at $500, but most consumers select more powerful models that cost between $1,000 and $1,500.

Terminology note: The term "personal computer" is sometimes abbreviated as "PC." However, "PC" is often used for a specific type of personal computer that's descended from the original IBM PC and runs Windows software. In this book, "PC" is used for these IBM PC descendants, not as an abbreviation for the term "personal computer."

Learn more about the latest PDA models, prices, software, and accessories by visiting the PDA InfoWeb.

What is a handheld? A **handheld computer**, such as a Palm, iPAQ, PocketPC, or Visor, is one that is designed to fit into a pocket, run on batteries, and be used while you are holding it. Also called a **PDA** (Personal Digital Assistant), a computer in this category is typically used as an electronic appointment book, address book, calculator, and notepad. Inexpensive add-ons make it possible to send and receive e-mail, use maps and global positioning to get directions, maintain an expense account, and make voice calls using cellular service.

With its slow processing speed and small screen, a handheld computer is not powerful enough to handle many of the tasks that can be accomplished by desktop or notebook personal computers. A handheld computer is designed to be a computing accessory, rather than your primary computer. Happily, it is possible to synchronize information between a handheld and a personal computer. For example, suppose that while traveling you add an e-mail address to your PDA's address book. When you return home, you can use the synchronization feature to automatically update the address book on your desktop computer.

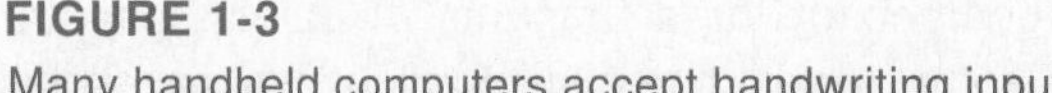

FIGURE 1-3

Many handheld computers accept handwriting input.

click to start

Some handheld computers accept input from a small—make that *tiny*—built-in keyboard. As Figure 1-3 illustrates, other handhelds accept handwriting input by means of a touch-sensitive screen.

What types of computers can be classified as workstations? The term "**workstation**" has two meanings. Computers advertised as workstations are usually powerful desktop computers designed for specialized tasks. A workstation can tackle tasks that require a lot of processing speed, such as medical imaging and computer-aided design. Some workstations contain more than one microprocessor, and most have circuitry specially designed for creating and displaying three-dimensional and animated graphics. Workstation prices range from $3,000 to $20,000. Because of its cost, a workstation is often dedicated to design tasks, and is not used for typical microcomputer applications, such as word processing, photo editing, and accessing the Web.

A second meaning of the term "workstation" applies to ordinary personal computers that are connected to a network. A **computer network** is two or more computers and other devices that are connected for the purpose of sharing data, programs, and hardware. A **LAN** (local area network) is simply a computer network that is located within a limited geographical area, such as a school computer lab or a small business.

Is a PlayStation a computer? A **videogame console**, such as Nintendo's® GameCube, Sony's PlayStation®, or Microsoft's XBox®, *is* a computer, but typically videogame consoles have not been considered a computer category because of their history as dedicated game devices that connect to a TV set and provide only a pair of joysticks for input. Today's videogame consoles contain microprocessors that are equivalent to any found in a fast personal computer, and they are equipped to produce graphics that rival those on sophisticated workstations. Add-ons, such as keyboards, DVD players, and Internet access, make it possible to use a videogame console to watch DVD movies, send and receive e-mail, and participate in online activities, such as multiplayer games. As with handheld computers, videogame consoles fill a specialized niche and are not considered a replacement for a personal computer—at least not yet.

FIGURE 1-4

This IBM S/390 mainframe computer weighs about 1,400 lbs. and is about 6.5 feet tall.

What's so special about a mainframe computer? A **mainframe computer** (or simply a "mainframe") is a large and expensive computer that is capable of simultaneously processing data for hundreds or thousands of users. Mainframes are generally used by businesses or governments to provide centralized storage, processing, and management for large amounts of data. Mainframes remain the computer of choice in situations where reliability, data security, and centralized control are necessary.

The price of a mainframe computer typically starts at several hundred thousand dollars and can easily exceed $1 million. Its main processing circuitry is housed in a closet-sized cabinet (Figure 1-4), but after additional large components are added for storage and output, a mainframe will fill a good-sized room.

How powerful is a supercomputer? A computer falls into the **supercomputer** category if it is, at the time of construction, one of the fastest computers in the world. Because of their speed, supercomputers can tackle complex tasks that just would not be practical for other computers. Typical uses for supercomputers include breaking codes, modeling worldwide weather systems, and simulating nuclear explosions. One impressive simulation designed to run on a supercomputer tracked the movement of thousands of dust particles as they were tossed about by a tornado.

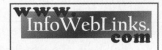

What's the latest news about supercomputers? Visit the Supercomputer InfoWeb to learn more about these amazing machines.

click

At one time, supercomputer designers focused on building specialized, very fast, and very large CPUs. Today, a supercomputer CPU is constructed from thousands of microprocessors. As an example, a $100 million supercomputer scheduled for completion in 2005 is designed to use 1 million microprocessors, which will enable it to operate at speeds exceeding 1 quadrillion operations per second.

What makes a computer a "server"? In the computer industry, the term "server" has several meanings. It can refer to computer hardware, to a specific type of software, or to a combination of hardware and software. In any case, the purpose of a **server** is to "serve" the computers on a network (such as the Internet or a LAN) by supplying them with data. A personal computer, workstation, or software that requests data from a server is referred to as a **client**. For example, on a network, a server might respond to a client's request for a Web page. Another server might handle the steady stream of e-mail that travels among clients from all over the Internet. A server might also allow clients within a LAN to share files or access a centralized printer.

Remarkably, just about any personal computer, workstation, mainframe, or supercomputer can be configured to perform the work of a server. That fact should emphasize the concept that a server does not require a specific type of hardware. Nonetheless, computer manufacturers categorize some of their computers as "servers" because they are especially suited for storing and distributing data on a network. Despite impressive performance on server-related tasks, these machines do not include features, such as sound cards, DVD players, and other fun accessories that consumers expect on their desktop computers. Most consumers would not want to buy a server to replace a desktop computer.

PERSONAL COMPUTER SYSTEMS

What's a personal computer system? The term "computer system" usually refers to a computer and all of the input, output, and storage devices that are connected to it. At the core of a personal computer system is a desktop or notebook computer, which probably looks like one of those in Figure 1-5.

FIGURE 1-5

Personal computer designs run the gamut from drab gray boxes to colorful curvy cases.

Despite cosmetic differences among personal computers, a personal computer system usually includes the following equipment:

- **Computer system unit.** The **system unit** is the case that holds the main circuit boards, microprocessor, power supply, and storage devices. The system unit for most notebook computers holds a built-in keyboard and speakers too.
- **Display device.** Most desktop computers use a separate **monitor** as a display device, whereas notebook computers use a flat panel **LCD screen** (liquid crystal display screen) that is attached to the system unit.
- **Keyboard.** Most computers are equipped with a keyboard as the primary input device.
- **Mouse.** A **mouse** is an alternative input device designed to manipulate on-screen graphical objects and controls.
- **Floppy disk drive.** A **floppy disk drive** is a storage device that reads data from and writes data to floppy disks (shown at right).
- **Hard disk drive.** A **hard disk drive** can store billions of characters of data. It is usually mounted inside the computer's system unit. A small external light indicates when the drive is reading or writing data.

- **CD-ROM or DVD drive.** A **CD-ROM drive** is a storage device that uses laser technology to read data that is permanently stored on computer or audio CDs. A **DVD drive** can read data from computer CDs, audio CDs, computer DVDs, or DVD movie disks. CD-ROM and DVD drives typically cannot be used to write data onto disks. "ROM" stands for "read-only memory," which means that the drive can read data from disks, but cannot be used to store new data on them.
- **CD-writer.** Many computers—especially desktop models—include a **CD-writer** that can be used to create and copy CDs.
- **Sound card and speakers.** Desktop computers have a rudimentary built-in speaker that's mostly limited to playing beeps. A small circuit board, called a **sound card**, is required for high-quality music, narration, and sound effects. A desktop computer's sound card sends signals to external speakers. A notebook's sound card sends signals to speakers that are built into the notebook system unit.
- **Modem.** Many personal computer systems include a built-in **modem** that can be used to establish an Internet connection using a standard telephone line.
- **Printer.** A computer printer is an output device that produces computer-generated text or graphical images on paper.

Figure 1-6 illustrates a typical personal computer system.

FIGURE 1-6

A typical personal computer system includes the system unit and a variety of storage, input, and output devices.

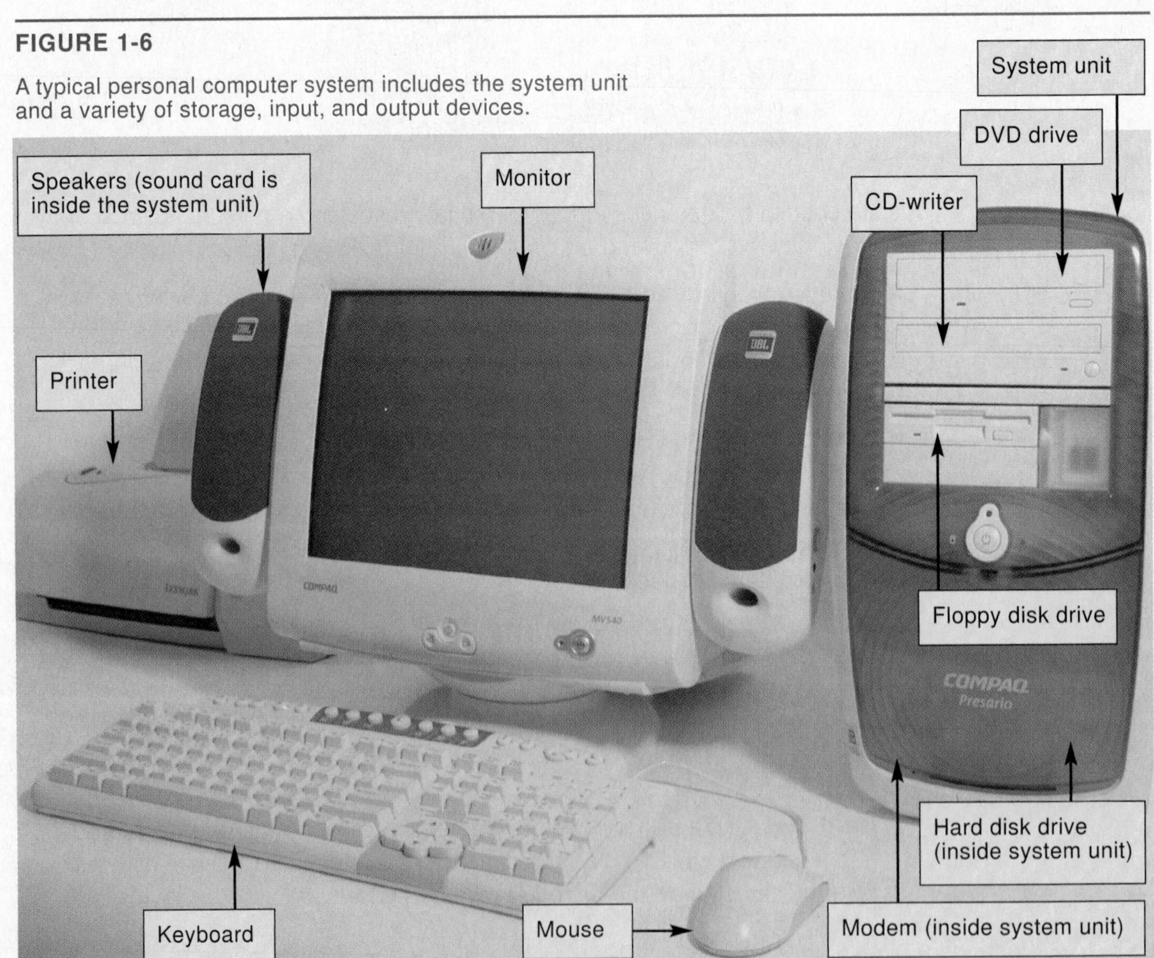

To establish a dial-up connection, your computer's modem dials a special access number, which is answered by an Internet modem. Once the connection is established, your computer is "on the Internet." When you complete an Internet session, your modem "hangs up" and the connection is discontinued until the next time you dial in.

Theoretically, the top speed of a dial-up connection is 56 Kbps, meaning that 56,000 bits of data are transmitted per second. Actual speed is usually reduced by distance, interference, and other technical problems, however, so the speed of most 56 Kbps dial-up connections is more like 45 Kbps. This speed is useable for e-mail, e-commerce, and chat. It is not, however, optimal for applications that require large amounts of data to be quickly transferred over the Internet. Watching an Internet-based video or participating in a teleconference over a 56 Kbps dial-up connection can be like watching a badly organized parade—the sound can be out of sync with the image, and the "show" can be interrupted by lengthy pauses as your computer waits for the next set of video frames to arrive.

Does a cable modem provide a faster Internet connection? Many cable TV companies offer Internet access in addition to the traditional roster of movie channels, network television, and specialty channels. This type of Internet access, often referred to as "cable modem service," is offered to a cable company's customers for an additional monthly charge. Cable modem service usually requires two pieces of equipment: a network card and a cable modem. A **network card** is a device that's designed to connect a personal computer to a local area network—when you get cable modem service, this card allows you to join a computer network that provides Internet access. Many of today's computers come equipped with a preinstalled network card. If not, one can be added for less than $50. A **cable modem** is a device that changes a computer's signals into a form that can travel over cable TV links (Figure 1-11.) Cable modems can be installed by consumers or installed (sometimes for a fee) by the "cable guy," and typically remain the property of the cable company.

FIGURE 1-11

A cable modem can be a standalone device, or it can be integrated with the other electronic components of a cable TV set-top box. A standalone cable modem is usually set up close to a computer, whereas a set-top box is usually set up right next to a television.

Cable modem access is referred to as an **always-on connection**, because your computer is, in effect, always connected to the Internet, unlike a dial-up connection that is established only when the dialing sequence is completed. An always-on connection is convenient because you don't have to wait 30–40 seconds for the dial/answer sequence to be completed. A cable modem receives data at about 1.5 Mbps (1.5 million bits per second), which is more than 25 times faster than a dial-up connection. This speed is suitable for most Internet activities, including real-time video and teleconferencing.

What about access provided by a school or business network? The computers in a school lab or business are usually connected to a local area network that is connected to the Internet. These computers offer an always-on connection, similar to cable modem service, which does not require a dial/answer sequence to establish an Internet connection. School and business networks do not, however, typically access the Internet via a cable company. Instead they use a high-speed telecommunications link dedicated solely to Internet access.

What other high-speed Internet access options are available? Many telephone and independent telecommunications companies offer high-speed Internet access over ISDN and DSL lines. **ISDN** (Integrated Services Digital Network) provides data transfer speeds of either 64 Kbps or 128 Kbps. Given data transfer speeds that are only marginally better than a free 56 Kbps dial-up connection, and substantial monthly fees, ISDN ranks low on the list of high-speed Internet options for most consumers.

If you want a really "hot" Internet connection, consider DSL. **DSL** (Digital Subscriber Line) and xDSL are generic names for a family of high-speed Internet links, including ADSL, SDSL, and DSL lite. Each type of DSL provides different maximum speeds—from twice as fast to approximately 125 times faster than a 56 Kbps dial-up connection. The faster types of DSL require professional installation, but DSL lite can be installed by consumers.

Both ISDN and DSL connections require proximity to a telephone switching station, which can be a problem for speed-hungry consumers in rural areas. Satellite dishes to the rescue! Once limited to only receiving Internet data (data flowing out of your personal computer had to travel over a dial-up connection), **DSS** (Digital Satellite Service) today offers two-way Internet access at an average speed of about 500 Kbps. Monthly fees for a DSS connection are typically less than DSL, but more than cable modem service. Consumers are required to rent or purchase a satellite dish and pay for its installation.

INTERNET SERVICE PROVIDERS

What's an ISP? To access the Internet, you do not typically connect your computer directly to the backbone. Instead, you connect it to an ISP, which in turn connects to the backbone. An **ISP** (Internet Service Provider) is a company that maintains Internet computers and telecommunications equipment in order to provide Internet access to businesses, organizations, and individuals. An ISP that offers dial-up connections, for example, maintains a bank of modems, which communicates with the modems in customers' computers.

An ISP, such as AOL (America Online), works in much the same way as a local telephone company. Just as a telephone company provides a point of access to telephones all over the world, an ISP is a point of access to the Internet. ISP customers arrange for service—in this case for Internet access—for which they pay a monthly fee. In addition to a monthly fee, an ISP might also charge an installation fee. Subscribers may also be required to pay per-minute fees for long-distance access.

What's the difference between a local ISP and a national ISP? A local ISP usually supplies Internet access within a limited geographical area, such as within a particular area code. A national ISP supplies access for customers spread throughout a large geographical area. A local ISP is a good choice unless you want to use your computer outside of your local dialing area. To access a local ISP while away from home, you'll probably have to dial long distance and pay minute-by-minute long-distance charges for the duration of your connect time. A national ISP, on the other hand, offers access in many different area codes. AT&T WorldNet, for example, offers access num-

History List. The Forward and Back buttons keep track of only the pages that you visited since you started your browser; however, they won't help you locate pages that you visited in previous sessions. To help you revisit sites from previous sessions, your browser provides a History list. You can display this list by clicking a button or menu option provided by your browser. To revisit any site in the History list, click its URL. Many browsers allow you to specify how long a URL will remain in the History list. Two or three weeks is usually sufficient.

Favorites or Bookmarks. Suppose that you found a great Web site and you suspect that you'll want to revisit it sometime in the future. Instead of writing down its URL, you can add the URL to a list, typically called "Favorites" or "Bookmarks." After adding a site to this list, you can simply click its URL to display it.

Stop button. Sometimes a Web page takes a very long time to appear on your screen. If you don't want to wait for a page, click the Stop button.

Find. A Web page is not necessarily the length of a standard piece of paper. Instead, some Web "pages" can be equivalent to 10 or even 100 typed pages. If you're looking for specific information on a "long" Web page, you can save yourself a lot of reading by using the Find option on your browser's Edit menu to locate a particular word or phrase.

SEARCH ENGINES

What is a search engine? The term **search engine** popularly refers to a Web site that provides a variety of tools to help you find information. They are an indispensible tool when it comes to finding information on the Web. Depending on the search engine that you use, you may be able to find information by entering a description, filling out a form, or clicking a series of links to drill down through a list of topics and subtopics. Based on your input, the search engine provides a list of Web pages like the one shown in Figure 1-19.

FIGURE 1-19

In response to your query, a search engine produces a list of relevant Web pages, along with a brief description of each page and a link to it.

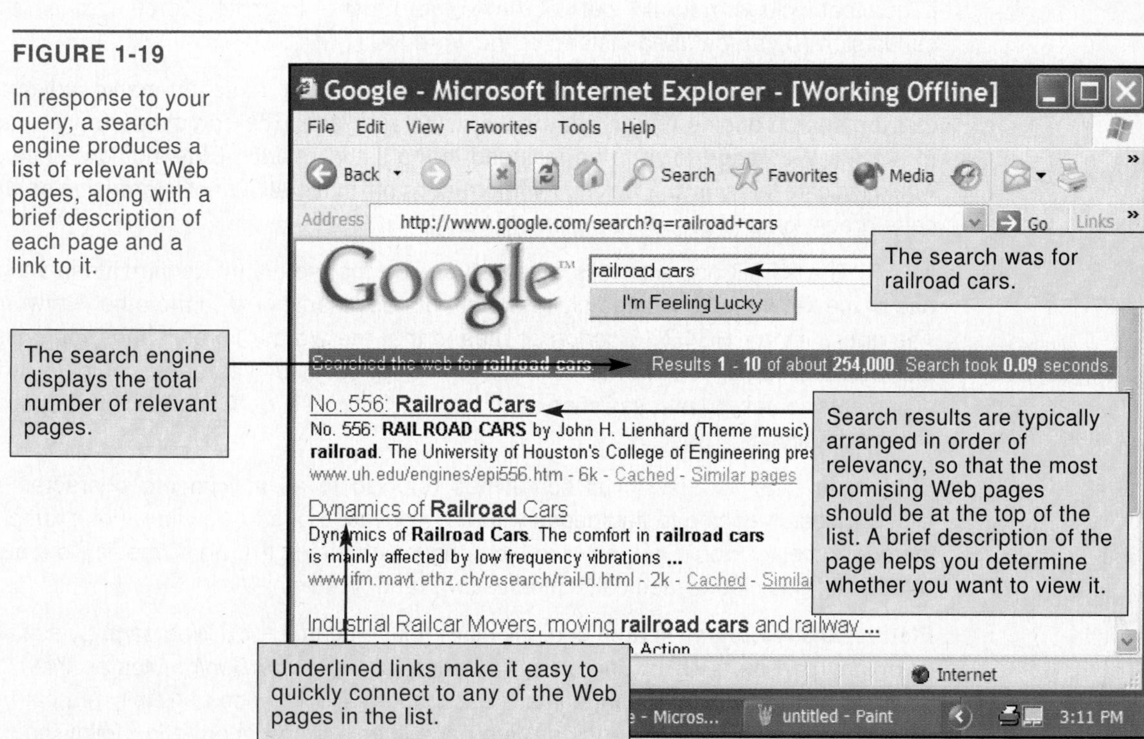

Exactly what is a query? A **query** describes the information that you want to find. It includes one or more keywords and may also include search operators. A **keyword** (sometimes called a "search term") is any word that describes the information that you're trying to find. For example, *gorp* could be used as a keyword in a query for information about tasty trail mixes. You can enter more than one search term. Separate each term with a space or a search operator.

Search engines change at an astonishing rate. Visit the Search Engine InfoWeb for a list of popular search engines and their URLs, some comparative statistics, and tips on finding the search engine that's right for you.

click

Search engines have a tendency to inundate you with possibilities—often finding thousands of potentially relevant Web pages. To receive a more manageable list of results, you need to formulate a more specific search. A **search operator** is a word or symbol that describes a relationship between keywords and thereby helps you create a more focused query. The search operators that you can use with each search engine vary slightly. To discover exactly how to formulate a query for a particular search engine, refer to its Help pages. Most search engines allow you to formulate queries with the search operators described below.

AND. When two search terms are joined by AND, both terms must appear on a Web page before it can be included in the search results. The query *railroad AND cars* will locate pages that contain both the words "railroad" and "cars." Your search results might include pages containing information about old railroad cars, about railroad car construction, and even about railroads that haul automobiles ("cars"). Some search engines use the Plus symbol (+) instead of the word AND.

OR. When two search terms are joined by OR, either one or both of the search words could appear on a page. Entering the query *railroad OR cars* produces information about railroad fares, railroad routes, railroad cars, automobile safety records, and even car ferries.

NOT. The keyword following NOT must not appear on any of the pages found by the search engine. Entering *railroad NOT cars* would tell the search engine to look for pages that include "railroad" but not the keyword "cars." In some search engines, the minus sign (-) can be used instead of the word NOT.

Quotation marks. Surrounding a series of keywords with quotation marks indicates that the search engine must treat the words as a phrase. The complete phrase must exist on a Web page for it to be included in the list of results. Entering *"green card"* would indicate that you are looking for information on immigration, not information on the color green, on golf greens, or greeting cards.

NEAR. The NEAR operator tells a search engine that you want documents in which one of the keywords is located close to but not necessarily next to the other keyword. The query *library NEAR/15 congress* means that the words "library" and "congress" must appear within 15 words of each other. Successful searches could include documents containing phrases such as "Library of Congress" or "Congress funds special library research."

Wildcards. The asterisk (*) is sometimes referred to as a "wildcard character." It allows a search engine to find pages with any derivation of a basic word. For example, the query *medic** would not only produce pages containing the word "medic," but also "medics," "medicine," "medical," "medication," and "medicinal."

Field searches. Some search engines allow you to search for a Web page by its title, or by any part of its URL. The query *T:Backcountry Recipe Book* indicates that you want to find a specific Web page titled "Backcountry Recipe Book." In this search, the *T:* tells the search engine to look at Web page titles and the information following the colon identifies the name of the title.

How do I use a topic directory? A **topic directory** is a list of topics and subtopics, such as Arts, Business, Computers, and so on, which are arranged in a hierarchy (Figure 1-20). The top level of the hierarchy contains general topics. Each successive level of the hierarchy contains more and more specific subtopics. A topic directory might also be referred to as a "category list," "index," or "directory."

FIGURE 1-20

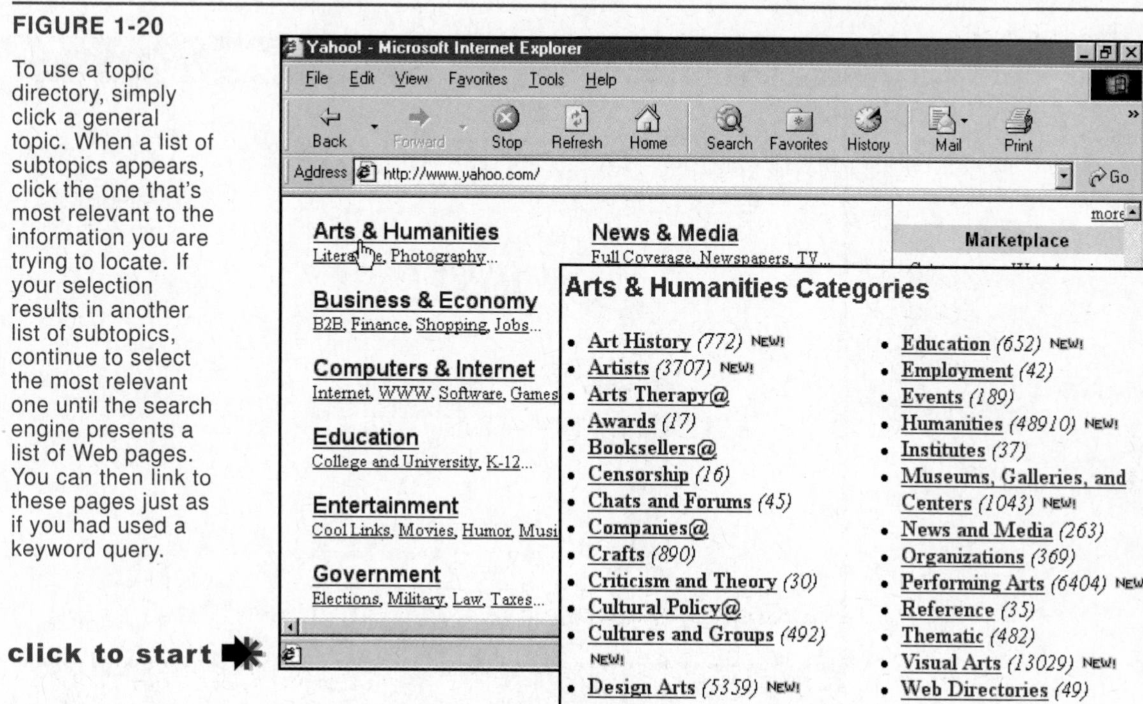

To use a topic directory, simply click a general topic. When a list of subtopics appears, click the one that's most relevant to the information you are trying to locate. If your selection results in another list of subtopics, continue to select the most relevant one until the search engine presents a list of Web pages. You can then link to these pages just as if you had used a keyword query.

How do I use a form to find information? Many search engines provide an advanced search form that helps you formulate a very targeted search. A search form, like the one shown in Figure 1-21, typically helps you enter complex queries. It also might allow you to search for pages that are written in a particular language, located on a specific Web server, or created within a limited range of dates.

FIGURE 1-21

Many search engines provide forms that are designed to simplify the search process. These forms are usually accessible by clicking an Advanced Search link, which often is located on the main page of the search engine Web site.

Advanced Web Search

Find results	with **all** of the words	railroad	10 results / Google Search
	with **any** of the words		
	with the **exact phrase**	Orient Express	
	without the words	American	
Occurrences	Return results where my terms occur	anywhere in the page	
Language	Return pages written in	French	
Domains	Only return results from the site or domain	e.g. google.com, .org More info	
SafeSearch	No filtering / Filter using SafeSearch		

Can't I just ask a simple question and get an answer? Instead of entering a cryptic query such as *movie+review+"The Matrix"* wouldn't it be nice to enter a more straightforward question like *Where can I find a review of The Matrix?* A few search engines specialize in natural language queries, which accept questions written in plain English (Figure 1-22).

FIGURE 1-22

Some search engines accept natural language queries.

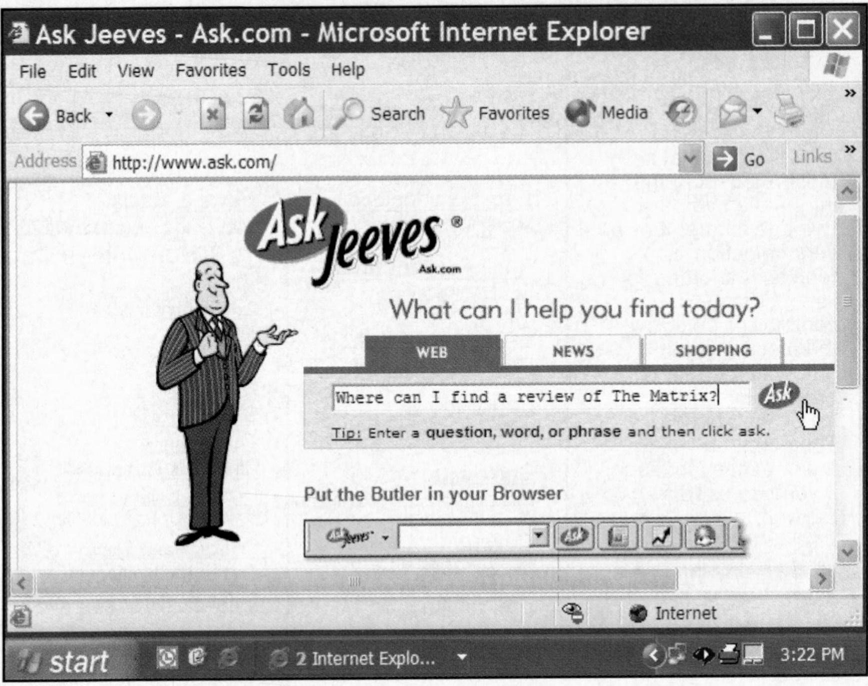

QUICKCheck Section C

1. Every Web page has a unique address called a(n) ________.
2. On a Web server that is ________ sensitive, an uppercase "E" is not the same as a lowercase "e".
3. A browser assembles a Web page on your computer screen according to the specifications contained in ________ tags.
4. Whenever you start your browser, it displays your ________ page.
5. Most browsers provide a way to save a copy of a Web page or media element. True or false? ________
6. A browser helps you find information by searching the Web for any pages that meet your specifications. True or false? ________
7. The ________ *railroad AND cars* will locate pages that contain both the words "railroad" and "cars."
8. A search engine's topic ________ helps you drill down through a hierarchy of topics and subtopics.

check answers

What is the order of events during the boot process? Six major events happen during the boot process:

1. **Power up.** When you turn on the power switch, the power light is illuminated, and power is distributed to the computer circuitry.
2. **Start boot program.** The microprocessor begins to execute the bootstrap program that is stored in ROM.
3. **Power-on self-test.** The computer performs diagnostic tests of several crucial system components.
4. **Identify peripheral devices.** The operating system identifies the peripheral devices that are connected to the computer and checks their settings.
5. **Load operating system**. The operating system is copied from the hard disk to RAM.
6. **Check configuration and customization.** The microprocessor reads configuration data and executes any customized startup routines specified by the user.

1

What if I turn on a computer and nothing happens? The first step in the boot process is the power-up stage. Power from a wall outlet or battery activates a small power light. If the power light does not come on when you flip the "on" switch, refer to the checklist in Figure 1-27.

FIGURE 1-27

Power Up Checklist

- ☑ Make sure that the power cable is plugged into the wall and into the back of the computer.
- ☑ Check batteries if you're using a notebook computer.
- ☑ Try to plug your notebook into a wall outlet.
- ☑ Make sure that the wall outlet is supplying power (plug a lamp into it and make sure that you can turn it on).
- ☑ If the computer is plugged into a surge strip, extension cord, or uninterruptible power supply, make sure that it is turned on and functioning correctly.
- ☑ Can you hear the fan in your desktop computer? If not, the computer's power supply mechanism might have failed.

What kinds of problems are likely to show up during the power-on self-test? The POST checks your computer's main circuitry, screen display, memory, and keyboard. It can identify when one of these devices has failed, but it cannot identify intermittent problems or impending failures.

The POST notifies you of a hardware problem by displaying an error message on the screen, or by emitting a series of beeps. A POST error message can help you pinpoint the source of a problem. Unfortunately, many computers display these error messages as numeric codes, such as "1790 Disk 0 Error." You can check the documentation or Web site for your computer to find the specific meaning of numeric error codes.

A **beep code** provides your computer with a way to signal a problem, even if the screen is not functioning. Two short beeps might mean a problem with the keyboard. Three long beeps might mean a problem with the screen display. Beep codes differ from one computer to another, depending on the ROM bootstrap program. The printed or online reference manual for a computer usually explains the meaning of each beep code.

Should I try to fix these problems myself? If a computer displays error messages, emits beep codes, or seems to "freeze up" during the boot process, you can take some simple steps that might fix it. First, turn the computer off, wait five seconds, then try to start the computer again and hope that the boot process proceeds smoothly. If the boot problem reoccurs, turn the computer off again and check all of the cables that run between your computer and peripheral devices, such as the keyboard, mouse, and monitor. After checking the cables, try to boot again. If you still encounter a boot error, contact a technical support person.

What's the long list of stuff that appears on my screen during the boot process? After the POST, the bootstrap program tries to identify all of the devices that are connected to the computer. Depending on the make and model of your computer, the settings for each device may appear on the screen, creating a list of rather esoteric information, as shown in Figure 1-28.

FIGURE 1-28

During the boot process, your computer tries to identify its storage devices, display devices, and other peripheral devices.

```
Award Medallion BIOS v6.0
Copyright (C) 1984-98, Award Software, Inc.

Copyright 1999 by Hewlett Packard, Inc
  Rev. 1.01

Intel(R) Pentium(R) III 500MHz Processor
Memory Test :  1310725 OK

Award Plug and Play BIOS Extension v1.0A
Initialize Plug and Play Cards . . .
PNP Init Completed

Detecting Primary Master          Maxtor 53073H6
Detecting Primary Slave           IOMEGA ZIP 100    ATAPI
Detecting Secondary Master        R/RW 4x4x24
Detecting Secondary Slave         FX482IT
```

On occasion, a device gets skipped or misidentified during the boot process. An error message is not produced, but the device won't seem to work properly. To resolve this problem, shut down the computer and reboot it again. If a device is causing persistent problems, you may need to check the manufacturer's Web site to see if a new software "patch" will improve its operation.

Do computers have trouble loading the operating system or applying customization settings? Problems during the last stages of the boot process are rare, except when a disk has been inadvertently left in the floppy disk drive. Before computers were equipped with hard disk drives, floppy disks were used to store the operating system and application software. As a legacy from these early machines, today's computers first check the floppy disk drive for a disk containing the operating system. If it doesn't find a disk in the drive, it merrily proceeds to look for the operating system on the hard disk. However, if a floppy disk happens to be hanging around in drive A, the computer will assume that you want to boot from it and will look for the operating system on that disk. The error message "Non-system disk or disk error" is the clue to this problem. Remove the floppy disk and press any key to resume the boot process.

How do I know when the boot process is finished? The boot process is complete when the computer is ready to accept your commands. Usually, the computer displays an operating system prompt or main screen. The Windows operating system, for example, displays the Windows desktop when the boot process is complete.

If Windows cannot complete the boot process, you are likely to see a menu that contains an option for Safe Mode. **Safe Mode** is a limited version of Windows that allows you to use your mouse, monitor, and keyboard, but not other peripheral devices. This mode is designed for troubleshooting, not for real computing tasks. If your computer enters Safe Mode at the end of the boot process (Figure 1-29 on the next page), you should use the Shut Down command on the Start menu to properly shut down and turn off your computer. You can then turn on your computer again. It should complete the boot process in regular Windows mode. If your computer enters Safe Mode again, consult a technician.

FIGURE 1-29

Windows enters Safe Mode as a response to a problem—usually to problems caused by the device driver software that controls a particular piece of peripheral equipment. You can also force a computer into Safe Mode by pressing the F8 key during the boot sequence.

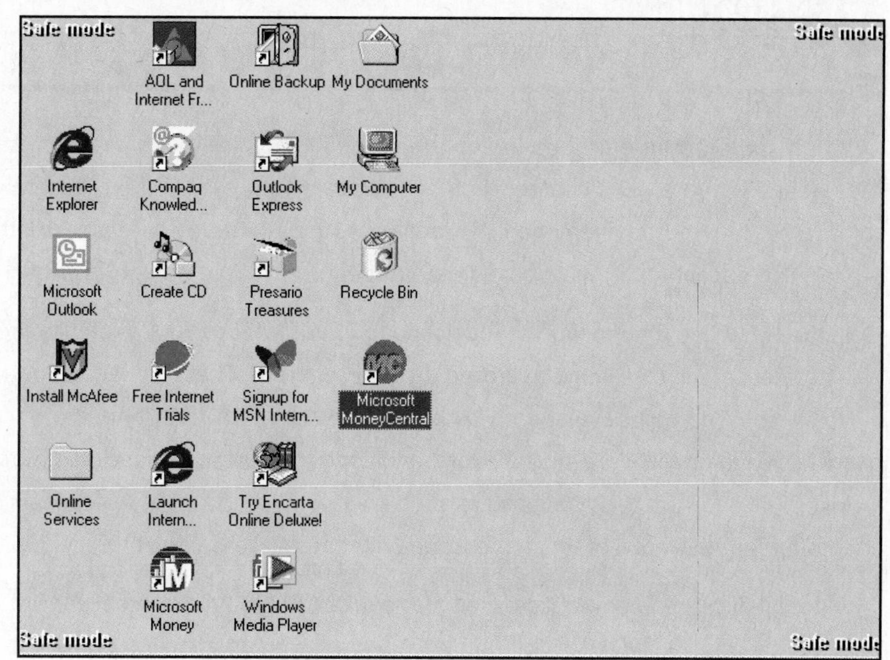

1

Safe Mode can help technically savvy computer owners identify and fix a number of problems caused by installing new hardware devices. To learn more, check out the Safe Mode InfoWeb.

click

When a computer is behaving erratically, does rebooting help? Sometimes—especially if a computer has been left on for a few weeks straight—the operating system seems to forget how to handle part of its job. Such problems can be caused by transient, "soft errors" in the memory circuits that are supposed to hold the operating system instructions. In other cases, areas of memory that are supposed to be reserved for the operating system somehow get overwritten by snippets of application programs. The end effect is the same—parts of the operating system are missing and can't control a particular input, output, or storage function. As a result, a computer might begin to behave erratically. The remedy for this problem is to restore the operating system back to full functionality. Usually, rebooting does the trick. If not, consider the possibility that your computer might have contracted a virus. (More information on the topic of viruses can be found in Chapter 4.)

QUICKCheck TechTalk

1. The boot process loads the ________ from the hard disk into memory.
2. During the boot process, the ________ checks your computer's main circuitry, screen display, memory, and keyboard.
3. Windows ________ mode provides a limited version of Windows that allows you to troubleshoot, but not use most peripheral devices.
4. If a computer is behaving erratically, rebooting might restore functionality. True or false? ________

check answers

ISSUE
HOW PRIVATE IS E-MAIL?

When you drop an envelope in the corner mailbox, you probably expect it to arrive at its destination unopened, and with its contents kept safe from prying eyes. When you make a phone call, you might assume that your conversation will proceed unmonitored by wiretaps or other listening devices. Can you also expect an e-mail message to be read only by the person to whom it is addressed?

In the U.S., The Electronic Communications Privacy Act of 2000 prohibits the use of intercepted e-mail as evidence unless a judge approved a search warrant. That doesn't mean the government isn't reading your mail. The FBI developed a technology called Carnivore that scans through messages entering and leaving an ISP's e-mail system and looks for e-mail associated with a person who is under investigation. Privacy advocates are concerned because Carnivore scans all of the messages that pass through an ISP, not just those messages destined for a particular individual.

Although law enforcement agencies are required to obtain a search warrant before intercepting e-mail, no such restriction exists for employers who want to monitor employee e-mail. According to the American Management Association, 27 percent of U.S. businesses monitor employee e-mail. But this intentional eavesdropping is only one way in which the contents of your e-mail messages might become public. The recipient of your e-mail can forward it to one or more people—people you never intended for it to reach. Your e-mail messages could pop up on a technician's screen in the course of system maintenance or repairs. Also, keep in mind that e-mail messages—including those that you delete from your own PC—can be stored on backups of your ISP's e-mail server. You might wonder if such open access to your e-mail is legal. The answer in most cases is yes.

The United States Omnibus Crime Control and Safe Streets Act of 1968 and the Electronic Communications Privacy Act of 1986 prohibit public and private employers from engaging in surreptitious surveillance of employee activity through the use of electronic devices. However, two exceptions to these privacy statutes exist. The first exception permits an employer to monitor e-mail if one party to the communication consents to the monitoring. An employer must inform employees of this policy before undertaking any monitoring. The second exception permits employers to monitor their employees' e-mail if a legitimate business need exists, and the monitoring takes place within the business-owned e-mail system.

Employees have not been successful in defending their rights to e-mail privacy. For example, in 1996, a Pillsbury employee was fired from his job for making unprofessional comments in an e-mail to his supervisor. The employee sued because he claimed that the company repeatedly assured its employees that e-mail was private. The court ruled that the employee's right to privacy did not outweigh the interests of the company. Although it would seem that the company violated the requirement to inform employees according to the first exception to the privacy statutes, the fact that the company owned the e-mail system gave it the right to monitor any correspondence carried out over that system. In more recent cases, Dow Chemical fired more than 90 people for sending pornographic e-mail, and the New York Times fired 23 people for sending offensive e-mail.

Like employees of a business, students who use a school's e-mail system cannot be assured of e-mail privacy. When a CalTech student was accused of sexually harassing a female student by sending lewd e-mail to her and her boyfriend, investigators retrieved all of the student's e-mail from the archives of the e-mail server. The student was expelled from the university even though he claimed that the e-mail had been "spoofed" to make it look as though he had sent it, when it had actually been sent by someone else.

You'll find lots more information about e-mail privacy (and lack of it) at the E-mail Privacy InfoWeb.

click

Why would an employer want to know the contents of employee e-mail? Why would a school be concerned with the correspondence of its students? It is probably true that some organizations simply snoop on the off chance that important information might be discovered. Other organizations have more legitimate reasons for monitoring e-mail. An organization that owns an e-mail system can be held responsible for the consequences of actions related to the contents of e-mail messages on that system. For example, a school has a responsibility to protect students from harassment. If it fails to do so, it can be sued along with the author of the offending e-mail message. Organizations also recognize a need to protect themselves from false rumors and industrial espionage. For example, a business wants to know if an employee is supplying its competitor with information on product research and development.

Many schools and businesses have established e-mail privacy policies, which explain the conditions under which you can and cannot expect your e-mail to remain private. Court decisions, however, seem to support the notion that because an organization owns and operates its e-mail system, the organization owns the e-mail messages that are generated on its system. The individual who authors an e-mail message does not own it and therefore has no rights related to it. A company can, therefore, legally monitor your e-mail. You should use your e-mail account with the expectation that some of your mail will be read from time to time. Think of your e-mail as a postcard, rather than a letter, and save your controversial comments for face-to-face conversations.

What Do You Think?

1. Do you think most people believe that their e-mail is private? ❍ Yes ❍ No ❍ Not sure
2. Do you agree with CalTech's decision to expel the student who was accused of sending harassing e-mail to another student? ❍ Yes ❍ No ❍ Not sure
3. Should the laws be changed to make it illegal for employers to monitor e-mail without court approval? ❍ Yes ❍ No ❍ Not sure
4. Would you have different privacy expectations regarding an e-mail account at your place of work as opposed to an account that you purchase from an e-mail service provider? ❍ Yes ❍ No ❍ Not sure

click to save your responses

INTERACTIVE SUMMARY

The Interactive Summary helps you review important concepts from this chapter. Fill in the blanks to best complete each sentence. When using the NP6 BookOnCD, you can click the Check Answers buttons to automatically score your answers. Place your Tracking Disk in the floppy disk drive if you want to save your scores.

A computer is a device that accepts input, ______ data, stores data, and produces output according to a series of stored instructions. Before a computer processes data, it is temporarily held in ______. This data is then processed in the ______ (CPU). The idea of a ______ program means that a series of instructions for a computing task can be loaded into a computer's memory.

Computers are grouped into categories, such as personal computers, handhelds, mainframes, supercomputers, servers, workstations, and videogame consoles. A ______ computer is a type of microcomputer that is designed to meet the needs of an individual. Computers process, store, and transmit data in ______ format as a series of 1s and 0s. Each 1 or 0 is called a ______. Eight bits, called a ______, represent one character—a letter, number, or punctuation mark. Data becomes ______ when it is presented in a format that people can understand and use.

An ______ system, such as Windows, UNIX, or Mac OS, is essentially the master controller for all of the activities that take place within a computer. ______ software is any set of computer programs that helps a person carry out a task. Although "Windows" is the name of an operating system, the term "Windows software" refers to application software that is designed for computers that run the Windows operating system.

check answers

The Internet is a collection of local, regional, national, and international computer ______ that are linked together to exchange data and distribute processing tasks. The main routes of the Internet are referred to as the Internet ______. Communications between all of the devices on the Internet is made possible by a standard set of rules called ______. To transmit data, files are divided into small chunks called ______ and sent to the IP address of their destination. The Internet hosts a wide variety of activities, such as Web browsing, e-commerce, e-mail, bulletin boards, chat groups, instant messaging, Internet telephony, digital broadcasts, remote access, downloads, uploads, and peer-to-peer connections.

Most people access the Internet using a dial-up connection that simply requires a telephone line and a ______. Faster access methods include cable modem service, ISDN, DSL, and satellite service. Regardless of the access method, individuals cannot typically connect directly to the Internet backbone and, therefore, need to use an ______ as an intermediary. Both national ISPs and local ISPs have advantages that cater to different computing lifestyles.

Access to the Internet is not restricted, but access to some areas requires a ______ and password. Passwords are most secure when they consist of two non-related words, or a word and a number. Managing multiple passwords can be simplified by selecting a low-security password and a high-security password, then applying them as necessary.

check answers

Composed of millions of files that are stored on Web ________ all over the world, the Web is one of the most popular aspects of the Internet. Many of these Web-based files are documents that a browser displays as Web ________. Other files contain photos, videos, animations, and sound clips that can be incorporated into specific Web pages. Web pages also contain text or graphics ________ to related documents and media files. Every Web page has a unique address called a ________. Most of them begin with "http", which stands for Hypertext ________ Protocol, the communications standard that's instrumental in ferrying Web documents to all corners of the Internet. A group of Web pages is usually referred to as a Web ________.

A ________ is a software program that runs on your computer and helps you access Web pages. It fetches Web pages and interprets HTML ________ in order to properly display the page on your computer screen. Current browsers simply fetch information from a given URL, but they do not have the capability to search for specific information based on your search specifications. A search ________ provides the tools that you need to search for specific information on the Web. These tools include keyword search input areas, advanced search forms, category lists, and "agents" that understand queries entered as simple questions.

check answers

E-mail, short for "electronic mail," can refer to a single electronic message, or to the entire system of computers and software that transmits, receives, and stores digital e-mail messages. Any person with an e-mail ________ can send and receive electronic mail. Basic e-mail activities include composing, reading, replying to, sending, forwarding, and deleting messages. More advanced activities include adding attachments, using HTML format, and maintaining an address book. Most e-mail messages are created in a plain and simple format called ________ text. It is also possible to create messages in ________ format, which includes underlining, fancy fonts, colored text, and embedded graphics.

E-mail has similarities and differences from other forms of communications, but it is the differences that spawned a collection of online communications guidelines called ________.

An e-mail system consists of e-mail servers, which are accessible to e-mail account holders. Today, consumers can choose between three types of e-mail. ________ mail holds your incoming mail on an e-mail server until you download it to your computer using e-mail ________ software. ________ mail gives you the option of downloading your mail or storing it on the e-mail server. Web-based e-mail operates exclusively from the Web. ________-based mail allows you to use a browser as e-mail client software.

check answers 

INTERACTIVE KEY TERMS

Make sure that you understand all of the boldfaced key terms presented in this chapter. If you're using the NP6 BookOnCD, you can use this list of terms as an interactive study activity. First, try to define a term in your own words, then click the term to compare your definition with the definition that is presented in the chapter.

Always-on connection, 19
Application software, 12
Beep code, 45
Bit, 11
Boot process, 44
Browser, 28
Byte, 11
Cable modem, 19
Case sensitive, 23
CD-ROM drive, 10
CD-writer, 10
Central processing unit (CPU), 4
Chat group, 17
Client , 8
Computer, 4
Computer network, 7
Computer program, 4
Data, 4, 11
Data file, 11
Desktop computer, 6
Dial-up connection, 18
Digital, 11
Downloading, 17
DSL, 20
DSS, 20
DVD drive, 10
E-commerce, 16
Electronic mail, 36
E-mail, 16
E-mail account, 36
E-mail attachment, 37
E-mail client software, 41
E-mail message, 36
E-mail servers, 40
E-mail system, 40
Executable file, 11
File, 11
Filename extension, 11
Floppy disk drive, 9
Handheld computer,7
Hard disk drive, 9
Home page, 30
HTML, 27
HTML tags, 29
HTTP, 27
Hypertext, 26
IMAP, 40
Information, 11
Input, 4
Instant messaging, 17
Internet, 15
Internet backbone, 15
Internet telephony, 17
IP address, 16
ISDN, 20
ISP, 20
Keyword, 32
LCD screen, 9
Links, 26
Local area network (LAN), 7
Macs, 13
Mailing list server, 16
Mainframe computer, 8
Memory, 5
Message header, 36
Microcomputer, 6
Microprocessor, 6
MIME, 37
Minicomputer, 6
Modem, 10
Monitor, 9
Mouse, 9
Netiquette, 39
Network card, 19
Newsgroups, 16
Notebook computer, 6
Operating system, 12
Output, 5
Packets, 16
Password, 22
PCs, 13
PDA, 7
Peer-to-peer, 18
Peripheral device, 11
Personal computer, 6
Platform, 13
POP, 40
POP server, 41
Power-on self-test (POST), 44
Processing, 4
Proprietary services, 22
Query, 32
Router, 16
Safe Mode, 46
Search engines, 16, 31
Search operator, 32
Server, 8
Smileys, 39
SMTP server, 41
Software, 4
Sound card, 10
Storage, 5
Store-and-forward technology, 40
Stored program, 5
Supercomputer, 8
System software, 12
System unit, 9
TCP/IP, 15
Telnet, 18
Topic directory, 33
Uploading, 17
URL, 27
Usenet, 16
User ID, 22
Videogame console, 7
Voice band modem, 18
Web, 26
Web pages, 26
Web servers, 27
Web site, 27
Web sites, 16
Web-based e-mail, 40
Workstation, 7

INTERACTIVE
SITUATION QUESTIONS

Apply what you've learned to some typical computing situations. When using the NP6 BookOnCD, you can type your answers, then use the Check Answers button to automatically score your responses. Place your Tracking Disk in the floppy disk drive if you want to save your scores.

1

1. You walk into an office and see the computer pictured to the right. You would probably assume that it would be categorized as a(n) ________ computer, but it might also be a(n) ________ or a server.

2. You receive a floppy disk from a friend and it contains a file called *Quake.exe*. Because of the filename extension, you assume that the disk contains a(n) ________ file that is some type of computer program, rather than a data file.

3. You are a musician and you use your Gateway PC to compose music. Your friend, who has an iMac computer, wants to try your software. If you loan the composition software to your friend, can she use it on her iMac? Yes or no? ________

4. You are a computer technician hired by Ben and Jerry's Ice Cream to set up a Web server. You know that your server will need a unique ________ address that pinpoints its location in cyberspace, and your server will need to use ________, the standard Internet protocol that transports data between all sorts of computer platforms over the Internet.

5. You want the cheapest Internet connection. You don't mind if the connection is limited to speeds under 56 Kbps and doesn't provide very good video performance. You would probably select an ISP that provides a(n) ________ connection.

6. You need to select a password for your online bank account. Which of the following passwords would be the LEAST secure: hddtmrutc, gargantuan, brickcloset, high348? ________

7. You want to look at the latest Nike athletic shoes. The URL that will probably get you to Nike's home page is ________.

8. You want to find some Web pages that contain information about snowboarding competitions. You know that your ________ can only fetch and display Web pages, so you'll need to connect to a(n) ________ site and enter a query, such as "snowboard competition."

9. If your ISP does not supply you with an e-mail account, you can get a free ________ e-mail account from a site such as Hotmail or Excite.

10. You receive an e-mail message that contains colored text and underlining. You assume that the person who sent the message had his mail software set for ________ format.

check answers

INTERACTIVE PRACTICE TESTS

When you use the NP6 BookOnCD, you can take Practice Tests that consist of 10 multiple-choice, true/false, and fill-in-the-blank questions. The questions are selected at random from a large test bank, so each time you take a test, you'll receive a different set of questions. Your tests are scored immediately, and you can print study guides that help you find the correct answers for any questions that you missed. If you are using a Tracking Disk, insert it in the floppy disk drive to save your test scores.

click to start

STUDY TIPS

Study Tips help you to organize and consolidate the information in a chapter by making lists, outlines, charts, and sketches. You can use paper and pencil or word processing software to complete most of the Study Tips activities.

1. Make sure that you can use your own words to correctly answer each of the green focus questions that appear throughout the chapter.
2. Explain how a computer makes use of input, processing, storage, memory, output, and the stored program concept.
3. List, briefly describe, and rank (in terms of computing capacity) the characteristics of each computer category described in Section A of this chapter.
4. Identify, list, and describe each of the components of a basic personal computer system.
5. Describe the difference between a data file and an executable file.
6. Describe the difference between an operating system and application software.
7. Discuss what makes two computer platforms compatible or incompatible.
8. Describe the significance of packets, IP addresses, TCP/IP, and routers on the Internet.
9. List at least five resources that are provided by the Internet, and identify those that are most popular.
10. Explain why so many people need the services of an ISP.
11. Make a list of the Internet connections presented in this chapter, and specify typical data transport speeds for each.
12. Describe how to select a password that is secure, yet easy to remember.
13. Describe the similarities and differences between a URL and an e-mail address.
14. Make sure that you can explain the difference between HTML, HTTP, and hypertext.
15. Make a list of the rules that you should follow when typing a URL.
16. Describe the difference between a browser and a search engine.
17. Explain the role of MIME as it relates to e-mail attachments.
18. Describe how e-mail is stored and transmitted by POP and SMTP servers.

How can a computer represent numbers using bits? Numeric data consists of numbers that might be used in arithmetic operations. For example, your annual income is numeric data, as is your age. The price of a Razor scooter is numeric data. So is your car's average gas mileage. Computers represent numeric data—like 24 (your car's average gas mileage)—using the **binary number system**, also called "base 2."

The binary number system has only two digits: 0 and 1. No "squiggle" like "2" exists in this system, so the number "two" is represented in binary as "10" (pronounced "one zero"). You'll recognize the similarity to what happens when you're counting from 1 to 10 in the familiar decimal system. After you reach 9, you run out of digits. For "ten," you have to use "10"—zero is a placeholder and the "1" indicates "one group of tens." In binary, you just run out of digits sooner—right after you count to 1. To get to the next number, you have to use the zero as a placeholder and the "1" indicates "one group of 2s." In binary then, you count 0 ("zero"), 1 ("one"), 10 ("one zero"), instead of counting 0, 1, 2 in decimal. If you need to brush up on binary numbers, refer to Figure 2-2 and to the lab at the end of Section A.

2

The important point to understand is that the binary number system allows computers to represent virtually any number simply by using 0s and 1s, which conveniently translate into electrical "on" and "off" signals. Your average gas mileage (24) is 11000 in binary, and can be represented by "on" "on" "off" "off" "off."

FIGURE 2-2

The decimal system uses ten symbols to represent numbers: 0, 1, 2, 3, 4, 5, 6, 7, 8, and 9. The binary number system uses only two symbols: 0 and 1.

Decimal (Base 10)	Binary (Base 2)
0	0
1	1
2	10
3	11
4	100
5	101
6	110
7	111
8	1000
9	1001
10	1010
11	1011
1000	1111101000

01001000 01001001 00100001

How can a computer represent words and letters using bits? Character data is composed of letters, symbols, and numerals that will not be used in arithmetic operations. Examples of character data include your name, address, and hair color. Just as Morse code uses dashes and dots to represent the letters of the alphabet, a digital computer uses a series of bits to represent letters, characters, and numerals. (See "HI!" at left, along with the bits that a computer can use to represent each character.)

Computers employ several types of codes to represent character data, including ASCII, EBCDIC, and Unicode. **ASCII** (American Standard Code for Information Interchange, pronounced "ASK ee") requires only seven bits for each character. For example, the ASCII code for an uppercase "A" is 1000001. ASCII provides codes for 128 characters, including uppercase letters, lowercase letters, punctuation symbols, and numerals. A superset of ASCII, called **Extended ASCII**, uses eight bits to represent each character. The eighth bit provides codes for 128 additional characters, which are usually boxes, circles, and other graphical symbols. **EBCDIC** (Extended Binary-Coded Decimal Interchange Code, pronounced "EB seh dick") is an alternative 8-bit code, usually used by older, IBM mainframe computers. **Unicode** (pronounced "YOU ni code") uses 16 bits and provides codes for 65,000 characters—a real bonus for representing the alphabets of multiple languages. Most personal computers use Extended ASCII code (shown in Figure 2-3), although Unicode is becoming increasingly popular.

FIGURE 2-3

The extended ASCII code uses a series of eight 1s and 0s to represent 256 characters, including lowercase letters, uppercase letters, symbols, and numerals. The first 63 ASCII characters are not shown in this table because they represent special control sequences that cannot be printed. The two "blank" entries are space characters.

	00100000	>	00111110	\	01011100	z	01111010	ÿ	10011000	╢	10110110	╘	11010100	≥	11110010
!	00100001	?	00111111	]	01011101	{	01111011	Ö	10011001	╖	10110111	╒	11010101	≤	11110011
"	00100010	@	01000000	^	01011110	¦	01111100	Ü	10011010	╕	10111000	╓	11010110	⌠	11110100
#	00100011	A	01000001	_	01011111	}	01111101	¢	10011011	╣	10111001	╫	11010111	⌡	11110101
$	00100100	B	01000010	`	01100000	~	01111110	£	10011100	║	10111010	╪	11011000	÷	11110110
%	00100101	C	01000011	a	01100001	⌂	01111111	¥	10011101	╗	10111011	┘	11011001	≈	11110111
&	00100110	D	01000100	b	01100010	Ç	10000000	₧	10011110	╝	10111100	┌	11011010	°	11111000
'	00100111	E	01000101	c	01100011	ü	10000001	ƒ	10011111	╜	10111101	█	11011011	∙	11111001
(	00101000	F	01000110	d	01100100	é	10000010	á	10100000	╛	10111110	▄	11011100	·	11111010
)	00101001	G	01000111	e	01100101	â	10000011	í	10100001	┐	10111111	▌	11011101	√	11111011
*	00101010	H	01001000	f	01100110	ä	10000100	ó	10100010	└	11000000	▐	11011110	ⁿ	11111100
+	00101011	I	01001001	g	01100111	à	10000101	ú	10100011	┴	11000001	▀	11011111	²	11111101
,	00101100	J	01001010	h	01101000	å	10000110	ñ	10100100	┬	11000010	α	11100000	■	11111110
-	00101101	K	01001011	i	01101001	ç	10000111	Ñ	10100101	├	11000011	ß	11100001		11111111
.	00101110	L	01001100	j	01101010	ê	10001000	ª	10100110	─	11000100	Γ	11100010		
/	00101111	M	01001101	k	01101011	ë	10001001	º	10100111	┼	11000101	π	11100011		
0	00110000	N	01001110	l	01101100	è	10001010	¿	10101000	╞	11000110	Σ	11100100		
1	00110001	O	01001111	m	01101101	ï	10001011	⌐	10101001	╟	11000111	σ	11100101		
2	00110010	P	01010000	n	01101110	î	10001100	¬	10101010	╚	11001000	µ	11100110		
3	00110011	Q	01010001	o	01101111	ì	10001101	½	10101011	╔	11001001	τ	11100111		
4	00110100	R	01010010	p	01110000	Ä	10001110	¼	10101100	╩	11001010	Φ	11101000		
5	00110101	S	01010011	q	01110001	Å	10001111	¡	10101101	╦	11001011	Θ	11101001		
6	00110110	T	01010100	r	01110010	É	10010000	«	10101110	╠	11001100	Ω	11101010		
7	00110111	U	01010101	s	01110011	æ	10010001	»	10101111	═	11001101	δ	11101011		
8	00111000	V	01010110	t	01110100	Æ	10010010	░	10110000	╬	11001110	∞	11101100		
9	00111001	W	01010111	u	01110101	ô	10010011	▒	10110001	╧	11001111	φ	11101101		
:	00111010	X	01011000	v	01110110	ö	10010100	▓	10110010	╨	11010000	ε	11101110		
;	00111011	Y	01011001	w	01110111	ò	10010101	│	10110011	╤	11010001	∩	11101111		
<	00111100	Z	01011010	x	01111000	û	10010110	┤	10110100	╥	11010010	≡	11110000		
=	00111101	[	01011011	y	01111001	ù	10010111	╡	10110101	╙	11010011	±	11110001		

Why does ASCII provide codes for 0, 1, 2, 3, 4, 5, 6, 7, 8, and 9? Computers represent numeric data with binary equivalents, so it might seem as if there would be no need for ASCII codes that represent numbers. Computers, however, sometimes distinguish between numeric data and numerals. For example, you don't typically use your social security "number" in calculations, so a computer typically considers it character data, composed of *numerals*, not numbers. Likewise, the "numbers" in your street address are treated as character data, not numeric data. A computer uses the ASCII code numerals for your social security number and street address, whereas it uses a binary number to code numeric data such as your age.

How does a computer convert sounds and pictures into codes? Sounds and pictures are not small, discrete objects like numbers or the letters of the alphabet. To work with sounds and pictures, a computer must somehow **digitize** colors, notes, and instrument sounds into 1s and 0s. Computers convert colors and sounds into numbers, which can be represented by bits. For example, a red dot on your computer screen might be represented by 1100, a green dot by 0010.

When a computer works with a series of 1s and 0s, how does it know which code to use? All of the "stuff" that your computer works with is stored in files as a long—make that really long—series of 1s and 0s. Your computer needs to know whether to interpret those 1s and 0s as ASCII code, binary numbers, or the code for a picture or sound. Imagine the mess if your computer thought that your term paper, stored as ASCII, was an accounting file that contained a series of numbers stored in binary format. It would never be able to reconstruct the words and sentences of your term paper.

To avoid confusion, most computer files contain a **file header** with information on the code that was used to represent the file data. A file header is stored along with the file and can be read by the computer, but never appears on the screen. By reading the header information, a computer can tell how a file's contents were coded.

QUANTIFYING BITS AND BYTES

How can I tell the difference between bits and bytes? Computer ads include lots of abbreviations relating to bits and bytes. A few key concepts will help you understand what these abbreviations mean. Even though the word "bit" is an abbreviation for "binary digit," it can be further abbreviated, usually as a lowercase "b." A byte, on the other hand, is composed of eight bits and is usually abbreviated as an uppercase "B." By the way, halfway between a little "bit" and a big "byte" is a thing called a nibble (four bits).

Transmission speeds are usually expressed in bits, whereas storage space is usually expressed in bytes. In Chapter 1, for example, you learned that the speed of most voice band modems is 56 Kbps—56 kilo*bits* per second. In a computer ad, you might see the capacity of a hard disk drive described as 8 GB—8 giga*bytes*.

What do the prefixes kilo- mega- and giga- mean? "Kilo" is usually a prefix that means 1,000. For example, $50 K means $50,000. When it refers to bits or bytes, a "kilo" is 1,024 because computer engineers measure everything in base 2, and 2^{10} turns out to be 1,024, not 1,000. So a **kilobit** (abbreviated Kb or Kbit) is 1,024 bits and a **kilobyte** (abbreviated KB or Kbyte) is 1,024 bytes.

The prefix "mega" refers to a million, or in the context of bits and bytes, precisely 1,048,576 (the equivalent of 2^{20}). Mb or Mbit is the abbreviation for **megabit**. MB or Mbyte is the abbreviation for **megabyte**. The prefixes **giga-** (billion), **tera-** (trillion), and **exa-** (quintillion) work the same way.

DIGITAL ELECTRONICS

How does a computer store and transport all of those bits? Because most computers are electronic devices, bits take the form of electrical pulses that can travel over circuits, much in the same way that electricity flows over a wire when you turn on a light switch. All of the circuits, chips, and mechanical components that form a computer are designed to work with bits. Most of these essential components are housed within the computer's system unit.

Does a typical computer owner need to mess around inside the system unit? If it weren't for the miniaturization made possible by digital electronic technology, computers would be huge, and the inside of a computer's system unit would contain a complex jumble of wires and other electronic gizmos. Instead, today's computers contain relatively few parts. Desktop computers are designed with the expectation that owners will forage around inside the system unit to add or replace various components. Notebook computers, on the other hand, usually provide access for expansion and replacement from outside of the case. In Figure 2-4, you can see what's inside a typical desktop computer.

FIGURE 2-4

A computer's system unit typically contains circuit boards, storage devices, and a power supply that converts current from an AC wall outlet into the DC current used by computer circuitry.

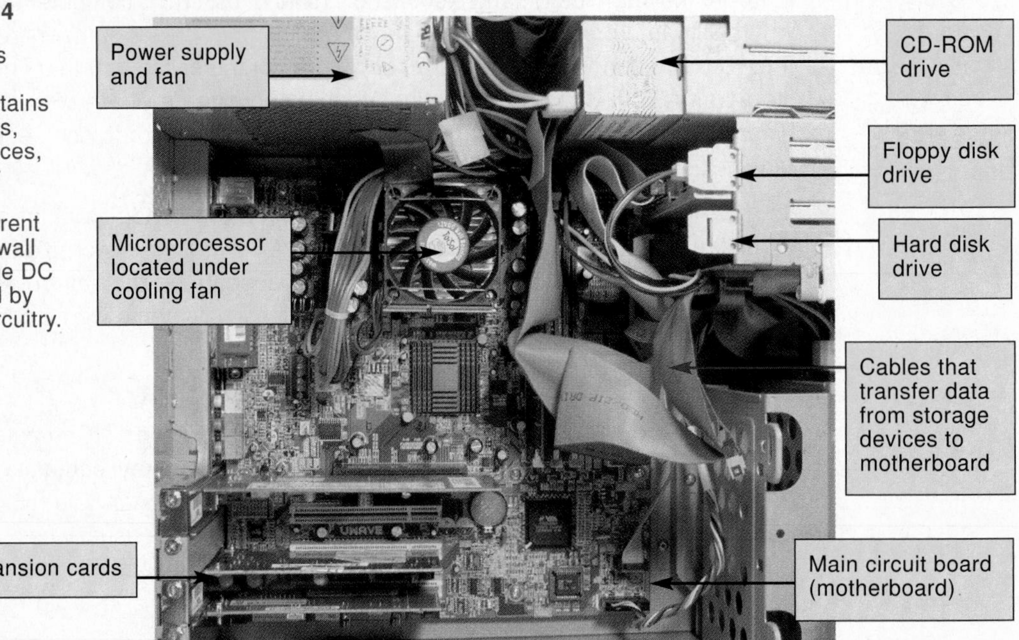

FIGURE 2-5

Chips are classified by the number of miniaturized components they contain—from small-scale integration (SSI) of less than 100 components per chip to "ultra large-scale integration" (ULSI) of more than 1 million components per chip.

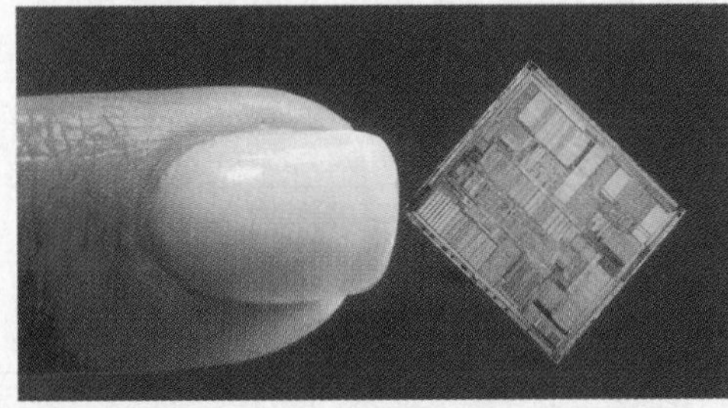

What's a computer chip? The terms "computer chip," "microchip," and "chip" originated as technical jargon for "integrated circuit." An **integrated circuit** (IC), such as the one pictured in Figure 2-5, is a super thin slice of semiconducting material packed with microscopic circuit elements such as wires, transistors, capacitors, logic gates, and resistors.

Semiconducting materials (or "semiconductors"), such as silicon and germanium, are substances with properties between those of a conductor (like copper) and an insulator (like wood). To fabricate a chip, the conductive properties of selective parts of the semiconducting material can be enhanced to essentially create miniature electronic pathways and components, such as transistors.

Find out how thousands of miles of wires and millions of components can be miniaturized to the size of a baby's fingernail at the Integrated Circuits InfoWeb.

click

The assortment of chips inside of a computer includes the microprocessor, memory modules, and support circuitry. These chips are packaged in a protective carrier that also provides connectors to other computer components. Chip carriers vary in shape and size—including small rectangular **DIPs** (dual in-line package) with caterpillar-like legs protruding from a black, rectangular "body;" long, slim **DIMMs** (dual in-line memory modules); pin-cushion-like **PGAs** (pin-grid arrays); and cassette-like **SEC cartridges** (single edge contact cartridges). Terms like DIMM and PGA frequently appear in computer ads. Figure 2-6 helps you visualize these components.

2

FIGURE 2-6

Integrated circuits can be used for microprocessors, memory, and support circuitry. They are housed within a ceramic carrier. These carriers exist in several configurations, or "chip packages," such as DIPs, DIMMs, PGAs, and SECs.

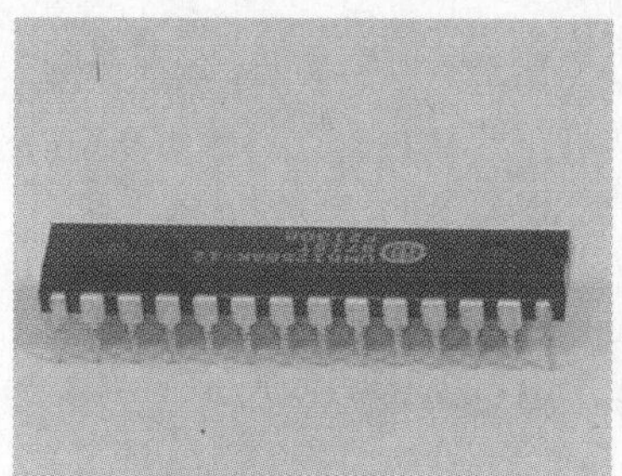

A DIP has two rows of pins that connect the IC circuitry to a circuit board.

A DIMM is a small circuit board containing several chips, typically used for memory.

A PGA is a square chip package with pins arranged in concentric squares, typically used for microprocessors.

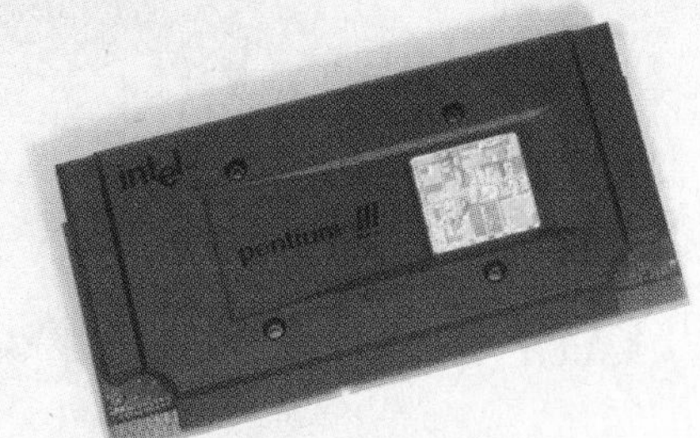

An SEC cartridge is a popular chip package for microprocessors.

How do chips fit together to make a computer? The computer's main circuit board, called a **motherboard** or "main board," houses all essential chips and provides connecting circuitry between them. If you look carefully at a motherboard, you'll see that some chips are permanently soldered in place. Other chips are plugged into special sockets and connectors, which allow chips to be removed for repairs or upgrades. When multiple chips are required for a single function, such as generating stereo-quality sound, the chips might be gathered together on a separate small circuit board, which can then be plugged into a special slot-like connector. Figure 2-7 on the next page provides a handy guide that can help you identify the components on your computer's motherboard. You will learn more about the components of a motherboard in this and subsequent chapters.

FIGURE 2-7

A computer motherboard provides sockets for chips, slots for small circuit boards, and the circuitry that connects all of these components.

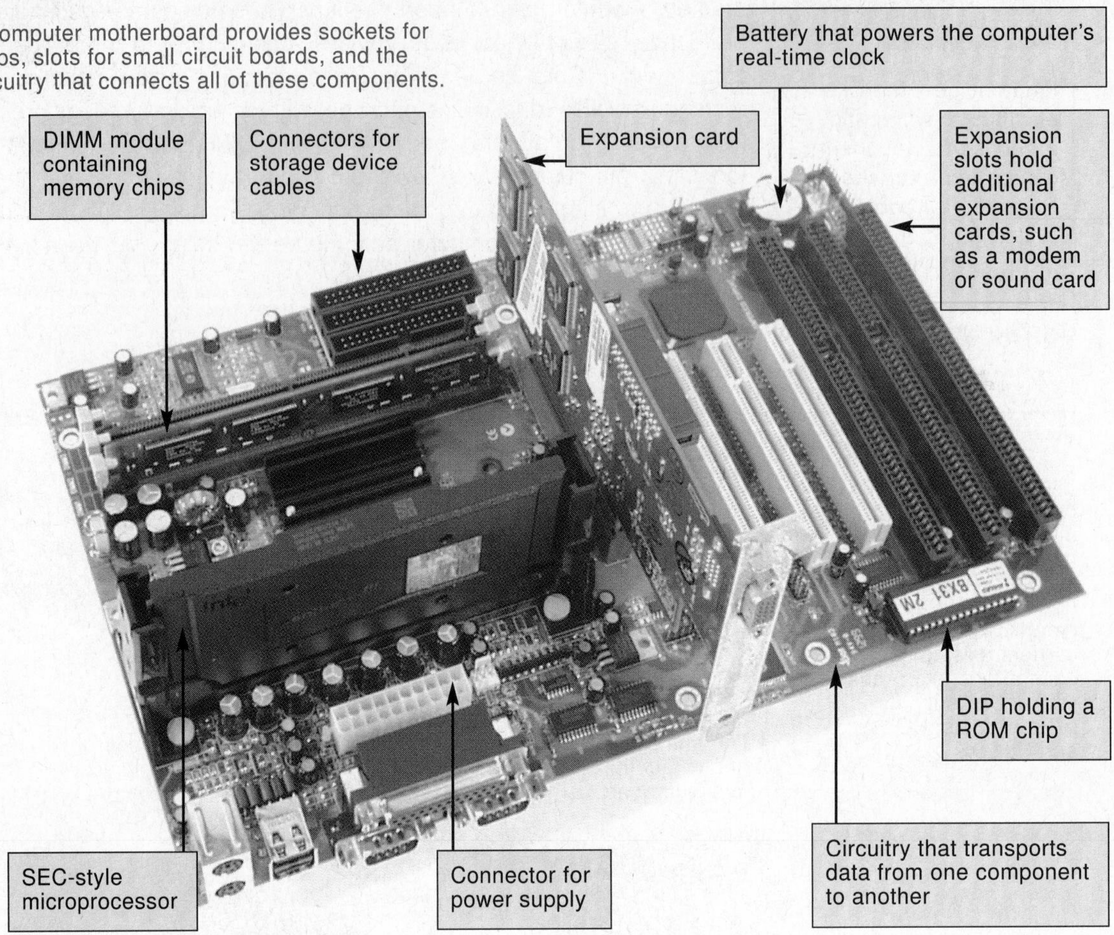

QUICKCheck Section A

1 A(n) ______ device works with discrete numbers, whereas a(n) ______ device works with continuous data.

2 The ______ number system represents numeric data as a series of 0s and 1s.

3 ASCII provides codes for numerals 0 through 9. True or false? ______

4 Most personal computers use the ______ code to represent character data.

5 A computer uses ______ code numerals for your social security number and street address, whereas it uses a(n) ______ number to code numeric data such as your age.

6 100 MB is larger than 100 Mbit. True or false? ______

7 A(n) ______ contains microscopic circuit elements, such as wires, transistors, and capacitors, that are packed onto a very small square of semiconducting material.

check answers

LAB 2-A WORKING WITH BINARY NUMBERS

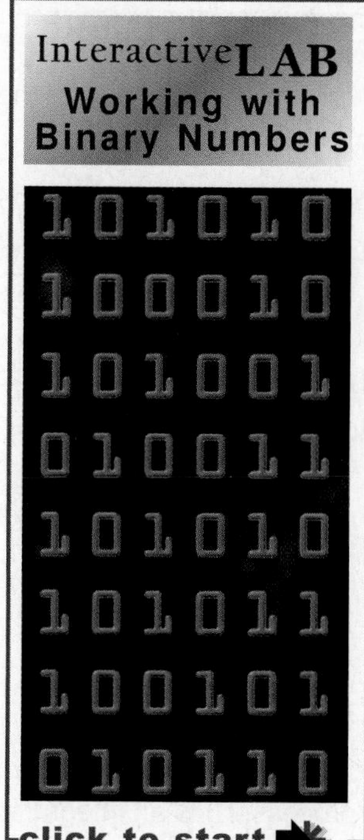

InteractiveLAB
Working with Binary Numbers
click to start

In this lab, you'll review and learn:

- The difference between the binary number system and the decimal number system
- How to count in binary
- How to convert decimal numbers into binary numbers
- How to convert binary numbers into decimal numbers
- How to use the Windows Calculator to convert numbers
- How to work with "powers of two"

2

LAB Assignments

1. Start the interactive part of the lab. Insert your Tracking Disk if you want to save your QuickCheck results. Perform each of the lab steps as directed, and answer all of the lab QuickCheck questions. When you exit the lab, your answers are automatically graded and your results are displayed.

2. Using paper and pencil, manually convert the following decimal numbers into binary numbers. Your instructor might ask you to show the process that you used for each conversion.

   a. 100 b. 1,000 c. 256 d. 27
   e. 48 f. 112 g. 96 h. 1,024

3. Using paper and pencil, manually convert the following binary numbers into decimal numbers. Your instructor might ask you to show the process that you used for each conversion.

   a. 100 b. 101 c. 1100 d. 10101
   e. 1111 f. 10000 g. 1111000 h. 110110

4. Describe what is wrong with the following sequence:

   10 100 110 1000 1001 1100 1110 10000

5. What is the decimal equivalent of 2^0? 2^1? 2^8?

Section B
MICROPROCESSORS AND MEMORY

A typical computer ad contains a long list of specifications that describe a computer's components and capabilities (Figure 2-8.) Savvy shoppers must have a good understanding of these specifications, including their effect on the price of a computer system. Most computer specifications begin with the microprocessor type and speed. Computer manufacturers want consumers to think that faster is better, but is there a point at which you can pay for speed that you won't need?

Computer ads also contain information about a computer's memory capacity. Lots of memory can add hundreds of dollars to the cost of a computer. Consumers are right to ask, "How much RAM is enough?"

The microprocessor and memory are two of the most important components in a computer. To understand how they affect computer performance and price, it is handy to know a little bit about how they work. Along the way, you'll learn to decipher computer ad terminology, such as MHz, SDRAM, and cache.

FIGURE 2-8

A typical computer ad is sprinkled liberally with acronyms and computer jargon. In this section of the chapter, you'll learn how to decipher the microprocessor and memory specifications highlighted in yellow.

- **Intel Pentium 4 processor 2.53 GHz**
- **1 GB RDRAM (max. 2 GB)**
- **8 K L1 cache, 512 K L2 cache**
- **80 GB UltraATA-100 HD (5400 rpm)**
- **48 X Max CD-RW**
- **3.5" 1.44 MB floppy disk drive**
- **19" (18.0" vis.) 26 dp. monitor**
- **64 MB AGP graphics card**
- **Sound Blaster Live! PCI sound card**
- **Altec Lansing speakers**
- **U.S. Robotics 56 Kbps modem**
- **Mouse & keyboard**
- **Windows XP Home Edition**
- **External drive bays: 3 5.25" bays for diskette, tape, or CD drives; 1 3.5" bay for a floppy drive**
- **Internal drive bays: 2 HDD bays**
- **4 USB ports**
- **1 serial, 1 parallel port, and 1 video port**
- **1 network port (RJ45 connector)**
- **5 PCI slots and 1 AGP slot**
- **Home/small business software bundle**
- **3-year limited warranty**

MICROPROCESSOR BASICS

Exactly what is a microprocessor? A **microprocessor** (sometimes simply referred to as a "processor") is an integrated circuit designed to process instructions. It is the most important component of a computer, and usually the most expensive single component. Although a microprocessor is sometimes mistakenly referred to as "a computer on a chip," it can be more accurately described as "a CPU on a chip" because it contains—on a single chip—circuitry that performs essentially the same tasks as the central processing unit of a classic mainframe computer.

What does it look like? Looking inside a computer, you can usually identify the microprocessor because it is the largest chip on the motherboard, although it might be hidden under a cooling fan. Depending on the brand and model, a microprocessor might be housed in an SEC cartridge or in a square PGA, like those shown in Figure 2-6, earlier in the chapter on page 63.

Inside the chip carrier, a microprocessor is a very complex integrated circuit, containing as many as 300 million miniaturized electronic components. Some of these components are only 30 nanometers thick. A **nanometer** is one billionth of a meter. Thirty nanometers are about the thickness of three atoms. You could stack 5,000 of them, one on top of another, and they would be only the thickness of a single sheet of notebook paper! The miniaturized circuitry in a microprocessor is grouped into important functional areas, such as the ALU and the control unit.

The **ALU** (arithmetic logic unit) performs arithmetic operations, such as addition and subtraction. It also performs logical operations, such as comparing two numbers to see if they are the same. The ALU uses **registers** to hold data that is being processed, just as you use a mixing bowl to hold the ingredients for a batch of brownies. The microprocessor's **control unit** fetches each instruction, just as you get each ingredient out of a cupboard or the refrigerator. The computer loads data into the ALU's registers, just as you add all of the ingredients to the mixing bowl. Finally, the control unit gives the ALU the green light to begin processing, just as you flip the switch to your electric mixer to begin blending all of the brownie ingredients.

Where does the microprocessor get its instructions? The simple answer is that a microprocessor executes instructions that are provided by a computer program. However, a microprocessor can't follow just any instructions. A program that contains an instruction to "self destruct" won't have much effect because a microprocessor can perform only a limited list of instructions—"self destruct" isn't one of them.

The list of instructions that a microprocessor can perform is called its **instruction set**. These instructions are hard-wired into the processor's circuitry and include basic arithmetic and logical operations, fetching data, and clearing registers. A computer can perform very complex tasks, but it does so by performing a combination of simple tasks from its instruction set.

MICROPROCESSOR PERFORMANCE FACTORS

What makes one microprocessor perform better than another? The performance of a microprocessor is affected by several factors, including clock speed, word size, cache size, instruction set, and processing techniques.

What do MHz and GHz have to do with computer performance? The speed specifications that you see in a computer ad indicate the speed of the **microprocessor clock**—a timing device that sets the pace for executing instructions. Most computer ads specify the speed of a microprocessor in megahertz (MHz) or gigahertz (GHz). **Megahertz** means a million cycles per second. **Gigahertz** means a billion cycles per second.

A cycle is the smallest unit of time in a microprocessor's universe. Every action that a processor performs is measured by these cycles. It is important, however, to understand that the clock speed is not equal to the number of instructions that a processor can execute in one second. In many computers, some instructions occur within one cycle, but other instructions might require multiple cycles. Some processors can even execute several instructions in a single clock cycle.

A specification such as 2.53 GHz means that the microprocessor's clock operates at a speed of 2.53 billion cycles per second. All other things being equal, a computer with a 2.53 GHz processor is faster than a computer with a 1.5 GHz processor or a 933 MHz processor.

Which is faster, an 8-bit processor or a 64-bit processor? Word size refers to the number of bits that a microprocessor can manipulate at one time. Word size is based on the size of the registers in the ALU, and the capacity of circuits that lead to those registers. A microprocessor with an 8-bit word size, for example, has 8-bit registers, processes eight bits at a time, and is referred to as an "8-bit processor." Processors with a larger word size can process more data during each processor cycle, a factor that leads to increased computer performance. Today's personal computers typically contain 32-bit or 64-bit processors.

How does the cache size affect performance? Cache (pronounced "cash") is sometimes called "RAM cache" or "cache memory." It is special high-speed memory that allows a microprocessor to access data more rapidly than from memory located elsewhere on the motherboard. Some computer ads specify cache type and capacity. A **Level 1 cache** (L1) is built into the processor chip, whereas a **Level 2 cache** (L2) is located on a separate chip and takes a little more time to get data to the processor. Cache capacity is usually measured in kilobytes.

In theory, a large cache increases processing speed. In today's computers, however, cache size is usually tied to a particular processor brand and model. It is not of particular significance to consumers because cache is not configurable. For example, you can't add more L1 cache to your computer without replacing the microprocessor.

What's the difference between CISC and RISC? As chip designers developed various instruction sets for microprocessors, they tended to add increasingly more complex instructions that each required several clock cycles for execution. A microprocessor with such an instruction set uses **CISC** (complex instruction set computer) technology. A microprocessor with a limited set of simple instructions uses **RISC** (reduced instruction set computer) technology. A RISC processor performs most instructions faster than a CISC processor. It might, however, require more of these simple instructions to complete a task than a CISC processor requires for the same task.

In theory, a RISC processor should be faster than a CISC processor. In practice, CISC processors excel at some processing tasks, while RISC processors excel at others. Most of the processors in today's Macs use RISC technology; most PCs use CISC technology. In fact, it is the availability of specialized, multiple clock-cycle graphics processing instructions in your PC's microprocessor that makes computer games perform at dizzying speeds.

Can a microprocessor execute more than one instruction at a time? Some processors execute instructions "serially"—that is, one instruction at a time. With **serial processing**, the processor must complete all of the steps in the instruction cycle before it begins to execute the next instruction. However, using a technology called **pipelining**, a processor can begin executing an instruction before it completes the previous instruction. Many of today's microprocessors also perform **parallel processing**, in which multiple instructions are executed at the same time. Pipelining and parallel processing enhance processor performance.

To get a clearer picture of serial, pipelining, and parallel processing techniques, consider an analogy in which computer instructions are pizzas. Serial processing executes only one instruction at a time, just like a pizzeria with one oven that holds only one pizza. Pipelining is similar to a pizza conveyor belt. A pizza (instruction) starts moving along the conveyor belt, but before it reaches the end, another pizza starts moving along the belt. Parallel processing is similar to a pizzeria with many ovens. Just as these ovens can bake more than one pizza at a time, a parallel processor can execute more than one instruction at a time.

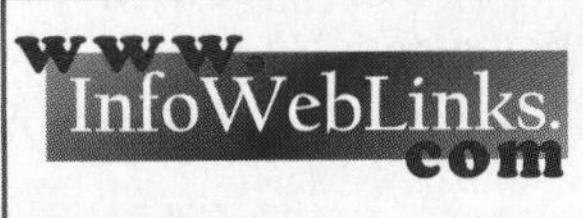

Test your own computer's performance by trying some of the tests at the Benchmark InfoWeb.

click

With so many factors to consider, how can I compare various microprocessors? Various testing laboratories run a series of tests to gauge the overall speed of a microprocessor. The results of these tests—called **benchmarks**—can then be compared to the results for other microprocessors. The results of benchmark tests are usually available on the Web, and are published in computer magazine articles.

What's the downside of hard disk storage? Hard disks are not as durable as many other storage technologies. The read-write heads in a hard disk hover a microscopic distance above the disk surface. If a read-write head runs into a dust particle or some other contaminant on the disk, it might cause what is called a **head crash**. A head crash damages some of the data on the disk. To help eliminate contaminants from contacting the platters and causing head crashes, a hard disk is sealed in its case. A head crash can also be triggered by jarring the hard disk while it is in use. Although hard disks have become considerably more rugged in recent years, you should still handle and transport them with care.

Can I use a second hard disk drive as a backup? Yes. Because of the ever-present possibility of a head crash, it is a good idea to make a backup copy of the data stored on your hard disk. One strategy is to use a second hard disk, which can be installed internally or connected externally. A more typical strategy is to use a removable hard disk, tape drive, or CD-writer. Other supplementary storage devices, such as RAID, are used in situations where data is critical.

Removable hard disks or hard disk cartridges contain platters and read-write heads that can be inserted and removed from the drive much like a floppy disk. Removable hard disks increase the potential storage capacity of your computer system, although the data is available on only one disk at a time. Removable hard disks also provide security for data by allowing you to remove the hard disk cartridge and store it separately from the computer.

A **RAID** (redundant array of independent disks) storage device contains many disk platters, provides redundancy, and achieves faster data access than conventional hard disks. The redundancy feature of RAID technology protects data from media failures by recording the same data on more than one disk platter. RAID is a popular option for mainframe and server storage, but is less popular for personal computers.

TAPE STORAGE

What's the purpose of a tape drive? New computers are rarely outfitted with a tape drive, which is a bit puzzling considering the fact that many experts consider it the best device for backing up data.

As you have learned in this chapter, hard disk data can be easily destroyed as a result of a head crash. Protecting the data on the hard disk is of particular concern because it contains so much data—data that would be difficult and time-consuming to reconstruct. A **tape backup** is a copy of the data on a hard disk, which is stored on magnetic tape and used to restore lost data. A tape backup is relatively inexpensive and can rescue you from the overwhelming task of trying to reconstruct lost data. If you have a tape backup of your hard disk, you can copy the data from the tape to any functional hard disk.

Despite its value as a backup device, a tape drive is not suitable for everyday storage tasks. To find out why, you need to understand how a tape drive works.

How does a tape drive work? A tape is a sequential, rather than a random-access, storage medium. Essentially, data is arranged as a long sequence of bits that begins at one end of the tape and stretches to the other end. The beginning and end of each file are marked with special "header labels." To locate a file, the tape drive must start at one end of the tape and read through all of the data until it finds the right header label. A tape may contain hundreds or—in the case of a mainframe—thousands of feet of tape. Access time is measured in slow seconds, not in milliseconds as for a hard disk drive.

Tape is simply too slow to be practical as your computer's main storage device. Its pokey nature doesn't, however, diminish its effectiveness as a backup device. When you make a backup, you're simply copying lots of data onto the tape. You don't need to locate specific data, or jump back and forth between different files. For a backup device, access time is less important than the time it takes to copy data from your hard disk to tape. Manufacturers do not always supply such performance specifications, but most users can expect a tape drive to back up 1 GB in 15-20 minutes. Chapter 4 provides more details on the process and equipment for making backups.

Is it easy to install a tape drive? Yes, and you should consider adding one to your computer system if it doesn't already include one. Tape drives are available in either internal or external models. An internal tape drive fits into a standard drive bay. An external model is a standalone device that you can tether to your computer with a cable. This model is preferred by notebook owners because it can be left at home and connected only when it is time to make a backup. Figure 2-20 shows several different kinds of tape used with personal computer tape drivers.

FIGURE 2-20

A tape cartridge is a removable magnetic tape module similar to a cassette tape. The most popular types of tape drives for personal computers use tape cartridges, but there are several tape specifications and cartridge sizes, including (from top to bottom) ADR (advanced digital recording), Ditto, Travan, and DDS (digital data storage). Check the tape drive manual to make sure that you purchase the correct type of tape for your tape drive.

CD TECHNOLOGY

Why would I want a CD-ROM drive in addition to a hard disk drive? Today, most computers come equipped with some type of optical drive—often a CD-ROM drive (sometimes called a "CD player"). CD-ROM (compact disc read-only memory, pronounced "cee dee rom") is based on the same technology as the audio CDs that contain your favorite music. A computer CD-ROM disk, like its audio counterpart, contains data that was stamped on the disk surface when it was manufactured.

Before CD-ROM drives became popular, and before software programs required megabytes of storage space, software manufacturers distributed software on floppy disks. Today, when you purchase software from a computer store, the box typically contains CDs. Therefore, unless you plan to download all of your new software from the Internet, your computer should have a CD drive so that you can install new software.

Furthermore, some software—particularly reference CDs and games—requires you to place the CD in the drive and leave it there while you use it. Without a CD drive, you would not be able to use this type of software.

What's the capacity and speed of a CD? CD-ROM technology provides storage capacity that far exceeds that of a floppy or Zip disk. A single CD-ROM disk holds up to 680 MB—equivalent to more than 300,000 pages of text. The surface of the disk is coated with a clear plastic, making the disk quite durable. Unlike magnetic media, a CD-ROM is not susceptible to humidity, fingerprints, dust, or magnets. If you spill coffee on a CD-ROM disk, you can just rinse it off and it will be as good as new. The useful life of a CD-ROM disk is estimated to exceed 500 years. Wow!

www.InfoWebLinks.com

For additional information about current CD and DVD technology, plus tips on how to handle and clean your CDs, connect to the CD & DVD InfoWeb.

click

Although a CD-ROM disk provides pretty good storage capacity, you can't store any of your own data on one. The "RO" in ROM means "read only." Your computer can read data from a CD-ROM, but cannot record or store data on it.

The original CD-ROM drives were able to access 150 KB of data per second. The next generation of drives doubled the data transfer rate and were consequently dubbed "2X" drives. Transfer rates seem to be continually increasing. A 24X CD-ROM drive, for example, would transfer data at a rate of 24 X 150 KB, or 3,600 KB per second. Refer to the CD & DVD InfoWeb for the latest specifications.

2

What's the difference between CD-ROM and ROM BIOS? Even though both contain the word "ROM," they refer to quite different technologies. As you should recall from earlier in the chapter, ROM BIOS refers to a chip on the motherboard that contains permanent instructions for the computer's boot sequence. A CD-ROM drive is an optical storage device that's usually installed in one of the system unit's drive bays. (See Figure 2-21.) To avoid confusion, a CD-ROM probably should have been called a "CD-ROS" for "read-only storage."

FIGURE 2-21

A CD-ROM drive is similar to a floppy disk drive, but uses a laser to read data, instead of a magnetized read-write head.

Drive spindle spins disk
Laser lens directs a beam of light to the underside of the CD-ROM disk
Laser pickup assembly senses the reflectivity of pits and lands
Tracking mechanism positions a disk track over the laser lens

Can I create my own CDs? Two CD-writer technologies called CD-R and CD-RW allow you to create your own CDs. A **CD-R** (compact disc recordable) drive records data on a special CD-R disk. The drive mechanism includes a laser that changes the reflectivity of a dye layer on a blank CD-R disk. As a result, the data on the disk is not actually stored in pits. Dark spots in the dye layer, however, play the same role as pits to represent data and allow the disks that you create to be read by not only a CD-R drive, but also by a standard CD-ROM drive or a DVD drive.

As with regular CD-ROM disks, the data on a CD-R cannot be erased or modified once you record it. However, most CD-R drives allow you to record your data in multiple sessions. For example, you can store two files on a CD-R disk today, then add the data for a few more files to the disk tomorrow.

CD-RW (compact disc rewritable) technology allows you to write data on a CD, then change that data at a later time. The process requires special CD-RW disks and a CD-RW drive, which uses **phase change technology** to alter the crystal structure on the disk surface. Altering the crystal structure creates patterns of light and dark spots similar to the pits and lands on a CD-ROM disk. The crystal structure can be changed from light to dark and back again many times, making it possible to record and modify data much like on a hard disk.

Is CD-RW a viable replacement for a hard disk? Unfortunately, the process of accessing, saving, and modifying data on a CD-RW disk is relatively slow compared to the speed of hard disk access. Therefore, CD-RW is a fine addition to a computer system, but is not a good replacement for a hard disk drive. Both CD-R and CD-RW technologies are quite useful for creating music CDs, storing graphics files, making backups, archiving data, and distributing large files. **Archiving** refers to the process of moving data off a primary storage device when that data is not accessed frequently. For example, a business might archive its accounting data for previous years, or a hospital might archive billing records once the accounts are paid. Archived data does not generally change, so even a CD-R is suitable. If you have some large files, such as photos or videos that you want to send to friends, clients, or colleagues, you can create a CD using either a CD-R or CD-RW drive. You might have a little better luck with a CD-R drive, however, because some optical devices tend to have trouble reading the data that's been stored on a CD-RW disk.

DVD TECHNOLOGY

How is DVD different from CD technology? DVD ("digital video disc" or "digital versatile disk") is a variation of CD technology that was originally designed as an alternative to VCRs, but was quickly adopted by the computer industry to store data. A computer's DVD drive can read disks that contain computer data (often called **DVD-ROM** disks), as well as disks that contain DVD movies (sometimes called **DVD-Video** disks).

Originally designed to provide enough storage capacity for a full-length movie, a DVD holds much more data than a CD—about 4.7 GB (4,700 MB) on a DVD compared with 680 MB on a CD-ROM. Like a CD-ROM disk, a DVD-ROM disk is stamped with data at the time of manufacture. The data on these disks is permanent, so you cannot add or change data.

The speed of a DVD drive is measured on a different scale than a CD drive. A 1X DVD drive is about the same speed as a 9X CD drive. The table in Figure 2-22 provides additional speed equivalents.

FIGURE 2-22 DVD and CD Drive Speed Comparison

DVD Drive Speed	Data Transfer Rate	CD Speed
1X	11.08 Mbps	9X
2X	22.16 Mbps	18X
4X	44.32 Mbps	36X
5X	55.40 Mbps	46X

Is my computer DVD drive the same as the one that's connected to my television set? Not exactly. Even with the large storage capacity of a DVD, movie files are much too large to fit on a disk unless they are compressed, or shrunk, using a special type of data coding called MPEG-2. The DVD player that you connect to your television includes MPEG decoding circuitry, which is not included on your computer's DVD drive. When you play DVD movies on your computer, it uses the CPU as an MPEG decoder. The necessary decoder software is included with Windows, or can be located on the DVD itself.

Are CDs and DVDs interchangeable? If you have to choose between a CD-ROM drive and a DVD drive, go with DVD. You cannot play DVDs on your CD-ROM drive, but you can play CD-ROM, most CD-R, and most CD-RW disks on your DVD drive.

Is there a DVD equivalent to CD-RW? DVD manufacturers have introduced several competing technologies that make it possible to write data on DVD disks. All of these technologies can read DVD-ROM and DVD-Video discs, but each uses a different type of disk for recording. DVD-R can record data once, uses a disk medium that's very similar to CD-R technology, and can be read by most DVD drives and players. Read/write formats include **DVD-RAM**, **DVD-RW**, and **DVD+RW**, which can be rewritten hundreds of times. Disks written with these devices can always be read by the same type of device that created them. Reading them with other devices might sometimes be a problem, however. Most experts predict that eventually today's multiple CD and DVD devices will be replaced by a single DVD device that reads CDs and DVD-ROMs, plays DVD movies, and writes DVDs that can be read by any other DVD device.

2

QUICKCheck Section C

1. Data on an optical storage medium is stored as ________ and lands.
2. ________ time is the average time that it takes a computer to locate data on a storage medium and read it.
3. A computer can move directly to any file on a(n) ________ access device, but must start at the beginning and read through all of the data on a(n) ________ access device.
4. Higher disk ________ provides increased storage capacity.
5. "HD DS" means "hard disk double-sided." True or false? ________
6. EIDE, Ultra ATA, and SCSI refer to the type of ________ used by a hard disk drive.
7. CD-R technology allows you to write data on a disk, then change that data. True or false? ________
8. A(n) ________ drive stores 4.7 GB on a disk, but does not allow you to change the data once it has been stored.

check answers

Section D INPUT AND OUTPUT DEVICES

Some computer manufacturers and retailers bundle a monitor, printer, and other peripheral devices with new computers. Are these bundles a good value? Typically, the cost of the bundle is less than purchasing everything separately, but the real value of the bundle depends on your computing needs.

Even after you purchase a computer, you can be fairly certain that you will want to add more equipment to expand or update its capabilities. How can you tell which peripheral devices are compatible with your computer? How do you install them and get them to work?

In this part of the chapter, you'll get a general overview of the computer's expansion bus—the components in a computer that carry data to peripheral devices. With that knowledge in hand, you'll be able to select, install, and use all kinds of peripherals. The section ends with a look at two of the most popular categories of peripherals: display devices and printers. You'll learn about other peripherals as they fit into the topics discussed in later chapters.

EXPANSION SLOTS, CARDS, AND PORTS

How does a computer get data from RAM to a peripheral device? Within a computer, data travels from one component to another over circuits called a **data bus**. One part of the data bus runs between RAM and the microprocessor. Another part of the data bus runs between RAM and various storage devices. The segment of the data bus that extends between RAM and peripheral devices is called the **expansion bus**. As data moves along the expansion bus, it may travel through expansion slots, cards, ports, and cables.

FIGURE 2-23
An expansion card simply slides into an expansion slot, then it can be secured with a small screw.

click to start

What's an expansion slot? An **expansion slot** is a long, narrow socket on the motherboard into which you can plug an expansion card. An **expansion card** is a small circuit board that provides a computer with the ability to control a storage device, an input device, or an output device. Expansion cards are also called "expansion boards," "controller cards," or "adapters." Figure 2-23 shows how to plug an expansion card into an expansion slot.

Most desktop computers have four to eight expansion slots, but some of the slots usually contain expansion cards. A graphics card (sometimes called a "video card") provides a path for data traveling to the monitor. A modem provides a way to transmit data over phone lines or cable television lines. A sound

tion to their high cost, LCD monitors have a limited viewing angle. The brightness and color tones that you see depend on the angle from which you view the screen because of the way that light reflects off the LCD elements. For this reason, graphic artists prefer CRT technology, which displays uniform color from any viewing angle.

Which display device produces the best image? Image quality is a factor of screen size, dot pitch, resolution, and color depth. Screen size is the measurement in inches from one corner of the screen diagonally across to the opposite corner. Typical monitor screen sizes range from 13" to 21". On most monitors, the viewable image does not stretch to the edge of the screen. Instead, a black border makes the image smaller than the size specified. Many computer ads now include a measurement of the **viewable image size** (vis). A 15" monitor has an approximately 13.9" vis. **Dot pitch** (dp) is a measure of image clarity. A smaller dot pitch means a crisper image. Technically, dot pitch is the distance in millimeters between like-colored **pixels**—the small dots of light that form an image. A dot pitch between .26 and .23 is typical for today's monitors.

Your computer's graphics card sends an image to the monitor at a specific **resolution**, defined as the maximum number of horizontal and vertical pixels that are displayed on the screen. The standard for many of the earliest PC graphics cards was called **VGA** (Video Graphics Array), which provided a resolution of 640 x 480. A succession of graphics card standards allowed higher resolutions. **SVGA** (Super VGA) provides 800 x 600 resolution, **XGA** (eXtended Graphics Array) provides 1024 x 768 resolution, **SXGA** (super XGA) provides 1280 x 1024 resolution, and **UXGA** (Ultra XGA) provides up to 1600 x 1200 resolution.

At higher resolutions, text and other objects appear smaller, but the computer can display a larger work area, such as an entire page of a document. The two screen shots in Figure 2-28 help you compare a display set at 640 x 480 resolution with a display set at 1024 x 768 resolution.

FIGURE 2-28

The upper-left screen shows a computer display set at 1024 x 768 resolution. Notice the size of text and other screen-based objects. The lower-right screen shows 640 x 480 resolution. Text and other objects appear larger than on the high-resolution screen, but you see a smaller portion of the screen-based desktop.

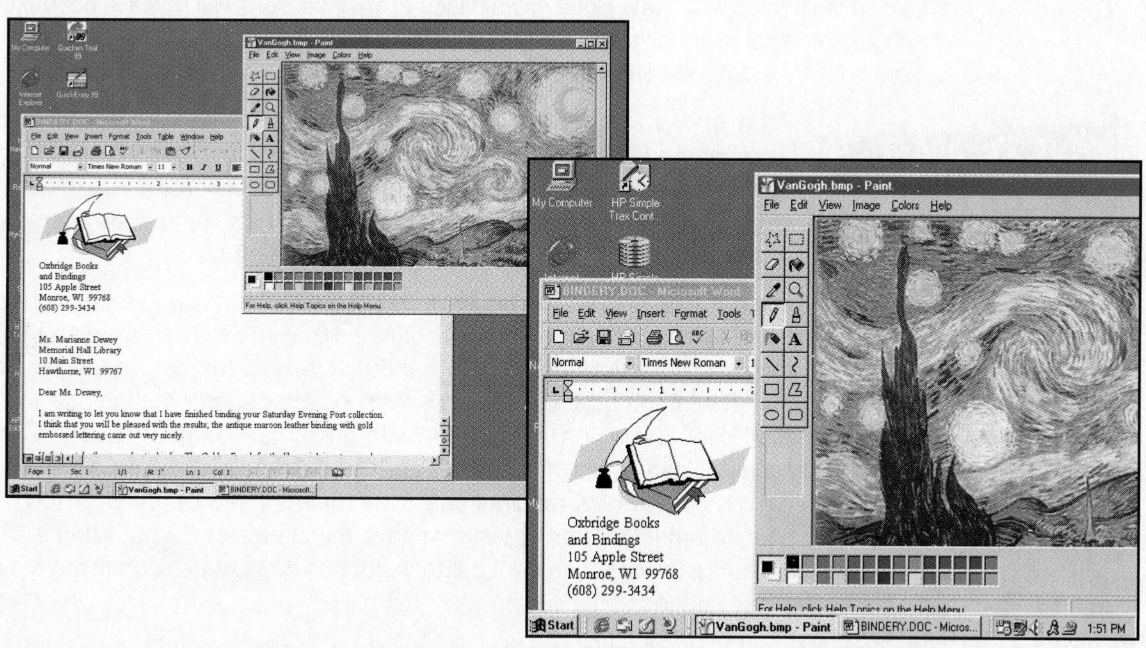

The number of colors that a monitor and graphics card can display is referred to as **color depth** or "bit depth." Most PCs have the capability to display millions of colors. When set at 24-bit color depth (sometimes called "True Color") your PC can display more than 16 million colors—and produce what are considered to be photographic-quality images. Windows allows you to select resolution and color depth. Most desktop owners choose 24-bit color at 1024 x 768 resolution.

What about notebook computer display systems? Many older notebooks had passive matrix screens, sometimes referred to as "dual-scan." A **passive matrix screen** relies on timing to make sure the liquid crystal cells are illuminated. As a result, the process of updating the screen image does not always keep up with moving images, and the display can appear blurred. Newer notebooks feature an **active matrix screen**, sometimes referred to as "TFT" (thin film transistor), which updates rapidly and is essential for a crisp display of animations and video.

Although you can set the color depth and resolution of your notebook computer display, you might not have as many options as with a desktop computer. LCD displays look their best at their "native resolution"—the resolution that is set by the computer's manufacturer. While a notebook might allow you to change to a different resolution, images and characters tend to appear grainy or blurry.

Typically, graphics card circuitry is built into the motherboard of a notebook computer, making it difficult to upgrade and gain more video memory for additional resolution and color depth. Inexpensive notebook computers, which feature VGA displays, provide a maximum resolution of 640 x 480. Mid-priced notebooks typically feature SVGA displays. More expensive notebooks feature XGA, SXGA, or UXGA displays.

PRINTERS

What features should I look for in a printer? Today's printer technologies include ink jet, solid ink, thermal transfer, dye sublimation, laser, and dot matrix. These printers differ in resolution and speed, which affect the print quality and price.

Resolution. The quality or sharpness of printed images and text depends on the printer's resolution—the density of the gridwork of dots that create an image. Printer resolution is measured by the number of dots it can print per linear inch, abbreviated as dpi. At normal reading distance, a resolution of about 900 dots per inch appears solid to the human eye, but a close examination of color sections will reveal a dot pattern. Although 900 dpi might be considered sufficient for some magazines, expensive coffee-table books are typically produced on printers with 2,400 dpi or higher.

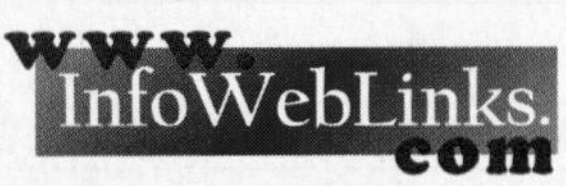

Before you shop for a printer, take a look at the buying tips listed at the Printer Buyer's Guide InfoWeb.

click

Print speed. Printer speeds are measured either by pages per minute (ppm) or characters per second (cps). Color printouts typically take longer than black-and-white printouts. Pages that contain mostly text tend to print more rapidly than pages that contain graphics. Ten pages per minute is a typical speed for a personal computer printer.

What's the most popular type of printer? Ink jet printers outsell all of the others because they print in color and they are inexpensive. An **ink jet printer** has a nozzle-like print head that sprays ink onto paper to form characters and graphics. Today's most popular printer technology, ink jet printers produce low-cost color or black-and-white printouts. The print head in a color ink jet printer consists of a series of nozzles, each with its own ink cartridge. Most ink jet printers use CMYK color, which requires only cyan (blue), magenta (pink), yellow, and black inks to create a printout that appears to have thousands of colors. Alternatively, some printers use six ink colors to print midtone shades that create slightly more realistic photographic images.

Operating costs for an ink jet printer are reasonable. You must periodically replace the black ink cartridge and a second cartridge that carries the colored inks. Each replacement ink cartridge costs between $25 and $35. Under realistic use, the cost for color printing will be between 5 and 15 cents per page. A potential hidden cost of operating an ink jet printer is special paper. Although you can satisfactorily print documents with small graphics and line art on the same type of inexpensive paper that you might use in a photocopier, photo printouts look best on special paper that can cost between $0.08 and $1.50 per sheet. Typically, this special paper has a super-smooth finish that prevents the ink from bleeding and creating dull colors.

Today's ink jet printers (Figure 2-29) have excellent resolution, which can range from 600 dpi to 2,880 dpi, depending on the model. If you want camera-store quality when printing photographic images, you need a printer with high resolution. Some ink jet printers can produce ultra-high resolution by making multiple passes over the paper. Although it might seem logical that this technique would slow down the printing process, multiple-pass ink jet printers produce a respectable five pages per minute.

FIGURE 2-29

Most ink jet printers are small, lightweight, and inexpensive, yet produce very good quality color output.

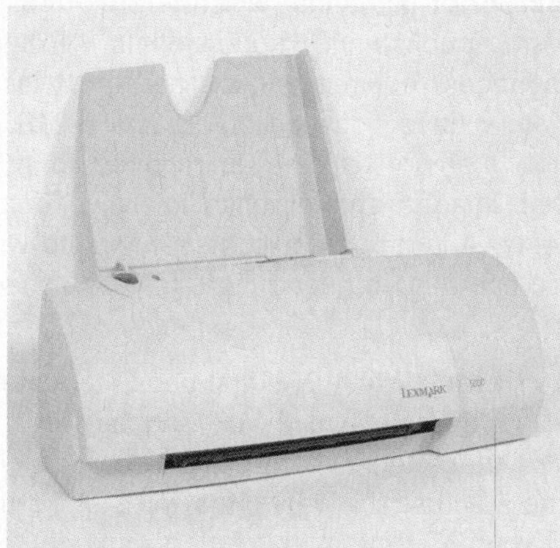

What's the difference between an ink jet printer and a solid ink printer? A **solid ink printer** melts sticks of crayon-like ink and then sprays the liquefied ink through the print head's tiny nozzles. The ink solidifies before it can be absorbed by the paper, and a pair of rollers finishes fusing the ink onto the paper. A solid ink printer produces vibrant colors on most types of paper, so unlike an ink jet printer, it does not require special, expensive paper to produce photographic-quality images.

What about thermal wax transfer and dye sublimation printers? A **thermal transfer printer** uses a page-sized ribbon that is coated with cyan, magenta, yellow, and black wax. The print head consists of thousands of tiny heating elements that melt the wax onto specially coated paper or transparency film (the kind that's used for overhead projectors). This type of printer excels at printing colorful transparencies for presentations, but the fairly expensive per-page costs and the requirement for special paper make this a niche market printer used mainly by businesses.

A **dye sublimation printer** uses technology similar to wax transfer. The difference is that the page-sized ribbon contains dye instead of colored wax. Heating elements in the print head diffuse the dye onto the surface of specially coated paper. Dye sublimation printers produce excellent color quality—perhaps the best of any printer technology. At $3 to $4 per page, however, these printers are a bit pricey for most personal computer owners.

Is a laser better than an ink jet? A **laser printer** uses the same technology as a photocopier to paint dots of light on a light-sensitive drum. Electrostatically charged ink is applied to the drum, then transferred to paper.

As with other printer technologies, print speed and resolution will be key factors in your purchase decision. Personal laser printers produce six to eight ppm (pages per minute) at a resolution of 600 dpi. Professional models pump out 15 to 25 ppm at 1,200 dpi. A personal laser printer has a duty cycle of about 3,000 pages per month—that means roughly 100 pages per day. You wouldn't want to use it to produce 5,000 campaign brochures for next Monday, but you would find it quite suitable for printing 10 copies of a five-page outline for a meeting tomorrow.

FIGURE 2-30

Laser printers are a popular technology for situations that require high-volume output or good quality printouts.

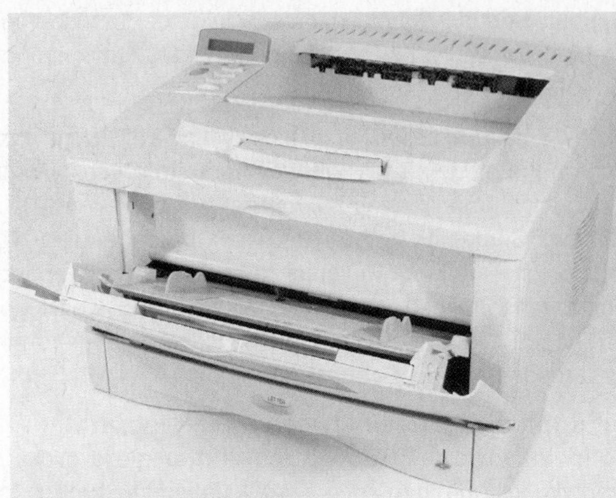

click to start

Some people are surprised to discover that laser printers are less expensive to operate than ink jet printers. On average, you can expect to pay about 2 cents per page for black-and-white laser printing. This per-page cost includes periodically replacing the toner cartridge and drum.

Laser printers (Figure 2-30) accept print commands from a personal computer, but use their own printer language to construct a page before printing it. **Printer Control Language** (PCL) is the most widely used printer language, but some printers use the **PostScript** language, which is preferred by many publishing professionals. Printer languages require memory, and most laser printers have between 2 MB and 8 MB. A large memory capacity is required to print color images and graphics-intensive documents. A laser printer comes equipped with enough memory for typical print jobs. If you find that you need more memory, check the printer documentation for information.

Why would anyone want a dot matrix printer? When PCs first began to appear in the late 1970s, dot matrix printers were the technology of choice, and they are still available today. A **dot matrix printer** produces characters and graphics by using a grid of fine wires. As the print head noisily clatters across the paper, the wires strike the ribbon and paper in a pattern prescribed by your PC. Dot matrix printers can print text and graphics—some even print in color using a multicolored ribbon.

With a resolution of 140 dpi, a dot matrix printer produces low-quality output with clearly discernible dots forming letters and graphics. Dot matrix speed is typically measured in characters per second (cps). A fast dot matrix device can print at speeds up to 455 cps—about five pages per minute. Today, dot matrix printers, like the one in Figure 2-31, are used primarily for "back-office" applications that demand low operating cost and dependability, but not high print quality. A $4 ribbon can print more than 3 million characters before it must be replaced.

FIGURE 2-31

A dot matrix printer uses a grid of thin wires to strike a ribbon and create an image on paper. Unlike laser and ink jet technologies, a dot matrix printer actually strikes the paper and, therefore, can print multipart carbon forms.

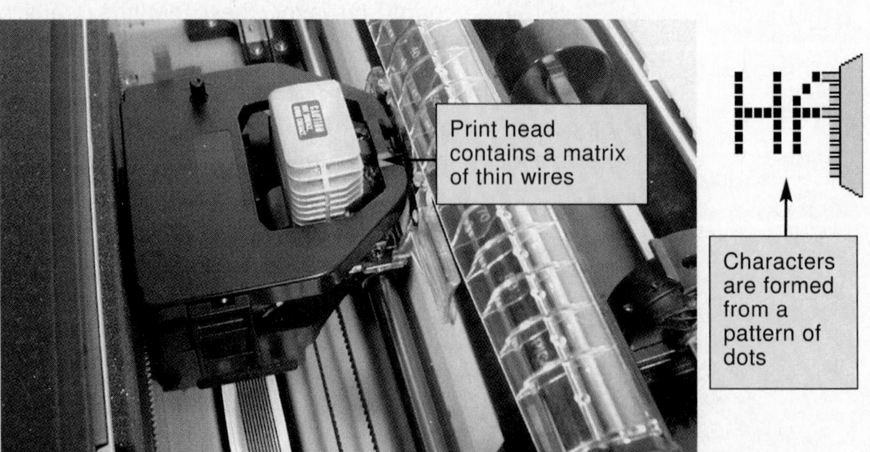
Print head contains a matrix of thin wires
Characters are formed from a pattern of dots

Currently, taxpayers pick up the tab for electronic waste disposal through municipal trash pick-up fees or local taxes. But is this approach fair to individual taxpayers who generate very little electronic waste?

To make consumers responsible for the cost of recycling the products that they buy, some lawmakers suggest adding a special recycling tax to computers and other electronic devices. A proposal in South Carolina, for example, would impose a $5 fee on the sale of each piece of electronic equipment containing a CRT, and require the state treasurer to deposit the fees into a recycling fund for electronic equipment.

Other lawmakers propose to make manufacturers responsible for recycling costs and logistics. "Extended producer responsibility" refers to the idea of holding manufacturers responsible for the environmental effects of their products through the entire product life cycle, which includes taking them back, recycling them, or disposing of them. Proposed legislation in Europe would require manufacturers to accept returns of their old equipment free of charge, then take appropriate steps to recycle it. The economics of a mandatory take-back program are likely to increase the costs of products because manufacturers would typically pass on recycling costs to consumers.

www.InfoWebLinks.com

You'll find much more information about how you can recycle an old computer at the Computer Recycling InfoWeb.

click

Some companies currently participate in voluntary extended producer responsibility programs. Hewlett-Packard, Dell, 3M, Apple, Nokia, IBM, Sony, Gateway, and Xerox, for example, provide recycling options for some products and components. Sony recently implemented a takeback program in Minnesota that allows residents to recycle all Sony products at no cost for the next five years. Using IBM's PC Recycling Service you can ship any make of computer including system units, monitors, printers, and optional attachments, to a recycling center for $29.99. Such programs are important steps in the effort to keep our planet green.

WHAT DO YOU THINK?

1. Have you ever thrown away an old computer or other electronic device? ○ Yes ○ No ○ Not sure
2. Are you aware of any options for recycling electronic equipment in your local area? ○ Yes ○ No ○ Not sure
3. Would it be fair for consumers to pay a recycling tax on any electronic equipment that they purchase? ○ Yes ○ No ○ Not sure

click to save your responses

INTERACTIVE SUMMARY

The Interactive Summary helps you to review important concepts from this chapter. Fill in the blanks to best complete each sentence. When using the NP6 BookOnCD, you can click the Check Answers buttons to automatically score your answers. Place your Tracking Disk in the floppy disk drive if you want to save your scores.

Most of today's computers are electronic, digital devices that work with data coded as binary digits, also known as ________. To represent numeric data, a computer can use the ________ number system. To represent character data, a computer uses ________, EBCDIC, or Unicode. These codes also provide digital representations for the numerals 0 through 9 that are distinguished from numbers by the fact that they are not typically used in mathematical operations. Computers also ________ sounds, pictures, and videos into 1s and 0s.

A ________ is a single 1 or 0, whereas a ________ is a sequence of eight 1s and 0s. Transmission speeds are usually measured in ________, but storage space is usually measured in ________ or gigabytes. In the context of computing, the prefix "kilo" means exactly 1,024. Kb stands for ________, while the abbreviation KB stands for ________. The prefix ________ means precisely 1,048,576, or about 1 million. The prefix "giga" means about 1 billion; "tera" means about 1 trillion; and "exa" means about 1 quintillion.

The terms "computer chip," "microchip," and "chip" originated as techie jargon for ________ circuits. These chips are made from a super-thin slice of semiconducting material and are packed with millions of microscopic circuit elements. In a computer, these chips include the ________, memory modules, and other support circuitry. They are housed on a large circuit board inside of the computer's system unit called the ________.

check answers

The microprocessor and memory are two of the most important components in a computer. The microprocessor is an ________ circuit, which is designed to process data, based on a set of instructions. Its miniaturized circuitry is grouped into important functional areas. The ________ unit performs arithmetic and logical operations. The ________ unit fetches each instruction, interprets it, loads data into the ALU's registers, and directs all of the processing activities within the microprocessor. In computer ads, microprocessor performance is usually measured in megahertz or ________—the number of cycles per second, or clock rate. Other factors affecting overall processing speed include word size, cache size, instruction set complexity, parallel processing, and pipelining.

RAM is a special holding area for data, program instructions, and the ________ system. It stores data on a temporary basis while it waits to be processed. In most computers, RAM is composed of integrated circuits called ________ or RDRAM. The speed of RAM circuitry is measured in ________ or in megahertz (MHz). RAM is different from disk storage because it is ________, which means that it can only hold data when the computer power is turned on. Computers also contain ________, which is a type of memory that provides a set of "hard-wired" instructions that a computer uses to boot up. A third type of memory, called ________, is battery powered and contains configuration settings.

check answers 

Is the data that I create classified as software? "Software" is a slippery term. In the early days of the computer industry, it became popular to use the term "software" for all non-hardware components of a computer. In this context, software referred to computer programs and to the data used by the programs. It could also refer to any data that existed in digital format, such as documents or photos. Using today's terminology, however, the documents and photos that you create are usually classified as "data" rather than as "software."

Why does software require so many files? You might be surprised by the number of files that are necessary to make software work. Most software packages, like the one in Figure 3-2, include at least one user-executable program plus several support programs and data files.

FIGURE 3-2

The files required by the VideoFactory software contain user-executable programs, support programs, and data.

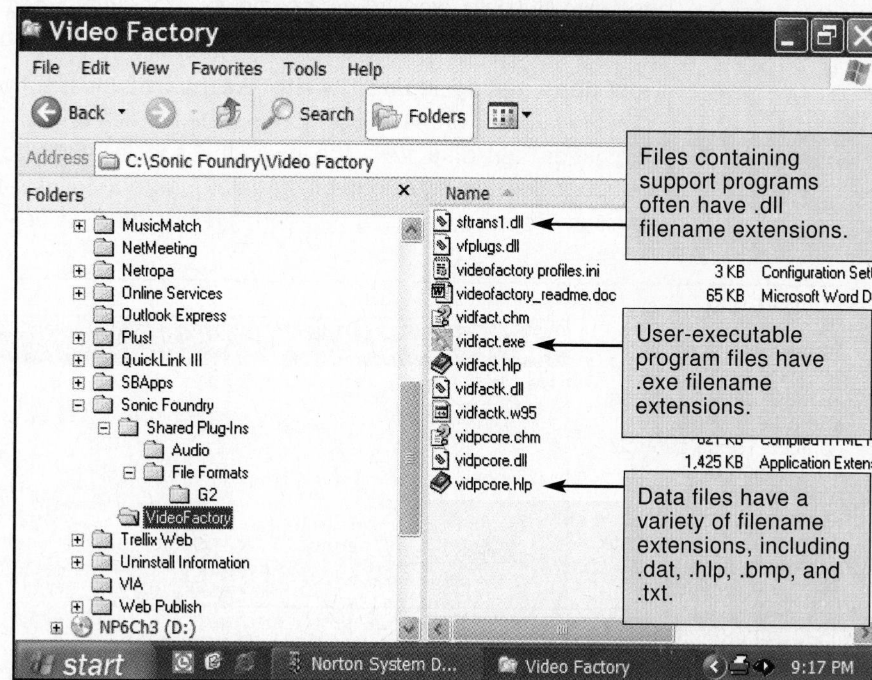

The use of a main user-executable file plus several support programs and data files provides a great deal of flexibility and efficiency for programmers. Support programs and data files can usually be modified without changing the main executable file. This modular approach can save programmers many hours of programming and testing within the main executable file, which is usually long and fairly complex. The modular approach also allows programmers to reuse their support programs and adapt preprogrammed support modules for use in their own software.

Modular programming techniques would be of only passing interest to people who use computer programs, except for the fact that such techniques affect the process of installing and uninstalling software, discussed later in this section. It is important, therefore, to remember that computer software typically consists of many files that contain user-executable programs, support programs, and data.

3

PROGRAMMERS AND PROGRAMMING LANGUAGES

Who creates computer software? Computer programmers write the instructions for the computer programs that become the components of a computer software product. The finished software product is then distributed by the programmers themselves, or by **software publishers**—companies that specialize in packaging, marketing, and selling commercial software.

At one time, businesses, organizations, and individuals had to write most of the software that they wanted to use. Today, however, most businesses and organizations purchase commercial software (sometimes referred to as "off-the-shelf software") to avoid the time and expense of writing their own. Individuals rarely write software for their personal computers, preferring to select from thousands of software titles available in stores, from catalogs, and on the Internet. Although most computer owners do not write their own software, working as a computer programmer and writing software for a government agency, business, or software publisher can be a challenging career.

How does a programmer "write" software? Most software is designed to provide a task-related environment, which includes a screen display, a means of collecting commands and data from the user, the specifications for processing data, and a method for displaying or outputting data. Figure 3-3 illustrates a very simple software environment that converts a Fahrenheit temperature to Celsius and displays the result.

FIGURE 3-3

Today's graphical software environments include menus, buttons, and other control objects. These controls are defined by a programmer, who designates their properties. For example, one of the properties of the Convert button specifies how to convert Fahrenheit temperatures to Celsius.

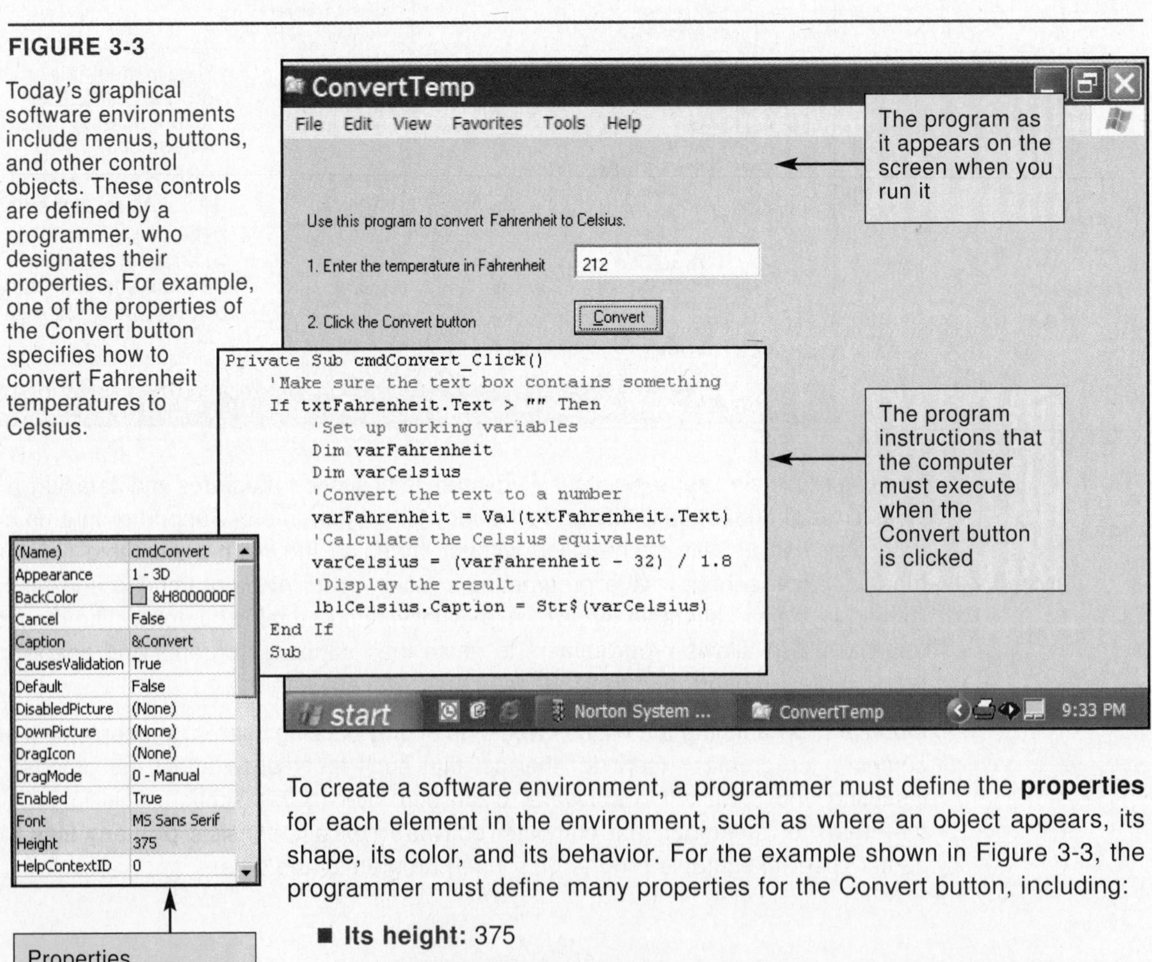

To create a software environment, a programmer must define the **properties** for each element in the environment, such as where an object appears, its shape, its color, and its behavior. For the example shown in Figure 3-3, the programmer must define many properties for the Convert button, including:

- **Its height:** 375
- **Its label (caption):** Convert
- **What happens when you click it:** Subtract 32 from Fahrenheit, divide by 1.8, and then display the answer

A **programming language** (sometimes referred to as a "computer language") provides the tools that a programmer uses to create software and produce a lengthy list of instructions, called **source code**, that defines the software environment in every detail—how it looks, how the user enters commands, and how it manipulates data. Most programmers today prefer to use **high-level languages**, such as C++, Java, COBOL, and Visual Basic, which have some similarities to human languages, and produce programs that are fairly easy to test and modify.

HOW SOFTWARE WORKS

How does a high-level language relate to the microprocessor's instruction set? A computer's microprocessor only understands **machine language**—the instruction set that is "hard wired" within the microprocessor's circuits. Therefore, instructions written in a high-level language must be translated into machine language before a computer can use them. Figure 3-4 gives you an idea of what happens to a high-level instruction when it is converted into machine language instructions.

FIGURE 3-4

High-level Language Instruction	Machine Language Equivalent	Description of Machine Language Instructions
Answer = FirstNumber + SecondNumber	10001000 00011000 010000000	Load FirstNumber into Register 1
	10001000 00010000 00100000	Load SecondNumber into Register 2
	00000000 00011000 00010000	Perform ADD operation
	10100010 00111000	Move the number from the accumulator to the RAM location called Answer

3

The process of translating instructions from a high-level language into machine language can be accomplished by two special types of programs: compilers and interpreters. A **compiler** translates all of the instructions in a program as a single batch, and the resulting machine language instructions, called **object code**, are placed in a new file (see Figure 3-5). Most of the program files that you receive on the distribution CD for commercial software are compiled so that they contain machine language instructions that are ready for the processor to execute.

FIGURE 3-5

A compiler converts high-level instructions into a new file containing machine language instructions.

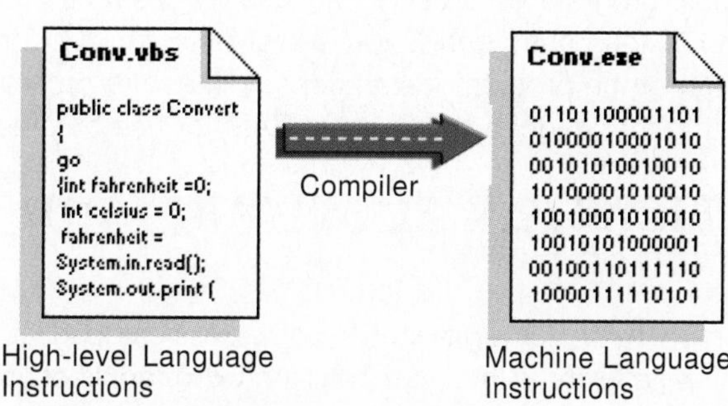

As an alternative to a compiler, an **interpreter** converts one instruction at a time while the program is running. This method of converting high-level instructions into machine language is more common with Web-based programs called **scripts**, written in languages such as JavaScript and VBScript. These scripts contain high-level instructions, which arrive as part of a Web page. An interpreter reads the first instruction in a script, converts it into machine language, and then sends it to the microprocessor. After the instruction is executed, the interpreter converts the next instruction, and so on (see Figure 3-6).

FIGURE 3-6

An interpreter converts high-level instructions into machine language instructions while the program is running.

An interpreted program runs more slowly than a compiled program because the translation process happens while the program is running.

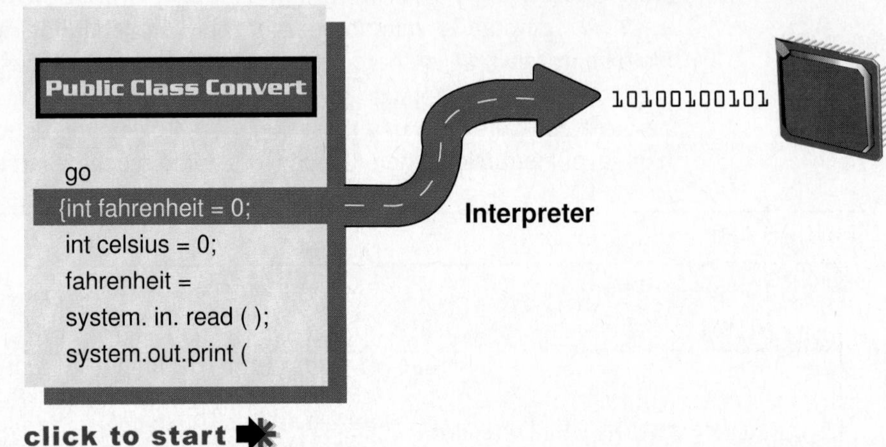
Public Class Convert
go
{int fahrenheit = 0;
int celsius = 0;
fahrenheit =
system. in. read ( );
system.out.print (
10100100101
Interpreter

click to start

To run a script, your computer must have the corresponding interpreter program. These programs are typically supplied with Web browser software, or are available as downloads from the Web.

So how does software work? Let's assume that a video editing program, such as VideoFactory, was installed on your computer, which is running Windows. You click the Start button, then select VideoFactory from the Programs menu. Your selection activates the main executable file called *Vidfact.exe*, which exists in compiled format on your computer's hard disk. The instructions for this program are loaded into RAM and then sent to the microprocessor. As processing begins, the VideoFactory window opens and the graphical controls for video editing tasks appear. The program waits for you to select a control by clicking it with the mouse. Based on your selection, the program follows its instructions and performs a specified action. Many of the instructions for these actions are included in the main executable file, but it might be necessary to call a support program in order to access its instructions. The program continues to respond to the controls that you select until you click the Close button, which halts execution of the program instructions, closes the program window, and releases the space that the program occupied in RAM for use by other programs or data.

APPLICATION SOFTWARE AND SYSTEM SOFTWARE

How is software categorized? Software is categorized as either application software or system software. When you hear the word "application," your first reaction might be to envision a financial aid application, or some other form that you would fill out to apply for a job, a club membership, or a driver's license. The word "application" has other meanings, however. One of them is a synonym for the word "use." A computer certainly has many uses, such as creating documents, crunching numbers, drawing designs, and editing photographs. Each of these uses is considered an "application," and the software that provides the computer with instructions for each of these uses is called **application software**, or simply an "application." The primary purpose of application software is to help people carry out tasks using a computer.

In contrast, the primary purpose of **system software**—your computer's operating system, device drivers, and utilities—is to help the computer carry out its basic operating functions. Figure 3-7 illustrates the division between system software and application software. You'll learn more about these software categories in Sections B and C.

FIGURE 3-7

Software can be classified into categories.

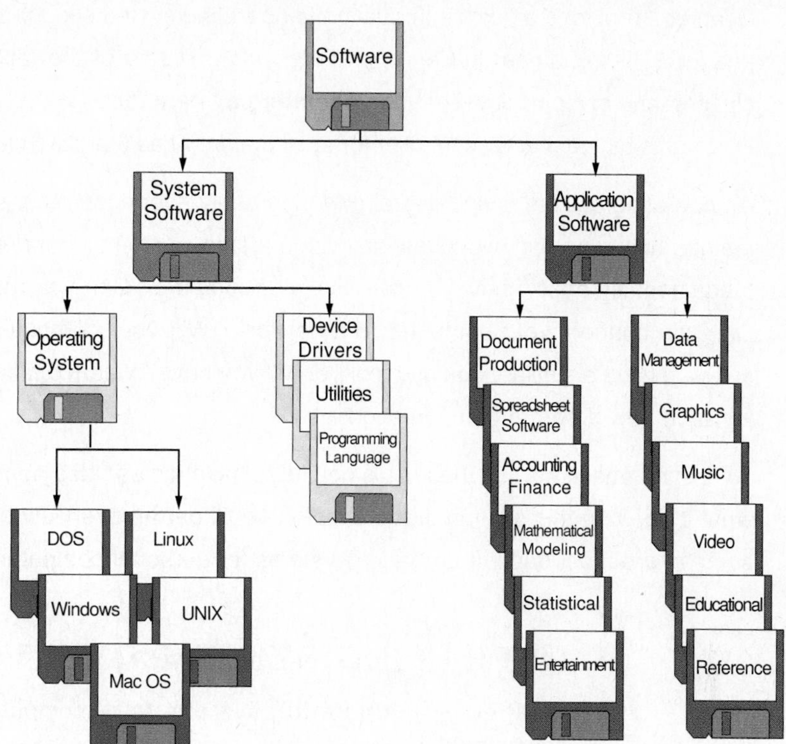

QUICKCheck Section A

1. Software usually contains support programs and data files, in addition to a user-[ ] file that you run to start the software.
2. To create a software environment, a programmer must define the [ ] for each element in the environment.
3. Instructions that are written in a [ ]-level language must be translated into [ ] language before a computer can use them.
4. A(n) [ ] translates all of the instructions in a program as a single batch, and the resulting machine language instructions are placed in a new file.
5. Software can be divided into two major categories: application software and [ ] software.

check answers

Section B PERSONAL COMPUTER OPERATING SYSTEMS

Chapter 1 provided a quick introduction to operating systems, such as Windows, Mac OS, Linux, UNIX, and DOS. It explained that an operating system is one of the factors that determines a computer's platform and compatibility. The term **operating system** (abbreviated OS) is defined as system software, which acts as the master controller for all of the activities that take place within a computer system.

An operating system is an integral part of virtually every computer system, including supercomputers, mainframes, servers, workstations, video game systems, handhelds, and personal computers. It fundamentally affects how you can use your computer. Can you run two programs at the same time? Can you connect your computer to a network? Will your computer run dependably? Will all of your software have a similar "look and feel," or will you have to learn a different set of controls and commands for each new program that you acquire?

To answer questions like these, it is helpful to have a clear idea about what an operating system is and what it does. In this section of the chapter, you'll get an overview of operating systems, and compare some of the most popular operating systems for personal computers.

OPERATING SYSTEM OVERVIEW

What does an operating system do? A computer's software is similar to the chain of command in an army. You issue a command using application software. Application software tells the operating system what to do. The operating system tells the device drivers, device drivers tell the hardware, and the hardware actually does the work. Figure 3-8 illustrates this chain of command for printing a document or photo.

FIGURE 3-8

Your command to print a document is relayed through various levels of software, including the operating system, until it reaches the printer.

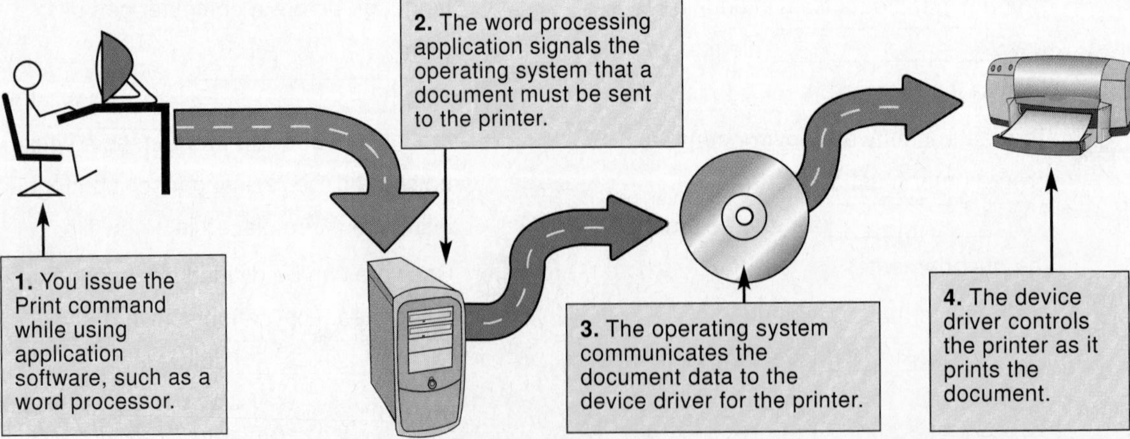

2. The word processing application signals the operating system that a document must be sent to the printer.
1. You issue the Print command while using application software, such as a word processor.
3. The operating system communicates the document data to the device driver for the printer.
4. The device driver controls the printer as it prints the document.

The operating system interacts with application software, device drivers, and hardware to manage a computer's resources. In the context of a computer system, the term **resource** refers to any component that is required to perform work. For example, the processor is a resource. RAM, storage space, and peripherals are also resources. While you interact with application software, your computer's operating system is busy behind the scenes with tasks such as identifying storage space, allocating memory, and communicating with your printer.

Many operating systems also influence the "look and feel" of your software—what kinds of menus and controls are displayed on the screen, and how they react to your input. Let's take a closer look at how an operating system manages resources and affects "look and feel."

How does the OS manage processor resources? Chapter 2 explained how the control unit directs activities within the microprocessor. The operating system also controls the microprocessor—just at a slightly higher level. Every cycle of a computer's microprocessor is a resource for accomplishing tasks. Many activities—called "processes"—compete for the attention of your computer's microprocessor. Commands are arriving from programs that you're using, while input is arriving from the keyboard and mouse. At the same time, data must be sent to the display device or printer, and Web pages are arriving from your Internet connection. To manage all of these competing processes, your computer's operating system must ensure that each one receives its share of microprocessor cycles. Ideally, the operating system should be able to help the microprocessor switch tasks so that, from the user's vantage point, everything seems to be happening at the same time. The operating system also must ensure that the microprocessor doesn't "spin its wheels" waiting for input, while it could be working on some other processing task.

Why does an operating system need to manage memory? A microprocessor works with data and executes instructions that are stored in RAM—one of your computer's most important resources. When you want to run more than one program at a time, the operating system has to allocate specific areas of memory for each program, as shown in Figure 3-9. While multiple programs are running, the OS must ensure that instructions and data from one area of memory don't "leak" into an area allocated to another program. If an OS falls down on the job and fails to protect each program's memory area, data can get corrupted, programs can "crash," and your computer will display error messages, such as "General Protection Fault." Your PC can sometimes recover from memory leak problems if you use the Ctrl-Alt-Del key sequence to close the corrupted program.

FIGURE 3-9

The operating system allocates a specific area of RAM for each program that is open and running.

The operating system is itself a program, and so it requires RAM space, too.

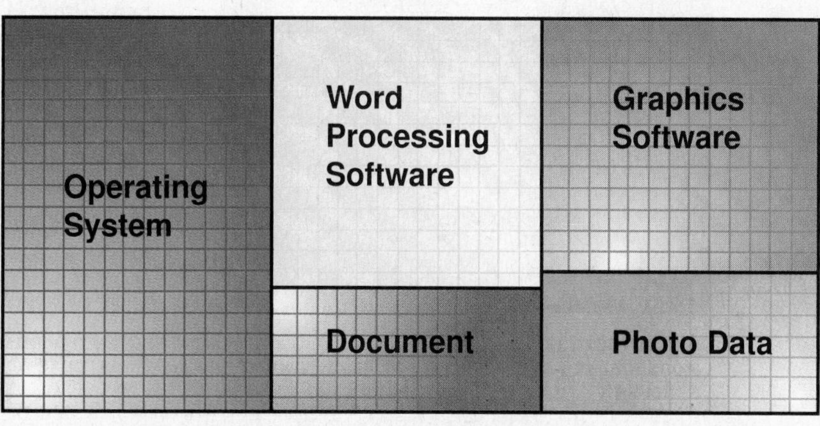

How does the OS keep track of storage resources? Behind the scenes, an operating system acts as a filing clerk that stores and retrieves files from your disks and CDs. It remembers the names and locations of all your files, and keeps track of empty spaces where new files can be stored. Chapter 4 explores file storage in more depth because this aspect of the operating system directly affects the way that you create, name, save, and retrieve files.

Why does the operating system get involved with peripheral devices? Every device that's connected to a computer is regarded as a resource. Your computer's operating system communicates with device driver software so that data can travel smoothly between the computer and these peripheral resources. If a peripheral device or driver is not performing correctly, the operating system makes a decision about what to do—usually it displays an on-screen message to warn you of the problem.

Your computer's operating system ensures that input and output proceed in an orderly manner, using "queues" and "buffers" to collect and hold data while the computer is busy with other tasks. By using a keyboard buffer, for example, your computer never misses one of your keystrokes, regardless of how fast you type, or what else is happening within your computer system at the same time.

How does the operating system affect the "look and feel" of application software? A **user interface** can be defined as the combination of hardware and software that helps people and computers communicate with each other. Your computer's user interface includes the mouse and keyboard that accept your input and carry out your commands, as well as the display device that provides cues to help you use software, and displays error messages that alert you to problems. An operating system typically provides user interface tools, such as menus and toolbar buttons, that define the "look and feel" for all of its compatible software.

Most computers today feature a graphical user interface. Sometimes abbreviated "GUI" and referred to as a "gooey," a **graphical user interface** provides a way to point and click a mouse to select menu options and manipulate graphical objects that are displayed on the screen. The original GUI concept was conceived at the prestigious Xerox PARC research facility. A few years later, in 1984, Apple Computer turned the idea into a commercial success with the launch of its popular Macintosh computer, which featured a GUI operating system and applications. GUIs didn't really catch on in the PC market until 1992 when Windows 3.1 became standard issue on most PCs, replacing a **command-line interface**, which requires users to type various memorized commands to run programs and accomplish tasks (see Figure 3-10).

FIGURE 3-10

A graphical user interface features menus and icons that you can manipulate with the click of a mouse.

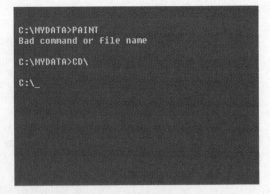

A command-line interface requires you to memorize and type commands.

FIGURE 3-16

Document production software makes it easy to get your ideas down on your screen-based "paper." Start the video to see word wrap and the spelling checker in action.

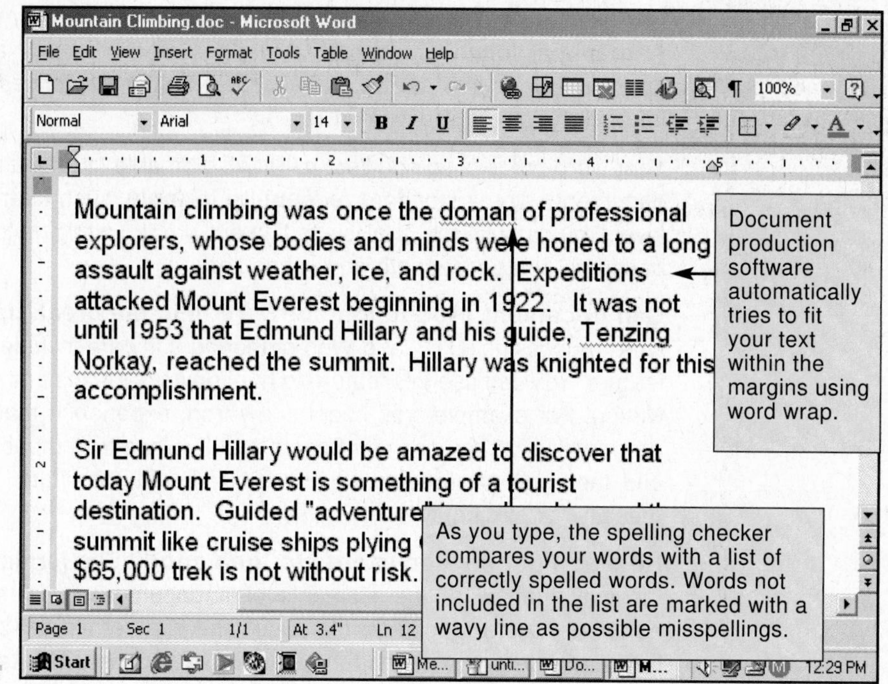
Mountain Climbing.doc - Microsoft Word
File Edit View Insert Format Tools Table Window Help
Mountain climbing was once the doman of professional explorers, whose bodies and minds were honed to a long assault against weather, ice, and rock. Expeditions attacked Mount Everest beginning in 1922. It was not until 1953 that Edmund Hillary and his guide, Tenzing Norkay, reached the summit. Hillary was knighted for this accomplishment.
Sir Edmund Hillary would be amazed to discover that today Mount Everest is something of a tourist destination. Guided "adventure"
summit like cruise ships plying
$65,000 trek is not without risk.
Document production software automatically tries to fit your text within the margins using word wrap.
As you type, the spelling checker compares your words with a list of correctly spelled words. Words not included in the list are marked with a wavy line as possible misspellings.
Page 1 Sec 1 1/1 At 3.4" Ln 12
Start
12:29 PM

click to start

3

What if I'm a bad speller? Most document production software includes a **spelling checker** that marks misspelled words in a document. You can easily correct a misspelled word as you type, or you can run the spelling checker when you finish entering all of the text. Some software even has an autocorrecting capability that automatically changes a typo, such as "teh," to the correct spelling ("the").

Although your software's spelling checker helps you correct misspellings, it cannot guarantee an error-free document. A spelling checker works by comparing each word from your document to a list of correctly spelled words that is stored in a data module called a **spelling dictionary**. If the word from your document is in the dictionary, the spelling checker considers the word correctly spelled. If the word is not in the dictionary, the word is counted as misspelled. Sounds OK, right? But, suppose your document contains a reference to the city of "Negaunee." This word is not in the dictionary, so the spelling checker considers it misspelled, even though it is spelled correctly. Proper nouns and scientific, medical, and technical words are likely to be flagged as misspelled, even if you spell them correctly, because they do not appear in the spelling checker's dictionary. Now suppose that your document contains the phrase "a pear of shoes." Although you meant to use "pair" rather than "pear," the spelling checker will not catch your mistake because "pear" is a valid word in the dictionary. Your spelling checker won't help if you have trouble deciding whether to use "there" or "their," "its" or "it's," or "too" or "to." Remember, then, that a spelling checker cannot substitute for a thorough proofread.

Will document production software help improve my writing? Because word processing software tends to focus on the writing process, it offers several features that can improve the quality of your writing. These features may not be available in desktop publishing software or Web authoring software, which put more focus on the format, rather than the content, of a document.

Your word processing software is likely to include a **thesaurus**, which can help you find a synonym for a word so that you can make your writing more varied and interesting. A **grammar checker** "reads" through your document and points out potential grammatical trouble spots, such as incomplete sentences, run-on sentences, and verbs that don't agree with nouns.

Your word processing software might also be able to analyze the reading level of your document using a standard **readability formula**, such as the Flesch-Kincaid reading level. You can use this analysis to find out if your writing matches your target audience, based on sentence length and vocabulary.

Can document production software help me break bad writing habits? Most word processing, DTP, and Web authoring software includes a **Search and Replace** feature. You can use this feature to hunt down mistakes that you typically make in your writing. For example, you might know from experience that you tend to overuse the word "typically." You can use Search and Replace to find each occurrence of "typically," and then you can decide whether you should substitute a different word, such as "usually" or "ordinarily."

How do I get my documents to look good? The **format** for a document refers to the way that all of the elements of a document—text, pictures, titles, and page numbers—are arranged on the page. The final format of your document depends on how and where you intend to use it. A school paper, for example, simply needs to be printed in standard paragraph format—perhaps double spaced and with numbered pages. Your word processing software has all of the features you need for this formatting task. A brochure, newsletter, or corporate report, on the other hand, might require more ambitious formatting, such as columns that continue on noncontiguous pages and text labels that overlay graphics. You might consider transferring your document from your word processing software to your desktop publishing software for access to more sophisticated formatting tools. For documents that you plan to publish on the Web, Web authoring software usually provides the most useful set of formatting tools.

You can add to your font collection by downloading font files from the Font InfoWeb.

The "look" of your final document depends on several formatting factors, such as font style, paragraph style, and page layout. A **font** is a set of letters that share a unified design. Font size is measured as **point size**, abbreviated pt. (one point is about 1/72 of an inch). Figure 3-17 illustrates several popular fonts that are included with document production software.

FIGURE 3-17

You can vary the font style by selecting character formatting attributes such as bold, italics, underline, superscript, and subscript. You can also select a color and size for a font. The font size for the text in a typical paragraph is set at 8, 10, or 12 pt. Titles can be as large as 72 pt.

Times New Roman Font	8 pt.
Times New Roman Font	10 pt.
Times New Roman Font	12 pt.
Times New Roman Font	16 pt.
Times New Roman Font	**16 pt. Bold**
Times New Roman Font	16 pt. Green
Arial Font	16 pt.
Comic Sans MS	16 pt.
Georgia Font	**16 pt. Bold Gold**
Serpentine Font	16 pt. Orange

Paragraph style includes the alignment of text within the margins, and the space between each line of text. **Paragraph alignment** refers to the horizontal position of text—whether it is aligned at the left margin, aligned at the right margin, or fully justified so that the text is aligned evenly on both the right and left margins. Your document will look more formal if it is **fully justified**, like the text in this paragraph, rather than if it has an uneven or "ragged" right margin. **Line spacing** (also called **leading**, pronounced "LED ing") refers to the vertical spacing between lines. Documents are typically single spaced or double spaced, but word processing and DTP software allow you to adjust line spacing in 1 pt. increments.

Instead of individually selecting font and paragraph style elements, document production software typically allows you to define a **style** that lets you apply several font and paragraph elements with a single click. (See Figure 3-18.) For example, instead of applying bold to a title, changing its font to Times New Roman, and then adjusting the font size to 24 pt., you can simply define a Title style as 24 pt., Times New Roman, bold. You can then apply all three style elements at once simply by selecting the Title style.

FIGURE 3-18

By defining a style, you can apply multiple font attributes with a single click.

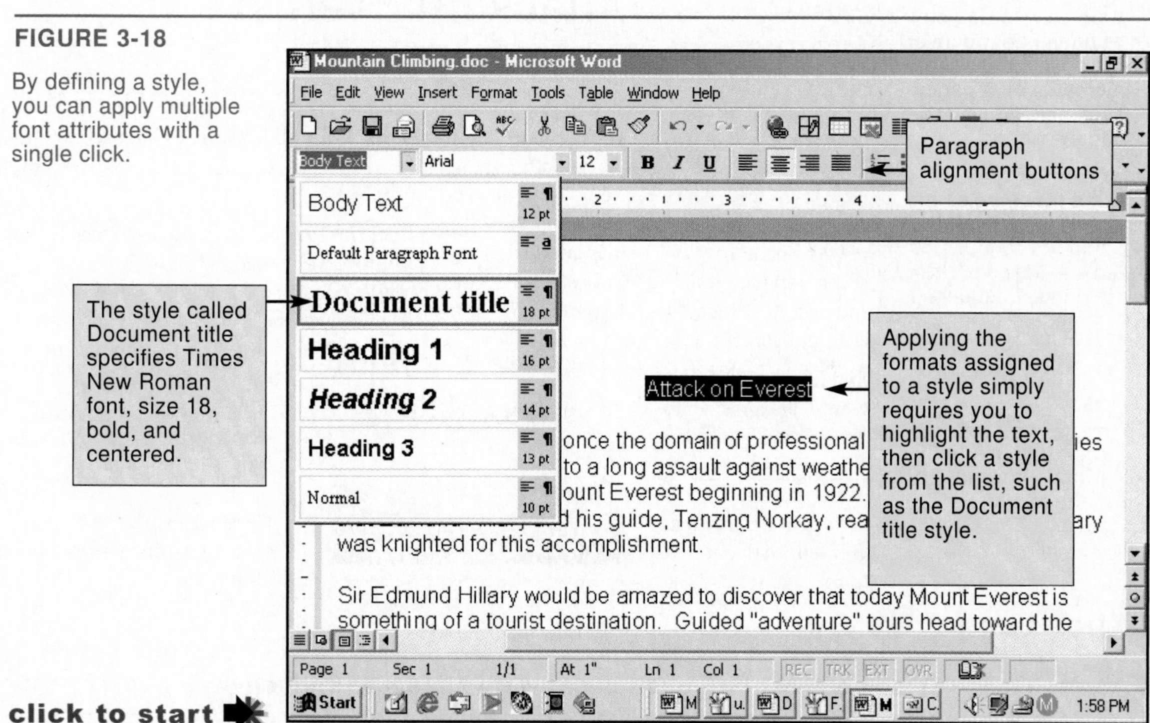
Mountain Climbing.doc - Microsoft Word
File Edit View Insert Format Tools Table Window Help
Body Text
Arial
12
Paragraph alignment buttons
Body Text 12 pt
Default Paragraph Font
Document title 18 pt
Heading 1 16 pt
Heading 2 14 pt
Heading 3 13 pt
Normal 10 pt
The style called Document title specifies Times New Roman font, size 18, bold, and centered.
Attack on Everest
Applying the formats assigned to a style simply requires you to highlight the text, then click a style from the list, such as the Document title style.
once the domain of professional
to a long assault against weathe
ount Everest beginning in 1922.
d his guide, Tenzing Norkay, rea
was knighted for this accomplishment.
Sir Edmund Hillary would be amazed to discover that today Mount Everest is
something of a tourist destination. Guided "adventure" tours head toward the
Page 1 Sec 1 1/1 At 1" Ln 1 Col 1 REC TRK EXT OVR
Start
1:58 PM

click to start

Page layout refers to the physical position of each element on a page. In addition to paragraphs of text, these elements might include:

- **Headers and footers.** A **header** is text that you specify to automatically appear in the top margin of every page. A **footer** is text that you specify to automatically appear in the bottom margin of every page. You might put your name and the document title in the header or footer of a document so that its printed pages won't get mixed up with those of another printed document.

- **Page numbers.** Word processing and DTP software automatically number the pages of a document according to your specifications, usually placing the page number either within a header or footer. A Web page, no matter what its length, is all a single page, so page numbering is not typically provided by Web authoring software.

- **Graphical elements.** Photos, diagrams, graphs, and charts can be incorporated in your documents. **Clip art**—a collection of drawings and photos designed to be inserted in documents—is a popular source of graphical elements.
- **Tables.** A **table** is a grid-like structure that can hold text or pictures. For printed documents, tables are a popular way to provide easy-to-read columns of data, and to position graphics. It may sound surprising, but for Web pages, tables provide one of the few ways to precisely position text and pictures. As a result, Web page designers make extensive and very creative use of tables.

Most word processing is page-oriented, because it treats each page as a rectangle that can be filled with text and graphics. Text automatically flows from one page to the next. In contrast most DTP software is frame-oriented because it allows you to divide each page into several rectangular-shaped **frames** that you can fill with either text or graphics. Text flows from one frame to the next, rather than from page to page. (See Figure 3-19.)

FIGURE 3-19

Frames provide you with finer control over the position of elements on a page, such as a figure and a caption on top of it.

Attack on Everest
by Janell Chalmers
Mountain climbing was once the domain of professional explorers, whose bodies and minds were honed to a long assault against weather, ice, and rock. Expeditions attacked Mount Everest beginning in 1922. It was not until 1953 that Edmund Hillary and his guide, Tenzing Norkay, reached the summit. Hillary was knighted for this accomplishment.
Sir Edmund Hillary would be amazed to discover that today Mount Everest has become something of a tourist destination. Guided "adventure" tours head toward the summit like cruise ships plying Caribbean ports. This $65,000 trek is not without risk. In 1996 a sudden storm killed eight climbers.
Back in 1923, British mountaineer, George Mallory was asked, why climb Everest? His reply, "Because it's there." A new answer to this question, "Because we can" may be largely attributable to new high... Nyl... Gor... ligh... fron... Ultraviolet lenses protect eyes from dangerous "snow-blindness."
"Because it's there."
George Mallory
One frame holds the centered title and author's byline. This text is linked to the text in subsequent frames.
Wrapping text around a frame adds interest to the layout.
Text can link to frames on the next page, or any page of the document.

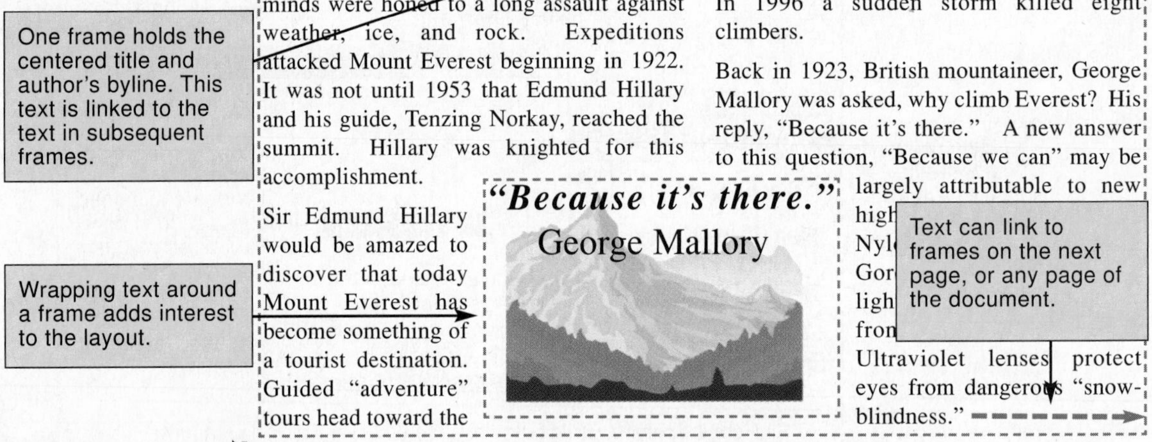

click to start

Does document production software increase productivity? Word processing software, in particular, provides several features that automate tasks and allow you to work more productively. For example, suppose that you want to send prospective employers a letter and your resume. Rather than composing and addressing each letter individually, your software can perform a **mail merge** that automatically creates personalized letters by combining the information in a mailing list with a form letter. Some of the additional capabilities of word processing software include:

- Automatically generating a table of contents and index for a document
- Automatically numbering footnotes and positioning each footnote on the page where it is referenced
- Providing document templates and document wizards that show you the correct content and format for a variety of documents, such as business letters, fax cover sheets, and memos
- Exporting a document into HTML format

DATA MANAGEMENT SOFTWARE

What is data management software? Data management software helps you to store, find, organize, update, and report information. Some data management software is tailored to special applications. A **personal information manager**, for example, is a specialized data management application that keeps track of daily appointments, addresses, and To Do lists. Other data management software allows you to work with any type of data you like. Two main types of data management software exist: file management software and database management software.

What's the difference between file management software and database management software? To better understand the difference between file and database management software, you'll need a little background on flat files and databases.

Within the context of computing, a file can contain many different types of data, arranged in a variety of ways. You are familiar with files that contain word processing documents. The data in these documents is typically arranged in a free-form manner. For example, a document about African-American literature might contain a reference to Alex Haley' s novel, *Roots*, but this reference would be embedded within a paragraph and could be difficult to find.

In contrast to free-form files, structured files contain data that is organized in much the same way as an old-fashioned library card file. A **structured file** is a collection of records, which are composed of fields that can hold data. A **record** holds data for a single entity—a person, place, thing, or event. A **field** holds one item of data relevant to a record. Figure 3-25 illustrates records and fields in a structured file.

3

FIGURE 3-25

In a file of library books, data for each book is stored as a record in the file. The record for each book contains a standard set of fields, filled with data that pertains to the book.

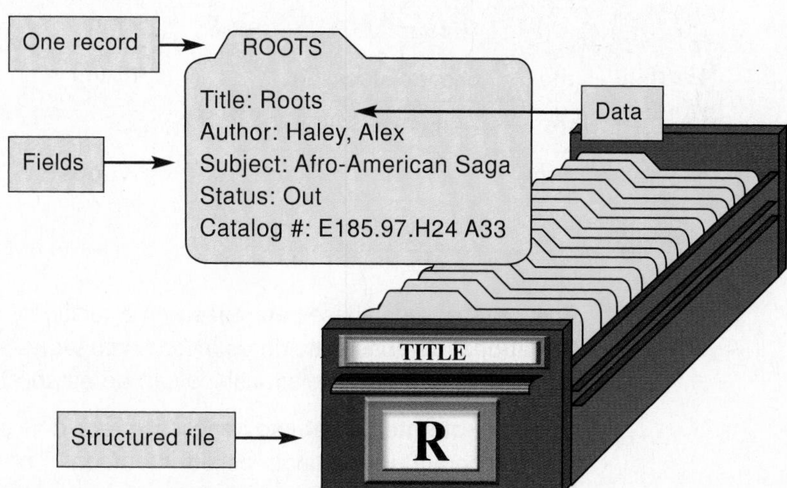

A structured file in which all of the records conform to the same set of fields is called a **flat file**. Flat files can be a useful repository for simple lists of information, such as e-mail addresses, holiday card addresses, doctor visits, appointments, or household valuables. **File management software** is designed to help you create, modify, search, sort, and print the data in flat files.

It might seem odd, but spreadsheet software provides quite an adequate set of file management tools. It includes special data handling features that allow you to enter data, sort data, search for data that meets specific criteria, and print reports. As a rule of thumb, spreadsheet software can handle any data that you could put on a set of index cards or in a Rolodex.

Although the term **database** can be used to refer to a flat file, it also encompasses a collection of data in which records may have different fields. For example, MTV might maintain a database of information pertaining to musicians and rock videos. One series of records might contain biographical data about the musicians, including name, birth date, and home town. The other series of records might contain data about the videos, including title, artist, and release date. A database allows you to store these diverse records in a single file and establish relationships between them. In the MTV database, for example, it would be possible to establish relationships between biographical data about the musicians and data about their videos, as shown in Figure 3-26.

FIGURE 3-26

A database allows you to work with different types of records and establish relationships between them.

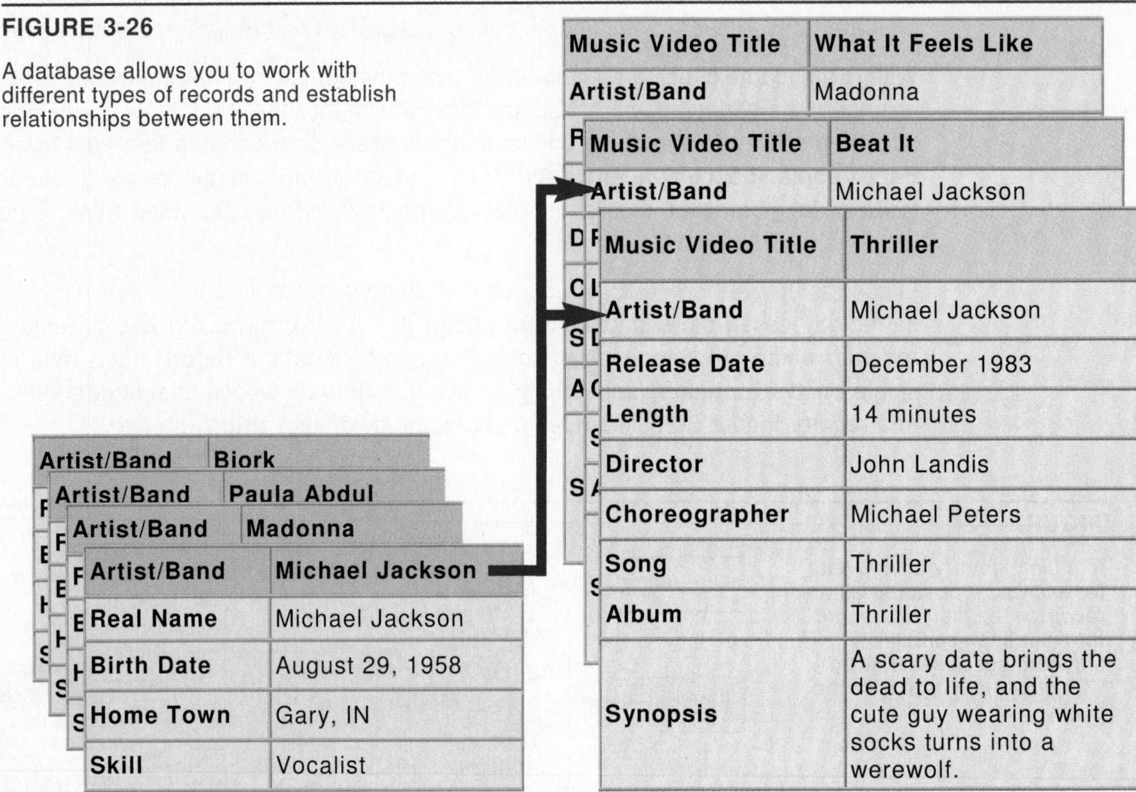

Most of today's databases are based on a relational model or an object-oriented model. A **relational database** structures records into tables in which each column is a field, and each row is a record. Relationships can be established between tables.

An **object-oriented database** treats each record as an object, which can be manipulated using program instructions called methods. For example, a university database containing information about its students might include an object called "Course Grades" and a method called "Calculate GPA."

For more information about file and database management software, connect to the Data Management Software InfoWeb.

Database management software (DBMS) is designed for creating and manipulating the records that form a database. It is an important tool for business, government, and educational institutions. Individuals, who have much less data to manipulate, tend to use file management software, rather than DBMS. Most of today's database management software, such as Microsoft Access, is designed for creating and manipulating relational databases. Object-oriented database management software is required for creating and manipulating object-oriented databases.

How do I use data management software? Whether you are using file management software or database management software, you must have a file of data to work with—such as a collection of information about jazz recordings. You might obtain a file with the data you need from a reference CD or from a Web site. More typically, you would create your own file by first defining the record structure, then entering the data. A **record structure** defines a list of fields and their data types. Simple tools like the form in Figure 3-27 help you to define the record structure for a database.

FIGURE 3-27

Your data management software provides the tools that you need to create the record structure for your data.

The *Jazz Recordings* file, shown at right, contains fields for Song Title, Performing Artist, Composer, Date, Record Label, and Length.

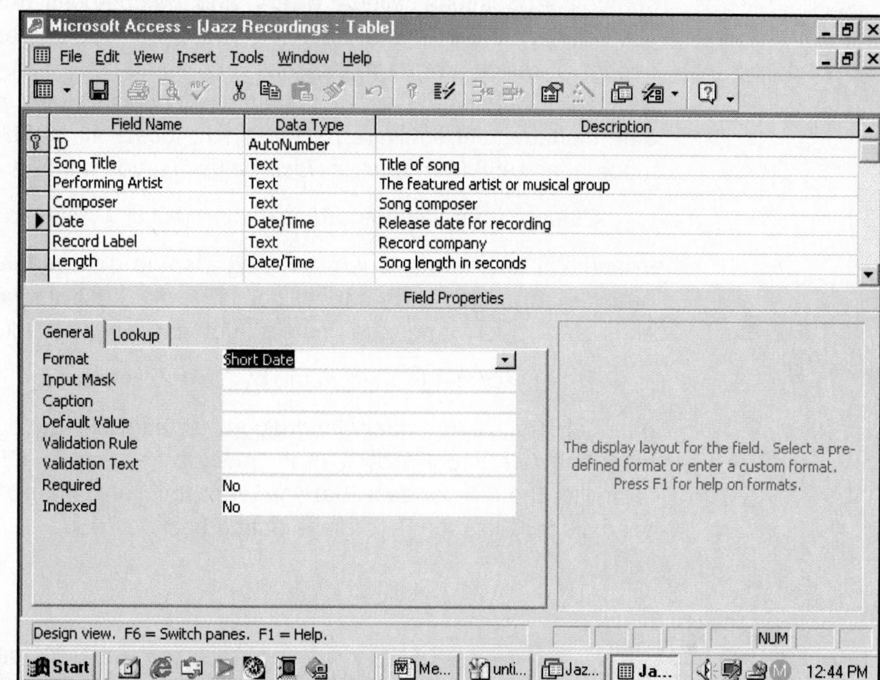

click to start

When you define a field, you can specify its data type as either character, numeric, date, logical, hyperlink, or memo. For example, if you're creating a file to hold personal data about your friends, you might define the Name field as character data, the Birthday field as date data, and the E-mail Address field as hyperlink data. Different data types are treated in different ways. For example, numeric data can be used in calculations, whereas character data cannot. The table in Figure 3-28 provides more information about how you might use data types.

FIGURE 3-28 Using Data Types

Data Type	Uses	Examples
Character	Use for fields that contain text-based data and will not be used for calculations	Names, addresses, social security numbers, phone numbers, products
Numeric	Use for fields that contain numeric data that might be used in calculations	Price, quantity, tax rate, test scores, miles per gallon
Date	Use for fields that contain dates	Birth date, date hired, current year
Logical	Use for fields that can have one of two values	True/false, yes/no, 0/1
Hyperlink	Use for fields that contain a URL that you would like to link to by clicking the field	www.cnn.com, www.excite.com
Memo	Use for fields that contain long sections of text	Descriptions, evaluations, diagnoses, notes
Currency	Use for fields that contain monetary amounts	Hourly wage, price, rental fee

3

After I design the record structure, what next? Once you create a record structure, you can enter the data for each of your records. With the data in place, you can modify the data in individual records to keep it up to date. You can also sort the records in a variety of ways, using any field as the **sort key**—that is, the field that is used to alphabetize or otherwise sort the records.

How do I locate specific data? Many flat files and databases contain hundreds or thousands of records. If you want to find a particular record or a group of records, scrolling through every record is much too cumbersome. Instead, you can enter search specifications called a **query**, and the computer will quickly locate the records you seek. Most data management software provides one or more methods for making queries. A **query language** provides a set of commands for locating and manipulating data. **SQL** (Structured Query Language) is a popular query language used by numerous data management software packages. To locate all of the Duke Ellington recordings made after 1958 from a *Jazz Recordings* file, you might enter an SQL query such as:

Select * from JazzRecordings where Artist = 'Ellington' and Date => '1958'

In addition to a formal query language, some data management software provides **natural language query** capabilities. To make such queries, you don't have to learn an esoteric query language. Instead, you can simply enter questions, such as:

What recordings were made by Duke Ellington from 1958 to the present?

As an alternative to a query language or a natural language query, your data management software might allow you to **query by example** (QBE), simply by filling out a form with the type of data that you want to locate. Figure 3-29 illustrates a query by example for Ellington recordings dating back to 1958.

FIGURE 3-29

When you query by example, your data management software displays a blank form on the screen, and you enter examples of the data that you want to find.

As you might guess from this example, QBE requires you to learn a few "tricks." The asterisk is used as a "wild card" so that the software will locate recordings made by anyone with a last name of Ellington: Duke Ellington, D. Ellington, and so on. The dash following 1958 means include any subsequent dates.

How can I use search results? Your data management software will typically help you print reports, export data to other programs (such as to a spreadsheet where you can graph the data), convert the data to other formats (such as HTML so that you can post the data on the Web), and transmit data to other computers.

Whether you print, import, copy, save, or transmit the data you find in databases, it is your responsibility to use it appropriately. Never introduce inaccurate information into a database. Respect copyrights, giving credit to the person or organization that compiled the data. You should also respect the privacy of the people who are the subject of the data. Unless you have permission to do so, do not divulge names, social security numbers, or other identifying information that may compromise someone's privacy.

GRAPHICS SOFTWARE

What kind of software do I need to work with drawings, photos, and other pictures? In computer lingo, the term **graphics** refers to any picture, drawing, sketch, photograph, image, or icon that appears on your computer screen. **Graphics software** is designed to help you create, display, modify, manipulate, and print graphics. Some graphics software packages specialize in a particular type of graphic, while others allow you to work with multiple graphics formats. If you are really interested in working with graphics, you will undoubtedly end up using more than one graphics software package.

Paint software (sometimes called "image editing software") provides a set of electronic pens, brushes, and paints for painting images on the screen. Graphic artists, Web page designers, and illustrators use paint software as their primary computer-based graphics tool.

Photo editing software includes features specially designed to fix poor-quality photos by modifying contrast and brightness, cropping out unwanted objects, and removing "red eye." Photos can also be edited using paint software, but photo editing software typically provides tools and wizards that simplify common photo editing tasks.

Drawing software provides a set of lines, shapes, and colors that can be assembled into diagrams, corporate logos, and schematics. The drawings created with this type of software tend to have a "flat" cartoon-like quality, but they are very easy to modify, and look good at just about any size. Figure 3-30 provides more information on paint, photo editing, and drawing software.

FIGURE 3-30

Paint software works well with realistic art and photos.

Photo editing software includes special features for touching up photographs.

Drawing software tends to create two-dimensional "cartoon-like" images.

3-D graphics software provides a set of tools for creating "wireframes" that represent three-dimensional objects. A wireframe acts much like the framework for a pop-up tent. Just as you would construct the framework for the tent, then cover it with a nylon tent cover, 3-D graphics software can cover a wireframe object with surface texture and color to create a graphic of a 3-D object. (See Figure 3-31).

FIGURE 3-31

3-D graphics software provides tools for creating a wireframe that represents a three-dimensional object.

Some 3-D software specializes in engineering-style graphics, while other 3-D software specializes in figures.

For links to information about specific graphics software packages, visit the Graphics Software InfoWeb.

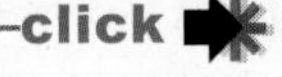

CAD software (computer-aided design software) is a special type of 3-D graphics software designed for architects and engineers who use computers to create blueprints and product specifications. Scaled-down versions of professional CAD software provide simplified tools for home-owners who want to redesign their kitchens, examine new landscaping options, or experiment with floor plans.

Presentation software provides the tools you need for combining text, photos, clip-art, graphs, animations, and sound into a series of electronic **slides**. You can display the electronic slides on a color monitor for a one-on-one presentation, or use a computer projection device, like the one shown in Figure 3-32, for group presentations. You can also output the presentation as overhead transparencies, paper copies, or 35 mm slides.

FIGURE 3-32

A computer-based presentation consists of a series of slides, created with presentation software. A presentation can be displayed for a group by using a projection device like the one pictured.

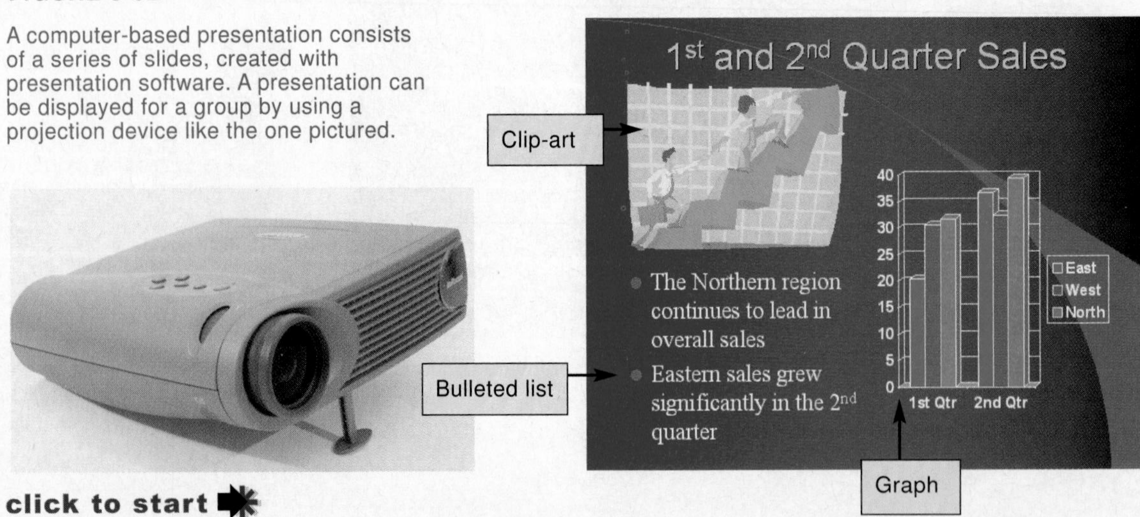

click to start

MUSIC SOFTWARE

Why would I need music software? You don't have to be a musician or composer to have a use for music software. Many types of music software are available. You might be surprised to find how many of them come in handy.

It is possible—and easy—to make your own digital voice and music recordings, which you store on your computer's hard disk. Windows and Mac OS operating system utilities typically supply the necessary **audio editing software**—Sound Recorder on PCs (Figure 3-33), and iTunes on Macs.

FIGURE 3-33

Audio editing software, such as Sound Recorder, provides controls much like those on a tape recorder. Menus provide additional digital editing features, such as speed control, volume adjustments, clipping, and mixing.

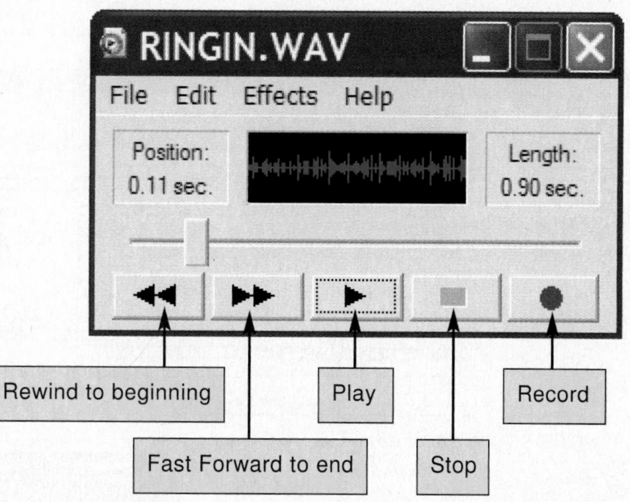

Audio editing software typically includes playback as well as recording capabilities. A specialized version of this software called Karaoke software integrates music files and on-screen lyrics—everything you need to sing along with your favorite tunes.

MP3 is a music compression file format that stores digitized music in such a way that the sound quality is excellent, but the file size remains relatively small—small enough to be easily downloaded from the Web. To listen to MP3 music on your computer, you need an **MP3 player**. Versions of MP3 player software are available for many handheld computers, and for personal computers running Windows, Mac OS, and Linux. With two additional types of MP3 software (sometimes combined into a single package), you can convert the tracks from standard audio CDs into MP3 format. To do so, you first use software called a **CD ripper** to pull the track off of the CD and store it in "raw" digital format on your computer's hard disk. Next, you use **MP3 encoding software** to convert the file into MP3 format. Once the file is in MP3 format, you can listen to it on your computer, or you can transfer it to a portable MP3 player.

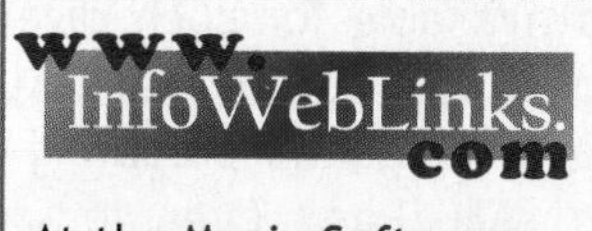

At the Music Software InfoWeb, you'll find detailed information on popular software in this category.

click

Ear training software targets musicians and music students who want to learn to play by ear, develop tuning skills, recognize notes and keys, and develop other musical skills. **Notation software** is the musician's equivalent of a word processor. It helps musicians compose, edit, and print the notes for their compositions. For non-musicians, **computer-aided music software** is designed to generate unique musical compositions simply by selecting the musical style, instruments, key, and tempo. **MIDI sequencing software** and software synthesizers are an important part of the studio musician's toolbox. They're great for sound effects, and for controlling keyboards and other digital instruments.

VIDEO EDITING SOFTWARE

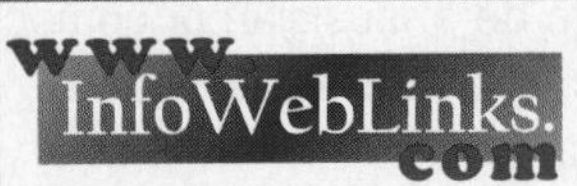

Learn more about Apple iMovie and Adobe Premiere at the Video Editing Software InfoWeb.

click

Is video editing software difficult to use? The growing popularity of computer-based video editing can be attributed to video editing software, such as Windows Movie Maker and Apple iMovie, now included with Windows computers and Macs. **Video editing software** provides a set of tools for transferring video footage from a camcorder to a computer, clipping out unwanted footage, assembling video segments in any sequence, adding special visual effects, and adding a sound track. Despite an impressive array of features, video editing software is relatively easy to use, as explained in Figure 3-34.

FIGURE 3-34

Video editing software, such as Adobe Premiere, helps you import a series of video clips from a camera or VCR, arrange the clips in the order of your choice, add transitions between clips, and add an audio track.

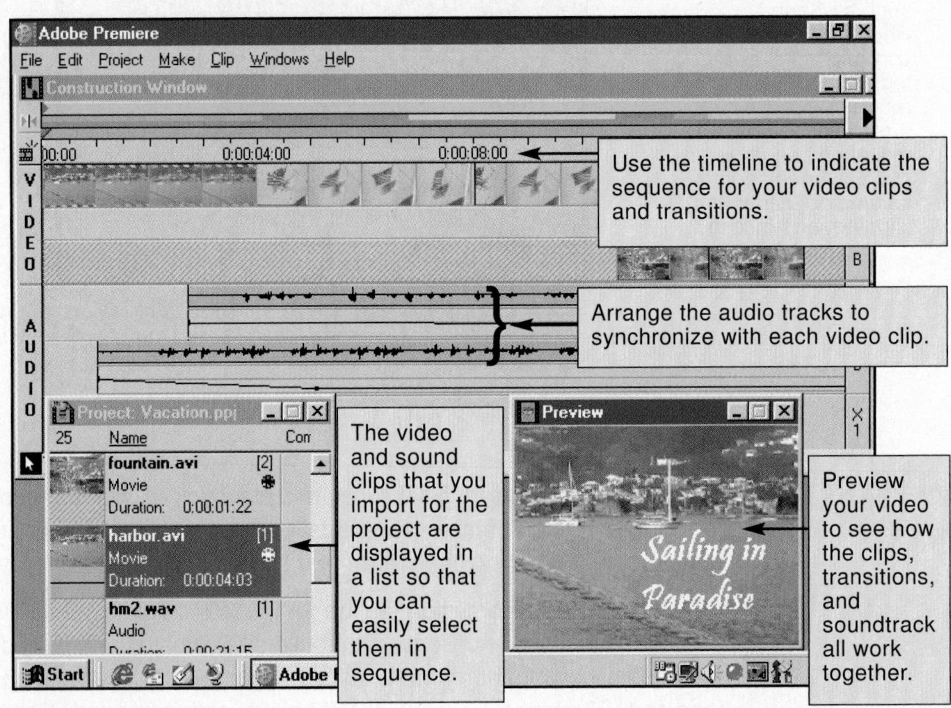
Adobe Premiere
File Edit Project Make Clip Windows Help
Construction Window
0:00:04:00
0:00:08:00
VIDEO
AUDIO
Use the timeline to indicate the sequence for your video clips and transitions.
Arrange the audio tracks to synchronize with each video clip.
Project: Vacation.ppj
Name
fountain.avi
Movie
Duration: 0:00:01:22
harbor.avi
Movie
Duration: 0:00:04:03
hm2.wav
Audio
The video and sound clips that you import for the project are displayed in a list so that you can easily select them in sequence.
Preview
Sailing in Paradise
Preview your video to see how the clips, transitions, and soundtrack all work together.
Start

EDUCATIONAL AND REFERENCE SOFTWARE

How can I use my computer to learn new things? Educational software helps you learn and practice new skills. For the youngest students, educational software, such as MindTwister Math and 3-D Froggy Phonics, teaches basic arithmetic and reading skills. Instruction is presented in game format, and the levels of play are adapted to the player's age and ability.

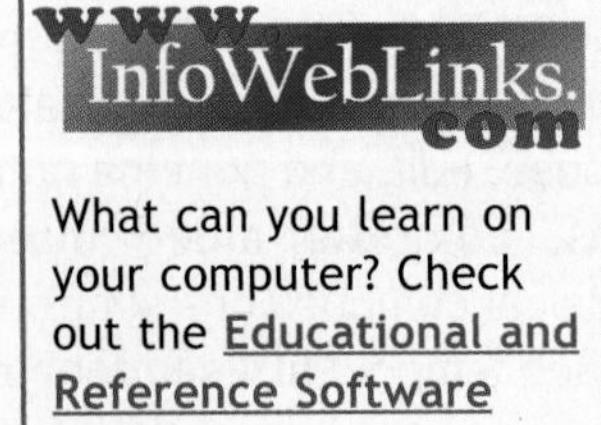

What can you learn on your computer? Check out the Educational and Reference Software InfoWeb.

click

For older students and adults, software is available for such diverse educational endeavors as learning languages, training yourself to use new software, learning how to play the piano or guitar, preparing for standardized tests, improving keyboarding skills, and even learning managerial skills for a diverse workplace. Exam preparation software is available for standardized tests such as the SAT, GMAT, and LSAT. Although little research is available on the effectiveness of this software, experts believe that the results should be similar to those of in-person coaching courses that improve composite SAT scores by about 100 points.

What's reference software? Reference software provides you with a collection of information and a way to access that information. This type of software includes massive amounts of data—unlike data management software, which is shipped without any data. The reference software category spans a wide range of applications—from encyclopedias to medical references, from map software to trip planners, and from cookbooks to telephone books. The options are as broad as the full range of human interests.

Reference software is generally shipped on a CD-ROM because of the quantity of data it includes. Many of these products provide links to Web sites that contain updates for the information on the CD-ROM. Other software publishers have eliminated the CD-ROM entirely and have placed all of their reference materials on the Web. Access to that information often requires a fee or a subscription.

The most popular software packages in this category—encyclopedias—contain text, graphics, audio, and video on a full range of topics from apples to zenophobia. Best-sellers include Microsoft's Encarta, Grolier's encyclopedia, Compton's encyclopedia, IBM's World Book encyclopedia, and Britannica's CD. All of these titles contain the standard information you would expect in an encyclopedia, such as articles written by experts on various topics, maps, photographs, and timelines. An encyclopedia on CD-ROM or the Web has several advantages over its printed counterpart. Finding information is easier, for example. Also, electronic formats take up less space on your bookshelf, and include interesting video and audio clips. A single CD is cheaper to produce than a shelf full of hard-bound printed books. These lower production costs translate to more affordable products, and allow an average person to own a comprehensive encyclopedia.

3

ENTERTAINMENT SOFTWARE

What's the best-selling entertainment software? Although some people might get a kick out of watching an animated screen saver, computer games are the most popular type of entertainment software. Over $6 billion of computer and video games, like those in Figure 3-35, are sold each year in the U.S. alone. Contrary to popular belief, teenage boys are not the only computer game enthusiasts. According to the Interactive Digital Software Association, 90 percent of all computer games are purchased by people 18 and older. Thirteen percent of gamers are over 50, and about 43 percent are women.

FIGURE 3-35

Computer games provide many different challenges. Some require fast reflexes, while others require careful planning and good problem-solving ability.

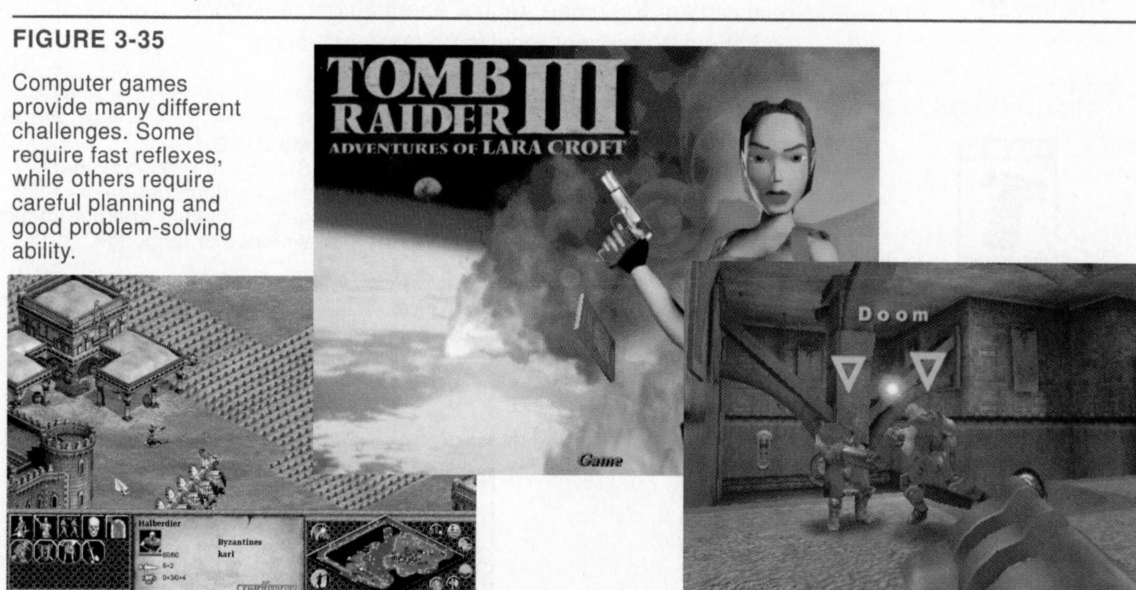

Computer games are generally classified into subcategories, such as role-playing, action, adventure, puzzles, simulations, and strategy/war games. **Role-playing games** are based on a detailed story line—often one that takes place in a medieval world populated with dastardly villains and evil monsters. The goal is to build a character into a powerful entity that can conquer the bad guys and accumulate treasure. Some of the most popular role-playing games include Diablo, EverQuest, Icewind Dale, and Planescape.

www.InfoWebLinks.com

The Entertainment Software InfoWeb is your link to the best game sites on the Internet.

click 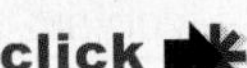

Action games, like arcade games, require fast reflexes as you maneuver a character through a maze or dungeon. Popular action games include Quake, Unreal Tournament, Half-life, Doom, and Tomb Raider.

Adventure games are similar to role-playing games except that the focus is on solving problems, rather than building a character into a powerful wizard or fighter. Popular games in this category include Myst, The Longest Journey, and Return to Monkey Island.

Puzzle games include computerized versions of traditional board games, such as Monopoly or cards, and Rubick's cube-like challenges, such as the classic Tetrus, and the wildly popular Lemmings.

Simulation games provide a realistic setting, such as the cockpit of an airplane. A player must learn to manipulate controls using the keyboard, a joystick, or a special-purpose input device. These games are great for people who want to learn to fly an airplane or drive a race car without the associated expenses or risks.

Sports games place participants in the midst of action-packed sports events, such as a football game, baseball game, hockey final, soccer match, or golf tournament. Most sports games offer arcade-like action and require quick reflexes.

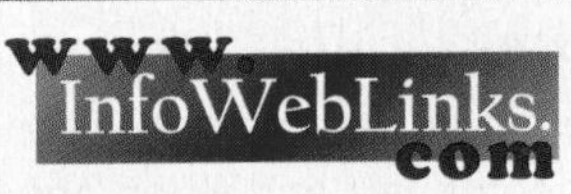

Who rates software and how do they do it? Find out at the Software Ratings InfoWeb.

click 

Strategy games, such as Age of Empires and the Sims, have their roots in chess. Players (one player might be the computer) take turns moving characters, armies, and other resources in a quest to capture territory.

Are computer games rated like movies and music? Since it was established in 1994, the Entertainment Software Rating Board (ESRB) has rated more than 7,000 video and computer games. Rating symbols, shown in Figure 3-36, can usually be found in the lower-right corner of the game box. In past years, about 70 percent of the top 20 computer games received an "Everyone" rating. About 20 percent received a "Teen" rating, and about 10 percent received a "Mature" rating.

FIGURE 3-36 ESRB Software Ratings and Symbols

	**TEEN** Suitable for 13 and older. May contain violent content, mild or strong language, and/or suggestive themes.	 	**MATURE** Suitable for 17 and older. May contain mature sexual themes or more intense violence or language.
	**EARLY CHILDHOOD** Suitable for ages 3 and older. Contains no material that parents would find inappropriate.	 	**EVERYONE** Suitable for ages 6 and older. May contains minimal violence, some comic mischief, or crude language.
 	**ADULTS ONLY** Content suitable only for adults. May include graphic depictions of sex and/or violence.		**RATING PENDING** Product has been submitted, but a rating has not yet been assigned.

BUSINESS SOFTWARE

Do businesses use specialized software? The term "business software" provides a broad umbrella for several types of software, which are designed to help businesses and organizations accomplish routine or specialized tasks. **Vertical market software** is designed to automate specialized tasks in a specific market or business. Examples include patient management and billing software that is specially designed for hospitals, job estimating software for construction businesses, and student record management software for schools. Today, almost every business has access to some type of specialized vertical market software designed to automate, streamline, or computerize key business activities.

Horizontal market software is generic software that can be used by just about any kind of business. **Payroll software** is a good example of horizontal market software. Almost every business has employees and must maintain payroll records. No matter what type of business uses it, payroll software must collect similar data and make similar calculations in order to produce payroll checks and W-2 forms. Accounting software and project management software are additional examples of horizontal market software. **Accounting software** helps a business keep track of the money flowing in and out of various accounts. **Project management software** is an important tool for planning large projects, scheduling project tasks, and tracking project costs.

"Groupware" is another umbrella term in the world of business software. **Groupware** is designed to help several people collaborate on a single project using network or Internet connections. It usually provides the capability to: maintain schedules for all of the group members, automatically select meeting times for the group, facilitate communication by e-mail or other channels, distribute documents according to a prearranged schedule or sequence, and allow multiple people to contribute to a single document.

QUICKCheck Section C

1 Various kinds of document ________ software provide tools for creating and formatting printed and Web-based documents.

2 ________ software provides a sort of "blank canvas" on which you can create numeric models by simply "painting" values, labels, and formulas.

3 ________ management software is useful for working with flat files, whereas ________ management software works well if you want to establish relationships between different types of records.

4 ________ software helps you work with wireframes, CAD drawings, photos, and slide presentations.

5 Audio editing software allows you to make ________ voice and music recordings, which you store on your computer's hard disk.

6 ________ market software is designed to automate specialized tasks in a specific market or business.

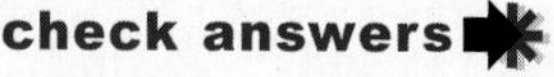

Section D

SOFTWARE INSTALLATION AND COPYRIGHTS

Software is sold in some surprising places. You might find graphics software at your local art supply store. Your favorite beauty salon might carry *Cosmopolitan's* makeup and hairstyle makeover software. You might even find homeopathic medicine software on sale at a health food store. Of course, software is also available from traditional sources, including office stores, computer superstores, electronics superstores, and discount stores, as well as local computer stores. You can buy software from mail-order catalogs, the software publisher's Web site, and software download sites.

However you obtain a new software package, you must install it on your computer before you can use it. That is the first topic in Section D. From time to time, you might want to eliminate some of the software that exists on your computer. The procedure for uninstalling software is the second topic in this section. The section ends with a discussion of software copyrights—important information that will help you understand the difference between legal and illegal software copying.

INSTALLATION BASICS

What's included in a typical software package? The key "ingredients" necessary to install new software are the files that contain the programs and data. These files might be supplied on **distribution disks**—one or more CDs or a series of floppy disks—that are packaged in a box, along with an instruction manual. Software downloaded over the Internet typically arrives as one huge file that contains the program modules and the text of the instruction manual.

How do I know if a software program will work on my computer? Tucked away at the software publisher's Web site or printed on the software package (as shown in Figure 3-37), you'll find **system requirements**, which specify the operating system and minimum hardware capacities necessary for a software product to work correctly.

FIGURE 3-37

System requirements typically can be found on the software box, or posted on the software download site.

System Requirements:
- Operating Systems: Windows® 95/98/2000, Me & NT® 4.0
- Processor: Pentium class computer
- Memory: 16 MB or more
- Hard Drive Space: 10 MB free
- Network Protocol: TCP/IP
- Network Connection: 10/100 Ethernet LAN/WAN, cable modem, DSL router, ISDN router, or dial-up modem

BLACKICE™ Defender 2.1

©2000 Network ICE Corporation. All rights reserved.
©2000 Macmillan USA, Inc. and its licensors. All rights reserved. Network ICE and BlackICE Defender are trademarks of Network ICE. All other companies and products listed herein are trademarks or registered trademarks of their respective holders.

Distributed by:
Macmillan USA, Inc.
201 West 103rd Street
Indianapolis, IN 46290

www.networkice.com www.macmillansoftware.com

Why is it necessary to install most software? When you **install** software, the new software files are placed in the appropriate folders on your computer's hard disk, and then your computer performs any software or hardware configurations that are necessary to make sure that the program is ready to run. During the installation process your computer usually performs the following activities:

- Copies files from distribution disks or CDs to specified folders on the hard disk
- Uncompresses files if they have been distributed in a compressed format
- Analyzes the computer's resources, such as processor speed, RAM capacity, and hard disk capacity, to verify that they meet or exceed the minimum system requirements
- Analyzes hardware components and peripheral devices to select appropriate device drivers
- Looks for any system files and players, such as Internet Explorer or Windows Media Player, which are required to run the program, but not supplied on the distribution disk
- Updates necessary system files, such as the Windows Registry and the Windows Program menu, with information about the new software

Are all of the files for the software provided on the distribution disks? With Windows and other operating systems, application software programs share some common files. These files are often supplied by the operating system and perform routine tasks, such as displaying the Print dialog box, which allows you to select a printer and specify how many copies of a file you want to print. These "shared" files are not typically provided on the distribution disks for a new software program because the files should already exist on your computer. The installation routine attempts to locate these files, and will notify you if any of them are missing.

Are all of the files for the new software installed in the same folder? The main executable files and data files for the software are placed in the folder that you specify. Some support programs for the software, however, might be stored in other folders, such as Windows/System. The location for these files is determined by the software installation routine. Figure 3-38 maps out the location of files for a typical Windows software installation.

FIGURE 3-38

When you install software, its files might end up in different folders.

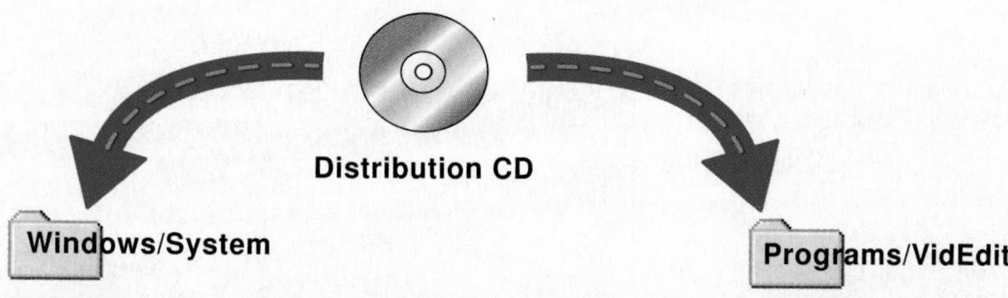

Filename	Size	Type
Vidmdbg.dll	20 KB	Support Program
Vidodec32.dll	92 KB	Support Program
Vidwave.dll	37 KB	Support Program
Version.dll	24 KB	Support Program
Vidpodbc.dll	955 KB	Support Program
Vidgain.dll	116 KB	Support Program
Vgateway.ocx	42 KB	Support Program

Filename	Size	Type
Videdit.exe	5,500 KB	Main Executable Program
Vidfact.hlp	275 KB	Help File
Vidcore.hlp	99 KB	Help File
Vidcore.dll	1,425 KB	Support Program
Vidfact.dll	1,517 KB	Support Program
Readme.doc	65 KB	Data File
Vdplugin.dll	813 KB	Support Program
vdtrans.dll	921 KB	Support Program

INSTALLING FROM DISTRIBUTION DISKS OR CDS

How do I install software from distribution disks or CDs? Installation procedures vary, depending on a computer's operating system. Let's take a look at the installation process on a computer running Windows.

Windows software typically contains a **setup program** that guides you through the installation process. Figure 3-39 shows you what to expect when you use a setup program.

FIGURE 3-39 Using the setup program to install video capture software from distribution CDs.

1 Insert the first distribution disk, CD, or DVD. The setup program should start automatically. If it does not, look for a file called *Setup.exe* and then run it.

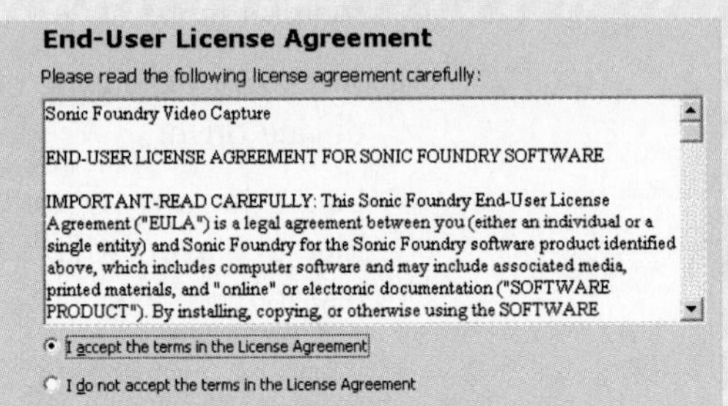

End-User License Agreement

Please read the following license agreement carefully:

Sonic Foundry Video Capture

END-USER LICENSE AGREEMENT FOR SONIC FOUNDRY SOFTWARE

IMPORTANT-READ CAREFULLY: This Sonic Foundry End-User License Agreement ("EULA") is a legal agreement between you (either an individual or a single entity) and Sonic Foundry for the Sonic Foundry software product identified above, which includes computer software and may include associated media, printed materials, and "online" or electronic documentation ("SOFTWARE PRODUCT"). By installing, copying, or otherwise using the SOFTWARE

I accept the terms in the License Agreement

I do not accept the terms in the License Agreement

2 Read the license agreement, if one is presented on the screen. By agreeing to the terms of the license, you can proceed with the installation.

Full Installation

Custom Installation

3 Select the installation option that best meets your needs. If you select a full installation, the setup program copies all files and data from the distribution medium to the hard disk of your computer system. A full installation provides you with access to all features of the software.

If you select a custom installation, the setup program displays a list of software features for your selection. After you select the features you want, the setup program copies only the selected program and data files to your hard disk. A custom installation can save space on your hard disk.

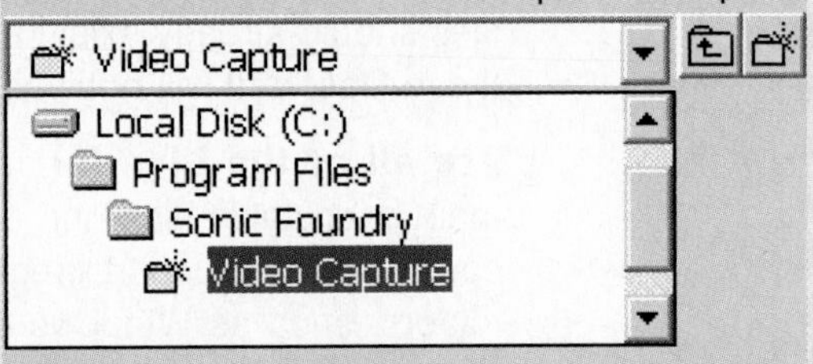

4 Follow the prompts provided by the setup program to specify a folder to hold the new software program. You can typically create a new folder during the setup process, if you did not prepare a folder ahead of time.

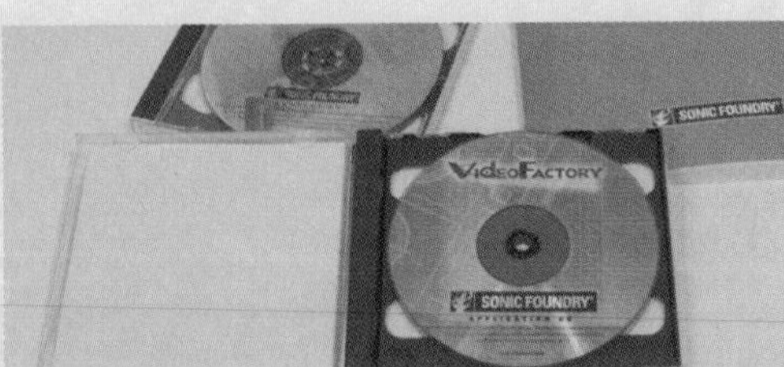

5 If the software includes multiple distribution disks, insert each one in the specified drive when the setup program tells you to do so.

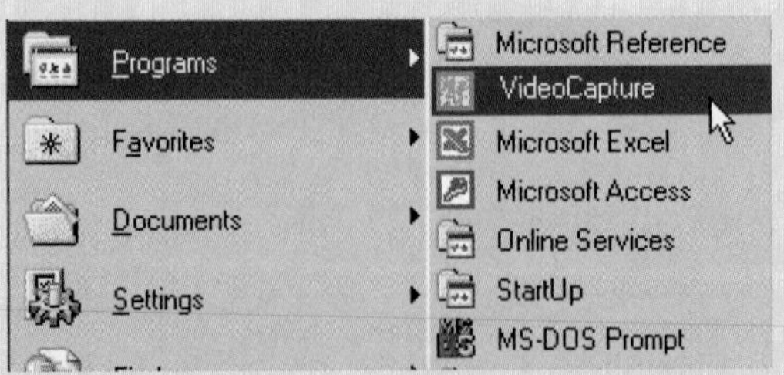

6 When the setup is complete, start the program that you just installed to make sure it works.

INSTALLING DOWNLOADED SOFTWARE

Is the installation process different for downloaded software? The installation process is slightly different for Windows software that you download. Usually all of the files needed for the new software are **zipped** to consolidate them into one large file, which is compressed to decrease its size and reduce the download time. As a first step in the installation process, this large, downloaded file must be reconstituted, or **unzipped**, into the original collection of files. Depending on the software, one or more parts of the installation process might be automated. You could encounter any of the following compressed file types for downloaded software:

- **Self-installing executable file.** Under the most automated installation system, the process of downloading the new software automatically initiates the entire installation process. The software download is packaged as one large file with an .exe extension. This **self-installing executable file** automatically unzips itself and starts the setup program. You simply have to follow the setup program prompts to acknowledge the license agreement, indicate the folder for the software files, and complete the installation.
- **Self-executing zip file.** Downloaded files with .exe extensions do not always install themselves. Some are simply **self-executing zip files**, which automatically unzip the software's files, but do not automatically start the setup program. Under this installation system, you start the executable file to unzip the files for the new software. One of these files will be the *Setup.exe* program. Next, you manually start the setup program and follow its prompts to complete the installation.
- **Manual download and install.** If you download the software and it arrives as one huge file with a .zip extension, you must locate this file on your hard disk and then use a program such as WinZip to unzip it. You then must run the setup program to acknowledge the license agreement, indicate the folder for the software files, and complete the installation. Windows XP includes built-in support for .zip files, so a third-party program like WinZip is not required, but you must still locate the .zip file and run it to initiate the installation process.

3

Is installing a software upgrade different from installing a full version? Installing a software upgrade, either from a distribution CD or from a download, is very similar to installing a full version of the software. The update usually provides a setup program that checks to make sure your computer contains a valid version of the program that you want to upgrade, then it guides you through the rest of the upgrade process.

UNINSTALLING SOFTWARE

How do I get rid of software? With some operating systems, such as DOS, you can remove software simply by deleting its files. Other operating systems, such as Windows and Mac OS, provide access to an **uninstall routine**, which deletes the software's files from various directories on your computer's hard disk. The uninstall routine also removes references to the program from the desktop and from operating system files, such as the file system and, in the case of Windows, from the Windows Registry.

With Windows software, you can typically find the uninstall routine on the same menu as the program (see Figure 3-40). If an uninstall routine is not provided by the software, you can use the one provided by the operating system. In Windows, the Add/Remove Programs icon is located in the Control Panel, accessible from the Start menu.

FIGURE 3-40

To uninstall any Windows application software, first look for an Uninstall option listed on the same menu that you use to start the program (top). If that option is not available, use the Add/Remove Programs option from the Control Panel (bottom).

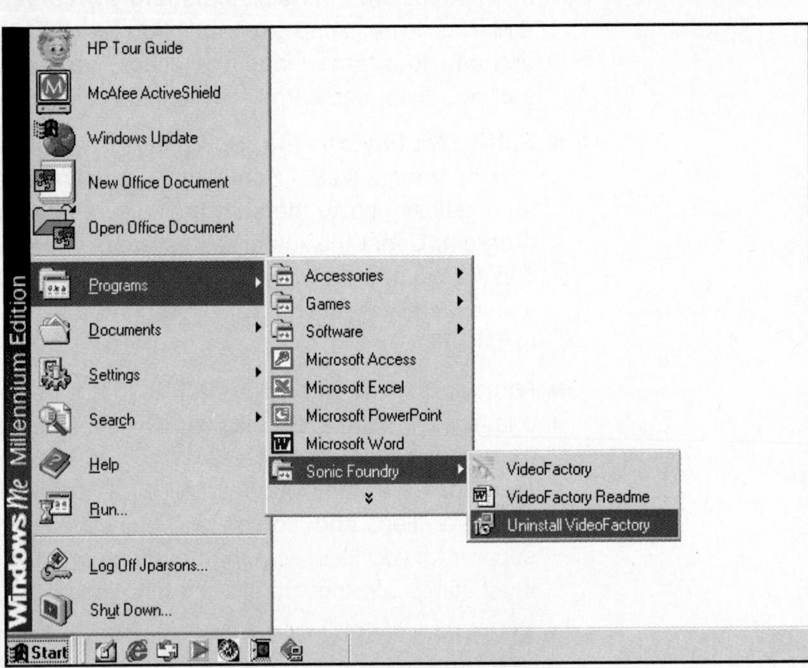

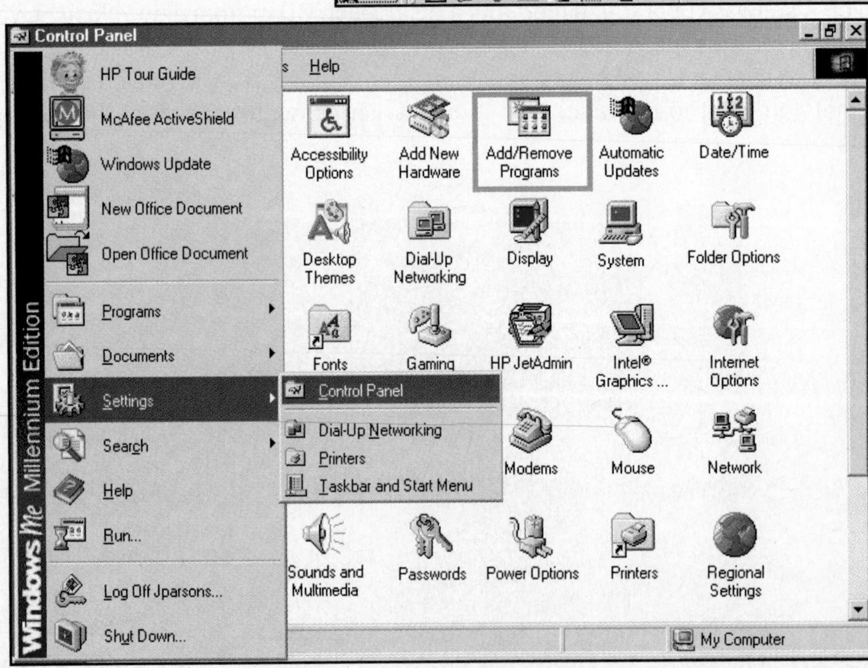

To read the actual text of software copyright laws, connect to the Software Copyright InfoWeb.

click

SOFTWARE COPYRIGHTS

Is it legal to copy software? Once you purchase a software package, you might assume that you can install it and use it in any way that you like. In fact, your "purchase" entitles you to use the software only in certain prescribed ways. In most countries, computer software, like a book or movie, is protected by a copyright. A **copyright** is a form of legal protection that grants the author of an original "work" an exclusive right to copy, distribute, sell, and modify that work, except under special circumstances described by copyright laws. These exceptions include:

1. The purchaser has the right to copy software from a distribution disk or Web site to a computer's hard disk in order to install it.
2. The purchaser can make an extra, or backup, copy of the software in case the original copy becomes erased or damaged.
3. The purchaser is allowed to copy and distribute sections of a software program for use in critical reviews and teaching.

Most software displays a **copyright notice**, such as "© 2001 eCourseWare," on one of its screens. This notice is not required by law, however, so programs without a copyright notice are still protected by copyright law. People who circumvent copyright law and illegally copy, distribute, or modify software are sometimes called software pirates, and their illegal copies are referred to as pirated software.

3

FIGURE 3-41

When software has a shrink-wrap license, you agree to the terms of the software license by opening the package. If you do not agree with the terms, you should return the software in its unopened package.

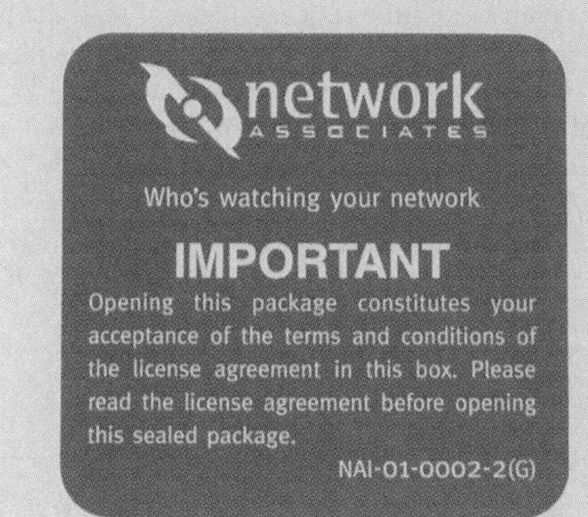

SOFTWARE LICENSES

What is a software license? In addition to copyright protection, computer software is often protected by the terms of a software license. A **software license**, or "license agreement," is a legal contract that defines the ways in which you may use a computer program. For personal computer software, you will find the license on the outside of the package, on a separate card inside the package, on the CD packaging, or in one of the program files.

Most legal contracts require signatures before the terms of the contract take effect. This requirement becomes unwieldy with software—imagine having to sign a license agreement and return it before you can use a new software package. To circumvent the signature requirement, software publishers typically use two techniques to validate a software license: shrink-wrap licenses and installation agreements.

When you purchase computer software, the distribution disks, CDs, or DVDs are usually sealed in an envelope, plastic box, or shrink wrapping. A **shrink-wrap license** goes into effect as soon as you open the packaging. Figure 3-41 explains more about the mechanics of a shrink-wrap license.

An **installation agreement** is displayed on the screen when you first install the software. After reading the software license on the screen, you can indicate that you accept the terms of the license by clicking a designated button—usually labeled "OK," "I agree," or "I accept."

Software licenses are often lengthy and written in "legalese," but your legal right to use the software continues only as long as you abide by the terms of the software license. Therefore, you should understand the software license for any software you use. To become familiar with a typical license agreement, you can read through the one in Figure 3-42.

FIGURE 3-42

When you read a software license agreement, look for answers to the following questions:

Am I buying the software or licensing it?

When does the license go into effect?

Under what circumstances can I make copies?

Can I rent the software?

Can I sell the software?

What if the software includes a distribution CD and a set of distribution disks?

Does the software publisher provide a warranty?

Can I loan the software to a friend?

Software License Agreement

Important - READ CAREFULLY: This License Agreement ("Agreement") is a legal agreement between you and eCourseWare Corporation for the software product, eCourse GraphWare ("The SOFTWARE"). By installing, copying, or otherwise using the SOFTWARE, you agree to be bound by the terms of this Agreement. The SOFTWARE is protected by copyright laws and international copyright treaties. The SOFTWARE is licensed, not sold.

GRANT OF LICENSE. This Agreement gives you the right to install and use one copy of the SOFTWARE on a single computer. The primary user of the computer on which the SOFTWARE is installed may make a second copy for his or her exclusive use on a portable computer.

OTHER RIGHTS AND LIMITATIONS. You may not reverse engineer, decompile, or disassemble the SOFTWARE except and only to the extent that such activity is expressly permitted by applicable law.

The SOFTWARE is licensed as a single product; its components may not be separated for use on more than one computer. You may not rent, lease, or lend the SOFTWARE. You may permanently transfer all of your rights under this Agreement, provided you retain no copies, you transfer all of the SOFTWARE, and the recipient agrees to the terms of this Agreement. If the software product is an upgrade, any transfer must include all prior versions of the SOFTWARE.

You may receive the SOFTWARE in more than one medium. Regardless of the type of medium you receive, you may use only one medium that is appropriate for your single computer. You may not use or install the other medium on another computer.

WARRANTY. eCourseWare warrants that the SOFTWARE will perform substantially in accordance with the accompanying written documentation for a period of ninety (90) days from the date of receipt. TO THE MAXIMUM EXTENT PERMITTED BY APPLICABLE LAW, eCourseWare AND ITS SUPPLIERS DISCLAIM ALL OTHER WARRANTIES AND CONDITIONS EITHER EXPRESS OR IMPLIED, INCLUDING, BUT NOT LIMITED TO, IMPLIED WARRANTIES OF MERCHANTABILITY, FITNESS FOR A PARTICULAR PURPOSE, TITLE, AND NON-INFRINGEMENT, WITH REGARD TO THE SOFTWARE PRODUCT.

Are all software licenses similar? Copyright laws provide fairly severe restrictions on copying, distributing, and reselling software; however, a license agreement may offer additional rights to consumers. The licenses for commercial software, shareware, freeware, open source, and public domain software provide different levels of permission for software use, copying, and distribution.

Commercial software is typically sold in computer stores or at Web sites. Although you "buy" this software, you actually purchase only the right to use it under the terms of the software license. A license for commercial software typically adheres closely to the limitations provided by copyright law, although it might give you permission to install the software on a computer at work and on a computer at home, provided that you use only one of them at a time.

Shareware is copyrighted software marketed under a "try before you buy" policy. It typically includes a license that permits you to use the software for a trial period. To use it beyond the trial period, you must pay a registration fee. A shareware license usually allows you to make copies of the software and distribute them to others. If they choose to use the software, they must pay a registration fee as well. These shared copies provide a low-cost marketing and distribution channel. Registration fee payment relies on the honor system, so unfortunately many shareware authors collect only a fraction of the money they deserve for their programming efforts. Thousands of shareware programs are available, encompassing just about as many applications as commercial software.

Freeware is copyrighted software that—as you might expect—is available for free. Because the software is protected by copyright, you cannot do anything with it that is not expressly allowed by copyright law or by the author. Typically, the license for freeware permits you to use the software, copy it, and give it away; but does not permit you to alter it or sell it. Many utility programs, device drivers, and some games are available as freeware.

Open source software makes the uncompiled program instructions—the source code—available to programmers who want to modify and improve the software. Open source software may be sold or distributed free of charge, but it must, in every case, include the source code. Linux is an example of open source software, as is FreeBSD—a version of UNIX designed for personal computers.

Public domain software is not protected by copyright because the copyright has expired, or the author has placed the program in the public domain, making it available without restriction. Public domain software may be freely copied, distributed, and even resold. The primary restriction on public domain software is that you are not allowed to apply for a copyright on it.

3

QUICKCheck Section D

1. A(n) ________ program typically handles the process of copying files from a distribution disk or CD to the hard disk.
2. Software that you download is usually ________ into a single, compressed file, so it must be reconstituted to its original files as part of the installation process.
3. You should ________ unwanted software, instead of simply deleting the folder that contains the software files.
4. ________ laws provide software authors with the exclusive right to copy, distribute, sell, and modify their work, except under special circumstances.
5. ________ is copyrighted software that is marketed with a "try before you buy" policy.
6. Linux is an example of open ________ software.
7. Public ________ software is not copyrighted, making it available for use without restriction, except that you cannot apply for a copyright on it.

check answers

LAB 3-D INSTALLING AND UNINSTALLING SOFTWARE

In this lab, you'll learn:

- How to use a setup program to install Windows application software from a distribution CD
- What to do if the setup program doesn't automatically start
- The difference between typical, compact, and custom installation options
- How to specify a folder for a new software installation
- How to install downloaded software
- How to install an upgrade
- How to uninstall a Windows application
- What happens in addition to deleting files when you uninstall a software application
- How to locate the program that will uninstall a software application
- Why you might not want to delete all of the files associated with an application

LAB Assignments

1. Start the interactive part of the lab. Insert your Tracking Disk if you want to save your QuickCheck results. Perform each of the lab steps as directed, and answer all of the lab QuickCheck questions. When you exit the lab, your answers are automatically graded and your results are displayed.

2. Browse the Web and locate a software application that you might like to download. Use information supplied by the Web site to answer the following questions:

   a. What is the name of the program and the URL of the download site?

   b. What is the size of the download file?

   c. According to the instructions, does the download file appear to require manual installation, is it a self-executing zip file, or is it a self-installing executable file?

3. On the computer that you typically use, look through the list of programs (click Start, then select Programs to see a list of them). List the names of any programs that include their own uninstall routines.

4. On the computer that you typically use, open the Control Panel and then open the Add/Remove Programs dialog box. List the first 10 programs that are currently installed on the computer.

As a justification of high piracy rates, some observers point out that people in many countries simply might not be able to afford software that is priced for the U.S. market. This argument would make sense in China, where the average annual income is equivalent to about $3,500, and in North Korea, where the average income is only $900. A Korean who legitimately purchases Microsoft Office for $250 would be spending more than one-quarter of his or her annual income. Most of the countries with a high incidence of software piracy, however, have strong economies and respectable per capita incomes. To further discredit the theory that piracy stems from poverty, India—which has a fairly large computer-user community, but a per capita income of only $1,600—is not among the top 10 countries with high rates of software piracy.

You can read the GNU Manifesto and other thought-provoking articles about software piracy at the Copyright and Piracy InfoWeb.

click

If economic factors do not account for the pervasiveness of software piracy, what does? Some analysts suggest that people need more education about software copyrights and the economic implications of piracy. Other analysts believe that copyright enforcement must be increased by supporting and implementing more vigorous efforts to identify and prosecute pirates.

3

WHAT DO YOU THINK?

1. Do you believe that software piracy is a serious issue? ○ Yes ○ No ○ Not sure
2. Do you know of any instances of software piracy? ○ Yes ○ No ○ Not sure
3. Do you think that most software pirates understand that they are doing something illegal? ○ Yes ○ No ○ Not sure
4. Should software publishers try to adjust software pricing for local markets? ○ Yes ○ No ○ Not sure

click to save your responses

INTERACTIVE SUMMARY

The Interactive Summary helps you to select and remember important concepts from this chapter. Fill in the blanks to best complete each sentence. When using the NP6 BookOnCD, you can click the Check Answers buttons to automatically score your answers. Place your Tracking Disk in the floppy disk drive if you want to save your scores.

__________ consists of computer programs and data files that work together to provide a computer with the instructions and data necessary for carrying out a specific type of task, such as document production, video editing, graphic design, or Web browsing. Computer __________ write the instructions for the programs that become the components of a computer software product. To understand how software is installed and uninstalled, it is important for computer owners to recognize that today's software typically consists of many files.

To create a software environment, a programmer must define the __________ for each element in the environment, such as where an object appears, its shape, its color, and its behavior. A computer __________ provides the tools that a programmer uses to create software. Most programmers today prefer to use __________ languages, such as C++, Java, COBOL, and Visual Basic. A computer's microprocessor only understands __________ language, however, so a program that is written in a high-level language must be compiled or interpreted before it can be processed. A __________ translates all of the instructions in a program as a single batch, and the resulting machine language instructions, called __________ code, are placed in a new file. An alternative method of translation uses an __________ to translate instructions one at a time while the program runs.

check answers

A computer's software is like the chain of command in an army. __________ software tells the operating system what to do. The operating system tells the device drivers, device drivers tell the hardware, and the hardware actually does the work. The operating system interacts with application software, device drivers, and hardware to manage a computer's __________. In addition, many operating systems also influence the "look and feel" of your software, or what's known as the user __________.

The core part of an operating system is called the __________. In addition to this core, many operating systems provide helpful tools, called __________, which you can use to control and customize your computer equipment and work environment. Operating systems are informally categorized and characterized using one or more of the following terms: A __________ operating system expects to deal with one set of input devices—those that can be controlled by one person at a time. A __________ operating system is designed to deal with input, output, and processing requests from many users. A __________ operating system provides process and memory management services that allow two or more programs to run simultaneously. A __________ operating system is one that's designed for a personal computer—either a desktop or notebook computer. Popular desktop operating systems include Windows 95/98/Me/XP and Mac OS. Popular __________ operating systems include Windows NT/2000, Linux, and UNIX.

PROJECTS

An NP6 Project is an open-ended activity that will help you apply the concepts you have learned. Many projects require resources in addition to your textbook, such as current magazines, library materials, or Web access. When you tackle a project, be prepared to use your critical thinking skills, logical analysis skills, and creativity.

1 Issue Research: Software Piracy The Issue section of this chapter focused on copyrights and software piracy. For this project, you will write a two–five page paper about this issue based on information that you gather from the Internet. To begin this project, consult the Copyright and Piracy InfoWeb (see page 161), and link to the recommended Web pages to get an in-depth overview of the issue. Armed with this background, select one of the following viewpoints and statements and argue for or against it:

a. Free software advocates: As an enabling technology, software should be freely distributed, along with its modifiable source code.

b. Librarians: Copyright laws, especially the Digital Millennium Copyright Act, minimize the needs of the public, and go too far in their efforts to protect the rights of software authors.

c. Software Publishers Association: Strong copyright laws and enforcement are essential in order for companies to publish and support high-quality software.

Whatever viewpoint you decide to present, make sure that you back it up with facts and references to authoritative articles and Web pages. You can place citations to these pages (including the author's name, article title, date of publication, and URL) at the end of your paper as endnotes, on each page as footnotes, or along with the appropriate paragraphs using parentheses. Follow your professor's instructions for submitting your paper via e-mail or as a printed document.

2 Legal Beagle: Analyzing a License Agreement When you use a software package, it is important to understand the legal restrictions on its use. For this project, make a photocopy of the license agreement for any software package. Read the license agreement, then answer these questions:

a. Is this a shrink-wrap license? Why or why not?

b. After you pay your computer dealer for the program covered by this license, who owns the program?

c. Can you legally have one copy of the program on your computer at work and another copy of the program on your computer at home if you use the software only in one place at a time?

d. Can you legally sell the software? Why or why not?

e. Under what conditions can you legally transfer possession of the program to someone else?

f. If you were the owner of a software store, could you legally rent the program to customers if you were sure they did not keep a copy after the rental period was over?

g. Can you legally install this software on one computer, but give more than one user access to it?

h. If you use this program for an important business decision and later find out that a mistake in the program caused you to lose $500,000, what legal recourse is provided by the license agreement?

3

ADDITIONAL PROJECTS

TIP

Click  to access the Web for additional projects.

FILE MANAGEMENT, VIRUS PROTECTION, AND BACKUP

CONTENTS

InfoWebLinks

The InfoWebLinks, located in the margins of this chapter, show the way to a variety of Web sites that contain additional information and updates to the chapter topics. Your computer needs an Internet connection to access these links. You can connect to the Web links for this chapter by:

- clicking the InfoWeb links in the margins
- clicking this underlined link
- starting your browser and entering the URL *www.infoweblinks.com/np6/chapter4.htm*

TIP

When using the **BookOnCD**, the  symbols are "clickable."

CHAPTER PREVIEW

What do you associate with the word "retro"? Maybe it conjures up images of fashionably nostalgic styles from the past—curvatious diners and chrome-laden automobiles, peace symbols and bell bottoms, or disco lights and leisure suits. For the troops on the front lines of the computer virus battlefield, "retro" means a nightmare—a virus that disables antivirus software and leaves computer files open to attack. The topics in Chapter 4 target computer files from several angles, including what they are, how you can keep them organized, and how you can protect them.

Section A launches the chapter with a general introduction to computer files—the storage bins for all of the "stuff" on your computer. It begins with some very practical information about filenames, helps you understand the importance of filename extensions in the Windows environment, and guides you through the tricky maze of devices, folders, and filenames that form a path to a file.

Section B explains techniques for organizing computer files so that they are easy to access, update, and back up. It also explains how an operating system stores, deletes, and tracks files—good background for understanding when and why to use a file shredder or defragmentation utility.

Section C delves into the fascinating world of computer viruses. You'll discover why you shouldn't open e-mail attachments like LOVE-LETTER-FOR-YOU, and where you might expect the Ping of Death to strike. This section also helps you distinguish between real virus alerts and hoaxes—a skill that can help you avoid the embarrassment of sending your friends panicky e-mails about a non-existent virus.

Section D focuses on one of the most important aspects of computing—backup. You'll learn how to evaluate different backup options, such as tapes, CDs, a network, or a Web site. You'll also discover the pitfalls of depending on the Restore CD provided with your computer.

When you complete this chapter you should be able to:

- Create valid names for files and folders, plus demonstrate that you can construct and trace file paths
- Demonstrate how to use file management features of application software and operating system utilities
- Describe how a computer physically stores data on disks, but represents this storage system with a logical model
- Explain how file viruses, boot sector viruses, macro viruses, Trojan horses, worms, and Denial of Service attacks affect files and disrupt computer operations
- Describe how a computer owner can use antivirus software to avoid, find, and remove viruses
- Demonstrate that you can implement a viable backup and restore plan
- Compare the advantages and disadvantages of using tapes, floppy disks, a second hard disk, CDs, Zip disks, networks, and Web sites for backups

4

TIP Click  to access the Web for a complete list of learning objectives for Chapter 4.

Section A

FILE BASICS

The term "file" was used for filing cabinets and collections of papers long before it became part of the personal computer lexicon. Today, a **computer file**—or simply "a file"— is defined as a named collection of data that exists on a storage medium, such as a hard disk, floppy disk, CD, DVD, or tape. A file can contain a group of records, a document, a photo, music, a video, an e-mail message, or a computer program.

Computer files have several characteristics, such as a name, format, location, size, and date. To make effective use of computer files, you'll need a good understanding of these file basics, and that is the focus of Section A.

FILENAMES, EXTENSIONS, AND FORMATS

What are the rules for naming files? Every file has a name and might also have a filename extension. When you save a file, you must provide it with a valid filename that adheres to specific rules, referred to as **file-naming conventions**. Each operating system has a unique set of file-naming conventions. You can use Figure 4-1 to determine whether filenames, such as *Nul*, *My File.doc*, *Report:2002*, and *Bud01/02.txt*, are valid under the operating system that you use.

<table>
<tr><th>FIGURE 4-1</th><th colspan="4">File-Naming Conventions</th></tr>
<tr><th></th><th>DOS and Windows 3.1</th><th>Windows 95/98/ME/XP/NT/2000</th><th>Mac OS (Classic)</th><th>UNIX/Linux</th></tr>
<tr><td>Maximum length of filename</td><td>8-character filename plus an extension of 3 characters or less</td><td>Filename and extension cannot exceed 255 characters</td><td>1-31 characters</td><td>14-256 characters (depending on UNIX/Linux version) including an extension of any length</td></tr>
<tr><td>Spaces allowed</td><td>No</td><td>Yes</td><td>Yes</td><td>No</td></tr>
<tr><td>Numbers allowed</td><td>Yes</td><td>Yes</td><td>Yes</td><td>Yes</td></tr>
<tr><td>Characters not allowed</td><td>* / [ ] ; " = \ : , | ?</td><td>* \ : < > | " / ?</td><td>:</td><td>* ! @ # $ % ^ & ( ) { } [ ] " \ ? ; < ></td></tr>
<tr><td>Filenames not allowed</td><td>Aux, Com1, Com2, Com3, Com4, Con, Lpt1, Lpt2, Lpt3, Prn, Nul</td><td>Aux, Com1, Com2, Com3, Com4, Con, Lpt1, Lpt2, Lpt3, Prn, Nul</td><td>Any filename is allowed</td><td>Depends on the version of UNIX or Linux</td></tr>
<tr><td>Case sensitive</td><td>No</td><td>No</td><td>No</td><td>Yes (use lowercase)</td></tr>
</table>

FIGURE 4-8

You can visualize the directory of a disk as a tree on its side. The trunk corresponds to the root directory, the branches to folders, and the leaves to files.

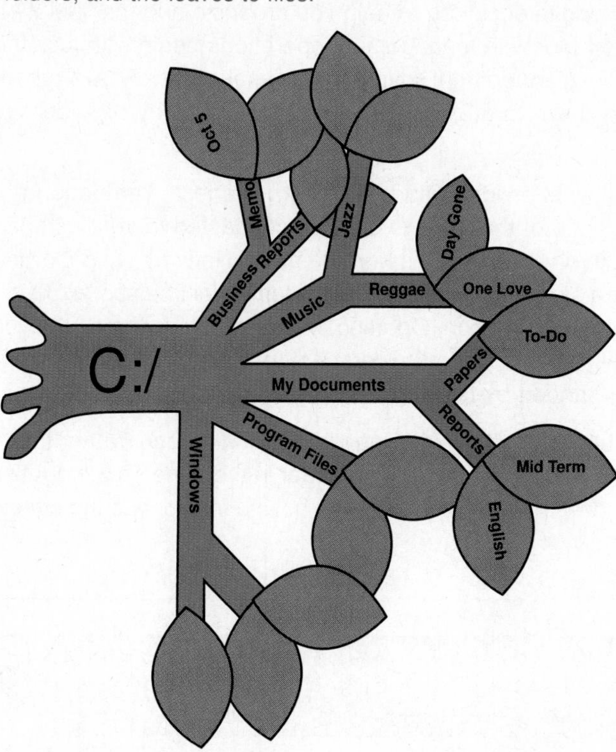

FIGURE 4-9

Windows Explorer borrows the folders from the filing cabinet metaphor, and places them in a hierarchical structure similar to a tree on its side.

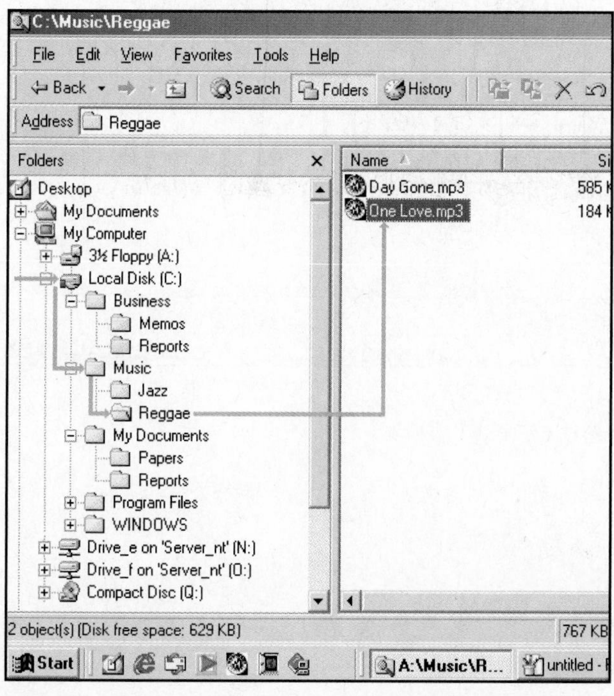

FILE MANAGEMENT METAPHORS

How does a metaphor help me visualize the "big picture" for my file storage? File management utilities often use some sort of **storage metaphor** to help you visualize and mentally organize the files on your disks and other storage devices. These metaphors are also called **logical storage models** because they are supposed to help you form a mental (logical) picture of the way in which your files are stored.

What storage metaphors are typically used for personal computers? After hearing so much about files and folders, you might have guessed that the filing cabinet is a popular metaphor for computer storage. In this metaphor, each storage device of a computer corresponds to one of the drawers in a filing cabinet. The drawers hold folders and the folders hold files.

Another storage metaphor is based on a hierarchical diagram that is sometimes referred to as a "tree structure." In this metaphor, a tree represents a storage device. The trunk of the tree corresponds to the root directory. The branches of the tree represent folders. These branches can split into small branches representing folders within folders. The leaves at the end of a branch represent the files in a particular folder. Figure 4-8 illustrates the tree lying on its side so that you can see the relationship to the metaphor shown in the next figure, Figure 4-9.

The tree structure metaphor provides a useful mental image of the way in which files and folders are organized. It is not, however, particularly practical as a user interface. Imagine the complexity of the tree diagram from Figure 4-8 if it were expanded to depict branches for hundreds of folders and leaves for thousands of files.

For practicality, storage metaphors are translated into more mundane screen displays. Figure 4-9 shows how Microsoft programmers combined the filing cabinet metaphor with the tree structure metaphor within the Windows Explorer file management utility.

WINDOWS EXPLORER

How do I use a file management utility? As an example of a file management utility, let's take a closer look at **Windows Explorer**, a utility program that is bundled with the Windows operating system, and is designed to help you organize and manipulate the files stored on your computer. Most file management operations begin with locating a particular file or folder. A file management utility should make it easy to find what you're looking for by drilling down through your computer's hierarchy of folders and files.

The Windows Explorer window is divided into two "window panes." The pane on the left side of the window lists each of the storage devices connected to your computer, plus several important system objects, such as My Computer, Network Neighborhood, and the Desktop. An icon for a storage device or other system object can be "expanded" by clicking its corresponding plus-sign icon. Opening an icon displays the next level of the storage hierarchy—usually a collection of folders. Any of these folders that contain subfolders can be further expanded by clicking their plus-sign icons.

A device icon or folder can be "opened" by clicking directly on the icon, rather than on the plus sign. Once an icon is opened, its contents appear in the pane on the right side of the Windows Explorer window. Figure 4-10 illustrates how to manipulate the directory display.

FIGURE 4-10

Windows Explorer makes it easy to drill down through the levels of the directory hierarchy to locate a folder or file.

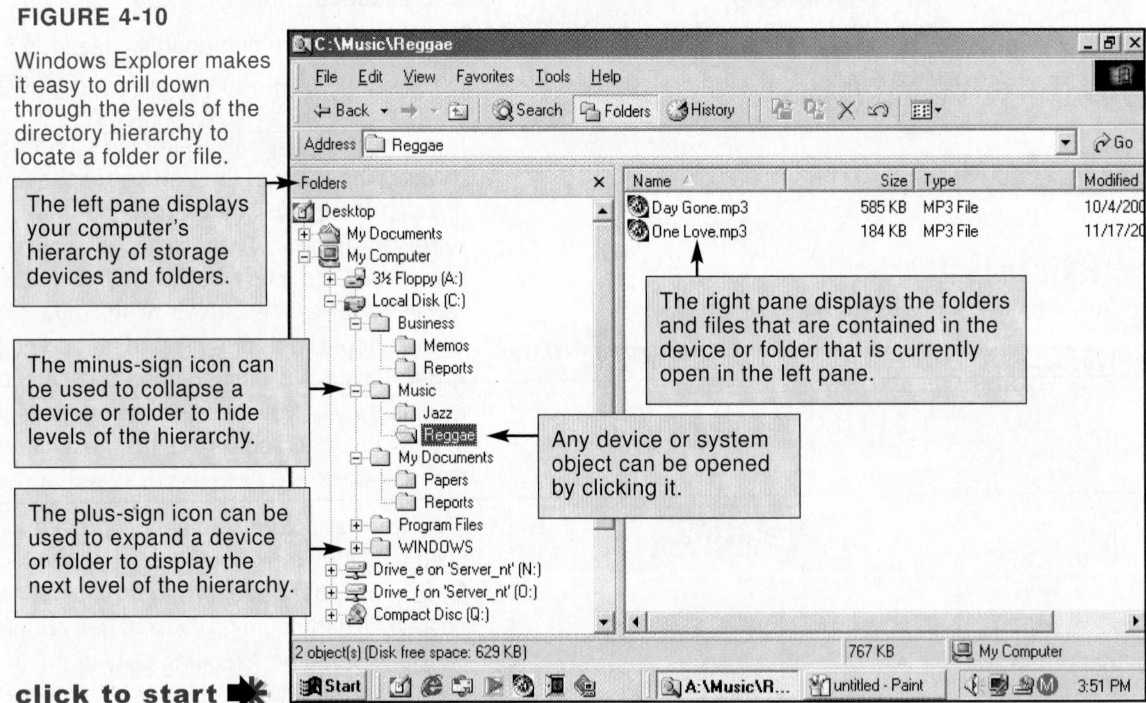

click to start

What can I do with the folders and files that are listed in Windows Explorer? In addition to locating files and folders, Windows Explorer provides a set of tools that will help you manipulate files and folders in the following ways:

- **Rename.** You might want to change the name of a file or folder to better describe its contents. When renaming a file, you should be careful to keep the same filename extension so that you can open it with the correct application software.
- **Copy.** You can copy a file or folder—for example, you can copy a file from your hard disk to a floppy disk if you want to send it to a friend or colleague. You might also want to make a copy of a document so that you can revise the copy and leave the original intact. Remember to adhere to copyright and license restrictions when you copy files.
- **Move.** You can move a file from one folder to another, or from one storage device to another. When you move a file, it is erased from its original location, so make sure that you remember the new location of the file. You can also move folders from one storage device to another, or move them to a different folder.
- **Delete.** You can delete a file when you no longer need it. You can also delete a folder. Be careful when you delete a folder, because most file management utilities also delete all the files that a folder contains.

FIGURE 4-11

Windows Explorer helps you to delete, copy, move, and rename files.

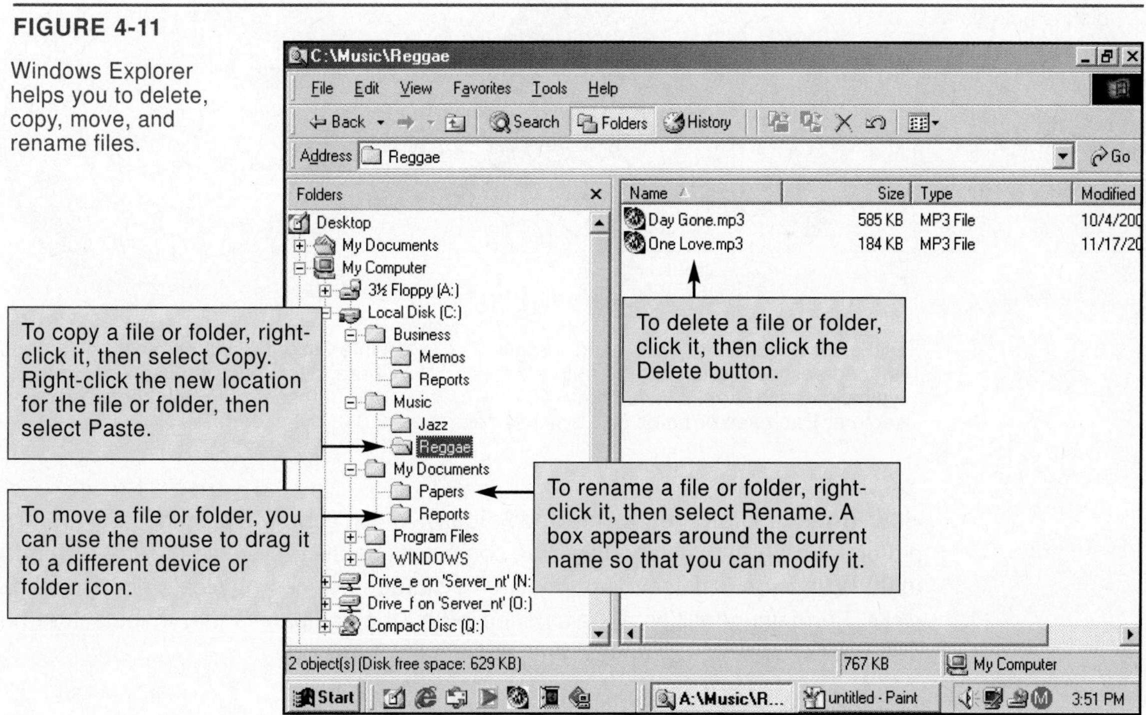

4

How can I work with more than one file at a time? To work with a group of files or folders, you must first select them. You can accomplish this task in several ways. You can hold down the Ctrl key as you click each item. This method works well if you are selecting files or folders that are not listed consecutively. As an alternative, you can hold down the Shift key while you click the first item and the last item that you want to select. By using this method, you select the two items that you clicked, and all the items in between. Windows Explorer displays all of the items that you selected by highlighting them. Once a group of items is highlighted, you can use the same copy, move, or delete procedure that you would use for a single item.

PHYSICAL FILE STORAGE

Is data stored in specific places on a disk? So far, you've seen how an operating system like Windows can help you visualize computer storage as files and folders. This pretty picture, however, has little to do with what actually happens on your disk. The structure of files and folders that you see in Windows Explorer is what's called a "logical" model—logical because it is supposed to help you create a mental picture. The **physical storage model** describes what actually happens on the disks and in the circuits. As you will see, the physical model is quite different from the logical model.

Before a computer can store a file on a disk, CD, or DVD, the storage medium must be formatted. The **formatting** process creates the equivalent of electronic storage bins by dividing a disk into **tracks**, and then further dividing each track into **sectors**. Tracks and sectors are numbered to provide addresses for each data storage bin. The numbering scheme depends on the storage device and the operating system. On CDs and DVDs, one or more tracks spiral out from the center of the disk; on floppy, Zip, and hard disks, tracks are arranged as concentric circles (Figure 4-12).

FIGURE 4-12

A process called formatting prepares the surface of a disk to hold data.

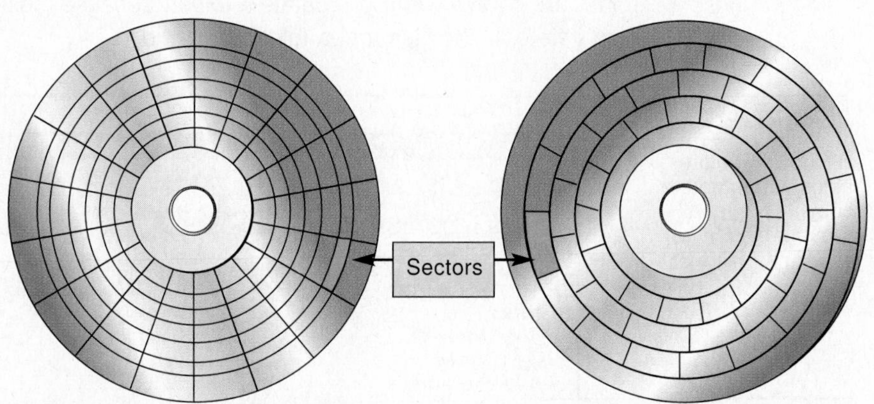

Disks are divided into tracks and wedge-shaped sectors—each side of a floppy disk typically has 80 tracks divided into 18 sectors. Each sector holds 512 bytes of data.

On a typical CD, a single track is about three miles long and is divided into 336,000 sectors. Each sector holds 2,048 bytes of data.

How does a disk get formatted? Today, most floppy, Zip, and hard disks are preformatted at the factory; however, computer operating systems provide **formatting utilities** that you can use to reformat some storage devices—typically floppy and hard disks. Formatting utilities are also supplied by the companies that manufacture hard disk drives, writable CD drives, and writable DVD drives.

COMPUTER VIRUSES

Computer viruses cause sensational headlines. They also cause an estimated $1.6 billion in lost productivity every year. Last year, in North America alone, businesses lost more than 7,000 person-years of productivity while responding to viruses, Denial-of-Service glitches, and other cyber attacks.

Viruses are one of the biggest threats to the security of your computer files. The number of computer viruses is increasing at an unprecedented rate. In 1986, there was one known computer virus. By 1990, the total had jumped to 80. Today, the count exceeds 58,000, and between 10 and 15 new viruses appear every day. Viruses are spreading more rapidly than ever. The Michelangelo virus took seven months to reach 75,000 people; the Melissa virus took 10 hours to reach 3.5 million people; and a virus called I-love-you took only three hours to reach 72 million.

Computer viruses invade all types of computers, including mainframes, servers, personal computers, and even handheld computers. Spreading a virus is a crime in the U.S. and in many other countries, but a battery of laws has not prevented viruses from "accidentally" escaping from a hacker's computer, or from being intentionally released. Although technically, the term virus refers to a type of program that behaves in a specific way, it has become a generic term that refers to a variety of destructive programs. To defend your computer against viruses, you should understand what they are, how they work, and how to use antivirus software.

VIRUSES, TROJAN HORSES, AND WORMS

What's the technical definition of a virus? A **computer virus** is a set of program instructions that attaches itself to a file, reproduces itself, and spreads to other files. It can corrupt files, destroy data, display an irritating message, or otherwise disrupt computer operations. A common misconception is that viruses spread themselves from one computer to another. They can only replicate themselves on the host computer. Viruses spread because people distribute infected files by exchanging disks and CDs, sending e-mail attachments, and downloading software from the Web.

A computer virus generally infects the files executed by your computer—files with extensions such as .exe, .com, or .vbs. When your computer executes an infected program, it also executes the attached virus instructions. These instructions then remain in RAM, waiting to infect the next program that your computer runs, or the next disk that it accesses. In addition to replicating itself, a virus might perform a **trigger event**, sometimes referred to as a "payload," which could be as harmless as displaying an annoying message, or as devastating as corrupting the data on your computer's hard disk. Trigger events are often keyed to a specific date. For example, the Michelangelo virus is designed to damage hard disk files on March 6, the birthday of artist Michelangelo.

A key characteristic of viruses is their ability to "lurk" in a computer for days or months, quietly replicating themselves. While this replication takes place, you might not even know that your computer has contracted a virus; therefore it is easy to inadvertently spread infected files to other people's computers.

Viruses can be classified by the types of files they infect. A virus that attaches to an application program, such as a game, is known as a **file virus**. One of the most notorious file viruses, called Chernobyl, can infect just about any EXE files, including games and productivity software. Its payload can overwrite sections of your hard disk.

A **boot sector virus** infects the system files that your computer uses every time you turn it on. These viruses can cause widespread damage and reoccurring problems. The old, but persistent, Stoned virus infects the boot sector of floppy and hard disks, for example. In various versions of this virus, the payload can display a message, such as "Your computer is now stoned!" or it can corrupt some of the data on your computer's hard disk.

A **macro virus** infects a set of instructions called a "macro." A **macro** is essentially a miniature program that usually contains legitimate instructions to automate document and worksheet production. A hacker can create a destructive macro, attach it to a document or worksheet, and then distribute it on a floppy disk or over the Internet—often as an e-mail attachment. When anyone views the document, the macro virus duplicates itself into the general macro pool, where it is picked up by other documents. The two most common macro viruses are the Melissa virus, which attaches itself to Microsoft Word documents, and Codemas, which attaches itself to Microsoft Excel spreadsheets.

How is a Trojan horse different from a virus? A **Trojan horse** is a computer program that seems to perform one function while actually doing something else. Technically, it is not the same as a virus because, unlike a virus, a Trojan horse is not designed to make copies of itself. Trojan horses are notorious for stealing passwords. For example, a Trojan horse called PictureNote.Trojan (alias Trojan Horse, Backdoor.Note, Picture.exe, and URLSnoop) usually arrives as an e-mail attachment named Picture.exe, which leads you to believe that you've received some type of graphics software. If you open this file, however, it searches for America Online (AOL) user information, and tries to steal your login and e-mail passwords.

Some Trojan horses delete files and cause other trouble. Although a Trojan horse is not defined as a program that replicates itself, some Trojan horses do contain a virus or a worm, which can replicate and spread.

What's a worm? With the proliferation of network traffic and e-mail, worms have become a major concern in the computing community. Unlike a virus, which is designed to spread from file to file, a **worm** is designed to spread from computer to computer. Most worms take advantage of communications networks—especially the Internet—to travel within e-mail and TCP/IP packets, jumping from one computer to another. Some worms are happy simply to spread throughout a network. Others also deliver payloads that vary from harmless messages to malicious file deletions.

www.InfoWebLinks.com

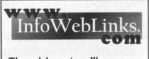

The old saying "know thy enemy" applies to viruses. To learn more details about the viruses that are high on the list of current threats, visit the Virus Descriptions InfoWeb.

Klez, for example, is a mass-mailing worm that sends itself to every address in the address book of an infected computer. To make the virus difficult to track, the "From" line of the infected message contains the e-mail address of a randomly selected person from the address book, rather than the address of the computer that actually sent the mail. The infected e-mail message typically claims to contain an attachment that can be used to protect your computer against Klez, but it actually contains the worm, which can infect your computer when the message—not the attachment—is opened or previewed.

Another notorious worm known as "Love Bug" arrives as an e-mail attachment called LOVE-LETTER-FOR-YOU.TXT.vbs. Once you open the attachment, the worm overwrites most of the music, graphics, document, spreadsheet, and Web files on your disk. After trashing your files, the worm automatically mails itself to everyone in your e-mail address book, looking for other victims.

Notice that the attachment LOVE-LETTER-FOR-YOU.TXT.vbs appears to have two filename extensions. That's a clue that should arouse your suspicions. The second extension, .vbs, is the real filename extension and it means that the file contains an executable program—potentially a virus. Remember that you can set Windows to hide filename extensions. If you do so, the worm-harboring attachment appears simply as LOVE-LETTER-FOR-YOU.TXT. It looks like the attachment has an innocent .txt extension. You might increase your chances of identifying "bad" e-mail attachments if you make sure that Windows is set to display all filename extensions.

Some worms are designed to generate a lot of activity on a network by flooding it with useless traffic—enough traffic to overwhelm the network's processing capability and essentially bring all communications to a halt. These **Denial of Service attacks** have colorful names like Ping of Death, Smurf, and Teardrop, but network users cut off from e-mail and Web browsing have other names for them, like disruptive and obnoxious.

How are viruses spread? Viruses can slip into your computer from a variety of sources. Be cautious of floppy disks, homemade CDs, and Web sites that contain games and other supposedly fun stuff. They are a common source of file viruses, boot sector viruses, and Trojan horses. Figure 4-16 illustrates how a single disk can easily infect many computers.

FIGURE 4-16

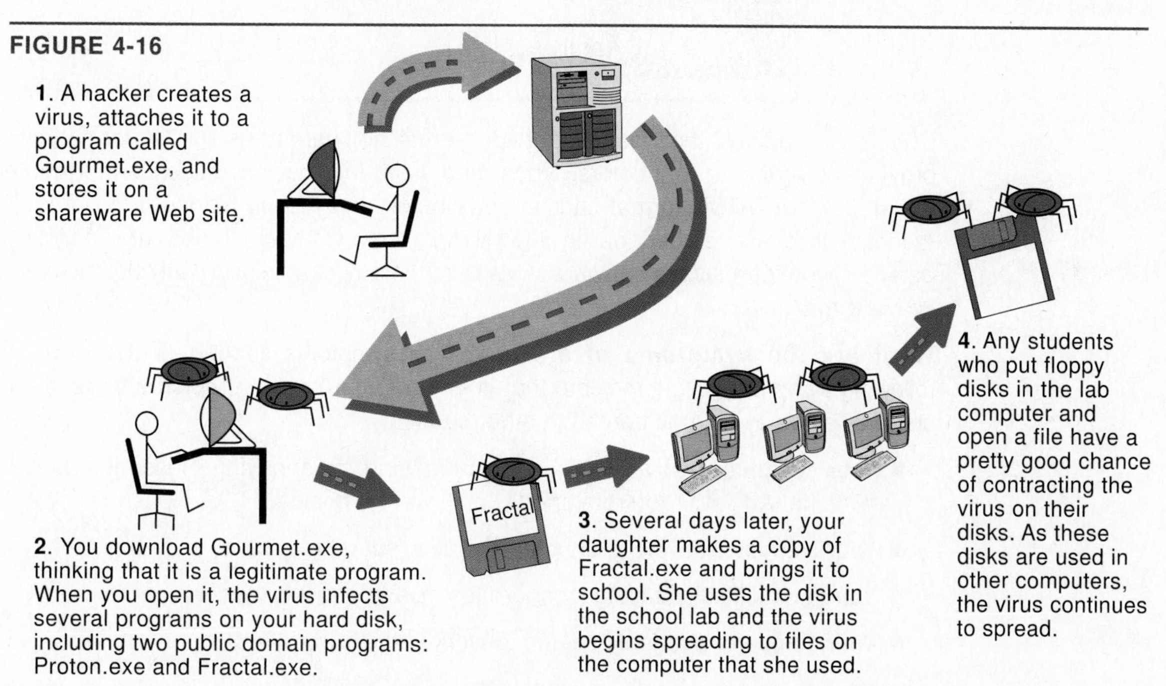

1. A hacker creates a virus, attaches it to a program called Gourmet.exe, and stores it on a shareware Web site.
2. You download Gourmet.exe, thinking that it is a legitimate program. When you open it, the virus infects several programs on your hard disk, including two public domain programs: Proton.exe and Fractal.exe.
Fractal
3. Several days later, your daughter makes a copy of Fractal.exe and brings it to school. She uses the disk in the school lab and the virus begins spreading to files on the computer that she used.
4. Any students who put floppy disks in the lab computer and open a file have a pretty good chance of contracting the virus on their disks. As these disks are used in other computers, the virus continues to spread.

4

A common misconception is that write-protecting your floppy disks by opening the small hole in the corner of the disk prevents virus infection. Although a virus cannot "jump" onto your disk when it is write-protected, you must remove the write protection each time you save a file on the disk. With the write protection removed, your disk is open to a virus attack.

E-mail attachments are another common source of viruses. A seemingly innocent attachment could harbor a file virus or a boot sector virus. Typically, infected attachments look like executable files, usually with .exe filename extensions, although in some cases they can have .sys, .drv, .com, .bin, .vbs, .scr, or .ovl extensions. These files cannot infect your computer unless you open them, thereby executing the virus code that they contain. You should follow the experts' advice about e-mail attachments. Never open a suspicious attachment without first checking it with antivirus software (discussed on the next page).

Macro viruses tend to hang out in documents created with Microsoft Word and spreadsheets created with Microsoft Excel. You might receive files infected with macro viruses on a disk, as a Web download, or as an e-mail attachment. The infected files display the usual .doc or .xls extensions—there are no outward clues to the virus lurking within the file. Today, most software that executes macros includes security features that help protect your computer from macro viruses. As shown in Figure 4-17, Microsoft Word allows you to disable macros.

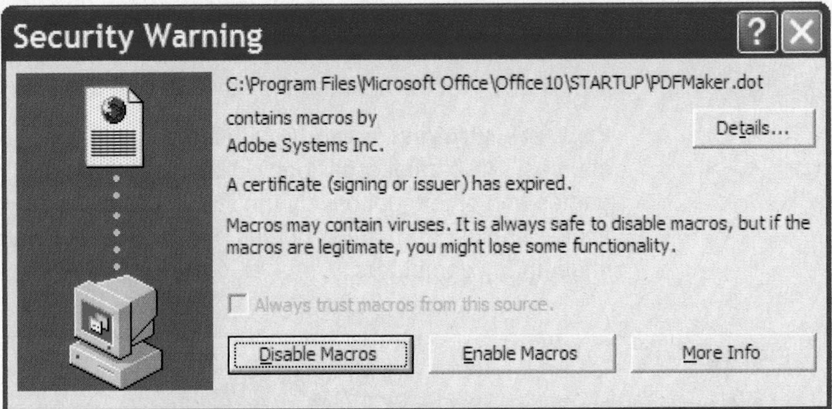

FIGURE 4-17

Macro security features may allow you to disable macros, or warn you if a document contains a macro. Macro security warnings do not necessarily mean that a document contains a macro infected with a virus. Scanning the macro with antivirus software, however, can detect the presence of a virus.

Chapter 1 explained that you can set your e-mail software to use HTML format, which provides a variety of font colors, types, and sizes for your messages. Unfortunately, e-mail that's in HTML format can harbor viruses and worms hidden in program-like "scripts" that are embedded in the HTML tags. These viruses are difficult to detect—even for antivirus software. As a result, many people stick with plain text, non-HTML e-mail.

What are the symptoms of a virus? The symptoms depend on the virus. The following symptoms might indicate that your computer has contracted a virus, though some of these symptoms can have other causes:

- Your computer displays vulgar, embarrassing, or annoying messages, such as "Gotcha! Arf Arf," "You're stoned!," or "I want a cookie."
- Your computer develops unusual visual or sound effects.
- You have difficulty saving files, or files mysteriously disappear.
- Your computer suddenly seems to work very slowly.
- Your computer reboots unexpectedly.
- Your executable files unaccountably increase in size.
- Your computer starts sending out lots of e-mail messages on its own.

It is important to remember, however, that some viruses, worms, and Trojan horses have no recognizable symptoms. Your computer can contract a worm, for example, that never displays an irritating message or attempts to delete your files, but which merrily replicates itself through your e-mail until it eventually arrives at a server where it can do some real damage to a network communication system. To avoid being a pawn in some hacker's destructive plot, you should use antivirus software to evict any viruses, worms, or Trojan horses that try to take up residence in your computer.

Section D DATA BACKUP

Have you ever mistakenly copied an old version of a document over a new version? Has your computer's hard disk drive gone on the fritz? Did a virus wipe out your files before you discovered that it had taken up residence in your computer? Has lightning "fried" your computer system? These kinds of data disasters are not rare; they happen to everyone. You can't always prevent them, so you need a backup plan that helps you recover data that's been wiped out by operator error, viruses, or hardware failures.

Computer experts universally recommend that you make backups of your data. It sounds pretty basic, right? Unfortunately, this advice tells you what to do, not how to do it. It fails to address some key questions, such as: Do I need special backup equipment and software? How often should I make a backup? How many of my files should I back up? What should I do with the backups?

In this last section of Chapter 4, you'll find the answers to your questions about backing up data that's stored on a personal computer. We'll begin by looking at how to devise a backup plan that's right for you, then we'll discuss your equipment and software options. Along the way, you should pick up lots of practical tips that will help you keep your data safe.

4

BACKUP AND RESTORE PROCEDURES

How do I make a backup? A **backup** is a copy of one or more files that has been made in case the original files become damaged. A backup is usually stored on a different storage medium from the original files. For example, you can back up files from your hard disk to a different hard disk, a writable CD or DVD, tape, floppy disk, or Web site. The exact steps that you follow to make a backup depend on your backup equipment, the software you use to make backups, and your personal backup plan. That said, the list in Figure 4-20 should give you a general idea of the steps that are involved in a typical backup session.

FIGURE 4-20 The steps in a typical backup session

click to start

1. Insert the disk, CD, or tape on which you'll store the backup.
2. Start the software you're using for the backup.
3. Select the folders and files that you want to back up.
4. Give the "go ahead" to start copying data.
5. Feed in additional disks, CDs, or tapes if prompted to do so.
6. Clearly label each disk, CD, or tape that you use.
7. Test your backup.

FIGURE 4-21

The steps in a typical restore session

1. Start the software you used to make the backup.
2. Select the file or files that you want to restore.
3. Insert the appropriate backup tape or disk.
4. Wait for the files to be copied from the backup to the hard disk.

How do I restore data? In technical jargon, you **restore** data by copying files from a backup to the original storage medium or its replacement. As with the procedures for backing up data, the process that you use to restore data to your hard disk varies, depending on your backup equipment and software. It also depends on exactly what you need to restore.

After a hard disk crash, for example, you'll probably need to restore all of your backup data to a new hard disk. On the other hand, if you inadvertently delete a file, or mistakenly copy one file over another, you might need to restore only a single file from the backup. Most software designed to back up and restore data allows you to select which files you want to restore. A typical session to restore data would follow the steps in Figure 4-21.

What's the best backup plan? A good backup plan allows you to restore your computing environment to its pre-disaster state with a minimum of fuss. Unfortunately, no single backup plan fits everyone's computing style or budget. You must devise your own backup plan that's tailored to your particular computing needs.

The checklist in Figure 4-22 outlines the factors you should consider as you formulate your own backup plan.

FIGURE 4-22

Backup tips

- ☑ Decide how much of your data you want, need, and can afford to back up.
- ☑ Create a realistic schedule for making backups.
- ☑ Make sure that you have a way to avoid backing up files that contain viruses.
- ☑ Find out what kind of boot disks you might need to get your computer up and running after a hard disk failure or boot sector virus attack.
- ☑ Make sure that you have a procedure for testing your restore procedure so that you can successfully retrieve the data that you've backed up.
- ☑ Find a safe place to store your backups.
- ☑ Decide what kind of storage device you'll use to make backups.
- ☑ Select software to handle backup needs.

Do I have to back up every file? A **full-system backup** contains a copy of every program, data, and system file on a computer. The advantage of a full system backup is that you can easily restore everything to its pre-disaster state simply by copying the backup files to a new hard disk. A full-system backup takes a lot of time, however, and fully automating the process requires a large-capacity tape backup device.

A pretty good alternative to a full system backup is a "selective" backup that contains only your most important data files. A backup of your important data files ensures that your computer-based documents and projects are protected from many data disasters. You can back up these files on floppy disks, Zip disks, removable hard disks, external hard disk, CDs, or DVDs. The disadvantage of this backup strategy is that because you backed up only data files, you must manually reinstall all of your software, in addition to restoring your data files.

If your strategy is to back up your important data files, the procedure can be simplified if you've stored all of these files in one folder or its subfolders. For example, Windows users might store their data files in folders contained in the *My Documents* folder. A folder called *My Documents\Music* might hold MP3 files, a *My Documents\Reports* folder can hold reports, a *My Documents\Art* folder can hold various graphics files, and so on. With your data files organized under the umbrella of a single folder, you will be less likely to omit an important file when you make backups.

Unfortunately for Mitnick, the jail term and $4,125 fine were, perhaps, the most lenient part of his sentence. Mitnick, who had served most of his jail term while awaiting trial, was scheduled for a supervised release soon after sentencing. The additional conditions of Mitnick's supervised release included a ban on access to computer hardware, software, and any form of wireless communication. He was prohibited from possessing any kind of passwords, cellular phone codes, or data encryption devices. And just to make sure that he didn't get into any trouble with technologies that are not specifically mentioned in the terms of his supervised release, Mitnick was prohibited from using any new or future technology that performs as a computer or provides access to one. Perhaps worst of all, he could not work for a company with computers or computer access on its premises.

The Mitnick case illustrates our culture's ambivalent attitude toward hackers. On the one hand, they are viewed as evil cyberterrorists who are set on destroying the glue that binds together the Information Age. From this perspective, hackers are criminals who must be hunted down, forced to make restitution for damages, and prevented from creating further havoc.

From another perspective, hackers are viewed more as Casper, the friendly ghost, in our complex cybermachines—as moderately bothersome entities whose pranks are tolerated by the computer community, along with software bugs and hardware glitches. Seen from this perspective, a hacker's pranks are part of the normal course of study that leads to the highest echelons of computer expertise. "Everyone has done it," claim devotees, "even Bill Gates (founder of Microsoft) and Steve Jobs (founder of Apple Computer)."

www.InfoWebLinks.com

Who's in cybercrime news? What happened to Mafiaboy? Where is Kevin Mitnick today? How are cybercriminals caught? The Computer Crime InfoWeb provides answers to these questions and more.

click 

4

Which perspective is right? Are hackers dangerous cyberterrorists or harmless pranksters? Before you make up your mind about computer hacking and cracking, you might want to further investigate the Mitnick case and similar cases by following the Computer Crime InfoWeb links.

WHAT DO YOU THINK?

1. Should it be a crime to steal a copy of computer data while leaving the original data in place and unaltered? ❍ Yes ❍ No ❍ Not sure
2. Was Mitnick's sentence fair? ❍ Yes ❍ No ❍ Not sure
3. Should hackers be sent to jail if they cannot pay restitution to companies and individuals who lost money as the result of a prank? ❍ Yes ❍ No ❍ Not sure
4. Do you think that a hacker would make a good consultant on computer security? ❍ Yes ❍ No ❍ Not sure

click to save your responses

INTERACTIVE SUMMARY

The Interactive Summary helps you to select and remember important concepts from this chapter. Fill in the blanks to best complete each sentence. When using the NP6 BookOnCD, you can click the Check Answers buttons to automatically score your answers. Place your Tracking Disk in the floppy disk drive if you want to save your scores.

A computer ________ is a named collection of data that exists on a storage medium, such as a hard disk, floppy disk, CD, DVD, or tape. Every file has a name and might also have a filename extension. The rules for naming a file are called file-naming ________. These rules typically do not allow you to use certain characters or ________ words in a filename. A filename ________ is usually related to a file format, which is defined as the arrangement of data in a file and the coding scheme that is used to represent the data. A software program's ________ file format is the default format that is used for storing the files created with that program.

A file's location is defined by a file ________ (sometimes called a "path"), which includes the storage device, folder(s), filename, and extension. In Windows, storage devices are identified by a drive letter, followed by a ________. An operating system maintains a list of files called a directory for each storage disk, tape, CD, or DVD. The main directory of a disk is sometimes referred to as the ________ directory, which can be subdivided into several smaller lists called subdirectories. Subdirectories often are depicted as ________.

check answers

File ________ encompasses any procedure that helps you organize your computer-based files so that you can find and use them more effectively. ________-based file management uses tools provided from within a software program to open and save files. Additional tools might also allow you to create new folders, rename files, and delete files. The Save and Save As dialog boxes are examples of application-based file management tools.

Most operating systems provide file management ________ that give you the "big picture" of the files that you have stored on your disks. The structure of folders that you envision on your disk is a logical model, which is often represented by a storage ________, such as a tree structure or filing cabinet. Windows Explorer is an example of a file management utility that is provided by an operating system. Windows Explorer allows you to find, rename, copy, move, and delete files and folders. In addition, it allows you to perform these file management activities with more than one file at a time.

The way that data is actually stored is referred to as the ________ storage model. Before a computer stores data on a disk, CD, or DVD, it creates the equivalent of electronic storage bins by dividing the disk into ________, and then further dividing each track into ________. The process of creating tracks and sectors is called ________. Each sector of a disk is numbered, providing a storage address that can be tracked by the operating system. Many computers work with a group of sectors, called a ________, to increase the efficiency of file storage operations. An operating system uses a file system to carry out your computer's actual storage activities and maintain a file, such as the File Allocation Table (FAT), which keeps track of every file's physical location.

check answers

A computer virus is a set of program instructions that attaches itself to a file, reproduces itself, and spreads to other files. You may encounter several types of viruses. A virus that attaches itself to an application program, such as a game, is known as a ________ virus. A boot ________ virus infects the system files that your computer uses every time you turn it on. A ________ virus infects a set of instructions that automates document and worksheet production.

A Trojan horse is a computer program that seems to perform one function while actually doing something else. Such programs are notorious for stealing ________, though some delete files and cause other problems. A ________ is a program that is designed to spread from computer to computer. Most take advantage of communications networks—especially the Internet—to travel within e-mail and TCP/IP packets, jumping from one computer to another.

Viruses can slip into your computer from a variety of sources, such as floppy disks, homemade CDs, and Web sites that contain games and other supposedly fun stuff. E-mail ________ are another common source of viruses. HTML-formatted e-mail is susceptible to viruses and worms hidden in program-like "scripts" that are embedded in the HTML tags. ________ software can help prevent viruses from invading your computer system, and can root out viruses that take up residence.

check answers

A backup is a copy of one or more files that has been made in case the original files become damaged. For safety, a backup is usually stored on a different storage medium from the original files. A good backup plan allows you to ________ your computing environment to its pre-disaster state with a minimum of fuss. Unfortunately, no single backup plan fits everyone's computing style or budget. Your personal backup plan depends on the files that you need to back up, the hardware that you have available to make backups, and your backup software. In any case, it is a good idea to back up the Windows ________ and make a ________ disk that contains the operating system files needed to start your computer without accessing the hard disk.

Before backing up your data, make sure that it is free of ________. Part of your backup routine should be to ________ your backup to make sure that you can successfully restore data from the backup to your hard disk. Backups can be recorded on tape, floppy disks, a second hard disk, a CD-R, a CD-RW, or a writable DVD. Backups should be stored in a safe place, away from the computer. Online backup, provided by a Web site, might be part of your backup strategy.

check answers

INTERACTIVE KEY TERMS

Make sure that you understand all of the boldfaced key terms presented in this chapter. If you're using the NP6 BookOnCD, you can use this list of terms as an interactive study activity. First, try to define a term in your own words, then click the term to compare your definition with the definition that is presented in the chapter.

Antivirus software, 189
Backup, 193
Backup software, 200
Boot disk, 197
Boot sector virus, 186
Checksum, 189
Cluster, 181
Computer file, 170
Computer virus, 185
Copy Disk utility, 200
Defragmentation utility, 183
Denial of Service attacks, 187
Differential backup 196
Directory, 172
File Allocation Table (FAT), 181
File date, 173
File format, 171
File management utilities, 176
Filename extension, 171
File management, 174
File-naming conventions, 170
File shredder software, 182
File size, 173
File specification, 172
File system, 181
File virus, 186
Folders, 172
Formatting, 180
Formatting utilities, 180
Fragmented files, 183
Full backup, 196
Full-system backup, 194
Incremental backup, 196
Logical storage models, 177
Macro, 186
Macro virus, 186
Multi-partite viruses, 190
Native file format, 171
Path, 172
Physical storage model, 180
Polymorphic viruses, 190
Recovery CD, 197
Rescue disk, 198
Reserved words, 171
Restore, 194
Retro viruses, 190
Root directory, 172
Sectors, 180
Stealth viruses, 190
Storage metaphor, 177
Subdirectories, 172
Tracks, 180
Trigger event, 185
Trojan horse, 186
Virus hoax, 191
Virus signature, 189
Windows Explorer, 178
Windows Startup Disk, 197
Worm, 186

INTERACTIVE SITUATION QUESTIONS

Apply what you've learned to some typical computing situations. When using the NP6 BookOnCD, you can type your answers, then use the Check Answers button to automatically score your responses. Place your Tracking Disk in the floppy disk drive if you want to save your scores.

1. Suppose you are using Microsoft Word and you want to open a file. When your software lists the documents that you can open, you can expect them to be in Word's [ ] file format, which is DOC.

2. Can you use a Windows application, create a document, and store it using the filename *I L*ve NY*? (Yes or No) [ ]

3. When you want to work with a group of your files—to move them to different folders, for example—it would be most efficient to use an operating system utility, such as Windows [ ].

4. When specifying a location for a data file on your hard disk, you should avoid saving it in the [ ] directory.

5. Suppose that you have a floppy disk that contains data you no longer need. You can use a(n) [ ] utility to erase the data on the disk and re-create all of the tracks and sectors on the disk.

6. You have an old computer that you will donate to a school, but you want to make sure that its hard disk contains no trace of your data. To do so, you should use file [ ] software that overwrites "empty" sectors with random 1s and 0s.

7. You receive an e-mail attachment called *Read this.txt.vbs*. Because it appears to have two filename [ ], you should assume that this file harbors a virus.

8. You receive an e-mail message from a friend that says, "My antivirus software says that an attachment I received from you contains the Klez virus." Would you assume that this message from your friend is a hoax? Yes or no? [ ]

9. You just bought a tape drive and you make a full-system backup. Before you depend on this backup, you should [ ] it to make sure that you can successfully restore the data in the event of a hard disk crash.

10. Your hard disk crashed for some unknown reason. Now when you switch on the computer power all you get is an "Error reading drive C:" message. Your first reaction should be to reach for a(n) [ ] disk that contains the operating system files needed to start your computer without accessing the hard disk.

check answers

4

INTERACTIVE PRACTICE TESTS

When you use the NP6 BookOnCD, you can take Practice Tests that consist of 10 multiple-choice, true/false, and fill-in-the-blank questions. The questions are selected at random from a large test bank, so each time you take a test, you'll receive a different set of questions. Your tests are scored immediately, and you can print study guides that help you find the correct answers for any questions that you missed. If you are using a Tracking Disk, insert it in the floppy disk drive to save your test scores.

click to start

STUDY TIPS

Study Tips help you to organize and consolidate the information in a chapter by making lists, outlines, charts, and sketches. You can use paper and pencil or word processing software to complete most of the Study Tips activities.

1. Make sure that you can use your own words to answer each of the green focus questions that appear throughout the chapter.
2. Make a list of five filenames that are valid under the file-naming conventions for your operating system. Also create a list of five filenames that are not valid, and explain the problem with each one.
3. Pick any five files on the computer that you typically use, and write out the full path for each one.
4. Describe the difference between the Save and the Save As options provided by an application.
5. In your own words, describe the difference between a logical storage model and a physical storage model.
6. Explain the kinds of file management tasks that might best be accomplished using a file management utility such as Windows Explorer, instead of the Save As or Open dialog box provided by a software application.
7. Explain the differences between an operating system and a file system.
8. Describe the difference between a sector and a cluster.
9. Make sure that you can describe what happens in the FAT when a file is stored or deleted.
10. Describe the characteristics of viruses, Trojan horses, worms, and Denial of Service attacks.
11. List the filename extensions of files that might typically harbor a virus.
12. Explain how multi-partite, stealth, polymorphic, and retro viruses work.
13. Explain how anitvirus software works, and how it is able to catch new viruses that are created after the software is installed on your computer.
14. Describe the various types of boot disks that might help you recover from a hard disk crash.
15. Discuss the pros and cons of each type of backup hardware.
16. Make a list of backup tips that you think would help people devise a solid backup plan.

The Minutemen could have positioned 20 or 30 lanterns on a hillside to spell out the words "LAND" or "SEA." Instead, they coded their message using a maximum of two lanterns—one lantern meant that the British were coming by land; two lanterns meant that they were coming by sea. It seems that the Minutemen selected a fairly efficient way to convey information.

Computers use bits to convey information. A bit, like a lantern, has two states: on (1) and off (0). So, a single bit can represent two messages, each called a unit of information. Figure 5-2 helps you visualize how increasing the number of bits increases the units of information that can be conveyed.

FIGURE 5-2

When you use one bit (one lantern)...	 ...you can convey up to two (2^1) units of information.	Unit one: 0 Unit two: 1	
When you use two bits (two lanterns)...	 ...you can convey up to four (2^2) units of information.	Unit one: 00 Unit two: 01 Unit three: 10 Unit four: 11	
When you use three bits (three lanterns)...	 ...you can convey up to eight (2^3) units of information.	Unit one: 000 Unit two: 001 Unit three: 010 Unit four: 011	Unit five: 100 Unit six: 101 Unit seven: 110 Unit eight: 111

The number of units of information that you can convey is simply the number of different combinations that you can make with a given number of bits. Let's look at the pattern: with one bit, you can convey two units of information; with two bits, you can convey four units; with three bits, you can convey eight units. The pattern is 2, 4, 8; these numbers are all powers of two, as shown in Figure 5-3.

FIGURE 5-3

Powers of two help you determine the maximum number of units of information that you can convey with a given number of bits.

$$2^1 = 2$$
$$2^2 = 2x2 = 4$$
$$2^3 = 2x2x2 = 8$$
$$2^4 = 2x2x2x2 = 16$$
$$2^5 = 2x2x2x2x2 = 32$$
$$2^6 = 2x2x2x2x2x2 = 64$$
$$2^7 = 2x2x2x2x2x2x2 = 128$$
$$2^8 = 2x2x2x2x2x2x2x2 = 256$$

You now have a rule about conveying information with bits: The maximum number of different units of information that you can convey with *n* bits is 2^n. The *2* represents the two states "on" and "off," and the *n* represents the number of bits. The extended ASCII code uses eight bits, which can represent 256 (that's 2^8) unique units of information: enough for uppercase letters, lowercase letters, punctuation symbols, numerals, and assorted other symbols and control characters. (Refer to Figure 2-3 on page 60.)

Computers use several coding schemes that are based on binary digits, including ASCII, EBCDIC, UNICODE, and binary numbers. As you think about how computer communications systems work, it is important to remember the underlying principle that computer data is digital and boils down to a series of 0s and 1s.

Exactly what is transmitted when I send a message? When data is transmitted, it usually takes the form of an electromagnetic signal. You can think of these signals as waves that ripple through cables or through the air. On a communications network, your data might be converted into several different types of waves before it reaches its destination. It might originate in your computer as electrical voltages, get converted into analog tones by a modem, and then undergo another conversion into bursts of laser light, radio waves, or infrared light. Electromagnetic waves are characterized by their amplitude, wavelength, and frequency, as shown in Figure 5-4.

FIGURE 5-4

Frequency is the number of times that a wave oscillates per second. Short wave lengths have high frequencies–many of them get packed into a one-second interval. Signals with shorter wavelengths tend to travel farther. That's why a 2.4 GHz cordless phone with a wavelength of 4.8" has a longer range than a 900 MHz phone with a 12" wavelength.

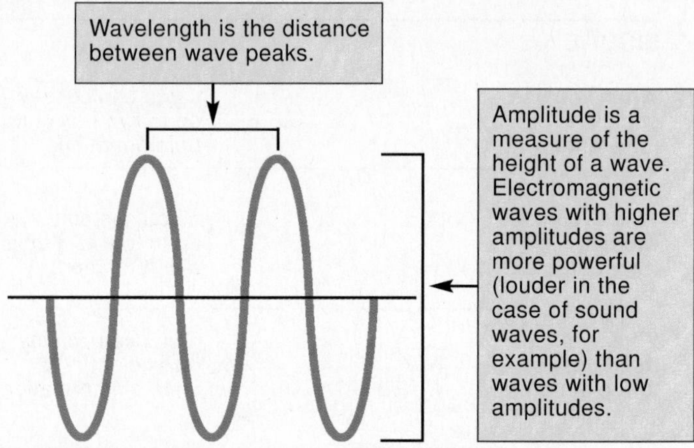

Wavelength is the distance between wave peaks.
Amplitude is a measure of the height of a wave. Electromagnetic waves with higher amplitudes are more powerful (louder in the case of sound waves, for example) than waves with low amplitudes.

Although you usually see a wave depicted as a smooth curve, waves can have different shapes, referred to as "waveforms" or "wave patterns." Analog signals typically represent an unlimited range of values and, therefore, have a smooth, curved waveform. Digital signals, on the other hand, represent discrete values within a limited range and, therefore, have a square or "stepped" waveform. Compare the analog and digital waveforms shown in Figure 5-5.

FIGURE 5-5

Analog waveforms are curved, whereas digital waveforms are squared or "stepped."

Analog waveform

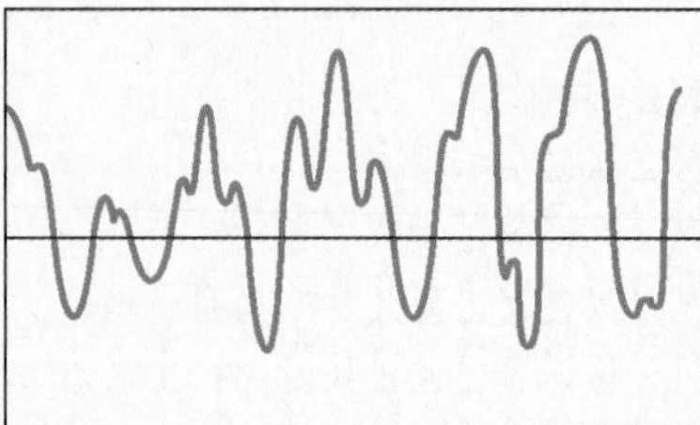

Digital waveform

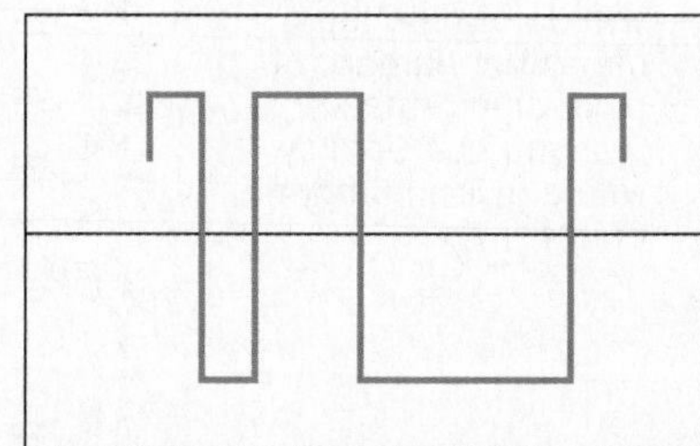

Are digital signals better than analog signals? The beauty of digital signals is that they require simple circuitry and are easy to "clean up" after being affected by noise.

At its most primitive level, digital equipment must be sensitive to only two frequencies—one that represents 1s and one that represents 0s. In contrast, analog equipment—a telephone or a microphone, for example—must be sensitive to a wide range of audible frequencies, or else it will not be able to pick up and transport very high or very low sounds.

Networks also have a **logical topology**, which corresponds to the way that messages flow. Logical topologies fall into the same three categories as physical topologies: star, bus, and ring. Contrary to what you might assume, however, a network's physical topology and its logical topology don't have to match! Figure 5-8 illustrates how data can flow in a logical ring over a network that is wired as a physical star.

FIGURE 5-8

A network might appear to be configured in a star topology, like the one shown in the first illustration. If you follow the lines, however, you will see that the data flows in a circular path because its logical topology is a "ring."

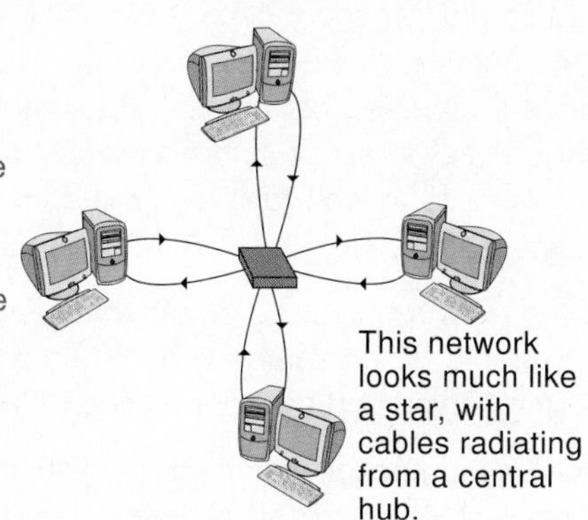

This network looks much like a star, with cables radiating from a central hub.

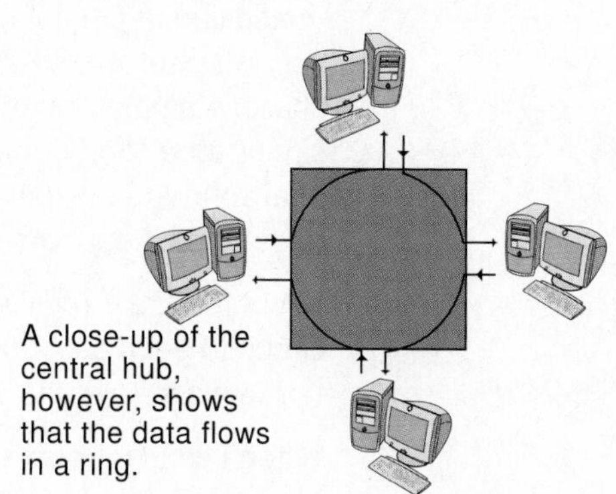

A close-up of the central hub, however, shows that the data flows in a ring.

PACKET AND CIRCUIT SWITCHING TECHNOLOGY

What's a packet? When you send a file or an e-mail message, you might suppose that it is transmitted as an entire unit to its destination. This is not the case. Your file is actually chopped up into small pieces called packets. A **packet** is a "parcel" of data that is sent across a computer network. Each packet contains the address of its sender, the destination address, a sequence number, and some data. When packets reach their destination, they are reassembled back into the original message according to the sequence number.

Why not just send an entire message? The short answer is that by dividing messages into equal-size packets, they are easier to handle than an assortment of small, medium, large, and huge files. The long answer is steeped in an old controversy between the engineers who built the technology that was eventually used on the Internet, and the moguls who ran the telephone company.

5

The telephone network uses a technology called **circuit switching**, which essentially establishes a private link between one telephone and another for the duration of a call. This type of switching provides callers with a direct pipeline over which streams of voice data can flow. At the time when the Internet was evolving, circuit switching was the only game in town. (See Figure 5-9.)

FIGURE 5-9

The telephone company operates a circuit switching network that provides a continuous link (in red) between the sender and receiver.

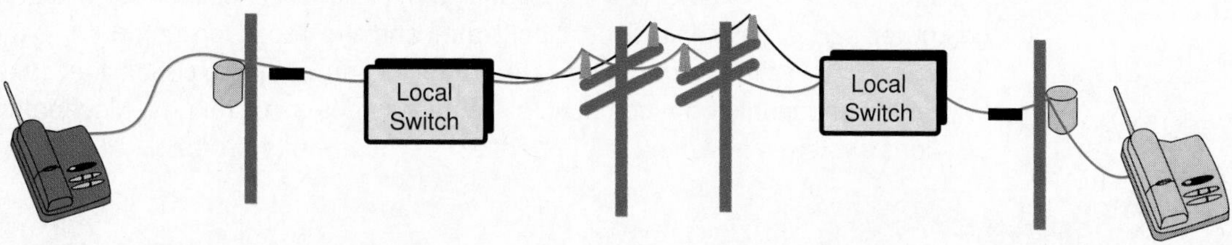

Engineers working on the blueprints for computer networks wanted a more robust communications link than was possible through circuit switching. To these engineers, it was essential that data reach its destination even if one communications link was cut. They devised a technology called **packet switching** in which a message was divided into several packets that can be routed independently to their destination to avoid out-of-service or congested links.

In addition to providing reliable data transport, packet switching was designed to make very efficient use of available bandwidth. Packets from many different messages can share a single communications channel, or "circuit." Packets are shipped over the circuit on a "first come, first served" basis. If some packets from a message are not available, the system does not need to wait for them. Instead, the system moves on to send packets from other messages. The end result is a steady stream of data.

In contrast, a circuit switching network, like the telephone system, devotes an entire circuit to each call. So, for example, when someone is "on hold," no communication is taking place—yet the circuit is reserved and cannot be used for other communications.

When it was introduced, the idea of packet switching met with skepticism—especially from the telephone establishment. Despite the skeptics, however, packet switching proved to be an efficient and dependable technology. Today, it is the technology used for virtually every computer network.

COMMUNICATIONS PROTOCOLS

What is a communications protocol? In general, a "protocol" is a set of rules for interacting and negotiating. In some respects, it is like the signals that pass between the pitcher and catcher in a baseball game. Before the ball is thrown, the catcher and the pitcher use hand signals to negotiate the speed and style of the pitch.

In the context of networks, the term "protocol," or **communications protocol**, refers to a set of rules for efficiently transmitting data from one network node to another. Protocols, such as TCP/IP, allow two devices to negotiate and agree on how data will be transmitted.

Among their many duties, communications protocols provide rules for starting and ending transmissions, recognizing transmission errors, determining the speed at which data is sent, and specifying how packets are addressed and formatted.

How does a protocol initiate a transmission? A major challenge of network communications is coordinating the transmission and reception of each packet. The transmitting computer sends a series of bits, but if the receiving device is not ready, data can get lost and messages can become hopelessly garbled. Protocols help two communications devices negotiate and establish communications through a process called **handshaking**. The transmitting device sends a signal that means, "I want to communicate." It then waits for an acknowledgement signal from the receiving device. The two devices then "negotiate" a transmission speed that both can handle. The devices also decide on how to coordinate the transmission. Using a **synchronous protocol**, the sender and the receiver are synchronized by a signal called a clock. The transmitting computer sends data at a fixed clock rate, and the receiving computer expects the incoming data at the same fixed rate. Much of the communication that takes place between components on a computer's motherboard is synchronous. Most data communications systems, however, implement an asynchronous protocol.

The rules for an **asynchronous protocol** require the transmitting computer to send a start bit that indicates the beginning of a packet. Data is then transmitted as a series of bytes—the number of bytes is specified by the protocol. A stop bit marks the end of the data.

Does data travel in both directions over the same channel? Communications channels, protocols, and devices provide different capabilities for sending and receiving data. For example, you use a walkie-talkie differently from the way that you use a telephone. A walkie-talkie requires you to press a button when you are ready to send, and release the button when you are ready to receive. In contrast, a telephone does not require any special action to switch between talking and listening.

Simplex refers to a type of communication in which a signal travels in only one direction. A radio transmitter uses simplex communication—it can transmit, but not receive, signals.

Half duplex refers to a type of communication that allows you to send and receive data, but not at the same time. A walkie-talkie is an example of half-duplex communication, because only one party can talk at a time.

Full duplex refers to a type of communication in which it is possible to send and receive at the same time, over the same channel—for example, a telephone conversation.

Most data communications networks operate in half-duplex or full-duplex mode. But you don't have to worry about holding down the "Talk" button, even if your network operates in half-duplex mode. Communications protocols usually take care of the flow of data.

How does a protocol make sure that data arrives without errors? Computers use error-checking protocols to ensure accurate delivery of data. As an example, one error-checking protocol adds a **parity bit** to a sequence of bits to keep track of the number of 1s and 0s it should contain. The **even parity protocol** requires the number of 1 bits, including the parity bit, to be an even number. Let's see how this works.

Suppose that your computer is sending the sequence 01000011. It contains three 1s. That's an odd number. To make even parity, your computer must add another 1 to the sequence, making the sequence 010000111. On the other hand, suppose that your computer is sending the sequence 01000001. It contains two 1s. That's an even number—just right under even parity, so your computer simply adds a parity bit of 0 to the sequence.

5

When a device receives the data that you sent, it counts the number of 1s. If the count reveals an even number of 1s, the device assumes that the data is correct. If it finds an odd number of 1s, it assumes that some type of interference changed one of the bits during transmission. Study Figure 5-10 for an overview of how computers use parity to detect transmission errors.

FIGURE 5-10

Under even parity, the receiving device expects an even number of 1s. If that is not the case, a transmission error probably occurred and the data must be sent again.

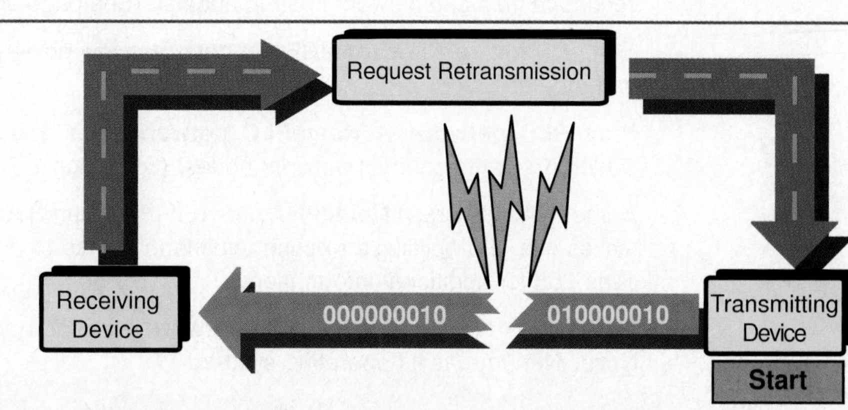

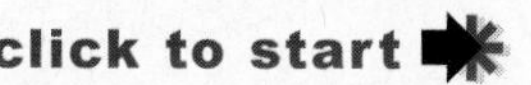

What part of a network specifies protocols? Some protocols are handled by hardware, whereas other protocols are handled by software. For example, physically changing a signal, say from the +5 volt pulse that emanates from a computer's motherboard to a 1,233 Hz "tone" that can travel over a telephone line, takes place in the circuitry of a modem. On the other hand, the specification for creating packets typically is provided by software.

NETWORK CLASSIFICATIONS

How are networks classified? In the press and in casual conversation, a network is often categorized by some distinguishing characteristics, such as its wiring technology, protocol, operating system, or geographical coverage. The following list contains brief definitions of the technical and not-so-technical terms used to refer to network categories:

An internetwork. An **internetwork**, or "internet" (with a lowercase "i"), is a network that is composed of many smaller networks.

The Internet. When spelled with an uppercase "I," the Internet refers to a global, public network that uses the TCP/IP protocol and includes servers that handle e-mail, Web sites, file downloads, and so on.

Intranet. An **intranet** is a network that uses TCP/IP protocols and provides many of the same services as the Internet, but has two differences. First, an intranet is usually owned by a private business and its use is limited to the business's employees. Second, as a protection against hackers, an intranet typically does not provide remote access, such as dial-up connections.

Extranet. An **extranet** is similar to a private intranet, except that it allows password-protected access by authorized outside users. A business or organization might use an extranet to provide remote access for branch offices, for example, or for employees who are working at home.

WAN. A **WAN** (wide area network) covers a large geographical area and may consist of several smaller networks. WANs can use any protocol, but today TCP/IP is the norm for wide area computer networks. The Internet is the largest example of a WAN.

MAN. A **MAN** (metropolitan area network) is a public high-speed network capable of voice and data transmission within a range of about 50 miles (80 km). A local ISP is a good example of a MAN.

LAN. A **LAN** (local area network) is a data communications network that typically connects personal computers within a very limited geographical area—usually a single building. (See Section D for more information.)

Wireless network. A **wireless network** uses radio frequencies, instead of cables, to send data from one network node to another. (See page 256 for additional information.)

HomeRF network. A **HomeRF network** is a low-power, wireless network designed for home use.

HomePLC network. A **HomePLC network** uses a building's existing power line cables (PLCs) to connect network nodes. (See page 256 for additional information.)

HomePNA network. A **HomePNA network** (PNA stands for Phone Networking Alliance) makes use of a building's existing telephone cables to connect network nodes. (See page 255 for additional information.)

Novell network. The term **Novell network** refers to a local area network that uses Novell NetWare as its operating system.

Ethernet. One of the most widely implemented network technologies, an **Ethernet** can be configured as a physical star or bus. Each packet is broadcast over the entire network, but is accepted only by the workstation to which it was addressed. Occasionally, two devices attempt to send packets at the same time and a collision occurs. Ethernets use a protocol called **CSMA/CD** (carrier sense multiple access with collision detection) to deal with these collisions, as shown in Figure 5-11.

FIGURE 5-11

On an Ethernet, data travels on a "first come, first served" basis. If two workstations attempt to send data at the same time, a collision occurs. That data must be resent.

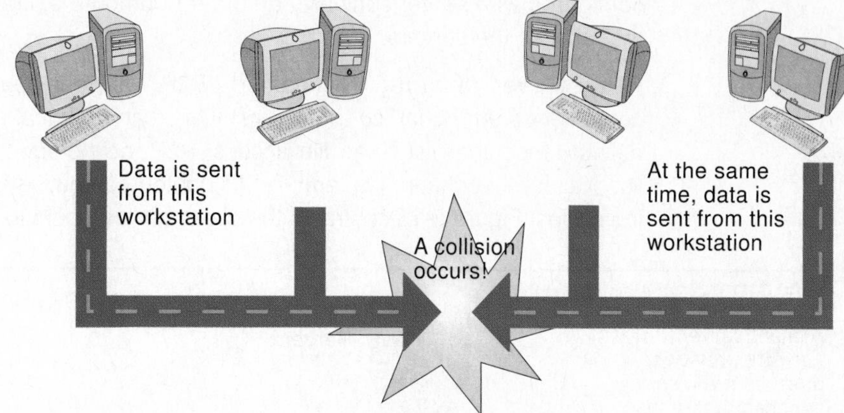
Data is sent from this workstation
At the same time, data is sent from this workstation
A collision occurs!

click to start

"10Base" networks. 10BaseT and 100BaseT refer to two of the most popular cabling options for Ethernet networks. A **10BaseT network** is techie jargon for an Ethernet network that uses a type of twisted-pair cable called "10BaseT" and transmits data at 10 Mbps. A **100BaseT network**, often referred to as "Fast Ethernet," supports transfer rates up to 100 Mbps.

Token Ring. A **Token Ring network** connects nodes in a physical star configuration, but passes data around a logical ring using a technology called a "token." Tokens prevent collisions. Therefore, in contrast to an Ethernet network, a Token Ring network needs no collision detection routines. (See Figure 5-12.)

5

FIGURE 5-12

To send data on a Token Ring network, a workstation must wait for the token to become available. A packet is then attached to the token and circles around the network until it reaches its destination.

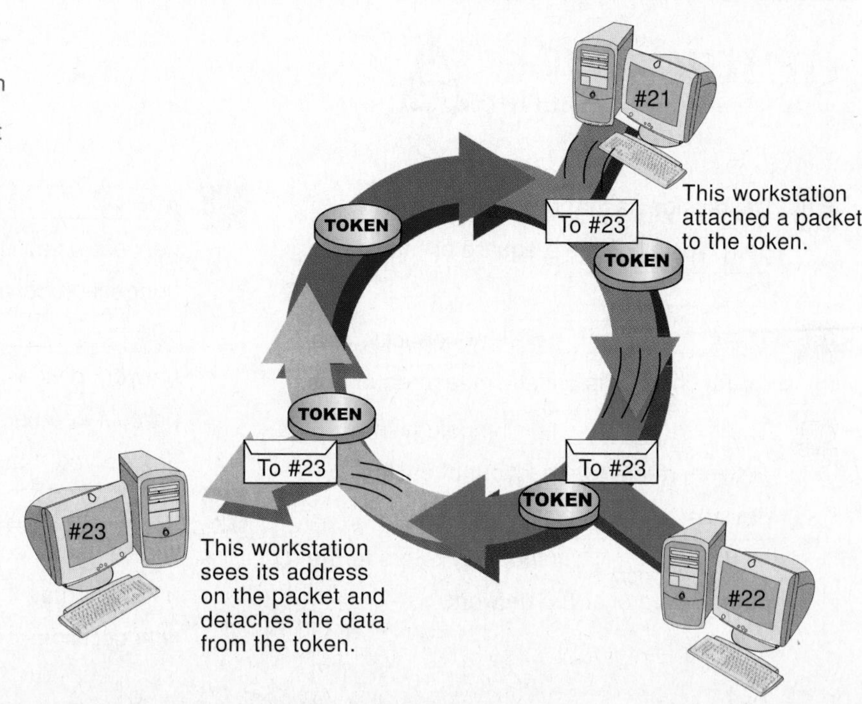
#21
This workstation attached a packet to the token.
TOKEN
To #23
TOKEN
TOKEN
To #23
To #23
TOKEN
#23
This workstation sees its address on the packet and detaches the data from the token.
#22

click to start

FDDI. FDDI (Fiber Distributed Data Interconnect) is a specification for a type of high-speed network that uses fiber-optic cable to link workstations.

ATM network. ATM (asynchronous transfer mode) is a network technology that has the capability to transmit all of the packets in a message over the same channel in order to provide smooth transmission of high-bandwidth files, such as those containing music and video.

Client/server network. A **client/server network** contains one or more computers configured with server software, and other computers, configured with client software, that access the servers.

Peer-to-peer network. Nicknamed "P2P," a **peer-to-peer network** treats every computer as an "equal" so that workstations can run local applications and also provide network resources, such as file access. P2P technology forms the basis for networks, like Kazaa, that share files, and for distributed computing networks that share processing cycles. Figure 5-13 contrasts the client/server model to the peer-to-peer model.

FIGURE 5-13

A client/server network provides more centralized services than a peer-to-peer network.

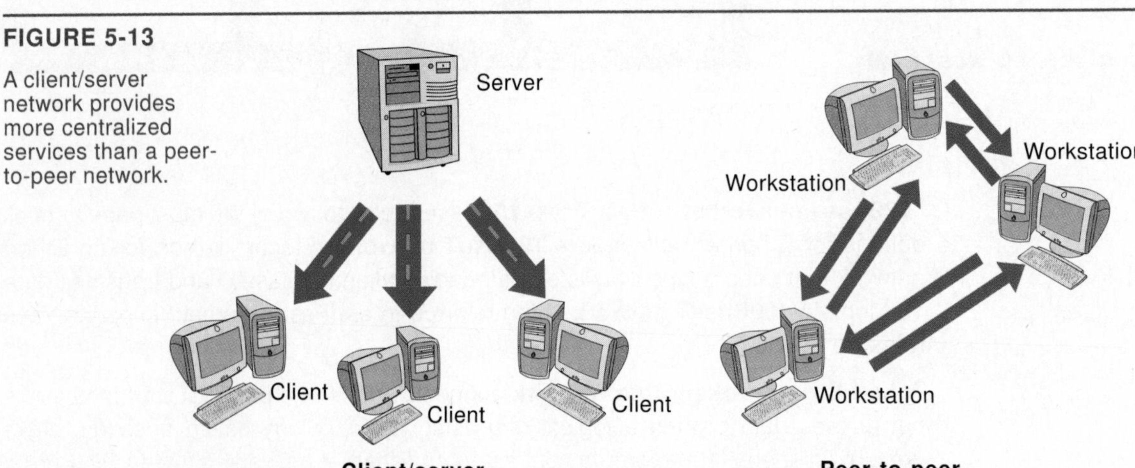

QUICKCheck Section A

1 Digital signals that represent computer data typically have a square or "stepped" [ ].

2 The [ ], or capacity, of a digital channel is usually measured in bps.

3 The [ ] topology of a network refers to the layout of cables, devices, and connections; the [ ] topology refers to the path of data over the network.

4 A(n) [ ] switching network establishes a dedicated connection between two devices, whereas a(n) [ ] switching network divides messages into small parcels and handles them on a "first come, first served" basis.

5 [ ] is one of the most widely used network technologies, and it uses a protocol called CSMA/CD to deal with collisions. **check answers**

Section B
INTERNET BUILDING BLOCKS

To most people, the Internet seems like "old hat." Even people who haven't used the Internet know a lot about it from watching the news, reading magazines, and watching movies. Using the Internet is actually pretty easy. Browsing Web sites, shopping at the Net mall, sending e-mail, and chatting online? No problem.

But what makes the Internet "tick?" How is it that one network can provide so much information to so many people? In this section of the chapter, we'll pull back the curtain and give you a glimpse of what happens in the hidden pathways of the Net.

BACKGROUND

How did the Internet get started? The history of the Internet begins in 1957 when the Soviet Union launched Sputnik, the first man-made satellite. In response to this display of Soviet superiority, the U.S. government resolved to improve its scientific and technical infrastructure. One of the resulting initiatives was the Advanced Research Projects Agency (ARPA).

ARPA swung into action with a project designed to help scientists communicate and share valuable computer resources. The ARPANET, created in 1969, connected computers at UCLA, Stanford Research Institute, University of Utah, and University of California at Santa Barbara. In 1985, the National Science Foundation (NSF) used ARPANET technology to create a similar, but larger, network, linking not just a few mainframe computers, but entire local area networks at each site. Connecting two or more networks creates an "internetwork" or "internet." The NSF network was an internet (with a lowercase "i"). As this network grew throughout the world, it became known as the Internet (with an uppercase "I").

www.InfoWebLinks.com

The history of ARPANET, NSFNET, and the Internet is three parts legend, one part fiction, and the rest–well, the rest is history. You can read about the people and events that shaped the Internet at the Internet History InfoWeb.

click

Early Internet pioneers—mostly educators and scientists—used primitive command-line user interfaces to send e-mail, transfer files, and run scientific calculations on Internet supercomputers. Finding information was not easy. Without search engines, Internet users relied on word of mouth and e-mail to keep informed about new data and its location. "The data that you need is on the Stanford computer in a file called Chrome.txt." was typical of messages between colleagues.

In the early 1990s, software developers created new user-friendly Internet access tools, and Internet accounts became available to anyone willing to pay a monthly subscription fee. Today, the Internet connects computers all over the globe and supplies information to people of all ages and interests.

5

INTERNET HARDWARE AND CONNECTIONS

What type of hardware populates Internet nodes? With an estimated 200 million nodes and 500 million users, the Internet is huge. A diagram of so many nodes would be impossible to construct. It's even difficult to envision a thing so vast. It is, however, possible to construct a somewhat simplified model that reflects how your own little computer niche fits into the sprawling, global Internet communications network.

How big is the Internet? Several organizations keep track of Internet statistics. Link to them from the Internet Stats InfoWeb.

click

The computer that you use is the starting point in the model. It typically connects to an ISP (Internet Service Provider) over a telephone line, cable TV line, or personal satellite link. Your computer can, alternatively, connect to a local area network, which usually provides a single Internet access point for all of its workstations. (See Figure 5-14.)

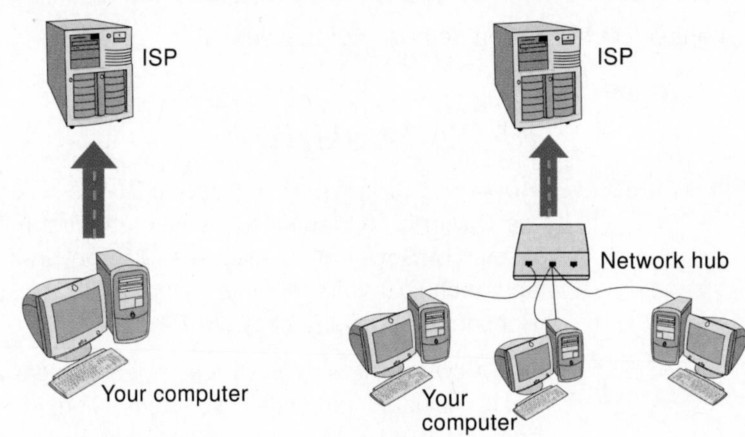

FIGURE 5-14

Your computer can connect directly to an ISP (left), or it can be part of a local area network that connects to the Internet (right).

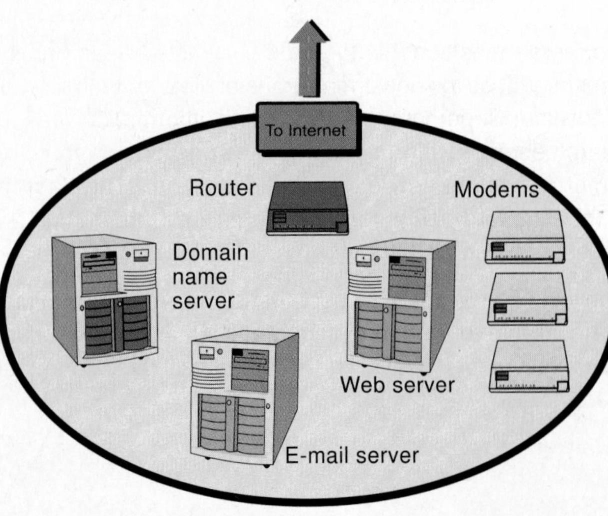

FIGURE 5-15

An ISP typically maintains the devices that provide subscribers with e-mail and access to the Web.

What kinds of network devices are part of an ISP? An ISP operates network devices that handle the physical aspects of transmitting and receiving data from your computer. For example, an ISP that offers telephone modem connections must maintain a bank of modems that answer when your computer dials the ISP's access number. An ISP might also operate an e-mail server to handle incoming and outgoing mail for its subscribers, and a Web server for subscriber Web sites. Your ISP might also operate a domain name server that translates an address, such as www.google.com, into a valid, numeric Internet address, such as 208.50.141.12. You'll learn more about this topic later in the chapter. The last piece of essential ISP equipment is a router that sends your data to the next "hop" toward its destination. Figure 5-15 illustrates the equipment at a typical ISP.

An ISP links to other ISPs in a sort of ISP network, which makes it easy to route data among subscribers. **Network service providers** (NSPs), such as MCI, Sprint, UUNET, or AT&T, supply ISPs with access to high-speed transmission lines that form the backbone of the Internet. NSPs also provide routers at network connection points.

Are Internet nodes all connected by cables? Although the Internet backbone is primarily composed of high-bandwidth fiber-optic cables, connections for the "last mile" between ISPs and subscribers call into play just about every modern communications technology. Your data might flow over simple telephone cables or on the cable TV infrastructure. It might also be beamed up to a satellite or flashed through fiber-optic cables.

www.InfoWebLinks.com

Would you like a color map of your data's path through cyberspace? Check out the Traceroute Utilities InfoWeb.

click

Can I trace the route of the data that I send and receive? An Internet utility called **Ping** (Packet Internet Groper) sends a signal to a specific Internet address and waits for a reply. If a reply arrives, Ping reports that the computer is online and displays the elapsed time, or **latency**, for the round-trip message. Ping is useful to find out if a site is up and running. Ping is also useful for determining whether the connection is adequate for online computer games or videoconferencing.

A utility called **Traceroute** records a packet's path—including intermediate routers—from your computer to its destination. Figure 5-16 contains a Traceroute report.

FIGURE 5-16

In this example, a Traceroute utility is used to monitor a connection between a small lakeside cabin in Northern Michigan and the HotWired Web site. The satellite connection has extremely high latency, and timed out before the Web site could be accessed.

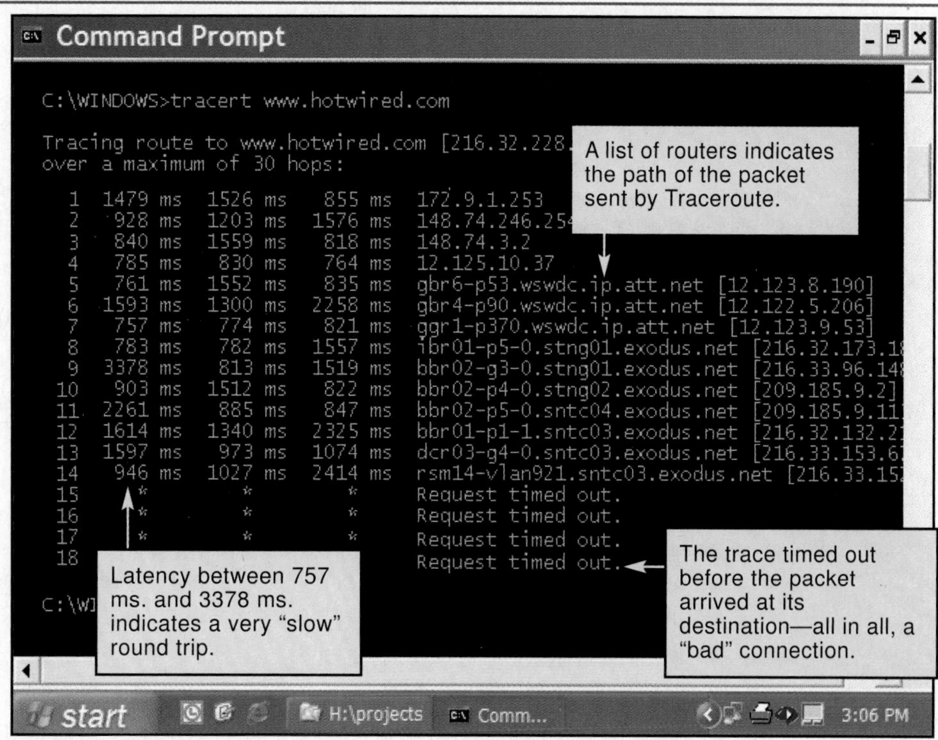

How fast does data travel over the Internet? Using Ping or Traceroute, you can discover how long data is in transit from point A to point B. On average, data within the continental U.S. usually arrives at its destination 110-120 ms. (milliseconds) after it is sent. Overseas transmission usually requires a little more time.

What's the capacity of the Internet? The Internet as a whole offers a tremendous amount of capacity. Although exact figures cannot be determined, it is estimated that Internet traffic exceeds 100 terabytes each week. A **terabyte** is 2 to the 40th power (1,099,511,627,776) bytes—about 1 trillion bytes. That's about ten times the amount of data stored in the entire printed collection of the U.S. Library of Congress.

INTERNET PROTOCOLS

Why does the Internet use TCP/IP? When the Internet was still the ARPANET, its communications protocols were slow and prone to crashes. Improvements were definitely in order, and by 1977, new protocols, including TCP/IP, were implemented.

From a practical perspective, TCP/IP provides a standard that is fairly easy to implement, public, free, and extensible. The Internet is not owned, operated, or controlled by any single business, government, or organization. In a sense, TCP/IP is the glue that holds the Internet together.

How does TCP/IP work? TCP/IP is a suite of protocols, which includes TCP, IP, ICMP, and others. **TCP** (Transmission Control Protocol) breaks a message or file into packets. **IP** (Internet Protocol) is responsible for addressing packets so that they can be routed to their destination. **ICMP** (Internet Control Message Protocol) provides error correction and routing information used by utilities such as Ping and Traceroute.

Is TCP/IP the only Internet protocol? No. Several other protocols are used in conjunction with TCP/IP on the Internet. Figure 5-17 briefly describes some of them.

FIGURE 5-17 Protocols Used on the Internet

Protocol	Name	Function
HTTP	Hypertext Transfer Protocol	Exchanges information over the Web
FTP	File Transfer Protocol	Transfers files between local and remote host computers
POP	Post Office Protocol	Transfers mail from an e-mail server to a client Inbox
SMTP	Simple Mail Transfer Protocol	Transfers e-mail messages from client computers to an e-mail server
IMAP	Internet Mail Access Protocol	An alternative to POP
TELNET	Telecommunication Network	Allows users who are logged on to one host to access another host
SSL	Secure Sockets Layer	Provides secure data transfer over the Internet

IP ADDRESSES

Does the Internet use a special addressing scheme? The "IP" part of TCP/IP defines the format for the addresses that identify computers on the Internet. As a result, these addresses are referred to as **IP addresses**; however, you may also see them referred to as "TCP/IP addresses."

An IP address is a series of numbers, such as 204.127.129.001. When written, an IP address is separated into four sections by periods for the convenience of human readers. The number in a section cannot exceed 255. In binary representation, each section of an IP address requires 8 bits, so the entire address requires 32 bits.

LAB 5-B TRACKING PACKETS

In this lab, you'll learn:

- How Ping and Traceroute work
- How to use the Ping and Tracert utilities supplied by Windows
- How to interpret Ping and Tracert reports with regard to the speed and reliability of your Internet connection
- How to access and use a graphical Traceroute utility
- What's on the Boardwatch Web site
- How to find and use Web-based Ping and Traceroute utilities
- The advantages and disadvantages of Web-based Ping and Traceroute utilities
- How to access the Internet Traffic Report Web site
- The meaning of a "traffic index"
- How to interpret data and graphs at the Internet Traffic Report Web site
- How to use Internet traffic data in conjunction with Ping and Traceroute reports to pinpoint problems with your Internet connection

LAB Assignments

5

1. Start the interactive part of the lab. Insert your Tracking Disk if you want to save your QuickCheck results. Perform each of the lab steps as directed, and answer all of the lab QuickCheck questions. When you exit the lab, your answers are automatically graded and your results are displayed.

2. Use the Ping utility that's supplied by Windows to ping *www.abcnews.com*. Record the IP address for the ABC News site, plus the minimum, maximum, and average times. For each time, indicate whether it would be considered poor, average, or good.

3. Use the Tracert utility that's supplied by Windows to trace a packet between your computer and *www.excite.com*. Print the Traceroute report. Circle any pings on the report that indicate high latency.

4. Locate a Web-based Ping utility and use it to ping *www.gobledegok.com*. Indicate the URL for the Web site where you found the Ping utility. Explain the results of the ping.

5. Connect to the Internet Traffic Report Web site, make a note of the date and time, and then answer the following questions:

   a. What is the traffic index for Asia?

   b. How does the index for Asia compare with the traffic index for North America?

   c. During the previous 24 hours in Europe, what was the period with the worst response time?

INTERNET ACCESS

The most difficult aspect of the Internet is getting connected. Although most people begin with a dial-up connection, many soon explore high-speed Internet access options, such as cable modems, DSL, personal satellite dishes, and ISDN. All high-speed access options are not created equal. So, if you have a choice, it is a good idea to compare access speed and costs.

In this section of the chapter, you'll discover why online interactive game players shun direct satellite connections. You'll learn why cable and DSL modems leave your computer open to hackers who cruise the Internet searching for user IDs, passwords, and launching points for bothersome viruses. And you won't be left in suspense—we'll tell you how to close up those security holes to prevent unwanted intrusions.

DIAL-UP CONNECTIONS

How does a dial-up connection work? A dial-up connection uses **POTS** (plain old telephone service) to transport data between your computer and your ISP. To understand how it works, you'll need a little background on telephone communications.

The telephone communications system uses a tiered network to transport calls locally, cross-country, and internationally. At each level of the network, a switch creates a connection so that a call eventually has a continuous circuit to its destination. The first tier of this network uses a star topology to physically connect each telephone in a city to a switch in what's called a "switching station," "local switch," or "central office."

The second tier of the telephone network links several local switching stations. Connections then fan out to switches maintained by many different local and long-distance telephone companies, as shown in Figure 5-21.

FIGURE 5-21

The telephone system connects your telephone to a local switch. Local switches are connected to other nearby local switches and to long-haul communications links.

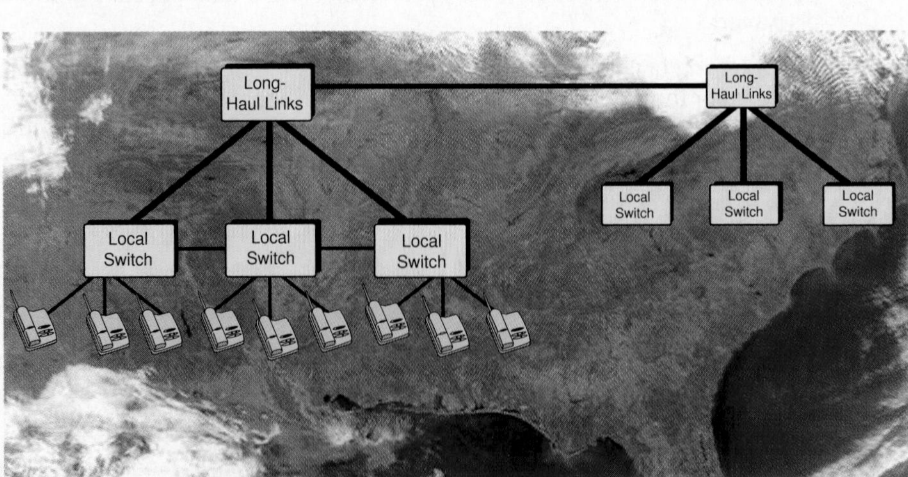

When you use a dial-up connection, your computer's modem essentially places a regular telephone call to your ISP. Your call is routed through the telephone company's local switch and out to the ISP. When the ISP's computer "answers" your call, a dedicated circuit is established between you and your ISP—just as if you had made a voice call and someone at the ISP had "picked up" the phone. The circuit remains connected for the duration of your call, and provides a communications link that carries data between your computer and the ISP. As your data arrives at the ISP, a router sends it out over the Internet. Figure 5-22 illustrates the path of your data when you use a dial-up connection.

FIGURE 5-22

When you use an ISP to access the Internet, your data travels through the local telephone switch to your ISP, which sends it onto the Internet.

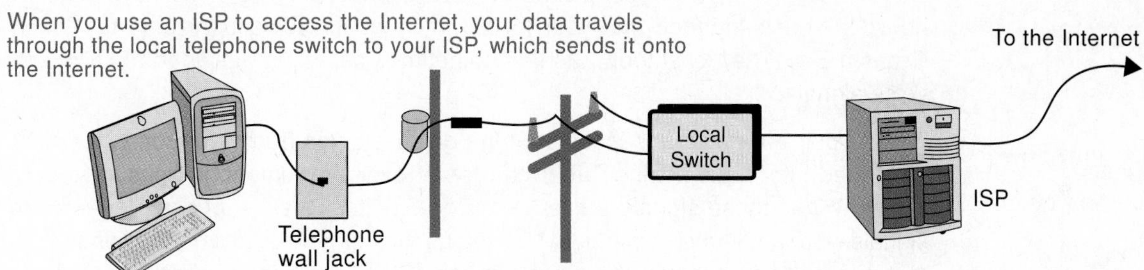
To the Internet
Local Switch
ISP
Telephone wall jack
Your computer

How does a modem work? The signals that represent data bits exist in your computer as digital signals. The telephone system, however, expects to work with human voices, so the "stuff" that it carries must be in the format of analog audio tones. It's as if you are trying to move a bunch of ice cubes through a tube. If the cubes won't fit through the tube, you can melt them into water, which can flow through the tube. A voiceband modem—usually referred to simply as a "**modem**"—converts the signals from your computer into signals that can travel over telephone lines. A modem transmits a 1,070 hertz tone for a 0 and a 1,270 hertz tone for a 1.

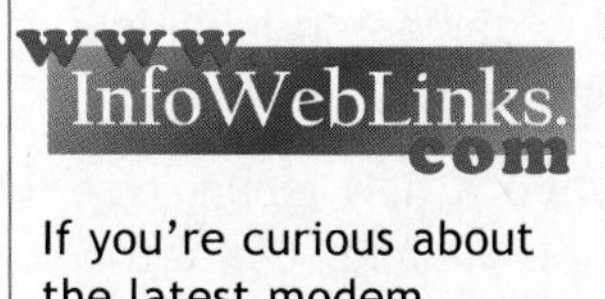
www InfoWebLinks.com

If you're curious about the latest modem technology, speed, and prices, check out the Modem InfoWeb.

click

The word "modem" is derived from the words "modulate" and "demodulate." In communications terminology, **modulation** means changing the characteristics of a signal, as when a modem changes a digital pulse into an analog audio signal. **Demodulation** means changing a signal back to its original state, as when a modem changes an audio signal back to a digital pulse. See Figure 5-23.

FIGURE 5-23

When you send data, your modem modulates the signal that carries your data. A modem at the other end of the transmission demodulates the signal.

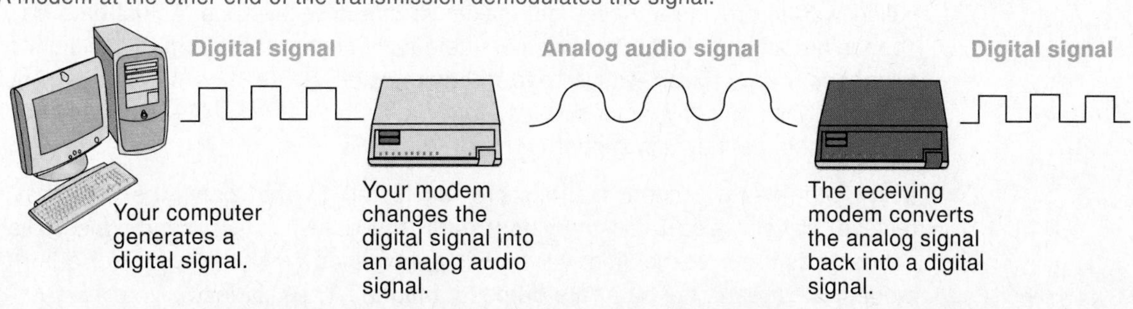
Digital signal
Analog audio signal
Digital signal
Your computer generates a digital signal.
Your modem changes the digital signal into an analog audio signal.
The receiving modem converts the analog signal back into a digital signal.

When your computer's modem initiates a connection, it sends a signal that is equivalent to picking up the receiver of a telephone to get a dial tone. It then dials the ISP by emitting a series of tones—the same tones that you'd produce if you punched in the ISP's number using a phone keypad. The modem then waits for the ISP's modem to answer the call. After the ISP's modem answers, the two modems begin to negotiate communications protocols, such as transmission rate. The series of beeps, tones, and whooshing sounds that you hear when you connect to your ISP is the sound of your modem "talking" to the ISP's modem. When the negotiation or "handshaking" is complete, data transmission can begin.

Why doesn't new digital telephone technology eliminate the need for a modem? Although telephone companies "went digital" long ago, their digital switches kick into action only after your call arrives at the local switching station. The technology between your telephone and your local switch would be recognizable to Alexander Graham Bell. The "local loop," as it is sometimes called, is designed to carry analog voice signals.

To transport data over this local loop, the digital signals from your computer must be converted into analog "tones" that can travel over the telephone lines to your local switch. When these signals arrive at the local switch, they are converted into digital signals—but not in the same digital format as they originated from your computer—so that they can be sent over the digital section of the telephone network. With all of this conversion, it seems amazing that data actually reaches its destination!

Can I talk and send data at the same time? When your computer is connected to your ISP via dial-up, data is transmitted over the same frequencies that are normally used for voice conversations. If you have only one telephone line, you cannot pick up your telephone receiver, dial your friend, and carry on a voice conversation while you are sending data. Some modems use technology, similar to call waiting, that allows you to remain connected to your ISP and temporarily suspend data transfers while answering a voice call. It is also possible to use the Internet to carry voice signals from your computer's microphone to the sound card of another computer. This technology, called **voice over IP** (VoIP) allows you to play games, for example, and chat about your moves all while you are online.

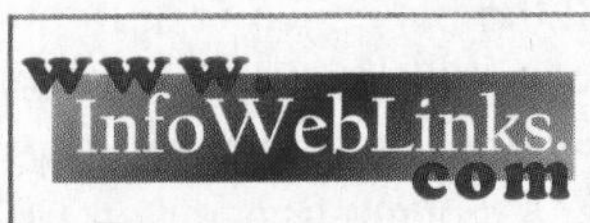

At the Voice over IP InfoWeb you'll find links to software downloads and more information about using the Internet as a voice channel.

How fast is a modem? When modems were a new technology, their speed was measured as **baud rate**—the number of times per second that a signal in a communications channel varies, or makes a transition between states. An example of such a transition is the change from a signal representing a 1 bit to a signal representing a 0 bit. A 300-baud modem's signal changes state 300 times each second, but—and this is the tricky part—each baud doesn't necessarily carry one bit. So, a 300-baud modem might be able to transmit more than 300 bits per second.

To help consumers make sense of modem speeds, they are now measured in bits per second. (If you're a stickler for details, you'll realize that this is actually a measure of capacity, but everyone calls it "speed.") Since 1998, most modems use a standard called **V.90** to provide a theoretical maximum speed of 56 Kbps. Actual data transfer speeds are affected by factors such as the quality of your local loop connection to the telephone switch. Even with a "perfect" connection, a 56 Kbps modem tops out at about 44 Kbps. Slightly faster speeds may be possible with new **V.92** and **V.44** modem standards, once they are supported by dial-up ISPs.

Many Internet connection methods provide faster **downstream** (the data that you receive) transmission rates than **upstream** (the data that you send) rates. Dial-up connections are no exception; 44 Kbps is a typical downstream speed for a 56 Kbps modem. Upstream, the data rate drops to about 33 Kbps, or less.

CABLE TELEVISION CONNECTIONS

How can the cable TV system provide Internet access? The cable television system was originally designed for remote areas where TV broadcast signals could not be received in an acceptable manner with an antenna. These systems were called "community antenna television," or CATV. The CATV concept was to install one or more large, expensive satellite dishes in a community, catch TV signals with these dishes, and then send the signals over a system of cables to individual homes.

The satellite dish "farm" at which television broadcasts are received and retransmitted is referred to as the **head-end**. From the head-end, a cabling system branches out and eventually reaches consumers' homes, as shown in Figure 5-24.

The topology of a CATV system looks a lot like the physical topology for a computer network. And that is just what is formed when your cable TV company becomes your Internet provider. A router and high-speed connection from the head-end to the Internet provide the potential for Internet connectivity over every cable in the system. Your computer becomes part of a neighborhood local area network like the one depicted in Figure 5-25.

FIGURE 5-24

Cables from the CATV head-end extend out as a series of "trunks." The trunks are then connected to "feeders" that serve neighborhoods. The connection from a feeder to a consumer's home is referred to as a "drop."

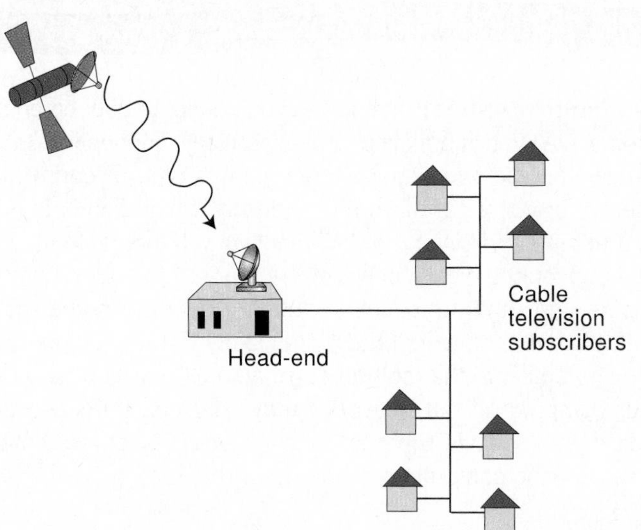

FIGURE 5-25

When a cable TV company becomes your Internet Service Provider, your computer becomes part of a "neighborhood network."

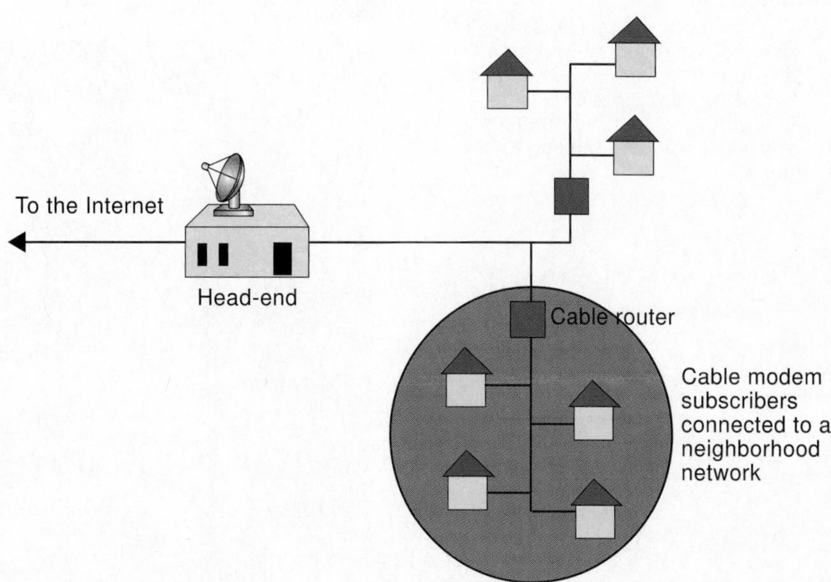

5

Are television and data signals carried over the same cable? The lowest-capacity coaxial cable that's used by the CATV system has a far greater carrying capacity than POTS lines. To offer both television and Internet access, the cable's bandwidth is divided among three activities. As shown in Figure 5-26, a CATV cable must provide bandwidth for television signals, incoming data signals, and outgoing data signals.

FIGURE 5-26
A CATV cable has enough bandwidth to support TV channels and data flowing downstream, as well as data flowing upstream.

How do I set up a cable modem connection? When you configure your computer to access the Internet over a CATV system, you are essentially connecting to an Ethernet-style local area network. The two requirements for this type of connection are circuitry to handle Ethernet protocols and a **cable modem**, which converts your computer's signal into one that can travel over the CATV network. If the cable modem includes Ethernet circuitry, you would typically connect the modem to your computer using a USB cable. Otherwise, the Ethernet circuitry must be installed in your computer. If your computer was originally "network ready," it is likely to be equipped with the necessary Ethernet circuitry built into the motherboard, as a PC card, or as a network interface card. If your computer is not network ready, you can purchase and install just about any standard, inexpensive Ethernet card. Figure 5-27 shows how to connect a cable modem to a desktop computer's Ethernet card.

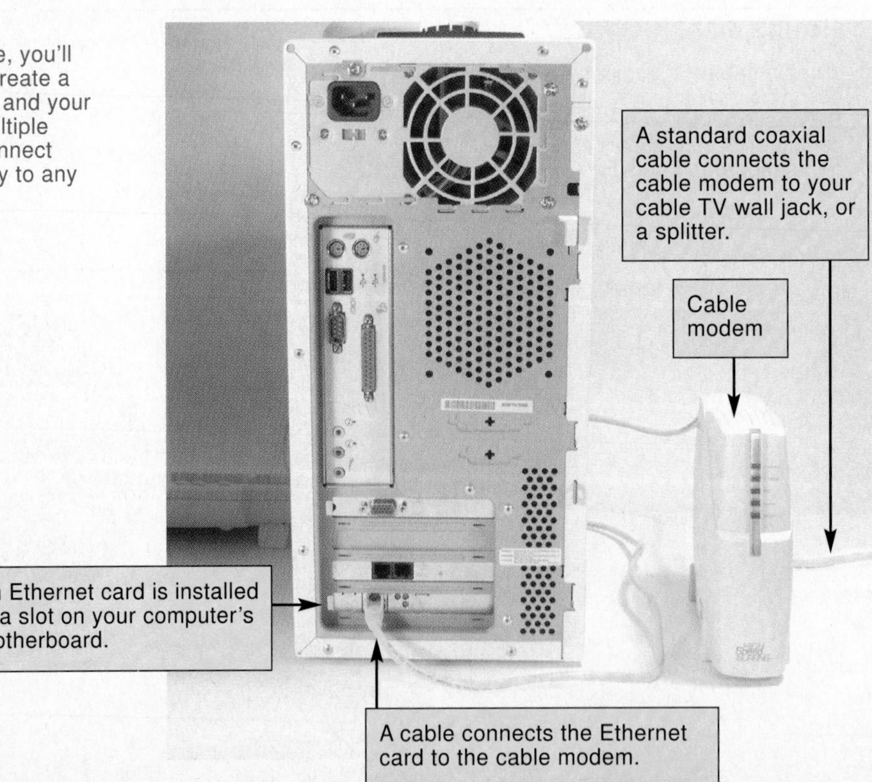

A standard coaxial cable connects the cable modem to your cable TV wall jack, or a splitter.
Cable modem
An Ethernet card is installed in a slot on your computer's motherboard.
A cable connects the Ethernet card to the cable modem.

FIGURE 5-27
With only one CATV cable, you'll need to use a splitter to create a link to your cable modem and your television. If you have multiple CATV cables, you can connect your cable modem directly to any one of them.

What's the significance of becoming part of a "neighborhood network"? When your CATV connection is up and running, your computer becomes part of a neighborhood data network because the cable from your computer and the cables from your neighbors' computers essentially connect at a centralized point. Two issues become significant: bandwidth and security.

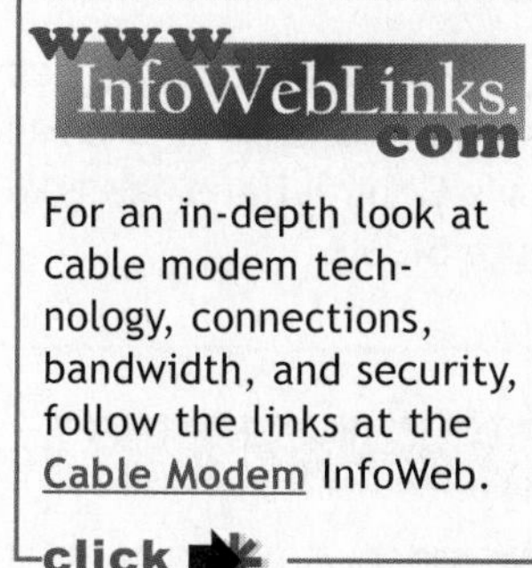

For an in-depth look at cable modem technology, connections, bandwidth, and security, follow the links at the Cable Modem InfoWeb.

click

The cable that you share with your neighbors has a certain amount of bandwidth. As more and more neighbors use the service, it might seem to get slower and slower. As an analogy, consider the luggage conveyor belt in an airport, which moves at a constant speed. If you have three pieces of luggage and you are the only passenger on the plane, your bags will arrive one right after another. However, if you just arrived on a full 747, your bags will be intermixed with those of hundreds of other passengers, and it will take longer to collect them. A communications channel like your CATV cable carries packets at a constant speed. However, if many of your neighbors are sending and receiving packets at the same time, those packets will seem to arrive more slowly.

As for the security issue, in the early days of cable modem service, some cable modem users were unpleasantly surprised when they happened to open the Windows Network Neighborhood only to be greeted with a list of their neighbors' computers! When you have an Ethernet card in your PC, Windows automatically takes inventory of the local area network during boot up. It looks for any computers on the network that have file and print sharing activated, and then lists them in the Network Places window, as shown in Figure 5-28.

FIGURE 5-28

If your PC is part of a network, and has file and printer sharing activated, other network users might be able to access your files by opening the *My Network Places* window.

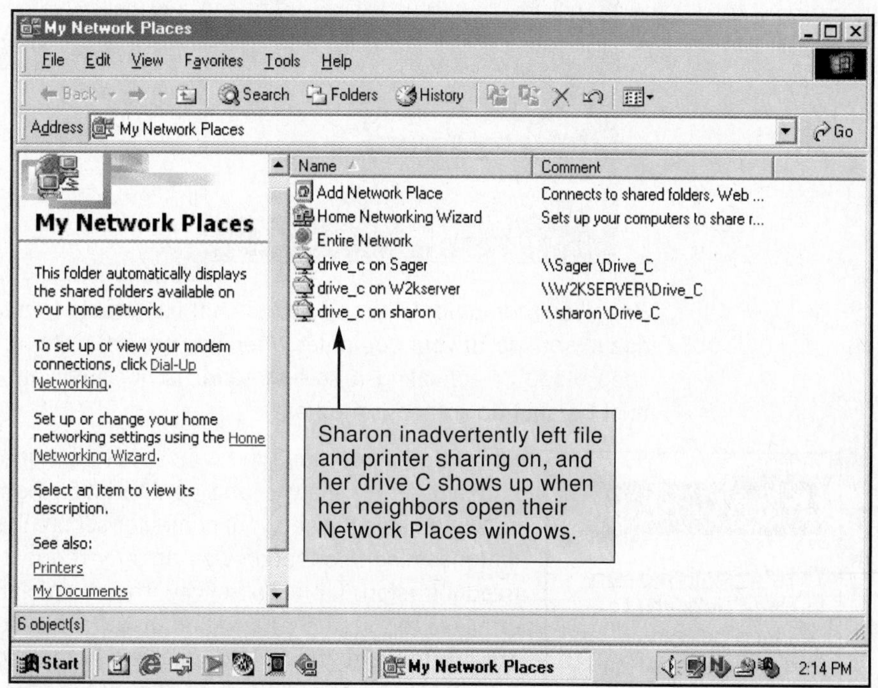

Today, many cable companies use DOCSIS-compliant cable modems to block this "crossover" access among computers owned by their cable modem subscribers. **DOCSIS** (Data Over Cable Service Interface Specification) is a security technology that filters packets to certain ports, including the port that Windows uses for networking. DOCSIS secures your computer from your neighbors, but it does not close up all of the security holes that are opened when you use an always-on connection, such as a cable modem or DSL.

5

Unlike a dial-up connection that's only connected for the duration of your call, an **always-on connection** is always connected, and it is "on" whenever your computer is powered up. With an always-on connection, you might have the same IP address for days, or even months, depending on your ISP. A hacker who discovers that your computer has a security weakness can easily find it again, and its high-speed access makes it a very desirable target.

How do I secure an always-on connection? If your PC is connected to a cable modem, you should take steps to protect it from hackers. The first step is to disable file and printer sharing. The Networking icon in the Windows Control Panel leads to a dialog box that allows you to adjust this setting. (See Figure 5-29.)

FIGURE 5-29

When you turn off file and printer sharing, your files and printer cannot be accessed by other network users.

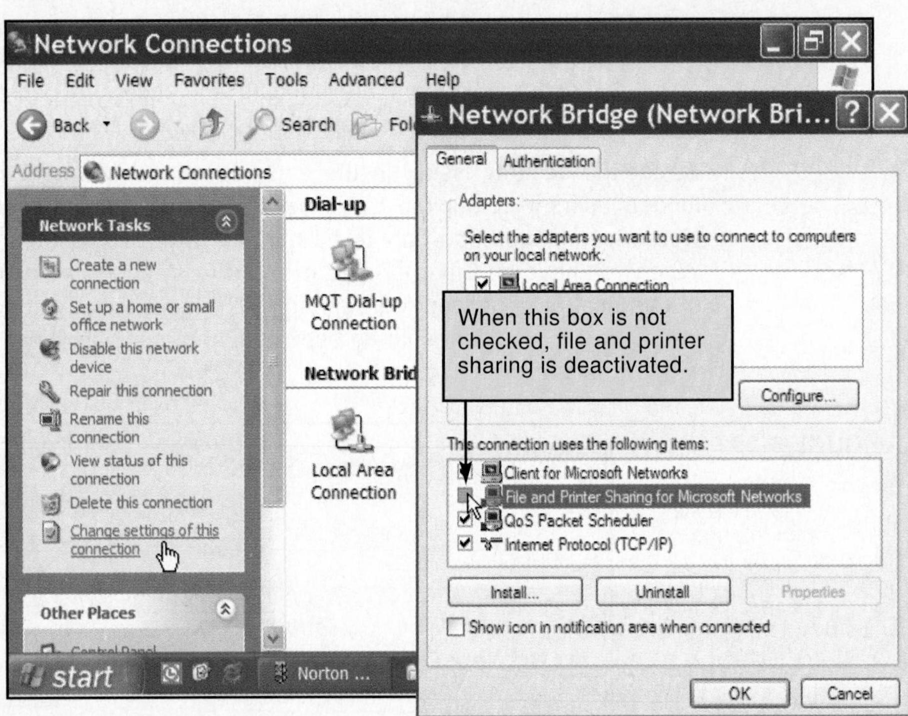

When your computer is turned off, it is not vulnerable to attack. Therefore, it is a good idea to shut down your computer when you are not using it. Putting your computer into sleep mode or activating a screen saver is not sufficient protection. Your computer must be shut down and turned off.

The Firewall Software InfoWeb links you to vendors, downloads, and in-depth information about how this software can protect your computer from hackers, crackers, and things that go bump in the night.

click

For added protection, you can install **personal firewall software**, which is designed to analyze and control incoming and outgoing packets. This software helps to keep your computer secure in several ways. It makes sure that incoming information was actually requested and is not an unauthorized intrusion. It blocks activity from suspicious IP addresses and—best of all—it reports intrusion attempts so that you can discover if any hackers are trying to break into your computer. Most firewall software allows you to set up various filters to control the type of packets that your workstation accepts. And if you don't want to delve into the intricacies of TFTPD, LPD, and UUCPD, most packages allow you simply to select a level of security, such as high, medium, or low.

DSL, ISDN, T1, AND T3

What other options are available for high-speed Internet access? Although the standard equipment provided by telephone companies limits the amount of data that you can transmit and receive over a voiceband modem, the copper wire that runs from your wall jacks to the switching station actually has a fair amount of capacity. Several services, such as DSL, ISDN, T1, and T3 take advantage of this capacity to offer high-speed digital communications links for voice and data.

www.InfoWebLinks.com

Nationwide, DSL vendors are grouping and regrouping. How might this affect your Internet access? You'll find up-to-date consumer information at the DSL InfoWeb.

click

What is DSL? DSL (Digital Subscriber Line) is a high-speed, digital, always-on, Internet access technology that runs over standard phone lines. It is one of the fastest Internet connections that's affordable to the individual consumer. Several variations of this technology exist, including ADSL (asymmetric DSL with downstream speed faster than upstream speed), SDSL (symmetric DSL with the same upstream and downstream speed), HDSL (high-rate DSL), and DSL lite. The acronym xDSL is sometimes used to refer to this entire group of DSL technologies, but xDSL is not a separate variation of DSL.

DSL is digital, so data doesn't need to be changed into analog form and then back to digital as it does when you use a dial-up connection. Data is transmitted over your local loop in pure digital form, bypassing the bottleneck of analog-to-digital-to-analog conversion, and escaping the requirement to use the narrow bandwidth allocated to voice transmissions. The result is fast data transmission over standard copper telephone cable.

A DSL connection can carry both voice and data. If permitted by your DSL provider, you can use your DSL line for voice calls instead of your POTS line. The digital data and analog voice signals travel over the DSL line to the local switching station. There, the voice signals are transferred to the telephone company's regular lines. The data signals are interpreted by special equipment called a **DSLAM** (DSL Access Multiplexor) and routed over high-speed lines to a DSL provider, or directly to the Internet. In many areas, DSL is a joint venture between the telephone company and the DSL provider. The telephone company is responsible for the physical cabling and voice transmission. The DSL provider is responsible for data traffic. Figure 5-30 illustrates how DSL handles voice and data.

5

FIGURE 5-30

Voice and data signals travel over DSL to a special device at the local telephone switching station, where they are divided and routed either to an ISP or to the regular telephone network.

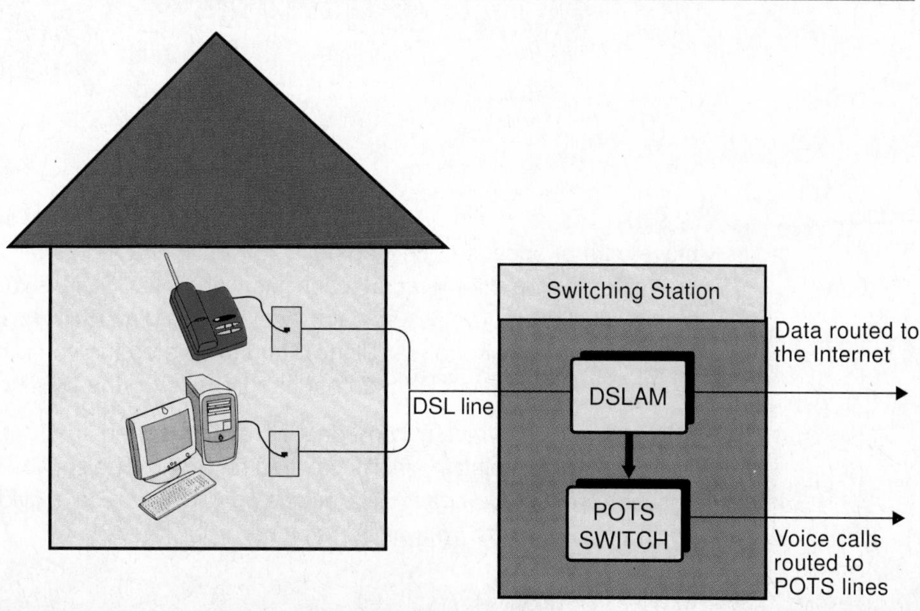

The speed of a DSL connection varies according to the characteristics of your telephone line, the equipment at your local switch, and your distance from the switching station. Most DSL modems are rated for 1.5 Mbps downstream. A DSL signal deteriorates over distance, however, which limits dependable DSL service to customers who live within three "cable" miles of a switching station. When shopping for a DSL connection, you should inquire about actual speed, find out if the upstream rate differs from the downstream rate, and check your distance from the switching station.

How do I install DSL? Most DSL installations require trained service technicians. A typical DSL installation begins when your DSL provider requests your local telephone company to designate a telephone line for the DSL connection. This line might utilize unused twisted pairs in your current telephone line, or it might require a new line from the nearest telephone pole to the telephone box outside of your house. This line is connected to a special type of DSL switch. Next, a technician from the DSL provider makes a service call to run cables and install a DSL wall jack, if necessary. The technician typically also installs a **DSL modem**, which manages the interface between your computer and a DSL line. If the modem includes Ethernet circuitry, a USB cable is used to connect the modem to your PC. Other types of DSL modems connect to your computer's Ethernet card. (See Figure 5-31.)

FIGURE 5-31

In a typical DSL installation, a twisted-pair cable connects your computer's Ethernet card to a DSL modem, which is plugged into a wall jack.

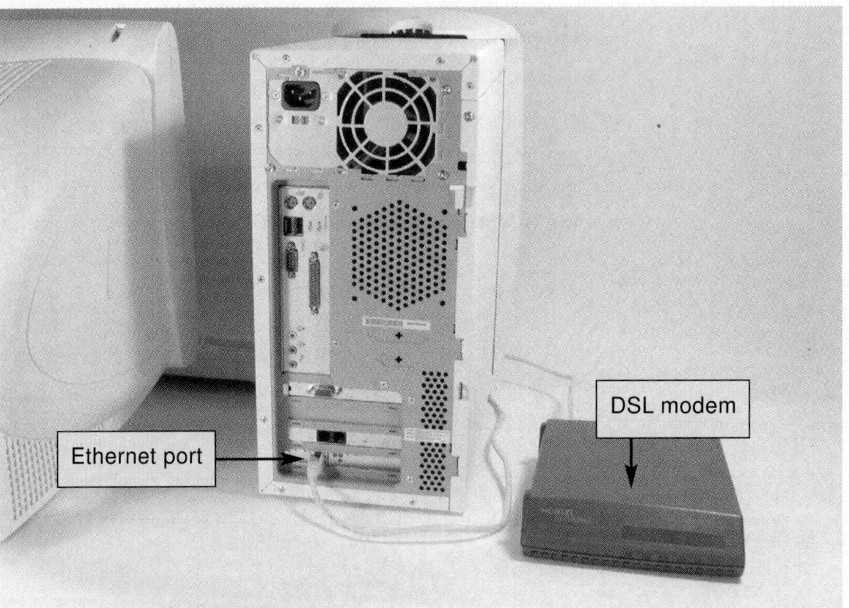

Is ISDN faster than DSL? ISDN (Integrated Services Digital Network) connections move data at speeds of 64 Kbps or 128 Kbps—not as fast as DSL or cable modems, but faster than a dial-up connection. As with DSL, ISDN is an all-digital service with the potential to carry voice and data. A device called an **ISDN terminal adapter** connects a computer to a telephone wall jack, and translates the computer's digital signals into a different kind of digital signal that can travel over the ISDN connection.

ISDN service is typically regarded as a high-speed Internet connection option for businesses that maintain small local area networks. The service is usually obtained from a local telephone company or a dedicated ISDN service provider. The availability and pricing of ISDN vary from place to place.

LAN HARDWARE

What's a typical LAN configuration? A LAN may connect as few as two computers, or it may encompass hundreds of devices, including computers, hubs, routers, printers, and modems.

On a typical network, each computer or peripheral device requires a network port and circuitry, which are usually supplied by a network interface card.

When connecting only two computers, you can simply use a single "cross-connect" cable between them. A hub or a hub/router is typically used to connect more than two computers. LAN hubs provide several connection ports. A small hub might provide four ports, as shown in Figure 5-36, whereas a larger hub would provide 64 ports.

FIGURE 5-36

On a typical Ethernet network, computers are connected to a centralized hub. The red and white cables lead to workstations. The yellow cable in the uplink port leads to another hub.

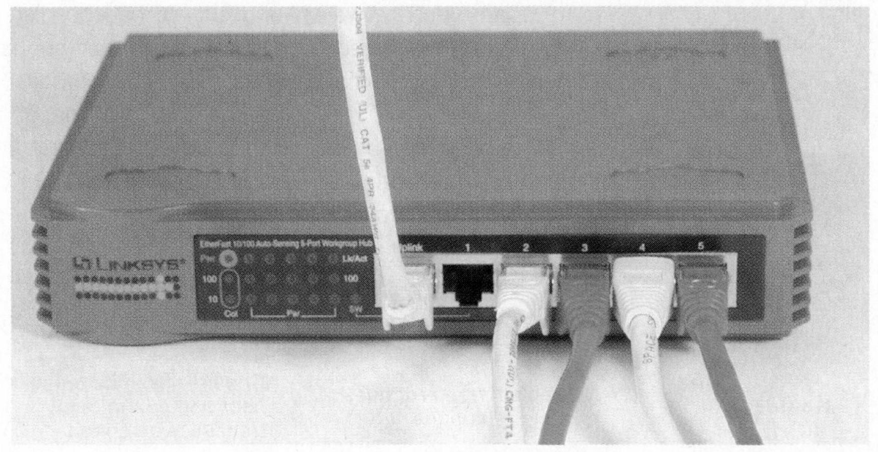

Each network device—computer, printer, or modem—requires one of the hub's ports. To expand a network beyond the capacity of a single hub, you can add other hubs. These hubs connect to each other via an **uplink port**.

What type of cable is used to connect LAN nodes? Most LANs use Category 5 ("cat 5") UTP (unshielded twisted pair) cables with plastic RJ-45 connections at both ends. These cables, sometimes referred to as "patch cables," are sold in various lengths, up to 100 feet. Category 5 cables are suitable for networks that transmit data at speeds up to 100 Mbps. An enhanced version—Category 5e—is suitable for 1 Gbps speeds.

Both "Cat 5" and "Cat 5e" cables look very similar. To differentiate between the two cables, you can read the specifications that appear on the package or are stamped on the cable itself.

Can a LAN use existing phone or electrical wiring? To avoid running unsightly cables throughout a house or office building, it is sometimes possible to use existing telephone or electrical wiring. The HomePNA network standard uses a special network interface card and cable to connect each computer to a standard telephone wall jack. The NICs contain circuitry that eliminates the need for hubs. When your computer is connected to a HomePNA network, you can typically use the phone to make a call and send information over the network at the same time because the network frequency is different from the voice frequency. You cannot, however, make a voice call while a dial-up Internet connection is active.

For the latest scoop on HomePNA and HomePLC networks, connect to the Home Network InfoWeb.

click 

Several companies offer wireless network kits for home installations. Businesses usually assemble a wireless network from a variety of off-the-shelf parts. For the latest information on equipment and pricing, check out the Wireless LAN InfoWeb.

click 

A HomePLC, or "powerline," network uses a special network interface card to connect a computer to a standard electrical outlet. Data, transmitted as low-frequency radio waves, travels along the electrical wiring until it reaches another network device. Unfortunately, powerline fluctuations caused by fluorescent lights, baby monitors, dimmer switches, amateur band radios, air conditioning units, or other major appliances can disrupt the signal and cause momentary loss of network connections.

Can LANs use wireless technology? In some home and business settings, running a cable between network devices is impractical. Most wireless LANs send and receive data as radio waves, which don't require cables. Each LAN device, including the hub, is equipped with a transceiver that both transmits and receives signals from other network devices.

Although wireless LANs eliminate unsightly wires, they are typically slower than wired networks, and signals can be disrupted by interference from large metal objects, metal wall studs, cell phones, pagers, and other wireless devices. The most popular wireless network standard is **802.11b** (sometimes called **Wi Fi** for "wireless fidelity"), which operates at 11 Mbps, spans distances of 300 feet, and can be used in conjunction with standard Ethernet networks. Another wireless standard, called **Bluetooth**, operates at speeds up to 700 Kbps with a maximum range of 35 feet. Figure 5-37 provides a quick comparison of home network technologies.

FIGURE 5-37 Home Network Technology Comparison

Network Type	Advantages	Disadvantages	Speed
HomePNA	No cables required; uses existing telephone wiring	Requires telephone jacks near computers; slow transmission speed	10 Mbps
Home PLC	No cables required; uses and standard electrical outlet	Susceptible to electrical Interference; very slow	2 Mbps
Ethernet	Inexpensive; reliable, standard technology; fast	Unsightly cables; may require running cables through walls, ceilings, and floors	10 Mbps, 100 Mbps, or 1 Gbps
Wireless	No cables required	Each devices requires a transceiver, which adds costs; susceptible to interference from large metal objects and other wireless devices	11 Mbps (802.11b) 700 Kbps (Bluetooth)

LAN STANDARDS AND PROTOCOLS

Do I have my choice of network standards? Several LAN standards exist, including Ethernet, Token Ring, ATM, FDDI, and LocalTalk. Each standard provides unique technology for sending data and preventing collisions. Today, Ethernet is the dominant standard for home and business networks.

www.InfoWebLinks.com

Ethernet is definitely cool. See what the "Ether" is all about at the Ethernet InfoWeb.

click

What's the most popular protocol used on small networks? Like the Internet, many LANs use TCP/IP because it is supplied with most personal computers, and it simplifies the process of transferring data from a LAN to the Internet. Alternative LAN protocols include **IPX/SPX**, a standard developed for Novell Networks, and **NetBIOS/NetBEUI**, a network standard developed by Microsoft.

LAN ADDRESSES

Does each LAN device have a unique address? When a NIC is manufactured, it is given a unique address called a **MAC address** (Media Access Control address), such as 00-E0-18-CD-6E-28. The first three bytes of this address indicate the company that manufactured the NIC. The remaining three bytes are the NIC's serial number.

Unfortunately, this 6-byte MAC address does not correspond to the address format that's required by TCP/IP, SPX/IPX, or other protocols. To send and receive packets of data over a network, your computer needs an address that conforms to the network protocol. For example, when connected to a network that uses TCP/IP, your computer will be assigned an IP address, such as 192.168.1.218. On a network that uses SPX/IPX, your computer will be assigned an IPX address, such as 4a.0000.0c00.23fe. These assigned addresses are used in packet headers to specify the packet's destination.

LAN SOFTWARE

Does a LAN require a special operating system? Special network operating systems (NOS), such as Novell NetWare, were quite popular at one time and are still used on some networks. The need for a special NOS has declined, however, because today's popular desktop and server operating systems include the software necessary to establish communication with the other computers and devices on a LAN.

Does a LAN require special application software? Most application software designed for standalone computers can be used on a network. Typically, your favorite word processing, spreadsheet, presentation, graphics, or other software works on a network workstation, just as it does when you use it on a standalone computer.

Theoretically, a network allows workstations to access application software that has been installed on network drives—those on a server or on a shared drive of a network workstation. Setting up such access is easy under some operating systems, but difficult in others. In order to run Windows software from a server, for example, you or your network manager must install the software on the server and complete a workstation installation of the software. A **workstation installation** copies some, but not all, of the program files to your local hard disk, then updates the Windows Registry and the Windows Start menu to include a listing for the new program.

How does copyright law affect program distribution on a LAN? Even though an application might run on a LAN, it is still subject to copyright law and the terms of the license agreement. A single-user license agreement typically allows one copy of the software to be in use at any given time. Using copies of the software on several workstations would violate the terms of this type of license agreement. Some software publishers provide special licenses designed for network use.

A **multiple-user license** allows more than one person to use a particular software package. It is beneficial in cases, such as electronic mail, where each person requires a personalized version of the software. Multiple-user licenses are generally priced per user, but the price for each user is typically less than the price of a single-user license.

A **concurrent-user license** allows a certain number of copies of the software to be used at the same time. This type of license is popular for application software that might be accessed through the day by 100 or more different people, but when no more than, say, 20 copies would be in use at any one time.

A **site license** generally allows software to be used on any and all computers at a specific location, such as within a corporate office or on a university campus. A site license is usually priced at a flat rate—for example, $5,000 per site.

LAN INSTALLATION

How do I set up a simple Ethernet LAN to connect several PCs? The first step in assembling your own LAN is to make sure that each PC contains an Ethernet port. If a computer does not supply one, you can install an Ethernet card. The Ethernet card for a desktop computer is usually installed in a slot on the motherboard. An Ethernet card for a notebook computer usually takes the form of a PC card. Both types feature a port (socket) for a network cable.

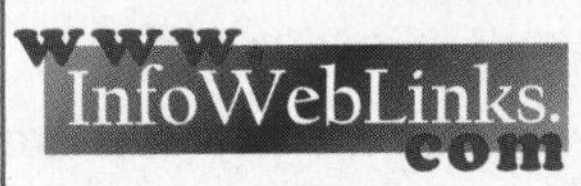

Your basic shopping list for a simple Ethernet LAN is at the Building a LAN InfoWeb.

After Ethernet ports are available in all of the workstations, the next step is to attach each workstation to a hub. To do so, simply connect a cable to a computer's Ethernet port, then connect the other end of the cable to one of the ports in the hub. If the hub requires power, plug it in. See Figure 5-38.

FIGURE 5-38

A LAN installation begins by making sure that every workstation contains an Ethernet port.

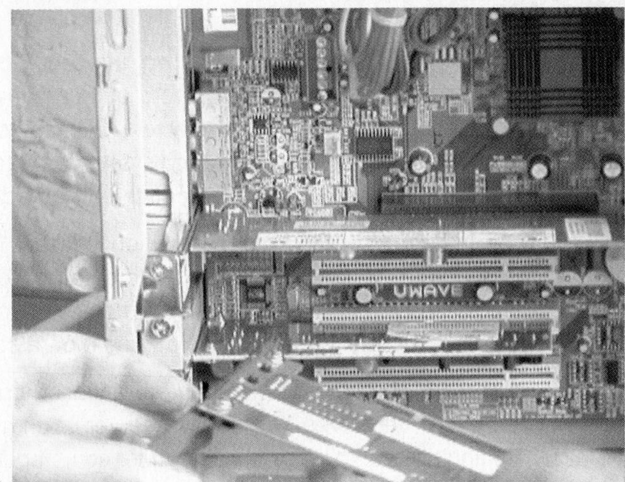

With all of the workstations connected, you can turn them on. Windows should automatically detect the Ethernet cards and establish a connection to the network.

How do I specify which resources can be shared by other workstations? For each workstation on the network, the workstation's owner can specify whether its files will be accessible to other workstations on the network. Earlier in the chapter, you learned how to turn off file and printer sharing. If you want the files on a workstation to be available to everyone on a network, you must turn on file sharing. Once file sharing is turned on, you can map connections to that workstation from other workstations on the network.

Drive mapping is Windows terminology for assigning a drive letter to a storage device that's located on a different workstation. Picture yourself sitting at your workstation—one of several connected to a LAN. Suppose that you want to access the hard drive of another workstation on a regular basis. You know that the owner of the drive has designated it as a shared resource that can be accessed by other network users. From your workstation, you can map the drive of the other computer as drive F. Once it has been mapped, you can access drive F, just as if it were one of the drives attached to your own workstation. For example, Windows Explorer would list drive F and all of the files that it contains, in addition to the files on your own workstation's drives.

Figure 5-39 explains how to use Windows Network Neighborhood to map the hard disk drive of another network computer to your own workstation.

FIGURE 5-39

In this example, drive C of a network server is mapped as drive F to a workstation. Once the mapping is complete, the server's hard disk will show up on the workstation's list of devices and folders as drive F, and can be used just as if it were a drive connected directly to the workstation.

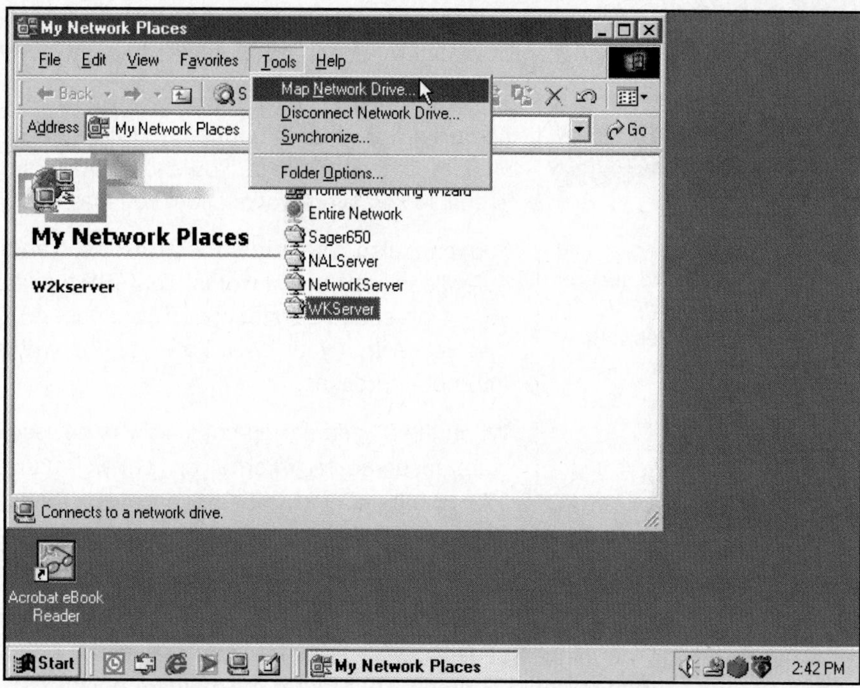

click to start

Can I connect my LAN to a high-speed Internet connection? One of the main reasons for creating a small LAN is to provide all the workstations with shared access to a single high-speed Internet connection, such as a cable modem or DSL line. The value of this distributed Internet access is so high that many non-technical computer owners are venturing into this somewhat "tricky" aspect of network installation.

To add high-speed Internet access to a LAN, you need a cable modem or DSL modem, and a corresponding ISP. You also need a router. You can purchase a router as a separate device, or you can purchase a hub with router capabilities to use instead of a plain non-router hub. Figure 5-40 illustrates how to connect a high-speed modem to a network that uses a combined hub/router.

FIGURE 5-40

Using a hub that also provides routing capability, all of the workstations in a LAN can gain access to a single high-speed Internet connection.

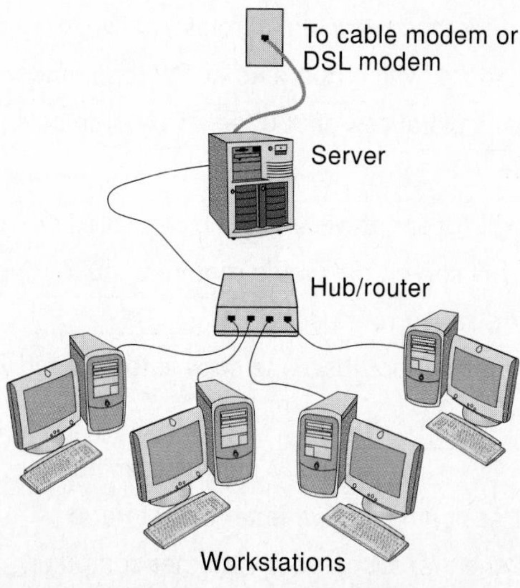

LAN SECURITY

What parts of a LAN are vulnerable to hackers? Local area networks are susceptible to internal security breaches, such as when a person at one workstation gains unauthorized access to the files on another workstation. If a LAN is equipped with an always-on Internet connection, it also becomes vulnerable to external attacks.

O.K. You set up a LAN with Internet access and now you want to secure it. The Network Security InfoWeb helps you evaluate firewall software and set up network address translation.

click

Should I bother with security measures on a home network? Any home network that is connected to an always-on Internet connection is vulnerable to intrusions. You should make sure that password protection is enabled on every workstation. You may want to use firewall software, too.

You can also use **network address translation** (NAT) as a line of defense. Here's how it works. Your ISP typically assigns an IP address to your high-speed connection. This address is visible to the rest of the Internet. Within your LAN, however, the workstations should use private Internet addresses.

When the IP addressing scheme was devised, three ranges of addresses were reserved for internal or "private" use: 10.0.0.0—10.255.255.255, 172.16.0.0—172.31.255.255, and 192.168.0.0—192.168.255.255. These **private IP addresses** cannot be routed over the Internet. If you've assigned private IP addresses to your workstations, they are essentially hidden from hackers, who see only the IP address for your router.

You might wonder how you can transmit and receive data from a workstation with a non-routable address. Your router maintains a network address translation table that keeps track of the private IP addresses assigned to each workstation. For outgoing packets, the router substitutes its own address for the address of the workstation. When a response to a packet arrives, the router forwards it to the appropriate workstation. In that way, only the router's address is publicly visible.

QUICKCheck Section D

1. Bluetooth is a popular wireless network standard, which operates at 11 Mbps, and spans distances of 300 feet. True or false? ______

2. Single-user software might be installed on a LAN server, but would require a multi-user, concurrent-user or ______ license if more than one copy is to be used at a time.

3. ______ is Windows terminology for assigning a drive letter to a storage device that's located on another computer.

4. To connect a LAN to a high-speed, always-on Internet connection, you need a DSL or cable modem, and a device called a(n) ______ that can be a standalone device or integrated into the hub.

5. Network address ______ provides a line of defense against hackers because it hides workstation IP addresses from the Internet.

check answers

Dial-up connections use POTS to transport data between your computer and your ISP over a "local loop" that carries ______, not digital, signals. A modem ______ your computer's digital signal so that it can travel over telephone lines. To restore a signal to its original state, it must be ______. Like many other Internet access technologies, a dial-up connection's ______ transmission rate is usually greater than the ______ rate. A cable modem provides Internet access over the same ______ cables that carry television signals from the cable company's head-end to your home. Some cable modems connect to a port provided by an ______ card, whereas other cable modems connect to a USB port. The cable connection is referred to as an ______ connection because it is active any time that your computer is turned on. With such a connection, security becomes an issue. To protect your files from hackers, you can turn off the Windows printer and ______ sharing, plus install personal ______ software.

DSL connections are similar to cable connections in several ways, except that a DSL connection uses specially conditioned telephone lines that carry ______ signals over the local loop. A similar, but slower, service is called ______. Two additional services are available from the telephone company, but typically they are too expensive for individual consumers. ______ is a high-speed digital network (1.544 Mbps) that supplies 24 channels, each with 64 Kbps capacity. ______ provides 672 channels with a total capacity of 43 Mbps. Direct ______ service provides another high-speed Internet access method that may be the only option in rural areas.

check answers

A LAN (local ______ network) connects computers, called workstations, within a limited geographical area. It provides workstations with access to resources, such as high-speed Internet connections, printers, and centralized storage and backup. Today, most LANs are based on the Ethernet standard, which features CSMA/CD ______ detection. Ethernet ______ in each workstation are connected to a centralized hub with twisted-pair cables. It is also possible to use existing telephone line and powerline wiring to connect workstations. Two standards, 802.11b and ______, provide wireless connections between network nodes. Each device on a LAN has a physical ______ address so that data can be routed to its destination. The physical address can be supplemented by a ______ address, such as an IP address, to correspond to the network protocol. Many of today's LANs use ______ protocol, just like the Internet. Alternative LAN protocols include SPX/IPX and NetBIOS/NetBEUI.

Standard single-user software applications run on workstations, just as they do on standalone computers. Applications can also be loaded onto a server or a shared hard disk and used by several workstations, if the software license permits such use. A ______ license allows more than one person to use a particular software package. A ______ license allows a certain number of copies of the software to be used at the same time. A ______ license generally allows the software to be used on any and all computers at a specific location.

Adding high-speed Internet access to a LAN requires a cable modem or DSL modem, and a corresponding ISP. You will also need a ______ to handle data traffic between the LAN and the Internet. When a LAN is connected to the Internet, it becomes more vulnerable to intrusions. In addition to firewall software, network ______ translation provides some measure of security because it allows you to "hide" the addresses of workstations from hackers on the Internet.

check answers

INTERACTIVE KEY TERMS

Make sure that you understand all of the boldfaced key terms presented in this chapter. If you're using the NP6 BookOnCD, you can use this list of terms as an interactive study activity. First, try to define a term in your own words, then click the term to compare your definition with the definition that is presented in the chapter.

INTERACTIVE
SITUATION QUESTIONS

Apply what you've learned to some typical computing situations. When using the NP6 BookOnCD, you can type your answers, then use the Check Answers button to automatically score your responses. Place your Tracking Disk in the floppy disk drive if you want to save your scores.

1. You're installing a LAN and you decide to go with Ethernet. You'll typically use Category ______ UTP cables to connect each workstation to a(n) ______.

2. You're finally ready to get a high-speed Internet connection. Because the cable modem provided by your CATV company contains Ethernet circuitry, you can simply connect the modem to your computer's ______ port.

3. Your Internet access seems very slow one day. You might be able to discover the location of the slowdown if you use a utility called ______.

4. Suppose that you decide to open a little Web store to sell handcrafted pottery. Your Web site will need a(n) ______ IP address, and you'll want to register a(n) ______ name.

5. Suppose that your computer contains a 56 Kbps modem that uses the V.90 standard. You can expect about 44 Kbps ______ speed, and about 33 Kbps as the maximum ______ speed.

6. Suppose that you just installed a cable modem. To secure your PC, you should first use the Control Panel's Network icon to turn off file and printer ______. You might also want to install personal ______ software.

7. Suppose that you live in a rural area that is not serviced by a cable TV company. Your best bet for high-speed Internet access is probably direct ______ service.

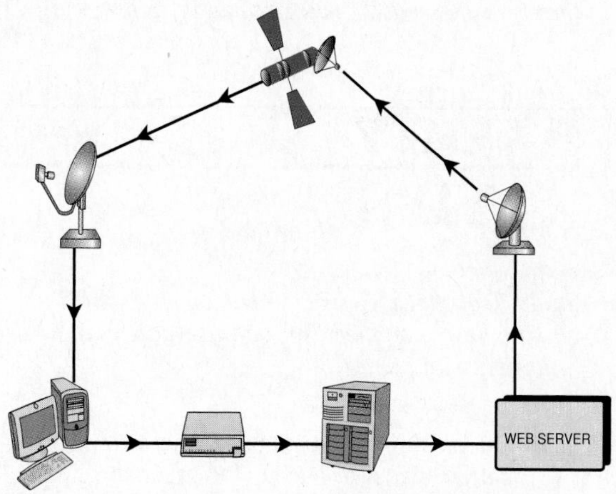

8. Suppose that you receive TV signals via satellite. You're thinking of subscribing to satellite Internet service, too. The company Web site features the diagram shown above. You can assume that the company provides ______-way satellite service.

9. Suppose that your PC is connected to a LAN, and you want to regularly access a file that's stored on one of the LAN workstations. You'd like to access that computer's hard disk as if it were connected to your own computer, so you decide to use Windows Network Places to ______ the workstation's hard disk drive as drive F.

10. Suppose that you arrive at work and one of your coworkers tells you that the "router is down." You can surmise that your workstation will not be able to access the ______ until the router is fixed.

check answers

5

INTERACTIVE PRACTICE TESTS

When you use the NP6 BookOnCD, you can take Practice Tests that consist of 10 multiple-choice, true/false, and fill-in-the-blank questions. The questions are selected at random from a large test bank, so each time you take a test, you'll receive a different set of questions. Your tests are scored immediately, and you can print study guides that help you find the correct answers for any questions that you missed. If you are using a Tracking Disk, insert it in the floppy disk drive to save your test scores.

click to start

STUDY TIPS

Study Tips help you organize and consolidate the information in a chapter by making lists, outlines, charts, and sketches. You can use paper and pencil or word processing software to complete most of the Study Tips activities.

1. Make sure that you can use your own words to correctly answer each of the green focus questions that appear throughout the chapter.
2. Draw a diagram of Shannon's communications model. Apply this model to an Internet dial-up connection by indicating which real-world devices would exist at various points in the model to originate data, encode it, transmit signals, and so on.
3. Suppose that you are a "big brother" or a "big sister" to a bright nine year old. How would you explain the idea that you can use four bits to convey 16 different messages?
4. Make a list of the networks discussed in this chapter, and then put them in order according to bandwidth.
5. Create a list of network devices mentioned in this chapter. Write a brief description of each one, and indicate whether it would typically be part of the Internet, a LAN, or both.
6. Draw diagrams of star, ring, and bus network topologies. Make sure that you can trace the route of data over a Token Ring network and an Ethernet. Discuss how collisions are detected and/or avoided.
7. Make a list of protocols mentioned throughout this chapter. For each one, indicate whether it would be associated with the Internet, a LAN, or both.
8. Begin with 0011010. Diagram a series of "comic strip" frames to describe how a computer would transmit this data under even parity, and what would happen when the data was received.
9. Make sure that you can list the Internet access methods in which upstream transmission rates differ from downstream rates.
10. Draw a diagram of the Internet that includes the following devices connected in a technically correct configuration so that data can flow from the personal computer to the Web server: personal computer, voiceband modem, ISP modem, e-mail server, ISP router, domain name server, two backbone routers, backbone repeater, and Web server.
11. Make a list of security concerns that are related to Internet access. Describe the steps that you would take to (a) secure an individual connection or (b) secure a network connection.
12. Draw a diagram of a LAN that connects three workstations, a network printer, and a high-speed DSL connection. Label each device, including the hub/router, workstations, NICs, and modem. Make up a MAC address for each device using the standard MAC address format. Indicate which devices would have private IP addresses and which would have public IP addresses, if you implemented NAT on your network.

Most HTML tags work in pairs. An opening tag begins an instruction, which stays in effect until a closing tag appears. Closing tags always contain a slash. For example, the following sentence contains opening and closing bold tags:

<B>Caterpillars</B> love sugar.

When displayed by a browser, the word "Caterpillars" will be bold, but the other words in the sentence will not be bold.

HTML is not a case-sensitive language, so tags may be entered as uppercase, lowercase, or a mixture of both. The tag <HR> is the same as <hr>. Some Web page authors like to use uppercase for opening tags and lowercase for closing tags, for example, <B> for the opening tag and </b> for the closing tag. In any case, it is the slash (/) that indicates the closing tag, not the fact that it is lowercase. In this book, both opening and closing tags will be presented in uppercase.

In addition to formatting, HTML tags can be used to specify how to incorporate graphics on a page. Some people are surprised to learn that HTML documents contain no graphics. Of course, graphics do appear on many of the Web pages displayed in your browser window, so how do they get there? The <IMG SRC> tag specifies the name and location of the graphics file that is to be displayed as part of a Web page. Figure 6-4 illustrates how graphics are incorporated into a Web page.

FIGURE 6-4

An <IMG SRC> tag in an HTML document (top) produces a graphic when the Web page (bottom) is displayed by your browser.

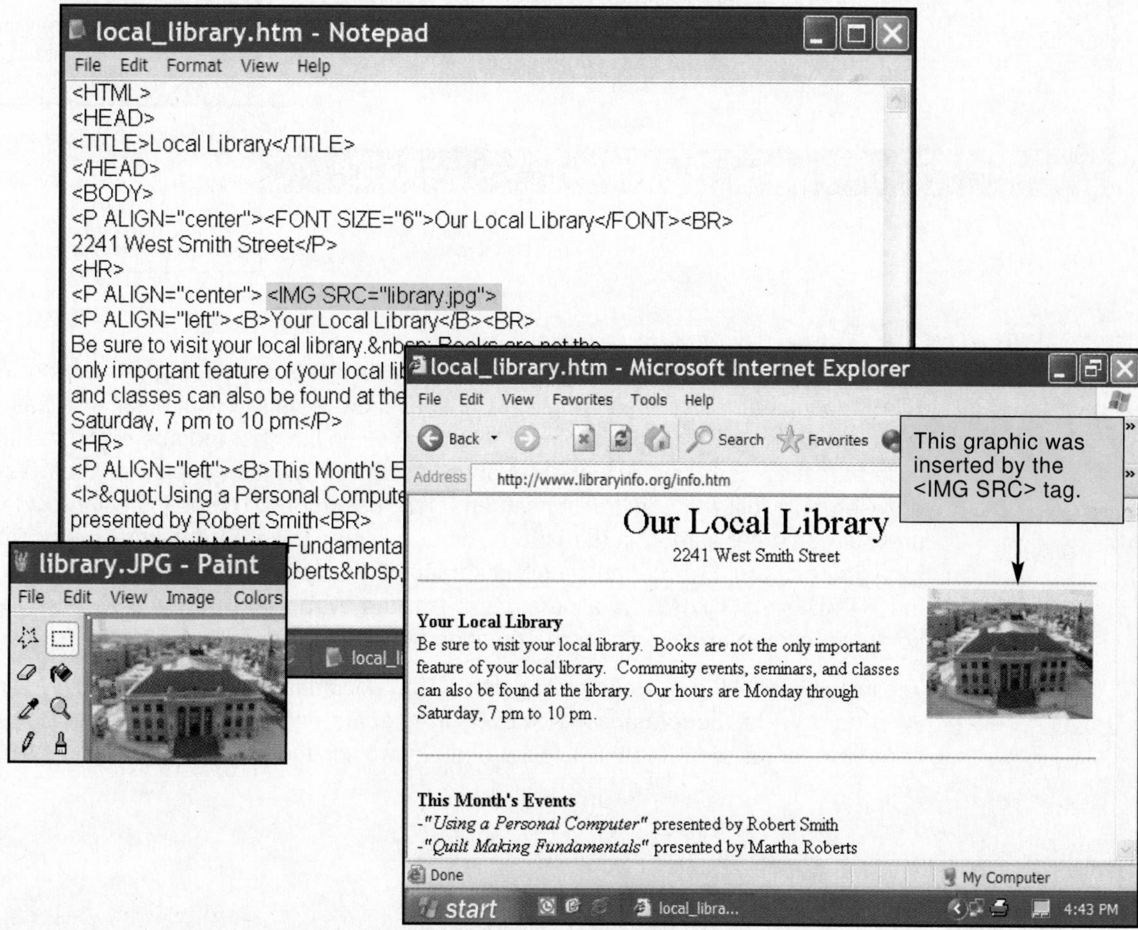

HTML tags do more than make a Web page look "pretty." They also produce the links that connect you to other Web documents. The <A HREF> tag specifies the information necessary to display the links that allow you to jump to related Web pages. Figure 6-5 explains.

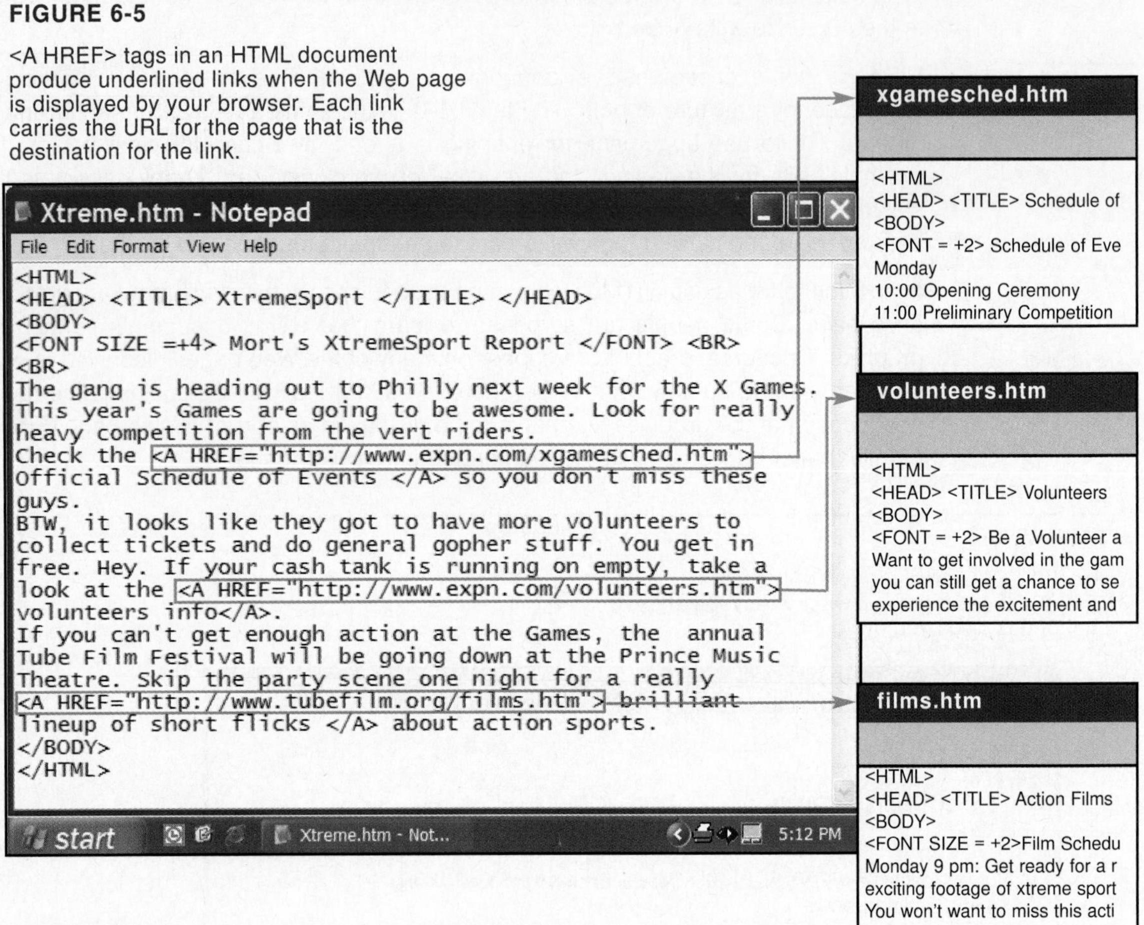

FIGURE 6-5

<A HREF> tags in an HTML document produce underlined links when the Web page is displayed by your browser. Each link carries the URL for the page that is the destination for the link.

So HTML documents look a lot different from Web pages, right? Exactly. An HTML document is like a screenplay, and your browser is like a director who has to make an author's screenplay come to life by assembling cast members and making sure that they correctly deliver their lines. As the HTML screenplay unfolds, your browser must follow the instructions in an HTML document to display the lines of text on your computer screen in the right color, size, and position. If the screenplay calls for a graphic, your browser must collect it from the Web server and display it. Although the HTML "script" exists as a permanent file, the Web page that you see on your computer screen exists only for the duration of the "performance."

Technically speaking, we can distinguish HTML documents—the "screenplay"—from Web pages—the performance. However, in everyday conversation, the term "Web page" is often used for the HTML document, as well as the Web page that you see on your screen.

Can I see the HTML tags used to create a Web page? Your browser is designed to display nicely formatted Web pages, not a messy "source" document filled with HTML tags. However, if you are curious about how a page was constructed, or if you would like to duplicate the features of a Web page, you can view the source document and its HTML tags by using a menu option on your browser. Figure 6-6 explains.

FIGURE 6-6

Most browsers include a menu option that allows you to view the HTML "source" document and the HTML tags it contains. The example at right illustrates how you would view source HTML while using the Internet Explorer browser.

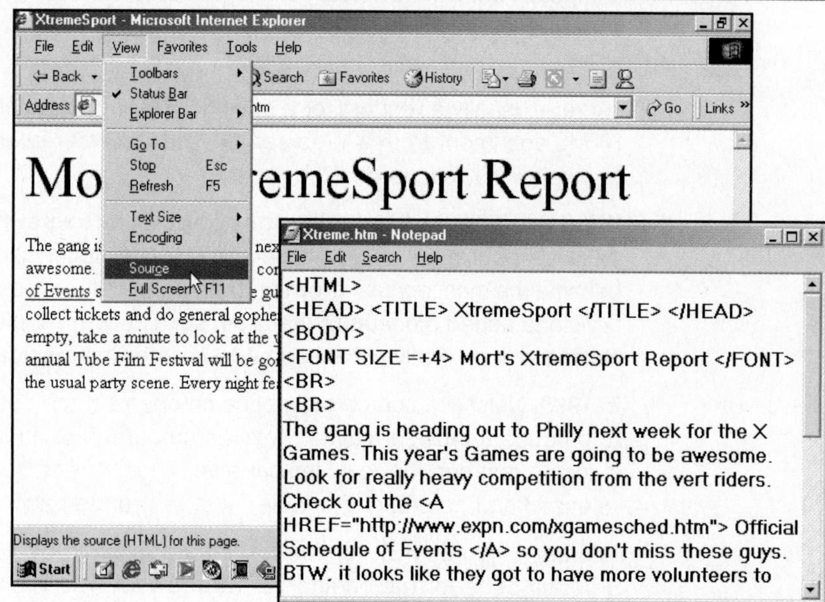

click to start

What are the most commonly used HTML tags? HTML includes hundreds of tags. For convenience, we can classify these tags into four groups. **Formatting tags** change the appearance of text, and work in much the same way as the formatting options in a word processor that create bold and italic text, adjust the size of text, change the color of text, arrange text in table format, or center text on a page. **Link tags** specify where and how to display links to other Web pages and e-mail addresses. **Media tags** specify how to display media elements, such as graphics, sound clips, or videos. **Operational tags** specify the basic setup for a Web page, provide ways for users to interact with a page, and offer ways for Web pages to incorporate information derived from databases. Figure 6-7 lists some of the most commonly used HTML tags, and indicates how they are categorized.

FIGURE 6-7 Basic HTML Tags

Tag	Description and Use	Category
<HTML> </HTML>	Place the <HTML> tag at the beginning of a document and place the </HTML> tag at the end of the document.	Operational
<TITLE> </TITLE>	Place immediately after the <HTML> tag. The text between the TITLE tags will appear on the title bar.	Operational
<FONT SIZE=+3> ... </FONT>	To specify a font size, use a positive or negative number in place of +3.	Formatting
 	The BR tag creates a line break.	Formatting
<A HREF = " "> ... </A>	To create an underlined link, place the URL for the link between the quotation marks, then type the link name between the tags.	Link
<IMG SRC=" " >	To display a graphic, place its filename between the quotation marks.	Media

WEB BROWSERS

Why do I need a browser to access the Web? In Chapter 1, you learned that a Web browser—usually referred to simply as a "browser"—is a software program that runs on your computer and helps you access Web pages. Technically, a browser is the client half of the client/server software that facilitates communication between a personal computer and a Web server. The browser is installed on your computer, and the Web server software is installed on a host computer somewhere on the Internet.

Your browser plays two key roles. First, it uses HTTP to send messages to a Web server—usually a request for a specific HTML document. Second, when it receives an HTML document from a Web server, your browser interprets the HTML tags in order to display the requested Web page.

What are some of today's most popular browsers? Netscape Navigator version 1.0 was published in December 1994. "Netscape," as it is generally called, quickly became the most popular browser, both on the Macintosh and PC platforms. Numerous revisions added pioneering features, such as frames, plug-ins, and JavaScript support. Netscape is currently published by Netscape Communications, a subsidiary of AOL.

In 1998, Netscape source code became open source software, which is currently used to produce a browser called Mozilla. Although Mozilla is a browser in its own right, it is also a test bed for new Netscape versions. After a new version of Mozilla has been released and determined "stable," it is re-branded and released as Netscape.

Internet Explorer (IE) version 1.0 was published by Microsoft in August 1995. The program code for the original IE 1.0 browser was licensed from a Netscape spin-off called Spyglass, which provided IE with many of the same features as Netscape. Until IE 4.0 appeared in 1997, however, Microsoft's browser was unable to match Netscape's popularity. Today, IE has supplanted Netscape as the dominant browser across the Mac and PC platforms. It is also available for Linux and several versions of UNIX. AOL's browser is a slightly modified version of IE.

A browser called NeoPlanet is technically an IE add-on, which allows you to customize the appearance of the browser window by selecting "skins" with various border and toolbar designs. To run Neoplanet, you must have IE installed on your computer.

Opera is one of the few real alternatives to IE and Netscape. First published in December 1996, Opera began as a Norwegian phone company project to develop a small and fast browser for computers with meager memory and processing resources. Unlike IE and Netscape, which descended from Mosaic, Opera was written from scratch, and as a result, it has some unique features, such as page zoom and a multi-document display. Versions of Opera are available for Windows, Linux, UNIX, and Mac OS.

Should I upgrade my browser when new versions become available? It is a good idea to upgrade when a new version of your browser appears. Both IE and Netscape updates are free. Therefore, you can get up-to-date browser functionality simply by spending a few minutes downloading and installing an update.

The problem with using an old version of a browser is that some Web pages may depend on new HTML features that are only supported by the latest browser versions. Without the latest upgrade, you might encounter errors as your browser tries to display a page, but cannot interpret some of the HTML. In other cases, your browser might display the Web page without errors, but you will not see all of the intended effects.

Another important reason to upgrade is for increased security. As hackers discover and take advantage of security holes, browser publishers try to patch the holes. Upgrades typically contain patches for known security holes, though new features might sometimes open new holes.

How long do cookies stay on my computer? A Web developer can program a cookie to "time out" after a designated period of time. When a cookie reaches the end of its pre-defined lifetime, your Web browser simply erases it.

You can also delete cookies, but you first must discover where they are stored. Netscape stores cookies in one large file called *Cookies.txt* on the PC or in *Magiccookie* on the Macintosh. IE stores each cookie in a separate file. Refer to your browser documentation to discover which folder holds your cookies. Most browsers allow you to delete unwanted cookies, as shown in Figure 6-13.

FIGURE 6-13

IE typically stores cookies as individual files on your computer's hard disk. You can view a list of cookies stored on your computer and delete those that you no longer want.

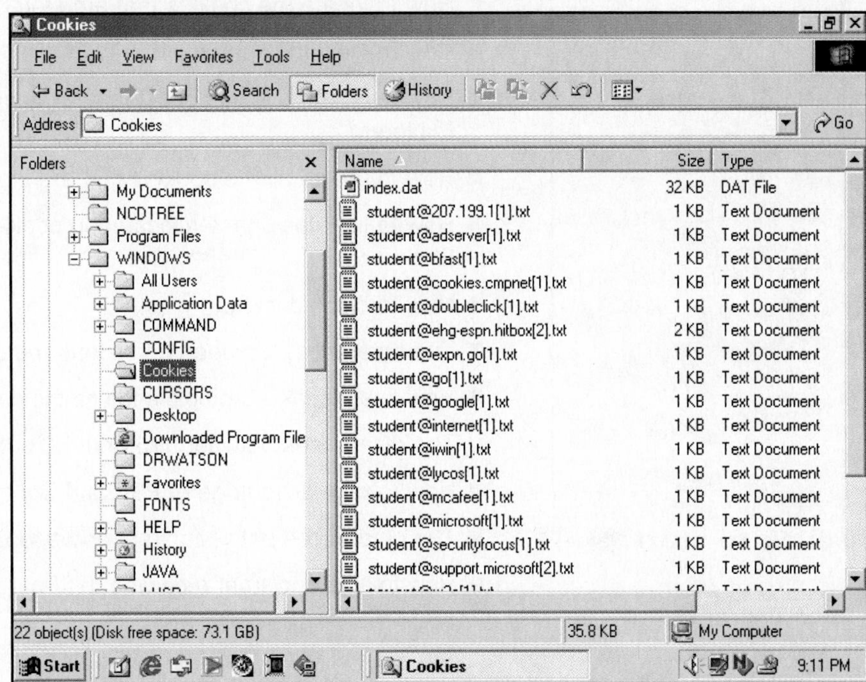

QUICKCheck Section A

1 The Web is based on the concept of ______—a collection of documents that can be related by links.

2 HTML is called a markup language because authors insert special instructions called HTML ______ that specify how a document should appear when displayed on a computer screen or printed.

3 A(n) ______ is the client half of the client/server software that facilitates communication between a personal computer and a Web server.

4 ______ is a protocol that works in conjunction with TCP/IP to get Web resources to your desktop.

5 A Web server usually listens for HTTP requests on ______ 80.

6 A(n) ______ helps a Web server track visitors and overcome some of the limitations of HTTP's stateless protocol.

check answers

LAB 6-A WORKING WITH COOKIES

Interactive LAB
Working With Cookies
click to start

In this lab, you'll learn:

- How Web servers use cookies
- Why cookies might pose a threat to your privacy
- How to locate the cookies that are stored on your computer
- How to view the contents of a cookie
- How to delete a single cookie that was created by Internet Explorer
- How to delete all the cookies that are stored on your computer
- How to limit the space allocated to cookies created by Internet Explorer
- How to block cookies
- The differences between persistent and session cookies
- How to set cookie prompts and use the cookie prompt dialog box
- The differences between IE5 and IE6 cookie settings
- How to take advantage of P3P and Compact Privacy Policies
- The differences between first-party and third-party cookies
- How to "opt out" from receiving third-party cookies

LAB Assignments

1. Start the interactive part of the lab. Insert your Tracking Disk if you want to save your QuickCheck results. Perform each of the lab steps as directed, and answer all of the lab QuickCheck questions. When you exit the lab, your answers are automatically graded and your results are displayed.

2. Use Windows Explorer to look at the cookies stored on your computer. Indicate how many cookies are currently stored. Examine the contents of one cookie, and indicate whether or not you think it poses a threat to your privacy.

3. Indicate the name and the version of the browser that you typically use.To find this information, open your browser, then select the About option from the Help menu. Next, look at the cookie settings provided by your browser. Describe how you would adjust these settings to produce a level of privacy protection that is right for your needs.

4. Adjust your browser settings so that you are prompted whenever a Web server attempts to send a cookie to your computer. Go to several of your favorite Web sites and watch for third-party cookies. When you receive a message from a third-party Web site, record the name of the third-party site and the contents of the cookie that it is attempting to send. Finally, indicate whether or not you would typically accept such a cookie.

Section B BASIC WEB PAGE AUTHORING

So you want to make your own Web pages. No problem. With today's Web-related software tools, creating a basic Web page has never been easier. In this section of the chapter, you'll learn about the basic components of a Web page, and you'll discover some tips for incorporating graphics, creating menus, adding navigation buttons, and posting your finished pages to a Web server.

WEB PAGE AUTHORING TOOLS

What software should I use to create Web pages? You have several choices when it comes to Web page authoring tools. The most difficult—and some would say the "old-fashioned"—way to create Web pages is to use a text editor, such as NotePad. A **text editor** is similar to word processing software. Unlike word processing software, however, a text editor creates an ASCII document with no hidden formatting codes. When you use a text editor to create an HTML document, you simply type the HTML tags along with the text that you want the browser to display on a Web page.

When saving the document that you create with a text editor, make sure that you specify an .html or .htm filename extension so that browsers will recognize it as an HTML document. If you want to create Web pages using a text editor, like the one shown in Figure 6-14, you will need a good HTML reference book.

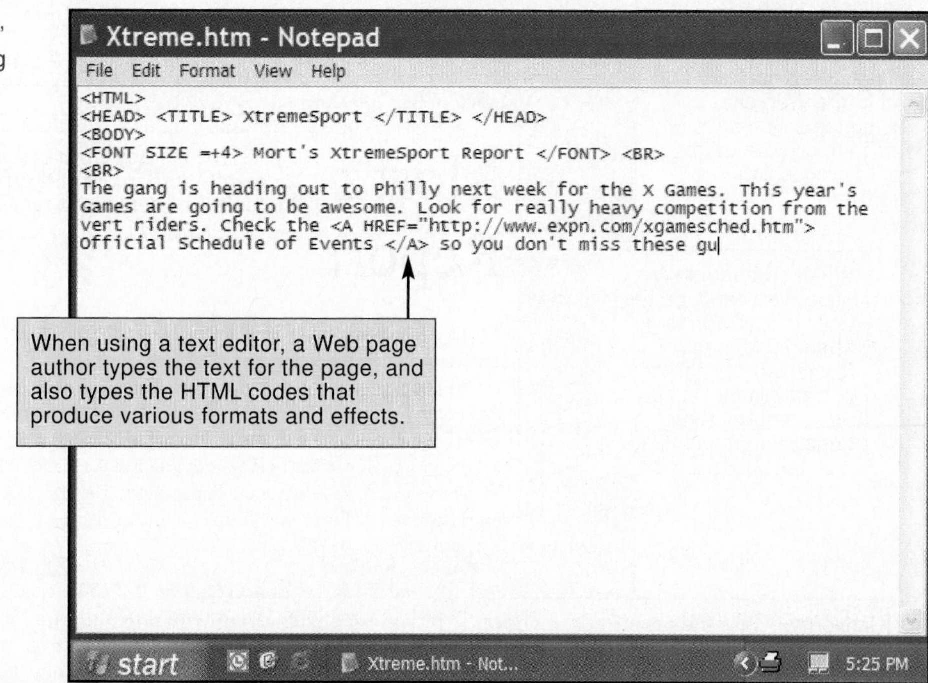

FIGURE 6-14

The most "primitive" Web page authoring tool is a simple text editor, such as NotePad.

Another way to create Web pages is to use the HTML conversion option that's included in many of the software applications you use every day. Microsoft Word, for example, allows you to create a standard DOC file and then use the File menu's *Save As Web Page* option to convert the document into HTML format. You might also find HTML capabilities in your spreadsheet, presentation, or desktop publishing software. To discover if an application has an HTML option, check the File, Save As, or Export menu options. You should be aware that converting a document into HTML format sometimes produces an unusual result, because some of the features and formatting in your original document might not be possible within the world of HTML.

For help in selecting software to design your own Web pages, connect to the Web Authoring Tools InfoWeb.

click

A third option for budding Web page authors is to use a set of online Web page authoring tools. These tools are provided by some ISPs and other companies that host Web pages for individuals and businesses. Working with these tools is typically quite simple—you type, select, drag, and drop elements onto a Web page. These simple tools are great for beginners, but they sometimes omit features that are included with more sophisticated authoring tools.

A fourth option for creating Web pages is a special category of software called **Web authoring software**, which provides tools specifically designed to enter and format Web page text, graphics, and links (Figure 6-15). Most of this software includes features that help you manage an entire Web site, as opposed to simply creating Web pages. Web site management tools include the capability to automatically link the pages within a site, and easily change those links. They are also capable of checking all of the external links at a site to make sure that they still link to valid Web pages—that's a really valuable feature for today's constantly changing Web!

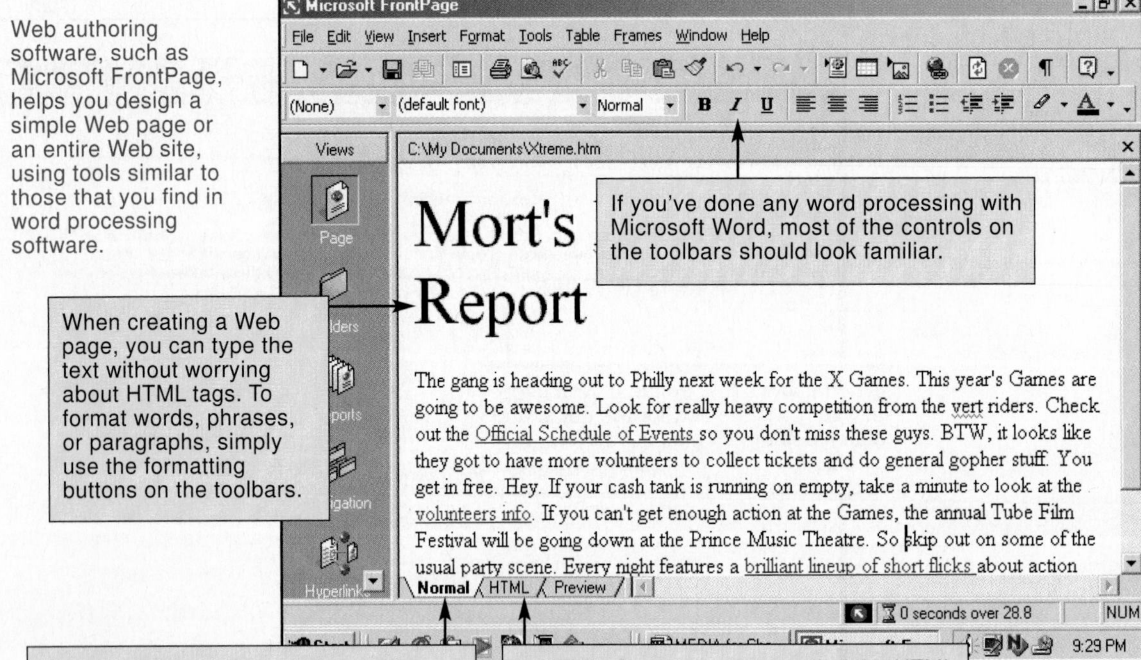

FIGURE 6-15

Web authoring software, such as Microsoft FrontPage, helps you design a simple Web page or an entire Web site, using tools similar to those that you find in word processing software.

Is DHTML a replacement for HTML? DHTML is not a replacement for HTML. In fact, DHTML is not a scripting language at all. It is simply a term that is used to describe a method for using HTML in combination with a few other technologies to make Web pages more, well, dynamic.

Do all browsers support DHTML? All of today's popular personal computer browsers support DHTML. However, each browser supports DHTML somewhat differently. As a result, the tags and scripts that a Web page author uses for dynamic effects to be displayed by the Netscape browser differ from the tags that are required to obtain the same effects with Internet Explorer.

If you ever noticed a message such as "This site is best when viewed with Netscape," you might have encountered a Web page that includes DHTML effects that only work when the page appears in the Netscape browser window. When you encounter Web pages such as these, it might be possible to obtain information from the site regardless of the browser that you use. You just may not be able to see all of the dynamic effects if you are not using the recommended browser.

XML, XSL, AND XHTML

What is XML? XML (eXtensible Markup Language) is a method for putting structured data, such as spreadsheet data or database records, into a text file. As with HTML, XML uses tags and attributes to mark up the contents of a file. Whereas HTML tags focus on the format or appearance of a document, XML tags essentially define fields of data. For example, whereas HTML provides a <B> tag that specifies how text is supposed to appear, XML tags, such as <PART NUMBER>, <PRICE>, and <WEIGHT>, explicitly identify a particular kind of information—much like a field heading in a database.

To learn more about DHTML, XML, XSL, and XHTML, you can access the Beyond HTML InfoWeb.

click

How does XML work? As the name suggests, XML is extensible, which means that individual users and groups of users can create their own tags. For example, suppose that an automobile manufacturing group wants to create an XML extension for Web pages that contain information about car prices. The group can specify new tags, such as <DEALER_PRICE> and <SUGGESTED_RETAIL_PRICE>, which can be inserted into XML documents along with corresponding data.

Of course, these new tags must be defined somewhere, so the XML specifications provide for **DTD files** (Document Type Definition files), which contain the tags used in an XML file. The DTD files can exist in the same location as the XML file, or they can exist on a server elsewhere on the Web. This flexibility makes it possible for an entire industry to define and use the same tags by referencing a DTD file on a known server. The tool for reading XML documents is referred to as an **XML parser**, and is included in all of today's popular browsers.

What is XSL? XSL (eXtensible Stylesheet Language) is a technology that's similar to XML, but can be used to create customized tags that control the display of the data that's contained in an XML document. The files that contain the definition for the new XSL tags can be stored in the same location as the XML file, or they can be referenced from a server anywhere on the Internet. XSL and XML work well together to produce customized, flexible, and platform-independent Web pages.

How does XHTML relate to HTML and XML? XHTML is the follow-up version to HTML 4. Rather than calling it HTML 5, the W3C preferred to name it XHTML 1.0 to reflect its extensibility. XHTML includes all of the HTML 4 tags, but like XML, it can be extended by the addition of customized tags. Web page authors can add new tags to those that already exist, and then incorporate those tags in HTML documents.

JAVASCRIPT AND VBSCRIPT

Is it possible to add programs to a Web page? Standard HTML provides a way to display text and graphics on a Web page, and to link to other Web pages, but because it isn't a programming language, HTML does not provide a way to perform complicated tasks or respond to user actions. Scripting languages, such as JavaScript and VBScript, allow a Web designer to embed simple program instructions, called "scripting statements," directly into the text of an HTML document. A series of these scripting statements is called a **script**. Scripting statements are not displayed by the browser; instead they instruct the browser to perform specific actions, or to respond to specific user actions.

How would a Web page author use a scripting language? Scripting languages allow Web pages to become more interactive, and incorporate activities that would otherwise require a computer program. Scripts allow e-commerce sites to verify credit card information. They also make possible interactive Web pages, such as loan payment calculators. Scripts work with cookies to deliver custom Web pages, such as those generated by Amazon.com, each time you return to the site. Scripts don't replace normal HTML—they extend and enhance it.

What are the most popular scripting languages? JavaScript and **VBScript** are the most popular scripting languages, but alternatives do exist, including PerlScript, Python, REXX, and Awk.

How do scripts work? Scripts can be executed on the client or the server. A **client-side script** consists of scripting statements embedded in an HTML document. The statements are executed by the browser, which must have the capability to deal with that scripting language. Most of today's browsers have built-in capability to execute JavaScript, but only IE has built-in capability to execute VBScript.

A **server-side script** consists of statements that are executed on the server. Server-side scripts typically accept data submitted by a form, process that data, then generate a custom HTML document that is sent to the browser for display. Because the server-side script is interpreted on the server, the browser receives only straight HTML code. The browser does not receive scripts that it needs to process, which eliminates many of the compatibility problems that can arise with client-side scripting.

What's a scripting error? If you've used the Web very much at all, you have almost certainly encountered your share of JavaScript error messages, similar to the one in Figure 6-24.

FIGURE 6-24

A JavaScript error means that your browser cannot execute the instructions in a JavaScript.

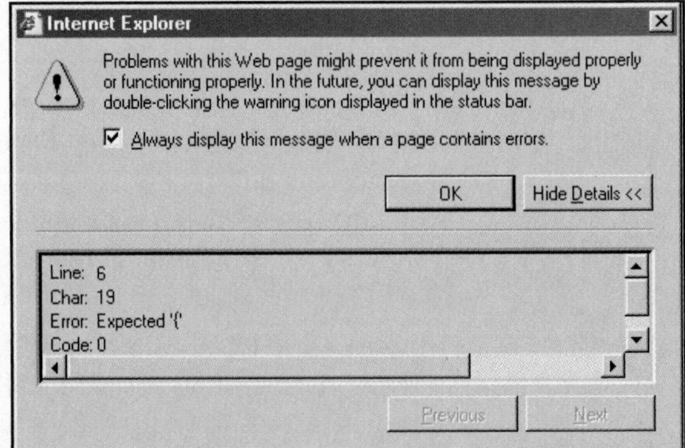

A **scripting error** occurs when a browser or server cannot execute one or more statements in a script. In some cases, scripting errors occur when one of the statements does not adhere to the rules of the scripting language. Usually, these "syntax" errors are caused by a careless Web page author who neglects to test pages before posting them. In other cases, scripting errors occur because the browser that's trying to execute the script does not support one of the commands.

Some browsers do not include support for a particular scripting language. For example, Internet Explorer 6.0 provides no support for JavaScript. Opera and Netscape version 6 do not support VBScript. If support for a scripting language is missing, you can download a player, provided that one is available for your browser. For example, Internet Explorer 6.0 users might find it necessary to download and install the Java Virtual Machine to correctly display Web pages that include JavaScript.

Whatever the cause, if you encounter a scripting error message, you can sometimes close the error message dialog box and then continue to access information from the Web site. In some instances, the script is tied to a key aspect of the Web site and you might have to use a different browser to view its pages.

JAVA APPLETS

What's a Java applet? Java is a high-level programming language that was developed by Sun Microsystems and has become a popular programming tool for Web-based projects. Small Java applications are called **Java applets**.

How do applets work? A programmer or Web page author can use the Java programming language to write Java applet source code, which is stored in a file with a .java filename extension. This source code is compiled into a format called **bytecode** with a .class filename extension. A reference to this bytecode file is included in an HTML document using the <APPLET> HTML tag. When an HTML document contains an <APPLET> tag, your browser downloads the specified bytecode file and then executes the applet using a **Java Virtual Machine** (JVM). Figure 6-25 helps you visualize this process.

FIGURE 6-25

Programmers create Java applet source code, compile it, and then include it in an HTML document, where it is executed by a browser.

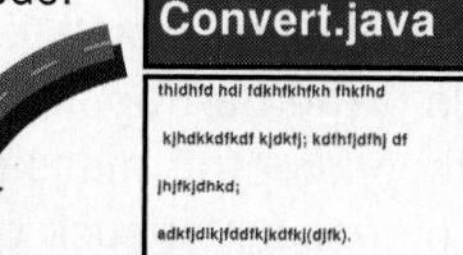
1. Programmer writes Java applet source code.
Convert.java

2. Source code is compiled into bytecode and stored in a file with a .class filename extension.
Convert.class

3. A reference to the bytecode file is placed in the HTML document, which is stored on a Web server.
Money.htm
<HTML>
<HEAD> <TITLE> Currency Conversion </TITLE> </HEAD>
<BODY>
Currency conversions are based on daily rates.
<APPLET CODE= "Convert.class">
</BODY> </HTML>

Money.htm
4. Your browser downloads the HTML document and sees the APPLET tag.

Convert.class
5. Your browser then downloads the file that contains the bytecode.

6. Your browser interprets and executes the bytecode file and displays the results.

6

What's the difference between Java applets and JavaScript? Although their names would lead you to believe that they are similar, Java applets and JavaScript are two very different technologies. The table in Figure 6-26 summarizes the differences between these two technologies.

FIGURE 6-26 Java Applet and JavaScript Comparison

Java Applets	JavaScript
Must be compiled into bytecode	Not compiled
Stored as a separate file	Entire script embedded within the HTML document
Referenced using the <APPLET> or <OBJECT> HTML tags	Identified by the <SCRIPT> HTML tag
Requires the browser to use a Java Virtual Machine	Requires a JavaScript interpreter
Programmers and Web page authors must use Java programming tools	No special programming tools required

How safe are Java applets? A Java applet is a program that your browser downloads and runs on your computer. You might wonder if a Java applet could contain a virus that would take up residence in your computer system, or a worm that would spread over your network. The technology for Java applets was designed with security in mind. The applets that you download from the Web have the following restrictions:

- They are not allowed to open, modify, delete, or create files on your computer.
- They are not allowed to make any network connections except to the originating site.
- They are not allowed to start other programs.

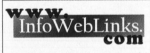

www.InfoWebLinks.com

Maybe you're interested in adding Java applets to your Web pages. You'll find links to online tutorials at the Java Applets InfoWeb.

click

You can see from the list that applets are prohibited from the activities that characterize viruses and worms. Because they cannot attach themselves to files (thereby modifying them), delete files on your hard disk, mail themselves to people in your address book, and so on, applets are considered a fairly safe technology.

The more troublesome aspect of Java applets is that they are sometimes blocked by network firewalls. When an applet is blocked, your browser might display a Security Exception error message, or you might see the broken graphic link icon. If you encounter such problems on your network, you should refer to your personal firewall documentation, or consult your network manager.

ACTIVEX CONTROLS

What is an ActiveX control? Sometimes, when you connect to a Web site, you might see a dialog box containing a security warning like the one in Figure 6-27. To better understand what this warning means, you'll need some background information about ActiveX controls.

FIGURE 6-27

Web surfers who use Internet Explorer sometimes encounter the Security Warning dialog box.

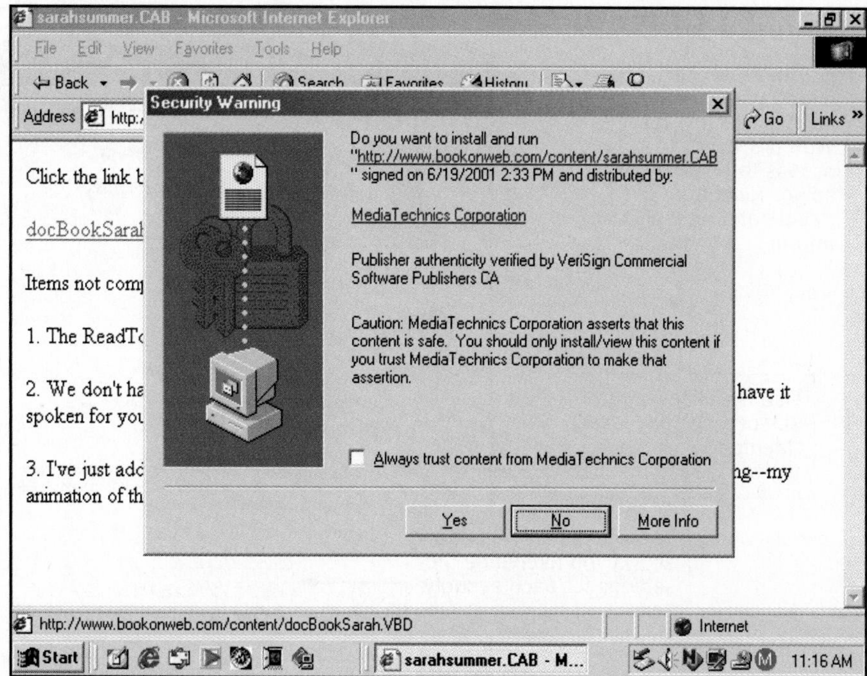

An **ActiveX control** is a compiled computer program that can be referenced from within an HTML document, downloaded, installed on your computer, and executed within the browser window. ActiveX controls can be used on the server side too. Programmers and Web page authors use programming languages, such as C++ and Visual Basic, to create these controls, which can be applied in a wide variety of ways to make Web pages interactive, and provide the functionality that many consumers now expect after using full-featured applications, such as word processing, graphics, and entertainment software.

How do ActiveX controls differ from Java applets? ActiveX controls are installed on your computer's hard disk, whereas Java applets are simply downloaded into memory and run. The advantage of installing an ActiveX control is that it will be available locally the next time you want to use it. Java applets cannot be installed on your computer—they are downloaded every time they are used.

Another key difference between the two technologies is that Java applets work on many computer platforms, but ActiveX controls are designed only for the Windows platform—in fact, ActiveX components only work on Windows PCs using the Internet Explorer browser. ActiveX, which is a Microsoft technology, is currently not supported by Netscape or by non-Windows operating systems, such as Linux or Mac OS.

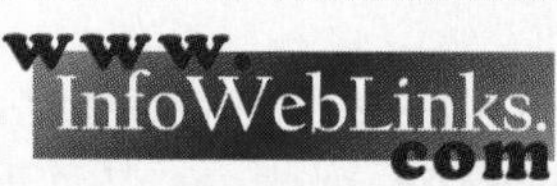

ActiveX controls are key components in all sorts of Windows software—not just Web-based applications. You can get the scoop on ActiveX controls, including how they affect security, by linking to the ActiveX InfoWeb.

click

Are ActiveX controls safe? Most ActiveX controls are safe. However, an ActiveX control is a full-fledged program, which gives it the potential to include routines that alter or delete data on your computer's hard disk. If you use IE as your browser, you can adjust its security settings so that it never downloads any ActiveX controls; it downloads and installs only those controls with signed digital certificates; or it downloads and installs any ActiveX controls. Figure 6-28 shows IE options for ActiveX security settings.

FIGURE 6-28

Internet Explorer allows you to select a level of security for Web browsing. To access the dialog box, select Tools from the menu bar, then select Internet Options.

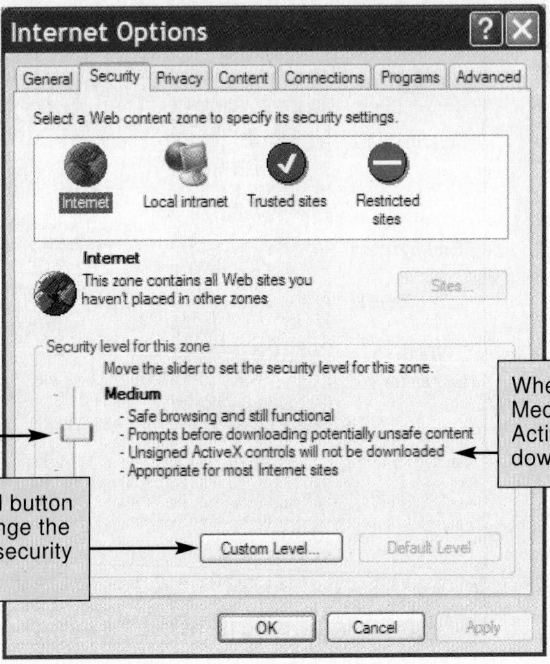

Internet Options

General | Security | Privacy | Content | Connections | Programs | Advanced

Select a Web content zone to specify its security settings.

Internet | Local intranet | Trusted sites | Restricted sites

Internet

This zone contains all Web sites you haven't placed in other zones

Sites...

Security level for this zone

Move the slider to set the security level for this zone.

Medium

- Safe browsing and still functional
- Prompts before downloading potentially unsafe content
- Unsigned ActiveX controls will not be downloaded
- Appropriate for most Internet sites

Custom Level... | Default Level

OK | Cancel | Apply

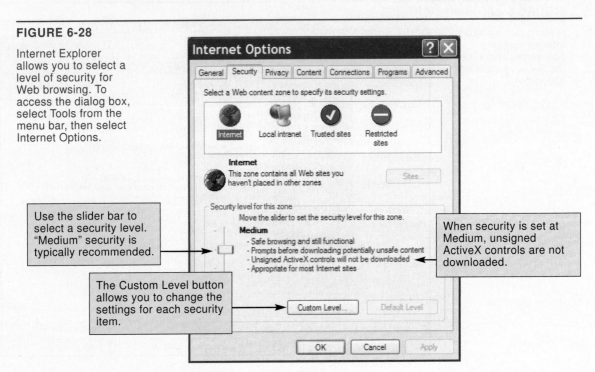

Use the slider bar to select a security level. "Medium" security is typically recommended.

When security is set at Medium, unsigned ActiveX controls are not downloaded.

The Custom Level button allows you to change the settings for each security item.

The Digital Certificates InfoWeb explains their use in monitoring ActiveX controls, and verifying consumer and merchant identities in an e-commerce transaction.

click

What is a digital certificate? In order to increase the security of ActiveX controls, they include digital certificates. A **digital certificate** is an electronic attachment to a file, such as an ActiveX control, that verifies the identity of its source. It is similar to a check cashing card, or to the stamp that you get on your hand when the "bouncer" checks your ID at the entry to a club. In the world of ActiveX controls, a digital certificate means that the control was created by an identifiable person or company, which can be held accountable for its contents.

An individual programmer, a Web author, or a company can apply for a digital certificate through a **certificate authority** such as VeriSign. Applicants must provide information to verify their identities. The certificate authority then confirms this information before issuing a certificate. Most certificates must be renewed annually for fees ranging from $20 for an individual certificate, to $3,000 for a corporate certificate.

A digital certificate can be electronically attached to any ActiveX control that is created by the applicant. That control is then referred to as "signed"—it is as if the programmer signed his or her name to it. The certificate authority never reviews the ActiveX control itself, so a digital certificate does not ensure that the control is virus-free. Instead, a certificate provides consumers with the name of the person who created the control—the theory being that malicious programmers would not put their names on the certificates that travel with an ActiveX control that is infected with a virus or worm.

FIGURE 6-29

A valid digital certificate contains the certificate holder's name. To ensure that the certificate is legitimate, you can click the underlined links to connect to the certificate holder's Web site, and the Web site of the certificate-issuing authority.

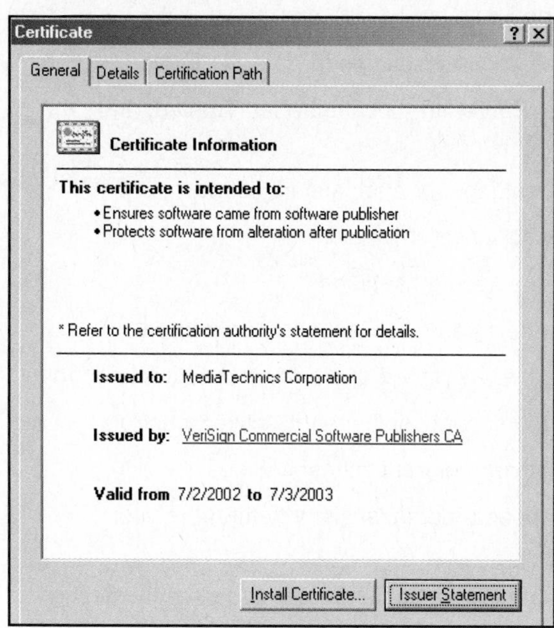

How does a digital certificate work? Suppose that you connect to a Web page that includes an ActiveX control, and your browser's security setting is "Medium"—the recommended setting for the average Web "surfer." When your browser encounters the HTML tag that references a signed ActiveX control, it displays a warning message to alert you that an ActiveX component is trying to install itself. Your browser reads the digital certificate, displays the name of the person or company that signed it, and verifies that the component was not altered since it was signed.

After examining this information, you can decide whether or not you want your browser to download and install the ActiveX control. To avoid viruses, you should not accept ActiveX controls that are unsigned, signed with "weird" names, or that have been changed since they were created. Figure 6-29 provides an example of a valid digital certificate.

QUICKCheck Section C

1 ________ is not a scripting language, but it is a method for using HTML in combination with a few other technologies to make Web pages less static.

2 ________ allows individual users and groups of users to enhance HTML with their own tags that define data.

3 The follow-up version to HTML 4 is ________.

4 ________-side scripts are typically embedded in an HTML document.

5 The source code for a Java applet is compiled into a format called ________.

6 A(n) ________ control can be "signed" with a digital certificate.

check answers 

LAB 6-C BROWSER SECURITY SETTINGS

In this lab, you'll learn:

- How to adjust the security settings for Internet Explorer
- The significance of Internet, Local Intranet, Trusted, and Restricted security zones
- How to view the settings for each security zone
- How to add sites to a security zone
- How to adjust zone security settings
- Why ActiveX controls pose a potential security threat
- The difference between signed and unsigned ActiveX controls
- The recommended security settings for ActiveX controls
- How to adjust ActiveX control security settings
- Why downloads pose a potential security threat to your computer
- How to activate the recommended download security settings
- Why Java applets pose a potential security threat to your computer
- The significance of Java permission levels
- How to activate the recommended Java security settings

LAB Assignments

1. Start the interactive part of the lab. Insert your Tracking Disk if you want to save your QuickCheck results. Perform each of the lab steps as directed, and answer all of the lab QuickCheck questions. When you exit the lab, your answers are automatically graded and your results are displayed.

2. Check the Internet zone security setting on the computer that you typically use. Indicate whether the setting is High, Medium, Medium-low, Low, or Custom. Describe how this setting handles ActiveX controls, downloads, and Java applets.

3. On the computer that you typically use, find out if any Web sites are listed in the Trusted or Restricted zones. Would you make changes to the list of sites for these zones? Explain why or why not.

4. Activate the "Prompt" setting for the "Download ActiveX controls" security setting. Use your browser to connect to *http://www.infoweblinks.com/np6/samples/activex.htm*, where you should encounter an ActiveX control security alert. Use your computer's PrtSc key to capture a screenshot of the warning. Paste the screenshot into Paint and then print it. Would you accept this ActiveX control? Why or why not?

E-COMMERCE

One of the most popular activities on the Web is shopping. It has the same allure as catalogs—you can shop at your leisure, anonymously, and in your pajamas. But the economics of the Web provide opportunities that go beyond retail catalogs. Even small businesses, individual artists, and isolated craftsmen can post Web pages that display their wares.

The Internet was opened to commercial use in 1991. Since then, thousands of businesses have taken up residence at Web sites. This section of the chapter focuses on e-commerce and the technologies that a typical shopper might encounter on the Web.

E-COMMERCE BASICS

What is e-commerce? Chapter 1 introduced e-commerce as Internet activities that include online shopping, electronic auctions, online banking, and online stock trading. Although the experts don't always agree on its definition, **e-commerce** is typically used to describe financial transactions that are conducted "electronically" over a computer network. It encompasses all aspects of business and market processes enabled by the Internet and Web technologies.

E-commerce "wares" include many kinds of physical products, digital products, and services. Physical products offered at e-commerce sites include such goods as clothing, shoes, skateboards, and cars. Most of these products can be shipped to buyers using the postal service or a parcel delivery service. Some products, like cars, must be picked up.

Increasingly, e-commerce goods include digital products such as news, music, video, databases, software, and all types of knowledge-based items. The unique feature of these products is that they can be transformed into bits and delivered over the Web. Consumers can get them immediately upon completing their orders, and no one must pay shipping costs.

E-commerce merchants also peddle services, such as arranging trips, online medical consultation, and remote education. Some of these services can be carried out by computers. Others require human agents. Services can be delivered electronically, as in the case of a distance education course, or they might produce some physical product, such as a cruise ship ticket.

Who is the typical e-commerce customer? The demographics of e-commerce have not yet stabilized. Whereas the typical e-commerce consumer in 1995 was a 30-something white male, in recent years, females and teens have entered the online shopping fray in droves.

Most of the e-commerce activities that the typical Web surfer enjoys are classified as **B2C** (business-to-consumer) e-commerce. In the B2C model, businesses supply goods and services to individual consumers. In another popular e-commerce model, consumers sell to each other. This **C2C** (consumer-to-consumer) model includes wildly popular online auctions and rummage sales.

But individuals are not the only e-commerce consumers. **B2B** (business-to-business) e-commerce involves one enterprise buying goods or services from another enterprise. **B2G** (business-to-government) e-commerce aims to help businesses sell to governments.

What makes e-commerce so special? E-commerce offers some unique advantages over "brick and mortar" stores and mail order catalogs. Customers can easily search through large catalogs. They can configure products online, see actual prices, and build an order over several days. Customers can easily compare prices between multiple vendors.

Merchants are always looking for ways to attract customers. The Web and its search engines provide merchants with a way to be found by customers without expensive, national advertising. Even small merchants can reach a global market. Web technology also allows merchants to track customer preferences and produce individually tailored marketing.

How does e-commerce work? E-commerce seems pretty simple from the perspective of a shopper who simply connects to an online store, browses the electronic catalog, selects merchandise, then pays for it. The screentour in Figure 6-30 walks you through a typical shopping session.

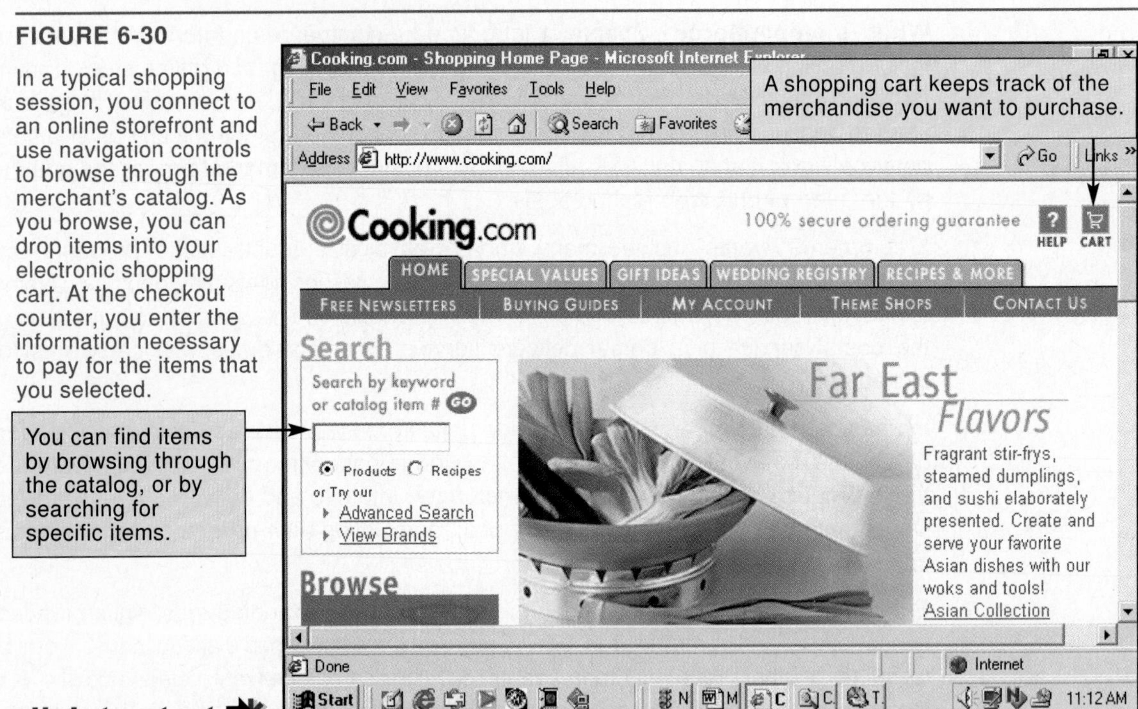

FIGURE 6-30

In a typical shopping session, you connect to an online storefront and use navigation controls to browse through the merchant's catalog. As you browse, you can drop items into your electronic shopping cart. At the checkout counter, you enter the information necessary to pay for the items that you selected.

click to start

Behind the scenes, e-commerce is based on a Web site and group of technologies that keep track of shoppers' selections, collect payment data, attempt to protect customers' privacy, and prevent credit card numbers from falling into the wrong hands.

A merchant establishes a Web site on a Web server. Depending on the volume of expected transactions, a merchant may decide to operate its own Web server, or outsource the site to a Web hosting service. Some ISPs provide "starter kits" for entrepreneurs who want to establish a small e-commerce site.

An e-commerce Web site is based on a domain name, such as *www.amazon.com*, which acts as the entry to the online store. A Web page at this location welcomes customers and provides links to various parts of the site. The goods and services that are for sale appear in a customer's browser window. For small e-commerce businesses, this online catalog might exist as a series of HTML documents. For large businesses, however, the online catalog is based on the information stored in a conventional database. This information can be pulled from the database by technologies such as XML, CGI, and ASP (discussed on page 314), and then displayed as Web pages.

An e-commerce site also typically includes some mechanism for customers to select merchandise and then pay for it. Customer orders might be processed manually in a small business. Most high-volume e-commerce businesses, however, use as much automation as possible; their order-processing systems automatically update inventories, and then print the packing slips and mailing labels that are used to pull ordered items off of the warehouse shelves. These printouts are used by company employees to pack orders into boxes and ship them to the customer's door.

SHOPPING CARTS

What's an online shopping cart? If you've done any shopping online, you've probably used an **online shopping cart**—a cyberspace version of the good old metal cart that you wheel around a store and fill up with merchandise.

How do shopping carts work? You should remember from reading earlier pages in this chapter that HTTP is a stateless protocol, which fulfills a single request for a Web resource, then immediately forgets about it. When you connect to an online retail site, for example, your browser requests and then receives the site's main page. A separate HTTP request might produce a picture of some merchandise. If you click the "Buy" button to purchase an item, your browser sends your click to the merchant's Web server. The Web server sends back some kind of response, but immediately breaks the connection and forgets about you. Under these circumstances, you might wonder how it is possible for an online retail store to "remember" the items that you put in your shopping cart.

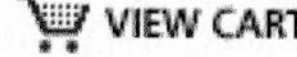

Most shopping carts work because they use cookies to store information about your activities on a Web site. Cookies work with shopping carts in one of two ways, depending on the e-commerce site. An e-commerce site might use cookies as a storage bin for all of the items that you load into your shopping cart, as shown in Figure 6-31.

6

FIGURE 6-31 Storing shopping cart items in a cookie

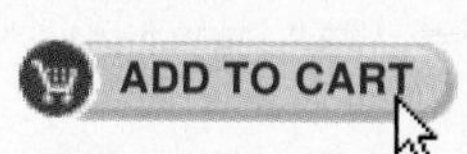

1. When you click the Add to Cart button, the merchant's server sends a message to your browser to add that item number to the cookie, which is stored on your computer.

ITEM #B7655

VIEW CART

2. When you check out, the server asks your browser for all of the cookie data that pertains to your shopping cart items.

3. Your browser sends those cookies along with a request for an order summary.

Your order:

1 Blender	29.95
1 Wok	38.49

4. The Web server uses the cookies to produce a Web page that lists the items you want to purchase.

Some e-commerce sites use cookies simply as a way to uniquely identify each shopper. These sites use your unique number to store your item selections in a server-side database (Figure 6-32).

FIGURE 6-32 Storing shopping cart items in a database

1. When you connect to a merchant's site, the server sends your browser a cookie that contains your unique shopping cart number.

WEB SERVER

CART # 2098-2

3. The Web server sends this number and your merchandise selection to the database, where it is stored in a record that corresponds to your shopping cart number.

DATABASE

CART # 2098-2

ITEM # B7655

WEB SERVER

CART # 2098-2

BUY IT

2. When you select an item to purchase, your browser reads your shopping cart ID number from the cookie, and then sends this number to the merchant's Web server.

Order for CART #2098-2

1 Blender	B7655	$29.95
1 Wok	GJK4-31	$38.49

4. When you check out, your browser sends your shopping cart number to the server, which retrieves all of your selections from the database.

ORDER FORMS AND SECURE TRANSACTIONS

What is an HTML form? After you wheel your cyber shopping cart over to the check-out line, you finalize the purchase by entering your name, address, and payment information into a series of blank boxes that are the screen-based equivalent of a paper form. An **HTML form**, (usually referred to simply as "a form"), is an on-screen form created using the HTML <FORM> and <INPUT> tags (Figure 6-33).

FIGURE 6-33

HTML forms are easy to create and are typically used to collect payment and shipping information at the "checkout counter" of e-commerce Web sites.

you're in Secure Shopping
Click for details

Billing Information

Cart Billing Shipping Review Payment

VISA MasterCard DISCOVER NOVUS

Name & Address

First Name	Janell	M.I.	B
Last Name	Tsukahara		
Address	43578 East 5oth St		
Address (line 2)			
City	Copell		
State/Other	Texas		
Zip/Postal Code	75019		

What happens to the data that's entered into a form? When you fill out a form, you might be concerned about the privacy and security of that data. You'll have a better sense about e-commerce privacy and security if you understand what happens to the data that's submitted from an HTML form.

The information that you enter into an HTML form is held in the memory of your computer, where your browser creates temporary storage bins that correspond to the input field names designated by the form's HTML tags. Your name, in the example from Figure 6-33, might be temporarily held in a memory location that's called "Customer." The information that you enter in a form is not stored on your computer's hard disk, so it is not left "hanging around" where it can be found by someone who uses your computer without your authorization. That in itself is a good start to keeping your information secure.

After you enter the information, you click a Submit button and your browser gathers the data from memory, and sends it to a specially designated program on an HTTP server. This server could be the one that sent the original HTML form to you, or it could be a different server that's set up exclusively to process form data.

Can the data in the HTTP message be intercepted in transit? A **packet sniffer** (officially called a "protocol analyzer") is a computer program that monitors data as it travels over networks. Within each segment of an Ethernet network—the architecture used for most of the Internet—packets flow to every device. Most network devices read only the packets addressed to them and ignore the packets addressed to other devices. However, a packet sniffer can observe and open any packet traveling on the network—even packets addressed to a different device. Packet sniffers have legitimate uses in system maintenance, but hackers also can use them to pilfer data as it travels from customers' computers to an HTTP server.

Two technologies can be used to protect the data in HTTP messages: SSL and S-HTTP. **SSL** (Secure Sockets Layer) is a protocol that encrypts the data that travels between a client computer and an HTTP server. This encryption protocol creates what's called an "SSL connection" using a specially designated port—typically Port 443 rather than Port 80, which is used for unsecured HTTP communication. Web pages that provide an SSL connection start with https: instead of http:.

S-HTTP (secure HTTP) is an extension of HTTP that simply encrypts the text of an HTTP message before it is sent. Although SSL and S-HTTP both use encryption techniques to securely transmit data, they are technically different. Whereas SSL creates a secure connection between a client and a server, over which any amount of data can be sent securely, S-HTTP is simply designed to encrypt and then transmit an individual message. From the consumer's perspective, however, either one of these security measures can do an excellent job of protecting the data that you ship over the Internet.

Securing your credit card number as it travels over the Internet solves only half of the security problem. In addition to avoiding sniffers, both parties in an e-commerce transaction must make sure that they are dealing with authorized and reputable entities. Consumers want to make sure that a merchant is legitimate. Merchants want to make sure that the credit card charges are authorized by the card's rightful owner.

SET (Secure Electronic Transaction) is a security method that relies on cryptography and digital certificates to ensure that transactions are legitimate as well as secure. SET has been endorsed by the major players in the e-commerce arena, including Microsoft, Netscape, Visa, American Express, and MasterCard. Because it uses digital certificates, SET enables merchants to verify a consumer's identity. It also uses secure connections to transfer consumers' credit card numbers directly to a credit card processing service for verification. This transfer method not only foils packet sniffers, it also keeps card numbers off a merchant's potentially unsecured computer.

What happens to my data once it arrives at a server? The HTTP message that contains your data also contains the name of a CGI script or ASP script that should accept the form data once it arrives at the server. **CGI** (Common Gateway Interface) is a set of specifications or standards for how servers can handle a variety of HTTP requests. Using these specifications, programmers and Web page authors can write CGI scripts that run on a server to handle data that is submitted as HTTP messages. These scripts can be written using a variety of programming and scripting languages, such as Perl, C, C++, C#, and Java.

ASP (Active Server Page) is a server-side technology developed by Microsoft as an alternative to CGI. ASP scripts, like CGI scripts, run on a server and deal with data that is submitted as HTTP messages. ASP scripts can be written in VBScript, Perl, REXX, or Jscript—Microsoft's version of JavaScript.

The CGI or ASP script that accepts the data from a form specifies how the server should deal with the data. In an e-commerce environment, the data is typically part of a purchase transaction, so it is processed to calculate the total price of the order and then stored in the company's database.

CREDIT CARD SECURITY

How can online credit card transactions get hacked? When you use your credit card for online transactions, it is vulnerable to several threats. Some threats are more likely to occur than others.

Fake storefronts. One of the most dangerous threats to your credit card security is a Trojan horse site. These sites appear to be online stores, but, in fact, they are fraudulent, "fake" storefronts, designed exclusively for the purpose of collecting credit card numbers from unwary shoppers. These sites might have all of the trappings of a real e-commerce site—they might even provide you with a secure connection for transmitting your credit card number. When your data is received, however, it is stored in a database that belongs to a hacker, who can use the data for illegitimate transactions.

Intercepted packets. Many shoppers worry that their credit card numbers might get intercepted as they travel over the Internet. Packet sniffer software makes it possible to intercept the packets that contain your credit card numbers, but the chance of your credit card number being stolen in this way is fairly low. Sniffing out packets is not an easy hack. Because each packet contains only a very small amount of data, a lot of painstaking work is required to reassemble all of the packets that contain your credit card number and billing data—the task is similar to reconstructing a paper document after it has been shredded. The use of secure connections and encryption further stymies packet theft—even if a hacker can reconstruct the packets that contain your payment data, this data must be decrypted before it could be used for illicit purposes.

Database break-ins. An increasing number of businesses report that their customer databases have been accessed without authorization. In some cases, thousands of credit card numbers were stolen. This area is a key concern for e-commerce security. Good business practices stipulate that databases should be protected by passwords, and that they should be encrypted. Unfortunately, not all businesses follow these practices. Even when databases seem secure, hackers might find security holes and retrieve sensitive data. Consumers really have no way of judging the security measures erected by businesses that collect and store credit card data.

Dishonest employees. An online "break-in" into the database of a merchant or credit card processing service is a fairly "high-tech" crime, but your credit card number can be compromised by low-tech methods as well. If a merchant collects your credit card number instead of routing it directly to a credit card processing service, a dishonest employee who works for the merchant may be able to obtain your card number while processing your order. Individual consumers can't do much to prevent this type of theft, but the likelihood of it occurring is low—you take a similar risk every time that you pay for a meal by allowing a waiter to take your credit card back to a cashier station, or when giving your credit card number over the phone.

Always-on connections. One additional security problem is worth noting. If your computer is connected to an always-on network connection, such as a DSL or a cable modem, unwanted intruders could find their way into the files stored on your computer's hard disk. If your credit card number exists in any file—for example, in an order confirmation sent to you in an e-mail message—a hacker could find it.

What steps can I take to safeguard my credit card number? Unfortunately, the only way to make your credit card "bulletproof" is to never use it. As that would be impractical, most people use their cards both for online and offline purchases, with the understanding that a chance exists for the card number to be stolen and used for unauthorized purchases. You can reduce the probability of online credit card fraud by making sure that you deal with legitimate merchants and use secure connections. If given the option, do not allow a merchant to store your billing data for future ordering convenience.

The Safeguarding Your Credit Card InfoWeb provides some tips on this important aspect of e-commerce.

As a consumer, you cannot prevent database break-ins, but you can take steps to insure that the credit card number stored in a merchant's database is of little use to a hacker. Several credit card companies provide **one-time-use credit card** numbers, which allow consumers to make purchases while keeping their actual card numbers hidden.

To obtain a one-time-use number, you log into your credit card provider's Web site and then enter your user ID and PIN. You will be given a one-time-use number that you can use for an online purchase. Your credit card company keeps track of all of the one-time-use numbers that correspond to your actual credit card number, and applies the one-time-use charges to your monthly statement. One-time-use numbers can never be used again, so even if a hacker gains access to the number, it will not be accepted for any additional purchases online or offline.

ELECTRONIC WALLETS

What is an electronic wallet? An **electronic wallet** (also called a "digital wallet") is software that stores and handles the information that a customer typically submits when finalizing an e-commerce purchase. Wallets, such as Microsoft's Passport and AOL's Screen Name service, typically hold your name; your shipping address; and the number, expiration date, and billing address for one or more credit cards. An electronic wallet might also hold a digital certificate that verifies your identity.

You can create an electronic wallet by subscribing at the wallet provider's site. Some online merchants give you the option of creating an electronic wallet by saving the information that you enter as you make purchases on their sites.

Once you create your electronic wallet, it pops up on your screen whenever you make a purchase at a participating merchant's site. When you use an electronic wallet, the data that it holds can be automatically transferred to the merchant so that you don't have to manually enter your name, credit card number, and other routine payment information. Figure 6-34 on the next page takes you on a tour of a typical electronic wallet.

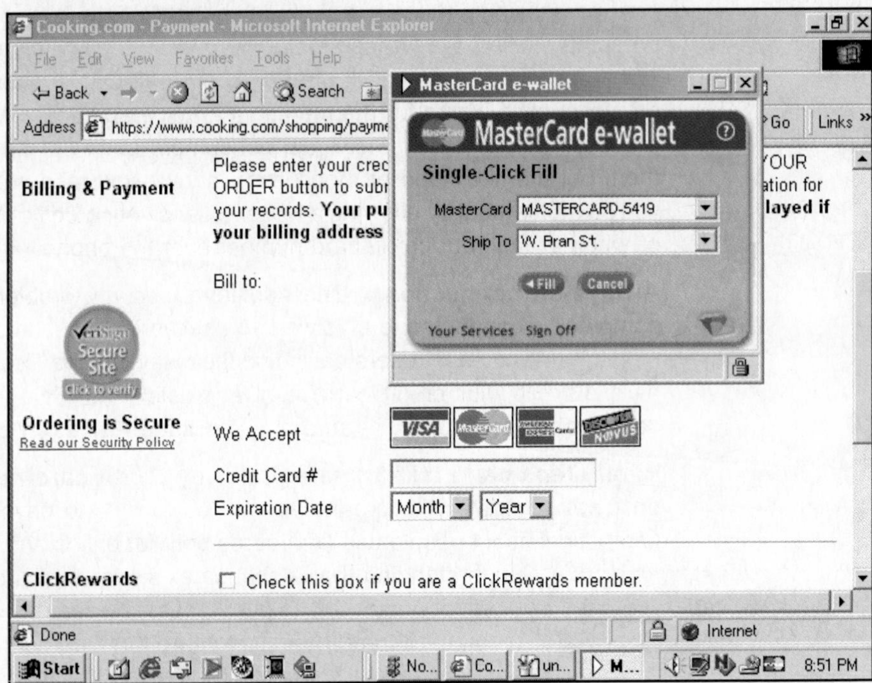

FIGURE 6-34

An electronic wallet transfers your billing and shipping information to an e-commerce Web server when you check out.

click to start

How does an electronic wallet work? The data for an electronic wallet can be stored on your computer, or on a server maintained by a wallet provider—usually a financial institution, such as a bank or credit card company. Server-side wallets are sometimes referred to as "thin wallets" because they don't require much storage space on your computer.

A wallet requires client-side and server-side software. The client-side software resides on your computer—usually in the form of a browser plug-in. The server-side wallet software resides on an HTTP server that is maintained by the merchant. Many "brands" of wallets exist, and a server only uses data from a compatible wallet.

When you proceed to an online checkout, software on the merchant's server sends an HTTP message to your PC that looks for and activates compatible wallet software. By clicking a Submit button, your payment data is transferred from your electronic wallet to the server.

How safe is an electronic wallet? Electronic wallets have several security features. As with other online payments, the data from an electronic wallet is transported over a secure connection, such as SSL. The data in an electronic wallet is also stored in an encrypted format. Even if a hacker gains access to your wallet file from your computer or a server, the data that it contains will be difficult to decode. Of course, you don't have to decode the contents of your electronic wallet before using it, so you might wonder if a hacker could simply copy your wallet and use the whole encrypted file just as you do. Your wallet should open only if you provide the correct password, which acts as a PIN number to prevent unauthorized use.

Electronic wallets are not totally secure, however. The technology has several vulnerabilities. Security analysts were stunned to discover that it is possible to steal credit card numbers from an electronic wallet simply by getting the victim to open an e-mail message. Hackers also may be able to snag data as it flows from an electronic wallet to a merchant's site by using Trojan horse technology to collect data that's entered at a supposedly trusted site. Consumers should carefully study current security bulletins before trusting their data to electronic wallets.

FIGURE 6-35

1. To use a person-to-person payment service, simply log into your account, enter the recipient's e-mail address, and indicate the payment amount.

2. The recipient immediately receives an e-mail notification of your payment.

3. The recipient connects to the payment site to "pick up" the money by transferring the funds to a checking account, requesting a check, or sending the funds to someone else.

PERSON-TO-PERSON PAYMENT SERVICES

What is a person-to-person payment? Most legitimate online businesses accept credit card purchases, but such a payment system requires merchants to set up an account with one or more credit card providers, get connected to a credit card verification service, and pay fees on each transaction. A **person-to-person payment** (sometimes called an "online payment") offers an alternative to credit cards. It can be used to pay for auction items and "wire" money over the Internet. A online service called PayPal pioneered person-to-person payments. PayPal's model has since been copied by several other service providers.

How does a person-to-person payment work? The process begins when you open an account at a person-to-person payment service. Some services require you to deposit some money in your account—just as if you were opening a bank account. Other services allow you to provide your credit card number, which is billed only as you make purchases. You receive a user ID and password that allow you to access your account to make purchases and deposit additional funds. Money can be sent to anyone who has an e-mail account, as shown in Figure 6-35.

Is person-to-person payment safe? The major advantage of person-to-person payments is that the payment service is the only entity that sees your credit card number—merchants, auction dealers, and other payment recipients never receive your credit card number and, therefore, can't misuse it or store it on an unsecured computer. Currently, however, the person-to-person payment industry is in its infancy, and companies are still scrambling to offer reliable, long-term service to customers. Unlike a bank, many of these companies are unregulated. They sometimes change their services or go out of business without providing much notice to consumers. Consumer advocates recommend using these services with caution, and keeping your account balances low.

QUICKCheck Section D

6

1 Increasingly, e-commerce goods include ________ products that can be transformed into bits and delivered over the Web.

2 Most shopping carts work because they use ________ to store information about your activities on a Web site.

3 A packet ________ is a computer program that monitors data as it travels over networks, and is sometimes used by hackers to intercept packets.

4 A one-time-use credit card number is included in an electronic wallet. True or false? ________

5 An electronic wallet can be stored client-side or server-side. True or false? ________

check answers

TECHTALK

ENCRYPTION

At one time, encryption was synonymous with spies, secret agents, and an assortment of cloak-and-dagger activities. The average person's exposure to encryption was pretty much limited to Captain Midnight decoder rings and pig Latin. Today, the situation is different. Encryption is one of the most important technologies for maintaining your privacy and the security of important information, such as your credit card number. This TechTalk is designed to provide you with a basic background in encryption, which you can apply when participating in e-commerce and other online activities.

Is encryption the same as coding? In the context of computers, the word "code" is bantered about in a variety of ways. Programmers write computer "code" to create software. ASCII and EBCDIC codes are used to represent the letters of the alphabet. These codes, however, are not the same as encryption. Encryption transforms a message in such as way that its contents are hidden from unauthorized readers. Encryption is designed to keep messages secret. Its purpose, therefore, is quite different from simple coding schemes, such as ASCII and EBCDIC, which are designed to transform data into formats that are publicly known and shared.

How does encryption work? An original message—one that has not yet been encrypted—is referred to as **plaintext** or "cleartext." An encrypted message is referred to as **ciphertext**. The process of converting plaintext into ciphertext is called **encryption**. The reverse process—converting ciphertext into plaintext—is called **decryption**. In an e-commerce transaction, for example, your credit card number exists as plaintext, which is encrypted into ciphertext for its journey over a secure connection to the merchant. When the ciphertext arrives at its destination, it is decrypted back into the original plaintext credit card number.

Messages are encrypted using a cryptographic algorithm and key. A **cryptographic algorithm** is a specific procedure for encrypting or decrypting a message. A **cryptographic key** (usually just called a "key") is a word, number, or phrase that must be known in order to encrypt or decrypt a message. Let's look at a simple example.

Julius Caesar made extensive use of an encryption method called simple substitution, which could have been used to turn the plaintext message "Do not trust Brutus" into GRQRWWUXVWEUXWXV. The cryptographic algorithm was to offset the letters of the alphabet. The key was 3. Anyone who knew this algorithm and key could set up a transformation table like the one in Figure 6-36 to encrypt or decrypt messages for Caesar.

FIGURE 6-36

The algorithm for Caesar's encryption technique was to offset the letters of the alphabet. A simple transformation table helped to encrypt or decrypt a message. For example, if a "G" appears in the encrypted message, it would be a "D" in the original, unencrypted message.

Ciphertext letters:

D E F G H I J K L M N O P Q R S T U V W X Y Z A B C

Equivalent plaintext letters:

A B C D E F G H I J K L M N O P Q R S T U V W X Y Z

What's the difference between strong and weak encryption? Caesar's simple substitution key is an example of **weak encryption** because it is easy to decrypt even without the algorithm and key. Unauthorized decryption is sometimes referred to as "breaking" or "cracking" a code. You could crack Caesar's code in several ways. For example, you could discover the key by making 25 different transformation tables, each with a different offset (assuming that the encryption method uses the letters of the alphabet in sequence and not at random). You could also analyze the frequency with which letters appear—in English documents those letters will be E, T, A, O, and N—and you can piece together the message by guessing how to fill in the blanks.

Strong encryption is loosely defined as "very difficult to break." Of course, with continuous advances in technology, strong encryption is a moving target. For example, several encryption methods that were considered "impossible" to break 10 years ago, have recently been cracked using networks of personal computers. The encryption methods that are used for most e-commerce transactions are considered "strong," but not unbreakable.

How long does it take to "break" strong encryption? Encryption methods can be "broken" by the use of expensive, specialized, code-breaking computers. The cost of these machines is substantial, but not beyond the reach of government agencies, major corporations, and organized crime. Encryption methods can also be broken by standard computer hardware—supercomputers, mainframes, workstations, and even personal computers. These computers typically break codes using a **brute force method**, which consists of trying all possible keys.

As an analogy, suppose that a criminal steals an ATM card. The card cannot be used, however, without the correct PIN number. A four-digit PIN number could be one of 10,000 possible combinations. If you're mathematically inclined, you'll realize that each digit of the PIN number could be one of 10 possibilities: 0, 1, 2, 3, 4, 5, 6, 7, 8, or 9. Because the PIN number consists of four digits, the number of possible PIN numbers is 10^4 or 10X10X10X10. To discover a PIN number by brute force, a criminal must try, at most, 10,000 possibilities. Of course, it would take a person quite a long time to figure out and try all 10,000 possibilities, but a computer could polish them off as quickly as the ATM would accept them.

The length of a computer-readable encryption key is measured in bits. A bit, as you know, can be either a 1 or a 0. Unlike the PIN example above in which each digit could be one of 10 possible numbers, in a computer-readable encryption key, each digit can be one of two possible numbers: 0 or 1. Figuring out how many numbers you must try in order to break a computer code requires a calculation using powers of two rather than powers of 10. A 32-bit key, therefore, could be one of about 4.2 billion (2^{32}) numbers. Surprisingly, it would be possible to try all of these numbers and discover the key using an average personal computer.

To discover a 40-bit key, you would have to try about 1 trillion possible combinations. A personal computer would require about a week's worth of continuous processing to discover a particular key. 56-bit encryption—once thought to be unbreakable by any computer in the private sector—requires a lot of computing power, but has been broken by combining the power of many personal computers connected over the Internet. 64-bit encryption can be broken by computing technology owned by government agencies, major corporations, organized crime, and research groups, but 80-bit encryption and 128-bit encryption are probably secure for several years.

6

For additional resources on using ciphertext to protect data, including PGP software that you can use on your PC, connect to the Encryption InfoWeb.

Another way to understand how the length of a key affects the strength of encryption is to consider this rule of thumb: Beginning with a 40-bit key, each additional bit doubles the time that it would take to discover the key. If a personal computer takes one week to crack a 40-bit key, it takes two weeks to crack a 41-bit key, four weeks to crack a 42-bit key, and eight weeks to crack a 43-bit key. A 128-bit key takes $2^{(128-40)}$ times longer to crack than a 40-bit key—that's 309,485,009,821,345,068,724,781,056 times longer!

What's public key encryption? Caesar's encryption method is an example of symmetric key encryption, which is also called "secret key" or "conventional" encryption. With **symmetric key encryption**, the key that is used to encrypt a message is also used to decrypt the message.

Symmetric key encryption is often used to encrypt stationary data, such as corporate financial records. It is not, however, a very desirable encryption method for data that's on the move. The person who encrypts the data must get the key to the person who decrypts the data, without the key falling into the wrong hands. On a computer network, key distribution is a major security problem because of the potential for the key to be intercepted by a packet sniffer.

To eliminate the key-distribution problem, in 1975, Whitfield Diffie and Martin Helman introduced a concept called **public key encryption** (PKE). It uses asymmetric key encryption in which one key is used to encrypt a message, but another key is used to decrypt the message. Figure 6-37 illustrates how public key encryption works.

FIGURE 6-37

Public key encryption uses two keys. A public key is used to encrypt a message. A private key is used to decrypt the message.

1. James sends the *public* key to JoBeth.
2. JoBeth uses the public key to encrypt a message, which she sends back to James.
GBDB001
FT20GB
3. James can decrypt the message using his *private* key.
"The new Product is ready"
? ? ?
4. If the message is intercepted by Draco, he cannot decrypt the message because he does not have the private key.

Public key encryption is a crucial technology on the Web and for e-commerce. When you use an SSL (secure socket layer) connection to transmit your credit card number, the server sends a public key to your browser. Your browser uses this public key to encrypt the credit card number. Once encrypted, no one—not even you—can use this public key to decrypt the message. The encrypted message is sent to the Web server, where the private key is used to decrypt it.

Public key encryption is not perfect. The mathematics of PKE make it easier to crack than symmetric key encryption. To get a level of security equal to 80-bit symmetrical encryption requires a 1024-bit public encryption key! As a result of these huge keys, PKE encryption and decryption usually require lots of processing time—about 1,000 times more than for symmetric encryption. For this reason, PKE is best used for short messages, such as e-commerce transactions and e-mail.

What are the most commonly used encryption methods? RSA (named for its inventors—Ron Rivest, Adi Shamir, and Leonard Adleman) is the most commonly used public key encryption algorithm. In addition to being the technology used for SSL connections, RSA is used to encrypt the data in most digital certificates. **DES** (Data Encryption Standard) is an encryption method based on an algorithm that was developed by IBM and the U.S. National Security Agency. It uses 56-bit symmetric key encryption. Although it was once the cornerstone of government encryption, DES is being replaced by AES, which offers stronger encryption. **AES** (Advanced Encryption Standard) is an encryption standard that uses three key sizes of 128, 192, or 256 bits. It is based on the Rijndael (pronounced "rain doll") encryption algorithm.

What kind of encryption can I use on my computer? When you engage in an e-commerce transaction, secure connections that encrypt your data are provided by the e-commerce site. In most cases, this is all the encryption necessary for the transaction. Even if you were to further encrypt your data, it is unlikely that the e-commerce server would be equipped to handle the decryption. You might, however, want to encrypt other data, such as your e-mail messages or your data files.

When personal computer users want to encrypt e-mail or other documents, they turn to Phillip Zimmerman's **PGP** (Pretty Good Privacy) software. In addition to encrypting data files, this software lets you digitally sign a message, which verifies to the recipient that you are the sender, and that no tampering is involved.

PGP is a type of public key encryption. When you first use PGP, the software generates a private key and a public key. You must keep your private key hidden. You typically e-mail the public key to the people who you authorize to send encrypted messages to you.

The people who receive your public key can store it in their PGP programs, which they will then use to encrypt messages. They will send these messages to you, and you will be able to decrypt them using your private key. PGP software is available as a free download from several Web sites. Figure 6-38 contains an example of a public key that's been generated by PGP.

FIGURE 6-38

PGP software generates a huge public key. Each person's public key is unique. You can send this key, via e-mail, to anyone who might want to send you an encrypted message.

-----BEGIN PGP PUBLIC KEY BLOCK-----

Version: 5.0

mQCNAi44C30AAAEEAL1r6BylvuSAvOKlk9ze9yCK+ZPPbRZrpXIRFBbe
+U8dGPMb9XdJS4L/cy1fXr9R9j4EfFsK/rgHV6i2rE83LjWrmsDPRPSaizz+
EQTIZi4AN99jiBomfLLZyUzmHMoUoE4shrYgOnkc0u101ikhieAFje77j/F3
596pT6nCx/9/AAURtCRBbmRyZSBCYBNhcmQgPGFiYWNhcmRAd2Vsb
C5zZi5jYS51cz6JAFUCBRAuOA6O7zYZz1mqos8BAXr9AgCxCu8CwGZR
dpfSs65r6mb4MccXvvfxO4TmPi1DKQj2FYHYjwYONk8vzA7XnE5aJmk5J
/dChdvflU7NvVifV6AF=GQv9

-----END PGP PUBLIC KEY BLOCK-----

QUICKCheck TechTalk

1 In an e-commerce transaction, your credit card number exists as ________, which is encrypted into ________.

2 ________ key encryption uses the same key to encrypt a message as it does to decrypt the message.

3 ________ key encryption uses one key to encrypt a message, but another key to decrypt the message.

4 ________ is public key encryption software that is popular with personal computer owners who want to encrypt e-mail and data files.

check answers

ISSUE

IS THE TRUTH OUT THERE?

In an episode of the "X-Files," Agent Scully warns Mulder about his search into the unexplored realm of extraterrestrial and paranormal phenomena: "The truth is out there, but so are lies." And so it is on the Internet, where truth mingles with lies, rumors, myths, and urban legends. The Internet is uncensored and unregulated. Anyone with a Web page or an e-mail account can rapidly and widely distribute information, which is often redistributed and forwarded like a chain letter on steroids. As an example, one e-mail message, circulated in the summer of 1999, contained this alarming first-person account: "When Zack was 2 years old, I put on the waterproof sunscreen. I don't know how, but he got some in his eyes. I called the poison control center and they told me to rush Zack to the ER now. I found out for the first time that many kids each year lose their sight to waterproof sunscreen. Zack did go blind for two days. It was horrible."

Worried parents forwarded this e-mail message to their friends, and many of them threw their sunscreen in the trash. In August of that year, members of an NBC television news team reported that they had researched the story, but failed to find evidence of any child becoming blind from sunscreen. They concluded their report by saying, "This is one of those stories that has spun out of control—touted as fact, when in reality, it's nothing more than a modern Internet myth."

The Internet has also been blamed for circulating reports that the U.S. Navy shot down TWA Flight 800. Pierre Salinger, an ex-TV reporter and a former advisor to President John F. Kennedy, made front-page headlines in November 1996 when he displayed documents that described how the Navy was testing missiles off Long Island and accidentally hit Flight 800. Although Salinger would not reveal the source of the documents, it turned out that they had been circulated on the Internet months earlier.

The *Chicago Tribune* described Salinger's error as "merely the latest outbreak of the disturbing new information-age phenomenon of bogus news," and went on to say that "America is awash in a growing and often disruptive avalanche of false information that takes on a life of its own in the electronic ether of the Internet, talk radio, and voice mail until it becomes impervious to denial and debunking."

In a more recent debacle, a seemingly legitimate news wire flashed over the Internet: "A city still mourning the death of punk rock innovator Joey Ramone has endured another tragedy as Velvet Underground leader Lou Reed was found dead in his apartment last night, apparently from an overdose of the painkiller demerol." Lou Reed was not dead, but the fake wire story fooled several radio stations, which reported it as hard news.

But is it fair to say that the Internet has a monopoly on false information? Probably not. Even well-established newspapers, magazines, and television news shows report stories that are later found to be misleading or untrue. In an article published online in *Salon*, Scott Rosenberg asks, "Who's more responsible for the spread of misinformation, the Internet or the news media? Well, ask yourself how you first heard of Salinger's memo: was it from the Net, or from a TV broadcast? The sad truth is that the old media are far more efficient disseminators of bogus news than the new."

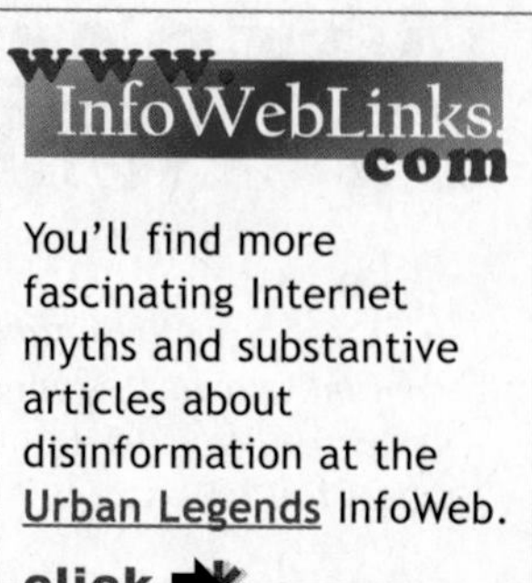

www.
InfoWebLinks.
com
You'll find more fascinating Internet myths and substantive articles about disinformation at the Urban Legends InfoWeb.
click

Before the Internet became a ubiquitous part of modern life, certain "rules of thumb" helped to distinguish truth from lies and fact from fiction. In *The Truth About URLs*, Robin Raskin writes, "When printed junk mail floods our overcrowded mailboxes we have some antennae for the bogus causes and the fly-by-night foundations. We've come to expect *The New York Times* to be a credible source of information; we're not as sure about *The National Inquirer*... It takes years to establish these sorts of cultural cues for knowing whether we're getting good information or a bum steer."

Perhaps the Internet has not been around long enough for us to establish the cultural cues we need to distinguish fact from fiction in Web pages, e-mails, online chats, and discussion groups. You can, however, get some help from the Web itself. Several sites keep track of the myths and so-called "urban legends" that circulate on the Internet. Before you spread dire warnings about sunscreen, or call a press conference to report a government coverup, you might want to check one of these sites for the real scoop.

Who should be responsible for the accuracy of information? Holding writers accountable for their "facts" does not seem to work, and governments, already overburdened with other problems, have scant resources available to sift through mountains of information and set the record straight. It seems, then, that the burden of verifying facts is ultimately left to the reader. Many people, however, do not have the time, motivation, expertise, or resources to verify facts before they pass them through the information mill.

We live in an information age. Ironically, much of the information that we hear and read just isn't true. False and misleading information is not unique to our time, but now it propagates more rapidly, fed by new technologies and nurtured by "spin doctors." As one commentator suggested, "The danger is that we are reaching a moment when nothing can be said to be objectively true, when consensus about reality disappears. The Information Age could leave us with no information at all, only assertions."

WHAT DO YOU THINK?

1. Would you agree that it sometimes seems difficult to determine if information is true or false? ❍ Yes ❍ No ❍ Not sure
2. Do older people tend to be more susceptible than younger people to false information that's disseminated over the Internet? ❍ Yes ❍ No ❍ Not sure
3. Have you ever received an e-mail that contained false information, or visited a Web site that provided inaccurate information? ❍ Yes ❍ No ❍ Not sure
4. Do you have your own set of rules to help you evaluate the truth of information that's disseminated over the Internet? ❍ Yes ❍ No ❍ Not sure

click to save your responses

INTERACTIVE SUMMARY

The Interactive Summary helps you to select and remember important concepts from this chapter. Fill in the blanks to best complete each sentence. When using the NP6 BookOnCD, you can click the Check Answers buttons to automatically score your answers. Place your Tracking Disk in the floppy disk drive if you want to save your scores.

The basic building blocks for today's Web were developed in 1990 by a British Scientist named Tim Berners-Lee. The Web did not "take off," however, until 1993 when Marc Andreessen and his colleagues developed a ________ called Mosaic. The Web is an abstract or imaginary space of information, whereas the ________ is the communications network that carries Web data. The Web is based on the concept of a ________—a series of documents that are stored electronically and linked together according to logical relationships. On today's Web, these documents are stored in ________ format and then displayed as Web ________ by a browser. HTML is a set of specifications for creating documents that contain special instructions called ________, which specify how the document should appear when displayed on a computer screen. In an HTML document, these tags are set apart from normal text by ________ brackets. In addition to HTML documents, Web browsers are designed to deal with ________ file formats, such as GIF, JPEG, and PNG. A browser can also work with other file formats if the necessary helper application, plug-in, or ________ has been installed.

HTML documents are transmitted from a Web server to a browser by means of the ________ protocol. This protocol is ________, which means that as soon as a request is fulfilled, the Web server "forgets" that your browser ever made a request. To keep track of an individual who clicks through several pages on a Web site, a Web server resorts to ________—a small chunk of data that is generated by a Web server, sent to a browser, and then stored on the client computer's hard disk.

check answers

Many software tools are available today that make it easy to create Web pages. A Web page author can use a ________, such as NotePad, to create Web pages "from scratch" by manually embedding HTML tags within the text of a document. It is also possible to use the HTML conversion routines that are included with many standard software applications. Another route is to use specialized Web page ________ software, such as Microsoft FrontPage. An HTML document is divided into two sections. The ________ section contains information that is used to define global properties for the document. The ________ section contains the text that you want the browser to display, the HTML tags that format the text, and a variety of links. In addition to embedding HTML tags within the text, a Web page can be formatted with a ________ style sheet, which allows Web page designers to change formats throughout an HTML document without modifying individual HTML tags. In addition to formatting specifications, HTML tags can be used to add graphics and links to Web pages. The <IMG SRC> tag can be used to specify a ________. The <A HREF> tag is used to specify a ________. Graphics and text links can be combined—for example, to create an ________ map that contains clickable ________ spots. To control the position of text and graphics on a Web page, many authors place these elements in the cells of a ________. In the context of Web pages, a ________ is part of a Web page that scrolls independently of other parts of the Web page.

check answers

HTML was designed to create static Web pages. With plain old HTML, once a Web page appeared in a browser window, the only way to change the appearance of the page was to download an update to the entire page. ________ is a method for updating Web pages "on the fly"—typically as the result of a mouseover or a mouse click. A technology called ________ can be used to incorporate structured data, such as spreadsheet data or database records, into a text file by adding special-purpose tags. These tags explicitly identify a particular kind of information, much like a field heading in a ________. A technology called ________ is similar to XML, but can be used to create customized HTML tags that control the appearance of an XML document. Extensible characteristics have been added to the next version of HTML, which is called ________.

Another way to add animation and interactivity to Web pages is to use ________ languages, such as JavaScript and VBScript. Unfortunately, browsers provide slightly different support for these languages, which sometimes results in a ________ error if the browser can't execute a particular instruction. In addition to JavaScript and VBScript, Java has become a popular programming tool for Web-based projects. Small Java programs are referred to as Java ________. ActiveX provides another Web development tool. An ActiveX ________ is a compiled computer program that can be referenced from within an HTML document, downloaded, installed on your computer, and executed within the browser window. This technology has potential security loopholes, which can be avoided by the use of digital ________.

check answers

The Internet was opened up to commercial use in 1991, and since that year, e-commerce has become one of the fastest growing activities on the Web. E-commerce "wares" include physical products, ________ products, and services. Most of the e-commerce activities that a typical Web surfer enjoys are classified as business-to-________, but with online auctions, consumer-to-________ e-commerce is also popular. An e-commerce site usually consists of a ________ name, such as *www.nike.com*, which acts as the entry to the online store. A Web page at this location welcomes customers and provides links to various parts of the Web site. A merchant's catalog might be stored as a series of HTML documents, but more likely, it is kept in a conventional database, from which it can be extracted by server-side technologies such as XML, CGI, and ________, before being displayed as Web pages. Customers use an electronic ________ cart to collect the items they want to purchase. These carts either store a customer's selections in a ________ on the client computer, or in a server-side database.

6

When it is time to check out, customers fill out an HTML ________ with shipping and billing information. A customer can use an electronic ________ at this stage of the transaction to automatically enter this information. The shipping and billing information is transmitted over a ________ connection using SSL or S-HTTP technology in order to avoid packet ________ software that could intercept it. Once the shipping and billing information arrives at a server, it is usually handled by a CGI or ASP script.

check answers 

INTERACTIVE KEY TERMS

Make sure that you understand all of the boldfaced key terms presented in this chapter. If you're using the NP6 BookOnCD, you can use this list of terms as an interactive study activity. First, try to define a term in your own words, then click the term to compare your definition with the definition that is presented in the chapter.

INTERACTIVE SITUATION QUESTIONS

Apply what you've learned to some typical computing situations. When using the NP6 BookOnCD, you can type your answers, then use the Check Answers button to automatically score your responses. Place your Tracking Disk in the floppy disk drive if you want to save your scores.

1. Suppose that you are about to check out at an online store, but you don't see any indication that your data will be protected by a secure connection. It would be best, under these circumstances, to use PGP software to encrypt your shipping and billing data. True or false? [ ]

2. Your friend, who is a little "computer phobic," is going to be creating his first Web page and asks you to recommend some software for the task. Which one would you recommend: NotePad or Microsoft Word? [ ]

3. Suppose that you visit a Web site that has eye-catching pages. You want to know how these pages were formatted, so you use one of the options on your browser's menu to view the [ ] HTML document.

4. Suppose that you click a link at a Web site and are provided with a message that the file cannot be displayed because it is in PDF format. To view the file, you need an updated version of your browser. True or false? [ ]

5. Suppose that you're performing a local test of a Web page that you created. All of the page elements appear to be correctly positioned and formatted. You're also happy to discover that your large graphics files are displayed quite quickly by your browser. Can you expect similar performance once you post the page on a Web site? (Yes or No) [ ]

6. You're poking around in an HTML document and you notice a tag that references a file with a .class filename extension. You assume that this file contains the bytecode for a Java [ ].

7. Suppose that your browser's security setting is "Medium." You can expect your browser to display a security warning message any time that a(n) [ ] control tries to install itself on your computer.

8. One of your relatives wants to try online shopping, but is suspicious that her credit card number might get stolen from a merchant's server by a hacker or a dishonest employee. Is it correct to tell her that she can best avoid these potential rip-offs by a secure connection, such as SSL? (Yes or No?) [ ]

9. Suppose that you're the high bidder in an online auction for a handmade quilt. The person who is selling the quilt does not accept credit cards, and instead suggests that you use a(n) [ ] payment service to, in effect, "wire" your payment electronically.

10. Suppose that your friend asks you if it is a good idea to turn off cookies. You should reply that, although some people believe they are protecting their privacy by turning off cookies, it is quite possible that the [ ] at e-commerce sites will not work, and then it will not be possible to select and purchase multiple items at the site.

check answers 

6

INTERACTIVE PRACTICE TESTS

When you use the NP6 BookOnCD, you can take Practice Tests that consist of 10 multiple-choice, true/false, and fill-in-the-blank questions. The questions are selected at random from a large test bank, so each time you take a test, you'll receive a different set of questions. Your tests are scored immediately, and you can print study guides that help you find the correct answers for any questions that you missed. If you are using a Tracking Disk, insert it in the floppy disk drive to save your test scores.

click to start

STUDY TIPS

Study Tips help you to organize and consolidate the information in a chapter by making lists, outlines, charts, and sketches. You can use paper and pencil or word processing software to complete most of the Study Tips activities.

1. Make sure that you can use your own words to correctly answer each of the green focus questions that appear throughout the chapter.
2. Draw a multi-panel "cartoon" that shows how a Web server and browser interact. Include the following terms: Web server, browser, HTTP, HTML, Port 80, socket, HTML document, graphic file, and URL.
3. Create a timeline of the history of HTML and browsers based on the information provided in this chapter. Your timeline should begin in 1990 and continue through 2001.
4. Make sure that you can explain the relationship between an HTML document and a Web page.
5. List and describe, in your own words, the four classifications of HTML formatting tags, as presented in this chapter.
6. In your own words, explain what the term "stateless protocol" means, then describe how it relates to cookies.
7. List the port numbers that are traditionally used for HTTP traffic, SMTP e-mail, and FTP.
8. List the major security and privacy features of cookies.
9. Describe the advantages and disadvantages of each type of Web page development tool that was discussed in this chapter.
10. Make sure that you can identify the following parts of a Web page: title, header, graphic, link, button, menu, and frame.
11. Explain how the term "header" is used in word processing, and how that differs from the way it is used in Web page authoring. Also explain how the use of the term "frame" in desktop publishing differs from its use in Web page authoring.
12. Describe some of the ways that Web page designers use links. Describe external links, mailto links, interpage links, and internal links.
13. In your own words, create definitions for HTML, DHTML, XML, XSL, and XHTML that clearly distinguish one technology from the others.
14. Explain the differences between a server-side script and a client-side script.
15. In your own words, create definitions for Java applet, ActiveX control, JavaScript, VBScript, CGI, and ASP that clearly distinguish one technology from the others.
16. Make a list of security technologies that were discussed in this chapter, then explain how each one works and why it is needed.

SCANNERS AND CAMERAS

www. InfoWebLinks.com

You'll find out more about scanning equipment at the Scanner Buyers Guide InfoWeb.

click

How do I convert a printed image into a bitmap? When you have a printed image, such as a photograph, a page from a magazine, or a picture from a book, you can use a **scanner** to convert the printed image into a bitmap graphic. A scanner essentially divides an image into a fine grid of cells, and assigns a digital value for the color of each cell. As the scan progresses, these values are transferred to your computer's hard disk and stored as a bitmap graphics file. Scanners, such as the one pictured in Figure 7-2, are inexpensive and easy to use.

FIGURE 7-2

To scan an image, turn on the scanner and start your scanner software. Place the image face down on the scanner glass, then use the scanner software to initiate the scan. The scanned image is saved in RAM, and can then be saved on your computer's hard disk.

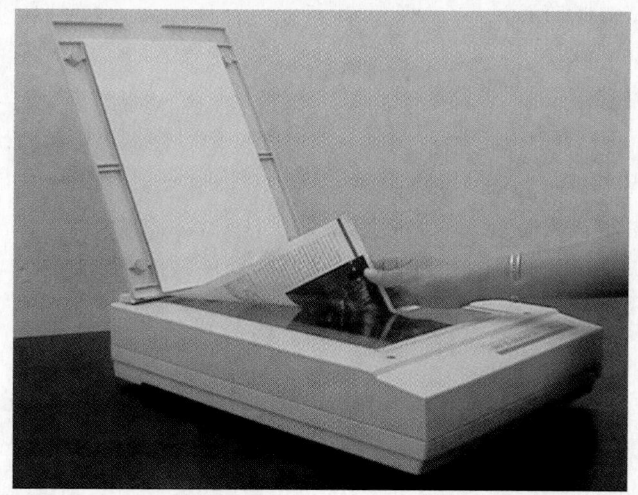

click to start

www. InfoWebLinks.com

Learn more about digital cameras and accessories by visiting the Digital Camera Buyers Guide InfoWeb.

click

When should I use a digital camera rather than a scanner? Whereas a scanner digitizes printed images, a **digital camera** digitizes real objects. Instead of taking a photo with a conventional camera, developing the film, then digitizing it with a scanner, a digital camera, such as the one in Figure 7-3, takes a photo in digital format, which you can then transfer directly to your computer.

FIGURE 7-3

The controls for a digital camera are very similar to those for an analog, or film, camera. To take a photo, you simply point and shoot.

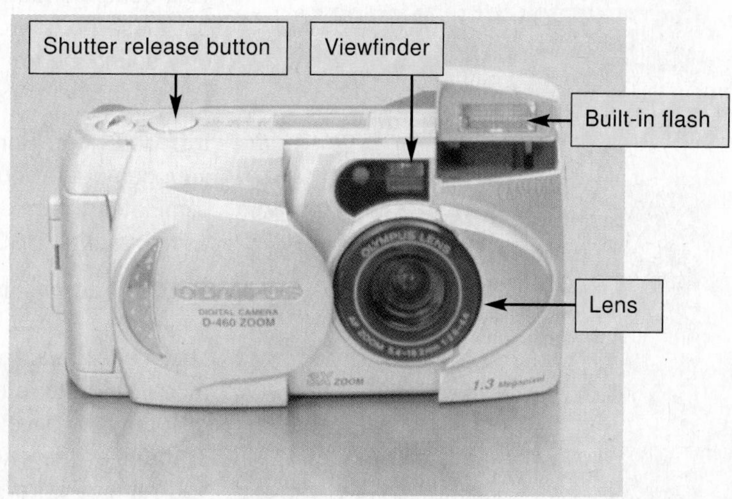

click to start

How does a digital camera store images? Some digital cameras store images on floppy disks, CDs, mini-CDs, or miniature hard disk drives. Other digital cameras store images in solid-state, removable, memory modules, sometimes called "memory cards." **Flash memory** is a popular technology for digital camera memory modules. Like RAM, it can be erased and reused. Unlike RAM, flash memory holds data without consuming power, so it doesn't lose data when the camera is turned off. Figure 7-4 describes the capacity of several digital camera storage options.

FIGURE 7-4

CompactFlash cards are available with capacities that range from 8 MB to 512 MB. Memory Sticks® range in capacity from 16 MB to 128 MB. SmartMedia Cards typically range in capacity from 16 MB to 128 MB. IBM's Microdrive provides up to 1 GB of storage on a miniature hard disk drive that slides into a slot in the camera.

CompactFlash

Microdrive

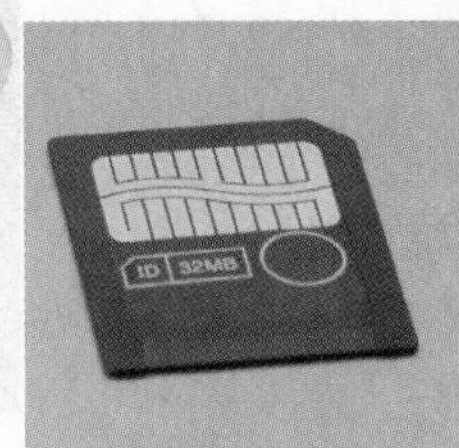

SmartMedia Card

Memory Stick

How can I get images out of the camera? Digital cameras allow you to preview images while they are still in the camera, and delete those that you don't want. The photos that you want to keep can be transferred directly to some printers, but typically, you'll transfer the photo data to your computer's hard disk. This transfer can be achieved in several ways, depending on your camera:

Media transfer. If your camera stores data on floppy disks or CDs, you can simply remove the media from your camera and insert it into the appropriate drive of your computer.

FIGURE 7-5

A memory card reader transfers photo data from a flash memory card to your computer's hard disk.

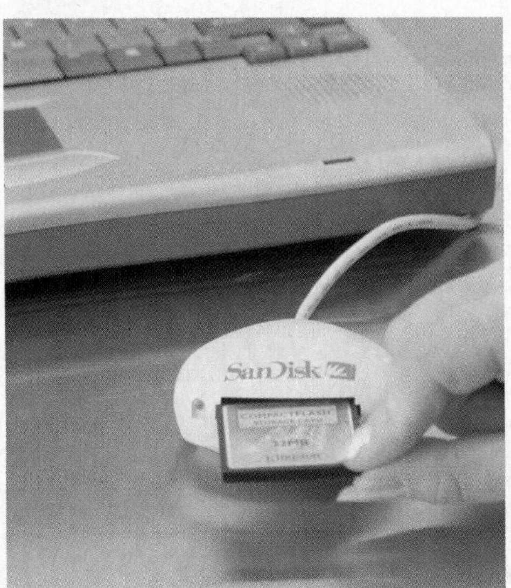

Direct cable transfer. If your computer and your camera have FireWire ports (also called IEEE-1394 ports), you can connect a cable between these two ports to transfer the photo data. You can use a similar transfer method if your computer and camera have USB ports or serial ports, but these ports are slower. The cable must be connected only during the transfer, then it can be disconnected so that you can carry the camera with you on vacation, or wherever.

Infrared port. Some cameras can "beam" the data from your camera to your computer's infrared port. This method eliminates the need for a cable, but is much slower than using a serial, USB, or FireWire port.

Card readers. A **memory card reader** is a small device connected to your computer's USB or serial port, and designed to read the data that's contained in a flash memory module. A card reader acts in the same way as an external disk drive by treating your flash memory like floppy disks. To transfer the photo data from a flash memory module, you remove it from the camera and insert it into the card reader, as shown in Figure 7-5.

Floppy disk adapters. A **floppy disk adapter** is a floppy disk-shaped device that contains a slot for a flash memory module. You simply insert the memory module into the floppy disk adapter, then insert the adapter into your computer's floppy disk drive.

Regardless of the technology that you use, transferring photo data from your camera to your computer requires software, which may be supplied along with your camera, with your memory card reader, or by a standalone graphics software package, such as Adobe Photoshop. This software allows you to select a file format, specify a filename, and determine the location for each image file. You'll learn about your choices for graphics file formats later in this section, but most cameras store photographic images in JPEG or TIFF formats.

After you store your digital photos on your computer's hard disk, you can modify them, send them as e-mail attachments, print them, post them on Web pages, or archive them onto a CD.

MODIFYING BITMAP GRAPHICS

What characteristics of a bitmap can I modify? Because bitmap graphics are coded as a series of bits that represent pixels, you can use graphics software to modify or edit this type of graphic by changing individual pixels. You can retouch or repair old photographs to eliminate creases, spots, and discoloration. You can modify photos to wipe out red eye, or erase the "rabbit ears" that ruined an otherwise good family portrait. You can even design eye-catching new pictures using images that you cut and paste from several photos or scanned images.

Whether you acquire an image from a digital camera or from a scanner, bitmap graphics tend to require quite a bit of storage space. While a large graphics file might provide the necessary data for a high-quality printout, these files take up space on your hard disk, and can require lengthy transmission times that clog up mailboxes and make Web pages seem "sluggish." The size of the file that holds a bitmap depends on its resolution and color depth. Let's see how these factors affect file size, and how you can alter them to create smaller graphics files, suitable for e-mail attachments and Web pages.

IMAGE RESOLUTION

How does resolution pertain to bitmap graphics? The dimensions of the grid that forms a bitmap graphic are referred to as its **resolution**. The resolution of a graphic is usually expressed as the number of horizontal and vertical pixels that it contains. For example, a small graphic for a Web page might have a resolution of 150 x 100 pixels—150 pixels across and 100 pixels high.

How does resolution relate to image quality? High-resolution graphics contain more data than low-resolution graphics. With more data, it is possible to display and print high-quality images that are smoother and cleaner than images produced using less data. For example, a photograph of a cat taken with an inexpensive digital camera might produce a graphic with a resolution of 1,600 x 1,200. Camera manufacturers sometimes express the resolution of digital cameras as **megapixels** (millions of pixels)—the total number of pixels in a graphic. A resolution of 1,600 x 1,200 would be expressed as 1.9 megapixels (1,600 multiplied by 1,200). If you take a photo of the same cat using a more expensive 3.5 megapixel digital camera with 2,160 x 1,440 resolution, the resulting bitmap graphic will contain more pixels. The high-resolution graphic will look better than the low-resolution graphic, at any given size.

How does resolution relate to the file size of a graphic? Each pixel in a bitmap graphic is stored as one or more bits. The more pixels in a bitmap, the more bits needed to store the file.

How does resolution relate to the physical size of an image? A bitmap graphic is simply a collection of data. Unlike a printed photograph, a bitmap has no fixed physical size. The size at which a bitmap is displayed or printed depends on the density, as well as the resolution, of the image grid.

Imagine that each bitmap image and its grid come on a surface that you can stretch or shrink. As you stretch the surface, the grid maintains the same number of horizontal and vertical cells, but each cell becomes larger and the grid becomes less dense. As you shrink the surface, the grid becomes smaller and more dense. The graphic retains the same resolution no matter how much you stretch or shrink the graphic's physical size, as shown in Figure 7-6.

FIGURE 7-6

The data that is contained in a bitmap graphic file retains the same resolution no matter how large it is displayed or printed.

24 x 24 resolution

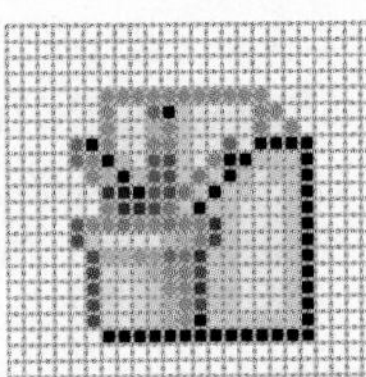

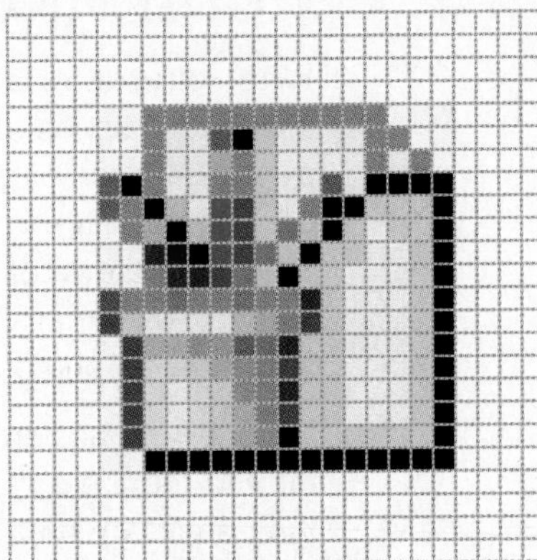

24 x 24 resolution

This concept of stretching and shrinking without changing resolution is important for understanding what happens when bitmaps are displayed and printed. As a rule of thumb, the denser the grid, the smaller the image will appear. The density of an image grid can be expressed as dots per inch (dpi) for a printer or scanner, or as pixels per inch (ppi) on a monitor.

How do I specify the size of a printed image? Most graphics software allows you to specify the size at which an image is printed without changing the resolution of the bitmap graphic. You'll get the highest print quality if the resolution of the graphic meets or exceeds the printer's dpi. An ink jet printer with a resolution of 1,440 x 720 dpi produces a very dense image grid. If each pixel of a 1,600 x 1,200 graphic was printed as a single dot on this printer, the resulting image would be very high quality, but just a bit wider than 1 inch. You can specify a larger size for the printout, in which case the printer must create additional data to fill the print grid. This process can produce a fuzzy and blocky image if the printed image gets very large.

As a rule of thumb, when you incorporate an image in a desktop-published document, or when you print photographs, you should work with high-resolution bitmaps so that you can produce high-quality output. To capture high-resolution bitmaps, use the highest resolution provided by your digital camera. When scanning an image, choose a dpi setting on your scanner that is at least as high as the dpi for the printout.

How does a bitmap's resolution relate to what I see on the screen? In an earlier chapter, you learned that you can set your computer monitor to a particular resolution, such as 1,024 x 768. When you display a bitmap graphic on the screen, each pixel of the graphic typically corresponds to one pixel on the screen. If the resolution of your graphic is 1,024 x 768 and your monitor is set at 1,024 x 768 resolution, the image will appear to fill the screen. If you view a 3.1 megapixel image on the same monitor, the image will be larger than the screen.

When viewing an image that is larger than the screen, you must scroll to see all parts of the image, or set the zoom level of your graphics software to less than 100 percent. You should take note, however, that changing the zoom level only stretches or shrinks the size of the image grid. It has no effect on the size at which a graphic is printed, or the size of the file in which the graphic is stored.

Can I change a graphic's file size? Sometimes the resolution and corresponding file size of a graphic might not be right for your needs. For example, if you take a photo with a 3.1 megapixel camera, it is unsuitable for a Web page. Not only would it take a long time to download, but it would be larger than most screens. A 3.1 megapixel graphic is also not suitable for an e-mail attachment. Uploading and downloading such a large file—especially over a dial-up connection—would take much too long. Reducing the resolution of a bitmap can reduce its file size, and the size at which it is displayed on a computer screen. Most experts recommend that Web graphics not exceed 100 KB, and that e-mail attachments not exceed 500 KB.

You can reduce the size of a bitmap by cropping it. **Cropping** refers to the process of selecting part of an image—just like cutting out a section of a photograph. Cropping decreases resolution and file size by reducing the number of pixels in a graphic. You can also reduce file size by removing pixels from the entire graphic; however, this process changes the quality of the image. Bitmap graphics are **resolution dependent**, which means that the quality of the image depends on its resolution. If you reduce the resolution, the computer eliminates pixels from the image, reducing the size of the image grid. For example, if you reduce the resolution from 2,160 x 1,440 (3.1 megapixels) to 1,080 x 720 (.8 megapixels), the image grid becomes a quarter of its original size. The file size is reduced by a similar amount. However, the computer threw away data with the pixels, which can reduce image quality.

If you attempt to enlarge a bitmap by increasing its resolution, your computer must somehow add pixels because no additional picture data exists. But what colors should these additional pixels become? Most graphics software uses a process called **pixel interpolation** to create new pixels by averaging the colors of nearby pixels. For some graphics, pixel interpolation results in an image that appears very similar to the original. Other images—particularly those that contain strong curved or diagonal lines—develop an undesirable **pixelated**, or "bitmappy," appearance (Figure 7-7).

FIGURE 7-7

When you increase the resolution of an existing graphic, the file size increases, but the quality might deteriorate.

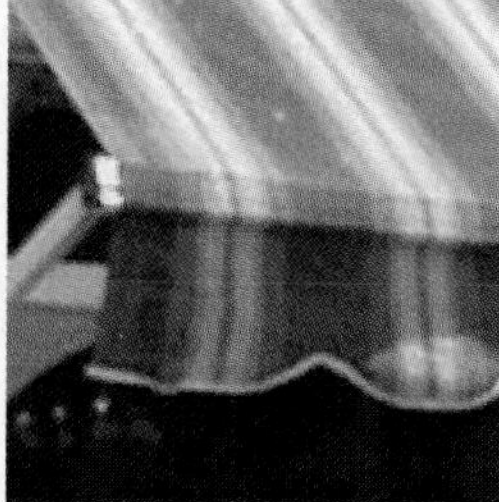

The figure above has a resolution of 130 x 130. The figure at right was enlarged to a resolution of 260 x 260, but it has a rough, pixelated appearance.

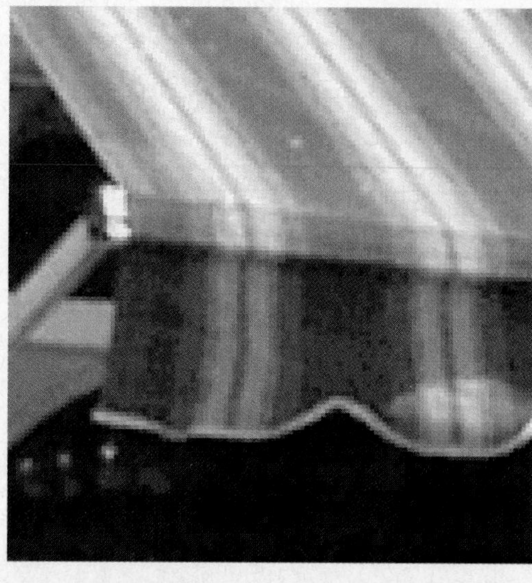

COLOR DEPTH AND PALETTES

What is color depth? Color depth is the number of colors that are available for use in an image. As the number of colors increases, image quality improves, but file size also increases. You can limit color depth to decrease the size of the file required for a graphic. To find out how this works, let's look at the storage requirements for various color depths. Then we can turn to the procedures for reducing color depth.

How does color depth relate to file size? To answer this question, let's go back to the old days of computing when monitors were simple monochrome devices. Each screen pixel could be either "on" or "off." A **monochrome bitmap** would be displayed by manipulating the pattern of "off" and "on" pixels displayed on the screen. To store the data for a monochrome bitmap, an "on" pixel is represented by a 1 bit. An "off" pixel is represented by a 0 bit. Each row of the bitmap grid is stored as a series of 0s and 1s, as shown in Figure 7-8.

FIGURE 7-8 Each pixel in a monochrome bitmap graphic is stored as a bit.

1. The image can originate as a black-and-white silhouette, as a black-and-white photograph, or even as a color photo.

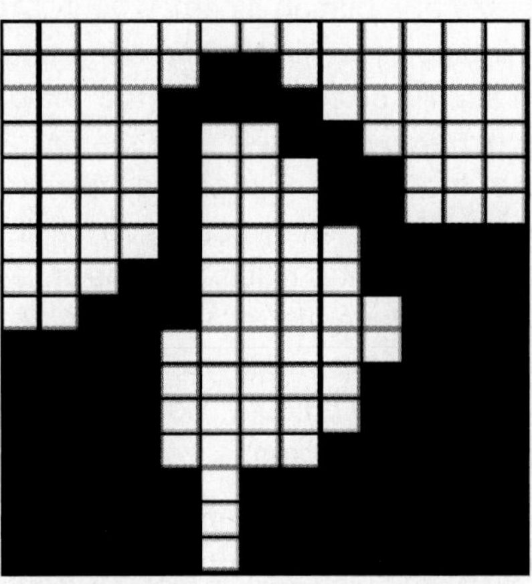

2. The computer divides the picture into a matrix.

1	1	1	1	1	1	1	1	1	1	1	1	1
1	1	1	1	1	0	0	1	1	1	1	1	1
1	1	1	1	0	0	0	0	1	1	1	1	1
1	1	1	1	0	1	1	0	0	1	1	1	1
1	1	1	1	0	1	1	1	0	0	1	1	1
1	1	1	1	0	1	1	1	0	0	1	1	1
1	1	1	1	0	1	1	1	1	0	0	0	0
1	1	1	0	0	1	1	1	1	0	0	0	0
1	1	0	0	0	1	1	1	1	1	0	0	0
0	0	0	0	1	1	1	1	1	1	0	0	0
0	0	0	0	1	1	1	1	1	0	0	0	0
0	0	0	0	1	1	1	1	1	0	0	0	0
0	0	0	0	1	1	1	1	0	0	0	0	0
0	0	0	0	0	1	0	0	0	0	0	0	0
0	0	0	0	0	1	0	0	0	0	0	0	0
0	0	0	0	0	1	0	0	0	0	0	0	0

3. If a cell is white, it is coded as a 1. If the cell is black, it is coded as a 0.

Monochrome bitmaps require very little storage space. Suppose that you create a full-screen monochrome bitmap with your monitor's resolution set to 640 x 480. Your screen displays 307,200 pixels (that's 640 multiplied by 480). Each pixel is set to display either a black dot or a white dot. When you store the graphic, each dot requires only one bit. Therefore, the number of bits required to represent a full-screen picture is the same as the number of pixels on the screen. At a resolution of 640 x 480, a full-screen graphic requires 307,200 bits of storage space. The number of bytes required to store the image is 307,200 divided by 8 (remember that there are eight bits in a byte). Your full-screen monochrome bitmap would, therefore, require only 38,400 bytes of storage space.

Today's color monitors require a more complex storage scheme. Each screen pixel displays a color based on the intensity of red, green, and blue signals that it receives. A pixel appears white if the red, green, and blue signals are set to maximum intensity. If red, green, and blue signals are equal, but at a lower intensity, the pixel displays a shade of gray. If the red signal is set to maximum intensity, but the blue and green signals are off, the pixel appears in brilliant red. A pixel appears purple if it receives red and blue signals. You get the idea.

The parts of a vector graphic are created as separate objects. For example, the Stonehenge image in Figure 7-12 was created with a series of roughly rectangular objects for the stones, and a circular object for the sun.

How can I identify vector graphics? It is difficult to accurately identify a vector graphic just by looking at an on-screen image. One clue that an image might be a vector graphic is a flat, cartoon-like quality. Think of clip art images—they are typically stored as vector graphics. For a more definitive identification, however, you should check the filename extension. Vector graphics files have filename extensions such as .wmf, .dxt, .mgx, .eps, .pict, and .cgm.

What are the advantages and disadvantages of vector graphics? Vector graphics are suitable for most line art, logos, simple illustrations, and diagrams that might be displayed and printed at various sizes. When compared to bitmaps, vector graphics have several advantages and disadvantages. You should take the following distinctions into account when deciding which type of graphic to use for a specific project.

Vectors resize better than bitmaps. When you change the physical size of a vector graphic, the objects change proportionally and maintain their smooth edges. Whereas a circle in a bitmap graphic might appear to have jagged edges after it is enlarged, a circle in a vector graphic appears as a smooth curve at any size, as shown in Figure 7-13.

FIGURE 7-13

Unlike bitmaps, vector graphics can be resized without becoming pixelated.

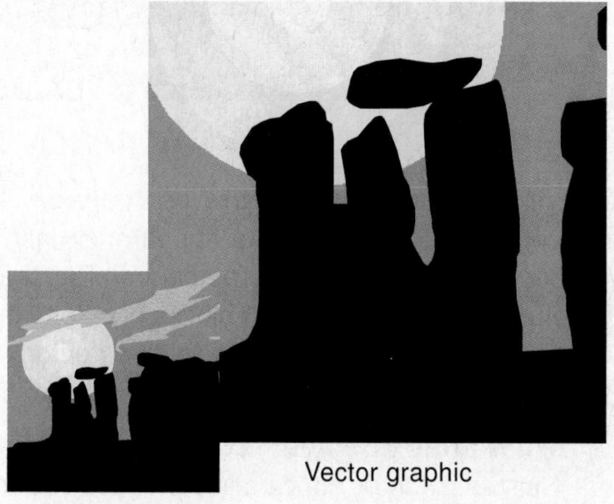

Vector graphic

Bitmap graphic

Vector images usually require less storage space than bitmaps. The storage space required for a vector graphic reflects the complexity of the image. Each instruction requires storage space, so the more lines, shapes, and fill patterns present in the graphic, the more storage space it requires. The Stonehenge vector graphic used as an example in this chapter requires less than 4 KB of storage space. A True Color photograph of the same image requires 1,109 KB.

7

It is easier to edit an object in a vector graphic than an object in a bitmap graphic. In some ways, a vector graphic is like a collage of objects. Each object can be layered over other objects, but moved and edited independently. You can individually stretch, shrink, distort, color, move, or delete any object in a vector graphic. For example, if you delete the sun from the Stonehenge vector image, the background and cloud layers remain. In contrast, most bitmap graphics are constructed as a single layer of pixels. If you erase the pixels for some of the stones in the Stonehenge photograph, you'll create a "hole" of white pixels. (See Figure 7-14.)

FIGURE 7-14

Vector graphic objects are layered, so it is easy to move and delete objects without disrupting the rest of the image. In contrast, deleting a shape from a bitmap image leaves a "hole" because the image is only one layer of pixels.

Vector graphics tend not to produce images that are as realistic as bitmap images. Most vector images tend to have a cartoon-like appearance instead of the realistic appearance that you expect from a photograph. The cartoon-like characteristic of vector images results from the use of objects filled with blocks of color. Your options for shading and texturing objects are limited, which tends to give vector graphics a "flat" appearance.

FIGURE 7-15

A digitizing tablet allows you to trace line drawings for a vector graphic.

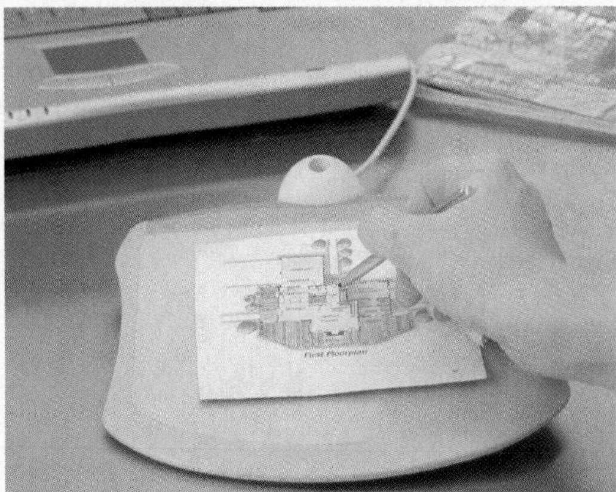

What tools do I need to create vector graphics? Neither scanners nor cameras produce vector graphics. Architects and engineers sometimes use a digitizing tablet, like the one in Figure 7-15, to turn a paper-based line drawing into a vector graphic. A **digitizing tablet** is a device that provides a flat surface for a paper-based drawing, and a pen or "puck" that you can use to click the endpoints of each line on the drawing. The endpoints are converted into vectors and stored.

Usually, vector graphics are created "from scratch" using vector graphics software, referred to as **drawing software**. Drawing software is sometimes packaged separately from the paint software used to produce bitmap graphics. In other cases, it is included with bitmap software as a graphics software suite.

Vector graphics software provides an array of drawing tools that you can use to create objects, position them, and fill them with colors or patterns. For example, you can use the filled circle tool to draw a circle that is filled with a solid color. You can create an irregular shape by connecting points to outline the shape. Figure 7-16 illustrates how to use drawing tools to create a vector graphic.

FIGURE 7-16

To draw a circle, select the filled circle tool, then drag the mouse pointer to indicate the location and size of the circle. A color palette at the bottom of the window allows you to select the circle color. Once you create the circle object, you can move it and change its size or color. You can draw irregularly shaped objects, such as clouds, by connecting short line segments.

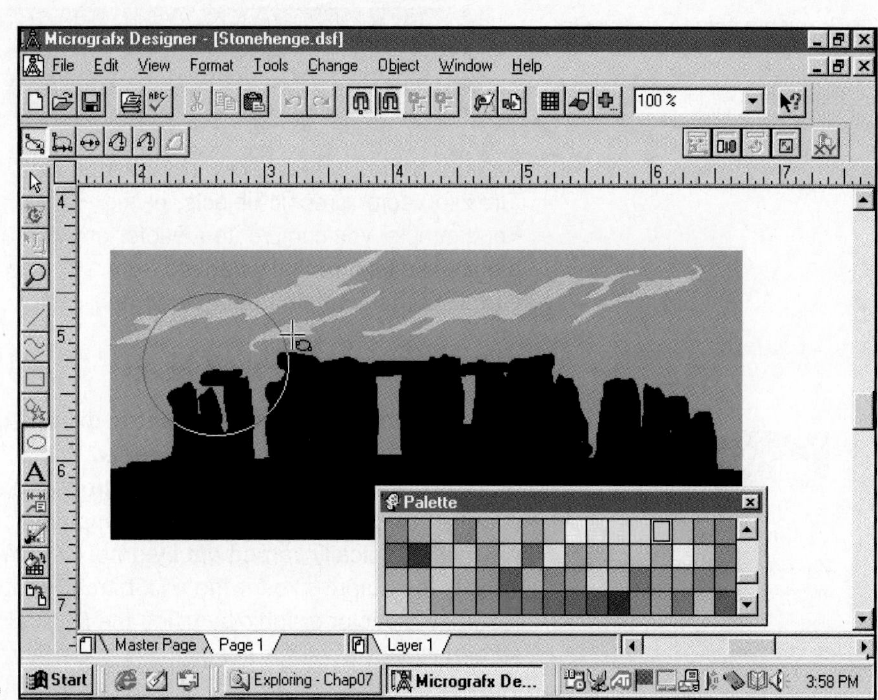
Micrografx Designer - [Stonehenge.dsf]
File Edit View Format Tools Change Object Window Help
100 %
Palette
Master Page Page 1 Layer 1
Start Exploring - Chap07 Micrografx De...
3:58 PM

click to start

The sun is a circle filled with a gradient.
The background is a filled rectangle.
The clouds are created as a series of short line segments and filled with color.
The stones are created as a series of short line segments and filled with black.

7

www InfoWebLinks.com

To learn more about popular vector graphics software, visit the Vector Graphics Software InfoWeb.

click

Vector graphics software helps you easily edit individual objects within a graphic by changing their sizes, shapes, positions, or colors. For example, the data for creating the circle is recorded as an instruction, such as CIRCLE 40 Y 200 150, which means create a circle with a 40-pixel radius, color it yellow, and place the center of the circle 200 pixels from the left of the screen and 150 pixels from the top of the screen. If you move the circle to the right side of the image, the instruction that the computer stores for the circle changes to something like CIRCLE 40 Y 500 150—500 pixels from the left instead of 200.

When filling in a shape with color, your graphics software might provide tools for creating a gradient. A **gradient** is a smooth blending of shades from one color to another, or from light to dark. Gradients, like those shown in Figure 7-17, can be used to create shading and three-dimensional effects.

FIGURE 7-17

Gradients help to give vector graphics a more lifelike appearance, such as making this shape appear to be a tube.

Some vector graphics software provides tools that apply bitmapped textures to vector graphic objects, giving them a more realistic appearance. For example, you can create a vector drawing of a house, and then apply a brick-like texture that's derived from a bitmap photograph of real bricks. Graphics that contain both bitmap and vector data are called **metafiles**.

VECTOR-TO-BITMAP CONVERSION

Looking for software to convert between vector images and bitmaps? You'll find helpful links at the Vector-Bitmap Conversion InfoWeb.

Is it possible to convert a vector graphic into a bitmap? A vector graphic can quite easily be converted into a bitmap graphic through a process called rasterizing. **Rasterization** works by superimposing a grid over a vector image, and determining the color for each pixel. This process is typically carried out by graphics software, which allows you to specify the output size for the final bitmap image. On a PC, you can also rasterize a vector graphic by using the PrtSc (Print Screen) key to take a screenshot of a vector image. It is important to output your rasterized images at the size you will ultimately need. If, instead, you rasterize a vector image at a small size, and then try to enlarge the resulting bitmap image, you will likely get a poor-quality pixelated image like the one in Figure 7-18.

FIGURE 7-18

When vector images are rasterized, they become bitmaps and can't be enlarged without becoming pixelated.

Once a vector graphic is converted to a bitmap, the resulting graphic no longer has the qualities of a vector graphic. For example, if you convert the Stonehenge vector graphic into a bitmap, the sun is no longer an object that you can easily move or assign a different color.

How about converting a bitmap graphic into a vector? Converting a bitmap graphic into a vector graphic is more difficult than converting from a vector to a bitmap. To change a bitmap graphic into a vector graphic, you must use special tracing software. **Tracing software** locates the edges of objects in a bitmap image and converts the resulting shapes into vector graphic objects. This software works best on simple images and line drawings. It does not typically provide acceptable results when used on photos. Tracing capabilities are included in some general-purpose graphics software, but standalone tracing software provides more flexibility and usually produces better results.

In computer jargon, compressing a file is called zipping; decompressing a file is called unzipping. You can zip any kind of file, including program or data files. The advantage of file compression is that zipped files can often fit on a single removable disk, and they take less time to upload or e-mail. The disadvantage of file compression is that you might be required to manually unzip the files before you use them. Figure 7-43 walks you through the process of zipping and unzipping files using the popular WinZip software.

FIGURE 7-43

Popular compression utilities, such as WinZip, zip one or more files into a new, compressed file.

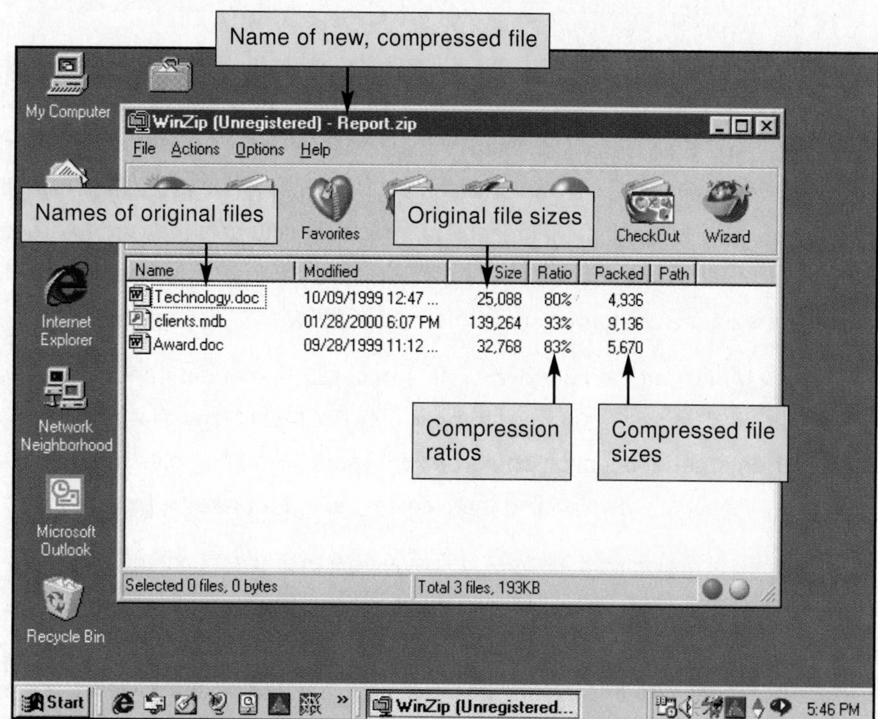

click to start

Before sending text, database, executable, and Windows bitmap (.bmp) files as e-mail attachments, it is a good idea to compress them. Using a file compression utility, you can shrink these files by as much as 70 percent. Other non-compressed file formats, such as Wave, may compress by about 20 percent. File formats such as GIF, MP3, MPEG, and JPEG hardly shrink at all when you zip them because they are already stored in a compressed format.

QUICKCheck
TechTalk

1. A compression [ ] is a measurement of the amount of shrinkage—the original file size compared to the compressed file size.
2. A compression [ ] is the set steps required to shrink the data in a file and reconstitute the file back to its original state.
3. Dictionary-based and statistical text compression are examples of [ ] compression, which loses no data during the compression process.
4. JPEG is an example of [ ] compression, in which data is eliminated during the compression process.

check answers

7

ISSUE
WHO'S GOT THE RIGHTS?

In early 1999, an 18-year-old student named Shawn Fanning developed a Web-based technology for sharing MP3 music files. This technology, dubbed "Napster" after Shawn's nickname, quickly became one of the hottest applications on the Internet. In less than a year, its user base exceeded 25 million.

Almost immediately, Napster ran afoul of the Recording Industry Association of America (RIAA), a watchdog organization that represents record companies, such as Columbia Records, Motown Records, and Epic Nashville. The RIAA compiled a list of 12,000 copyrighted songs that Napster technology made available as free downloads. In December of 1999, the RIAA filed suit, accusing Napster of contributing to copyright infringement, which considerably reduced the revenues of record companies and artists. The ensuing court battle stirred up a caldron of issues that relate to the use and abuse of digital media, including music, photos, and videos.

To get a handle on the controversy, it is necessary to understand how file-sharing technology works. Napster was created as a peer-to-peer network technology that could run over the Internet. Anyone with an Internet connection could become part of the Napster network simply by registering at the Napster Web site, downloading the Napster client software called MusicShare, and installing it.

Registered users make their MP3 files available over the Napster Network by placing the files in a "user library" folder on their own computers' hard disks. Whenever one of these users logs in at the Napster Web site, the names of his or her MP3 files are uploaded to the Napster server and incorporated in a master database. These MP3 filenames only remain in the database and accessible while the user is logged in.

Any Napster member can search the master database to find the name of a specific music file. Once found, the file is transferred directly between the hard disks of the users. No MP3 files are stored on Napster servers, nor do these files travel through Napster servers as they are transferred from one user to another. No copyrighted material is ever in Napster's possession. So how can Napster be held responsible for copyright violation? The argument went something like the following:

RIAA: Napster is providing technology that is infringing on copyrights held by record companies and recording artists.

Napster: No copyrighted material was ever stored on our servers.

RIAA: But you knew that your registered users were using your technology to illegally exchange copyrighted music files.

Napster: What's illegal about it? The Audio Home Recording Act of 1992 allows people to make recordings and lend them out to people, provided it is not done for commercial purposes. Our members were not getting paid for allowing others to copy their MP3 files, so our network has nothing to do with commercial use.

RIAA: Even though money is not changing hands, Napster-style copying is commercial use for two reasons: First, Napster users are distributing files, not to their friends, but to Napster users they have never met. Second, by getting files for free, Napster users don't buy the music through legitimate channels, and that has tangible commercial repercussions.

Napster: But Napster can't be held responsible for users who break the law. Remember that the courts refused to hold video tape recorder manufacturers and retailers responsible when their machines were used to make tapes of copyrighted television shows. Also, remember that the Digital Millennium Copyright Act protects Internet Service Providers from being liable for illegal actions on the part of their subscribers.

RIAA: Ah, but ISPs are only protected if they have no knowledge of their subscribers' illegal actions. We asked the court to subpoena your e-mail records, and there is clear evidence that you knew what your members were doing! Just look at the names of the files in your database—"Yellow Submarine by the Beatles," "Celebrity - N Sync," and "Loverboy - Carey."

Napster: Even if we knew, how could we stop them? Suppose that instead of calling a file "Yellow Submarine by the Beatles," one of our users named it "Light-Colored Underwater Craft by a Famous British Rock Group?" We would have no way to screen that file out of our database.

RIAA: If you can't find a way to police your network, we'll ask for damages to the tune of $5 million.

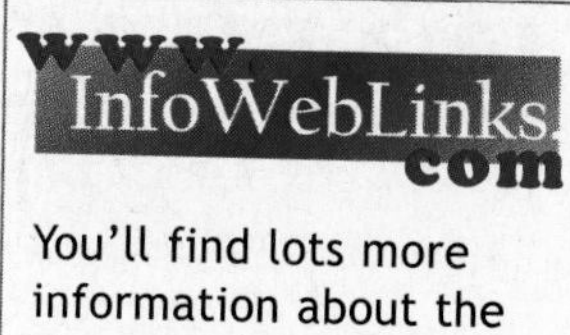

You'll find lots more information about the Napster controversy at the Intellectual Property InfoWeb.

click

In 2001, U.S. courts suspended Napster activity, and in 2002, the file-sharing site officially closed. Despite this setback, similar sites have appeared. Some operate legally by making sure that the files, especially MP3 files, are in the public domain, or posted with permission from the artist and record company.

Other music-sharing networks, such as Morpheus, Kazaa, and Grokster, provide access to copyrighted material, but use file-sharing technology called Gnutella, which is subtly different from the technology used by Napster. Unlike Napster, Gnutella networks require no central database. In true peer-to-peer fashion, client software installed on one user's computer searches for other similar clients. For example, as soon as a Gnutella client comes online, it sends a signal to another Gnutella client. That client then tells eight other clients that it has established contact with the new client. Each of those eight then tells seven others, who tell six others, and so on. In this way, each client tells many other clients it is online, and what content it has available.

P2P utilities that employ this decentralized approach provide another unique set of legal challenges. Because there is no central server maintaining an index of users, there is no easy way to target and stop the use of the network and its software. Many content developers in music, video, and similar creative industries are beginning to realize that fundamental changes are on the horizon. Shutting down Napster might stop the first wave of digital pirates, but will it have much effect on the tidal wave of digital distribution issues that are yet to come?

What Do You Think?

1. Do you think that most people realize that copyright law gives musicians and record companies the exclusive right to distribute their music? ○ Yes ○ No ○ Not sure
2. Do you believe that music-sharing networks should not allow their members to swap copyrighted music without the permission of the copyright holder? ○ Yes ○ No ○ Not sure
3. Can you envision any way to monitor Gnutella networks to make sure that they don't contribute to illegal activities? ○ Yes ○ No ○ Not sure

click to save your responses

7

INTERACTIVE SUMMARY

The Interactive Summary helps you to select and remember important concepts from this chapter. Fill in the blanks to best complete each sentence. When using the NP6 BookOnCD, you can click the Check Answers buttons to automatically score your answers. Place your Tracking Disk in the floppy disk drive if you want to save your scores.

A ________ graphic is composed of a grid of dots, and the color of each dot is stored as a binary number. Both scanners and cameras produce images in bitmap format. The ________ of the grid that forms a bitmap graphic is referred to as its resolution. High-resolution graphics typically produce better image quality than low-resolution graphics, but require more storage space. It is possible to change the resolution and/or the file size of a bitmap graphic, but because bitmaps are resolution ________, these changes can reduce image quality. For example, enlarging a bitmap requires your computer to fill in missing pixels, which often results in a jagged or ________ image. As a rule of thumb, images that you intend to print should remain at full size and resolution. When sending bitmap files as e-mail attachments, they can be ________ in size or resolution to produce a file that is less than 500 KB.

Color ________ refers to the number of colors available for use in an image. It is related to file size because the number of bits needed to describe the color of a pixel depends on the total number of colors available in an image. For example, a bitmap composed of 256 colors requires only ________ bits to store the data for each pixel in an image, whereas 24 bits are required for each pixel in a ________ Color graphic. Grayscale, system, and Web palettes use eight bits to represent each pixel. If a particular palette does not contain the right selection of colors for an image, graphics software can ________ the graphic using scattered or patterned techniques. Popular bitmap graphics formats include BMP, PCX, TIFF, GIF, JPEG, and PNG. Of these formats, GIF, JPEG, and PNG are supported by most Web browsers.

check answers

Unlike a bitmap graphic, created by superimposing a grid of pixels over an image, a ________ graphic consists of a set of instructions for creating a picture. These graphics are created using a type of graphic software called ________ software. They are stored as a collection of ________ and their corresponding sizes, colors, and positions. You can identify these graphics by their flat "cartoon-like" appearance and their filename extensions: .wmf, .dxt, .mgx, .eps, .pict, and .cgm. Vector graphics are suitable for most line art, logos, simple illustrations, and diagrams. They are frequently used for clip art. Vector graphics have several advantages over bitmaps: they resize better, require less storage space, and are easier to edit.

A vector graphic can be converted into a bitmap by a process called ________. Once converted, however, the resulting graphic loses all of the object-editing qualities that it had in its vector state. In contrast, changing a bitmap image to a vector graphic is not easy. It requires the help of ________ software, which works best on simple line drawings. Vector graphics have not been popular on the Web because they have not been supported by browsers. Two vector graphics formats, ________ and Flash, are gaining popularity, despite the fact that they require browser plug-ins or players.

check answers

Like vector graphics, 3-D graphics are stored as a set of instructions. For a 3-D graphic, however, the instructions contain the locations and lengths of lines that form a __________ for a three-dimensional object. These lines form a framework that can be covered by colored, patterned, and textured surfaces. This process, called __________, produces a bitmap image of the three-dimensional object. For additional realism, __________ tracing adds highlights and shadows to the image. 3-D graphics can be animated to produce special effects for movies and the animated characters for 3-D computer games.

Whereas animated 3-D graphics are created "from scratch" by an artist, digital video is usually based on footage of real objects, filmed and then stored as bits. Videos that are constructed and played on a personal computer are called __________ videos. The videos are typically stored on a computer's __________ disk for editing, and then they can be transferred to CDs, DVDs, or videotape. A video is composed of a series of bitmap graphics. Each one is called a __________. Popular desktop video file __________ include AVI, QuickTime, MPEG, Real Media, and ASF. When video footage is filmed using an analog camera, it must be converted into digital format by a video __________ device. Footage from a digital video camera requires no conversion and can be streamed directly from camera to computer through a __________ or USB port. Once footage is stored on a __________-access device, such as a hard disk, it can be easily edited. Raw video footage contains a huge amount of data. The size of a video file can be reduced by three techniques: reducing the size of the video window, reducing the __________ rate, and __________ the video data. A codec is the software that __________ files, such as graphics and videos. Videos can be added to Web pages, typically using __________ video, which transmits the first segment of a video, begins to play it, and then continues to transfer additional segments. **check answers**

Music, voice, and sound effects can all be recorded and digitally stored as __________ audio. To digitally record sound, __________ of the sound are collected at periodic intervals and stored as numeric data. High-quality sound is usually sampled at 44.1 __________, and each stereo sample requires 32 bits of storage space. To conserve space, "radio-quality" recordings of speaking voices are often recorded at lower sampling rates. A computer's __________ card is responsible for transforming the bits stored in an audio file into music, sound effects, and narrations. It contains digital __________ processing circuitry that transforms bits into analog sound, records analog sounds as digital bits, and deals with audio compression. Waveform audio file formats include Wave, Audio Interchange Format, RealAudio, and MP3.

MIDI music is __________ sound that is artificially created or "synthetic." Unlike waveform sound files, which contain digitized recordings of real sound passages, MIDI files contain __________ for creating the pitch, volume, and duration of notes made by musical instruments. MIDI files are typically much smaller than waveform audio files for similar musical passages, so they are ideal for Web pages. However, MIDI music tends to lack the full resonance of symphony-quality sound that can be achieved with waveform audio.

Speech __________ is the process by which machines, such as computers, produce sound that resembles spoken words. Speech __________ refers to the ability of machines to "understand" spoken words.

INTERACTIVE KEY TERMS

Make sure that you understand all of the boldfaced key terms presented in this chapter. If you're using the NP6 BookOnCD, you can use this list of terms as an interactive study activity. First, try to define a term in your own words, then click the term to compare your definition with the definition that is presented in the chapter.

24-bit bitmap, 339
32-bit bitmap, 339
3-D graphics, 350
Analog video camera, 355
ASF, 354
Audio Interchange Format, 366
AVI, 354
Bitmap graphic, 332
BMP, 341
CD ripper, 367
Codec, 359
Color depth, 338
Color palette, 339
Compression algorithm, 371
Compression ratio, 371
Cropping, 337
Data compression, 371
Desktop video, 353
Dictionary-based compression, 372
Digital camera, 333
Digital signal processor, 366
Digital video camera, 355
Digitizing tablet, 346
Dithering, 340
Drawing software, 346
External video, 361
File compression utility, 374
Flash graphics, 349
Flash memory, 334
Floppy disk adapter, 335
Frame rate, 353
GIF, 342
Gradient, 348
Grayscale palette, 340
Internal video, 361
JPEG, 342
Key frame, 374
Linear editing, 358
Lossless compression, 373
Lossy compression, 373
Megapixels, 335
Memory card reader, 334
Metafiles, 348
MIDI, 368
MIDI sequence, 368
Monochrome bitmap, 338
MP3, 366
MP3 encoder, 367
MPEG, 354
Non-linear editing, 358
Paint software, 332
PCX, 341
Phonemes, 369
Pixel interpolation, 337
Pixelated, 337
PNG, 342
QuickTime, 354
Rasterization, 348
Ray tracing, 350
RealAudio, 366
RealMedia, 354
Rendering, 350
Resolution, 335
Resolution dependent, 337
Run-length encoding, 373
Sampling rate, 365
Scanner, 333
Sound card, 365
Spatial compression, 373
Speech recognition software, 370
Speech recognition, 369
Speech synthesis, 369
Statistical compression, 372
Streaming video, 361
SVG, 349
Synthesized sound, 368
System palette, 340
Temporal compression, 374
Text-to-speech software, 369
TIFF, 341
Tracing software, 348
True Color bitmap, 339
Vector graphics, 344
Video capture device, 357
Video capture software, 357
Video editing software, 358
Videoconferencing camera, 355
Wave, 366
Waveform audio, 364
Wavetable, 368
Web palette, 340
Wireframe, 350

INTERACTIVE
SITUATION QUESTIONS

Apply what you've learned to some typical computing situations. When using the NP6 BookOnCD, you can type your answers, then use the Check Answers button to automatically score your responses. Place your Tracking Disk in the floppy disk drive if you want to save your scores.

1 You have an old photograph that you want to incorporate in a brochure for your antiques business. To convert the photo into digital format, you use a(n) [ ].

2 Suppose that you receive a bitmap image from one of your friends, but it seems curiously "blocky" or pixelated. Either this image was captured using a very low-resolution camera, or the size of the image was [ ].

3 Suppose that you are preparing a series of bitmap graphics for a Web site. To decrease the download time for each graphic, you can remove pixels or reduce the color [ ].

4 Suppose that you are designing a logo for a client. You know that the design will undergo several revisions, and you understand that the logo will be used at various sizes. You decide that it would be best to use drawing software to create the logo as a(n) [ ] graphic.

5 Suppose that you created a diagram as a vector graphic, but you want to post it on the Web as a bitmap so that it can be viewed without a plug-in or player. You can convert the vector into a bitmap using a process called [ ].

6 Suppose that you download a video from the Web with an .avi filename extension. You attempt to open it using Microsoft Media Player, but the video window remains blank. A likely cause of this problem is that you do not have the correct [ ].

7 Suppose that you click a Web page link to a video, but it is barely watchable because it is so jerky, and the sound doesn't coordinate with the images. You would expect this type of problem if you are using a slow, [ ] Internet connection.

8 Suppose that you are creating an English-as-a-Second-Language Web page and you want to add links to sound files that pronounce English phrases. If you want the sound files to play without the aid of a plug-in or player, you should use either the Audio Interchange Format or [ ] file format.

9 Suppose that you're a musician and you are asked to synthesize some music for the opening screen of a Web site. For this project, you would most likely work with [ ] music.

10 Suppose that you visit a Web site that allows you to enter sentences, and then it reads the sentences back to you. The site even gives you a choice of a female voice or a male voice. You assume that this site uses speech [ ] technology.

check answers

7

INTERACTIVE PRACTICE TESTS

When you use the NP6 BookOnCD, you can take Practice Tests that consist of 10 multiple-choice, true/false, and fill-in-the-blank questions. The questions are selected at random from a large test bank, so each time you take a test, you'll receive a different set of questions. Your tests are scored immediately, and you can print study guides that help you find the correct answers for any questions that you missed. If you are using a Tracking Disk, insert it in the floppy disk drive to save your test scores.

click to start 

STUDY TIPS

Study Tips help you to organize and consolidate the information in a chapter by making lists, outlines, charts, and sketches. You can use paper and pencil or word processing software to complete most of the Study Tips activities.

1. Make sure that you can use your own words to correctly answer each of the green focus questions that appear throughout the chapter.
2. Make a list of the file extensions that were mentioned in this chapter and group them according to digital media type: bitmap graphic, vector graphic, digital video, waveform audio, and MIDI. Circle any formats that are used on the Web.
3. Make a list of the software mentioned in this chapter, indicating the type of task that it helps you accomplish.
4. Describe the devices that transfer photos from a digital camera to a computer.
5. Make a list that includes the approximate file size for: a full-screen high-res bitmap graphic, a vector graphic, a commercial audio CD, five minutes of waveform audio, a five-minute MIDI file, a feature-length uncompressed movie, and one minute of compressed desktop video.
6. Describe how resolution and color depth contribute to the size of a graphics file.
7. Summarize how you would prepare bitmap graphics for the following uses: e-mail attachment, Web page, desktop publishing, and printed photo.
8. Explain how a computer monitor displays color, and how that relates to the way it stores a color palette.
9. Describe the effects of applying different types of dithering to a bitmap graphic.
10. Explain how the concept of layering relates to your ability to modify a vector graphic.
11. Make a list of the advantages and disadvantages of bitmaps and vector graphics.
12. Make a series of quick sketches that illustrates the evolution of a 3-D graphic from wireframe to rendered image, and to ray-traced image.
13. Explain the different procedures required to transfer analog or digital video from camera to computer.
14. Define the differences between linear and non-linear editing.
15. List three ways in which you can reduce the file size of a desktop video.
16. Explain how streaming audio and video work, and contrast them to non-streaming technology.
17. Calculate the storage space required for the following:

    A True Color 640 x 480 bitmap image

    A grayscale 640 x 480 bitmap image

    A True Color 1,024 x 768 image

    A 1,024 x 768 bitmap image that uses the system palette

    An uncompressed desktop video that uses a 256-color palette, 15 fps, and a 320 x 240 window

    One minute of uncompressed stereo music recorded at a sampling rate of 44.1 KHz

PROJECTS

An NP6 Project is an open-ended activity that will help you apply the concepts you have learned. Many projects require resources in addition to your textbook, such as current magazines, library materials, or Web access. When you tackle a project, be prepared to use your critical thinking skills, logical analysis, and your creativity.

1 **Issue Research: Who's Got the Rights** The Issue section of this chapter focused on the Napster controversy, but this issue has widespread implications for all types of digital media, including graphics, animations, MIDI music, and videos. For this project, write a two–five page paper about one aspect of copying and distribution of digital media. To begin this project, consult the Intellectual Property InfoWeb (see page 377) and link to the recommended Web pages to get an in-depth overview of the issue. Next, determine the viewpoint that you will present in your paper. You might, for example, decide to present the viewpoint of a student who made extensive use of Napster-like sites, such as Kazaa, Morpheus, and Grokster, and continues to exchange MP3 music files with others. Or, you might present the viewpoint of a recording artist who suspects that royalties would be higher if it somehow became technically or legally impossible for people to freely exchange music. Whatever viewpoint you decide to present, make sure that you can back it up with facts and references to authoritative articles and Web pages. You can place citations to these pages (including the author's name, article title, date of publication, and URL) at the end of your paper as endnotes, on each page as footnotes, or along with the appropriate paragraphs using parentheses. Follow your professor's instructions for submitting your paper.

2 **Digital Cameras** Use the Web to research the latest offerings in digital cameras, and find out how prices relate to megapixels. Assume that you are required to purchase a digital camera for use in one of your courses. Which cameras fit within your budget? Of those cameras, which one gives you the best selection of features?

3 **Explore the GIF Controversy**

The GIF file format is extraordinarily popular for graphics—especially for graphics on the Web. Unfortunately, its use is controversial due to the fact that the GIF format uses the LZW compression technology, which is owned by Unisys. For this project, you should use library and Internet resources to explore the history of the GIF controversy by answering the following questions:

- Who invented LZW compression and when was information about it first published?
- When was the LZW compression technique incorporated into the GIF format?
- Why did the GIF format become so popular?
- Are there any alternative non-proprietary graphics formats that could replace GIF?
- What information about GIF usage restrictions has been provided by Unisys?
- What is the current status of the GIF controversy?

Make sure that you incorporate specific bibliographic information to indicate the source of your answers. If possible, cite at least two sources for each answer, showing that you were able to confirm the accuracy of your facts from more than one source.

7

ADDITIONAL PROJECTS

TIP

Click ✱ to access the Web for additional projects.

8 THE COMPUTER INDUSTRY

CONTENTS

LAB

InfoWebLinks

The InfoWebLinks, located in the margins of this chapter, show the way to a variety of Web sites that contain additional information and updates to the chapter topics. Your computer needs an Internet connection to access these links. You can connect to the Web links for this chapter by:

- clicking the InfoWeb links in the margins
- clicking this underlined link
- starting your browser and entering the URL ***www.infoweblinks.com/np6/chapter8.htm***

TIP

When using the **BookOnCD**, the symbols are "clickable."

CHAPTER PREVIEW

8

The automobile industry operates on a predictable annual cycle of new models. In comparison, the computer industry seems somewhat chaotic. In this chapter, you'll delve into the computer industry's past, present, and future to find out what makes it tick.

Section A takes a brief look at the development of computers, beginning with very basic counting devices, and progressing to today's small, powerful, and efficient computers. When reading the material about computer prototypes, you'll gain some insights into the process of invention. You'll also discover what changed personal computers from simple kits for hobbyists into wildly popular productivity and communications tools.

Section B provides an overview of the computer and IT industries, along with their rapid emergence as a global economic force. In this section, you will get a glimpse of the way companies plan, build, and market computer-related products.

Section C focuses on the computer profession and answers your questions about careers in the computer and IT industries. You'll learn about working conditions, salaries, educational preparation, and certification options.

Section D provides lots of practical advice for job hunters, including tips about using the Internet, and creating resumes that command attention in today's technology-driven job market. Information in this section, though directed to those entering computer careers, has broader applications to job seekers in other fields as well. The TechTalk section revisits Moore's law and how it might "run out of steam" in the future. What technologies could replace silicon-based integrated circuits? The answer might surprise you.

When you complete this chapter you should be able to:

- Outline the development of calculating and computer devices, beginning with simple counting aids, and continuing through the developments that led to today's computer technology
- Describe the hardware, software, and operating system characteristics for computer prototypes, and each of the four generations of computers
- List the factors that changed personal computers from hobbyists' kits to widely used productivity and communications tools
- Describe the role of the computer and IT industries with respect to the global economy
- Explain the life cycle of typical hardware and software products
- Discuss the advantages and disadvantages of various marketing channels for consumers who want to purchase computers and related products
- Describe the job outlook, working conditions, and salaries for computer professionals
- Differentiate between computer engineering, computer science, and information systems degree programs
- Demonstrate how to create a resume that works in today's technology-driven job market

TIP Click ➧ to access the Web for a complete list of learning objectives for Chapter 8.

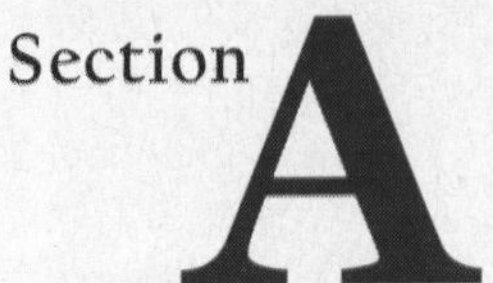

Section A COMPUTER HISTORY

Like so many inventions throughout history, the computer evolved as inventors tinkered with various devices. As a result, it is difficult for historians to point to one development and say that it represents the first calculator or the first computer. Keeping that uncertainty in mind, it is, nonetheless, interesting to trace the development of computers. Knowing the history of computers helps you understand the design and capabilities of today's digital computers. It also helps you understand how the computer industry of today came into being.

MANUAL CALCULATORS

What came before computers? Even before recorded history, humans used **counting aids**, such as pebbles and notched sticks, to keep track of quantities—the number of sheep in a flock, for example, or the number of oil jars purchased from a merchant. Many transactions, however, required calculations.

A calculation is based on an algorithm—the step-by-step process by which numbers are manipulated. Even simple paper-and-pencil addition requires an algorithm. The steps include adding the rightmost digits first, carrying a 1 if necessary, and then moving left to any remaining digits, where the process is repeated. A **manual calculator** is a device that assists in the process of numeric calculations, but requires the human operator to keep track of the algorithm.

A manual calculator called an **abacus** first appeared around 1200 in China, and then in Japan around 1600. An abacus, like the one in Figure 8-1, consists of beads mounted on sticks within a rectangular frame. Each bead represents a quantity—1, 5, 10, 50 and so on. To use an abacus, you must learn the algorithm for manipulating the beads.

FIGURE 8-1

An abacus uses beads to represent numbers. This abacus shows the number 17. Using an algorithm, the beads on an abacus can be manipulated to perform arithmetic operations.

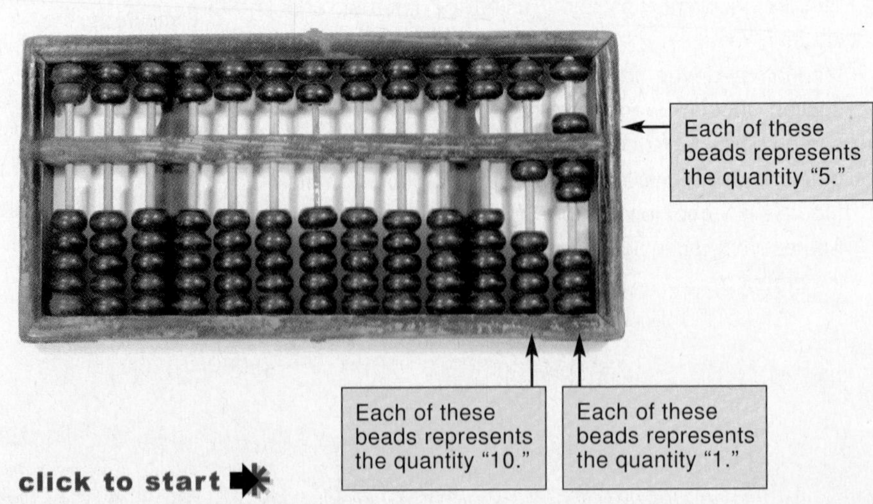
Each of these beads represents the quantity "5."
Each of these beads represents the quantity "10."
Each of these beads represents the quantity "1."

click to start

Other manual calculators include the oddly-named **Napier's Bones**, and the slide rule. John Napier, the Scottish Laird of Merchiston, made two contributions to the field of mathematics. He invented logarithms and a device for multiplication and division. The device consisted of several rods, divided into ten squares, each labeled with two numbers. The rods were positioned according to the numbers in a calculation, and the result was determined by adding values shown in a specific location on the rods. These rods were often constructed out of bones, so they came to be called Napier's Bones (Figure 8-2).

Want to learn more about manual and mechanical computing devices? Connect to the Calculating Devices InfoWeb.

click

In 1621, an English mathematician named William Oughtred used Napier's logarithms to construct the first **slide rule**. Slide rules, like the one pictured in Figure 8-2, remained in use as an essential tool for students, engineers, and scientists through the 1960s.

8

FIGURE 8-2 Napier's Bones (left) evolved into the slide rule (right).

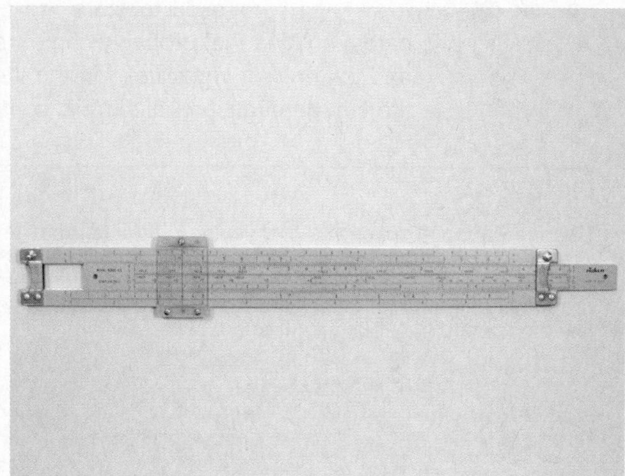

click to start

MECHANICAL CALCULATORS

When did machines begin to perform calculations? Manual calculators, such as the abacus and slide rule, require the operator to apply algorithms to perform calculations. In contrast, a **mechanical calculator** implements algorithms autonomously. To work a mechanical calculator, the operator simply enters the numbers for a calculation, and then pulls a lever or turns a wheel to carry out the calculation. No thinking—or at least very little—is required.

Mechanical calculators were developed as early as 1623, when a German professor named Wilhelm Schickard created a mechanical calculator (called **Schickard's Calculator**) with a series of interlocking gears. Each of the ten spokes on a gear represented a digit. Every time a gear completed a full circle, it activated the gear to the left, moving it one notch to "carry the 1."

In 1642, a Frenchman named Blaise Pascal developed the **Pascaline**, a mechanical device that could be used to perform addition, subtraction, multiplication, and division. Yet another mechanical calculator—now called the **Leibniz Calculator**—was created by a German baron named Gottfried Wilhelm von Leibniz in 1673. It was not until 1820, however, that Thomas **deColmar's Arithmometer** became the first mass-produced calculator.

When did calculating devices begin to operate without "human power?" In 1822, an English mathematician named Charles Babbage proposed a device called the **Difference Engine** that would operate using steam power. Although steam power might seem an unusual choice to us in these days of free-flowing electricity, steam power was cutting-edge technology during Babbage's lifetime. The Difference Engine was intended to quickly and accurately calculate large tables of numbers used for astronomical and engineering applications. The blueprints for the Difference Engine called for more than 4,000 precision-engineered levers, gears, and wheels. Babbage worked on the Difference Engine until 1833, but he was unable to fabricate gears with the necessary precision to create a working version of this complex mechanical device.

www InfoWebLinks.com

At the Charles Babbage InfoWeb, you'll find sketches, photos, and original documents describing the Analytical and Difference Engines, including programming notes by mathematician Ada Byron.

click

In 1834, Babbage began designing a new general-purpose calculating device, called the **Analytical Engine**. Computer historians believe that the Analytical Engine design embodies many of the concepts that define the modern computer, including memory, a programmable processor, an output device, and user-definable input of programs and data. Babbage proposed to store the programs and data for calculations on punched cards, an idea that probably came from the use of punched cards to control the color and patterns of yarns used in the Jacquard loom. Punched cards were later used in the first generation of electronic computing devices (Figure 8-3).

FIGURE 8-3

Charles Babbage conceived of a device called the Analytical Engine, which embodied many of the characteristics that define modern computers. For example, he proposed to store the programs and data for calculations on punched cards, much like those used in 1970s mainframes.

The U.S. Census provided incentive for the next generation of calculating machines. Compiling data from the 1880 census dragged on until 1887—just three years before the next census was to begin. With a surge in the population, Census Bureau administrators feared that the 1890 census could not be completed before the 1900 census would begin. Clearly a faster way of tabulating census results was required.

The U. S. Census Bureau held a competition to find a way to tabulate the 1890 census. Herman Hollerith won the competition with a design for an electronic punched card tabulating device. Each card contained areas to represent fields, such as "nationality." Once punched, the cards were fed into a card reader that used an array of metal rods to electronically read the data from the cards and tabulate the results. The **Hollerith Tabulating Machine** was successful. The 1890 census was tallied in six months, and only two additional years were required to complete all statistical calculations.

To alleviate inefficiencies in the software development process, computer manufacturers such as IBM developed operating systems that provided standardized routines for input, output, memory management, storage, and other resource management activities. Application programmers no longer were required to write resource management routines. These operating systems allowed programmers to write application software that "called" the operating system's standard routines.

Early proprietary operating systems were designed to work only on a particular computer. Each of these operating systems had a unique set of commands to call its routines. Early operating systems were a step in the right direction, but unfortunately, learning to use each one was like learning a new and unique programming language. It was not until the next generation of computers, however, that portable operating systems, such as CP/M and UNIX, provided programmers with similar operating system commands across hardware platforms.

In addition to operating systems, second-generation computers also ran programming language compilers that allowed programmers to write instructions using English-like commands, rather than the binary numbers of machine language. High-level languages, such as COBOL (Common Business-Oriented Language) and FORTRAN (Formula Translator), were available for use on second-generation computers and remain in use today. The availability of high-level computer programming languages made it possible for third parties to develop software, and that capability was instrumental in the birth of the software industry.

FIGURE 8-7
Jack Kilby's original integrated circuit

What are the characteristics of third-generation computers? Third-generation computers became possible in 1958, when Jack Kilby at Texas Instruments and Robert Noyce at Fairchild Semiconductor independently developed integrated circuits (Figure 8-7). Integrated circuit technology made it possible to pack the equivalent of thousands of vacuum tubes or transistors onto a single miniature chip, greatly reducing the physical size, weight, and power requirements for devices such as computers.

Two of the first computers to incorporate integrated circuits were the **RCA Spectra 70** and the wildly successful **IBM 360**. The first orders for these computers were filled in 1965—a date regarded by many historians as the advent of third-generation computers.

In 1965, Digital Equipment Corp. (DEC) introduced the **DEC PDP-8**, the first commercially successful minicomputer. As explained in Chapter 1, minicomputers were designed to be smaller and less powerful than mainframe computers, while maintaining the capability to simultaneously run multiple programs for multiple users. Thousands of manufacturing plants, small businesses, and scientific laboratories were attracted to the speed, small size, and reasonable cost of the PDP-8. DEC introduced a succession of minicomputers that stole a share of the mainframe market. Eventually IBM and other mainframe makers introduced their own minicomputers, but the "star" for minicomputers faded rapidly. Digital Equipment Corporation was purchased by Compaq in 1998. By 2000, the **IBM AS/400** (renamed the iSeries 400) was one of the few remaining devices that could be classified as a minicomputer. Today, demand for minicomputers is satisfied by high-end personal computers and servers, and the term "minicomputer" has generally fallen into disuse.

How did microprocessor technology affect the computer industry? The technology for **fourth-generation computers** appeared in 1971, when Ted Hoff developed the first general-purpose microprocessor. Called the Intel 4004, this microprocessor dramatically changed the computer industry, resulting in fourth-generation microprocessor-based computer systems that were faster, smaller, and even less expensive than third-generation computers.

FIGURE 8-8

The Intel 4004 microprocessor was small—only 1/8" by 1/16" compared to today's Pentium microprocessors. The 4004's 2,300 transistors provided much less processing power than the Pentium III with its 9.5 million transistors, or the Pentium 4 with 42 million transistors.

Microprocessor manufacturers soon flourished. Early industry leaders included Intel, Zilog, Motorola, and Texas Instruments. Intel's 4004 microprocessor (Figure 8-8) was smaller than a corn flake, but matched the computing power of ENIAC. The 4004 packed the equivalent of 2,300 transistors or vacuum tubes on a single chip, and was able to perform 60,000 instructions per second. The 4004 was followed by the 8008, the first commercial 8-bit microprocessor.

In 1974, Motorola released the 6800 8-bit microprocessor. A few months later, ex-Motorola engineers working at MOS Technologies created the 6502, an 8-bit microprocessor that was used in the Apple II and Commodore personal computer systems.

In 1976, Zilog introduced the Z80 microprocessor, an enhanced 8080 microprocessor that was used in many early computer systems. In the same year, Intel released the 8085, a further enhancement of the 8080.

Both Intel and Motorola continued development of advanced microprocessors. The Intel line, used in most Windows-compatible computers, included the 8086, 8088, 80286, 80386, 80486, Pentium, and Itanium microprocessors. The Motorola line of microprocessors grew to include the 68000 series processors used in Apple Macintosh computers, plus the PowerPC processors developed in the early 1990s, and used in current Macintosh computer systems.

Today, microprocessors are key components of computers—ranging from PDAs to supercomputers. Intel reigns as the world's leading microprocessor manufacturer, though microprocessors are also produced by companies such as Hitachi, Texas Instruments, Sun Microsystems, AMD, Toshiba, and Motorola.

PERSONAL COMPUTERS

Who invented the personal computer? In the early 1970s, many hobbyists used microprocessors to create their own computer systems. One such system was the **Mark-8** developed by Jonathan A. Titus, who was featured in the July 1974 issue of Radio-Electronics. These early personal computers were not commercially produced or widely available, but they are often considered forerunners of today's personal computer.

In 1975, Ed Roberts and the MITS (Micro Instrument and Telemetry Systems) company announced the **MITS Altair**, which many historians believe to be the first commercial microcomputer. The Altair was based on the Intel 8080 processor and sold as a kit for $395, or fully assembled for $650—about one-fourth the price of a 1975 Volkswagen Beetle. The Altair was a computer for the hobbyist. The kit came unassembled in a box containing a processor and 256 bytes of memory—not 256 K, just 256 bytes. It had no keyboard, no monitor, and no permanent storage device. Programming the Altair computer meant flipping individual switches on the front of the system unit. Output consisted of flashing lights, and the only programming language available was 8080 machine language. Although it was typically sold as a kit, required assembly, and was too limited to perform significant computational tasks, the Altair, shown in Figure 8-9, was snapped up by hobbyists.

FIGURE 8-9

The Altair computer made the cover of Popular Electronics in January 1975.

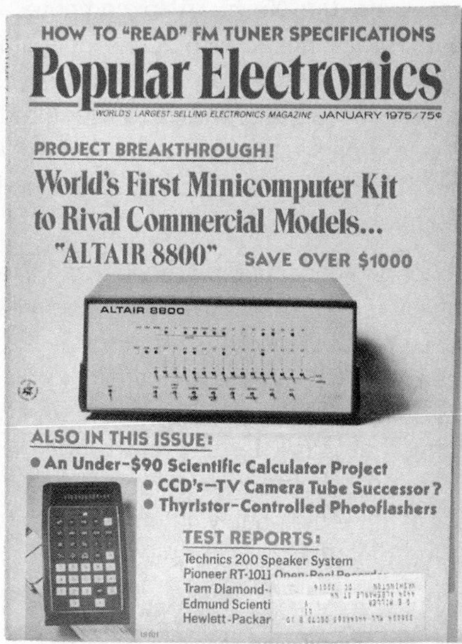

In 1977, Steve Jobs and Steve Wozniak founded Apple Computer Corporation and released the **Apple I**, a kit containing a motherboard with 4 K of RAM that sold for $666.66. Other companies, such as Commodore, Atari, and Radio Shack, also pursued the hobbyist market with preassembled computers.

How did personal computers become so successful? In 1978, Apple introduced the **Apple II** computer, which featured color graphics, expansion slots, a disk drive, a 1.07 MHz 6502 processor, and 16 KB of RAM for $1,195. The Apple II was a very successful computer. One of the main reasons behind its success was a commercial software program called **VisiCalc**—the first electronic spreadsheet. This program landed computers on the radar screen of business users, and clearly marked a turning point where personal computers appealed to an audience beyond hobbyists.

In 1981, IBM began marketing what it called a "personal computer" or "PC," based on the 8088 processor. When the PC version of VisiCalc became available, the IBM PC quickly became the top-selling personal computer, far surpassing IBM's expectations.

The $3,000 **IBM PC**, shown in Figure 8-10, shipped with a 4.77 MHz Intel 8088 processor, 16 KB of RAM, and single-sided 160 KB floppy disk drives. The IBM PC was soon followed by the **IBM PC XT**, which featured RAM upgradable to 640 KB, and a 10 megabyte hard disk drive.

FIGURE 8-10

The IBM PC, launched in 1981, evolved into today's popular Windows-based PCs.

IBM PCs were constructed with off-the-shelf parts that could be easily obtained from many electronics wholesalers. Within months, dozens of companies used these parts to produce "clones" of IBM-compatible computers that could run the same software and use the same expansion cards as the IBM PC and XT. These companies were also able to obtain essentially the same operating system used by IBM. The IBM PC used an operating system called PC-DOS that was created by a young programmer named Bill Gates, founder of a fledgling new software company called Microsoft. Microsoft marketed a similar operating system, called MS-DOS, to PC clone makers. Many of the companies that produced IBM clones failed, but some, such as recently merged Compaq and Hewlett-Packard, became major forces in the personal computer industry.

If you're interested in photos of old computers, check out the links at the Computer Museum InfoWeb.

click

Although hobbyists and the business community had embraced computers, these machines were still considered difficult for the average person to use. That perception began to change in 1983, when Apple introduced a product called the **Apple Lisa**. A key feature of the Lisa was its graphical user interface—an idea borrowed from the **Xerox Alto** computer. At $10,000, the Lisa proved too expensive for most consumers. Apple stuck to its commitment to graphical user interfaces, however, and in 1984, released the first **Apple Macintosh**. The $2,495 Macintosh featured a graphical user interface that made programs easier to use than those on the command-line-based IBM PC. The Macintosh became the computer of choice for graphical applications such as desktop publishing.

By the late 1980s, the computer industry had begun to consolidate around two primary platforms—the MS-DOS based IBM-compatible platform and the Apple Macintosh. Although dozens of companies produced IBM-compatible systems that ran the same software and used the same hardware as the IBM PC, Apple attempted to keep its system proprietary. As more IBM-compatible computers were sold, the market for IBM-compatible hardware and software continued to grow. By the mid-1990s, IBM-compatible computer systems accounted for over 90 percent of all personal computer sales. The Apple Macintosh accounted for most of the remainder, with other proprietary platforms accounting for a very small percentage of new computer sales.

Even as computer sales soared, and graphical user interfaces, such as Windows 3.1, made computers easier to use, many people simply could not think of any reason to own one. They preferred to write short notes on paper, rather than learn how to use a word processor. It seemed easier to punch numbers into a handheld calculator than tackle the complexities of electronic spreadsheets. Why buy a computer if it didn't offer some really enticing perks? That attitude began to change in the late 1980s when the Internet opened to public use. In a flurry of activity, graphical browsers appeared, ISPs provided inexpensive connections, e-mail began to fly, and e-commerce sites opened their doors. Personal computers had finally achieved mass popularity.

QUICKCheck Section A

1. Manual calculators, such as the abacus and slide rule, require the operator to apply a(n) ________ to perform calculations.

2. Charles Babbage designed a general-purpose calculating device, called the ________ Engine, that embodied many of the concepts that define the modern computer.

3. Herman Hollerith's Tabulating Machine Company later changed its name to ________ Business Machines, which eventually became the world's leading computer company.

4. Computers designed by Atanasoff, Zuse, and Aiken are usually considered to be computer ________ because they were experimental models.

5. The first generation of computers can be characterized by its use of ________ tubes to store individual bits of data, whereas second-generation computers used ________.

6. The key technology that characterizes fourth-generation computers is the ________.

check answers

Section B

THE COMPUTER AND IT INDUSTRIES

The industries that supply computer goods and services are in a continual state of change as new products appear and old products are discontinued; as corporations form, merge, and die; as corporate leadership shifts; as consumers' buying habits evolve; and as prices steadily decrease.

Before you venture out to buy computers, peripheral devices, or software; before you commit yourself to a computer career; or before you buy stock in computer companies, you should arm yourself with some basic knowledge about the computer and information technology industries. In this section of the chapter, you'll learn about the scope and economics of these dynamic industries.

INDUSTRY OVERVIEW

Is there a difference between the computer industry and the information technology industry? The term "computer industry" is used in a variety of ways. Narrowly defined, the **computer industry** encompasses those companies that manufacture handheld computers, personal computers, high-end workstations, servers, mainframes, and supercomputers. It is also used more broadly, however, to include software publishers and peripheral device manufacturers.

A broader term, **information technology industry** (or IT industry), is typically used to refer to the companies that develop, produce, sell, or support computers, software, and computer-related products. It includes some of the companies that you might think of immediately, such as IBM, Microsoft, Apple, and Intel. It also includes hundreds of parts manufacturers, communications service vendors, and other companies that might not be directly visible to consumers.

The terms "computer industry" and "IT industry" are sometimes used interchangeably in news reports and publications, leaving the reader to discern whether or not the subject is limited to computer manufacturers and distributors. In this textbook, we use the term "computer industry" in its more limited sense, and use "IT industry" when referring to the broader group of companies that provide computer, software, and telecommunications equipment and services.

Is every company that uses computers part of the IT industry? No. A bank uses computers, but it is classified as part of the banking industry. A clothing store might use computers to track inventory, but it is classified as part of the apparel industry. Such businesses make use of information technology, but they are definitely not part of the computer industry, and are not typically considered part of the IT industry either.

What kinds of companies are included in the IT industry? Companies in the IT industry can be separated into several broad categories, sometimes referred to as "sectors" or "segments," including equipment manufacturers, chipmakers, software publishers, service companies, and retailers.

Equipment manufacturers design and manufacture computer hardware and communications products, such as personal computers, mainframe computers, PDAs, mice, monitors, storage devices, routers, scanners, and printers. Examples of hardware companies are computer manufacturers IBM and Hewlett-Packard. Network hardware companies, such as Cisco and Cabletron, are also examples of hardware companies.

Chipmakers design and manufacture computer chips and circuit boards including microprocessors, RAM, motherboards, sound cards, and graphics cards. Intel, AMD, and Texas Instruments are examples of chipmakers.

Software publishers create computer software including applications, operating systems, and programming languages. Examples of software companies are Microsoft, Adobe Systems, and Computer Associates.

Service companies provide computer-related services including business consulting, Web site design, Web hosting, Internet connections, computer equipment repair, network security, and product support. Classic examples of service companies include AOL/TimeWarner and the computer consulting giant, EDS (Electronic Data Systems).

Retailers (sometimes called "resellers") include companies that sell products through retail stores, direct sales representatives, mail-order catalogs, and Web sites. Well-known resellers include CompUSA, which operates retail stores, and mail-order retailers, PC Connection and MicroWarehouse.

The computer industry makes a tremendous contribution to global financial resources. For links to information on company stock values, venture over to the NASDAQ InfoWeb.

click

Although some companies fit neatly into one of the above categories, other companies operate in two or more areas. For example, Dell manufactures hardware, but also resells that hardware directly to individuals and businesses. Sun Microsystems is known for its Sun servers and workstations, but also develops and sells software such as operating systems and the Java programming language. IBM designs and manufactures computer chips and circuit boards, as well as producing personal computers, servers, and mainframes.

The IT industry also encompasses large conglomerates with one or more divisions devoted to computer hardware, software, or services. As an example, Japanese-owned Hitachi produces a wide variety of electronic devices, but it is also one of the world's largest chipmakers.

What about "dot coms"? The 1990s spawned a group of Internet-based companies that came to be called "dot coms." The "dot com" moniker came from the companies' domain names, which inevitably ended with ".com"; many of the companies even incorporated ".com" into their official company names.

Amazon.com was one of the first Internet-based companies. Founded in 1995, the company mission—stated on its Company Information Web page—is to "use the Internet to transform book buying into the fastest, easiest, and most enjoyable shopping experience possible." The "transformation" meant buying books online, without walking into a "brick and mortar" store.

Unless a "dot com" sells computers, peripherals, or software online, it is probably not considered part of the computer industry, but experts disagree on whether "dot coms" rightfully belong to the IT industry. These Internet-based companies certainly make extensive use of computers—they could not exist if it weren't for computers and the Internet. As a result, some analysts group them under the IT industry umbrella. Other analysts classify "dot coms" by their core businesses. For example, "dot coms" that sell clothing would be in the apparel industry, music vendors would be in the entertainment industry, and an online stock broker would be in the financial industry.

Is the IT industry located in Silicon Valley? IT industry heavyweights such as Cisco, Intel, Sun Microsystems, Oracle, Hewlett-Packard, Palm, Handspring, Apple, AMD, 3Com, and Silicon Graphics all have headquarters in California's Silicon Valley (see Figure 8-11).

FIGURE 8-11

"Silicon Valley" is home to many companies in the IT industry.

Although Silicon Valley has a reputation as the home of the IT industry, many of the top IT players are located elsewhere. Microsoft is located near Seattle. Texas is also home to many IT companies—EDS is headquartered in Plano, and Dell is just outside Austin. North Carolina's Research Triangle (Raleigh-Durham-Chapel Hill) is the home base for IBM's largest hardware lab, and several small research startups. Colorado's Front Range (the Boulder-Denver-Longmont area) hosts tape manufacturer Exabyte and desktop publishing software vendor Quark, Inc. Software publisher Computer Associates is based in New York. Unisys, a high-end server manufacturer, has its headquarters near Philadelphia.

Many of the largest companies in the IT industry have branch offices all over the world. Manufacturing facilities are also found worldwide, with Asia and Mexico particularly popular because of the availability of skilled labor for relatively low wages. For similar reasons, India is an attractive source for programmers. Companies such as Microsoft and Oracle make extensive use of programmers based in India, who telecommute, when necessary, via the Internet.

The IT Sources InfoWeb contains a comprehensive list of links to IT industry information resources.

click

Despite the increasing globalization of the IT industry, it is still dominated by the U.S. Sixty-eight percent of IT workers are in the U.S., even though 62 percent of industry sales are to non-U.S. companies. Approximately 88 percent of all research and development jobs, and 70 percent of computer manufacturing jobs, are located in the U.S.

Where can I find information about the IT industry? Whether you are planning to purchase a computer, embark on a computing career, or invest in a computer company, you can dig up lots of information on IT and computer companies from a wide variety of computer and business publications. The type of computer publication you need depends on the kind of information you want. The IT Sources InfoWeb provides you with an up-to-date guide to publications and other IT industry resources.

ECONOMIC FACTORS

How has the IT industry affected the economy? The IT industry has been described as "the most dynamic, most prosperous, most economically beneficial industry the world has ever known." That statement might be a bit of an exaggeration, but the IT industry unquestionably has fueled the economies of many countries. By dollar value, the biggest computer hardware producing countries are the U.S., Japan, Taiwan, Singapore, and China.

Looking at individual countries, economists gauge the effect of an industry by its contribution to the gross domestic product (GDP), or gross national product (GNP), as it was referred to before 1991. **GDP** is defined as the total value of a nation's goods and services produced within a specific time period. In the U.S., for example, the IT industry accounted for about 5 percent of the growth in the 1985 GDP. By 1990, with the increasing popularity of personal computers, IT accounted for over 6 percent of the GDP growth. As shown in Figure 8-12, the Internet added more fuel to the fire, and by 2000, IT's total contribution to GDP growth was about 8.6 percent. In contrast, the U.S. automobile industry's contribution to the GDP was only 4 percent in the same year.

FIGURE 8-12 IT industry growth

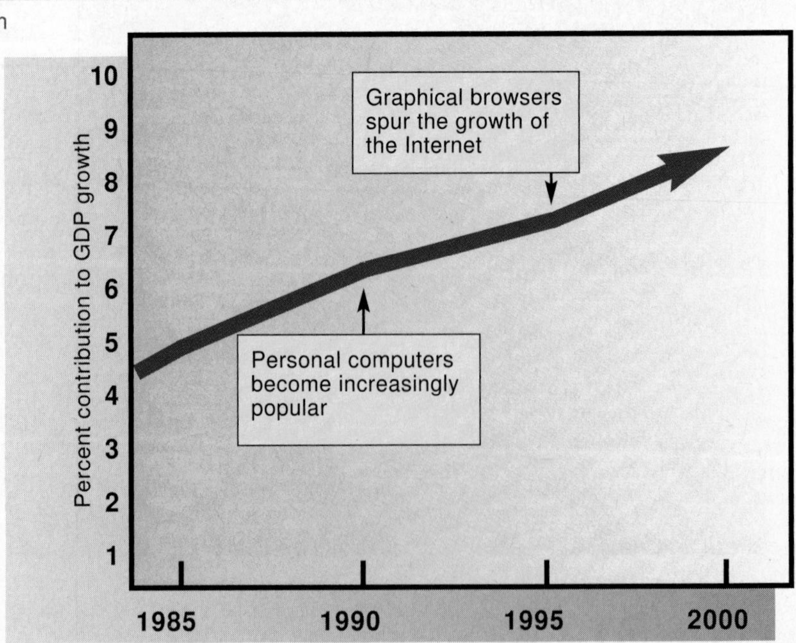

GDP is only part of the economic story. According to the U.S. Department of Commerce, the IT industry accounted for one-third of the real economic growth, and almost half of all productivity growth between 1995 and 1999. As another gauge of the increased affect of IT, nearly 45 percent of all business equipment investments are in the IT sector. That number in itself might not be surprising, but it reflects an increase from a mere 3 percent in the 1960s.

The effect of the IT industry is not limited to the U.S. The world IT market (hardware, software, and computer services) grew at an annual rate of 10 percent between 1987 and 1995—nearly twice the rate of the world GDP. By 1998, worldwide revenues of IT producers exceeded a whopping US$1 trillion.

In 2000, IT industry growth in the U.S. slowed as a result of a shakeout in the "dot com" sector. A high rate of "dot com" business failures meant a slowdown in equipment orders, Web site hosting contracts, and IT sector job openings. Nonetheless, strength in worldwide markets for IT equipment and services continues to buoy up the industry, and most analysts forecast steady, though not meteoric, future growth.

What accounts for the success of the IT industry? As with many situations involving the economy, the factors that account for the success of the IT industry cannot be pinpointed with certainty. It is likely, however, that population growth and business globalization are two important factors that contribute to huge investments in information technology.

The worldwide population more than doubled over the past 50 years, and a recent study predicts that the population will peak at 9 billion by the year 2070. Keeping track of the information relating to all these people—births, deaths, marriages, property ownership, taxes, purchases, banking records, and licenses—certainly seems impossible without the use of computers. Governments and private businesses have discovered that they can become much more efficient with a liberal application of computers and other information technologies.

FIGURE 8-13

The manual record-keeping systems of the past have gradually been replaced by computerized archives.

As a business globalizes, it encounters new competitors with technological advantages. Intense global competitive pressure keeps companies looking for ways to cut costs and raise productivity. Keeping up with the Joneses—or Muramotos, Cordobas, Faisals, and Orlovs—becomes a priority for survival. If your business competitor offers automated, online order tracking, for example, you might lose customers unless you can offer the same service. Bottom line: if your business competitors turn to technology, so must you. In our highly populated global economy, information technology products provide an effective alternative to manual record-keeping systems (Figure 8-13).

PRODUCT DEVELOPMENT

What's the reason for the amazing number of new computer products that appear each year? Automobile manufacturers introduce new models every year, which incorporate new features and give customers an incentive to buy. IT manufacturers and publishers introduce new products for the same reasons as their counterparts in the automotive industry. New products, such as a computer with a faster microprocessor, a DVD player, or an upgrade to Windows, are designed to attract customers and generate sales.

In contrast to the automotive industry, however, the IT industry is not on an annual cycle. As a result, the computer marketplace seems rather chaotic because new product announcements, availability dates, and ship dates all occur at irregular intervals.

The equipment manufacturing segment of the IT industry is relatively young, and technology, rather than marketing, is the major force that drives product development. New technologies spur a flurry of development activity, and generate new products designed to increase sales. For example, in 1997, a breakthrough in modem technology increased the maximum upstream capacity from 33.6 Kbps to 56 Kbps. Modem sales soared because most computer owners wanted to take advantage of this new breakthrough. Technological breakthroughs do not necessarily adhere to a schedule, however. Companies cannot always predict when a new technology will appear, or how it might be incorporated into new products. As a result, the life cycle of computer hardware and some computer products is short, whereas other products have a long life cycle.

What are the stages in the life cycle of a typical hardware product? In the computer industry, the life cycle of a new computer model typically includes five stages: product development, product announcement, introduction, maintenance, and retirement, as shown in Figure 8-14.

FIGURE 8-14 Five-stage life cycle of a computer product

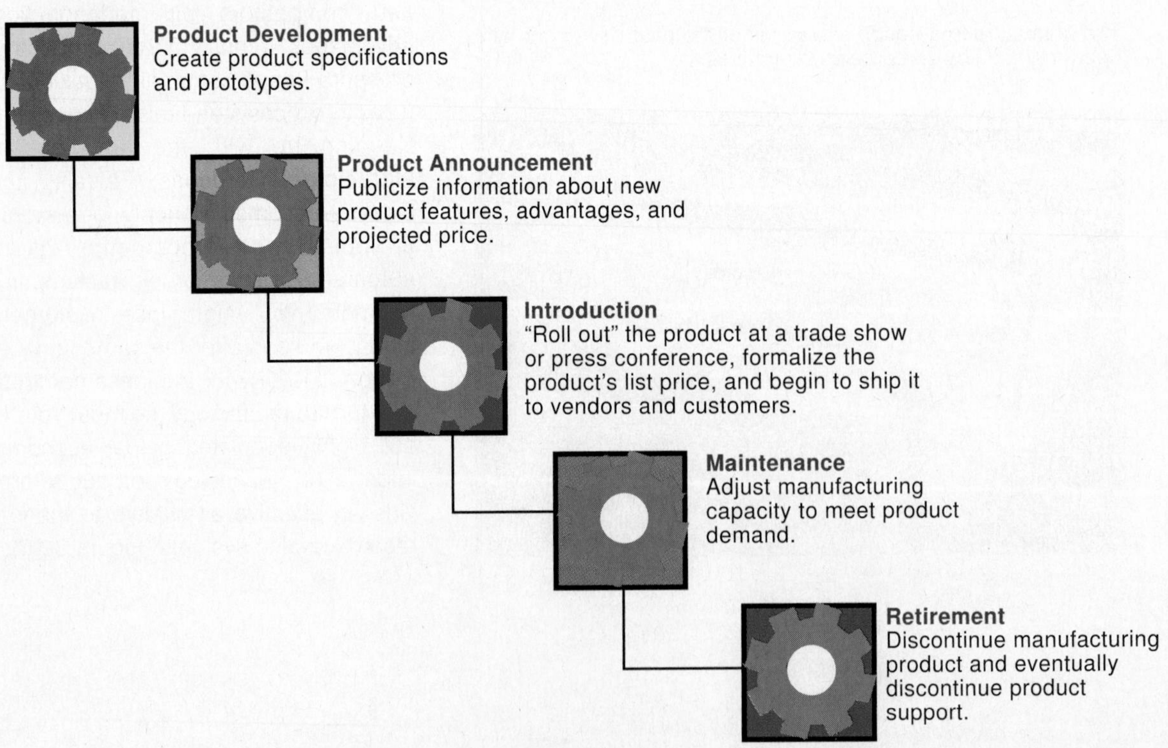

Product Development
Create product specifications and prototypes.
Product Announcement
Publicize information about new product features, advantages, and projected price.
Introduction
"Roll out" the product at a trade show or press conference, formalize the product's list price, and begin to ship it to vendors and customers.
Maintenance
Adjust manufacturing capacity to meet product demand.
Retirement
Discontinue manufacturing product and eventually discontinue product support.

Product development. Product development often takes place "under wraps." Developers use fanciful code names, such as Merced and Camelot, to refer to their products. Inevitably, news of these products leaks out and causes much speculation among industry analysts.

Product announcement. Sometime during the development process, a company makes a product announcement to declare its intention to introduce a new product. Products are often announced at trade shows and press conferences. As a consumer, you should be wary of making purchase or investment decisions based on product announcements. A product announcement can precede the actual launch of the product by several years. Some products, referred to as **vaporware**, are announced, but never produced.

Introduction. When a new product becomes available, it is usually added to the vendor's product line and featured prominently in advertisements. Initial supplies of the product generally remain low while manufacturing capacity increases to meet demand. Consumers who want a scarce product must pay a relatively high **list price**—sometimes called the "suggested list price" or "manufacturer's suggested retail price" (MSRP)—set by the manufacturer.

Maintenance. As supply and demand for a product reach an equilibrium, the price of the product decreases slightly. Usually the price decrease is due to discounting by retailers rather than a change to the manufacturer's list price. This discounted price is usually referred to as the **street price**. Over time, the manufacturer also reduces the list prices of products with older technology to keep them attractive to buyers.

Retirement. Gradually, a company's oldest products are discontinued as demand for them declines. As you can see from the ad in Figure 8-15, the least expensive products tend to have slower processors, less RAM, and lower-capacity hard disk drives. If your budget is not severely limited, a computer in the middle of a vendor's product line usually gives you the most computing power per dollar.

FIGURE 8-15 A typical manufacturer's product line

MTI

Edge 2500 Notebook

- 1.33 GHz Intel Celeron
- 14.1" XGA TFT Display
- 128 MB SDRAM
- 40 GB Ultra ATA HD
- 24X CD-RW Drive
- 32 MB Video RAM
- 56K Fax Modem

$1099

MTI

Edge 4200 Notebook

- 1.7 GHz Intel Pentium 4
- 15" XGA TFT Display
- 256 MB SDRAM
- 40 GB Ultra ATA HD
- 40XCD-RW Drive
- 32 MB Video RAM
- 56K Fax Modem

$1699

MTI

Edge 8200 Notebook

- 2.4 GHz Intel Pentium 4
- 15" UXGA TFT Display
- 512 MB SDRAM
- 60 GB Ultra ATA HD
- 40X CD-RW/DVD Drive
- 64 MB Video RAM
- 56K Fax Modem

$2499

Is the life cycle of a software product similar to that of a hardware product? Software, like hardware, begins with an idea that is shaped by a design team and marketing experts. A team of programmers then works to produce executable programs and support modules for the new software product.

Most software products undergo extensive testing before they are released. The first phase of testing, called an **alpha test**, is carried out by the software publisher's in-house testing team. Errors, or "bugs," found during the alpha test phase are fixed, and then the software enters a second testing phase called a **beta test**. Typically, a beta test is conducted by a team of off-site testers, such as a professional testing company. Sometimes a software publisher releases a "beta version" of the software to selected individuals and companies in the general public in order to expose the software to the widest possible variety of computers and operating environments. Although it can be exciting to test a yet-to-be-released software package, beta versions are typically "buggy" and can cause unexpected glitches in your computer. Beta testing requires a high tolerance for frustration.

A newly published software package can be an entirely new product, a new version (also called a "release") with significant enhancements, or a revision designed to add minor enhancements and eliminate bugs found in the current version.

When a new software product first becomes available, the publisher often offers a special introductory price that's designed to entice customers. For example, several software products that now carry a list price of $495 were introduced at a special price of $99. Even after the introductory price expires, most vendors offer sizable discounts. Expect software with a list price of $495 to be offered for a street price of about $299.

Unlike computer hardware products, older versions of software typically do not remain in the vendor's product line. Soon after a new version of a software product is released, the software publisher usually stops selling earlier versions. When a publisher offers a new version of the software that you are using, it is a good idea to upgrade, but you can wait for several months until the initial rush for technical support on the new product subsides. If you don't upgrade, you might find that the software publisher offers minimal technical support for older versions of the program. Also, if you let several versions go by without upgrading, you might lose your eligibility for special upgrade pricing.

FIGURE 8-16 Market share

Worldwide Personal Computer Vendors 2002

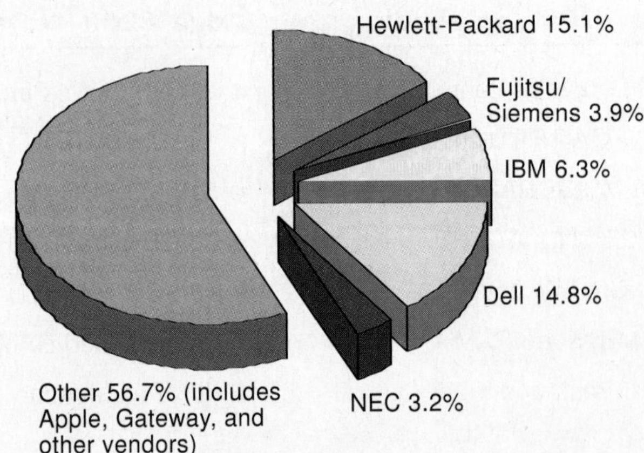

MARKET SHARE

How do computer companies stack up against each other? Industry analysts often use market share as a gauge of a company's success. **Market share** refers to a company's share, or percentage, of the total market "pie." For example, Microsoft's share of the total personal computer operating system market is about 80 percent. The remaining 20 percent share is distributed among Apple and several Linux vendors.

Among hardware vendors, Hewlett-Packard, which absorbed Compaq in 2002, leads the pack. Figure 8-16 shows the market shares of worldwide personal computer vendors in 2002.

Market share graphs for personal computer manufacturers, software publishers, operating system developers, Internet Service Providers, and handheld computer manufacturers provide a roadmap to the changing fortunes of companies in the computer industry. Competition is fierce in all segments of the industry, and market share is one indicator of a company's ability to "steal" sales from its rivals. The top companies are constantly challenged, not only by their peers, but by startup companies in lower tiers of the industry.

What's the relevance of market tiers? Since 1981, hundreds of companies have produced personal computers. Industry analysts have classified these companies into **market tiers**, or categories. Although analysts do not agree on which companies belong in each tier, the concept of tiers helps explain price differences and changing market shares.

The top (first) tier in any segment of the computer industry consists of large companies that have been in the computer business for many years, and have an identifiable share—usually more than 2 percent—of total computer sales. IBM and Hewlett-Packard are two venerable members of the top tier of the computer industry. The second tier includes newer companies with sales volume just below the cutoff level for identifiable market share, and somewhat fewer financial resources than companies in the first tier. Most analysts place companies such as Gateway in this tier. The third tier consists of smaller startup companies that sell primarily through mail order.

Computer prices vary by tier. Computers from top-tier vendors generally are more expensive than computers offered by second-tier or third-tier vendors. First-tier companies often have higher overhead costs, management is often paid higher salaries, and substantial financial resources are devoted to research and development. These companies are responsible for many of the innovations that make computers faster, more powerful, and more convenient. Also, many consumers believe that computers sold by first-tier companies offer better quality and are a safer purchasing decision—a stable first-tier company is likely to provide continuing support, honor warranties, and maintain an inventory of replacement parts.

Computers from second-tier companies are generally less expensive than those from first-tier firms, although the quality can be just as good. Most PCs are constructed from off-the-shelf circuit boards, cables, cases, and chips. Consequently, the components in the computers sold by second-tier companies are often the same as those in computers sold by first-tier firms. Second-tier companies typically maintain low prices by minimizing operating costs. These companies have limited research and development budgets. Also, they try to maintain a relatively small workforce by contracting with other companies to provide repair and warranty work.

Computers from third-tier companies often appear to be much less expensive than those in other tiers. Sometimes this difference reflects the low overhead costs of a small company, but other times it reflects poor-quality components. A consumer who is knowledgeable about the market and has technical expertise can often get a bargain on a good-quality computer from a third-tier company. But some consumers think it is risky to purchase computers from third-tier companies. Third-tier companies are smaller and perhaps more likely to go out of business, leaving their customers without technical support.

MARKETING CHANNELS

Why are computer equipment and software sold through so many outlets? Hardware manufacturers and software publishers try to reach consumers by making their products available through a variety of sources. Computer hardware and software are sold through marketing outlets called **marketing channels**. These channels, shown in Figure 8-17, include computer retail stores, mail-order/Internet outlets, value-added resellers, and manufacturer direct.

FIGURE 8-17

Computer hardware and software are sold through several marketing channels.

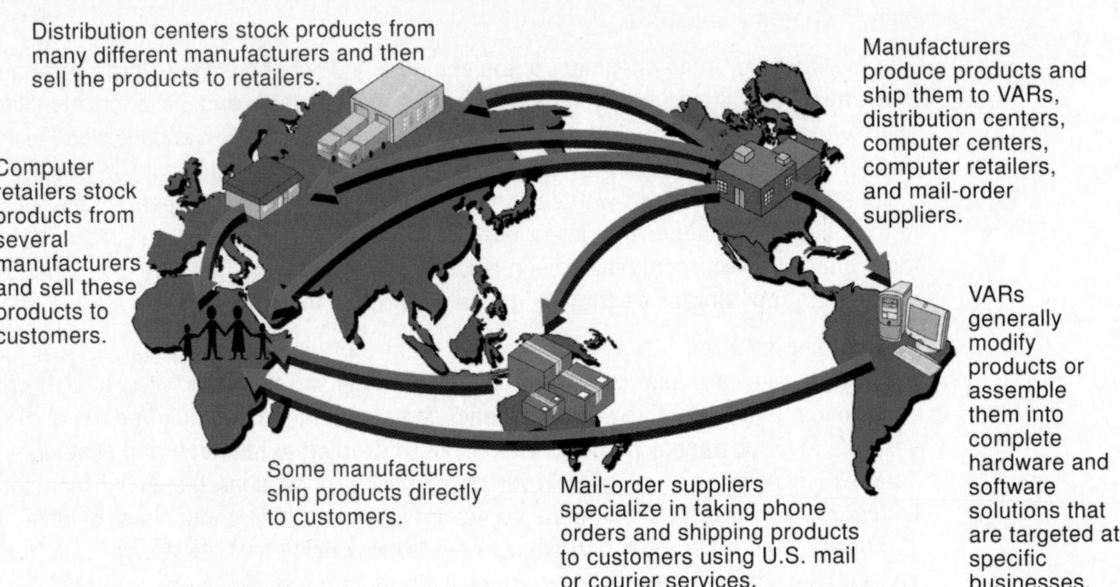

Distribution centers stock products from many different manufacturers and then sell the products to retailers.
Manufacturers produce products and ship them to VARs, distribution centers, computer centers, computer retailers, and mail-order suppliers.
Computer retailers stock products from several manufacturers and sell these products to customers.
VARs generally modify products or assemble them into complete hardware and software solutions that are targeted at specific businesses.
Some manufacturers ship products directly to customers.
Mail-order suppliers specialize in taking phone orders and shipping products to customers using U.S. mail or courier services.

Isn't a computer retail store the best channel for hardware and software products? A **computer retail store** purchases computer products from a variety of manufacturers, and then sells those products to consumers. Computer retail stores are either small local shops or nationwide chains that specialize in the sale of microcomputer software and hardware. Computer retail store employees are often knowledgeable about a variety of computer products, and can help you select a hardware or software product to fit your needs. Many computer retail stores also offer classes and training sessions, answer questions, provide technical support, and repair hardware products.

A computer retail store is often the best shopping option for buyers who are likely to need assistance after their purchases, such as beginning computer users, or those with plans for complex computer networks. Retail stores can be a fairly expensive channel for hardware and software, however. Their prices reflect the cost of purchasing merchandise from a distributor, maintaining a retail storefront, and hiring a technically qualified staff.

From the perspective of hardware manufacturers and software publishers, computer retail stores purchase products in bulk quantities, which provides economies of scale in terms of order processing and shipping. In addition, once products are shipped to a retail store, they are removed from the manufacturer's inventory. Selling slow-moving products then becomes the responsibility of the retail store, not the manufacturer. On the downside, a retail store may also carry competitors' products, which can reduce the sales of a particular manufacturer's product.

How does the mail-order channel compare to retail? Mail order is a special instance of retailing in which a vendor takes orders by telephone or from an Internet site, then ships the product directly to consumers. Mail-order suppliers generally offer low prices, but might provide only limited service and support. A mail-order supplier is often the best source of products for buyers who are unlikely to need support, or who can troubleshoot problems by calling a Help desk. Experienced computer users who can install components, set up software, and do their own troubleshooting are often happy with mail-order suppliers. Inexperienced computer users might not be satisfied with the assistance they receive from some of these suppliers. From a manufacturer's or software publisher's perspective, mail-order retailers are essentially the same as brick and mortar retail stores—mail-order vendors typically carry competing products, but order in bulk quantities, and are responsible for managing their own inventories.

Don't some manufacturers and publishers sell direct? Manufacturer direct refers to hardware manufacturers that sell their products directly to consumers without a "middleman," such as a retail store. IBM has a long tradition of direct sales, and that model has been emulated by several hardware manufacturers and some software publishers. A company's sales force usually targets large corporate or educational customers where large-volume sales can cover the sales representative's costs and commissions.

For computer hardware, Dell Computers pioneered Web-based direct sales to individual customers. Its innovative Web site allows customers to select from a variety of standard models, or configure their own custom builds. (See Figure 8-18.) A "just-in-time" inventory model allows Dell to build each customer's computer as it is ordered, which eliminates costly inventories of computers that quickly become outdated. The obvious advantage of direct sales is that by cutting out the retailer, a manufacturer can make more profit on each unit sold. The disadvantage is that the manufacturer must provide customers with technical support—a potentially costly service that requires large teams of technical support personnel.

FIGURE 8-18

At Dell's Web site, customers can order a custom-built computer by simply clicking to add various hardware options.

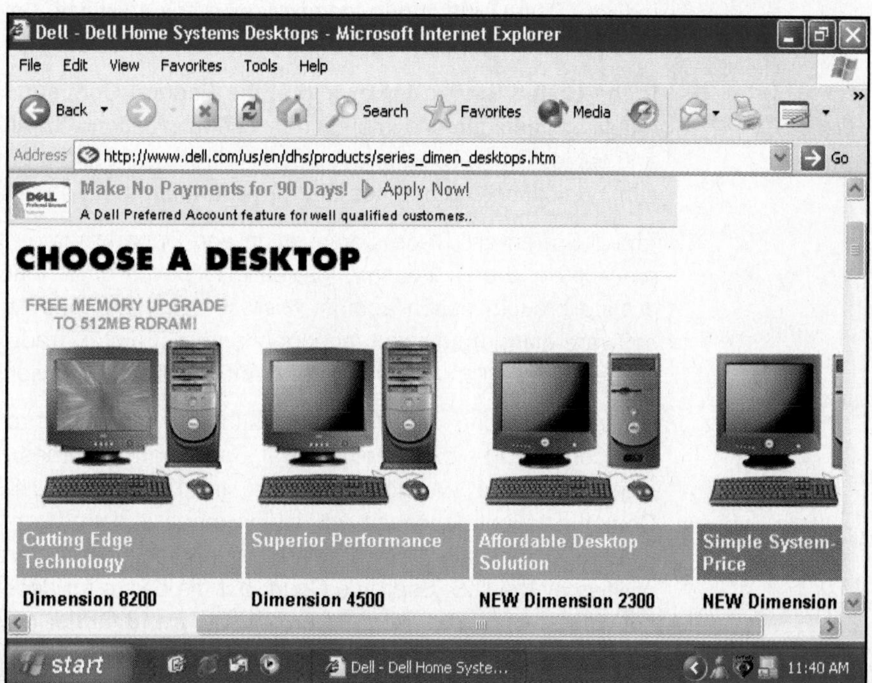

click to start

What's a VAR? VAR stands for value-added reseller. A value-added reseller combines commercially available products with specialty hardware or software to create a computer system designed to meet the needs of a specific industry. Although VARs charge for their expertise, they are often the only source for specialized computer systems. For example, if you own a video rental store and want to automate the rental process, the best type of vendor might be a VAR that offers a complete hardware and software package tailored to the video rental business. Otherwise, you must piece together the computer, scanner, printer, and software components yourself. VARs are often the most expensive channel for hardware and software, but their expertise can be crucial to ensure that the hardware and software work correctly in a specific environment.

Don't all those channels confuse consumers? Consumers can benefit from a variety of channels. Because the price of computer equipment and software tends to vary by channel, consumers can shop for the best price and the most appropriate level of support.

Although consumers benefit from a variety of channels, vendors within the channels often find that their sales are pirated by other channel vendors—a process referred to as **channel conflict**. In the early days of the IT industry, hardware manufacturers and software publishers awarded exclusive territories to their retail vendors. An Apple computer dealer in Spokane, for example, was assured of sales to any customers in the local area who wanted a Macintosh. Mail-order vendors, however, were also able to attract the business of Spokane customers, creating a channel conflict. To avoid such conflicts, Apple did not allow its computers to be sold through mail-order channels.

INDUSTRY REGULATION

Is the IT industry regulated in any way? Some aspects of the IT industry are regulated by government agencies, but many aspects are self regulated. Unlike the U.S. airline industry, which is regulated by the Federal Aviation Authority (FAA), most countries do not have a single government agency dedicated to regulating the IT industry. The IT industry encompasses many activities, however, and consequently, it is subject to regulation from a variety of broad-based government agencies.

In the United States, for example, the Federal Communications Commission (FCC) regulates interstate and international communications by radio, television, wire, satellite, and cable. The policies of this agency directly affect the Internet because of the many communications companies that provide telephone, satellite, and cable connections.

The U.S. Federal Trade Commission and Department of Justice police the business practices of the IT industry, just as they police other industries. The Department of Justice brought action against Microsoft in 1994, and again in 1998, accusing the software giant of unlawful monopoly and restraint of trade. In 1998, the U.S. Federal Trade Commission accused Intel of monopolistic behavior.

Many governments are enacting laws that restrict access to particular Internet activities and content. For example, several Caribbean countries recently enacted laws that regulate online casino operators. In 1996, the U.S. Congress enacted the Communications Decency Act, which made it illegal to put indecent material online where children might see it. Parts of this legislation were contested and ultimately nullified by the U.S. Supreme Court, but the desire for decency without censorship has not died among lawmakers. In an effort to avoid further government regulations, many Internet service companies are establishing their own policies for policing and monitoring their customers' online activity.

In many countries, export restrictions affect the type of technology that can be sold to foreign governments and individuals. For example, before being exported from the U.S., software and hardware products that contain certain encryption algorithms must be registered with the U.S. government. Additional government regulations that pertain to law enforcement, national security, e-commerce, and taxation can also affect the way the IT industry carries out business and engineers products.

How does the IT industry perceive government regulation? Most IT industry leaders oppose further regulation of their industry. They remain skeptical of government regulations that might limit their ability to explore new technologies and offer them to the public. To avoid further government intervention, the IT industry has taken steps toward self regulation.

Several organizations provide a forum for the IT industry to examine issues, express views, work out self-governing policies, and set standards. The Information Technology Industry Council has become one of the major trade associations for computer manufacturers, telecommunications suppliers, business equipment dealers, software publishers, and IT service providers. As part of its mission, this organization provides a powerful lobbying group, which works with lawmakers to minimize legislation that might curtail technology innovation and use.

The Software and Information Industry Association, formerly known as the Software Publishers Association, has 1,200 members. This organization focuses on protecting the intellectual property of members, and lobbying for a legal and regulatory environment that benefits the entire IT industry. Its anti-piracy program is instrumental in identifying and prosecuting software and Internet piracy cases.

Organizations such as the IEEE Standards Association help the IT industry standardize technology. Such organizations maintain standards for technologies, such as microprocessor architecture and network protocols, as well as programming languages and multimedia components.

QUICKCheck Section B

1 The IT industry's effect on the economy can be measured as a percentage of a country's ______ domestic product (GDP).

2 New ______ tend to drive product development in the IT industry, resulting in erratic introduction of new products.

3 In the computer industry, the life cycle of a new computer model typically includes five stages: product development, product announcement, introduction, maintenance, and ______.

4 Some products, referred to as ______, are announced but never produced.

5 As supply and demand for a product reach an equilibrium, its ______ price tends to decrease due to discounting by retailers.

6 The top ______ in any segment of the computer industry consists of large companies that have been in the computer business for many years, and have an identifiable share of total computer sales.

check answers

CAREERS FOR COMPUTER PROFESSIONALS

Today, it seems that just about everyone uses computers at work. Secretaries use computers for word processing; auto mechanics use computers for engine diagnostics; bartenders use computers for tracking drink orders; architects use computers to draw blueprints; teachers use computers to automate grade books; and the list goes on. In fact, it is difficult to find a job nowadays that does not make use of computers in some capacity.

But who writes the software that's used by all of these workers? Who designs their hardware, configures their networks, and troubleshoots their technical glitches? In this part of the chapter, you'll learn about a special cadre of workers within the IT industry called "computer professionals." You'll find out who they are, what they do, who employs them, and how much they're paid. Maybe you'll even get a glimpse of your own future, if you're considering a career in IT.

JOBS AND SALARIES

What is a "computer professional?" Despite the widespread deployment of computers, not everyone who uses a computer is considered a computer professional. In 1999, the U.S. Congress crafted an amendment to the Fair Labor Standards Act that essentially defines a **computer professional** as any person whose primary occupation involves the design, configuration, analysis, development, modification, testing, or security of computer hardware or software. The actual wording of the definition is provided in Figure 8-19.

FIGURE 8-19 Official U.S. definition of a computer professional

ANY EMPLOYEE WHO IS A COMPUTER SYSTEMS, NETWORK, OR DATABASE ANALYST, DESIGNER, DEVELOPER, PROGRAMMER, SOFTWARE ENGINEER, OR OTHER SIMILARLY SKILLED WORKER WHOSE PRIMARY DUTY IS:

(i) THE APPLICATION OF SYSTEMS OR NETWORK OR DATABASE ANALYSIS TECHNIQUES AND PROCEDURES, INCLUDING CONSULTING WITH USERS, TO DETERMINE HARDWARE, SOFTWARE, SYSTEMS, NETWORK, OR DATABASE SPECIFICATIONS (INCLUDING FUNCTIONAL SPECIFICATIONS);

(ii) THE DESIGN, CONFIGURATION, DEVELOPMENT, INTEGRATION, DOCUMENTATION, ANALYSIS, CREATION, TESTING, SECURING, OR MODIFICATION OF, OR PROBLEM RESOLUTION FOR, COMPUTER SYSTEMS, NETWORKS, DATABASES, OR PROGRAMS, INCLUDING PROTOTYPES, BASED ON AND RELATED TO USER, SYSTEM, NETWORK, OR DATABASE SPECIFICATIONS, INCLUDING DESIGN SPECIFICATIONS AND MACHINE OPERATING SYSTEMS;

(iii) THE MANAGEMENT OR TRAINING OF EMPLOYEES PERFORMING CERTAIN DUTIES DESCRIBED IN CLAUSE (I) OR (II);

(iv) A COMBINATION OF DUTIES DESCRIBED IN CLAUSES (I), (II), OR (III), THE PERFORMANCE OF WHICH REQUIRES THE SAME LEVEL OF SKILLS.

What kinds of jobs are typically available to computer professionals? The IT industry provides a wide range of jobs, each requiring different skill sets and personalities. Jobs exist for highly focused programming "hermits," as well as outgoing sales reps and technical support specialists. The following sketches of the most common IT jobs highlight typical job responsibilities and required skills:

Job titles and their descriptions vary from one company to another. At the IT Careers InfoWeb, you'll find links that help you decipher job titles and gather additional information about IT careers.

click

A **systems analyst** investigates the requirements of a business or organization, its employees, and its customers in order to plan and implement new or improved computer services. This job requires the ability to identify problems and research technical solutions. Good communications skills are essential for interacting with managers and other employees.

A **security specialist** analyzes a computer system's vulnerability to threats from viruses, worms, unauthorized access, and physical damage. Security specialists install and configure firewalls and antivirus software. They also work in conjunction with management and employees to develop policies and procedures to protect computer equipment and data. Computer security is punctuated by "crises" when a virus hits, or a security breach is discovered. A security specialist must have wide-ranging knowledge of computers, as well as communications protocols that can be applied for a quick resolution to any crisis that occurs.

A **computer programmer** designs, codes, and tests computer programs. In addition, programmers modify existing programs to meet new requirements or eliminate bugs. Computer programming requires concentration, and a good memory for the countless details that pertain to a programming project. Programming projects range from entertainment and games, to business and productivity applications. Programmers get satisfaction from devising efficient ways to make a computer perform specific jobs, tasks, and routines.

A **quality assurance specialist** participates in alpha and beta test cycles of software, looking for bugs or other usability problems. This job title sometimes refers to assembly line workers who examine and test chips, circuit boards, computers, and peripheral devices. An effective QA specialist has a good eye for detail and a passion for perfection.

A **database administrator** analyzes a company's data to determine the most effective way to collect and store it. Database administrators create databases, data entry forms, and reports. They also define backup procedures, provide access to authorized users, and supervise the day-to-day use of the databases.

A **network specialist/administrator** plans, installs, and maintains one or more local area networks. They also provide network accounts and access rights to approved users. They troubleshoot connectivity problems, and respond to requests from the network's users for new software. Network specialists/administrators may be responsible for maintaining the security of a network, plus they often pick up the duties of Webmaster to maintain an organization's Web site.

A **computer operator** typically works with minicomputers, mainframes, and supercomputers. Computer operators monitor computer performance, install software patches and upgrades, perform backups, and restore data as necessary.

A **computer engineer** designs and tests new hardware products, such as computer chips, circuit boards, computers, and peripheral devices.

A **technical support specialist** provides phone or online help to customers of computer companies and software publishers. These specialists also work at the help desks of businesses and organizations to troubleshoot hardware and software problems. Good interpersonal skills and patience are required for this job, and it is one of the most "social" jobs in the IT industry.

8

A **technical writer** creates documentation for large programming projects, and writes the online or printed user manuals that accompany computers, peripheral devices, and software. Some technical writers work for computer magazines where they write columns about the latest hardware products, software, and automated business solutions. Good writing and communications skills are valuable for this job, as is an ability to quickly learn how to use new computers and software.

A **computer salesperson**, or "sales rep," sells computers. Sales reps may pay personal visits to potential corporate customers, or they might staff the order desk of a mail-order computer company. Sales reps' starting salaries tend to be low, but typically are supplemented by commissions and bonuses. Effective sales reps tend to have good interpersonal skills, an ability to remember technical specifications, and an understanding of business problems and solutions.

A **Web site designer** creates, tests, posts, and modifies Web pages. A good sense of design and artistic talent are required for this job, along with an understanding of how people use graphical user interfaces. Familiarity with Web tools, such as HTML, XML, JavaScript, and ActiveX, is becoming more important for this job, as is a knowledge of computer programming and database management.

A **manufacturing technician** participates in the fabrication of computer chips, circuit boards, system units, or peripheral devices. Some of these jobs require basic screwdriver skills, whereas others require special training in microlithography.

These job titles are but a sample of those in the IT industry. Additional job titles are listed in Figure 8-20. You'll find even more at the IT Careers InfoWeb.

FIGURE 8-20 IT jobs

Account Representative
Applications Systems Analyst
Applications Programmer
Art Director - Web
Associate Editor - Web
Associate Producer -Web
Assoc. Product Manager - Web
Business Development Associate
Business Development Director
Business Development Manager
Business Systems Analyst
Client/Server Programmer
Computer Operations Manager
Computer Operations Supervisor
Computer Operator
Content Engineer - Web
Creative Director - Web
Data Architect
Data Control Clerk
Data Entry Clerk
Data Entry Supervisor
Data Security Analyst
Data Security Manager
Data Security Supervisor
Data Warehouse Specialist
Database Administrator
Database Analyst
Database Librarian
Documentation Specialist
E-commerce Manager
Electronic Data Interchange Specialist
Graphical User Interface Programmer
Hardware Engineer
Help Desk Support Technician
Information Systems Auditor
Information Technology Director
Interface Designer
Intranet Applications Manager
LAN Support Technician
Mail Server Administrator
Mainframe Programmer
Network Administrator
Network Analyst
Operating Systems Programmer
PC Maintenance Technician
Software Engineer
Software Quality Assurance
Technical Librarian
Trainer
Telecommunications Analyst
Webmaster Web Site Designer

What's the outlook for computer careers? The U.S. Bureau of Labor Statistics (BLS), which keeps track of employment trends in the United States, projects that the number of jobs in the computer industry will substantially increase between now and 2008. According to the BLS, the largest increases in available jobs will be for database administrators, computer support specialists, and computer engineers. Other industry observers agree, but suggest that the need for computer security specialists will also increase dramatically in response to threats from viruses, hackers, and terrorists.

Before making a career decision, it is important for you to research current industry trends and the general economic outlook. The Career Outlook InfoWeb will help you access Web resources on this topic.

click

Over the next few years, economic trends may cause significant changes in the job market. In preparing for an IT career, flexibility is the key. You should be willing to train and then retrain as new skills are needed to work with emerging technologies.

What can I expect as a salary for an IT industry job? Web sites, such as *www.bls.gov,* provide salary data for various IT industry jobs. In addition to data provided by BLS, you can find comparative IT industry salary averages using a standard Web search engine.

8

As with almost every industry, the compensation rates for jobs in the IT industry vary. Jobs that require college degrees and certification typically pay more than jobs that require a high school diploma and some on-the-job training. IT industry salaries also vary by geographic location. In the U.S., the highest salaries tend to be offered in the Northeast and on the West Coast. Figure 8-21 shows the range of salaries for selected IT jobs in the U.S.

FIGURE 8-21 Median IT Industry Salaries 2002

Job title	Southeast	Midwest	Northeast	Southwest	West Coast
Software Engineer	76,900	72,243	79,048	64,809	80,200
Database Administrator	107,734	105,009	117,585	98,931	108,677
Web Developer	81,036	84,445	90,095	83,666	89,608
Network Manager LAN/WAN	96,726	73,036	96,432	80,540	92,606
Systems Analyst/Project Leader	82,170	81,675	90,981	80,983	89,496
Programmer/Analyst	69,354	70,277	70,074	59,887	67,605
PC Applications Specialist	56,060	52,173	54,219	51,252	57,779
Quality Assurance Analyst	66,000	69,778	73,059	68,287	72,860
Security Specialist	87,591	90,214	92,836	86,647	101,753

WORKING CONDITIONS

What are the advantages of working in the computer industry? Many technology companies offer employee-friendly working conditions that include child care, flexible hours, and the opportunity to work from home. As in any industry, the exact nature of a job depends on the company and the particular projects that are in the works. Some jobs and projects are more interesting than others.

Are IT workers typically satisfied with their jobs? One indication of job satisfaction is **voluntary turnover rate**. A job "turns over" when an employee voluntarily leaves and is replaced by another person. High voluntary turnover rates tend to indicate that employees are not satisfied with their compensation, responsibilities, or working conditions. Low turnover rates tend to correspond with high levels of employee satisfaction.

Some companies in the IT industry have remarkably low turnover rates. Database giant Oracle and network powerhouse Cisco Systems have turnover rates that are less than 6 percent. Turnover rates at IBM and Microsoft are less than 10 percent, which seems to indicate higher-than-average employee satisfaction.

What about part-time or contract work? The typical IT industry employee works a 40-hour week, and often longer hours are required. Part-time workers are defined as those who are required to be on the job for fewer than 40 hours a week. The number of part-time workers in the computer industry is similar to other industries.

The IT industry has an unusually large number of contract and temporary workers. A **contract worker** is typically hired as a consultant. Contract workers are not official employees of a company. They may be paid by the job, rather than by the hour, and they are not eligible for a company's health insurance benefits or retirement plan. Approximately 300,000 of the 2 million IT workers in the U.S. are contract workers. Many IT workers prefer contract work. It provides variety and new challenges, plus the opportunity to learn new skills while working with different businesses. IT contract workers typically earn more than permanent full-time workers doing the same work. Contract workers command anywhere from $25 to $350 an hour, although health insurance and other benefits are not included.

IT businesses benefit from the ability to hire contract workers. The pool of IT contract workers provides a selection of people with specialized skills. Contract workers can be added to a company's staff when needed, instead of hiring full-time workers who might later be laid off if the company is forced to downsize. A few businesses, however, have been accused of misusing contract workers by hiring them for years at a time without paying benefits. Potential contract workers are advised to carefully read their contracts and understand the terms of employment.

Can I work at an IT job from home? Workers in many industries are interested in **telecommuting**—using available technology to work from home or an off-site location, at least part of the time. In recent years, businesses have begun to allow telecommuting because it makes financial sense. Telecommuters tend to be more productive than those who must commute to the company location. They tend to work longer hours because they have no commute time, and they are not interrupted by routine office chatter.

The Internet and telecommunications technologies have made an impact on the availability of telecommuting opportunities for workers. It has become common for employees to collaborate through e-mail, fax, groupware, and videoconferencing.

Although technology makes telecommuting possible, the Bureau of Labor Statistics reports that less than 7 percent of computer industry employees work at home—a figure far lower than the approximately 16 percent of all workers who work at home. Industry observers expect the number of telecommuting IT workers to increase, however. Telecommuting should be possible for many jobs in the IT industry.

How safe are IT jobs? Most people in the IT industry work at "desk jobs," and spend many hours of the workday gazing at a computer monitor and typing on a keyboard. According to the BLS, "Data entry keyers and others who work at video terminals for extended periods of time may experience musculoskeletal strain, eye problems, stress, or repetitive motion illnesses, such as carpal tunnel syndrome." To avoid these health hazards, workers should be aware of the ergonomics of their work areas.

Ergonomics is the study of work. The U.S. Occupational Safety and Health Administration (OSHA) further explains ergonomics as "the science of designing the job to fit the worker, rather than physically forcing the worker's body to fit the job." Ergonomics provides guidelines for making our work environments safer and healthier. For example, Figure 8-22 illustrates how to use ergonomic guidelines to set up your computer, desk, and chair to avoid potentially disabling musculoskeletal injuries.

8

FIGURE 8-22

OSHA guidelines help you set up your computer work area according to ergonomic principles.

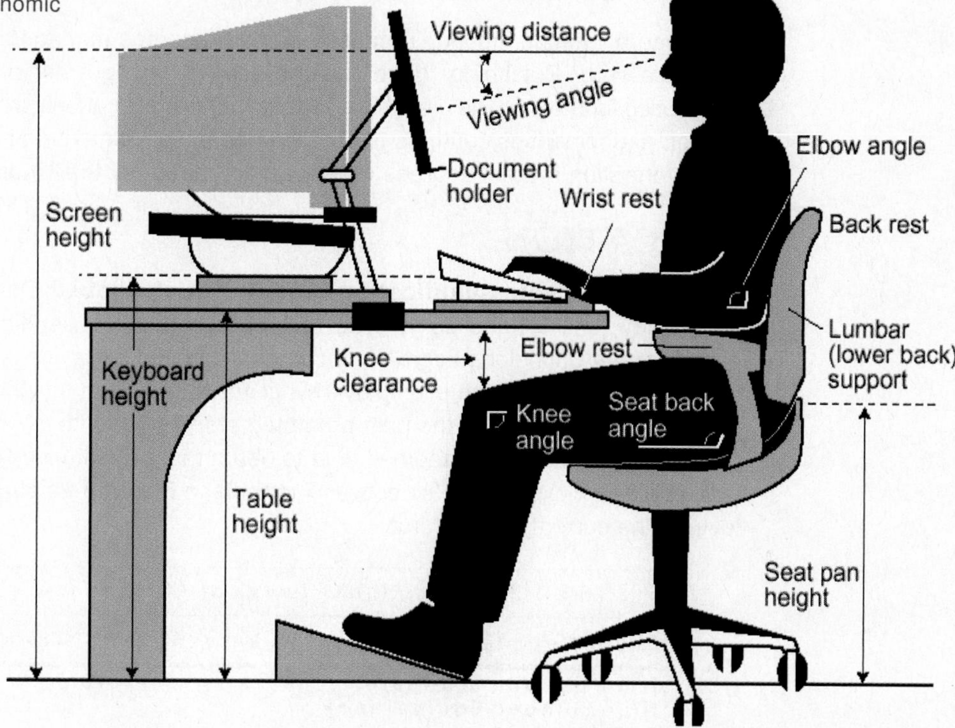

What are the demographics of the computer industry? As you might expect, IT industry workers are younger than their counterparts in most other industries. Figure 8-23 shows that about 35 percent of IT industry workers are 25-34 years old, whereas only 23 percent of all workers are in that age group.

FIGURE 8-23 Percent Distribution of IT Employees by Age Group

Age Group	IT Industry	All Industries
16-19	1.6	5.4
20-24	8.2	9.5
25-34	35.2	23.8
35-44	32.2	27.5
45-54	17.0	21.0
55-64	5.1	9.8
65 and older	.6	2.9

As with many technical occupations, men outnumber women in the IT industry. In the U.S. only 28 percent of programmers are women, though in India, that figure is 38 percent. Fewer than 20 percent of the members of the World Wide Web Consortium staff, which sets the standard for HTML and other Web protocols, are women. Only a handful of women head major IT corporations, even though IT is considered one of the industries with the fewest barriers to women.

Minorities are increasingly taking advantage of opportunities in the IT industry. The typical IT workplace in the U.S. is populated by a large percentage of people of Asian, European, and Indian descent. The number of African Americans in the IT industry is growing slowly. Although the Latino population is the fastest-growing segment of U.S. society, it remains the most underrepresented in the IT workforce.

The general attitude among IT industry human resource managers is, "If you're good, we'll hire you." But being "good" means having the right set of qualifications and experience for the job. The disturbing news is that despite various scholarship incentives, women and minorities continue to shy away from the engineering, computer science, and information system degrees necessary to gain entry to IT industry careers.

EDUCATION

What are the basic qualifications for IT industry jobs? Qualifications for most IT industry jobs include some type of higher education, certification, or computer experience. A Bachelor's degree in a computer-related discipline is the most prevalent job requirement, but some employers accept a two-year Associate's degree. High demand for IT workers in the past prompted employers to hire high school graduates and college students who seemed able to "learn fast." A maturing IT industry, however, has made employers more selective. The table in Figure 8-24 shows the educational level of the current IT workforce.

FIGURE 8-24 Educational Level of IT Workers

Level Completed	Percent of IT Workers
High School Graduate, High School Equivalency, or less	10.6
Some College, no degree	20.5
Associate's Degree	10.2
Bachelor's Degree	45.3
Graduate Degree	13.4

Do I need a computer science degree to work in the computer industry? Computer science is only one of the many computer-related degrees that are offered by colleges and universities. Each of these degrees emphasizes a particular aspect of information technology:

Computer engineering focuses on the design of computer hardware and peripheral devices, often at the chip level. The curriculum includes basic studies in calculus, chemistry, engineering, physics, computer organization, logic design, computer architecture, microprocessor design, and signal processing. Students learn how to design new computer circuits, microchips, and other electronic components; plus they learn how to design new computer instruction sets, and combine electronic or optical components to provide powerful, cost-effective computing. A degree in computer engineering provides excellent qualifications for working at a chip manufacturer, such as Intel, Motorola, IBM, or Texas Instruments.

Computer science focuses on computer architecture, and how to program computers to make them work effectively and efficiently. The curriculum includes courses in programming, algorithms, software development, computer architecture, data representation, logic design, calculus, discrete math, and physics. Students investigate the fundamental theories of how computers solve problems, and they learn how to write application programs, system software, computer languages, and device drivers. Computer science graduates generally find jobs as programmers, with good possibilities for advancement to software engineers, object-oriented/GUI developers, and project managers in technical applications development. Computer scientists work as theorists, inventors, and researchers in fields as diverse as artificial intelligence, virtual reality, and computer games.

Information systems, or "information technology," degree programs, typically offered by a university's College of Business, focus on applying computers to business problems. The curriculum includes course work in business, accounting, computer programming, communications, systems analysis, and human psychology. For students who want to become computer professionals but lack strong math aptitude, most academic advisors recommend the information systems degree. An information systems degree usually leads to a programming or technical support job, with good possibilities for advancement to systems analyst, project manager, database administrator, network manager, or other management positions.

What kinds of computer jobs require only an Associate's degree? Colleges, community colleges, and technical schools offer several computer-related Associate's degrees, ranging from computer programming to graphic design, networking, and telecommunications. The curriculum for these programs varies from one degree program to another, but all tend to require intensive course work. Graduates of two-year programs typically find employment as entry-level technicians, programmers, and support personnel. Advancement opportunities might be limited, however, without additional education or certification.

Do I need a graduate degree? Master's degrees in software engineering have been difficult to find except at large research universities with well-established computer science programs. The Master's degree in Computer Science is available at most four-year colleges and universities that offer graduate degrees. Another option at the graduate level is to pursue a Master's degree in Information Systems or a Master's degree in Business Administration (MBA). Any of these graduate degrees would help you get a management position in the computer industry.

Doctoral degrees are available in software engineering, applications software engineering, systems software development, and management information systems. A doctoral degree in any of these areas would qualify you for advanced technical research, or for a position as a college professor.

Where can I find information on computer-related degree programs? Peterson's is a comprehensive resource for educational services. Its Web site at *www.petersons.com* has become a primary resource for locating educational programs, as well as providing testing services for admissions and certification. Peterson's maintains a searchable database of two-year and four-year programs that prepare you for a variety of IT jobs. You can find additional information by connecting to the Web sites of various technical schools, community colleges, and universities.

CERTIFICATION

How important is certification? Certification alone is rarely sufficient to qualify you for a job in the IT industry. In conjunction with a college degree or extensive experience, however, several studies suggest that certification can improve your chances for employment, increase your credibility in the workplace, and lead to higher salaries. Many employers view certification with some degree of skepticism, so the value of a certificate depends on where, when, and how it is obtained. Critics of certification exams, for example, maintain that a multiple-choice test cannot accurately measure a person's ability to deal with real-world equipment and software. Bottom line: certification is only part of your total package of qualifications.

What type of certification is available? Certification falls into two broad categories: certificates of completion and certification exams. **Certificates of completion** are offered to students who successfully complete one or more courses on a specific topic. Community colleges and technical schools often offer certificates of completion in a variety of computer-related areas, such as Information Technology Specialist, LAN Administrator, User Support Specialist, PC/Hardware Support Specialist, and IT Operations Specialist.

FIGURE 8-25

Your local bookstore and the Internet provide sources for independent study materials that can help you prepare for an IT certification exam.

A **certification exam** is an objective test that verifies your level of knowledge about a particular technology or subject. Approximately 300 computer-related certification exams are offered in areas of specialty that range from desktop publishing to network installation. Most of these exams use multiple-choice format, last several hours, and require substantial testing fees. You can prepare for a certification exam with independent study materials (Figure 8-25), online tutorials, or an exam preparation class. Certification exams can be divided into several categories:

General computer knowledge. The Institute for Certification of Computing Professionals (ICCP) offers several generalized certification exams, including the CCP (Certified Computing Professional) exam. According to the ICCP Web site, "Professionals certified with ICCP serve as consultants, working with local, state, and federal government; in accounting and banking; in high schools, technical schools, and universities; in the manufacturing industry; in insurance and numerous other fields."

Software applications. Many certification exams allow you to demonstrate your prowess with a specific software application. The Microsoft Office User Specialist (MOUS) certification is perhaps the most popular. Autodesk offers the AutoCAD Certified Professional exam on the use of its 3-D design software. Certification is also available for popular Adobe software applications, such as Illustrator, PageMaker, and Premiere. Software application certification is of limited value to most computer professionals who are expected to be able to quickly learn applications on their own. This type of certification is most valuable for entry-level secretarial and clerical positions, as well as Help desk personnel.

www.InfoWebLinks.com

For a comprehensive list of certification exams and tips on how to prepare for them, connect to the Certification InfoWeb.

click

Database administration. Databases require a high level of expertise, not only in the use of database software, but in the conception and design of database structures. Many computer professionals have sought certification in database systems, such as Oracle, Access, Sybase, and DB2. The most popular database certification exams include the Microsoft Certified Database Administrator (MCDBA) and Oracle Certified Database Administrator.

Networking. Among computer professionals, network certification may be the most useful. One of the earliest network certification exams was offered by Novell, publisher of a network operating system called NetWare. Microsoft offers a corresponding MCSE certification (Microsoft Certified Systems Engineer). Network hardware certification includes the Cisco Certified Network Professional (CCNP), offered by network equipment supplier Cisco Systems.

Computer hardware. One of the most popular computer hardware certification exams is the A+ Certification, sponsored by the Computing Technology Industry Association. This exam is designed to certify the competency of entry-level computer service technicians for installing, configuring, upgrading, troubleshooting, and repairing personal computer systems. A+ Certification provides good credentials for employment in a computer store or computer repair shop.

8

QUICKCheck Section C

1. A computer ________ is any person whose primary occupation involves the design, configuration, analysis, development, modification, testing, or securing of computer hardware or software.
2. A computer ________ monitors computer performance, installs software patches and upgrades, performs backups, and restores data as necessary.
3. Most computer industry jobs are safe when ________ guidelines are followed to set up your computer, desk, and lighting to avoid potentially disabling musculoskeletal injuries.
4. Qualifications for most IT industry jobs include some type of higher education, ________, or computer experience.
5. Computer ________ degree programs focus on computer architecture, and how to program computers to make them work effectively and efficiently.
6. Information ________, or "information technology," degree programs focus on applying computers to business problems.

check answers

Section D JOB HUNTING RESOURCES

In earlier sections of this chapter, you learned of the events that created today's computer and IT industries. You then learned about becoming a computer professional and working in these industries. In this section of the chapter, you'll find out how to hunt for a job using up-to-date tools and techniques. Although the focus is hunting for jobs in the IT industry, you'll find that many of the tips and techniques apply to job hunting in any field.

JOB HUNTING BASICS

How do I find a job in the IT industry? In many ways, finding a job in the IT industry is just like finding a job in any other industry. Effective job seekers begin by taking stock of their qualifications, identifying job titles relevant to their skills, identifying potential employers, and considering the geographic area in which they want to work. They then create a carefully worded resume, look for job openings, contact potential employers, and work with employment agencies and recruiting firms. Figure 8-26 summarizes the steps in a job hunt.

FIGURE 8-26 Job hunting steps

Define the job that you want
Create your resume
Look for job openings
Supply potential employers with resume
Prepare for interviews
Evaluate job offers
Accept a new job

Conventional wisdom about job hunting applies to a broad spectrum of industries, such as financial, automotive, hospitality, and even entertainment. But one job hunting strategy is not necessarily effective for every job in every industry. Let's take a closer look at the job hunting process, and examine how hunting for an IT job might differ from a job search in other industries.

How can I use the Internet to find a job? The Internet has become an important tool for job hunters. In 1994, about 10,000 resumes were posted on the Web. By 1998, that number exceeded 1 million. Today, the Web plays host to an estimated 2.5 million resumes.

The Internet can figure into your job hunt in several ways, including researching potential jobs and employers, posting your resume, locating job leads, and corresponding with potential employers. Career counselors warn of placing too much emphasis on the online aspects of your job search. "Don't put all of your eggs in the online basket," is often-repeated advice. Job hunting experts advise IT job seekers to spend no more than 50 percent of their total job hunting efforts online. Rather than accept that advice outright, consider it with regard to your employment needs, geographical location, and current employment situation.

At the Online Job Hunting InfoWeb, you'll find lots of tips for using technology to find a job.

click 

To protect your privacy, you might consider removing most of the contact information, such as your address and phone number, from your online resume. You should provide an e-mail address, but not the address of the business e-mail account supplied by your employer. Also, make sure that your e-mail address is not linked to a personal profile, as it is on America Online and some other Internet provider sites. You can open a Web-based e-mail account specifically devoted to job hunting. By the way, consider your e-mail user ID carefully. Employers might respond better to an e-mail address like excellentprogrammer@hotmail.com rather than an address like bigbertha@hotmail.com.

Many job seekers are hesitant to post their resumes for fear that their current employers will learn that they are preparing to "jump ship." Some job banks allow you to block access to your resume by specific employers. If that is not possible, you can disguise the name of your employer by substituting a generic description of it. For example, Epson America might become "a multinational company specializing in digital printer technology."

HEAD HUNTERS AND EMPLOYMENT AGENCIES

What's a "head hunter?" The term **head hunter** refers to a recruitment firm. These firms are contacted by companies seeking new employees. A head hunter looks through its database of job seekers and attempts to find suitable candidates. Head hunters are continually searching for workers to add to their databases. They use a variety of techniques to find workers with high-demand skills—even workers who might not be actively seeking a new job.

Head hunter recruitment fees are usually paid by the companies that hire them. They are paid only if they make a placement. Fees are typically based on a percentage of the employee's salary—not because the employee pays the fees, but because head hunters command higher fees for finding scarce high-level executives.

Companies usually ask head hunters to help fill managerial and executive positions. However, during boom times in the IT industry, qualified applicants at all levels of the corporate ladder sometimes become scarce, and head hunters are asked to recruit even entry-level workers, such as junior programmers.

What about employment agencies? An **employment agency** (or placement service) works on behalf of employees, rather than employers. The focus of an employment agency is to find employers for people who seek work. State-run employment agencies and those operated by schools typically offer placement services for free. Most colleges and universities offer some type of placement service, and encourage students to tap into resources offered by career counselors, alumni, and on-campus recruiters. Private employment agencies, however, usually charge a fee for their services. At some agencies the fee is due up front, whereas other agencies charge only when a job offer is accepted.

EVALUATING JOB OPENINGS

What factors should I consider before responding to a job opening? A job application takes time—your time and a recruiter's time. Before you apply for a job, most career counselors suggest that you first gather some background information about the company and its location. This information can help you decide whether the job is worth pursuing. If you decide to go ahead with an application, the information that you gather can also help you formulate some intelligent questions to ask if you're invited for an interview. You also may be able to use the Web to find out about your prospective employer's financial status and corporate culture. And you might find Web resources that provide information about the town that could become your new home.

If you need to explore a company's finances, corporate culture, or geographical location, use the links provided by the Companies and Places InfoWeb.

click

How do I find information about a company's finances and corporate culture? To find information about a company, start at its Web site. Most companies provide a set of "About us" pages that describe the company's mission.

How do I find information about the quality of life in a particular city? Web sites such as *www.homefair.com* provide online tools that help you calculate the cost of moving, the cost of living, and the quality of life in a selected location. Such sites provide comparative information about crime rates, demographics, school systems, the local economy, air quality, and water quality, as well as cultural, sports, and leisure activities. You can also connect to the city's Chamber of Commerce Web site, which might provide additional information about lifestyles in the area.

QUICKCheck Section D

1. Non-standardized job [ ] can pose a problem for IT industry job hunters, especially those who use search engines to locate job openings.
2. You can demonstrate your ability to use technology for everyday tasks by preparing your [ ] in a variety of formats, suitable for different computer platforms and delivery methods.
3. For resumes that become part of a computer-searchable database, experts recommend that you focus on [ ], rather than verbs.
4. The largest job [ ] span just about every industry, but several specialize in the IT industry.
5. A job search [ ] is an automated program that searches one or more databases, and notifies you when it finds any leads that match your specified criteria.
6. Before posting your resume, you should check the job bank's privacy policy. True or false? [ ]

check answers

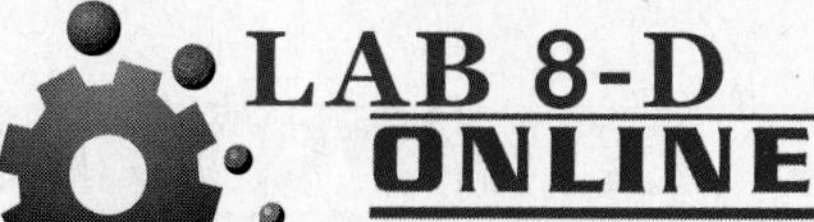

LAB 8-D ONLINE JOB HUNTING

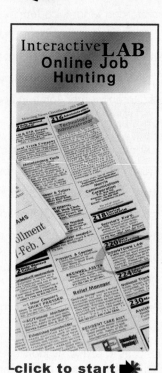

Interactive LAB Online Job Hunting

click to start

In this lab, you'll learn:

- How to register with an online job bank
- How to submit your resume online
- Why the file that you use for your printed resume might not be appropriate for posting online
- The characteristics of an ASCII document
- How to convert a formatted resume to an ASCII resume
- How to "fix" an ASCII resume so that it presents information in an easy-to-read format
- How to post an ASCII resume at a job bank
- How to enter a job search by keyword or category
- Creative ways to use keywords in a search specification
- How to configure a search agent
- How to find information on salaries, employers, and places to live

LAB Assignments

1. Start the interactive part of the lab. Insert your Tracking Disk if you want to save your QuickCheck results. Perform each of the lab steps as directed, and answer all of the lab QuickCheck questions. When you exit the lab, your answers are automatically graded and your results are displayed.
2. Write a paragraph that describes your ideal job. Next, create a list of search specifications that you could enter at an online job bank to find job openings for your ideal job. Connect to an online job bank and enter your search specifications. Describe the results. If your results were not satisfactory, try modifying your search specifications. Record what seems to be the most effective search, and, if possible, print the job listings that resulted from your search.
3. Using word processing or desktop publishing software, create a one-page resume that highlights your current skills and experience. Print this resume. Convert the resume into an ASCII document, tidy up the format, and then print it.
4. Use the Web to find information about the corporate culture at Microsoft. Summarize your findings, and list each Web site that you visited to find information.
5. Use the Web to compare Macon, GA to San Diego, CA. Write a one-page summary of the strengths and weaknesses of each city, then express which city you would prefer to live in. List the URLs for any Web sites that you used for this assignment.

TECHTALK
THE FUTURE OF COMPUTING

The computer industry has been running on Moore's law since 1965 when Gordon Moore, co-founder of Intel, predicted that the number of transistors per integrated circuit would double about every year. He originally forecasted that this trend would continue through 1975, but Moore's law is expected to hold true until at least 2012. By that year, Intel estimates that it can integrate 1 billion transistors onto a production chip that will operate at 10 GHz. After that, however, Moore's law is expected to encounter some major technological obstacles.

Current computer technology is silicon based. Chipmakers can now pack about 42 million transistors on a chip by shrinking components down to 130 nanometers (billionths of a meter). Making these features even smaller, however, requires new and expensive fabrication facilities. Many semiconductor experts believe that commercial fabrication methods cannot economically make silicon transistors much smaller than 100 nanometers. Even if chipmakers could figure out a cost-effective way to etch them onto a chip, ultrasmall silicon components might not work reliably. At transistor dimensions of around 50 nanometers, the electrons begin to obey quantum laws, which cause erratic behavior.

Researchers are experimenting with three technologies that might supplant silicon: molecular computing, biological computing, and quantum computing.

What's molecular computing? Molecular computing can be described as the use of individual molecules to build components that perform functions identical or analogous to those of transistors and other key components of today's microchips. Molecules are small—much smaller than even the microscopic components that populate today's highly miniaturized chips. To put the size differential in perspective, imagine a semiconductor-based transistor enlarged to the size of the printed page you're currently reading. A molecular device would be the size of the period at the end of this sentence. Put another way, molecular electronic devices are about 500 times smaller than today's silicon transistors.

FIGURE 8-31

A carbon nanotube is a cylindrical molecule.

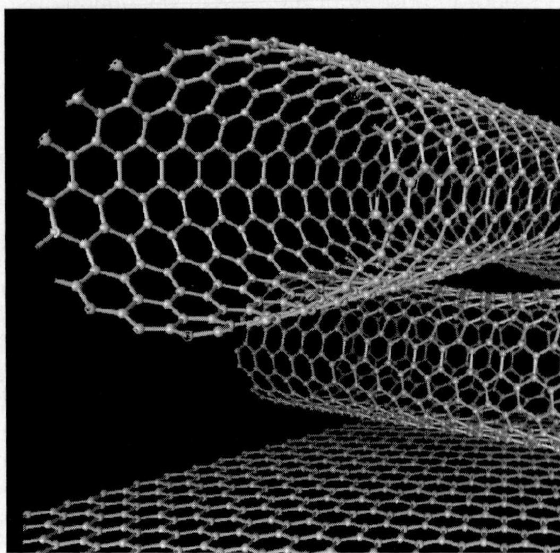

Some of the most promising research into molecular technologies involves carbon nano-tubes, first discovered by Japanese scientist Sumio Iijima in 1991. A carbon nanotube is a single, cylinder-shaped molecule that's about 50,000 times thinner than a human hair (Figure 8-31). The electrical properties of carbon nanotubes are similar to those of the semiconductors used in today's microprocessors. Because carbon nanotubes are so small, they could be used for microprocessors and memory, providing up to 30,000 times more memory capacity and 10,000 times more speed than today's DRAM chips.

In 2002, IBM researchers were able to construct a prototype carbon-nanotube transistor that outperformed today's silicon transistors. This technology is currently the computer industry's best chance for replacing silicon-based computer circuity. Researchers warn, however, that nanotube computers are not expected to be feasible for at least 10 years.

What is biological computing? Biological computing is a multidisciplinary field that integrates the work of computer scientists, molecular biologists, geneticists, mathematicians, physicists, and others. One much-talked-about application of biological computing focuses on using DNA strands. DNA (deoxyribonucleic acid) molecules are the basic building blocks of genes. Just as a string of binary data is encoded using 1s and 0s, a strand of DNA is encoded with four nucleotides represented by the letters A, T, C, and G. In the cell, DNA is modified biochemically by a variety of enzymes. For example, one enzyme cuts DNA and another enzyme pastes it back together. Other enzymes function as copiers. Even others function as repair units. Scientists have developed techniques for performing many of these cellular operations in a test tube.

How do these enzymatic operations relate to computing? Just as a microprocessor's ALU contains circuitry for addition, subtraction, and logical operations, DNA has cutting, copying, pasting, and repairing operations that can be harnessed to solve computational problems. In 1994, Leonard Adleman performed the first DNA computation to solve the classic Hamiltonian Path problem, which is popularly called the "traveling salesman" problem. As Figure 8-32 shows, the problem is to help the salesman find the most efficient way to visit each city, starting in LA and ending in NY.

FIGURE 8-32

The "traveling salesman" problem is solved by finding the best route for a visit to each city. Note that routes between cities are limited to those shown by arrows. The problem becomes more and more difficult to solve as the number of cities and routes increases.

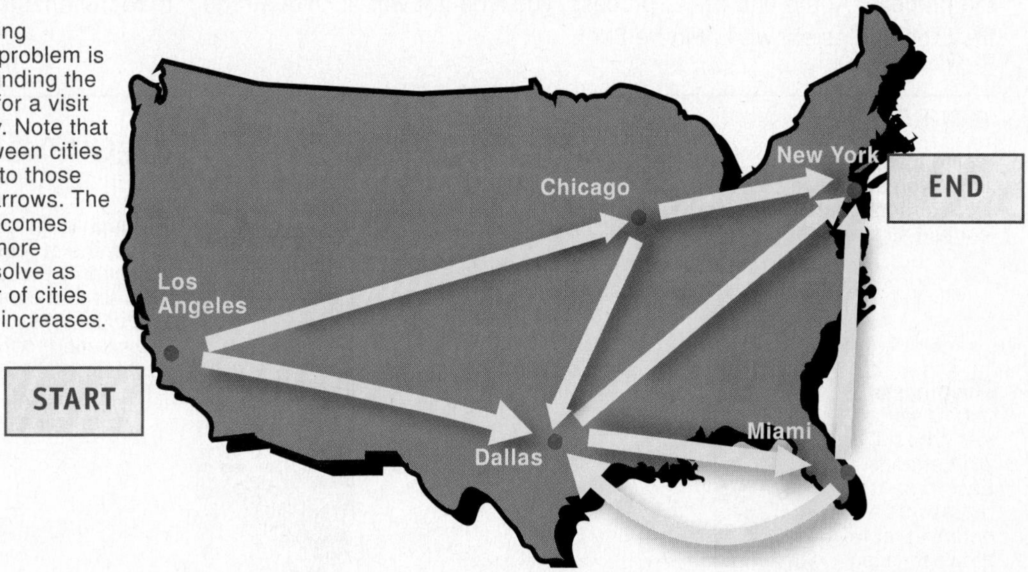

To solve the problem with DNA, you must first decide on city codes that can be represented by the A, T, C, and G nucleotides. For example, you could code each city as shown in Figure 8-33.

FIGURE 8-33

Patterns of nucleotides can be used to code information.

CITY NAME	NUCLEOTIDE CODE
Los Angeles	GCTACG
Chicago	CTAGTA
Dallas	TCGTAC
Miami	CTACGG
New York	ATGCCG

Your next step is to generate DNA molecules for every possible route. For example, the route LA -> Chicago -> Dallas -> Miami -> New York would simply be represented by the DNA strand:

GCTACGCTAGTATCGTACCTACGGATGCCG

This step results in a test tube full of DNA strands for all routes between the cities, but not all of these strands represent routes that begin in LA and end in NY, as required by the salesman. You can use a technique called Polymerase Chain Reaction to selectively amplify the DNA strands that begin in LA and end in NY. After using this technique, the test tube is filled with DNA strands of various lengths that represent itineraries between LA and NY, but you want the shortest route. To discover the shortest route, a process called Gel Electrophoresis forces the DNA through an electric field, which sorts the DNA by size. Once the sorting is complete, you can cut out the shortest strands for further analysis.

Unfortunately, some of these strands may not include all five cities—some might have the salesman travel back and forth between LA, Dallas, Miami, and NY, but never reach Chicago. The final step is to pull out the strands that include all five cities. A process called Affinity Purification allows you to match parts of a DNA strand with a "key" strand. For example, by using GCTACG as a key, you can first pull out all of the strands with LA. From those, you can use the same process to pull out all of the strands that contain Dallas, and so on. Any DNA strand that is missing a city will be left behind at one stage of the process. At the end of the process, you'll be left with a DNA strand that represents the solution to the problem, as shown in Figure 8-34.

FIGURE 8-34
Using a sequence of keys, you can sieve out DNA strands that do not contain all five cities.

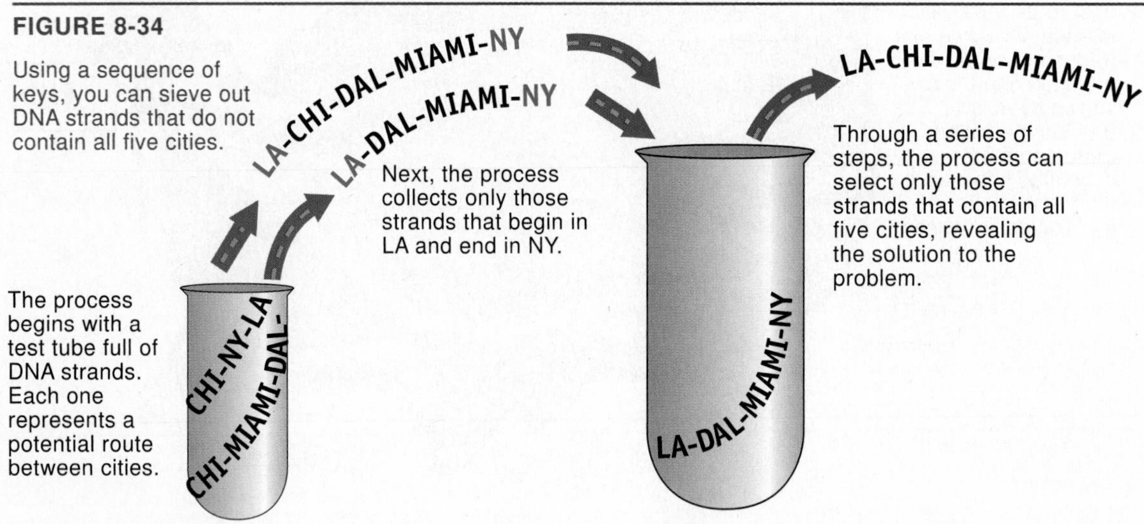

LA-CHI-DAL-MIAMI-NY
LA-DAL-MIAMI-NY
Next, the process collects only those strands that begin in LA and end in NY.
LA-CHI-DAL-MIAMI-NY
Through a series of steps, the process can select only those strands that contain all five cities, revealing the solution to the problem.
The process begins with a test tube full of DNA strands. Each one represents a potential route between cities.
CHI-NY-LA
CHI-MIAMI-DAL-
LA-DAL-MIAMI-NY

Is DNA computing practical? Applying DNA to solve the traveling salesman problem involved a complex algorithm and a variety of molecular biology techniques. Aldeman's initial attempt to solve the problem took seven days of "DNA computing time." Your standard desktop computer could solve the same problem in less than a second. Nevertheless, the potential of DNA computing is staggering. Nucleotides that can be used to represent data are spaced a mere 0.35 nanometers apart along the DNA molecule, giving DNA a remarkable storage density of nearly 18 Mbits per linear inch. In two dimensions, the data density is over 1 million gigabits per square inch. In comparison, your computer's hard disk drive stores only 7 gigabits per square inch. Significantly, the storage capacity of DNA matches its processing capacity because enzymes can work on many DNA molecules simultaneously. This parallel operating capacity could allow a DNA-based computer to solve a complex mathematical problem in hours, in contrast to the years of computing time required by today's silicon-based sequential processors.

What's quantum computing? Quantum computing is the application of quantum mechanics to computer systems. It has been described as "a bizarre, subatomic world in which two electrons can be two places at the same time." The description is fairly accurate. The principles of quantum computing certainly seem to stretch the limits of credibility.

Today's digital computers work with bits, and each bit can represent either a 0 or 1. Bits are easy to understand because they correspond to known characteristics of our physical world: electrical current that is on or off, particles magnetized with positive or negative polarity, and so on. Quantum computers, on the other hand, have their roots in quantum theory, which deals with atomic particles, such as electrons, protons, and neutrons. According to scientists, an isolated individual particle—an electron, for example—may exist in multiple states and locations until it is observed and measured. It further seems that a particle might be able to exist in more than one state at a time.

Suppose that a computer can be constructed to work with these atomic particles instead of conventional bits. A quantum bit, called a **qubit**, can theoretically exist in multiple states. A qubit would have the potential not just to represent a 1 or a 0, but to represent *both* 1 and 0 at the same time. A computer containing 500 qubits could represent as many as 2^{500} states. Unlike a classical digital computer, which would use 500 bits to represent ONE of these 2^{500} states at a time, a quantum computer could represent all of the 2^{500} states simultaneously. Then with one tick of the quantum computer's system clock, a calculation could be performed on all 2^{500} machine states. Eventually, observing the system causes it to coalesce into a single state corresponding to a single answer.

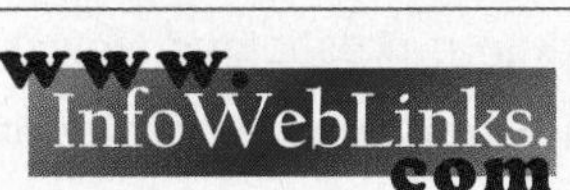

The **Future of Computing** InfoWeb provides links to information about quantum computing, molecular computing, and DNA computing.

click

Will quantum computers replace desktops? Quantum computers are at least 20 years down the road, according to most researchers, and they are probably not destined to tackle desktop tasks, such as word processing and e-mail. Large-scale cryptography, on the other hand, is ideal for quantum computing, and could provide security experts with tools for cracking encrypted data. Another potential use for quantum computers is modeling and indexing very large databases, an application that could become crucial if the Web continues to grow at its current rate.

QUICKCheck TechTalk

1. ______ law predicted that the number of transistors per integrated circuit would double every 18 months.
2. Carbon nanotubes are one of the most promising technologies for ______ computing.
3. Biological computing makes use of substances such as ______ (deoxyribonucleic acid) molecules for processing and storage.
4. In a quantum computer, data is represented by ______, instead of the 0 and 1 bits that are familiar to users of today's silicon-based electronic digital computers.

check answers

ISSUE

WHO NEEDS PROFESSIONAL ETHICS?

When discussing ethical issues, we often do so from the perspective of the victim. We imagine how it might feel if someone else—an employer, the government, cyberpunks, and so on—pilfered our original artwork from a Web site, read our e-mail, or stole our credit card number from an e-commerce site. It is quite possible, however, that at some time in your career, you will encounter situations in which you could become the perpetrator—the copyright violator, the snoop, or the thief.

Every day, computer professionals must cope with ethical dilemmas, in which the right course of action is not entirely clear, or in which the right course of action is clear, but the consequences—such as getting fired—are not easy to face.

Suppose, for example, that you are hired to manage a local area network in a prestigious New York advertising agency. On your first day of work, your employer hands you a box containing the latest upgrade for Microsoft Office, and asks you to install it on all the computers in the organization. When you ask if the agency owns a site license, your boss responds, "No, do you have a problem with that?" What would you reply? Would you risk your job by insisting that the agency order enough copies for all the computers before you install it? Or, would you go ahead and install the software, assuming that your boss would take responsibility for this violation of the software license agreement?

Now imagine that you're hired as a programmer for a local public school system. One day, the Superintendent of Schools calls you into her office and asks if you can write software that will monitor online access and provide reports to management. From your understanding of the school's network and Web access, you realize that it would be easy to write such monitoring software. You also realize, however, that the Superintendent could use the software to track individual teachers and students as they visit Web sites. You ask the Superintendent if faculty and students would be aware of the monitoring software, and she replies, "What they don't know won't hurt them." Should you write the program? Should you write the program, but start a rumor that monitoring software is being used to track faculty and student Web access? Should you pretend that it would be technically impossible to write such software?

A Code of Ethics is designed to help computer professionals thread their way through a sometimes tangled web of ethical decisions. Published by many professional organizations—such as the Association for Computing Machinery, the British Computer Society, the Australian Computer Society, and the Computer Ethics Institute—each code varies in detail, but supplies a similar set of overall guiding principles for professional conduct.

PROJECTS

An NP6 Project is an open-ended activity that will help you apply the concepts you have learned. Many projects require resources in addition to your textbook, such as current magazines, library materials, or Web access. When you tackle a project, be prepared to use your critical thinking skills, logical analysis, and your creativity.

8

1 **Issue Research: Professional Ethics** The Issue section of this chapter focused on professional ethics. In many courses, ethics are presented as a series of case studies that students try to "solve" by determining the pros and cons of various courses of action. For this project, create your own two–five page case study describing an IT industry scenario that involves an ethical dilemma. To begin this project, consult the Ethics in Computing InfoWeb (see page 435), and link to the recommended Web pages, where you can find some sample case studies. Next, write a one-page description of your case. You can create your own case from scratch, or you can create a variation on one of the cases that you read on the Web. If you create a variation, however, make sure that you provide a reference to the original case. In the remaining two pages of your case study, discuss the possible solutions to the dilemma. Use additional information from the InfoWeb links to various ethical codes to cite guidelines that might apply to a solution. You can place citations to these pages (including the author's name, article title, date of publication, and URL) at the end of your paper as endnotes, on each page as footnotes, or along with the appropriate paragraphs using parentheses. Follow your professor's instructions for submitting your paper via e-mail or as a printed document.

2 **Careers** Books, magazines, and the Web supply plenty of resources to help you choose a career. If you're considering a career change, these resources can help you decide if it is the right thing to do. Use the resources in your library and on the Web to gather information about a career in which you are interested. Unless your instructor requires it, you do not need to limit yourself to IT industry careers. After completing your research, answer the following questions:

a. In one paragraph, how would you describe the nature of work that you would perform in this career?

b. What types of businesses and organizations typically hire people in your chosen career?

c. What are the working conditions?

d. What is the employment outlook for this career?

e. What specific qualifications would you need to successfully compete in this career?

f. What is a typical starting salary? What is the top salary?

g. What sources did you use to locate information about this career?

3 **Web Resume** The Web provides a way to publish your resume so it might be seen by prospective employers. But what does it take today to create an effective online resume? Use the Web to locate information and tips about creating effective online resumes. Using the guidelines that you find, create a resume using word processing software or Web page authoring software. Show your initial draft to several friends, colleagues, or instructors. Collect their feedback and make any necessary revisions. Submit your completed resume in the format specified by your instructor, accompanied by a description of the features that you included to make your resume easy to find and understand.

ADDITIONAL PROJECTS

TIP

Click ➜ to access the Web for additional projects.

INFORMATION SYSTEMS ANALYSIS AND DESIGN

CONTENTS

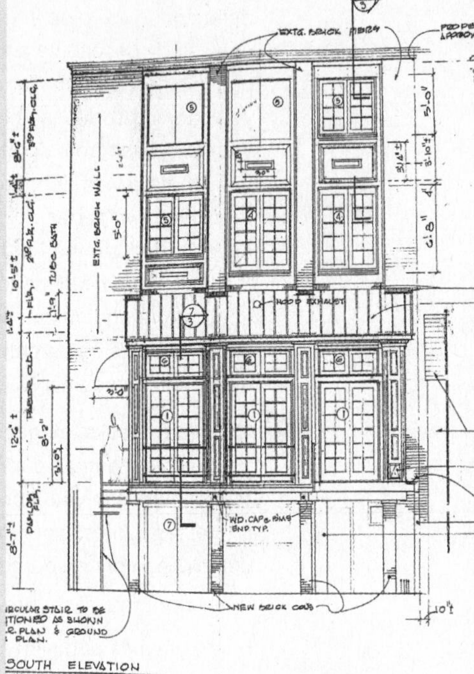

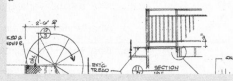

InfoWebLinks

The InfoWebLinks, located in the margins of this chapter, show the way to a variety of Web sites that contain additional information and updates to the chapter topics. Your computer needs an Internet connection to access these links. You can connect to the Web links for this chapter by:

- clicking the InfoWeb links in the margins
- clicking this underlined link
- starting your browser and entering the URL ***www.infoweblinks.com/np6/chapter9.htm***

TIP

When using the **BookOnCD**, the ➧✱ symbols are "clickable."

CHAPTER PREVIEW

9

Unlike a personal computer system, an information system rarely comes in a box with a simple page of setup instructions. Most information systems are carefully designed, crafted, and customized to meet the needs of a specific business, corporation, organization, or firm. These systems are expensive and failure is costly. The process of developing an information system requires careful planning, much like any large construction project. In this chapter, you'll learn about developing an information system, which will help you understand the information systems that you use in the course of day-to-day activities. And, if you one day find yourself working for an organization that is planning to replace its old information system, your understanding of the development process will make you a useful resource and project participant.

Section A begins with some basic material about organizations and how information systems can contribute to their success. Section B focuses on the initial planning and analysis that are required for a successful new information system. Section C delves into the intricacies of designing an information system—a task similar to creating the blueprints for a building or bridge. Section D begins with a description of the steps necessary to assemble the hardware and software components for an information system, test them, and then put the system to work. The section concludes by explaining what's required to keep an information system running.

When you complete this chapter you should be able to:

- Describe how information systems help organizations fulfill their missions, deal with threats, and take advantage of opportunities
- Contrast and compare the characteristics of office automation systems, transaction processing systems, management information systems, decision support systems, and expert systems
- Describe various models for the system development life cycle (SDLC), and explain the focus of the structured, information engineering, object-oriented, and rapid application development approaches to system development
- List the activities that take place in each phase of the system development life cycle
- Apply the PIECES framework to classify problems that reduce the effectiveness of an information system
- Describe alternative hardware and software solutions that a project team might typically consider
- Explain the differences between unit testing, integration testing, system testing, and acceptance testing
- Describe the advantages and disadvantages of direct conversion, parallel conversion, phased conversion, and pilot conversion
- Explain the feedback mechanism that helps system operators identify and fix "bugs"

TIP Click  to access the Web for a complete list of learning objectives for Chapter 9.

INFORMATION SYSTEMS

You are probably a member of an organization, such as a student club, fraternity or sorority, sports team, or political party. You also deal with all kinds of organizations every day: your school, stores, banks, and government agencies. Most organizations use information systems to operate more effectively, gather information, and accomplish tasks. In this section, you'll review some basic concepts about organizations, and find out how information systems enhance organizational activities.

INFORMATION SYSTEMS IN ORGANIZATIONS

What is an information system? An **information system** collects, stores, and processes data to provide useful, accurate, and timely information, typically within the context of an organization. Although an information system does not necessarily have to be computerized, today most information systems rely on computers and communications networks to store, process, and transmit information with far more efficiency than would be possible with a manual system. In this textbook, the term "information system" always refers to a system that uses computers, and usually includes communications networks.

What's the official definition of "organization"? An **organization** is a group of people working together to accomplish a goal. According to Peter Drucker, one of today's most influential writers about business and management, "the purpose of an organization is to enable ordinary people to do extraordinary things." Organizations have accomplished amazing feats, such as sending astronauts into space, providing live television coverage of global events, and inventing freeze-dried ice cream. They also accomplish all kinds of day-to-day, routine tasks, such as offering banking services, selling merchandise, and policing your neighborhood.

Any organization that seeks profit by providing goods and services is called a **business**. Some organizations are formed to accomplish political, social, or charitable goals that do not include amassing profit. These organizations are known as **nonprofit organizations**.

Every organization has a goal or plan that's often referred to as its **mission**. All activities that take place in an organization, including those that involve computers, should contribute to this mission. The written expression of an organization's mission is called a mission statement. A **mission statement** describes not only an organization's goals, but also the way in which those goals will be accomplished. Companies publish their mission statements in corporate reports and on the Web. (See Figure 9-1.)

FIGURE 9-1 A Web-based mission statement

Return to Home Page
About The Foundation
Our Mission
Become a Member
OUR MISSION
The mission of Pacific Whale Foundation, Pacific Whale foundation's Eco-Adventures and Pacific Whale Foundation's Marine Resource Centers is to inspire and promote appreciation, understanding and protection of whales, dolphins, coral reefs and our planet's oceans. We accomplish this through public environmental education, by supporting and conducting responsible marine research, and by addressing marine conservation issues through activism and education.

Who uses information systems? An information system is used by the people in an organization and its customers. You've undoubtedly used many information systems—for example, when registering for classes, getting cash from an ATM machine, and purchasing merchandise on the Web. You might even work for a business or nonprofit organization where you have access to an information system.

Not everyone in an organization uses an information system in the same way. An information system must support the needs of people who engage in many different organizational activities.

To coordinate the activities of their employees, most organizations use a hierarchical structure. An **organizational chart**, such as the one in Figure 9-2, depicts the hierarchy of employees in a typical organization.

FIGURE 9-2 An organizational chart

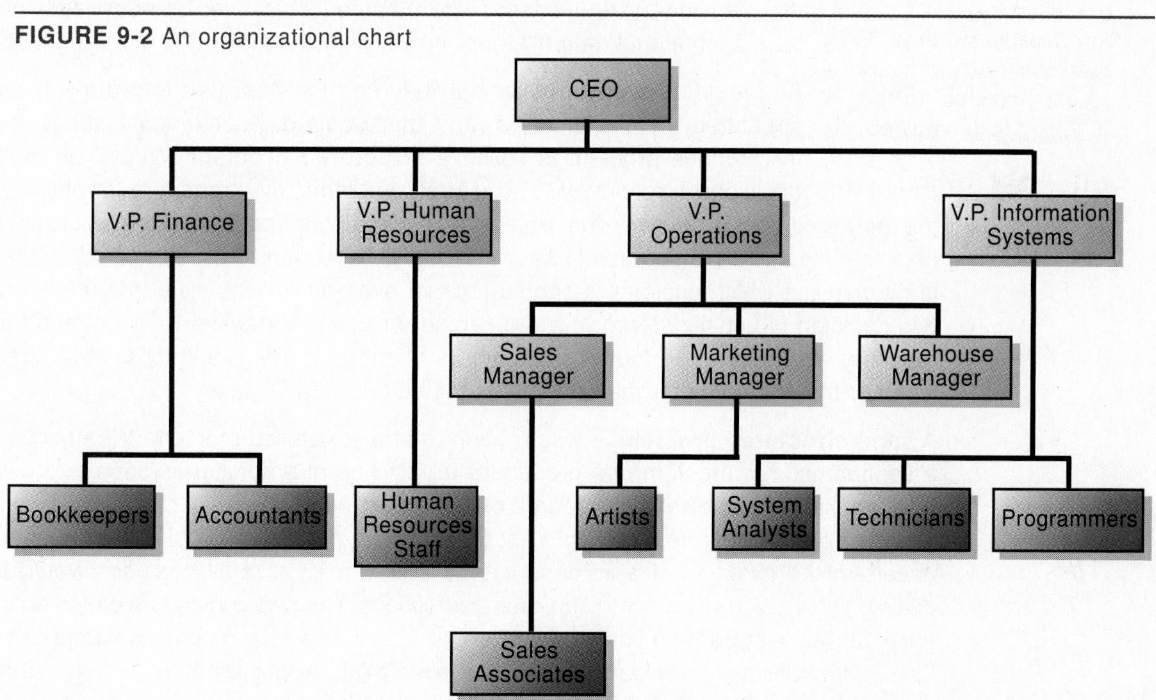

In many organizations, and most businesses, employees can be classified as either workers or managers. **Workers** are the people who carry out the organization's mission. For example, they assemble cars, write newspaper articles, sell merchandise, answer telephones, lay bricks, cut trees, or fix engines. Workers typically collect the data for information systems. For example, as a checkout clerk rings up sales, her cash register records each item in a database.

Managers determine organizational goals and plan how to achieve those goals. They approve new products, authorize new construction, and supervise workers. High-level, executive managers plan an organization's long-range goals for profitability, market share, membership levels, and so on. This emphasis on long-range and future goals is referred to as **strategic planning**. Mid-level managers are responsible for figuring out how to achieve those long-range goals through sales, marketing, or new product development. They set incremental goals that can be achieved in a year or less—a process referred to as **tactical planning**. Low-level managers are responsible for scheduling employees, ordering supplies, and other activities that make day-to-day operations run smoothly—a process referred to as **operational planning**. Information systems can provide some or all of the data needed for strategic, tactical, and operational planning.

How do information systems help the people in an organization? An information system can help the people in an organization perform their jobs more quickly and effectively by automating routine tasks, such as reordering inventory, taking customer orders, or sending out renewal notices. Information systems can also help people solve problems.

Many case studies provide detailed accounts of successful (and sometimes unsuccessful) information systems. To read some of these case studies, connect to the IS Case Study InfoWeb.

click

One of the major functions of an information system is to help people make decisions in response to problems. According to Herbert Simon, who is well known for his insights into organizational behavior and his pioneering role in artificial intelligence, the decision-making process has three phases. First, you must recognize a problem or a need to make a decision. Next, you devise and analyze possible solutions or actions to solve the problem. Finally, you select an action or solution. Sometimes, the decision-making phases are clearcut, objective, standardized, and based on factual data. At other times, decision making is more intuitive.

All problems are not alike, but they can be classified into three types: structured, semi-structured, and unstructured. An everyday, run-of-the-mill, routine problem is called a **structured problem**. When you make decisions in response to structured problems, the procedure for obtaining the best solution is known, the objective is clearly defined, and the information necessary to make the decision is easy to identify. An example of a structured problem is figuring out which customers should receive overdue notices. The information for this decision is usually stored in a file cabinet or computer system. The method for reaching a solution is to look for customers with outstanding balances, then check whether the due dates for their payments fall before today's date.

A **semi-structured problem** is less routine than a structured problem. When solving a semi-structured problem, the procedure for arriving at a solution is usually known; however, it might involve some degree of subjective judgment. Also, some of the information regarding the problem might not be available, might lack precision, or might be uncertain. An example of a semi-structured problem for a retail business would be deciding how much inventory to stock for the holidays. The decision can be based on the previous year's sales, with some adjustment for the current year's consumer confidence index. The consumer confidence index, however, might or might not accurately predict consumer spending over the holidays, so the holiday inventory problem would be classified as a semi-structured problem.

An **unstructured problem** requires human intuition as the basis for finding a solution. Information relevant to the problem might be missing, and few, if any, parts of the solution can be tackled using concrete models. If experts are presented with the same problem data, but they disagree on a solution, it is likely an unstructured problem. Global warming is an example of an unstructured problem. Although historic temperature data exists, even experts disagree on how to interpret this data.

Traditionally, information systems have contributed most to solving structured problems, but tools have emerged to help people tackle semi-structured and unstructured problems as well. Despite these tools and the data they provide, many semi-structured and unstructured problems continue to be resolved based on "guesstimates."

An information system's ability to assist with problem solving and decision making depends on the data that it collects and then makes available. Some information systems collect and store **internal information** generated by the organization itself. Other information systems store or provide access to **external information** generated by sources outside the organization. Later in this section, you'll learn how different types of information systems deal with internal and external information.

How do information systems help organizations carry out their missions? Most organizations exist in a rapidly changing and competitive environment, where many opportunities and threats can be effectively handled only by using computers. A well-known business analyst, Michael Porter, created the Five Forces model, shown in Figure 9-3, to illustrate the interaction between these opportunities and threats.

FIGURE 9-3

Michael Porter's Five Forces model illustrates the factors that affect competition among business rivals.

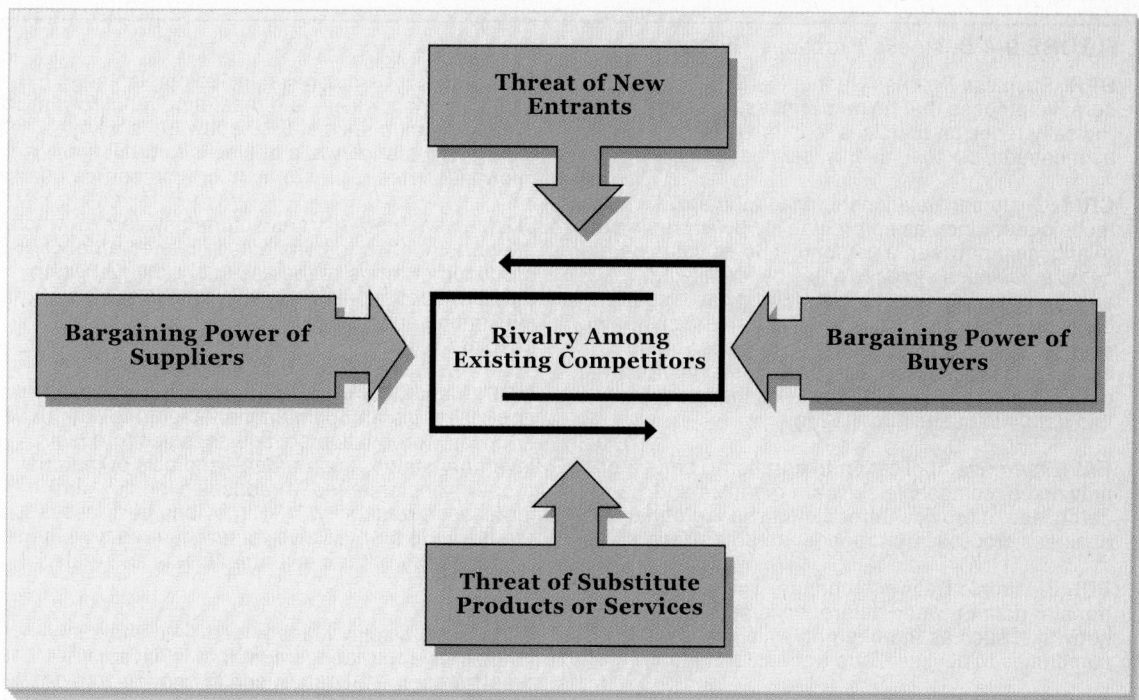

click to start

9

To be successful in its mission, an organization must respond effectively to opportunities and threats. An organization has a choice of three fundamental responses. First, it can become better at what it does by cutting costs, lowering prices, improving its products, offering better customer service, and so on. Computers often provide ways to make businesses run more efficiently, and they can provide timely information that helps improve customer service. For example, to keep up with other automakers, DaimlerChrysler developed a new information system, which uses the Internet to track vehicle design, manufacturing, and supply.

A second response is to change the structure of an industry. Computers and related technologies such as the Internet often make such changes possible. For example, Amazon.com pioneered the idea of selling books on the Web, which was a major change to an industry in which success depended on the number of store franchises that could be placed in shopping malls.

As a third response, an organization can create a new product, like flavored potato chips, or a new service, such as overnight package delivery. Although creativity and invention usually spring from the minds of people, computers can contribute to research and development efforts by collecting and analyzing data, helping inventors create models, explore simulations, and so on.

You'll find more in-depth information about terms such as BPR and CRM at the **Business Practices** InfoWeb.

click

As organizations respond to opportunities and threats, they change. Because these changes often affect the organization's members, employees, and customers, it can be important to understand the nature of coming changes. That's sometimes easier said than done. What does your boss mean when he says "We're putting in a new CRM system?" or "We're going to try BPR."? To help you make sense out of the acronyms that refer to changing business practices and new information systems, refer to Figure 9-4.

FIGURE 9-4 Business Practices Glossary

BPR (Business Process Reengineering) An ongoing iterative process that helps businesses rethink and radically redesign practices to improve performance, as measured by cost, quality, service, and speed.

CRM (Customer Relationship Management) A technique for increasing profitability by improving the relationship between a company and its customers. It helps a business increase sales by identifying, acquiring, and retaining customers. It can also cut costs by automating sales, marketing, and customer service. Information systems make it possible to collect and process the large volumes of customer data required for CRM, and to efficiently transform this data into useful information.

EAI (Enterprise Application Integration) The use of networked, compatible software modules and databases to provide unrestricted sharing of data and business processes throughout an organization.

EDI (Electronic Data Interchange) The ability to transfer data between different companies using networks, such as the Internet, which enables companies to buy, sell, and trade information.

ERP (Enterprise Resource Planning) A system of business management that integrates all facets, or "resources," of a business, including planning, manufacturing, sales, and marketing. An information system running special ERP software is a key technology that allows a business to track the information necessary to monitor its resource use.

JIT (Just In Time) A manufacturing system in which the parts needed to construct a finished product are produced or arrive at the assembly site just when they are needed. JIT typically reduces costs by eliminating substantial warehousing costs and obsolete parts.

MRP (Manufacturing Resource Planning) Calculates and maintains an optimum manufacturing plan based on master production schedules, sales forecasts, inventory status, open orders, and bills of material. If properly implemented, it reduces cash flow and increases profitability. MRP provides businesses with the ability to be proactive rather than reactive in the management of their inventory levels and material flow.

TQM (Total Quality Management) A technique initiated by top management that involves all employees and all departments, and focuses on quality assurance in every product and service offered to customers.

Do organizations require different kinds of information systems? Because organizations have different missions, face different threats, and encounter different opportunities, they require different kinds of information systems. An information system might have one or more of the following components: an office automation system, a transaction processing system, a management information system, a decision support system, an expert system, or a neural network. Let's take a closer look at each of these systems.

OFFICE AUTOMATION SYSTEMS

Can an information system automate routine office tasks? As its name suggests, an **office automation system** "automates," or computerizes, routine office tasks. Word processing, spreadsheet, scheduling, database, and e-mail software are integral parts of most office automation systems. LANs, intranets, and the Internet also play important roles in office automation by facilitating communications among workers, and providing centralized storage for documents, reports, memos, and other data. Office automation systems can be used by workers and managers at all levels of the organizational hierarchy.

9

TRANSACTION PROCESSING SYSTEMS

What's a transaction? In an information system context, a **transaction** is an exchange between two parties that is recorded and stored in a computer system. When you order a product at a Web site, buy merchandise in a store, or withdraw cash from an ATM, you are involved in a transaction.

What is a transaction processing system? Many activities of an organization involve transactions. A **transaction processing system** (TPS) provides a way to collect, process, store, display, modify, or cancel transactions. Most transaction processing systems allow many transactions to be entered simultaneously. The data collected by a TPS is typically stored in databases, and can be used to produce a regularly scheduled set of reports, such as monthly bills, weekly paychecks, annual inventory summaries, daily manufacturing schedules, or periodic check registers. Early transaction processing systems, such as banking and payroll applications of the 1970s, used **batch processing** to collect and hold a group of transactions for processing until the end of a day or pay period. An entire batch was then processed without human intervention, until all transactions were completed, or until an error occurred.

In contrast to batch processing, most modern transaction processing systems use **online processing**—an interactive method in which each transaction is processed as it is entered. Such systems are often referred to as **OLTP systems** (online transaction processing systems). OLTP uses a "commit or rollback" strategy to ensure that each transaction is processed correctly. This strategy is crucial because most transactions require a sequence of steps, and every step must succeed for the transaction to be complete. If you withdraw cash from an ATM, the bank's computer must make sure that your account contains sufficient funds before it allows the ATM to deliver cash, and deducts the withdrawal from your account. If the ATM is out of cash, however, the transaction fails, and the withdrawal should not be deducted from your account. A TPS can **commit** to a transaction and permanently update database records only if every step of the transaction can be successfully processed. If even one step fails, however, the entire transaction fails and the records must **roll back** to their original state. Figure 9-5 diagrams the processes that take place in a typical TPS, and the video that accompanies the figure provides additional information about commit and rollback.

FIGURE 9-5

A transaction processing system is characterized by its ability to:

- Collect, display, and modify transactions
- Store transactions
- List transactions

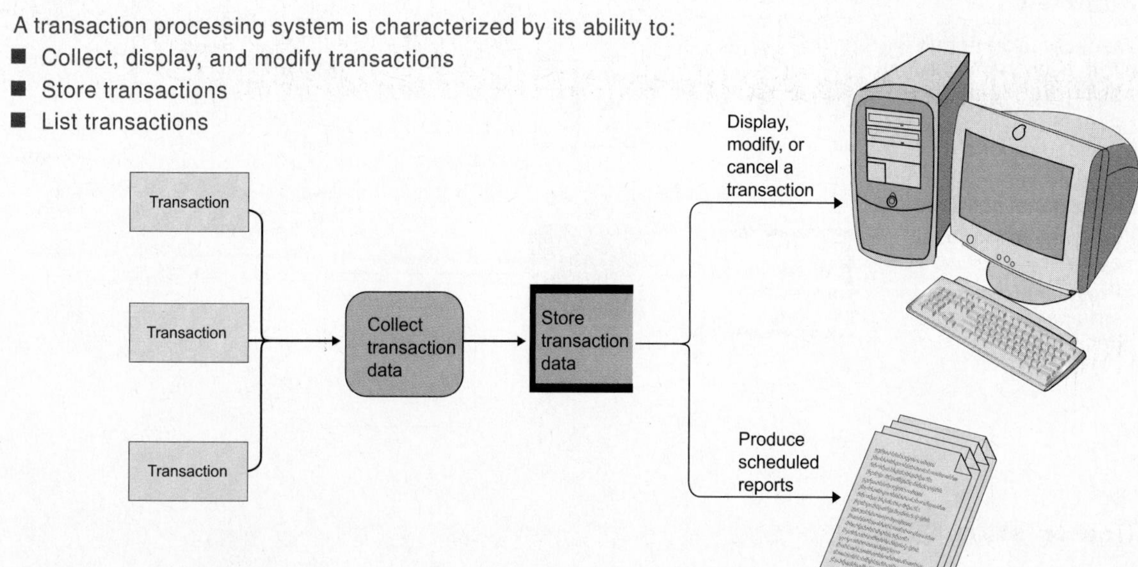

click to start

What are common examples of transaction processing systems? Examples of business transaction processing systems include the following:

- A point-of-sale (POS) system records items purchased at each cash register, and calculates the total amount due for each sale. Some POS systems automatically verify credit cards, calculate change, and identify customers who previously wrote bad checks.
- An order-entry/invoice system provides a way to input, view, modify, and delete customer orders. It helps track the status of each order, and it creates invoices.
- A general accounting system records the financial status of a business by keeping track of income, expenses, and assets.
- An e-commerce system collects online orders and processes credit card payments.

What are the limitations of transaction processing systems? Although a TPS excels at maintaining transaction data entered by clerical personnel and online customers, its reporting capabilities are limited. A typical TPS generates **detail reports**, which provide a basic record of completed transactions. However, managers need more sophisticated reports to help them understand and analyze data. These reports are usually created by a management information system.

MANAGEMENT INFORMATION SYSTEMS

What is a management information system? The term "management information system" is used in two contexts. It can be a synonym for the term "information system," or it can refer to a specific category or type of information system. We'll use the term **management information system** (MIS, pronounced EM EYE ESS) in this second context, to refer to a type of information system that uses the data collected by a transaction processing system, but manipulates that data to create reports that managers can use to make routine business decisions in response to structured problems. As Figure 9-6 shows, an MIS is characterized by the production of routine reports that managers use for structured and routine tasks.

FIGURE 9-6

A management information system is characterized by its ability to:

- Produce routine and on-demand reports
- Provide information for managerial activities
- Increase managerial efficiency
- Provide information for structured, routine decisions

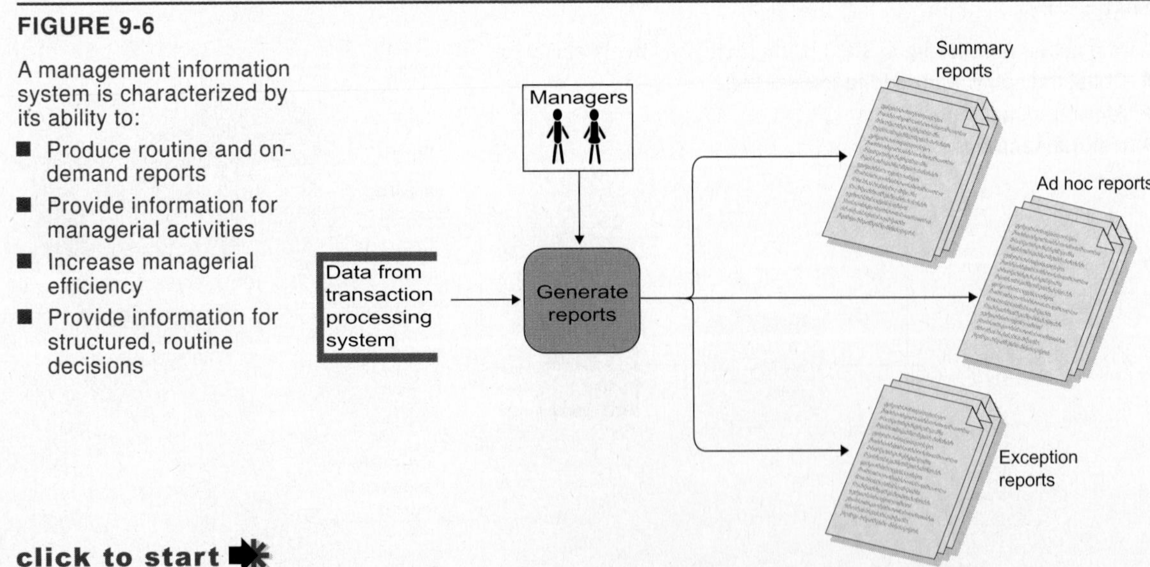

click to start

The original **waterfall SDLC**, shown on the previous page, approaches each phase as a discrete step in the development process. One phase is supposed to be completed before the next phase can begin. In reality, this model is impractical because it is not possible to neatly compartmentalize the development process. For example, it is difficult to complete the design phase until analysts and programmers have a chance to work with software tools that are to be purchased later in the implementation phase. A **modified waterfall SDLC** allows overlap between SDLC phases. An **iterative SDLC** allows phases to repeat, if necessary, as the project progresses. Figure 9-15 illustrates various SDLC models.

FIGURE 9-15 Modified waterfall and iterative SDLCs

The modified waterfall SDLC allows overlap between phases.

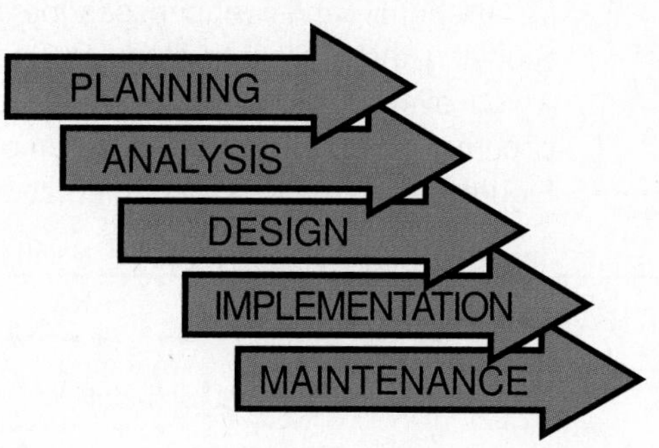

The iterative SDLC allows phases to repeat, if necessary.

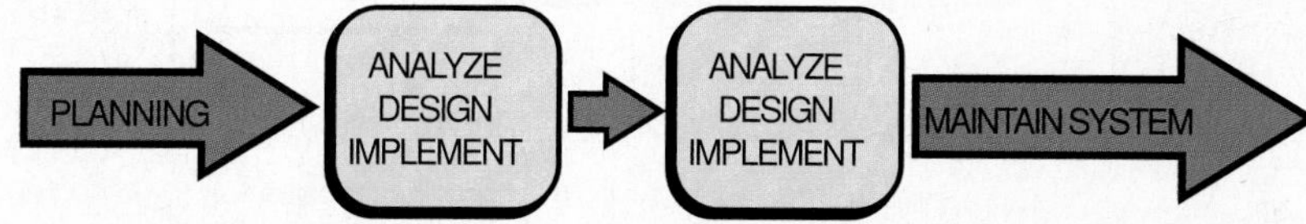

9

How do different SDLCs affect project development? An organization typically develops an information system according to a specific methodology and a set of related development tools. The **structured methodology** focuses on the processes that take place within an information system. The **information engineering methodology** focuses on the data that an information system collects before working out ways to process that data. The **object-oriented methodology** treats an information system as a collection of objects that interact with each other to accomplish tasks. A methodology called **rapid application development** (RAD) proceeds with the project team creating a series of prototypes that users can evaluate. User comments are incorporated into the next prototype, and the process continues until the system is acceptable. In many cases, RAD shortens the development schedule, which is why it is called "rapid" application development.

Different SDLCs also affect the project schedule. The experienced systems analysts on the project team typically map out a schedule during the planning phase, and refine it as the development process proceeds.

The tools for analyzing and designing an information system are directly related to the methodology. You'll learn more about diagrams, software packages, and other systems analysis and design tools in the Lab and TechTalk for this chapter.

FIGURE 9-16

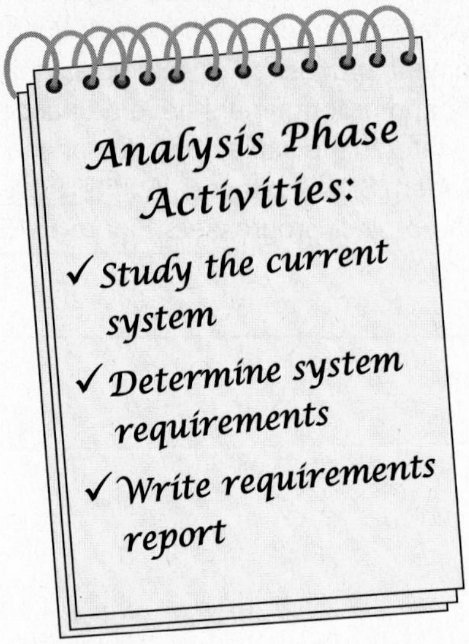

Analysis Phase Activities:

✓ Study the current system

✓ Determine system requirements

✓ Write requirements report

ANALYSIS PHASE

What happens in the analysis phase? The goal of the **analysis phase** is to produce a list of requirements for a new or revised information system. Project team tasks for the analysis phase are listed in Figure 9-16.

STUDY THE CURRENT SYSTEM

Is it really important to understand the current system before planning a new system? Typically, a new information system is designed to replace a system or process that is already in place. It is important to study the current system to understand its strengths and weaknesses before planning a new system. Studying the current system can be a very detailed process, in which every aspect of an organization's procedures and data is documented using data flow diagrams (DFDs), like the one shown in Figure 9-17, and other documentation tools.

FIGURE 9-17

A data flow diagram documents the origin, flow, storage, and processing of data.

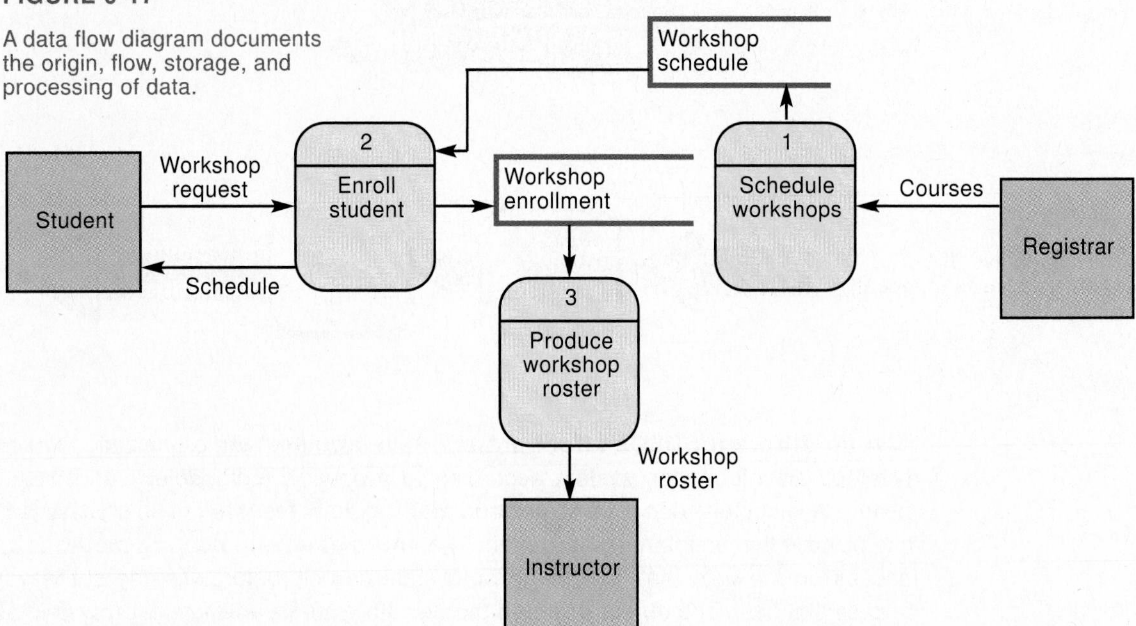

How does the project team discover what happens in the current system? Some members of the project team might have first-hand experience with the current system. They can often provide an overview of the system, and they might be able to give details about key features, strengths, and weaknesses. To obtain additional information about the current system, the project team members can interview the people who use the system, or observe the system in action. The purpose of these interviews and observations is twofold. First, the project team is looking for aspects of the current system that must be carried over to the new information system. Second, the team is looking for problems with the current system that must be solved by the new system. These requirements and problems are documented and incorporated into the requirements for the new system.

DETERMINE SYSTEM REQUIREMENTS

How does the project team determine what the new system should do? System requirements are the criteria for successfully solving the problem or problems identified in an information system. These requirements guide the design and implementation for a new or updated information system. They also serve as an evaluation checklist at the end of the development project, so they are sometimes called **success factors**. A new or updated information system should meet the requirements defined by the project team.

The project team determines requirements by interviewing users and studying successful information systems that solve problems similar to those found in the current system. Another way to determine requirements is to construct a prototype as an experimental or trial version of an information system. Often the prototype is not a fully functioning system because it is designed to demonstrate only selected features that might be incorporated into a new information system. A systems analyst shows the prototype to users, who evaluate which features of the prototype are important for the new information system.

How does the project team document system requirements? The project team can use a variety of tools to diagram the current system and specify what it does. These tools help the team produce documentation that is also useful in later phases of the SDLC. It can be difficult, however, to maintain this documentation as the project progresses. A **CASE tool** (computer-aided software engineering tool) is a software application that is designed for documenting system requirements, diagramming current and proposed information systems, scheduling development tasks, and developing computer programs. CASE tools automate many of the routine housekeeping tasks required by the systems analysis and design process, such as changing every instance of "ItemNumber" to "InventoryID." Figure 9-18 shows a screen from a CASE tool called PowerDesigner.

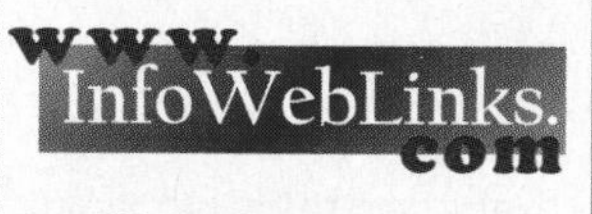

You'll find more information about CASE software, including links to downloads, at the CASE Tools InfoWeb.

click

FIGURE 9-18

CASE tools help the project team members manage all the details of system documentation. In this example, the project team initially assumed that merchandise was identified by an "item number." The team later realized that most employees refer to it as an "inventory ID." The CASE tool allows the team to make a global change that is applied to every diagram and narrative created with the CASE software.

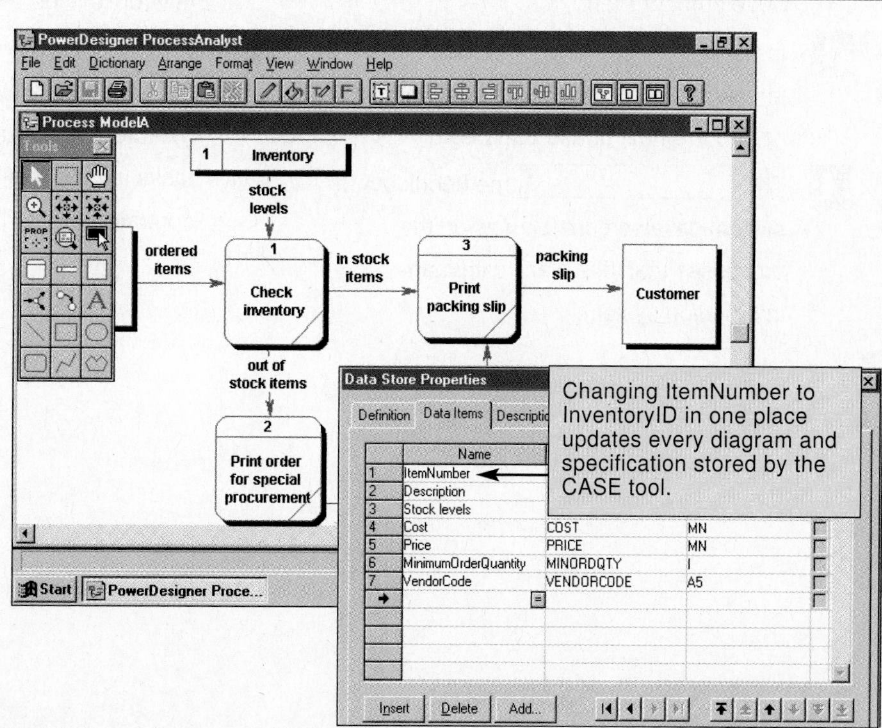

click to start

What marks the end of the analysis phase of the SDLC? After the project team studies the current system and determines system requirements, the analysis phase concludes when the project team produces a written report that documents its findings. The **System Requirements Report** typically contains diagrams that illustrate what the new information system should do. The report also includes narrative descriptions and diagrams showing the new system's users, data, processes, objects, and reports.

QUICKCheck Section B

1 Computer professionals who specialize in analyzing and designing information systems are referred to as [ ] analysts.

2 During the [ ] phase, a member of the IS staff creates a Project Development Plan.

3 In the [ ] SDLC, one phase of the process must be completed before the next phase can begin.

4 The [ ] methodology for system development focuses on the processes that take place within an information system.

5 A project team that uses rapid application development (RAD) methodology creates a series of prototypes that users can evaluate. True or false? [ ]

6 The goal of the [ ] phase is to produce a list of requirements for a new or revised information system.

7 A(n) [ ] tool helps the project team document the current system by automating many of the housekeeping tasks involved in diagramming and documenting an information system.

check answers

LAB 9-B WORKING WITH DFDs

Interactive LAB
Working with DFDs

B Student
A Registrar
0 Workshop registration system
C Workshop roster
Faculty member

click to start

In this lab, you'll learn:

- The purpose of data flow diagrams (DFDs) in the system development life cycle
- How to read a leveled set of DFDs
- The meaning of each DFD symbol
- The differences between Gane/Sarson DFD notation and Yourdon/Coad DFD notation
- How to label data flows, entities, data stores, and processes
- How to create a context DFD
- How to "explode" a DFD to show additional levels of detail
- Why "black holes" and "miracles" indicate DFD errors

LAB Assignments

1. Start the interactive part of the lab. Insert your Tracking Disk if you want to save your QuickCheck results. Perform each of the lab steps as directed, and answer all of the lab QuickCheck questions. When you exit the lab, your answers are automatically graded and your results are displayed.

2. Use paper and pencil, graphics software, or a CASE tool to create a context DFD for a video rental store. Use Gane/Sarson notation. Remember that the store purchases as well as rents videos and DVDs.

3. Explode the DFD that you created in Assignment 2 so that it represents the main processes and data stores for the video rental store. Make sure that you label data flows, processes, entities, and data stores. Before you finalize your DFD, make sure that it contains no black holes or miracles.

4. Convert the DFD that you drew in Assignment 3 to Yourdon/Coad notation.

SYSTEM DESIGN

Returning to our blueprint analogy, we can suppose that during the analysis phase, an architect determines the elements a new building will contain. A single-family home, for example, might require bedrooms, bathrooms, closets, a kitchen, living room, dining room, and laundry room. In the design phase, the architect must figure how to arrange these elements. Should all of the rooms be on the same floor? How many bedrooms? Where will the closets be located? Where will the doors be placed to make the best traffic pattern? As the architect answers these questions, the design for the house begins to emerge. In Section C, you'll learn how a project team designs a new information system.

FIGURE 9-19

Design Phase Activities:

- ✓ Identify potential solutions
- ✓ Evaluate solutions and select the best
- ✓ Select hardware and software
- ✓ Develop application specifications
- ✓ Obtain approval to implement the new system

DESIGN PHASE

What happens in the design phase? In the analysis phase, the project team determines WHAT the new information system must do. In the **design phase** of the SDLC, the project team must figure out HOW the new system will fulfill the requirements specified in the System Requirements Report. The activities that typically take place during the design phase for an information system are listed in Figure 9-19.

IDENTIFY POTENTIAL SOLUTIONS

How does the project team come up with solutions? There might be more than one way to solve the problems and meet the requirements identified in the analysis phase of the SDLC. Some potential solutions might be better than others—more effective, less costly, or less complex. Therefore, it is not a good idea to proceed with the first solution that comes to mind. The project team should, instead, identify several potential hardware and software solutions by "brainstorming" and researching case studies on Web sites and in computer magazines.

What kinds of hardware alternatives are available? A myriad of hardware options are available for information systems. Mainframes, servers, and personal computers are the most commonly used components, but in some information systems, handhelds, or even supercomputers, play a role. When evaluating hardware solutions for a new information system, the project team considers the overall architecture of the information system based on level of automation, processing methodology, and network technology.

Level of automation and computerization. Some information systems provide a higher level of automation than others. For instance, a point-of-sale system with a low level of automation might require the checkout clerk to enter credit card numbers from a keypad. At a higher level of automation, a magnetic strip reader automates the process of entering a credit card number. A further level of automation is achieved by using a pressure-sensitive digitizing pad and stylus to collect your signature (Figure 9-20). With your signature in digital format, the entire transaction record becomes electronic, and the business does not need to deal with paper credit card receipts.

FIGURE 9-20

Automation options, such as this device that digitizes signatures, might be considered by the project team as it brainstorms solutions.

Automation alternatives can affect many aspects of an information system. In our point-of-sale example, a credit card number can be stored using a few bytes. Storing a digitized signature, however, might require far more disk space and a special type of database software. The project team should consider the pros and cons of different levels of computerization and automation, as they affect all aspects of the planned information system.

Centralized or distributed processing. An information system can be designed for **centralized processing** in which data is processed on a centrally located computer. An alternative design option is **distributed processing** in which processing tasks are distributed to servers and workstations. Typically, centralized processing requires a more powerful computer—usually a mainframe—to achieve the same response speed as distributed processing. Distributed processing in a client/server or peer-to-peer environment (discussed in Chapter 5) is very popular today because it provides high levels of processing power at a low cost. However, these distributed architectures present more security problems than a single, centralized computer—a factor that the project team must consider within the context of selecting a solution.

Network technology. An information system, by its very nature, is designed to serve an entire organization. That organization includes many people who work in different rooms, different buildings, and perhaps even different countries. Virtually every information system requires a network, so the project team must examine network alternatives, such as LANs, extranets, intranets and the Internet. (For a review of network terminology, refer to Chapter 5.) Many information systems require a complex mixture of networks, such as a LAN in each branch office connected to a company intranet, with access to selected data provided to customers via the Internet.

What kinds of software alternatives are available? The project team might consider software alternatives, such as whether to construct the system "from scratch," use an application development tool, or purchase commercial software.

Creating an information system "from scratch" using a programming language can take many months or years. It is typically very costly, but provides the most flexibility for meeting the system requirements. As an analogy, baking a cake from scratch allows you some flexibility in the ingredients you choose—margarine instead of shortening, for example. However, baking from scratch requires a lot of time and work to sift the flour with the salt; mix the sugar, eggs, shortening, and milk; combine the dry and wet ingredients; and so forth. During the design phase, the project team can analyze the costs and benefits of developing information system modules from scratch.

Many programming languages are available, and the project team must decide which language works best based on the programming expertise available within the organization, and the design approach. For example, object-oriented design usually requires an object-oriented programming language.

An **application development tool** is essentially a type of software construction kit containing building blocks that can be assembled into a software product. An application development tool is the programmer's "cake mix," which contains many of the ingredients necessary for quickly and easily developing the modules for an information system. Application development tools include expert system shells and database management systems. Although application development tools usually speed up the development process, they might not provide the same level of flexibility as a programming language. Application development tools must be carefully selected by the project team. The right tools must match the available programming expertise and design approach.

Commercial software for an information system is usually a series of pre-programmed software modules, supplied by a software developer, consulting company, or value-added reseller (VAR). Following through with the cake analogy, commercial software is equivalent to buying a pre-made cake, which you simply slice and serve.

Commercial software eliminates much of the design work required with programming languages or application development tools. However, commercial software requires extensive evaluation to determine how well it meets the system requirements. Commercial software is available for standard business functions, such as human resource management, accounting, and payroll. It is also available for many vertical market businesses and organizations, such as law offices, video stores, medical offices, libraries, churches, e-commerce, and charities. Although most commercial software provides some customization options, in many cases, it cannot be modified to exactly meet every system requirement, which necessitates adjustments in an organization's procedures. The project team must decide if the benefits of commercial software can offset the cost and inconvenience of procedural changes.

A **turnkey system** is essentially an "information system in a box," which consists of hardware and commercial software designed to offer a complete information system solution. In terms of the cake analogy, a turnkey system is like going out to dinner and simply ordering your choice of cake for dessert. A turnkey system might seem like a quick and easy solution, and looks attractive to many project teams. Like commercial software, however, a turnkey system must be extensively evaluated to determine whether it can satisfy system requirements.

EVALUATE SOLUTIONS AND SELECT THE BEST

How does the team choose the best solution? To determine the best solution, the project team devises a list of criteria for comparing each of the potential solutions. This list includes general criteria relevant to costs, benefits, and development time. The list also includes technical criteria, such as the flexibility of the solution, and its adaptability for future modifications and growth. Finally, the list includes functional criteria that indicate how well the solution satisfies the specified requirements.

Each criterion is assigned a weight to indicate its importance. The project team then evaluates the criteria for each solution and assigns raw scores. The raw score for each criterion is multiplied by the weight, and these weights are added to produce a total score for each solution. Sound complicated? It isn't, especially if the project team uses a **decision support worksheet**. Take a few moments to study Figure 9-21, and you'll quickly see how it works.

FIGURE 9-21

A spreadsheet produces a decision support worksheet for comparing potential solutions.

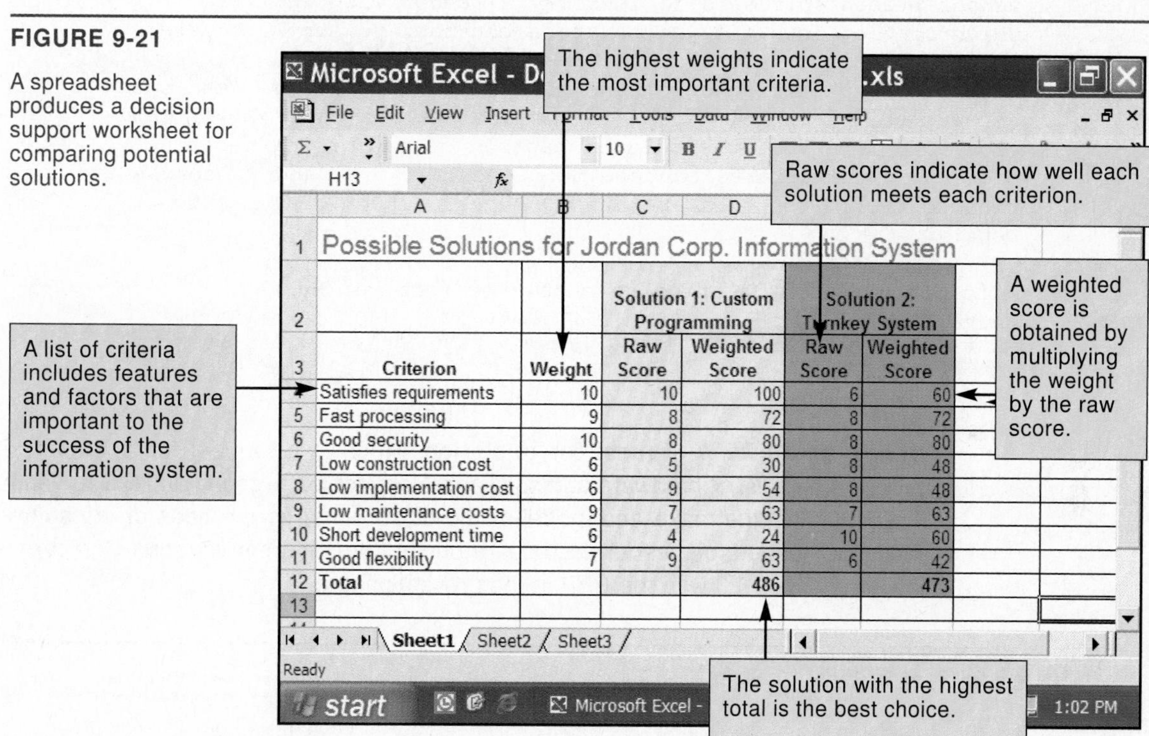

Possible Solutions for Jordan Corp. Information System

Criterion	Weight	Solution 1: Custom Programming Raw Score	Solution 1: Custom Programming Weighted Score	Solution 2: Turnkey System Raw Score	Solution 2: Turnkey System Weighted Score
Satisfies requirements	10	10	100	6	60
Fast processing	9	8	72	8	72
Good security	10	8	80	8	80
Low construction cost	6	5	30	8	48
Low implementation cost	6	9	54	8	48
Low maintenance costs	9	7	63	7	63
Short development time	6	4	24	10	60
Good flexibility	7	9	63	6	42
Total			486		473

The highest weights indicate the most important criteria.
Raw scores indicate how well each solution meets each criterion.
A weighted score is obtained by multiplying the weight by the raw score.
A list of criteria includes features and factors that are important to the success of the information system.
The solution with the highest total is the best choice.

SELECT HARDWARE AND SOFTWARE

How does the project team find the right hardware and software for the new information system? Once the project team selects a solution, the next task is to select the hardware and software needed to implement the solution. Sometimes more than one vendor sells the hardware and software necessary for the new system, so an organization might have a choice of vendors.

The method for selecting the hardware, software, and vendor depends on the project team's understanding of what is required for the solution. If the team members do not know exactly what hardware and software are needed, they can use an RFP to describe the problem and ask vendors how they would solve it. If the project team members know exactly what they want, they can use an RFQ to find a reputable vendor that sells the equipment at a reasonable price.

What's an RFP? A **request for proposal** (RFP) is a document that describes the information system problem and the requirements for the solution. An RFP essentially asks a vendor to recommend hardware and software for the solution, and to describe the vendor's qualifications for implementing the solution. A project team usually issues an RFP to vendors when its members believe that a vendor's knowledge and experience in the solution area are more comprehensive than that of the team members. Look at the sample RFP in Figure 9-22.

FIGURE 9-22 RFP excerpt

RFP for The University of Iowa Library Information System

The purpose of this request for proposal (RFP) and subsequent vendor presentations is to identify a vendor with whom The University of Iowa will negotiate a contract to supply, install, and support an integrated library system. This system must be capable of supporting an online public access catalog, cataloging and authority control, acquisitions and serials control, circulation, and reserve. It should be capable of supporting media booking, interlibrary loan and document delivery, and preservation control. Proposals are due 10 August 3:00pm, Purchasing Dept.

A letter of intent to propose should be received by the University of Iowa by 5:00pm CDT, July 13, 1998. Letters should be ...

What's an RFQ? A **request for quotation** (RFQ) is a request for a formal price quotation on a list of hardware and software. A project team issues an RFQ to vendors when it knows the make and model of the equipment and the titles of the software packages needed, but wants to compare prices from different vendors. Compare the RFQ in Figure 9-23 with the RFP in the previous figure.

FIGURE 9-23 RFQ excerpt

Fresno California City Hall Information System RFQ

The Information Technology Office is seeking qualified vendors for the quotation of network equipment required for the expansion of the city hall facility. A list of hardware and software is provided below. Prospective vendors MUST provide the total price including shipping charges and the applicable sales tax. Any deviation from the specifications MUST be noted on the quotation and a written explanation is strongly encouraged to support the substitutions. Bids submitted with equipment other than those stated in the specifications may be rejected.

Part Description	Part Number	Quantity	Price
1. Cisco Catalyst 4000 Chassis (6-Slot), WS-X4013 Supervisor II Engine, (2) AC PS, Fans, Rack-Mount Kit	CS-4000-WSX4013	1	
2.Cisco Catalyst 4000 E/FE/GE L3 Module, 2-GE (GBIC), 32-10/100 (RJ45)	WS-X4232-L3	1	
3. C...			

What does a DFD look like? In a completed DFD, data flow arrows show the path of data to and from external entities, data stores, and processes. Figure 9-30 explains how to read a DFD.

FIGURE 9-30 DFD for workshop registration system

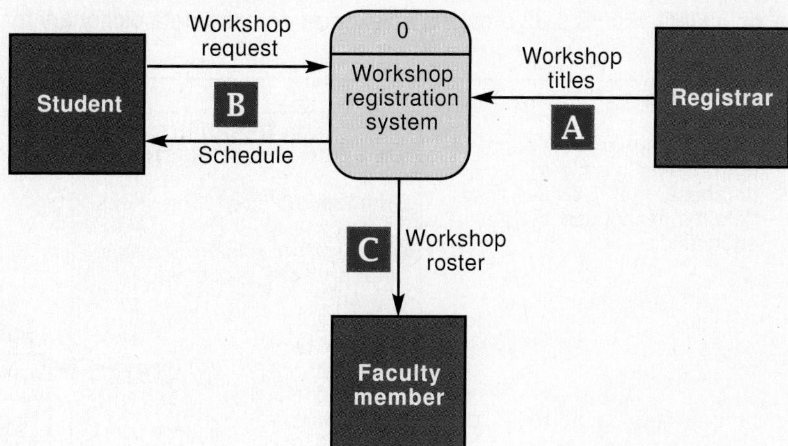

A The registrar produces the list of workshops offered, and submits it to the registration system.

B A student submits a request to enroll in a workshop. The workshop registration system processes the request and produces a schedule of workshops in which the student is enrolled.

C A faculty member receives a list of the students enrolled in a workshop.

Why doesn't the DFD show the detail of the system? The DFD in the previous figure is called a **context diagram**, and it simply provides an overview of the information system. This context DFD can be "exploded" to show more details. Figure 9-31 illustrates how the rectangle labeled 0 in the previous diagram is exploded to show the more detailed processes that take place within the system. It also shows the two data stores that can be accessed by processes.

FIGURE 9-31

In this exploded DFD for workshop registration, the yellow area corresponds to the single process depicted in the context diagram.

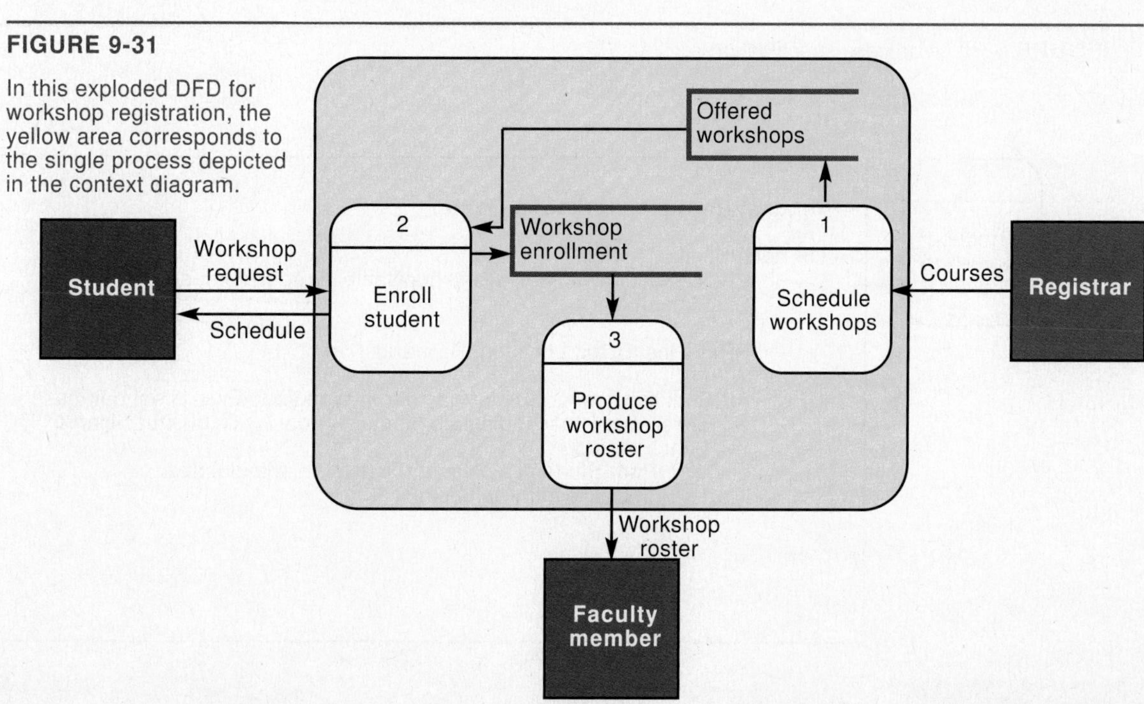

How do I find out what data is included in each data store? A DFD does not provide a direct mechanism for listing the data in a data store. For that purpose, a project team typically uses a **data dictionary**, which contains a detailed description of the records stored in a database. A complete data dictionary can provide the specifications necessary to construct the database for a new information system. CASE tools usually provide a way to attach the data dictionary to its corresponding data store on a DFD. Figure 9-32 provides an excerpt from the data dictionary for the Offered Workshops data store.

FIGURE 9-32

A data dictionary lists each of the fields in a file or database, then provides a detailed description of each field.

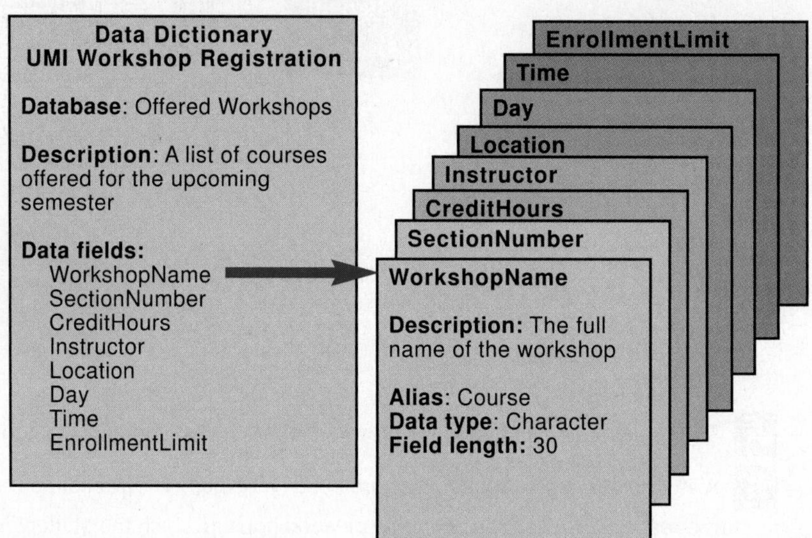

Can a DFD provide the specifications needed by programmers to write applications for an information system? Although DFDs can be exploded to show more and more detailed levels of processing activity, they do not typically provide enough detail for programmers. Instead, the project team provides programmers with **process specifications**, which explain exactly what happens in each process of a DFD. Many CASE tools provide a way to attach a process specification to its corresponding process on a DFD. For example, Figure 9-33 provides an excerpt from the process specification for the Produce Workshop Roster process.

FIGURE 9-33 A process specification

3

Produce workshop roster

Process: Produce Workshop Roster

```
FOR each SectionNumber
        PRINT SectionNumber, WorkshopName, CreditHours, and
        EnrollmentLimit

        PRINT Instructor, Location, Day, and Time

        FIND all records for SectionNumber in Workshop Enrollment database
        SORT records in ascending alphabetical order by StudentLastName
        FOR each record
                Print StudentLastName, FirstName, MiddleInitial,
                SocialSecurityNumber
```

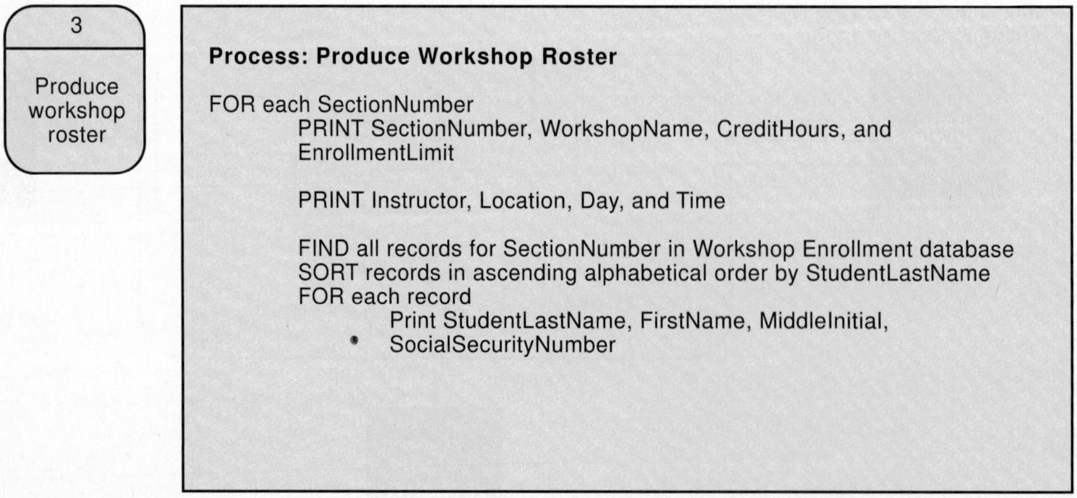

OBJECT-ORIENTED DOCUMENTATION TOOLS

How do documentation tools differ for object-oriented analysis and design? In structured design, the goal is to create documentation that indicates how to design databases and write the applications that allow people to interact with those databases. In contrast, object-oriented design tools provide the blueprints for creating data objects, and the routines that allow people to interact with those objects. The current standard for object-oriented documentation is called **UML** (Unified Modeling Language). Three of the most frequently used UML tools include use case diagrams, sequence diagrams, and class diagrams.

What is a use case diagram? A **use case diagram** documents the users of an information system and the functions that they perform. In object-oriented jargon, the people who use the system are called **actors**. Any task that an actor performs is called a **use case**. Figure 9-34 shows a simple use case diagram for a workshop registration system.

FIGURE 9-34

A use case diagram for a workshop registration system depicts two use cases—one in which a student enrolls in a workshop, and one in which the student drops the workshop.

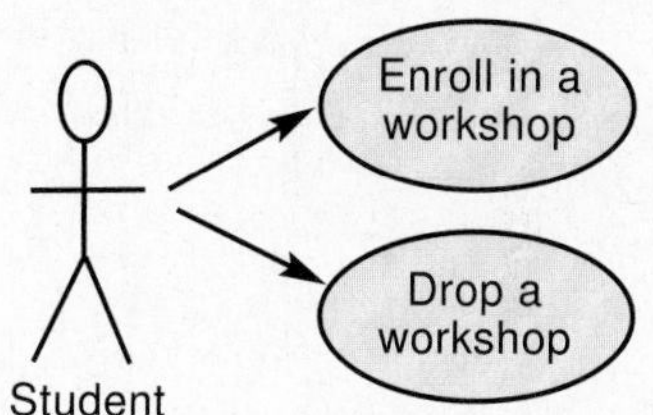

Does a use case diagram explode like a DFD? No. To fill in the detail for a use case, the project team uses a **sequence diagram**, which depicts the detailed sequence of interactions that take place. Figure 9-35 shows the sequence diagram for the Enroll in a Workshop use case, and explains how to interpret it.

FIGURE 9-35

Sequence diagram for Enroll in a Workshop use case

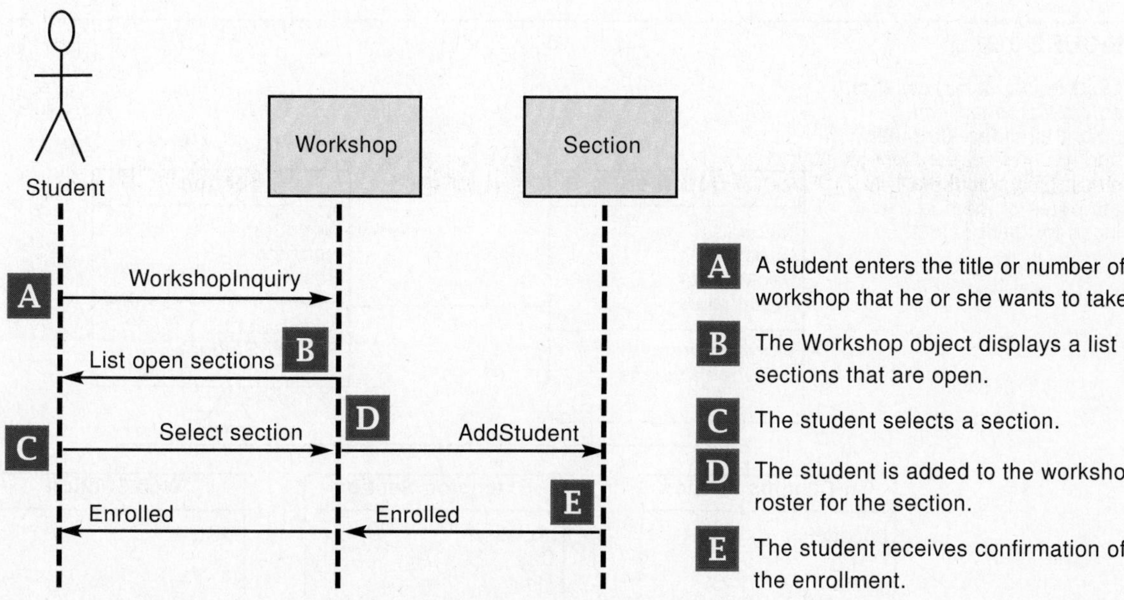

Student
Workshop
Section
A WorkshopInquiry
B List open sections
C Select section
D AddStudent
E Enrolled
Enrolled
A A student enters the title or number of a workshop that he or she wants to take.
B The Workshop object displays a list of sections that are open.
C The student selects a section.
D The student is added to the workshop roster for the section.
E The student receives confirmation of the enrollment.

What is the composition of an object? A key element of object-oriented development is defining objects. In the previous diagram, the student interacted with two objects: the Workshop object and the Section object. A **class diagram** provides the name of each object, a list of each object's attributes, a list of methods, and an indication of the cardinality between objects. An attribute is simply any data element that is stored as part of an object. A method is any behavior that an object is capable of performing. Cardinality refers to the number of associations that can exist between objects. You'll find detailed definitions of object-oriented terms, such as classes, attributes and methods, in Chapter 11. Figure 9-36 illustrates a class diagram for the workshop registration system.

FIGURE 9-36

This class diagram shows each object's attributes (in blue) and methods (in green). The cardinality between objects (indicated by 1 and 1..*) means that each workshop may have one or more sections.

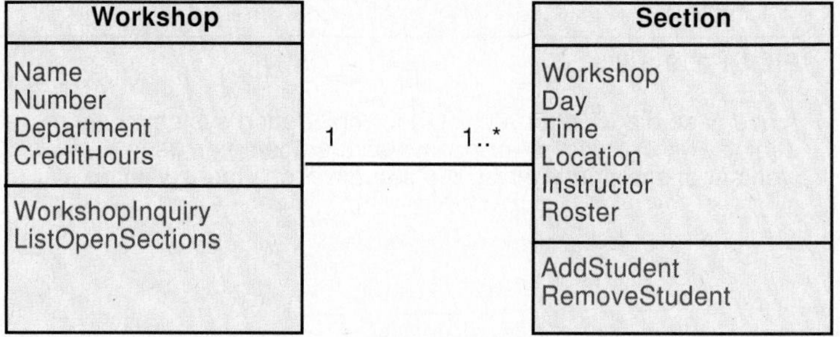

Class diagrams can be further refined to show inheritance—how objects inherit attributes and methods from a class. In objected-oriented terminology, a class is a group of objects with similar characteristics. For example, consider a school that offers sections of the same workshop on campus, at extension centers, and over the Web. All of these sections have common attributes, such as a name, scheduled day and time, instructor, and roster. However, extension center workshops might require additional fees, and self-paced, Web-based workshops might not meet on a particular date and time. Figure 9-37 shows a modified class diagram in which On-Campus Sections, Extension Sections, and Web Sections are subclasses of the Section object.

FIGURE 9-37

Objects in a subclass, such as On-Campus Section, inherit all of the attributes and methods of the Section class. Only additional attributes or methods are listed for each object.

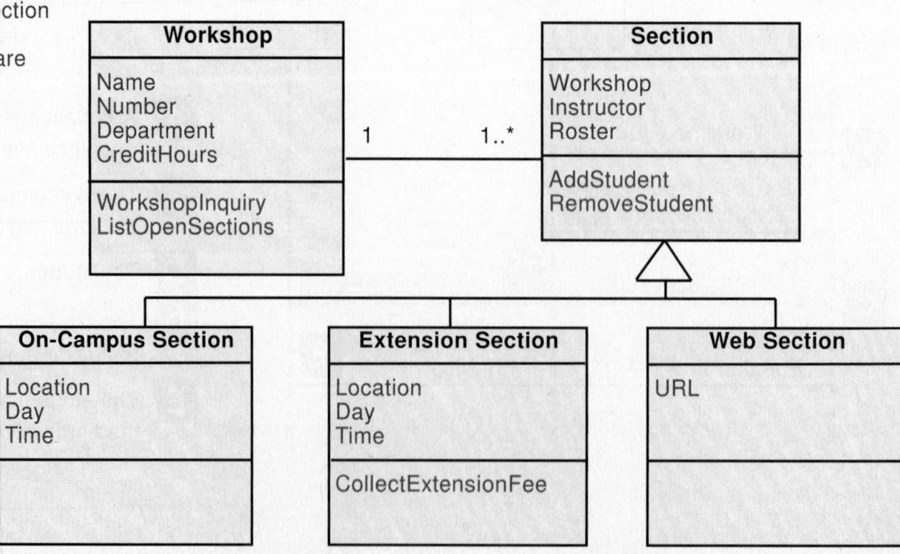

How do the various object-oriented diagrams fit together? A use case diagram provides an overview of the actors and use cases in an information system. A sequence diagram provides detailed steps showing how the actor interacts with objects. The objects are defined in detail in a class diagram. Figure 9-38 illustrates how these diagrams are linked conceptually, though a project team would not actually create such a linked diagram in practice.

FIGURE 9-38 Conceptual links among object-oriented diagrams

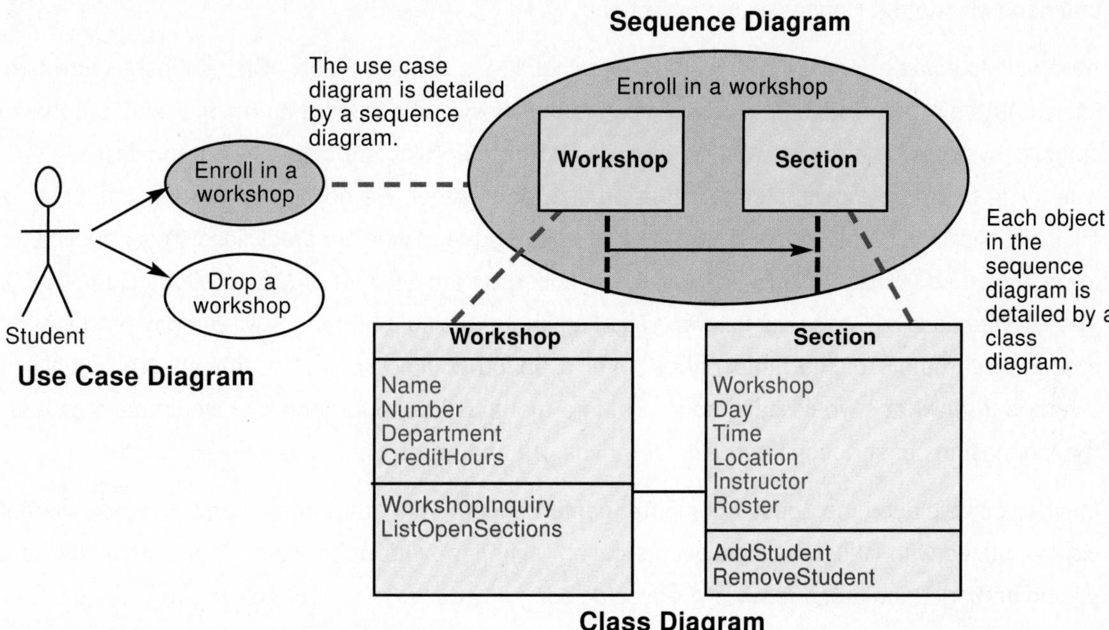

Is it necessary to document the methods associated with an object? Yes, the methods associated with an object can be documented using a technique similar to the process specifications produced as part of structured analysis and design.

QUICKCheck TechTalk

1 A(n) ______ is a diagramming tool used in the process of structured analysis and design that depicts the possible paths for data traveling from entities (such as customers) to processes (such as printing) or storage areas.

2 A(n) ______ dictionary can be used to describe the contents of a data store.

3 The current standard for object-oriented analysis and design diagramming is abbreviated as ______.

4 A(n) ______ case diagram documents the users of an information system and the functions that they perform.

5 A(n) ______ diagram provides the name of each object, a list of each object's attributes, a list of methods, and an indication of the cardinality between objects.

check answers

ISSUE
DO INFORMATION SYSTEMS WORK?

In Tolkien's book *The Hobbit*, Bilbo Baggins, alone and lost in a dark tunnel, gropes about in the dark, finds a small ring, and drops it in his pocket. That seemingly insignificant incident sets in motion events that soon plunge the Hobbits' world into chaos.

According to some scientists, our world—the real world—is already chaotic. Chaos theory, more formally known as the "theory of complex dynamical nonlinear systems," is the study of unstable behavior in complex systems. The theory was first introduced by meteorologist Edward N. Lorenz. In 1960, Lorenz was trying to create a computer model to predict the weather. He noticed that just a small change in the initial conditions of his model drastically altered its long-term weather predictions. This discovery came to be known as the Butterfly Effect, and is described by Ian Stewart, author of *Does God Play Dice? The Mathematics of Chaos*, as follows: "The flapping of a single butterfly's wing today produces a tiny change in the state of the atmosphere. Over a period of time, what the atmosphere actually does diverges from what it would have done. So, in a month's time, a tornado that would have devastated the Indonesian coast doesn't happen. Or maybe one that wasn't going to happen, does."

Maybe you've played the popular computer game SimCity. This game simulates a complex system—a city populated with little simulated people called "simmies" who go to work, have kids, build houses, pile up garbage, and grumble when the electric company builds a nuclear power plant next door. In the game, you become the city planner and try to keep the simmies happy. What you soon discover is that a seemingly insignificant event might set in motion other events that can turn your once-thriving city into a ghost town. That insignificant event is an element of chaos.

How does chaos theory apply to information systems in organizations? An organization is a complex system. The members of an organization—managers, stockholders, and employees—typically want it to succeed. They depend on transaction processing systems to gather data, management information systems to supply a steady stream of reports, and decision support systems to provide tools for analyzing data that can be used to plan strategic improvements. Although today's TPSs and MISs typically do their jobs dependably, some doubt exists about the effectiveness of decision support systems. Why? Most decision support systems do not account for the possible effects of chaotic events. Therefore, some experts assert that even with a powerful DSS, it is difficult to accurately predict the future, and determine whether organizational changes—new products, new markets, and so on—will succeed. Crossan, White, Lane, and Klus summarize this idea in an article that appeared in the journal *Organizational Dynamics*: "No matter how much we know..., no matter how powerful the computers are, specific long-range predictions are not feasible. We can know, but we cannot predict...."

If you accept this bleak assessment of DSS, it would seem that chaos theory essentially invalidates strategic planning and makes decision support systems obsolete. "Not so," says a hardy group of researchers who are trying to incorporate chaotic elements into the computer models used in decision support systems. They suggest that although a situation might be complex, much of the complexity results from a huge number of interactions between essentially simple entities. Chris Meyer, who heads the Ernst & Young Center for Business Innovation, provides a colorful example: "Suppose you come down from Mars and you see taxicabs working the streets of New York. You want to simulate that. Each yellow car has a simple brain following a few simple rules: Stop for anything that waves. Go where it says." Meyer suggests that a model containing these simple rules will closely simulate what actually happens as taxis buzz around Times Square.

You'll find lots more information about chaos theory and information systems at the Chaos InfoWeb.

click

9

Researchers are working on such simulations. For example, programmers at the accounting firm of Coopers & Lybrand developed a computer program designed to predict whether a new music CD will become a hit. The program contains 50,000 simmies who are fad-following music fans, and whose record-buying habits have been determined from market research. For example, some simmies are programmed to run right out and buy any CDs produced by their favorite musicians; others wait until they've heard songs from the CD a few times on the radio; and others have "random" purchasing habits. After requesting some background information on the current popularity of a musician, the program sets the simulated music fans in action to see how many purchase the CD. Managers can use the simulation to make decisions about which new CDs to include in their product lines.

Some experts believe that these simulations are accurate representations of a complex system, and they allow decision makers to account for the chaotic nature of complex situations. Other experts argue that we can never verify with certainty that a computer model represents the world because we don't know whether it includes all possible factors, or takes into account all possible starting values.

WHAT DO YOU THINK?

1. Does your intuition tell you that chaos theory is valid? ❍ Yes ❍ No ❍ Not sure
2. Does chaos theory invalidate deterministic tools, such as spreadsheet "what-if" analysis? ❍ Yes ❍ No ❍ Not sure
3. Is it possible to create an information system that is an accurate representation of a complex system? ❍ Yes ❍ No ❍ Not sure

click to save your responses

INTERACTIVE SUMMARY

The Interactive Summary helps you to select and remember important concepts from this chapter. Fill in the blanks to best complete each sentence. When using the NP6 BookOnCD, you can click the Check Answers buttons to automatically score your answers. Place your Tracking Disk in the floppy disk drive if you want to save your scores.

______ systems play a key role in helping organizations achieve goals, which are set forth in a ______ statement. Computers can be used by people at all levels of the organizational ______. Workers use information systems to produce and manipulate information. Managers depend on information systems to supply data that is essential for long-term ______ planning and short-term tactical planning.

Office ______ systems computerize routine tasks, such as producing form letters and tracking employee schedules. Transaction ______ systems provide an organization with a way to collect, display, modify, or cancel transactions. These systems encompass activities such as general accounting, inventory tracking, and e-commerce. ______ information systems typically build on the data collected by a TPS to produce reports that managers use to make the business decisions needed to solve routine, structured problems.

A decision ______ system helps workers and managers make non-routine decisions by constructing decision models that include data collected from internal and external sources. An ______ system is designed to analyze data and produce a recommendation or decision based on a set of facts and rules called a ______ base. These facts and rules can be written using an expert system shell or a programming language. An ______ engine evaluates the facts and rules in a knowledge base to produce answers to questions posed to the system. Using a technique called ______ logic, these systems can deal with imprecise data and problems that have more than one solution.

check answers

The process of planning and building an information system is referred to as systems ______ and design. The development process is supervised by an organization's Information Systems (IS) department, but the ______ team usually includes members from other departments as well. System development follows a system development ______ cycle (SDLC), which consists of several steps, or "phases." In the ______ SDLC, one phase of the SDLC must be completed before the next phase can begin. In practice, however, most project teams use a modification of this model in which phases can overlap or repeat. A project team can use one of several approaches to the system development process. For example, the ______ methodology focuses on the processes that take place in an information system. The information ______ methodology focuses on the data that an information system collects. The object-______ methodology treats an information system as a collection of interacting objects.

Project development begins with a short ______ phase in which a member of the IS department creates a Project Development Plan. The project team then proceeds to the ______ phase, with the goal of producing a list of requirements for a new or revised information system.

PROJECTS

An NP6 Project is an open-ended activity that will help you apply the concepts you have learned. Many projects require resources in addition to your textbook, such as current magazines, library materials, or Web access. When you tackle a project, be prepared to use your critical thinking skills, logical analysis, and your creativity.

9

1 **Issue Research: Controlling Chaos** The Issue section of this chapter focused on the extent to which an information system can accurately represent the processes, procedures, and decisions in an organization. For this project, write a two–five page paper that examines the limits of information systems. To begin this project, consult the Chaos InfoWeb (see page 485), and link to the recommended Web pages to get an in-depth overview of chaos theory. You should not, however, limit your discussion to chaos theory. Instead, look for additional ways in which an information system might fail to support the mission of an organization. In your paper, discuss whether or not you believe that information system failures can be prevented by better system development methods. Make sure that you document the information that you used to form an opinion. You can place citations to this information (including the author's name, article title, date of publication, and URL) at the end of your paper as endnotes, on each page as footnotes, or along with the appropriate paragraphs using parentheses. Follow your professor's instructions for submitting your paper via e-mail or as a printed document.

2 **Mission Statement** Suppose that you are a management consultant for one of the following well-known companies or nonprofit organizations. The company's managers want a new mission statement and it is your job to help. The managers also want to know what kind of information system would help deal with future opportunities and threats. Select one of the organizations in the following list. Use library or Internet resources to locate background information on the company, and write or revise its mission statement. After completing the mission statement, make a list to indicate how the organization would use an office automation system, a TPS, an MIS, a DSS, and an expert system.

Ziff-Davis	Nike	Black & Decker	Red Cross
Harley-Davidson	Mattel	Pier 1 Imports	Habitat For Humanity
Ben & Jerry's	Intel	Royal Carribean Cruise Line	United Way

3 **Decision Support Software** Assume that you are the information systems director for a manufacturer of trail bikes. The president of the company asks you to learn more about decision support software. Use library resources and the Web to search for information about available decision support software. Select three software packages and write a one paragraph description of each.

4 **Explore an Information System** Think about any transaction processing system that you have used for tasks such as banking or registering for classes. Make a list of the "entities" (people, offices, other businesses) that interact with the information system. Explain the nature of a transaction that's performed with the information system. Describe the data that is manipulated, and the databases that must be correctly updated to complete a successful transaction.

ADDITIONAL PROJECTS

TIP

Click ➡ to access the Web for additional projects.

10 DATABASES

CONTENTS

InfoWebLinks

The InfoWebLinks, located in the margins of this chapter, show the way to a variety of Web sites that contain additional information and updates to the chapter topics. Your computer needs an Internet connection to access these links. You can connect to the Web links for this chapter by:

- clicking the InfoWeb links in the margins
- clicking this underlined link
- starting your browser and entering the URL *www.infoweblinks.com/np6/chapter10.htm*

TIP

When using the **BookOnCD**, the  symbols are "clickable."

CHAPTER PREVIEW

10

Using a database is like viewing the tip of an iceberg. Only a small part of it is visible. The rest is hidden. To really understand how databases work, you've got to jump into the chilly water of database theory, and explore the hidden facets of data models, data management tools, database design, and query languages. This chapter will help you learn what happens beneath the tip of the database iceberg, and beyond the easy-to-use database interfaces provided by e-commerce sites, ATM machines, and course registration systems.

Section A focuses on basic database concepts and terminology, beginning with fields and records. It introduces the key concepts of record types and relationships, before ending with a description and comparison of hierarchical, network, relational, and object-oriented databases.

Section B looks at a variety of database tools—from simple word processing software, to entry-level database management software, to sophisticated database servers.

Section C delves into the process of designing relational databases, and provides tips that can come in handy when you need to create your own databases.

Section D focuses on SQL, one of today's most popular database query languages. An understanding of SQL provides you with valuable background about what goes on behind the facade of the menus and forms that you typically use to interact with databases both online and offline.

When you complete this chapter you should be able to:

- Define basic database terminology, such as fields, records, record types, and cardinality
- Describe the characteristics of hierarchical, network, relational, and object-oriented databases
- Explain the capabilities of various data management tools, such as commercial applications, word processing software, spreadsheet software, file management software, and database management software
- Describe various ways to provide access to databases via the Web
- Explain how to design an effective relational database
- Use your knowledge of SQL queries to describe how to add records, delete records, search for information, update fields, and simultaneously access data from multiple tables

TIP Click  to access the Web for a complete list of learning objectives for Chapter 10.

Section A FILE AND DATABASE CONCEPTS

In today's wired world, you probably interact directly with several databases, such as when you modify your e-mail address book, order a pay-per-view movie, register online for classes, or select merchandise from an e-commerce Web site. Most of the time, these databases are so easy to use that you don't even think about them as databases. Occasionally, however, databases can be frustrating. Why can't you find the e-mail address for Bob O'Neill? Why did your cable TV service bill you for a movie that you never watched? Why did you get an F in the course you thought you'd dropped? Why can't you find a way to cancel an order at *Nordstroms.com*? To understand the problems that sometimes crop up when you use databases, you need some background in database concepts and design.

Section A begins with a short review of basic database terminology pertaining to files, fields, and records, before tackling the key concept of record types. Once you understand record types, it is easy to grasp the last topic in this section, which describes hierarchical, network, relational, and object-oriented database models.

Beginning in Section A, and continuing throughout the chapter, most of the examples focus on the data maintained by WebMusic, a fictitious Web-based music store. WebMusic's information system stores data about CD prices, monitors inventory levels, maintains customer records, and reports which CDs are the top sellers. It also keeps track of customer orders, prints shipping labels, and produces quarterly sales reports. The characteristics of WebMusic's database are typical of many databases that you will encounter on and off the Web.

DATABASES AND STRUCTURED FILES

What is a database? In the broadest definition, a **database** is a collection of information. Today, databases are typically stored as computer files. The tasks associated with creating, maintaining, and accessing the information in these files are referred to as data management, file management, or database management.

Computer databases evolved from file processing technology, in which data is stored in a single structured file. A **structured file** is similar to a card file or Rolodex because it uses a uniform format to store data for each person or thing in the file.

FIELDS

What is the basic element of a structured file? A **field** contains the smallest unit of meaningful information, so you might call it the basic building block for a structured file or database. Each field has a unique **field name** that describes its contents. For example, in the WebMusic database, the field name ArtistName might describe a field containing the name of the artist or band that recorded the CD.

A field can be either variable length or fixed length. A **variable-length field** is like an accordion—it expands to fit the data you enter, up to some maximum number of characters. A **fixed-length field** contains a predetermined number of characters (bytes). The data that you enter in a fixed-length field cannot exceed the allocated field length. Moreover, if the data you enter is shorter than the allocated length, blank spaces are automatically added to fill the field. The fields in Figure 10-1 are fixed length. The underscores indicate the number of characters allocated for each field.

FIGURE 10-1

WebMusic uses fixed-length fields to store most of its data.

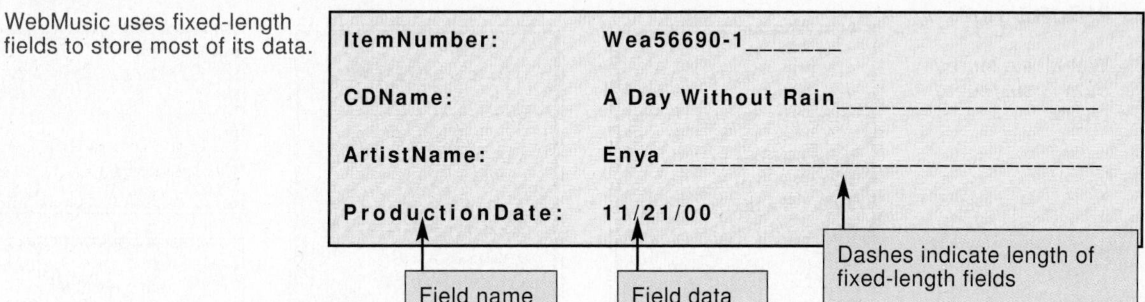

RECORDS

What is a record? Unlike the music world where a "record" refers to an old-fashioned recording medium that preceded cassette tapes and CDs, in the world of computing a **record** refers to a collection of data fields. Each record stores data about one entity—a person, place, thing, or event. For example, if you have a group of index cards and each index card lists information about a particular CD, then each index card is a record. You can visualize a record as a card, a form, or a row in a table, as Figure 10-2 illustrates.

FIGURE 10-2

Records can be displayed as rows in a table, or as forms.

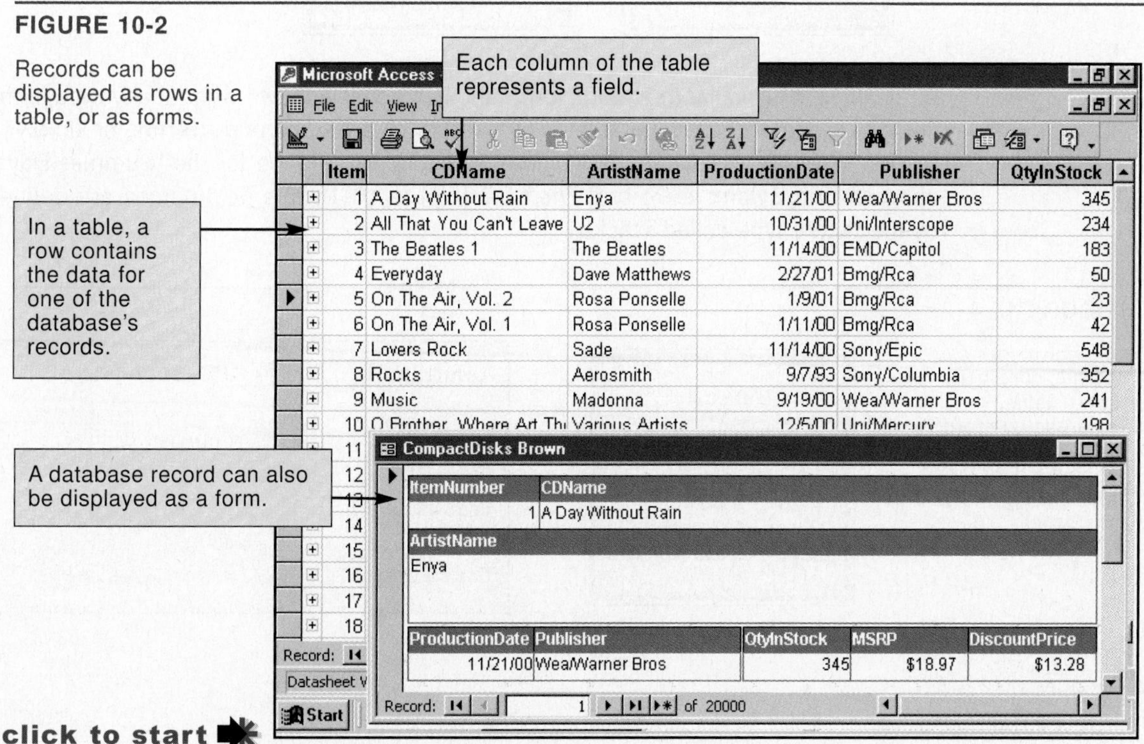

click to start

Who defines the structure for the records in a file? The person who creates a data file defines the fields it contains. This task is similar to designing a blank form for a manual record-keeping system or card file. Each kind of record is referred to as a **record type**. Different record types are necessary for storing data about different types of entities. For example, WebMusic uses one record type for storing information about customers, and another record type for storing information about music CDs. WebMusic uses four other record types for storing additional data. All six record types are illustrated in Figure 10-3.

FIGURE 10-3

WebMusic stores data in six record types.

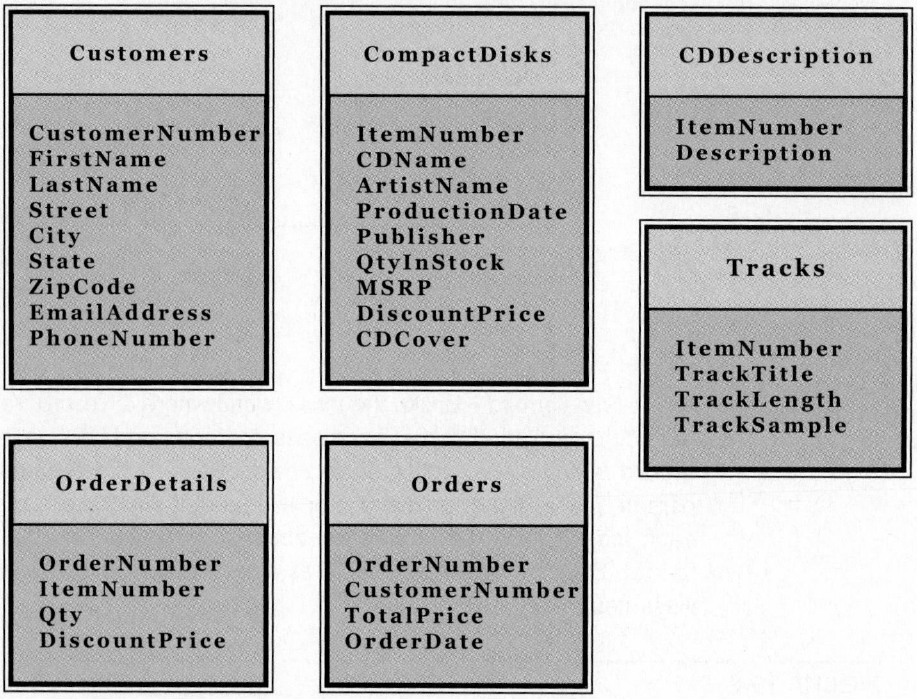

Customers
CustomerNumber FirstName LastName Street City State ZipCode EmailAddress PhoneNumber

CompactDisks
ItemNumber CDName ArtistName ProductionDate Publisher QtyInStock MSRP DiscountPrice CDCover

CDDescription
ItemNumber Description

Tracks
ItemNumber TrackTitle TrackLength TrackSample

OrderDetails
OrderNumber ItemNumber Qty DiscountPrice

Orders
OrderNumber CustomerNumber TotalPrice OrderDate

A record type is similar to a blank form, and it is usually shown without any data in the fields. A record that contains data is referred to as a **record occurrence**, or simply "a record." WebMusic's database includes a record occurrence for the "Summer Days" song on Bob Dylan's *Love and Theft* CD (Figure 10-4). The field names are defined by the record type called Tracks.

FIGURE 10-4

A record type (left) is simply a list of fields, whereas a record occurrence (right) contains data for a particular entity.

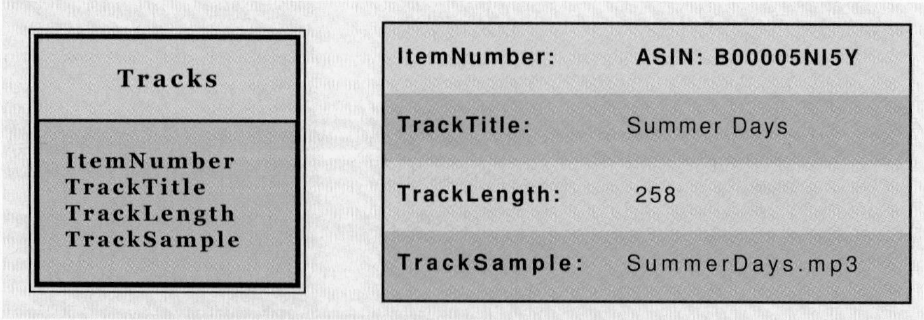

Tracks
ItemNumber TrackTitle TrackLength TrackSample

ItemNumber:	ASIN: B00005NI5Y
TrackTitle:	Summer Days
TrackLength:	258
TrackSample:	SummerDays.mp3

RELATIONSHIPS AND CARDINALITY

How do record types pertain to files and databases? A data file that contains only one record type is often referred to as a **flat file**. In contrast, a database can contain a variety of different record types. A key characteristic of a database is its ability to maintain relationships so that data from several record types can be consolidated or aggregated into essentially one unit for data retrieval and reporting purposes.

What are relationships? In database jargon, a **relationship** is an association between data that's stored in different record types. For example, WebMusic's Customers record type is related to the Orders record type because customers place orders. Figure 10-5 helps you visualize the relationship between these two record types.

FIGURE 10-5

For maximum efficiency, WebMusic stores general information about customers in one set of records, but stores the information about individual orders in a different set of records. WebMusic's database maintains a relationship between these records so that it is possible to find the orders placed by each customer.

CustomerNumber:	171109
FirstName:	Jorge
LastName:	Rodriguez
Street:	101 Las Vegas Court
City:	Taos
State:	NM
ZipCode:	87571
EmailAddress:	jrod@hotmail.com
PhoneNumber:	505-555-3412

The WebMusic database stores basic information about a customer, such as Jorge Rodriguez, in a single record.

OrderNumber:	02-3422901
CustomerNumber:	171109
TotalPrice:	$52.28

OrderNumber:	03-4873392
CustomerNumber:	171109
TotalPrice:	$23.89

OrderNumber:	03-9872655
CustomerNumber:	171109
TotalPrice:	$46.58
OrderDate:	09/30/03

The database also stores records for each of Jorge's orders.

10

One important aspect of the relationship between record types is cardinality. **Cardinality** refers to the number of associations that can exist between two record types. For example, a WebMusic customer can place more than one order. The reverse is not true, however. A particular order cannot be placed jointly by two customers. When one record is related to many records, the relationship is referred to as a **one-to-many relationship**.

In contrast, a **many-to-many relationship** means that one record in a particular record type can be related to many records in another record type, and vice versa. For example, a CD contains many songs. At the same time, a song could be included on several different CDs. For example, George Harrison's song "Something" was included in the Beatles *Abbey Road* album and the "best hits" release, *The Beatles 1*.

The Data Relationships InfoWeb provides more information on relationships and various ways to depict them in diagrams.

A **one-to-one relationship** means that a record in one record type is related to only one record in another record type. This kind of relationship is rare in the world of databases. It is sometimes used to conserve disk space when an item of information will not be stored for every record in the database. For example, the marketing director at WebMusic sometimes wants to include a description of a CD in the database, but only for top-selling CDs. If a Description field is included in the CompactDisks record type, it will be empty for most records. Empty fields take up space on the disk, so it's not desirable to have fields that will most likely be blank. Creating another record type, called CDDescription, allows this data to be stored efficiently. Only top-selling CDs would have a corresponding CDDescription record. The CD record and its corresponding description would have a one-to-one relationship.

Relationships between record types can be graphically depicted using diagramming techniques, such as an **entity-relationship diagram** (sometimes called an "ER diagram" or "ERD"). Figure 10-6 shows ERDs for one-to-many, many-to-many, and one-to-one relationships.

FIGURE 10-6

An entity-relationship diagram depicts each record type as a rectangle. Relationships and cardinality are shown by connecting lines.

Many-to-many relationship

CD SONG

One CD contains many songs, and a song may be included on several different CDs.

One-to-one relationship

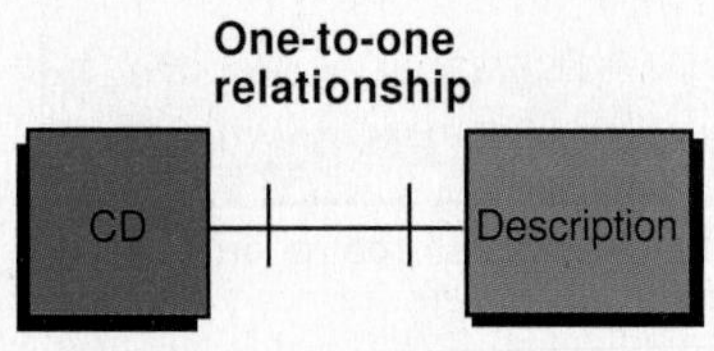

A CD has only one description.

One-to-many relationship

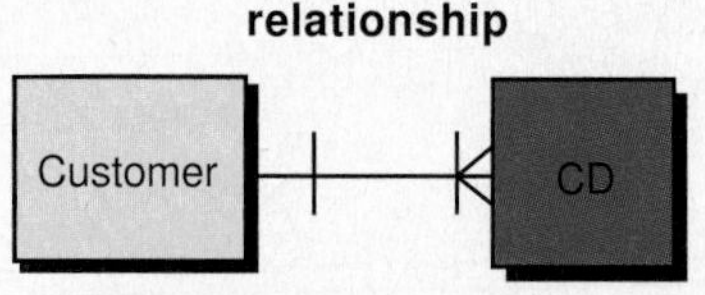

One customer can order many CDs.

KEY TO ERD SYMBOLS

The crossbar indicates exactly one occurrence.

The circle and crow's foot indicate zero or more occurrences.

The crossbar and circle indicate zero or one occurrence.

The crossbar and crow's foot indicate one or more occurrences.

HIERARCHICAL, NETWORK, RELATIONAL, AND OBJECT-ORIENTED DATABASES

Am I limited to one type of database? Several database models exist. Some models work with all of the relationships described earlier in this section, whereas other models work with only a subset of the relationships. The four main types of database models in use today are hierarchical, network, relational, and object oriented.

What's the simplest database model? The simplest database model arranges record types as a hierarchy. In a **hierarchical database**, a record type is referred to as a **node** or "segment." The top node of the hierarchy is referred to as the **root node**. Nodes are arranged in a hierarchical structure as a sort of upside-down tree. A **parent node** can have more than one **child node**. A child node, however, can have only one parent node. The relationship between a parent node and a child node in a hierarchical database is always one-to-many, as shown in Figure 10-7.

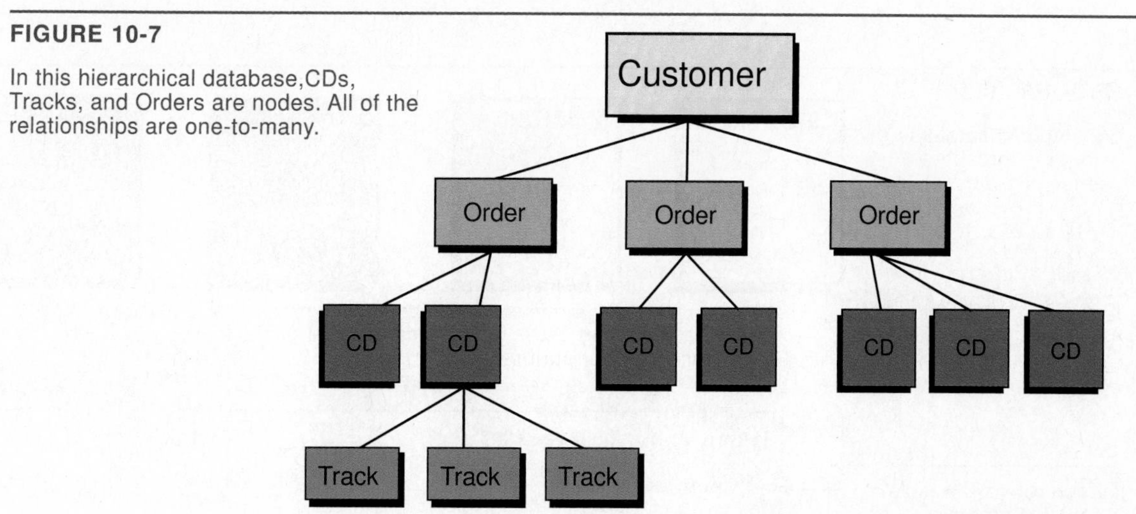

FIGURE 10-7

In this hierarchical database, CDs, Tracks, and Orders are nodes. All of the relationships are one-to-many.

10

Although the hierarchical database model is the earliest and simplest type of database, it remains in use today for storing data characterized by fairly simple relationships and routine, predictable search requirements. For example, Windows uses a hierarchical database to store Registry data that keeps track of the software and hardware configuration of your PC. In addition, databases created with XML (Extensible Markup Language) tags support a hierarchical database model. (For a review of XML, refer to Chapter 6.)

Which database model allows many-to-many relationships? The **network database** model allows many-to-many relationships in addition to one-to-many relationships. Related record types are referred to as a **network set**, or simply a "set." A set contains an owner and members. An **owner** is similar to a parent record in a hierarchical database. A **member** is roughly equivalent to the child records in a hierarchical database. (See Figure 10-8.)

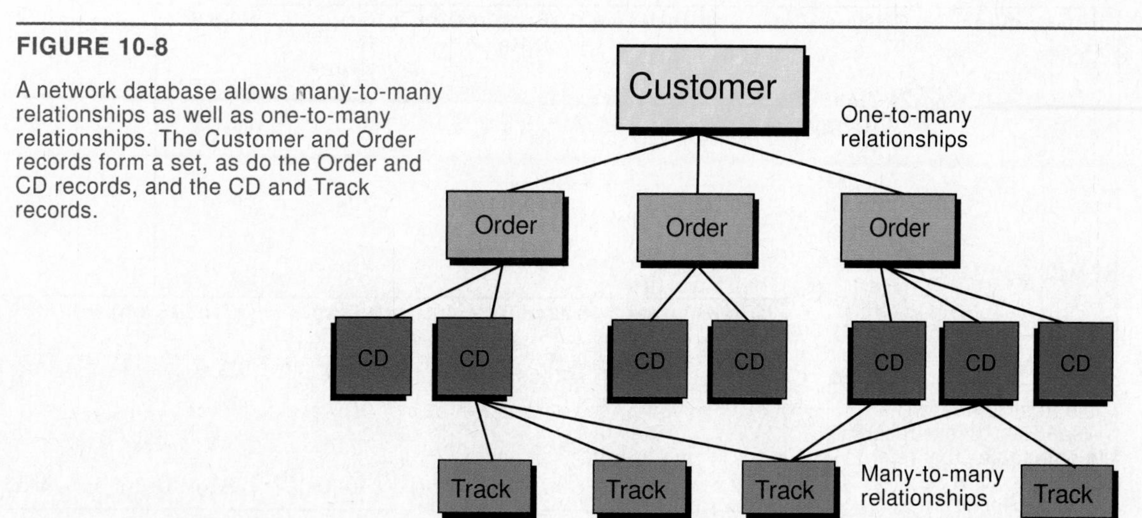

FIGURE 10-8

A network database allows many-to-many relationships as well as one-to-many relationships. The Customer and Order records form a set, as do the Order and CD records, and the CD and Track records.

What's a relational database? Although the network database model seems like a good idea, it produces databases that are difficult to create, manipulate, and maintain. The relational database model quickly replaced it, and is the most popular database model today. A **relational database** stores data in a collection of related tables. Each **table** (also called a "relation") is a sequence, or list, of records. All of the records in a table are of the same record type. Each row of a table is equivalent to a record and is sometimes called a **tuple**. Each column of the table is equivalent to a field, sometimes called an **attribute**. Figure 10-9 illustrates relational database terminology.

FIGURE 10-9

A relational database stores records in a series of tables.

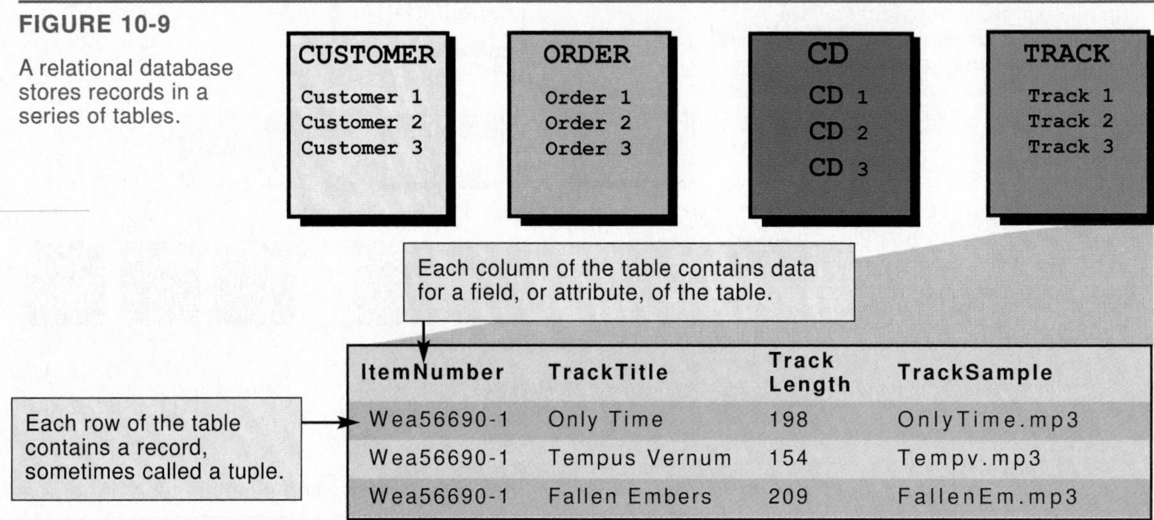

ItemNumber	TrackTitle	Track Length	TrackSample
Wea56690-1	Only Time	198	OnlyTime.mp3
Wea56690-1	Tempus Vernum	154	Tempv.mp3
Wea56690-1	Fallen Embers	209	FallenEm.mp3

In a relational database, relationships are specified through the use of common data stored in the fields of records in different tables. This method of establishing relationships allows the tables to be essentially independent, but the tables can be consolidated, when required, for a particular task. Relationships can be added, changed, or deleted on demand. Figure 10-10 illustrates how a relationship can be established using the ItemNumber field in two tables.

FIGURE 10-10

In a relational database, two tables are related by similar fields—in this example, by ItemNumber.

ItemNumber	CDName	ArtistName	Production Date	Qty In Stock	MSRP
Wea56690-1	A Day Without Rain	Enya	11/21/00	345	18.95
Umi983200	All that You Can't Leave	U2	10/31/00	234	19.95
EMD720167	The Beatles 1	The Beatles	11/14/00	183	24.95
RCA-00-134	Everyday				

ItemNumber	TrackTitle	Track Length	TrackSample
Wea56690-1	Only Time	198	OnlyTime.mp3
Wea56690-1	Tempus Vernum	154	Tempv.mp3
Wea56690-1	Fallen Embers	209	FallenEm.mp3
EMD720167	She Loves You	141	SheLovesYou.mp3

The ItemNumber Wea56690-1 links records in both tables that refer to the Enya CD *A Day Without Rain.*

What's an object-oriented database? An **object-oriented database** stores data as objects, which can be grouped into classes, and defined by attributes and methods. Chapter 11 covers object-oriented terminology in detail, but in the context of object-oriented databases, a class defines a group of objects by specifying the attributes and methods that these objects share. The attributes for an object are equivalent to fields in a relational database. A method is any behavior that an object is capable of performing. There is no equivalent to a method in a non-object-oriented database. Specifications for the object-oriented database model are provided by standards organizations, such as the Object Data Management Group (ODMG). Figure 10-11 explains how data is stored in an object-oriented database.

FIGURE 10-11

An object-oriented database can easily store data about different types of orders. A class called Orders holds data and methods common to all types of orders. An object called Phone Orders inherits all of the characteristics of Orders, but it has attributes and methods unique to orders placed by telephone. The Web Orders object has attributes and methods unique to orders placed via the Web.

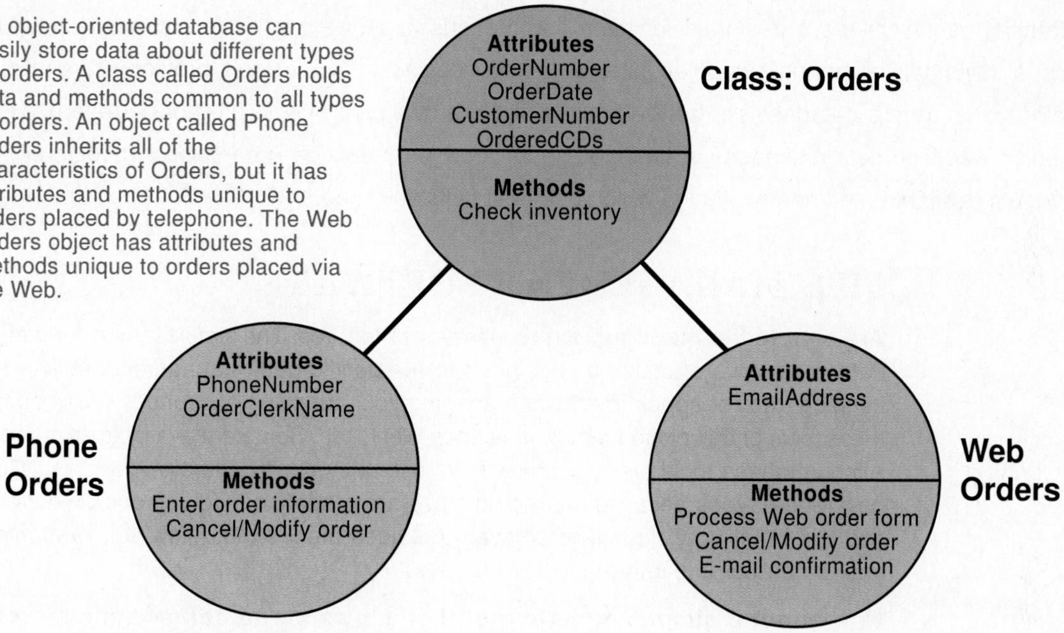

10

QUICKCheck Section A

1. A(n) ________ file uses a uniform format to store data in records and fields.
2. A(n) ________ holds the smallest unit of meaningful information, and is the basic building block of most databases.
3. A database consists of one or more record ________ that are like blank forms used to store information.
4. The number of associations that can exist between record types is referred to as ________.
5. A(n) ________ database is one that can link record types through shared fields on demand.

check answers 

Section B DATA MANAGEMENT TOOLS

One of the first decisions to make when designing a database is what type of data management tools to use. Different tools are designed for different uses. Simple tools that easily store address book information may not be well suited for managing a worldwide airline reservation system. On the other hand, database software that's designed for huge corporations might be overkill for keeping track of your social calendar, or storing customer data for a small business. Some tools provide ways to display information from a database on the Web, and some are designed only to print basic reports. How do you know which data management tools to use for a project? Section B describes the different types of tools available, and how to decide which one best suits your needs.

FILE MANAGEMENT SOFTWARE

Are simple file management tools available? Yes. The simplest tools for managing data are software packages designed for a specific data management task, such as keeping track of appointments or managing your checking account. You can purchase these tools or download them from various Web sites. Some are available as shareware. Although these tools are typically easy to use, they don't generally allow you to create new record types because the record types are predefined. To use one of these tools, you just enter your data. The software provides menus that allow you to manipulate your data after it is entered.

How about a simple, generic tool that allows me to define a file structure? Several popular applications provide simple file design and management capabilities. For example, your word processing software probably allows you to maintain data as a set of records, as shown in Figure 10-12.

FIGURE 10-12

Microsoft Word allows you to create a table of information, such as a mailing list, which you can edit, sort, search, and print. In addition, you can merge the data from the table with a template letter to create customized form letters, mailing labels, and envelopes.

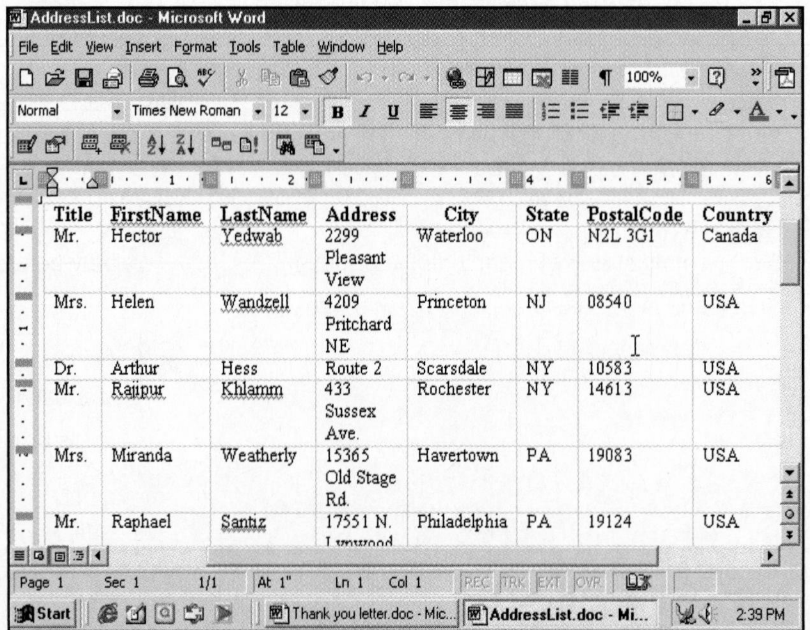

click to start

Some spreadsheet software also includes simple data management commands. It's quite easy to create simple flat files using a spreadsheet. Depending on the software, it may be possible to sort records, validate data, search for records, perform simple statistical functions, and generate graphs based on the data. Figure 10-13 illustrates the data functions provided by Microsoft Excel.

FIGURE 10-13

Spreadsheet software usually provides tools for working with flat files.

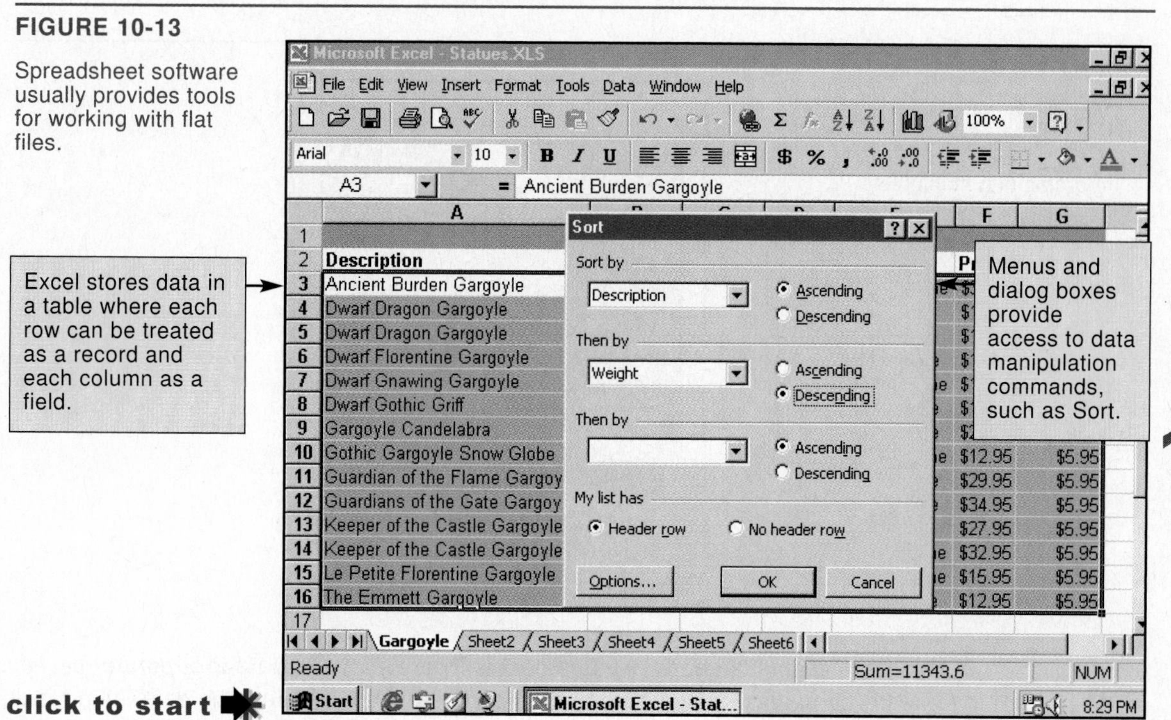

The simple file management tools provided by word processing and spreadsheet software are popular for individuals who want to maintain flat files that contain hundreds, not thousands, of records. They do not, however, provide database capabilities for establishing relationships between different record types, and they are not powerful enough to maintain the large volume of records required for business information systems.

Can I create my own file management software? It is possible to simply enter data as an ASCII text file, then use a programming language to write any routines required to access that data. Custom software can be created to accommodate hierarchical, network, relational, and object-oriented databases, as well as flat file management. It has the advantage of being tailored to the exact needs of a business or individual. This advantage is offset, however, by several disadvantages. Custom software requires skilled programmers. The development time for each module can be lengthy and costly. In addition, programmer efforts are sometimes redundant because similar modules are often required for different data files. For example, programmers who write a print routine for one data file might have to repeat their efforts a few weeks later for a different data file.

Poorly designed custom software can result in **data dependence**—a term that refers to the undesirable situation in which data and program modules are so tightly interrelated that they become difficult to modify. Imagine a file management system, like the one pictured in Figure 10-14, in which the programs and the data all exist in one large file! It would be impossible to access the data while editing the program. Furthermore, changing the file structure in any way might make the programs unusable.

FIGURE 10-14

Data dependence means that it is difficult to separate the data from the programs that manipulate the data.

Modern file and database management software supports **data independence**, which means separating the data from the programs that manipulate the data. As a result, a single data management tool can be used to maintain many different files and databases. In addition, standard search, sort, and print routines continue to function, regardless of changes to the database structure. Figure 10-15 illustrates the concept of data independence.

FIGURE 10-15

Data independence means that data is stored separately from the programs that are used to manipulate the data.

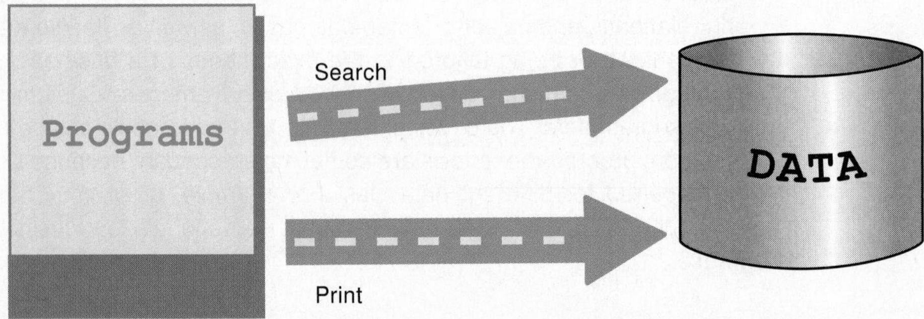

InfoWebLinks.com

Get the latest scoop on relational, object-oriented, and XML database software at the DBMS InfoWeb.

click

DATABASE MANAGEMENT SYSTEMS

What kinds of tools are specifically designed for creating and manipulating databases? The term **DBMS** (database management system) refers to software that is designed to manage data stored in a database. Each DBMS is typically optimized for one of the four database models or for a specific type of data.

An **XML DBMS**, for example, is optimized for handling data that exists in XML format. An **OODBMS** (object-oriented database management system) is optimized for the object-oriented database model, allowing you to store and manipulate data classes, attributes, and methods. An **RDBMS** (relational database management system) allows you to create, update, and administer a relational database. In addition, today's most popular RDBMS software also provides the capability to handle object classes and XML data, making it unnecessary to purchase a separate OODBMS or XML DBMS.

Which DBMS should I use for my projects? Today most database projects are implemented with a relational database management system. The particular RDBMS package that you choose, however, depends on the scope of your project, the number of people that will simultaneously access the database, and the expected volume of records, queries, and updates.

10

Entry-level RDBMS software, such as Microsoft Access, is designed for personal and small business uses, such as managing a diet-and-exercise log, or maintaining customer information. An entry-level DBMS typically includes all of the tools that you need to manipulate the data in a database, create data entry forms, query the database, and generate reports, as shown in Figure 10-16.

FIGURE 10-16

An entry-level DBMS usually includes all of the tools that you need to manipulate the data in a database.

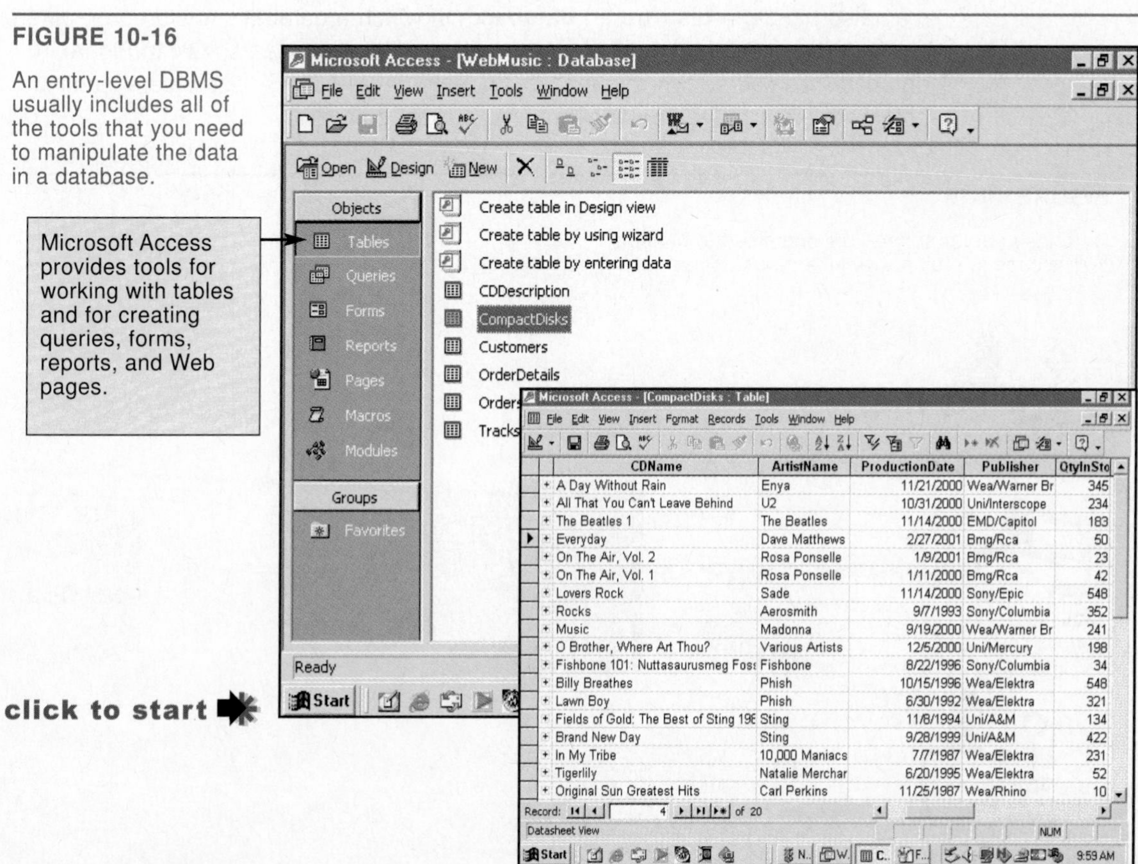

click to start

FIGURE 10-17

Multiple users can access a database using client software.

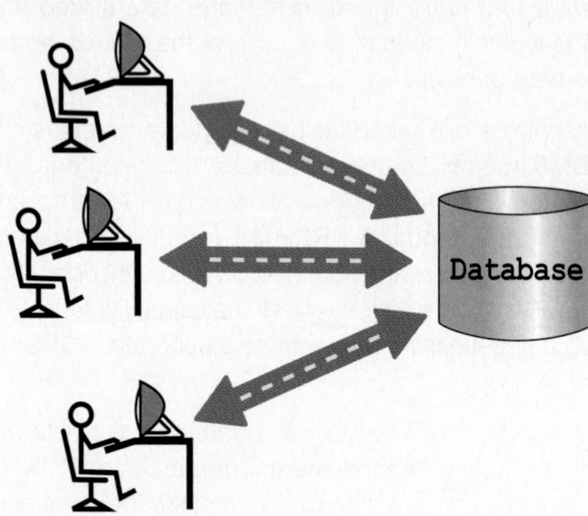

If an entry-level DBMS is located on a network, it is possible for multiple users to access the database at the same time. As shown in Figure 10-17, each workstation typically uses database client software to communicate with the DBMS. **Database client software** allows any remote computer or network workstation to access data in a database.

An entry-level DBMS that resides on a network server may be able to handle many simultaneous searches. However, these DBMSs have limited capabilities to deal with problems that arise when multiple users attempt to update the same record at the same time. This limited multiuser capability might be able to handle, for example, a civic center ticketing system operated by a box office clerk. It would not be sufficient, however, to handle the volume of simultaneous transactions for Ticketmaster's 3,800 retail ticket center outlets, 20 telephone call centers worldwide, and online Web site.

In situations with many users who make simultaneous updates, it is usually necessary to move to database server software, such as Oracle Database, IBM DB2 Universal Database, or Microsoft SQL Server. **Database server software** is designed to manage billions of records, and several hundred transactions every second. It provides optimum performance in client/server environments, such as LANs and the Internet. It may also handle a **distributed database**, in which a database is stored on different computers, on different networks, or in different locations. As shown in Figure 10-18, database server software replaces an entry-level DBMS, and users continue to communicate with the server by means of client software.

FIGURE 10-18

Database server software is optimized to provide fast access to multiple simultaneous users.

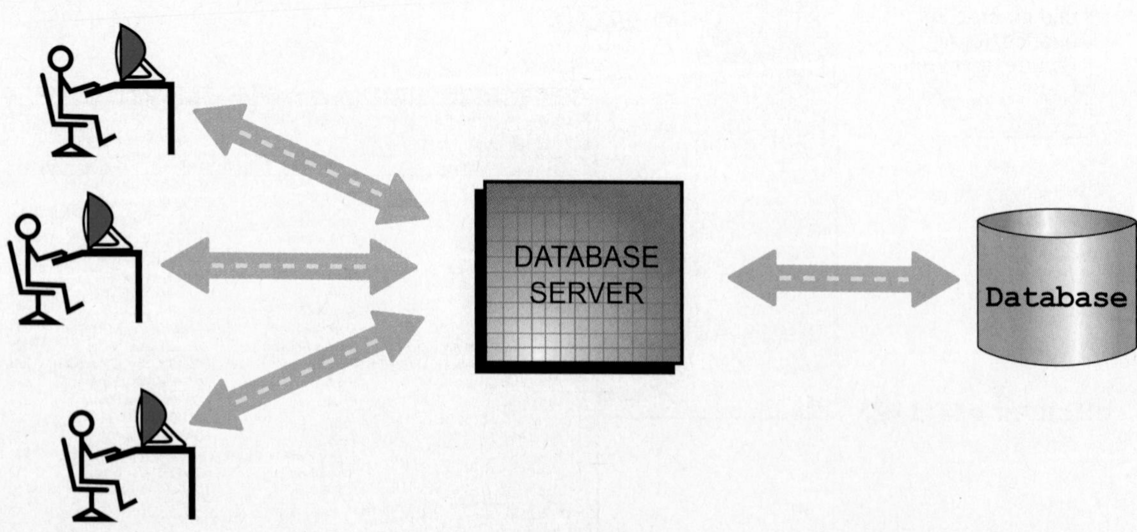

Wouldn't it be nice if King's speeches were stored in HTML documents that identified their contents as speeches, and their author as Martin Luther King, Jr.? XML provides tags that can be embedded in an XML document to put data in context, as shown in Figure 10-23.

FIGURE 10-23

A document with XML tags allows you to make a targeted search for AUTHOR = Martin Luther King, Jr. and DOCUMENTTYPE = SPEECH.

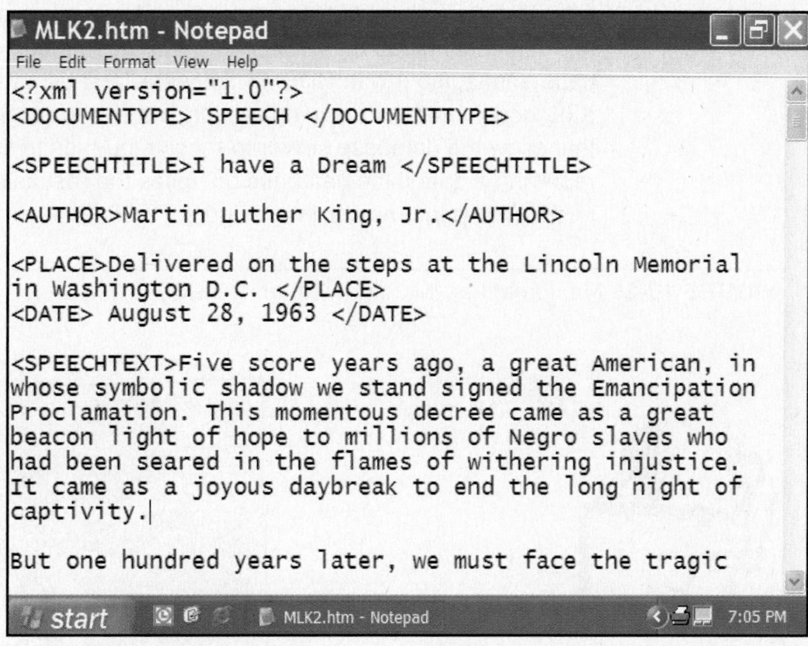

```
MLK2.htm - Notepad
File Edit Format View Help
<?xml version="1.0"?>
<DOCUMENTYPE> SPEECH </DOCUMENTTYPE>

<SPEECHTITLE>I have a Dream </SPEECHTITLE>

<AUTHOR>Martin Luther King, Jr.</AUTHOR>

<PLACE>Delivered on the steps at the Lincoln Memorial
in Washington D.C. </PLACE>
<DATE> August 28, 1963 </DATE>

<SPEECHTEXT>Five score years ago, a great American, in
whose symbolic shadow we stand signed the Emancipation
Proclamation. This momentous decree came as a great
beacon light of hope to millions of Negro slaves who
had been seared in the flames of withering injustice.
It came as a joyous daybreak to end the long night of
captivity.

But one hundred years later, we must face the tragic
start MLK2.htm - Notepad 7:05 PM
```

10

You can see how XML tags might make the free-form documents that currently exist on the Web much easier to manage. One of XML's most positive contributions to data management is the ability to add context to the information contained in a widely diverse pool of documents on the Web.

An XML document can also contain structured data organized into records and fields. Such a document replaces a traditional database in some respects. Figure 10-24 provides an example of an XML document that contains data similar to that in WebMusic's CompactDisks table.

FIGURE 10-24

This XML document contains data that looks similar to the fields and records from a table of a relational database.

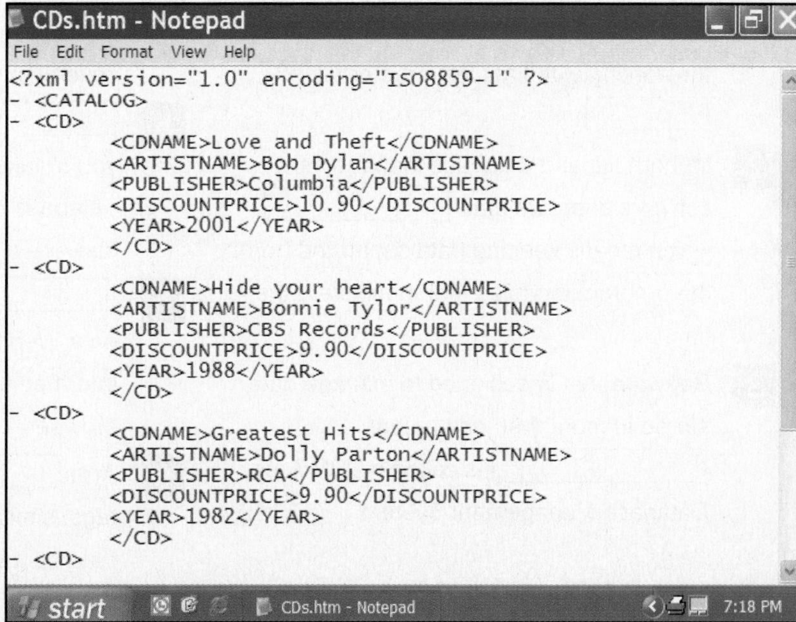

```
CDs.htm - Notepad
File Edit Format View Help
<?xml version="1.0" encoding="ISO8859-1" ?>
- <CATALOG>
- <CD>
        <CDNAME>Love and Theft</CDNAME>
        <ARTISTNAME>Bob Dylan</ARTISTNAME>
        <PUBLISHER>Columbia</PUBLISHER>
        <DISCOUNTPRICE>10.90</DISCOUNTPRICE>
        <YEAR>2001</YEAR>
        </CD>
- <CD>
        <CDNAME>Hide your heart</CDNAME>
        <ARTISTNAME>Bonnie Tylor</ARTISTNAME>
        <PUBLISHER>CBS Records</PUBLISHER>
        <DISCOUNTPRICE>9.90</DISCOUNTPRICE>
        <YEAR>1988</YEAR>
        </CD>
- <CD>
        <CDNAME>Greatest Hits</CDNAME>
        <ARTISTNAME>Dolly Parton</ARTISTNAME>
        <PUBLISHER>RCA</PUBLISHER>
        <DISCOUNTPRICE>9.90</DISCOUNTPRICE>
        <YEAR>1982</YEAR>
        </CD>
- <CD>
start CDs.htm - Notepad 7:18 PM
```

Storing data in an XML document provides several advantages. It is "portable" so that it can be easily accessed from virtually any computer platform—PCs, Macs, Linux computers, mainframes, and even handhelds. All that's required on the platform is an XML-enabled browser, such as Internet Explorer or Netscape Navigator. XML documents are not, however, optimized for many operations that you would customarily associate with databases, such as fast sorts, searches, and updates. To get the best out of XML and relational databases, some experts recommend storing data in a relational database, managing it with RDBMS software, and using server-side software to generate XML documents for exchanging data via the Web. Some RDBMSs provide methods that allow the database server to receive queries in the form of XML commands. After receiving a query, the database compiles the results and uses XML to format the data into a Web page, as shown in Figure 10-25.

FIGURE 10-25 Manipulating XML data with an RDBMS

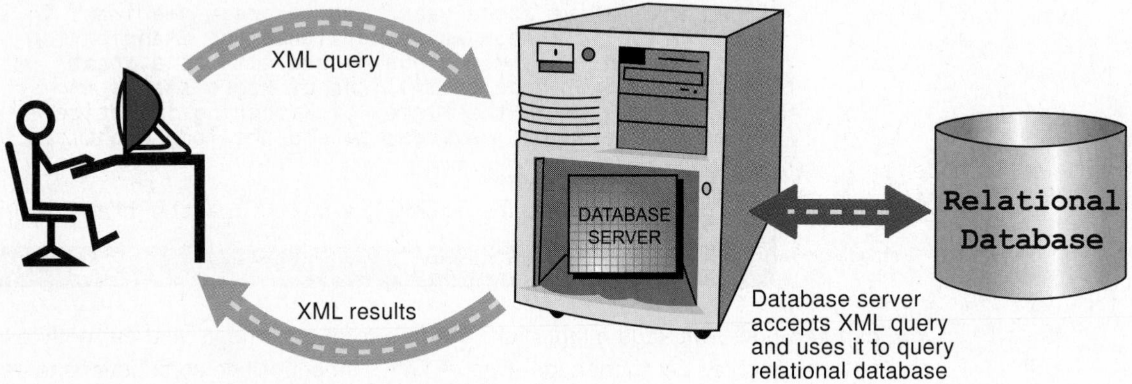

QUICKCheck Section B

1. Spreadsheet software typically includes some file management commands suitable for working with flat files. True or false? ________

2. Modern file and database management software supports data ________, which means keeping data separated from the program modules that manipulate the data.

3. Software that is designed to manage data stored in more than one record ________ is called a DBMS, or Database Management System.

4. Database ________ software is designed to manage billions of records and several hundred transactions per second.

5. ________ Web publishing allows you to take a snapshot of the data in a database by generating a report, which is converted into an HTML document.

6. ________-side programs reside on a Web server and act as an intermediary between a DBMS and a browser.

6. A(n) ________ document uses tags, similar to field names, that identify data contained in the document.

DATABASE DESIGN

The term **database structure** refers to the arrangement of the fields, tables, and relationships in a database. The key to an effective file or database is the initial design of its structure. With a good structure, the data can be flexibly manipulated to provide timely, meaningful, and accurate information for decision making. Bad database structures can lead to messy databases, lost records, and inaccurate data.

The goal of good database design is to store information so that it is easy to access and maintain, but concise enough to take up as little disk space as possible. Section C looks at databases from the perspective of the database designer, and describes how to create an efficient structure for a relational database.

DEFINING FIELDS

How does a database designer know what data to store? The first step in designing a relational database is to determine what data must be collected and stored. To do so, a database designer might begin by listing available data, as well as any additional data that is necessary to produce on-screen output or printed reports. If you are designing the database structure for WebMusic, for example, you would probably recognize that data such as CD Name, Artist Name, Production Date, Item Number, Publisher, Qty In Stock, MSRP (manufacturer's suggested retail price), Discount Price, and a photo of the CD Cover should be collected and stored.

Once the database designer determines what data to store, the next step is to organize that data into fields. It is usually easy to break data into fields just by using common sense and considering how people might want to access the data. Any data that people would want to search for, sort on, or use in a calculation should be in its own field.

Why are last names stored in a different field than first names? The treatment of first and last names illustrates the concept of breaking data into fields. A database designer could define a field called Name to hold an entire customer's name, such as Gilbert B. Grape. With the entire name in one field, however, the database would not be able to access individual parts of the name, making it difficult to alphabetize customers by last name, or produce a report in which names appear in a format like Grape, Gilbert B. (See Figure 10-26.)

FIGURE 10-26

If a field contains an entire name, it is difficult to individually manipulate the first name, last name, and middle initial. A more flexible design provides separate fields for each part of the name.

What makes each record unique? Although two people might have the same name or two paychecks might contain the same amount, a computer must have some way to differentiate between records. A **primary key** is a field that contains data unique to a record. When determining the fields for a database, designers commonly designate fields such as SocialSecurityNumber and PartNumber as primary keys.

How does a database designer know what data types to use? The data that can be entered into a field depends on the field's data type. From a technical perspective, a **data type** specifies the way data is represented on the disk and in RAM. From a user perspective, the data type determines the way data can be manipulated. When designing a database, each field is assigned a data type.

The two most common data types are numeric and character. A database designer can assign a **numeric data type** to fields containing numbers that will be manipulated mathematically by adding, averaging, multiplying, and so forth. As an example, the DiscountPrice field in Figure 10-27 is a numeric field, so the data in this field can be added to the prices for other CDs to calculate a total price when a customer buys more than one CD.

FIGURE 10-27

Data in numeric fields can be used for calculations.

DiscountPrice $12.97

INVOICE

Qty	CD Title	Discount Price
1	Tigerlily	$12.97
1	Cuttin' Heads	$18.97
1	Everyday	$18.97
	Total	$50.91

There are two main numeric data types: real and integer. A **real number** is formatted to include decimal places. An **integer** is a whole number. Computers store real numbers in a different format from integers. Real numbers typically require more storage space. The data in the DiscountPrice field is a real number because it contains a decimal point. The data in the Qty field is an integer because it does not contain a decimal point. Database designers typically use integer format unless the data requires decimal places.

For fields that contain data that would not be used for calculations, a database designer can specify a **character data type**, which is also referred to as a "string data type." Examples of character data include CD names and artist names.

Character fields sometimes hold data that looks like numbers, but doesn't need to be mathematically manipulated. Telephone "numbers" and ZIP codes are examples of data that looks numeric, but is stored in character fields because database users would never want to add two telephone numbers together, or find the average of a group of ZIP codes. As a rule of thumb, information such as telephone numbers, ZIP codes, Social Security numbers, and item numbers should be stored as character data.

Some file and database management systems provide additional data types such as date, logical, and memo. As you might expect, the **date data type** is used to store dates in a format that allows them to be manipulated, such as when you want to calculate the number of days between two dates. The **logical data type** is used to store true/false or yes/no data using minimal storage space. For example, a database designer might define a logical field called OnSale, which would contain a Y if a CD is on a special sale, or N if the CD is not on sale. A **memo data type** usually provides a variable-length field into which users can enter comments. For example, the WebMusic database might contain a memo field for storing comments about a particular CD like "Winner of the 2002 Best Compact Disk of the Year award!"

LAB 10-C WORKING WITH DATABASE SOFTWARE

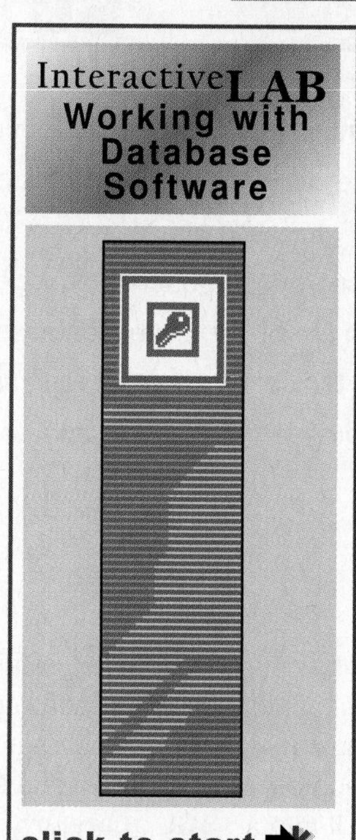

InteractiveLAB
Working with
Database
Software
click to start

In this lab, you'll learn:

- How relational database software depicts data as tables, records, and fields
- How to use tables and forms to view data
- How to create a table
- How to use primary keys
- How to enter and edit data
- Why relationships between tables are so important
- How to sort data and create an index
- How to search for data
- How to set filters
- How to create queries
- How to view the SQL code for a query
- How to create a report
- How to modify a report in Design view

LAB Assignments

1. Start the interactive part of the lab. Insert your Tracking Disk if you want to save your QuickCheck results. Perform each of the lab steps, as directed, and answer all of the lab QuickCheck questions. When you exit the lab, your answers are automatically graded and your results are displayed.
2. A friend wants to create a table to store information about a collection of old books. List the fields that you might include in the table to store information about the books. For each field, specify the field name, data type (text, numeric, date, etc.), and field length. Indicate the primary key(s), and describe how you would sort and/or index the data.
3. Use Microsoft Access or any available file or database management software to create the structure for the table you specified in Assignment 2. Enter at least ten records. Print a list of all your data.
4. Make a list of five queries that might be useful if your database had hundreds of records. Try these queries on your table. For each query, list the records that were selected.
5. Sketch a report on paper that uses some of the fields in your table. Make sure that your report contains a title and headings for each field. Specify whether you would like to align your data at the right, center, or left of each column. Use your software to generate and print the report.

SQL

Adding records, finding information, and making updates are all important aspects of database use. Most people who access a database on a "casual" basis—to shop online or withdraw cash from an ATM, for example—interact with very simple user interfaces. These user interfaces shield users from the intricacies of sophisticated query languages. Nevertheless, a little background in query languages can help you understand the power and capabilities of databases. In Section D, you'll explore a database query language called **SQL** (Structured Query Language) by working with SQL examples that illustrate major database functions, such as deleting records, adding records, searching for information, updating records, and joining tables.

SQL BASICS

How does a query language like SQL work? Query languages like SQL typically work behind the scenes as an intermediary between the database client software provided to users, and the database itself. Database client software provides an easy-to-use interface for entering search specifications, new records, data updates, and so on. The client software collects your input, then converts it into an **SQL query**, which can operate directly on the database to carry out your instructions, as shown in Figure 10-38.

FIGURE 10-38

Database client software provides database users with simple forms that can be used to enter search specifications or update data.

The client software converts these entries into SQL commands, which interact directly with the database to locate data, update records, and perform other functions requested by the user.

SELECT CDName FROM CompactDisks
WHERE ArtistName = 'Garth Brooks'

Search
Artist: Garth Brooks
Title:
Label:
Format: CD Cassette DVD Audio
Search Now Clear the Form

What does a simple SQL query look like? An SQL query is a sequence of words, much like a sentence. For example, an SQL query that searches for a song called "Fly Away" in WebMusic's database might look like this:

SELECT TrackTitle FROM Tracks WHERE TrackTitle = 'Fly Away'

The SQL query language provides a collection of special command words called **SQL keywords**, such as SELECT, FROM, INSERT, and WHERE, which issue instructions to the database. Although we use uppercase letters for the keywords in our examples, most implementations of SQL accept either uppercase or lowercase keywords.

Most SQL queries can be divided into three simple elements that specify an action, the name of a database table, and a set of parameters. Let's look at each of these elements.

How does SQL specify the action that I want carried out in the database? An SQL query typically begins with an action keyword, or command, which specifies the operation that you want carried out. For example, the command word **DELETE** removes a record from a table. Figure 10-39 lists some of the most commonly used SQL command words.

FIGURE 10-39 SQL Command Words

Command	Description	Example
CREATE	Create a database or table	CREATE TABLE CompactDisks
DELETE	Remove a record from a table	DELETE FROM Tracks WHERE TrackTitle = 'Yesterday'
INSERT	Add a record	INSERT INTO CDDescription (ItemNumber,Description) VALUES ('RCA8766098', 'In the Top 10 list for 28 weeks!')
JOIN	Use the data from two tables	SELECT FROM CompactDisks JOIN Tracks ON CompactDisks.ItemNumber = Tracks.ItemNumber
SELECT	Search for records	SELECT FROM CompactDisks WHERE ArtistName = 'Garth Brooks'
UPDATE	Change data in a field	UPDATE CompactDisks SET DiscountPrice = 15.95 WHERE ItemNumber = 'RCA6578988'

How does SQL specify which table to use? SQL keywords such as USE, FROM, or INTO can be used to construct a clause specifying the table that you want to access. The clause consists of the keyword followed by the name of the table. For example, the clause **FROM Tracks** indicates that you want to use WebMusic's Tracks table.

An SQL query that begins with **DELETE FROM Tracks** means that you want to delete something from the Tracks table. To complete the query, you provide the parameters that specify which record you want to delete.

How does SQL specify parameters? The term **parameter** is technical jargon that refers to the detailed specifications for a command. Keywords such as WHERE usually begin an SQL clause that contains the parameters for a command. Suppose that WebMusic's inventory manager wants to delete all the CDs in the WebMusic database recorded by Phish. The SQL looks like this:

DELETE	FROM CompactDisks	WHERE ArtistName = 'Phish'
SQL command word	FROM clause specifies the table to use	WHERE clause specifies the field name and its contents

Now that you've learned the basic structure of an SQL query, let's take a closer look at the SQL for specific database tasks, such as adding records, searching for information, updating fields, organizing records, and joining tables.

ADDING RECORDS

How are records added to a database? Suppose that you want to purchase a new CD from the WebMusic site. As a first-time customer, you fill out a form with your name, address, and so on. The client software that you use collects the data that you enter in the form and generates an SQL statement using the **INSERT** command, which adds your data to the Customers table of the WebMusic database. Figure 10-40 shows the Customer form, the SQL statement that adds the customer data to the database, and the data that is added to the Customers table.

FIGURE 10-40

Data from the Customer form is added to the database.

Customer form

First Name: Jorge
Last Name: Rodriguez
Address Line 1 (or company name): 101 Las Vegas Court
Address Line 2 (optional):
City: Taos
State/Province/Region: NM
ZIP/Postal Code: 87571
Phone Number: 5055553412

SQL statement

```
INSERT INTO Customers
(LastName, FirstName, Street, City,
State, ZipCode, PhoneNumber)
VALUES ('Rodriguez', 'Jorge', '101
Las Vegas Court', 'Taos', 'NM',
'87571', '5055553412')
```

Customers table

LastName	FirstName	Street	City	State	ZipCode	PhoneNumber
Rodriguez	Jorge	101 Las Vegas Court	Taos	NM	87571	505-555-3412
Bleuman	Jonathan	5022 Lake St.	Negaunee	MI	49866	906-555-2131
Wincheta	Daisy	499 Table Mesa	Boulder	CO	80301	303-555-6902
Venkata	Patel	872 Old York Way	Durango	CO	81301	970-555-4438
Wong	Joy	822 Park Place	New York	NY	10023	212-555-9903
Helwig	Nathaniel	5 Winsome Drive	Cheyenne	WY	82003	303-555-3223
Chen	Lu-Chi	2235 Overview Trail	San Francisco	CA	94118	415--555-9001
Walton	William	500 Vista Mesa [illegible]	[illegible]	NM	87504	505-555-1111
Bolduc	Luc	41 Rue [illegible]	[illegible]	[illegible]	[illegible]	[illegible]
[illegible]	Kallie	[illegible]	[illegible]	[illegible]	[illegible]	[illegible]

Does data analysis require a special type of information system? Most data analysis methods fall under the broader scope of decision support systems. As described in Chapter 9, a decision support system, or DSS, provides decision makers with tools to analyze information. Today's decision support systems vary in their sophistication. Some provide only rudimentary tools for summarizing and extracting data, whereas others provide tools for complex data analysis.

The Data Analysis InfoWeb provides links to case studies about OLAP, data mining, data warehouses, and multi-dimensional databases.

click

Today's most advanced data analysis method is referred to as **OLAP** (online analytical processing). An OLAP system consists of computer hardware, database software, and analytical tools that are optimized for summarizing, consolidating, viewing, and synthesizing data.

The architecture of an OLAP system is usually not the same as transaction processing architecture. Broadly speaking, a transaction processing system (TPS) is optimized to provide maximum performance for inserting, updating, and deleting information from a database. In contrast, an OLAP system is used to analyze existing data, generate summaries, and expose patterns and trends in the data. Because the data in an OLAP system rarely changes, it makes more sense for an OLAP system to be optimized to quickly perform complex searches and calculate summaries and aggregates.

10

What methods are used to analyze information in an OLAP system? Many OLAP systems support a data analysis technique called data mining. **Data mining** refers to the use of statistical tools for automated extraction of predictive information from large databases. For example, a store that sells kitchen equipment and cookbooks may notice that 50 percent of the people who buy *The New Sushi Cookbook* also buy rice cookers. Data mining is the method used to clarify some of these "hidden" relationships so that organizations can benefit from information that is not obvious. Data mining typically looks at the relationships between data along a single dimension. Decision makers who "mine data" seek an answer to the question, "How does X affect Y?" (or in our example, "How does a cookbook purchase affect the purchase of cooking implements?")

OLAP also allows decision makers to look for relationships between multiple data dimensions. For example, imagine a sales history database for a national bookstore. A typical OLAP query may retrieve the total sales of all non-fiction books for bookstores in Indiana in the month of January 2003. This query consists of three dimensions—the category of the book (non-fiction), the store location (Indiana), and the time period (January 2003).

The information used for OLAP queries is often represented as a data cube. A **data cube** is a three-dimensional model of the data in a database. Each dimension of a data cube corresponds to a dimension of the OLAP query. See Figure 10-45 for an example of a data cube.

FIGURE 10-45

A data cube represents data in multiple dimensions. This data cube has three dimensions—months, states, and book categories.

The black cube represents data for non-fiction books sold in Indiana in January 2003.

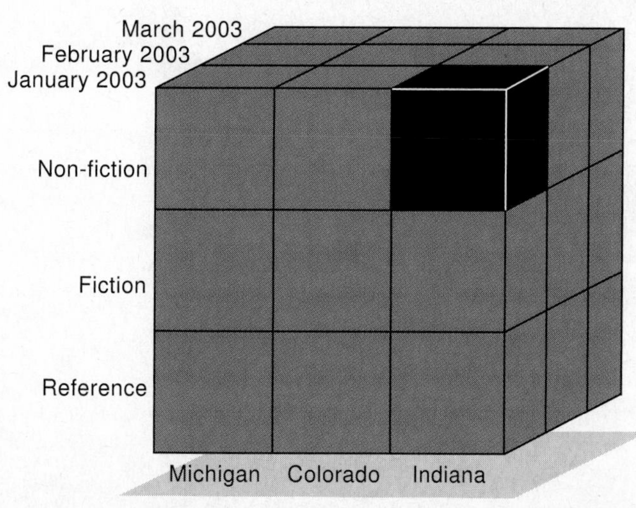

Does an OLAP system require a special type of database? The database used for an OLAP system is often referred to as a data warehouse. A **data warehouse**, or "information warehouse," is a collection of information organized for analysis. A data warehouse may contain data from only one particular database, but more often it contains information from a variety of sources. These sources include flat files, databases, spreadsheets, text files, and any other source of historical information an organization maintains. Data from these sources can be exported to a data warehouse, which is typically stored with the help of a relational database management system, or RDBMS.

The process of populating a data warehouse with data typically requires custom conversion routines. During the conversion, incomplete or inaccurate data is either corrected or eliminated. For example, suppose that customer information from a transaction processing system is being added to a data warehouse. If some customer records don't include a ZIP code, the conversion routine could attempt to find the correct ZIP code, or simply discard records without ZIP codes. This process ensures that the data warehouse receives only customer information that is complete and accurate.

Depending on how the data warehouse is used, sometimes the conversion routines summarize information rather than convert all of the raw data. For example, suppose a data warehouse is used to analyze sales by region. It may be necessary to store only the number of customers per ZIP code, in which case any "extra" customer information, such as name, address, and e-mail address, can be eliminated. Data may also be summarized by date. For example, a bookstore may include only the number of books sold per month by title, rather than the number of books on each particular invoice. These kinds of "shortcuts" in the conversion process make data analysis faster and more precise than if the analysis was performed on the raw data. Figure 10-46 summarizes the process of populating a data warehouse.

FIGURE 10-46

When data is moved into a data warehouse, conversion routines may summarize or change data before storing it.

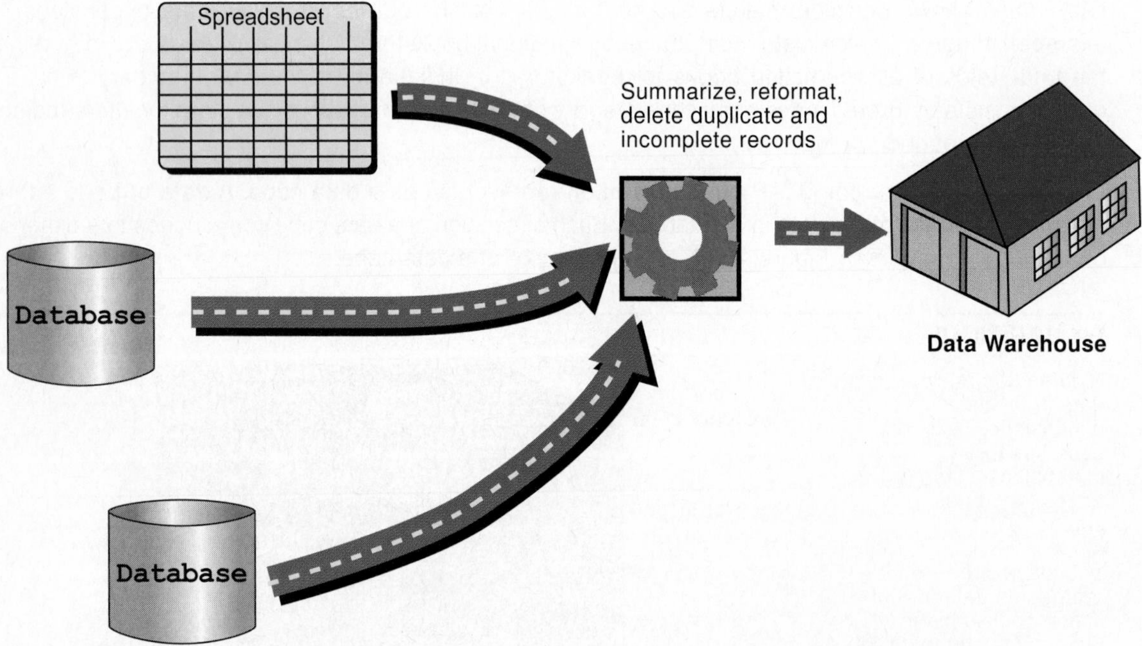

To facilitate the use of data cubes and multidimensional analysis, some OLAP systems are based on a **multidimensional database**, which provides built-in methods to display and store data in a multidimensional structure. Organizing data in a multidimensional database requires that all the data be converted into a multidimensional format. Because this process is often time consuming, many large OLAP systems retain information in an RDBMS. To support multidimensional analysis with an RDBMS, however, it is usually necessary to create additional tables to store aggregated and summarized data, as well as dimension-specific data. With these additional tables, an RDBMS can essentially "mimic" an MDBMS (multidimensional database management system) for purposes of data analysis.

Can I use any DBMS for data analysis? Data analysis usually involves large amounts of data and complex queries. As a result, entry-level DBMSs usually don't include sophisticated data analysis tools, nor do they supply the speed to adequately support a data warehouse. However, most professional DBMSs include tools for data analysis. These tools include sophisticated methods for converting and summarizing information from a variety of sources, and query languages optimized for working with OLAP systems.

QUICKCheck TechTalk

1. A(n) ______ system is optimized to quickly perform complex searches, summarize data, and calculate aggregates.
2. Data ______ refers to the use of statistical tools for automated extraction of predictive information from large databases.
3. A data ______ is a three-dimensional model of OLAP data.
4. A data ______ is a database that consists of information from a variety of sources organized and optimized for data analysis.
5. An entry-level DBMS does not typically include analysis tools, nor does it supply the speed to adequately support a data warehouse. True or false? ______

check answers 

ISSUE
WHAT HAPPENED TO PRIVACY?

You might be astonished by the amount of information stored about you in computer databases. Your bank has information on your financial status, credit history, and the people, organizations, and businesses to which you write checks. School records indicate something about your ability to learn and the subjects that interest you. Medical records indicate the state of your health. Credit card companies track the places you shop, and what you purchase in person, by mail, or on the Web. Your phone company stores your phone number, your address, and a list of the phone numbers you dial. The driver's license bureau has your physical description. Your Internet cookies track many of the Web sites that you frequent. By compiling this data—a process sometimes referred to as "profiling"—an interested person or company could guess some very private things about you, such as your political views, or even your sexual orientation.

When records were stored on index cards and in file folders, locating and distributing data constituted a laborious process that required hand transcriptions or photocopies of piles of papers. Today, this data appears in electronic format and is easy to access, copy, sell, ship, consolidate, and alter. Privacy advocates point out the potential for misusing data that has been collected and stored in computer databases. A University of Miami law professor, A. Michael Froomkin, writes, "The most important part of the emerging database phenomenon, however, arises from the combination of the growth in computer processing power with the likelihood that routine personal data collection will soon become nearly ubiquitous. As the cost of data storage plummets, these trends will make it possible to assemble an individual data profile of extraordinary detail by cross referencing multiple, extensive databases. These profiles have uses in commerce, in law-enforcement; some applications are benign, some less so."

Privacy advocates are encouraging lawmakers to restrict the sale and distribution of information about individuals. One proposal would require your permission before information about you could be distributed. Legislation passed by the U.S. Congress in 2001 established regulations to protect the confidentiality of medical records by requiring a patient's consent before medical information can be disclosed. Doctors, insurance companies, and other health care entities must comply with these regulations by 2003.

The issue of privacy is not simple. Information about you is not necessarily "yours." Although you might "reveal" information about yourself on an application form, other information about you is collected without your direct input. For example, suppose that you default on your credit card payments. The credit card company has accumulated information on your delinquent status. Shouldn't it have the freedom to distribute this information, for example, to another credit card company?

Furthermore, many individuals knowingly let companies gather profiling information to get free products. A trend that developed in 1999 was to swap a free PC or other merchandise for permission to collect information on people's "clickpaths"—the Web sites that they visit, their online spending habits, and so on. For one such offer, recipients of a free PC were required to agree to the terms of a lengthy contract, which included the following section on profiling: "The Free-PC System will monitor your use of the Free-PC System, and will construct personal profiles about your interests and characteristics from the information supplied directly or indirectly to us, whether from your use of the Free-PC System, the Internet, or otherwise, as well as through the use of data harvesting and mining techniques. Such collected information may be used for our marketing or promotional purposes, for providing services to you, and in administering the Free-PC System and our relationship with you."

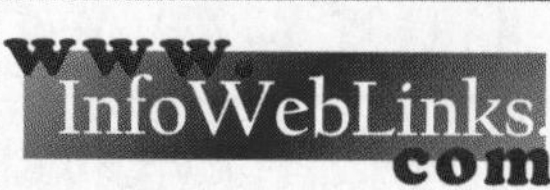

You'll find lots more information about privacy issues at the Privacy InfoWeb.

click

Unfortunately, private information can be garnered from your computer without your permission. Spyware is a type of software containing code that tracks personal information from your computer and passes it on to third parties, without your authorization or knowledge. Spyware may be embedded in an application that you download, or it can download itself from unscrupulous Web sites—a process called a "driveby download."

Databases that contain personal information do provide positive benefits. For example, many Web surfers appreciate the shortcuts offered by software agents that assemble a customer profile in order to recommend books, CDs, videos, news articles, and other targeted goods and services. These users may willingly give up some measure of privacy for the convenience afforded by these agents. For another example, the LEXIS-NEXIS database has been used for several socially beneficial activities, such as locating heirs to estates, reuniting family members, finding pension beneficiaries, and tracing the influence of personal donations in politics.

10

The electronic privacy issue appears to be heading toward some type of compromise between strict privacy and wholesale collection/distribution of personal data. Check out the Privacy InfoWeb for more information on the issue, as well as tips and computer programs that you can use to protect your privacy online.

WHAT DO YOU THINK?

1. Do you think that data about you should be distributed only after your permission is obtained? ○ Yes ○ No ○ Not sure
2. Can you identify an actual incident when you discovered that data about you was distributed without your approval? ○ Yes ○ No ○ Not sure
3. Do you think that the information you provide on paper forms is more private than information that you enter into Web-based forms? ○ Yes ○ No ○ Not sure
4. Have you thought about ways to protect your privacy? ○ Yes ○ No ○ Not sure

click to save your responses

INTERACTIVE SUMMARY

The Interactive Summary helps you to select and remember important concepts from this chapter. Fill in the blanks to best complete each sentence. When using the NP6 BookOnCD, you can click the Check Answers buttons to automatically score your answers. Place your Tracking Disk in the floppy disk drive if you want to save your scores.

A database is a collection of information, typically stored as computer files. Computer databases evolved from file processing technology in which data is stored in a single ________ file that uses a uniform format for each item in the file. A ________ contains the smallest unit of meaningful information. A series of data fields forms a ________, which stores data about one entity—a person, place, thing, or event. The blank structure of a record is referred to as a record ________. A record that contains data is sometimes referred to as a record ________. A ________ file contains only one record type. In contrast, a ________ can contain a variety of different record types.

In a database, records can be related by one-to-________ relationships, one-to-many relationships, or many-to-many relationships. The number of associations that can exist between two record types is referred to as ________. Relationships can be graphically depicted using diagramming techniques, such as ________-relationship diagrams. ________ databases allow only one-to-many relationships. ________ databases allow one-to-many and many-to-many relationships. ________ databases exist as a series of tables that can be related by common fields. The relationships between these tables can be added, changed, or deleted on demand. An object-oriented database stores data in objects that can be grouped into ________, and defined by attributes and methods.

check answers

Flat files can be created and manipulated using a variety of tools, including word processing and spreadsheet software. For databases composed of more than one record type, however, it is necessary to use a database management system, which is abbreviated as ________. An entry-level database management system typically handles many simultaneous searches, but has limited capability to deal with multiple simultaneous updates. Handling billions of records and performing hundreds of transactions every second require database ________ software.

The data in a database can be accessed via the Web. A simple process called ________ Web publishing converts a database report into an HTML document, which can be displayed by a browser. A more sophisticated technique called ________ Web publishing produces data from a database on demand. HTML forms and XForms provide not only search capabilities, but can also be used to add or modify data in a database with a Web browser. ________ documents provide a Web-based data management tool that uses special tags as field names within a document.

check answers

The first step in designing a relational database is to define its fields by specifying a field name and data type. The [ ] data type is used for fields that contain data that might be mathematically manipulated. The [ ] data type is used for fixed-length fields containing text that is not intended to be mathematically manipulated. The date data type is used when you want to store and manipulate dates. The [ ] data type is used to store true/false or yes/no data. The [ ] data type is a variable-length field for entering text. The [ ] data type is used to store binary data, such as MP3 files or graphics. When designing fields, a database designer can also include field formats, lookup routines and [ ] rules to reduce data entry errors.

The number of tables in a database can be determined by a process called [ ], which helps a database designer group fields into record types and avoid data redundancy. A database designer must also consider how to sort or index records. The [ ] key for a table specifies the order in which records are stored, and where new records are inserted in a table. A database [ ] provides an alternative way to organize records, using a series of keys and pointers to temporarily arrange data without affecting the physical sequence of records specified by the sort order. A database designer might also be responsible for designing the user interface and report templates for a database, as well as the conversion routines for loading the initial set of data into the database.

check answers

10

SQL is a database query language that typically works behind the scenes as an intermediary between the database [ ] software provided to users, and the database itself. Although the specifications for searches and other database tasks are collected by easy-to-use graphical user interfaces, those specifications are converted into an SQL [ ], which can communicate directly with the database.

An SQL query contains SQL [ ], such as SELECT, FROM, INSERT, JOIN, and WHERE, plus [ ] that specify the details of the command. Records can be removed from a database using the SQL [ ] command. Records are added using the SQL [ ] command. The SQL [ ] command is used to search for data. To change the data in a field requires the SQL [ ] command. SQL also provides a [ ] command that can be used to temporarily consolidate two tables so that data can be accessed simultaneously from both of them.

check answers

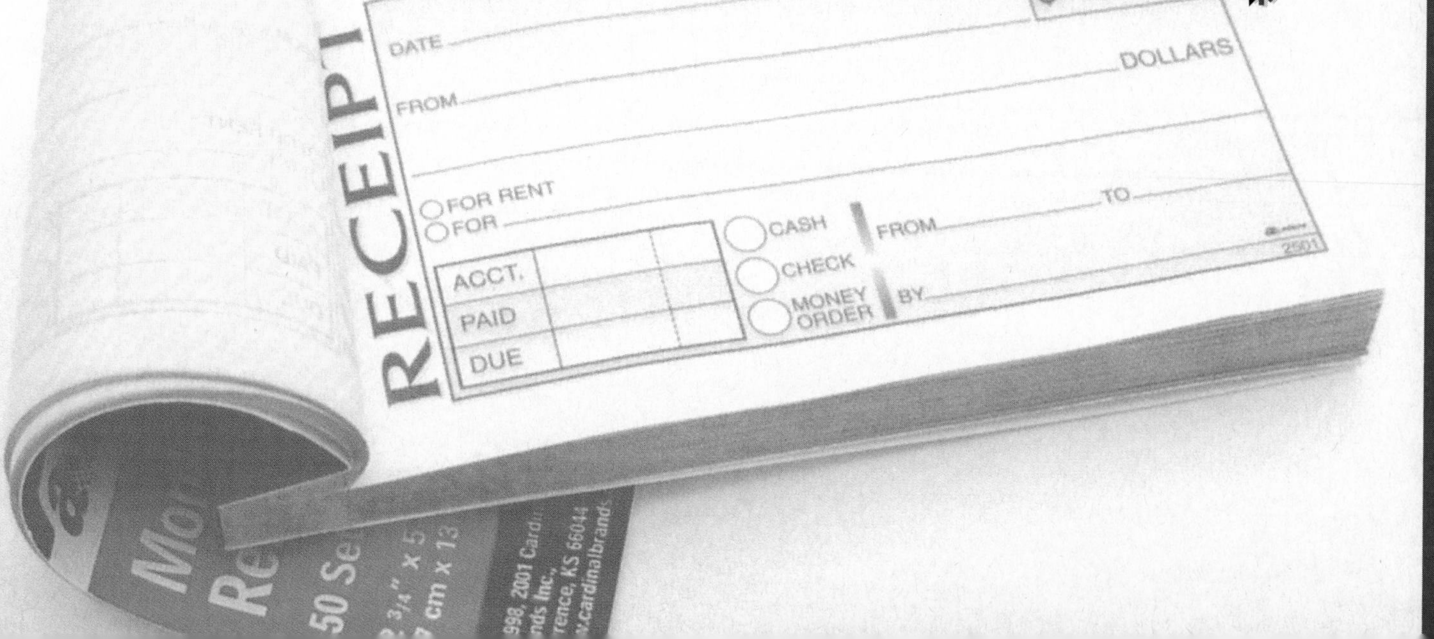

INTERACTIVE KEY TERMS

Make sure that you understand all of the boldfaced key terms presented in this chapter. If you're using the NP6 BookOnCD, you can use this list of terms as an interactive study activity. First, try to define a term in your own words, then click the term to compare your definition with the definition that is presented in the chapter.

INTERACTIVE
SITUATION QUESTIONS

Apply what you've learned to some typical computing situations. When using the NP6 BookOnCD, you can type your answers, then use the Check Answer buttons to automatically score your responses. Place your Tracking Disk in the floppy disk drive if you want to save your scores.

1 You're working for a company that's just getting started with a database project. The boss wants "the most standard kind of database," so you recommend that the company evaluate ________ database management software.

2 You are analyzing a company's customer and order information. Because each customer can place multiple orders, you know this is a(n) ________-to-many relationship.

3 You are designing a record type that holds customer information. You should use a(n) ________ data type to hold information such as telephone numbers and Social Security numbers, because although this data looks like numbers, you'll never need to use it to perform mathematical calculations.

4 You are creating a movie review database, and one field stores the "star rating" that a popular reviewer gave each particular movie. Movies are rated from one to four stars, so the "Stars" field is only valid if the number is between 1 and 4. To ensure that nobody enters a value below 1 or above 4, you use a field ________ rule to filter the data as it's entered into the table.

5 You want to print a professionally designed list of all the records in your database. To organize and format the list, you use a report generator to create a reusable report ________.

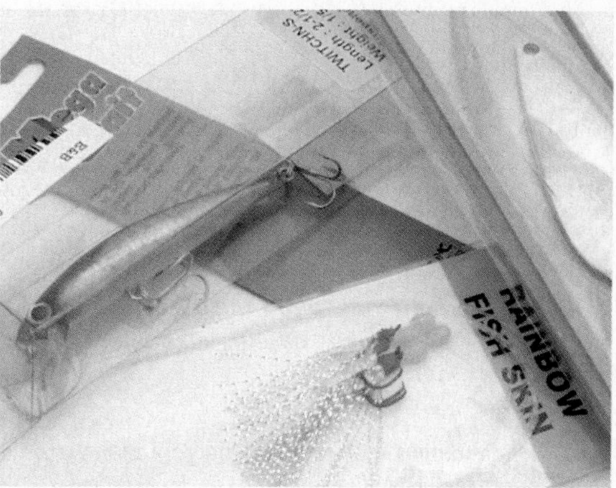

6 You own a fly fishing shop and maintain an inventory database that, along with inventory data, stores the names of the wholesalers from which you buy each item. Hot Rod Wholesalers just changed its name to Northern Rod and Reel, so you need to update your database. The best way to do this would be to perform a(n) ________ update that changes every instance of "Hot Rod Wholesalers" to "Northern Rod and Reel."

7 You are designing the structure for a mail-order catalog company. You recognize that a many-to-many relationship exists between an order and the items that are listed on the order. That clue indicates that you should separate the data into two ________, Orders and OrderDetails.

8 Your friend is working on some Web pages, and you notice that they contain tags such as <editor>Ella Ellison</editor>

<born>1960/05/26</born>

You surmise that your friend is using ________ instead of HTML.

INTERACTIVE PRACTICE TESTS

When you use the NP6 BookOnCD, you can take Practice Tests that consist of 10 multiple-choice, true/false, and fill-in-the-blank questions. The questions are selected at random from a large test bank, so each time you take a test, you'll receive a different set of questions. Your tests are scored immediately, and you can print study guides that help you find the correct answers for any questions that you missed. If you are using a Tracking Disk, insert it in the floppy disk drive to save your test scores.

click to start 

STUDY TIPS

Study Tips help you to organize and consolidate the information in a chapter by making lists, outlines, charts, and sketches. You can use paper and pencil or word processing software to complete most of the Study Tips activities.

1. Make sure that you can use your own words to correctly answer each of the green focus questions that appear throughout the chapter.
2. Explain the differences between a flat file and a database.
3. Make a list of the three different types of cardinality, and write down an example of each.
4. For each of the following pairs of record types, draw an ERD showing whether the relationship is one-to-one, one-to-many, or many-to-many.

   Author Book

   Musician CD

   Person Social Security number

   House Mailbox
5. Take a "real-world" entity, like a comic book collection or a recipe file, that you might want to store information about in a database, and divide the information into fields and record types.
6. Draw a hierarchy diagram showing the relationships among the following terms: file, program file, data file, structured data file, flat file, database, relational database, hierarchical database, network database, and object-oriented database.
7. Explain the differences between a record occurrence and a record type.
8. Provide five examples of data you would store in numeric, logical, date, memo, image, and BLOB data fields.
9. Describe the differences between hierarchical, network, relational, and object-oriented databases.
10. Create a chart that summarizes the terms used as synonyms for "record type," "record," and "field" in hierarchical, network, relational, and object-oriented databases.
11. Explain the advantages of using computed fields in a database application.
12. List the techniques that a database designer can use to reduce data entry errors.
13. Use your own words and examples to explain how normalization relates to the way you divide fields into records when designing a database.
14. Explain the differences between sorting and indexing.
15. Use diagrams to explain different ways of providing Web access to the data in a database.
16. Imagine that you must access a library card catalog using SQL. Write an SQL query that you would use to search for any books by J. K. Rowling in a table called Books, where authors' names are stored in a field called AuthorName.

A computer program is typically stored as a file and transferred into RAM when needed, but a computer program can also be embedded in computer hardware—in a ROM chip, for example. As explained in Chapter 3, a computer program can exist as a single module that provides all of the instructions necessary for a software application, device driver, or operating system. Alternatively, a computer program might consist of several modules that form a software application or operating system.

How big is a typical computer program? Compared to commercial application software, the programs that you'll work with in this chapter are relatively tiny. By Department of Defense standards, a "small" program is one with fewer than 100,000 lines of code. A "medium-sized" program is one with 100,000 to 1 million lines. A "large" program is one with more than 1 million lines. Research has shown that, on average, one person can write, test, and document only 20 lines of code per day. It is not surprising, then, that most commercial programs are written by programming teams and take many months or years to complete.

Who creates computer programs? The people who develop computer programs are referred to as computer programmers ("programmers" for short) or software engineers. A **computer programmer** typically focuses on coding computer programs. The term **coding** refers to entering the list of commands that become a computer program.

Creating a computer program that works, however, typically requires more than coding. The term **computer programming** encompasses a broad set of activities that include planning, coding, testing, and documenting computer programs. Most computer programmers participate to some extent in all of these phases of program development.

How does software engineering differ from computer programming? The term **software engineering** refers to a program development process in which mathematical, engineering, and management techniques are applied to reduce the cost and complexity of a computer program while increasing its reliability and modifiability. Software engineers frequently manage large software projects where cost overruns and software errors might have disastrous consequences.

Like a computer programmer, a **software engineer** designs, codes, tests, and documents software, but tends to focus on designing and testing activities. Software engineers approach these activities using formalized techniques based on mathematical proofs, computer science research, and engineering theory. For example, a computer programmer might code a search routine by simply instructing the computer to step through a list looking for a match. In contrast, a software engineer might consider several sophisticated methods for implementing the search, and select the one that provides the greatest efficiency based on the computer architecture and the data being processed.

Is software engineering the same as systems analysis? Some software engineering activities overlap with the systems analysis and design activities presented in Chapter 9. To distinguish between the two activities, remember that systems analysis and design typically encompass all aspects of an information system, including hardware, software, people, and procedures. In contrast, software engineering tends to focus primarily on software development.

PROGRAMMING LANGUAGES AND PARADIGMS

What is a programming language? A **programming language**, or "computer language," is a set of keywords and grammar rules designed for creating instructions that can ultimately be processed, or executed, by a computer. Most people are familiar with the names of programming languages, such as BASIC, C, Pascal, FORTRAN, Java, and COBOL. But many other programming languages, such as 8088 assembly, FORTH, LISP, and APL, remain relatively unknown to the general public.

Just as an English sentence is constructed from various words and punctuation that follow a set of grammar rules, each instruction for a computer program consists of keywords and parameters that are held together by syntax rules. A **keyword**, or "command," is a word that has a predefined meaning for the compiler or interpreter that translates each line of program code into machine language. Keywords for the Pascal computer language include WRITE, READ, IF...THEN, and GOSUB.

Keywords can be combined with specific **parameters**, which provide more detailed instructions for the computer to carry out. Keywords and parameters are combined with punctuation according to a series of rules called **syntax**, as shown in Figure 11-2.

FIGURE 11-2

An instruction for a computer program consists of keywords and parameters, formed into sentence-like statements according to a set of syntax rules.

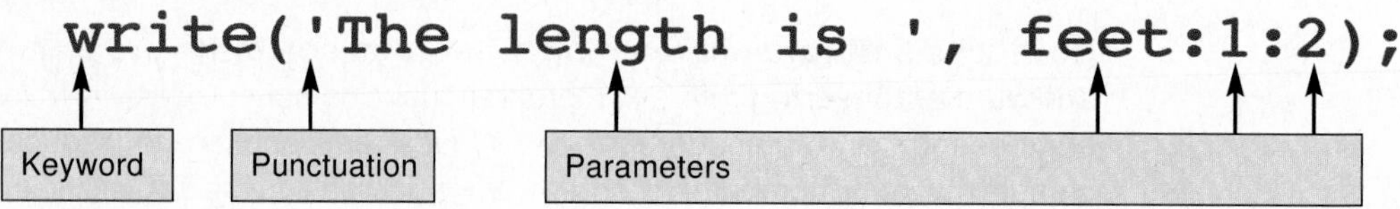

How are programming languages categorized? Programming languages are categorized in several ways. They can be divided into two major categories: low-level languages and high-level languages. They are also categorized by generation and by paradigm.

What is a low-level language? A **low-level language** typically includes commands that are specific to a particular CPU or microprocessor family. Low-level languages require a programmer to write instructions for the lowest level of the computer's hardware—that is, for specific hardware elements, such as the processor, registers, and RAM locations. Low-level languages include machine languages and assembly languages.

What is a high-level language? A **high-level language** provides what computer scientists call a "level of abstraction" that hides the underlying low-level assembly or machine language, and provides command words and grammar that are more like human languages. High-level languages, such as COBOL, BASIC, Java, and C, make the programming process easier by replacing unintelligible strings of 1s and 0s or cryptic assembly commands with understandable commands such as PRINT and WRITE. In addition, high-level language commands eliminate many lines of code by substituting a single high-level command for multiple low-level commands, as shown in Figure 11-3 on the next page.

FIGURE 11-3

A single high-level command typically does the work of multiple low-level commands.

High-level Pascal command	Low-level assembly commands
Total:=5+4	LDA 5 STA Num1 LDA 4 ADD Num1 STA Total END

How did programming evolve from low-level to high-level languages? The first computers were programmed without programming languages. Technicians rewired a computer's circuitry to prepare it for various processing tasks. The idea of storing programs in computer memory paved the way for computer programming languages, which allowed a programmer to write a series of commands and load them into the computer for execution. Programming languages were very primitive at first, but they evolved through many generations into the computer languages of today.

What was the first generation of programming languages? Machine languages were the first languages available for programming computers and, therefore, they are sometimes referred to as **first-generation languages**. A **machine language** provides a set of commands, represented as a series of 1s and 0s, corresponding to the instruction set that is hardwired into the circuitry of a microprocessor. A machine language is specific to a particular CPU or microprocessor family. For example, the machine language that is hardwired into a Pentium 4 processor includes many unique commands that are not wired into older PC 8088 microprocessors or Macintosh-based PowerPC microprocessors. Although machine languages still work on today's computers, programmers rarely use machine languages to write programs.

11

What is a second-generation language? An **assembly language** allows programmers to use abbreviated command words, called op codes, such as LDA for "load," rather than the 1s and 0s used in machine languages. At the time assembly languages were first introduced, they were hailed as a significant improvement over machine languages, and came to be known as **second-generation languages**.

Like a machine language, an assembly language is classified as a low-level language because it is machine specific—each assembly language command corresponds on a one-to-one basis to a machine language instruction. As you might expect, the assembly language instructions for a Pentium 4 microprocessor differ from those for an 8088 or a PowerPC microprocessor. An assembly language is useful when a programmer wants to directly manipulate what happens at the hardware level. Today, programmers typically use assembly languages to write system software, such as compilers, operating systems, and device drivers.

What is a third-generation language? When high-level languages were originally conceived in the 1950s, they were dubbed **third-generation languages** because they seemed a major improvement over machine and assembly languages. Third-generation languages used easy-to-remember command words, such as PRINT and INPUT, to take the place of several lines of assembly language op codes or endless strings of machine language 0s and 1s.

Many computer scientists believed that third-generation languages, such as COBOL, Fortran, Pascal, C, and BASIC, would eliminate programming errors. Errors certainly became less frequent, and program development time decreased significantly. Programmers using third-generation languages still made a variety of errors, however, so computer language development continued to progress.

What is a fourth-generation language? In 1969, computer scientists began to develop high-level languages, called **fourth-generation languages**, which more closely resemble human languages, or "natural languages," than do third-generation languages. Fourth-generation languages, such as SQL and RPG-I, eliminate many of the strict punctuation and grammar rules that complicate third-generation languages. Today, fourth-generation languages are typically used for database applications. A single SQL command, such as `SORT TABLE Kids on Lastname`, can replace many lines of third-generation code, as shown in Figure 11-4.

FIGURE 11-4

A single command written in a fourth-generation language can replace many lines of third-generation code.

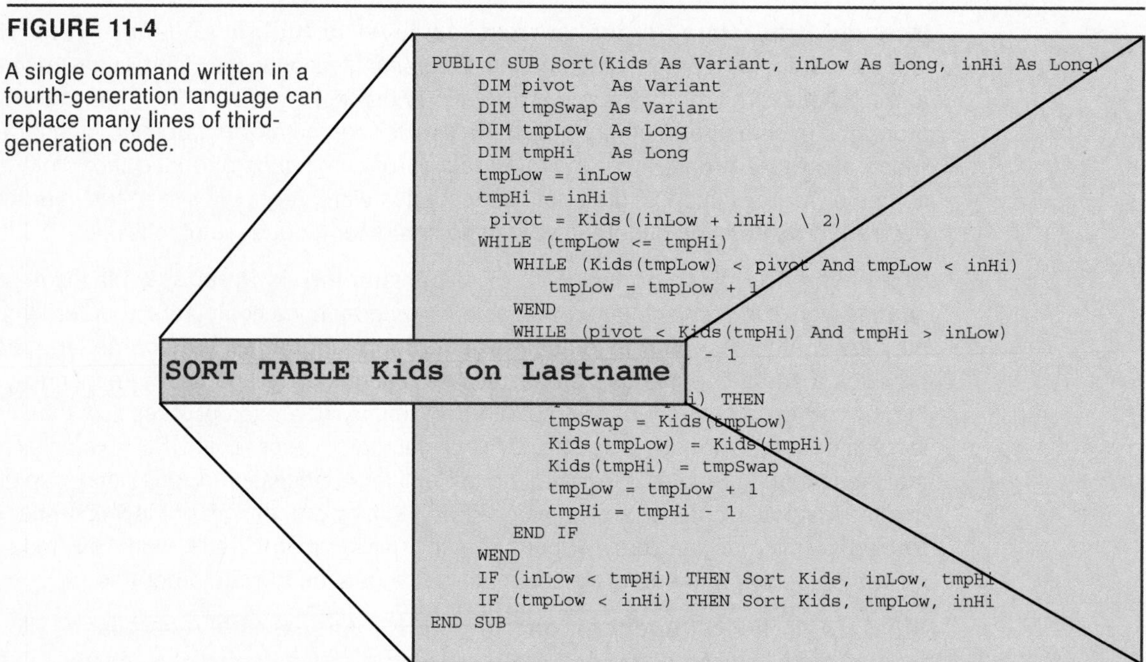

PUBLIC SUB Sort(Kids As Variant, inLow As Long, inHi As Long)
DIM pivot As Variant
DIM tmpSwap As Variant
DIM tmpLow As Long
DIM tmpHi As Long
tmpLow = inLow
tmpHi = inHi
pivot = Kids((inLow + inHi) \ 2)
WHILE (tmpLow <= tmpHi)
WHILE (Kids(tmpLow) < pivot And tmpLow < inHi)
tmpLow = tmpLow + 1
WEND
WHILE (pivot < Kids(tmpHi) And tmpHi > inLow)
- 1
i) THEN
tmpSwap = Kids(tmpLow)
Kids(tmpLow) = Kids(tmpHi)
Kids(tmpHi) = tmpSwap
tmpLow = tmpLow + 1
tmpHi = tmpHi - 1
END IF
WEND
IF (inLow < tmpHi) THEN Sort Kids, inLow, tmpHi
IF (tmpLow < inHi) THEN Sort Kids, tmpLow, inHi
END SUB
SORT TABLE Kids on Lastname

Do any fifth-generation languages exist? In 1982, a group of Japanese researchers began work on a fifth-generation computer project which used Prolog—a computer programming language based on a declarative programming paradigm that is described in detail later in the chapter. Prolog and other declarative languages became closely identified with the fifth-generation project and were classified by some experts as **fifth-generation languages**. Other experts disagree with this classification and instead define fifth-generation languages as those that allow programmers to use graphical or visual tools to construct programs, rather than typing lines of code. You'll learn more about visual programming later in the chapter.

Programmers can choose from a wide array of programming languages. To learn more about the most popular languages, visit the Programming Languages InfoWeb.

What is the best programming language? Hundreds of programming languages exist, and each has unique strengths and weaknesses. Although it might be possible to select the best language for a particular project, most computer scientists would find it difficult to agree on one all-time "best" language. The table in Figure 11-5 on the next page briefly describes some of the programming languages discussed in this chapter.

FIGURE 11-5 Selected Programming Languages

APL (A Programming Language) Scientific language used to manipulate tables of numbers.

BASIC (Beginner's All-purpose Symbolic Instruction Code) Developed by John Kemeny and Thomas Kurtz in the mid-1960s; simple, interactive programming language.

C Developed by Dennis Ritchie at Bell Laboratories in the early 1970s; used today for a wide range of commercial software

C++ and **C#** Languages derived from C that provide object-oriented capabilities.

COBOL (COmmon Business Oriented Language) Procedural language developed in the early 1960s and used extensively for mainframe business applications.

CPL (Combined Programming Language) Developed in the 1960s for scientific and commercial programming.

Eiffel An advanced OO language developed in 1988 with syntax similar to C.

FORTRAN (FORmula TRANslator) One of the original third-generation languages, FORTRAN was developed in the 1950s and is still used today for scientific applications.

Haskell A functional programming language named for the mathematician Haskell Brooks Curry.

Java A high-level C++ derivative developed by Sun Microsystems and used extensively for Web-based programming.

LISP (LISt Processing) Developed in 1959 by famed AI researcher John McCarthy, LISP is used for artificial intelligence applications.

Pascal Named in honor of Blaise Pascal, who invented one of the first mechanical adding machines, Pascal is a third-generation language developed to teach students programming concepts.

PL/1 (Programming Language 1) A complex business and scientific language developed in 1964 by IBM that combines FORTRAN, COBOL, and ALGOL.

Prolog (PROgramming in LOGic) Declarative language developed in 1972 and used for artificial intelligence applications.

RPG (Report Program Generator) and RPG-II An IBM programming platform introduced in 1964 for easily generating business reports.

Visual Basic Windows-based software development kit created by Microsoft in the early 1990s that assists programmers in developing Windows-based applications.

Scheme A dialect of LISP, used for computer research and teaching.

SIMULA (SIMUlation LAnguage) is believed to be the first object-oriented programming language.

Smalltalk Classic object-oriented programming language developed by Xerox researchers in 1980.

What is a programming paradigm? In addition to being classified by level and by generation, programming languages can also be classified by paradigm. Programmers approach problems in different ways. Whereas one programmer might focus on the steps required to complete a specific computation, another programmer might focus on the data that forms the basis for the computation. The phrase **programming paradigm** refers to a way of conceptualizing and structuring the tasks that a computer performs. Quite a number of programming paradigms exist, and they are not mutually exclusive. A programmer might use techniques from multiple paradigms while planning and coding a program.

Programming languages can be categorized by the programming paradigms that they support. Some languages support a single paradigm. Other programming languages—referred to as **multiparadigm languages**—support more than one paradigm. Figure 11-6 provides a brief description of today's most popular programming paradigms. Sections B, C, and D of this chapter provide a detailed look at three popular paradigms—procedural, object-oriented, and declarative.

FIGURE 11-6 Popular Programming Paradigms

Paradigm	Languages	Description
Procedural	BASIC, Pascal, COBOL, FORTRAN, Ada	Emphasizes linear, step-by-step algorithms that provide the computer with instructions on how to solve a problem or carry out a task
Object-oriented	Smalltalk, C++, Java	Formulates programs as a series of objects and methods that interact to perform a specific task
Declarative	Prolog	Focuses on the use of facts and rules to describe a problem
Functional	LISP, Scheme, Haskell	Emphasizes the evaluation of expressions, called "functions"
Event-driven	Visual Basic, C#	Focuses on selecting user interface elements and defining event-handling routines that are triggered by various mouse or keyboard activities

PROGRAM PLANNING

How does a programmer plan a computer program? Problems that you might try to solve using a computer often begin as questions—for example, "Which pizza place has the best deal?" But such questions might not be stated in a way that helps you devise a method for a computer to arrive at an answer. A question like "Which pizza place has the best deal?" is vague. It does not specify what information is available or how to determine the best deal. Do you know the price of several pizzas at different pizza places? Do you know the sizes of the pizzas? Do you know how many toppings are included in each price? What does "best deal" mean? Is it merely the cheapest pizza? Is it the pizza that gives you the most toppings for the dollar? Is it the biggest pizza you can get for the $24.63 that you and your friends managed to scrape together? The programming process begins with a problem statement that helps you clearly define the purpose of a computer program.

What is a problem statement? In the context of programming, a **problem statement** defines certain elements that must be manipulated to achieve a result or goal. A good problem statement for a computer program has three characteristics:

- It specifies any assumptions that define the scope of the problem.
- It clearly specifies the known information.
- It specifies when the problem has been solved.

Study Figure 11-7 and see if you can formulate a problem statement that is better than the initial vague question, "Which pizza place has the best deal?"

FIGURE 11-7 Which pizzeria offers the best deal?

What is an assumption? In a problem statement, an **assumption** is something that you accept as true in order to proceed with program planning. For example, with the pizza problem, you can make the assumption that you want to compare two pizzas. Furthermore, you can assume that some pizzas are round and others are square. To simplify the problem, you might make the additional assumption that none of the pizzas are rectangular—that is, none will have one side longer than the other. This assumption simplifies the problem because you need to deal only with the "size" of a pizza, rather than the "length" and "width" of a pizza. A fourth assumption for the pizza problem is that the pizzas you compare have the same toppings. Finally, you assume that the pizza with the lowest cost per square inch is the best buy.

A visual development environment is a very powerful tool for programming software applications for GUI environments, such as Windows. Most GUI applications are "event-driven," which means that when launched, the program's interface appears on the screen and waits for the user to initiate an event by clicking a menu, dragging an object, double-clicking an icon, typing text, or clicking a button. The fact that the sequence of user actions cannot be predicted introduces a level of complexity that doesn't fit well with traditional programming languages, which tend to approach programs as a fixed sequence of procedures.

Visual development environments have spawned an approach to programming that is sometimes referred to as the **event-driven paradigm**, in which a programmer develops a program by selecting user interface elements and specifying event-handling routines. The programmer is never required to deal with the overall program sequence because the development environment automatically combines user interface elements and event-handling routines into a file that becomes the final computer program. This event-driven paradigm can significantly reduce development time and simplify the entire programming process.

PROGRAM TESTING AND DOCUMENTATION

How does a programmer know if a program works? A computer program must be tested to ensure that it works correctly. Testing often consists of running the program and entering test data to see whether the program produces correct results. If testing does not produce the expected results, the program contains an error, sometimes called a "bug." This error must be corrected, and then the program must be tested again and again until it runs error-free.

11

What can cause program errors? When a program doesn't work correctly, it is usually the result of an error made by the programmer. A **syntax error** occurs when an instruction does not follow the syntax rules, or grammar, of the programming language. For example, the BASIC command `If AGE = 16 Then "You can drive."` produces a syntax error because the command word PRINT is missing. The correct version of the command is `If AGE = 16 Then Print "You can drive."`

Syntax errors are very easy to make, but they are typically also easy to detect and correct. A syntax error can be caused by omitting a keyword, misspelling a keyword, or using incorrect punctuation, such as a colon (:) where a semicolon (;) is required. Many program editors detect and point out syntax errors as the programmer enters each instruction.

Another type of program bug is a **runtime error**, which, as its name indicates, shows up when you run a program. Some runtime errors result from instructions that the computer can't execute. The BASIC instruction `DiscountPrice = RegularPrice/0` produces a runtime error, because dividing by 0 is a mathematically impossible operation that the computer cannot perform.

Some runtime errors are classified as logic errors. A **logic error** is an error in the logic or design of a program, such as using the wrong formula to calculate the area of a round pizza. Logic errors can be caused by an inadequate definition of the problem, or an incorrect formula for a calculation, and are usually more difficult to identify than syntax errors.

How do programmers find errors? Programmers can locate errors in a program by reading through lines of code, much like a proofreader. They can also use a tool called a **debugger** that allows programmers to step through a program and monitor the status of variables, input, and output. A debugger is sometimes packaged with a programming language, or can be obtained as an add-on.

Do computer programs contain any special documentation? Anyone who uses computers is familiar with program **documentation** in the form of user manuals and help files. Programmers also insert documentation called **remarks** or "comments" into the program code. Remarks are identified by language-specific symbols, such as // in Java, or keywords, such as Rem in BASIC. Remarks are useful for programmers who want to understand how a program works before modifying it. For example, suppose that you are assigned to make some modifications to a 50,000-line program that calculates income tax. Your task would be simplified if the original programmer included remarks that identify the purpose of each section of the program and explain the basis for any formulas used to perform tax calculations.

A well-documented program contains initial remarks that explain its purpose, and additional remarks in any sections of a program where the purpose of the code is not immediately clear. For example, in the pizza program, the purpose of the expression `3.142 * (size1 / 2) ^2` might not be immediately obvious. Therefore, it would be helpful to have a remark preceding the expression, as shown in Figure 11-13.

FIGURE 11-13

Remarks are embedded in program code by programmers. In the BASIC programming language, the keyword "Rem" indicates that a line of code is a remark, which should not be executed by the computer.

```
Rem The program calculates the number of square inches
Rem in a round pizza using the formula pi r squared
Rem pi = 3.142, size/2 = radius,
Rem and (size/2)^2 = radius squared
Rem SquareInches = 3.142*(size/2)^2
```

QUICKCheck Section A

1 Computer ______ focus on coding computer programs, whereas software ______ plan and develop computer software using formalized techniques based on mathematical proofs, computer science research, and engineering theory.

2 A programming language typically supports one or more programming ______, such as procedural, object-oriented, or declarative.

3 A computer program is based on a problem ______ that specifies assumptions, lists known information, and specifies when the problem has been solved.

4 To code a program, a programmer might use a(n) ______ editor, a(n) program ______, or a ______ development environment.

5 A(n) ______ error occurs when a line of code does not follow the grammar rules for a programming language.

check answers

LAB 11-A USING A VISUAL DEVELOPMENT ENVIRONMENT

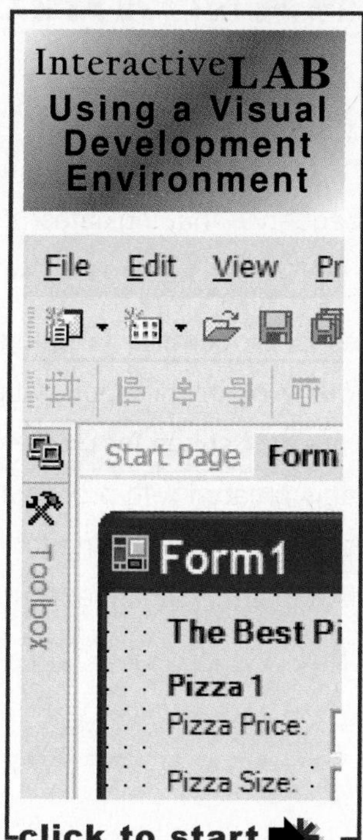

In this lab, you'll learn:

- To use the basic tools provided by the Visual Basic VDE
- How to work with a form design grid
- How to select controls, such as buttons, menus, and dialog boxes, for the graphical user interface of a computer program
- The way that a visual development environment displays the properties for a control
- How to set properties that modify the appearance and operation of a control
- About the variety of events that can affect a control
- How to add code that specifies how a control responds to events
- How to add a component to the Visual Basic toolbox, and then incorporate it into a program
- How to save and test a program
- How to compile a program and run the executable version

11

LAB Assignments

1. Start the interactive part of the lab. Insert your Tracking Disk if you want to save your QuickCheck results. Perform each of the lab steps as directed, and answer all of the lab QuickCheck questions. When you exit the lab, your answers are automatically graded and your results are displayed.

2. Draw a sketch of the main screen of your favorite word processing program. Identify five controls (such as menus, toolbars, lists, buttons, and scroll bars) provided by the programmer. Describe the external events (such as clicks, double-clicks, right-clicks, and mouseovers) to which each control responds.

3. Suppose that you are preparing to write a program that calculates the number of calories you burn while exercising. The program requires users to enter their weight, the distance travelled, and the elapsed time in minutes from the beginning of the exercise to the end. Users should also be able to select from the following types of exercises: jogging, walking, swimming, and bicycling. Once these calculations are entered, users should click a Calculate button to display the results of the calorie calculation. A Clear button should allow users to enter a new set of weight, distance, and time data. Sketch a form design grid like the one you used in the lab, and indicate where you would place each of the controls necessary for this program's user interface.

Section B
PROCEDURAL PROGRAMMING

The traditional approach to programming uses a **procedural paradigm** (sometimes called an "imperative paradigm") to conceptualize the solution to a problem as a sequence of steps. A program written in a procedural language typically consists of self-contained instructions in a sequence that indicates *how* a task is to be performed or a problem is to be solved.

A programming language that supports the procedural paradigm is called a **procedural language**. Machine languages, assembly languages, COBOL, FORTRAN, C, and many other third-generation languages are classified as procedural languages. Procedural languages are well suited for problems that can be easily solved using a linear, or step-by-step, algorithm. Programs created with procedural languages have a starting point and an ending point. The flow of execution from the beginning to the end of a program is essentially linear—that is, the computer begins at the first instruction and executes the prescribed series of instructions until it reaches the end of the program.

ALGORITHMS

What is an algorithm? An **algorithm** is a set of steps for carrying out a task, which can be written down and implemented. For example, the algorithm for making a batch of macaroni and cheese is a set of steps that includes boiling water, cooking the macaroni in the water, and making a cheese sauce. The algorithm is written down, or expressed, as instructions in a recipe. You can implement the algorithm by following the recipe instructions.

Donald Knuth's multivolume collection of programming algorithms, called *The Art of Computer Programming*, is considered one of the best scientific monographs of the twentieth century. You'll find information about this book and more at the Algorithms InfoWeb.

An important characteristic of a correctly formulated algorithm is that carefully following the steps guarantees that you can accomplish the task for which the algorithm was designed. If the recipe on a macaroni package is a correctly formulated algorithm, by following the recipe, you should be guaranteed a successful batch of macaroni and cheese.

How do I write an algorithm? An algorithm for a computer program is a set of steps that explains how to begin with known information specified in a problem statement, and how to manipulate that information to arrive at a solution. Algorithms are typically written in a format that is not specific to a particular programming language. This approach allows you to focus on formulating a correct algorithm, without becoming distracted by the detailed syntax of a computer programming language. In a later phase of the software development process, the algorithm is coded into instructions written in a computer programming language so that it can be implemented by a computer.

How do I figure out an algorithm? To design an algorithm, you might begin by recording the steps that you take to solve the problem yourself. If you take this route with the pizza problem, you must obtain initial information about the cost, size, and shape of each pizza. The computer also needs this initial information, so part of your algorithm must specify how the computer gets it. When the pizza program runs, it should ask the user to enter the initial information needed to solve the problem. Your algorithm might begin like this:

Ask the user for the shape of the first pizza and hold it in RAM as Shape1.

Ask the user for the price of the first pizza and hold it in RAM as Price1.

Ask the user for the size of the first pizza and hold it in RAM as Size1.

Next, your algorithm should specify how to manipulate this information. You want the computer to calculate the price per square inch, but a statement like "Calculate the price per square inch" neither specifies how to do the calculation, nor deals with the fact that you must perform different calculations for square and round pizzas. A more appropriate set of statements for the algorithm is shown in Figure 11-14.

FIGURE 11-14 An algorithm for calculating the price per square inch

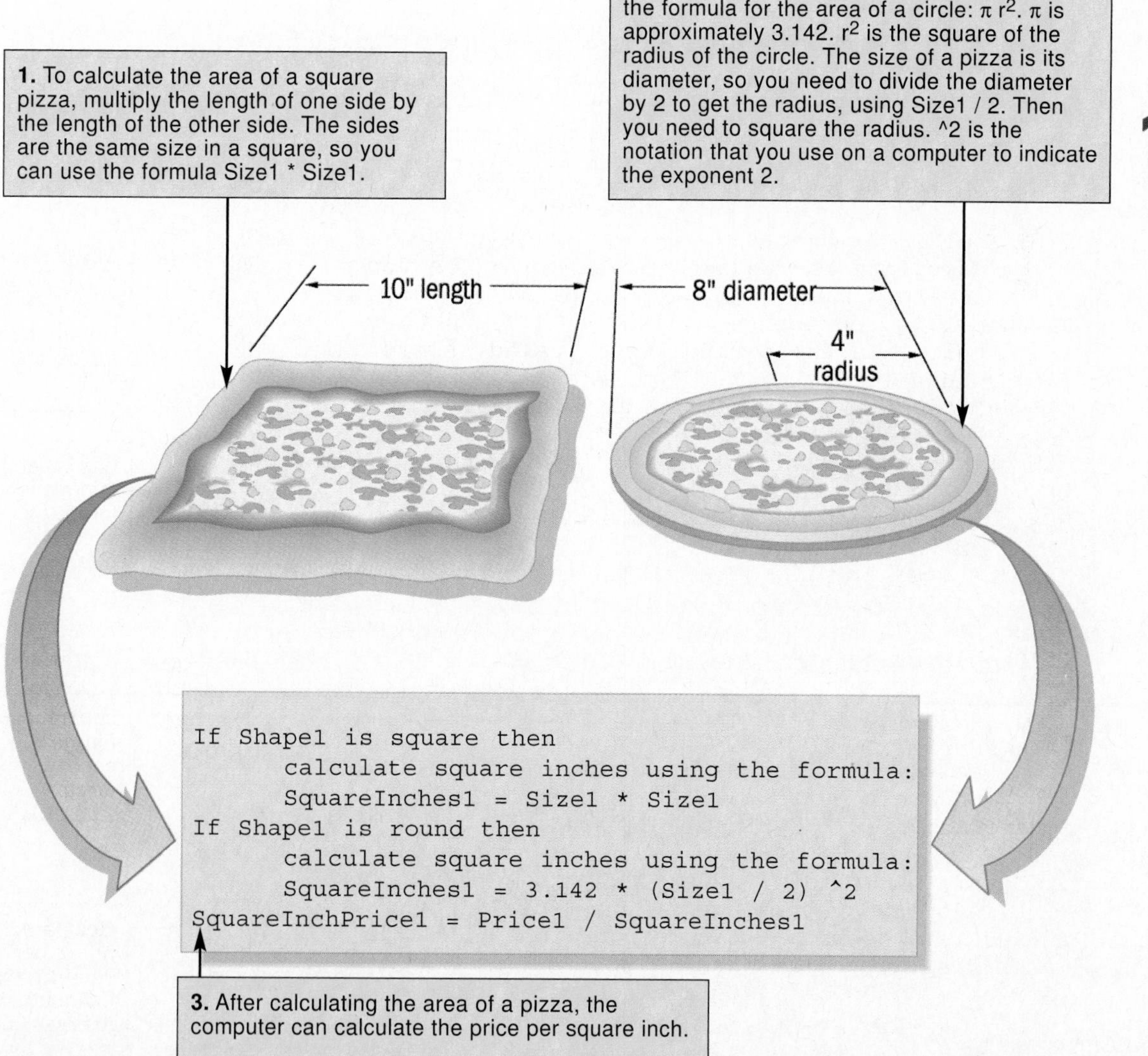

1. To calculate the area of a square pizza, multiply the length of one side by the length of the other side. The sides are the same size in a square, so you can use the formula Size1 * Size1.
2. To calculate the area of a round pizza, use the formula for the area of a circle: π r2. π is approximately 3.142. r2 is the square of the radius of the circle. The size of a pizza is its diameter, so you need to divide the diameter by 2 to get the radius, using Size1 / 2. Then you need to square the radius. ^2 is the notation that you use on a computer to indicate the exponent 2.
10" length
8" diameter
4" radius
If Shape1 is square then
calculate square inches using the formula:
SquareInches1 = Size1 * Size1
If Shape1 is round then
calculate square inches using the formula:
SquareInches1 = 3.142 * (Size1 / 2) ^2
SquareInchPrice1 = Price1 / SquareInches1
3. After calculating the area of a pizza, the computer can calculate the price per square inch.

11

So far, the algorithm describes how to calculate the price per square inch of one pizza. It should specify a similar process for calculating the price per square inch of the second pizza.

Finally, the algorithm should specify how the computer decides what to display as the solution. You want the computer to display a message indicating which pizza has the lowest square-inch cost, so your algorithm should include steps like the following:

If SquareInchPrice1 < SquareInchPrice2 then display the message "Pizza 1 is the best deal."

If SquareInchPrice2 < SquareInchPrice1 then display the message "Pizza 2 is the best deal."

But don't forget to indicate what you want the computer to do if the price per square inch is the same for both pizzas:

If SquareInchPrice1 = SquareInchPrice2 then display the message "Both pizzas are the same deal."

The complete algorithm for the pizza problem is shown in Figure 11-15.

FIGURE 11-15

The algorithm for the pizza problem, written in structured English, has five main sections.

```
Ask the user for the shape of the first pizza and hold it
     in RAM as Shape1.
Ask the user for the price of the first pizza and hold it
     in RAM as Price1.
Ask the user for the size of the first pizza and hold it
     in RAM as Size1.
```

Get initial information for the first pizza.

```
If Shape1 is square then
     calculate the square inches using the formula:
     SquareInches1 = Size1 * Size1
If Shape1 is round then
     calculate the square inches using the formula:
     SquareInches1 = 3.142 * (Size1 / 2) ^2
SquareInchPrice1 = Price1 / SquareInches1
```

Calculate the price per square inch for the first pizza.

```
Ask the user for the shape of the second pizza and hold it
     in RAM as Shape2.
Ask the user for the price of the second pizza and hold it
     in RAM as Price2.
Ask the user for the size of the second pizza and hold it
     in RAM as Size2.
```

Get initial information for the second pizza.

```
If Shape2 is square then
     calculate the square inches using the formula:
     SquareInches2 = Size2 * Size2
If Shape2 is round then
     calculate the square inches using the formula:
     SquareInches2 = 3.142 * (Size2 / 2) ^2
SquareInchPrice2 = Price2 / SquareInches2
```

Calculate the price per square inch for the second pizza.

```
If SquareInchPrice1 < SquareInchPrice2 then
     display the message "Pizza 1 is the best deal."
If SquareInchPrice2 < SquareInchPrice1 then
     display the message "Pizza 2 is the best deal."
If SquareInchPrice1 = SquareInchPrice2 then
     display the message "Both pizzas are the same deal."
```

Compare the prices per square inch, then output the results.

EXPRESSING AN ALGORITHM

What's the best way to express an algorithm? You can express an algorithm in several different ways, including structured English, pseudocode, and flowcharts. These tools are not programming languages, and they cannot be processed by a computer. Their purpose is to provide a way for you to document your ideas for program design.

For additional examples of ways to express algorithms, connect to the Pseudocode & Flowcharts InfoWeb.

Structured English is a subset of the English language with a limited selection of sentence structures that reflect processing activities. Refer to Figure 11-15 on the previous page to see how structured English can be used to express the algorithm for the pizza problem.

Another way to express an algorithm is with pseudocode. **Pseudocode** is a notational system for algorithms that has been described as "a mixture of English and your favorite programming language." Pseudocode is less formalized than structured English, so the structure and wording are left up to you. Also, when you write pseudocode, you are allowed to incorporate command words and syntax from the computer language that you intend to use for the actual program. Compare Figure 11-15 with Figure 11-16 and see if you can identify some of the differences between structured English and pseudocode.

FIGURE 11-16

The pseudocode for the pizza program mixes English-like instructions, such as "display prompts," with programming commands, such as "input."

```
display prompts for entering shape, price, and size
input Shape1, Price1, Size1
if Shape1 = square then
      SquareInches1 ← Size1 * Size1
if Shape1 = round then
      SquareInches1 ← 3.142 * (Size1 / 2) ^2
SquareInchPrice1 ← Price1 / SquareInches1
display prompts for entering shape, price, and size
input Shape2, Price2, Size2
if Shape2 = square then
      SquareInches2 ← Size2 * Size2
if Shape2 = round then
      SquareInches2 ← 3.142 * (Size2 / 2) ^2
SquareInchPrice2 ← Price2 / SquareInches2
if SquareInchPrice1 < SquareInchPrice2 then
      output "Pizza 1 is the best deal."
if SquareInchPrice2 < SquareInchPrice1 then
      output "Pizza 2 is the best deal."
if SquareInchPrice1 = SquareInchPrice2 then
      output "Both pizzas are the same deal."
```

11

A third way to express an algorithm is to use a flowchart. A **flowchart** is a graphical representation of the way that a computer should progress from one instruction to the next when it performs a task. The flowchart for the pizza program is shown in Figure 11-17 on the next page.

FIGURE 11-17

The pizza program flowchart illustrates how the computer will proceed through the instructions in the final program.

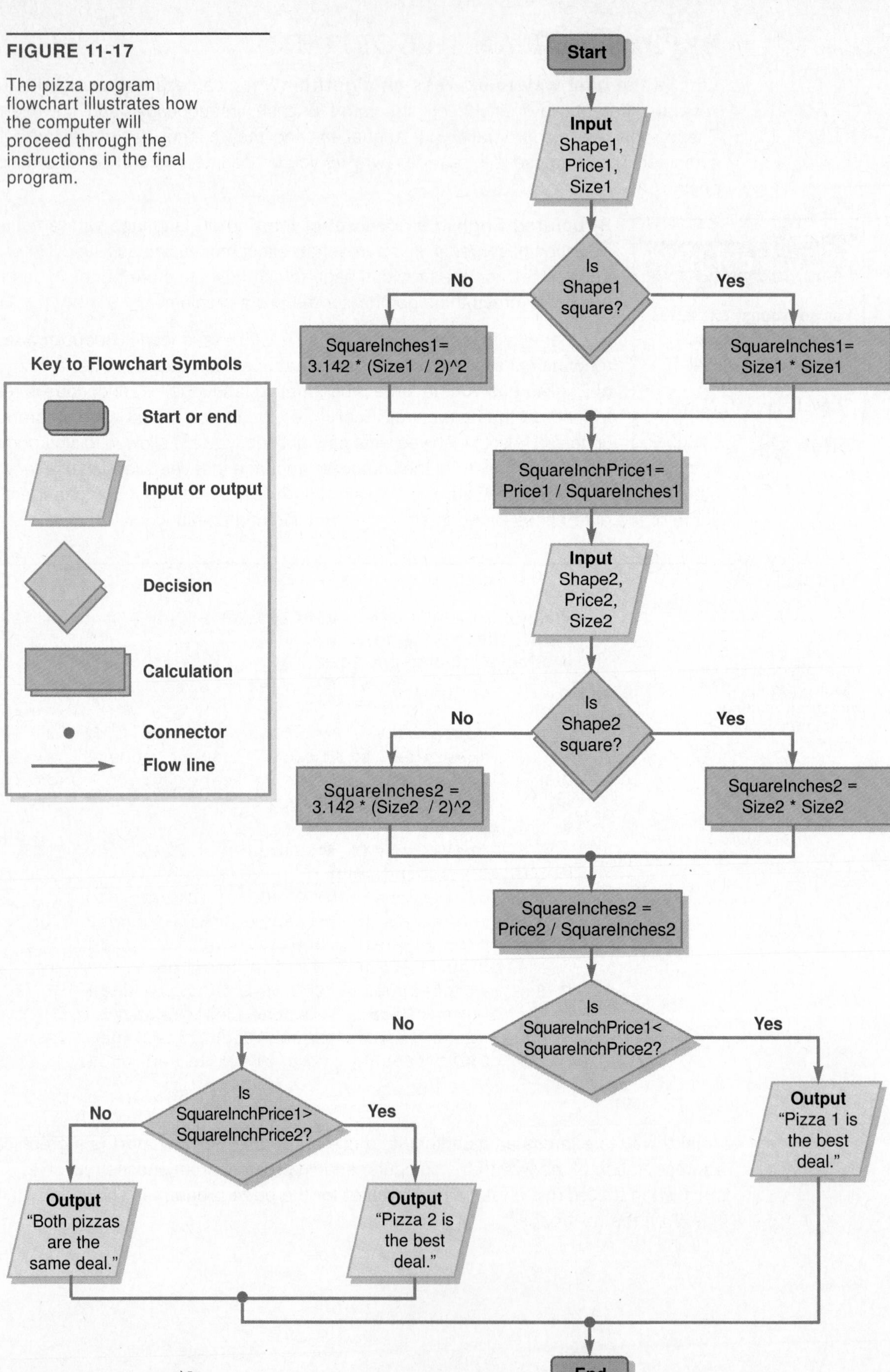

click to start

Section C
OBJECT-ORIENTED PROGRAMMING

The procedural paradigm forced programmers to view every problem in terms of a step-by-step algorithm. It soon became clear, however, that not every problem fit into the procedural pigeon hole. Alternative programming paradigms and languages were quick to appear, but none achieved the widespread popularity of the procedural paradigm until the emergence of "OO." The abbreviation "OO," which stands for object oriented, is used to describe a programming paradigm as well as a variety of computer programming languages.

In this section, you'll find out what OO is all about. Java is used for the examples in this section of the chapter because it is today's most popular language for implementing object-oriented programs.

OBJECTS AND CLASSES

What is the basic focus of the object-oriented paradigm? The **object-oriented paradigm** is based on the idea that the solution for a problem can be visualized in terms of objects that interact with each other. In the context of this paradigm, an **object** is a unit of data that represents an abstract or real-world entity, such as a person, place, or thing. For example, an object can represent a $10.99 small round pepperoni pizza. Another object can represent a pizza delivery guy named Jack Flash. Yet another object can represent a customer who lives at 22 W. Pointe Rd.

11

What's the difference between an object and a class? The real world contains lots of pizzas, customers, and delivery guys. These objects can be defined in a general way by using classes. Whereas an object is a single instance of an entity, a **class** is a template for a group of objects with similar characteristics. For example, a Pizza class defines a group of gooey Italian snacks that are made in a variety of sizes, crafted into rectangular or round shapes, and sold for various prices. A class can produce any number of unique objects, as shown in Figure 11-24.

FIGURE 11-24

A class, such as the Pizza class, is a general template for a group of objects with similar characteristics.

CLASS: Pizza

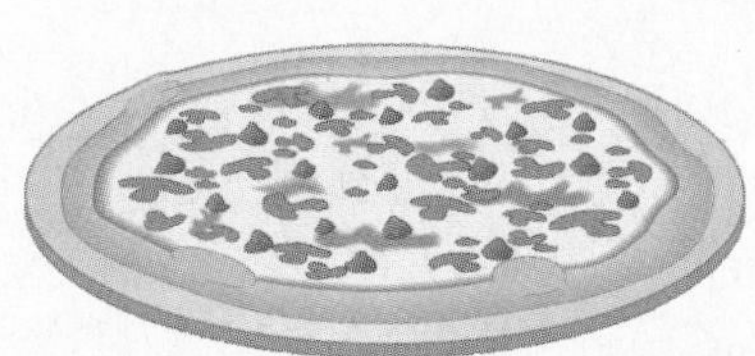

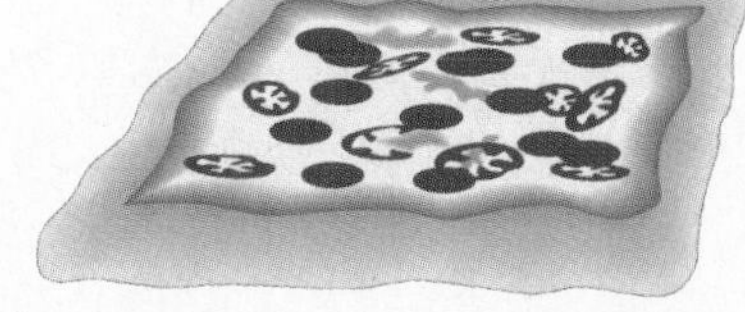

Pizza objects

How do I define the classes that I need to solve a problem? When taking the object-oriented approach to a problem, one of the first steps is to identify the objects that pertain to a solution. As you might expect, the solution to the pizza problem requires some pizza objects.

Certain characteristics of pizzas provide information necessary to solve the problem. This information—-the price, size, and shape of a pizza—provides the structure for the Pizza class. A class is defined by attributes and methods. A **class attribute** defines the characteristics of a set of objects. Each class attribute typically has a name, scope, and data type. One class attribute of the Pizza class might be "pizzaPrice." Its scope can be defined as public or private. A **public attribute** is available for use by any routine in the program. A **private attribute** can be accessed only from the routine in which it is defined. The pizzaPrice attribute's data type can be defined as "double," which means that it can be any decimal number, such as "12.98." Figure 11-25 describes the data types most typically used to describe class attributes.

FIGURE 11-25 Class Attribute Data Types

Data Type	Description	Example
Int	Integer whole numbers	10
Double	Numbers with decimal places	12.99
String	Multiple characters, symbols, and numerals	Square
Boolean	Limited to two values	T or F

OO programmers often use **UML** (unified modeling language) diagrams to plan the classes for a program. The UML diagram in Figure 11-26 shows one possible way to envision the Pizza class.

FIGURE 11-26

The core of a UML diagram is a rectangular shape that contains information about a class.

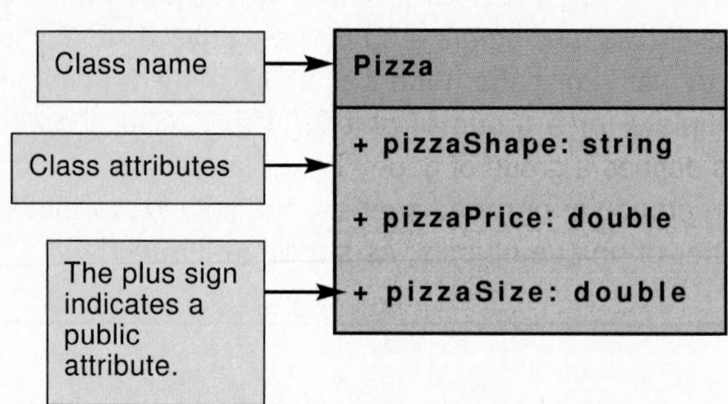

How do I code a class when writing a program? Although a programmer would typically complete the overall program plan before coding, let's jump ahead to take a quick look at the Java code for the attributes in the Pizza class. The first line of code defines the name of the class. Each subsequent line defines the scope, data type, and name of an attribute. The curly brackets simply define the start and end of the class.

```
class Pizza
{
  public string pizzaShape;
  public double pizzaPrice;
  public double pizzaSize;
}
```

INHERITANCE

How flexible are classes for defining different types of objects? The object-oriented paradigm endows classes with quite a bit of flexibility. For the pizza program, objects and classes make it easy to compare round pizzas to rectangular pizzas, rather than just to square pizzas. Suppose that you want to compare a 10-inch round pizza to a rectangular pizza that has a length of 11 inches and a width of 8 inches. The Pizza class in Figure 11-26 on the previous page holds only one measurement for each pizza—pizzaSize. This single attribute won't work for rectangular pizzas, which might have a different length and width. Should we modify the class definition to add attributes for pizzaLength and pizzaWidth? No, because these attributes are necessary only for rectangular pizzas, not for round pizzas. An OO feature called "inheritance" provides flexibility to deal with objects' unique characteristics.

FIGURE 11-27

The subclass attributes in yellow—pizzaShape and pizzaPrice—are inherited from the Pizza superclass. The attributes in blue are unique to the subclasses. The plus sign indicates that these attributes are public.

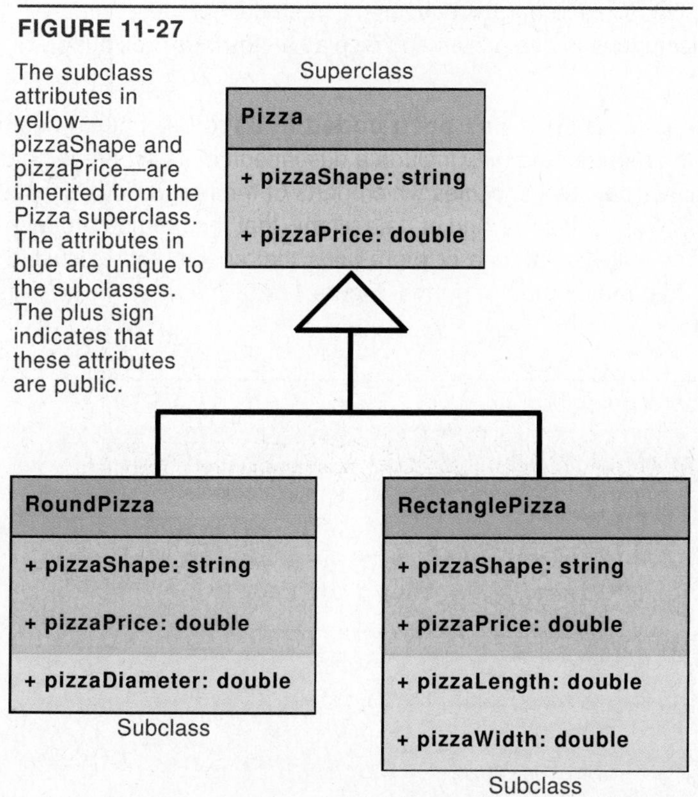

11

What is inheritance? In object-oriented jargon, **inheritance** refers to passing certain characteristics from one class to other classes. For example, to solve the pizza problem, a programmer might decide to add a RoundPizza class and a RectanglePizza class. These two new classes can inherit attributes from the Pizza class, such as pizzaShape and pizzaPrice. We can then add specialized characteristics to the new classes. The RectanglePizza class can have attributes for length and width. The RoundPizza class can have an attribute for diameter.

The process of producing new classes with inherited attributes creates a superclass and subclasses. A **superclass**, such as Pizza, is any class from which attributes can be inherited. A **subclass** (or "derived class"), such as RoundPizza or RectanglePizza, is any class that inherits attributes from a superclass. The set of superclasses and subclasses that are related to each other is referred to as a **class hierarchy**. The UML diagram in Figure 11-27 shows the Pizza class and its subclasses.

How do I code a subclass? Java uses the "extends" command to link a subclass to a superclass. The statement `class RectanglePizza extends Pizza` means "create a class called RectanglePizza that's derived from the superclass called Pizza." Figure 11-28 contains the Java code that creates attributes for the RectanglePizza class.

FIGURE 11-28

Using the extends command, the RectanglePizza class inherits the pizzaShape and pizzaPrice attributes from the Pizza superclass. The pizzaLength and pizzaWidth attributes are unique to the RectanglePizza class.

```
class RectanglePizza extends Pizza
{
        double pizzaLength;
        double pizzaWidth;
}
```

METHODS AND MESSAGES

How does an OO program use objects? Objects can be used by an OO program in a variety of ways. A basic way to use objects is to manipulate them with methods. A **method** is a segment of code that defines an action. The names of methods usually end in a set of parentheses, such as compare() or getArea().

What can a method do? A method can perform a variety of tasks, such as collecting input, performing calculations, making comparisons, executing decisions, and producing output. For example, the pizza program can use a method named compare() to compare the square-inch prices of two pizzas and display a message indicating which pizza is the best deal.

How does a method look when it has been coded in Java? A method begins with a line that names the method and may include a description of its scope and data type. The scope—public or private—specifies which parts of the program can access the method. The data type specifies the kind of data, if any, that the method produces. The initial line of code is followed by one or more lines that specify the calculation, comparison, or routine that the method performs. Figure 11-29 illustrates the code for the compare() method.

FIGURE 11-29 Java code for the compare() method

```
public compare( Pizza Pizza1, Pizza Pizza2 )
{
       if (Pizza1.SquareInchPrice < Pizza2.SquareInchPrice )
          System.out.println("Pizza 1 is the best deal!");

       if (Pizza1.SquareInchPrice > Pizza2.SquareInchPrice )
          System.out.println("Pizza 2 is the best deal!");

       if (Pizza1.SquareInchPrice == Pizza2.SquareInchPrice
          System.out.println("The pizzas are the same deal!");
}
```

The method manipulates pizza objects.

The method title includes its scope and name.

The body of the method contains logic statements that determine which pizza is the best deal and print the result.

How does a Java program begin? The computer begins executing a Java program by locating a standard method called main(), which contains code to send messages to objects by calling methods. For the pizza program, the main() method includes code that defines a few variables and then asks the user to enter the shape of the first pizza. If the shape entered is "Round" the program creates an object called Pizza1 that is a member of the RoundPizza class. If the shape entered is "Rectangle" the program creates an object called Pizza1 that is a member of the RectanglePizza class.

After the pizza object is created, the program uses the getArea() method to calculate its area. The program then uses the getSquareInchPrice() method to calculate the pizza's square-inch price. Once the calculations are complete for the first pizza, the program executes the same process for the second pizza. Finally, the program uses the compare() method to compare the square-inch prices of the two pizzas and output a statement about which one is the best deal.

Because it is not the goal of this section to teach you the particulars of Java programming, don't worry about the detailed syntax of the Java code. Instead, refer to Figure 11-34 to get an overview of the activity that takes place in the main() method for the pizza program.

FIGURE 11-34 Java code for the main section of the pizza program

```
public static void main(String[] args)
  {

     Pizza Pizza1;
     Pizza Pizza2;
     String pizzaShape;

    pizzaShape = Keyin.inString("Enter the shape of the first pizza: ");
     if (pizzaShape.equals("Round"))
      {
       Pizza1 = new RoundPizza();
      }
     else
        Pizza1 = new RectanglePizza();

     Pizza1.getArea();
     Pizza1.getSquareInchPrice();

    pizzaShape = Keyin.inString("Enter the shape of the second pizza: ");
     if (pizzaShape.equals("Round"))
        Pizza2 = new RoundPizza();
     else
        Pizza2 = new RectanglePizza();

     Pizza2.getArea();
     Pizza2.getSquareInchPrice();

     compare(Pizza1, Pizza2);
  }
```

1. Main() method title
2. Define variables used in the main() method.
3. Collect input for the shape of the first pizza, then create an object called Pizza1 that belongs to the RoundPizza or RectanglePizza class.
4. Use the getArea() and getSquareInchPrice() methods to calculate area and square-inch price for the first pizza.
5. Collect input for the shape of the second pizza, then create an object called Pizza2 that belongs to the RoundPizza or RectanglePizza class.
6. Use the getArea() and getSquareInchPrice() methods to calculate area and square-inch price for the second pizza.
7. Use the compare() method to determine which pizza is the best deal, then print results.

What happens when the completed pizza program runs? When you run the pizza program, it looks for the main() method. This method displays an onscreen prompt that asks for the pizza's shape. The getArea() method displays a prompt for the pizza's diameter (for a round pizza) or the pizza's length and width (for a rectangular pizza). A similar series of prompts appears for the second pizza. The program concludes when the compare() method displays a statement about which pizza is the best deal. The screentour for Figure 11-35 lets you see what happens when the OO pizza program runs.

FIGURE 11-35

When the pizza program runs, onscreen prompts ask for the shape, size, and price of each pizza, then the program displays a message indicating which pizza is the best deal.

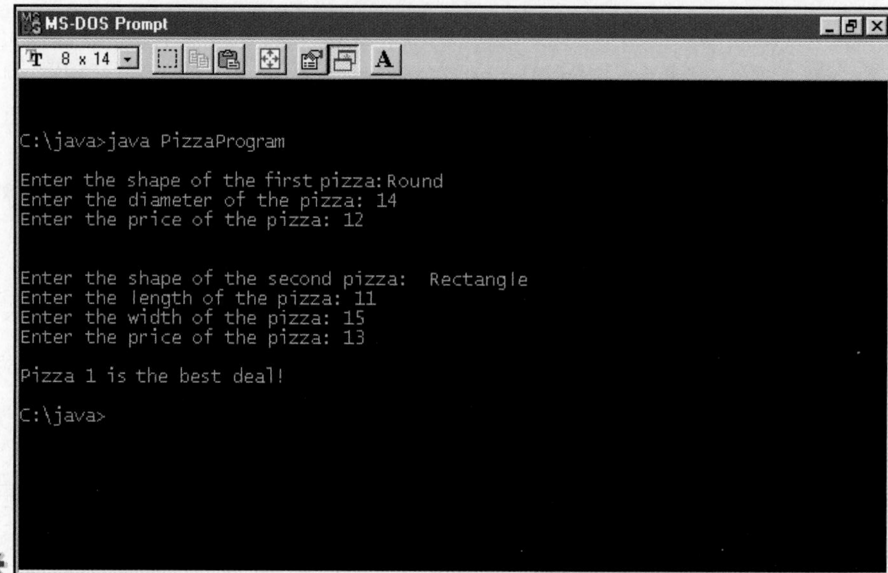

click to start

OBJECT-ORIENTED LANGUAGES AND APPLICATIONS

How did object-oriented languages originate? Computer historians believe that SIMULA (SIMUlation LAnguage) was the first computer language to work with objects, classes, inheritance, and methods. SIMULA was developed in 1962 by two Norwegian computer scientists for the purpose of programming simulations and models. SIMULA laid the foundation for the object-oriented paradigm, which was later incorporated into other computer languages, such as Eiffel, Smalltalk, C++, and Java.

The second major development in object-oriented languages came in 1972 when Alan Kaye began work on the Dynabook project at the Xerox Palo Alto Research Center (PARC). Dynabook was a prototype for a notebook-sized personal computer, intended to handle all the information needs of adults and children. Kaye developed a programming language called Smalltalk for the Dynabook that could be easily used to create programs based on real-world objects. The Dynabook never became a commercial product, but Smalltalk survived and is still in use today. Smalltalk is regarded as a classic object-oriented language, which encourages programmers to take a "pure" OO approach to the programming process.

Which object-oriented languages are popular today? As the object-oriented paradigm gained popularity, several existing programming languages were modified to provide programmers with the ability to work with objects, classes, inheritance, and polymorphism. The concept for the Ada programming language originated in 1978 at

Instantiation is one of the keys to understanding how Prolog works. Unlike a procedural programming language, which is designed to step through a series of statements in a path prescribed by the programmer, Prolog can autonomously run through every possible instantiation, backtracking if necessary to deal with multiple variables. **Backtracking** refers to a process by which every possible solution is tried. If you envision solutions as the branches on a tree, backtracking begins by following one branch seeking a solution. If the solution is not found, it backs up to the trunk and follows another branch. For example, backtracking would enable a Prolog program to analyze every possible move in a chess game. Instantiation and backtracking are very powerful tools when used by savvy programmers. They work in the context of Prolog facts and Prolog rules. Let's take a look at how a programmer codes Prolog rules; then we can see how those rules work.

PROLOG RULES

How does a programmer code Prolog rules? The pizza program requires a rule that states, "A pizza is a better deal if its price per square inch is less than the price per square inch of the other pizza." Translated into Prolog code, this rule becomes:

```
betterdeal(PizzaX,PizzaY) :-
        squareinchprice(PizzaX,AmountX),
        squareinchprice(PizzaY,AmountY),
        AmountX < AmountY.
```

Let's take a look at the logic behind this rule. A Prolog rule consists of a head, body, and connecting symbol, as described in Figure 11-40.

FIGURE 11-40

A Prolog rule consists of a head and one or more clauses that form the body of the rule.

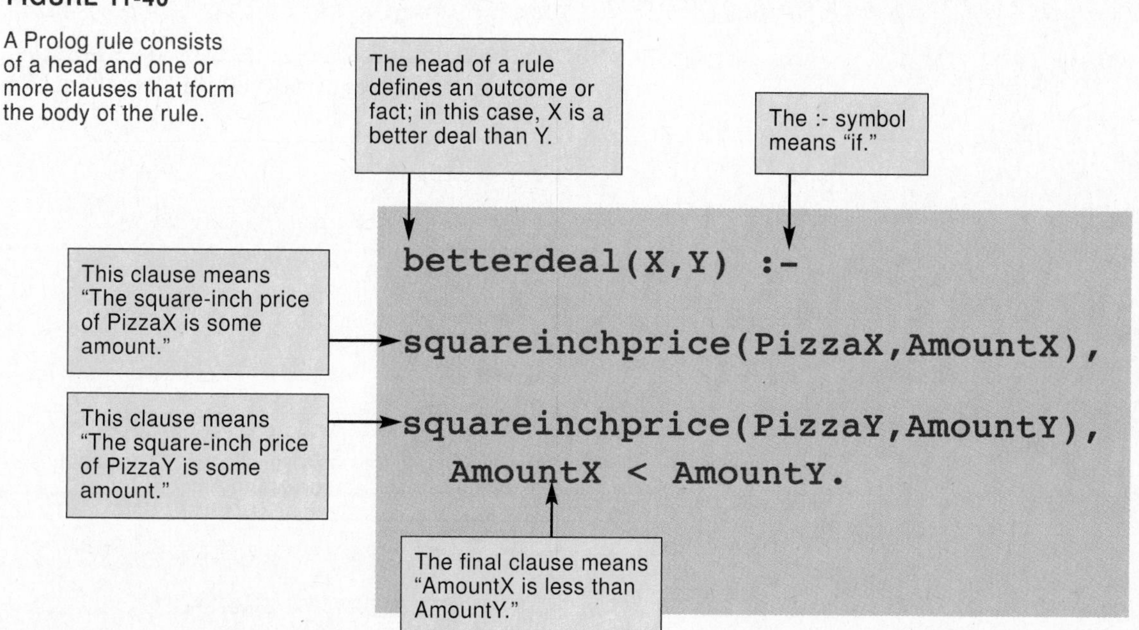
The head of a rule defines an outcome or fact; in this case, X is a better deal than Y.
The :- symbol means "if."
betterdeal(X,Y) :-
This clause means "The square-inch price of PizzaX is some amount."
squareinchprice(PizzaX,AmountX),
This clause means "The square-inch price of PizzaY is some amount."
squareinchprice(PizzaY,AmountY),
AmountX < AmountY.
The final clause means "AmountX is less than AmountY."

How do Prolog rules work? To understand how the betterdeal rule works, we'll need to perform a bit of "magic" to determine the price per square inch of each pizza. In the completed pizza program, the computer can calculate the square-inch price using a rule provided by the programmer. Because we don't yet have such a rule, let's temporarily assume that the square-inch price of the first pizza is .0694 (6.94 cents) and the square-inch price of the second pizza is .0612 (6.12 cents). These facts would be stated as `squareinchprice(pizza1,.069).` and `squareinchprice(pizza2,.0612).`

Now, suppose that you enter the query `?- betterdeal(pizza1,pizza2).`, which translates to "Is pizza1 a better deal than pizza2?" Figure 11-41 illustrates how Prolog uses the betterdeal rule to answer your query.

FIGURE 11-41 How Prolog executes the betterdeal rule

Facts for the pizza program

```
priceof(pizza1,10).
sizeof(pizza1,12).
shapeof(pizza1,square).
priceof(pizza2,12).
sizeof(pizza2,14).
shapeof(pizza2,round).
squareinchprice(pizza1,.069).
squareinchprice(pizza2,.0612).
```

The betterdeal rule

```
betterdeal(PizzaX,PizzaY) :-
    squareinchprice(PizzaX,AmountX),
    squareinchprice(PizzaY,AmountY),
    AmountX < AmountY.
```

The query

```
?- betterdeal(Pizza1,Pizza2)
```

1. Prolog instantiates pizza1 to PizzaX and pizza2 to PizzaY.

```
betterdeal(pizza1,pizza2) :-
    squareinchprice(pizza1,AmountX),
    squareinchprice(pizza2,AmountY),
    AmountX < AmountY.
```

2. Prolog looks through the facts to find the squareinchprice for pizza1 and pizza2. These prices are instantiated to AmountX and AmountY.

```
betterdeal(pizza1,pizza2) :-
    squareinchprice(pizza1,.0694),
    squareinchprice(pizza2,.0612),
    .0694 < .0612.
```

3. The last line now contains a statement that is not true—.0694<.0612—which invalidates the rule and produces "no" as a response to your query, "Is pizza1 a better deal than pizza2?"

What are the advantages and disadvantages of declarative languages? Declarative languages offer a highly effective programming environment for problems that involve words, concepts, and complex logic. As you learned in this chapter, declarative languages provide a great deal of flexibility for querying a set of facts and rules. These languages also allow you to describe problems using words rather than the abstract structures required by procedural and object-oriented languages.

Currently, however, declarative languages are not very popular and they are not commonly used for production applications. To some extent, today's emphasis on the object-oriented paradigm has pushed declarative languages out of the mainstream, both in education and in the job market. Many aspiring programmers are never introduced to declarative languages, so they are not included in the languages evaluated for a specific project.

Declarative languages have a reputation for providing minimal input and output capabilities. Although many of today's Prolog compilers provide access to Windows and Mac user interface components, programmers are often unaware of this capability.

A final disadvantage of declarative languages is their relatively poor performance on today's personal computer architecture, which is optimized for sequential processing. Declarative languages run much more efficiently on parallel architectures, which are only now emerging in the personal computer market.

QUICKCheck Section D

1. Whereas the procedural paradigm focuses on an algorithm that describes a(n) ______, the declarative paradigm focuses on describing the ______.

2. In the Prolog fact, `likes(dog, biscuits).`, "likes" is called the ______, whereas "dog" and "biscuits" are called ______.

3. A Prolog attribute can be a(n) ______, such as "pizza" (with a lowercase "p") or it can be a(n) ______, such as "Pizza" (with an uppercase "P").

4. A programmer can create a Prolog ______ for a statement such as "A pizza is a better deal if its price per square inch is less than the price per square inch of another pizza."

5. For debugging purposes, Prolog programmers use a(n) ______ feature that allows them to track through each instantiation and follow the execution sequence for facts and rules.

check answers

TECHTALK

PROGRAMMING TOOLS

The software tools shipped with today's personal computers typically do not include programming languages. If you want to try your hand at programming, your first step is to obtain some programming tools, such as an editor, compiler, components, and debugger. This TechTalk begins with an overview of basic programming tools. It concludes with information about how programming tools, such as SDKs and IDEs, are distributed.

What's the most important programming tool? Although programmers spend most of their time interacting with a program editor or VDE (visual development environment), coding tools are not the most important element of the programmer's toolbox. You can use the coolest program editor or visual development environment, but without a compiler or interpreter, your instructions cannot be executed by the computer. Because of their key role in translating high-level instructions into executable machine language, compilers and interpreters are the most important programming tools.

A microprocessor is designed to perform a repertoire of very basic activities, discussed in Chapter 2, such as add, load, and stop. These basic activities are defined in a microprocessor's built-in machine language instruction set. The programs that you write in a high-level language must be translated into machine language instructions that coincide with a microprocessor's instruction set. A program can be translated into executable code in one of two ways: it can be compiled or interpreted.

How does a computer compile a program? A **compiler** translates a program written in a high-level language into low-level instructions before the program is executed. The commands that you write in a high-level language are referred to as **source code**. The low-level instructions that result from compiling the source code are referred to as **object code**. Some compilers produce executable files that contain machine language instructions. Other compilers produce files that contain intermediate language instructions.

An **intermediate language** is a set of low-level instructions that can be converted easily and quickly into machine language. For example, when the source code for a Java program is compiled, it produces a file containing intermediate language instructions called **bytecode** (Figure 11-46). This bytecode can be distributed to PC or Mac owners. The bytecode is converted into machine language by software called a **Java Virtual Machine** (JVM) when the program is run. The JVM for a PC converts the bytecode into machine language instructions that work on a Pentium processor. The JVM for a Mac converts the bytecode into machine language for the PowerPC processor.

FIGURE 11-46

An intermediate language provides low-level instructions that can be compiled quickly for a specific computer platform.

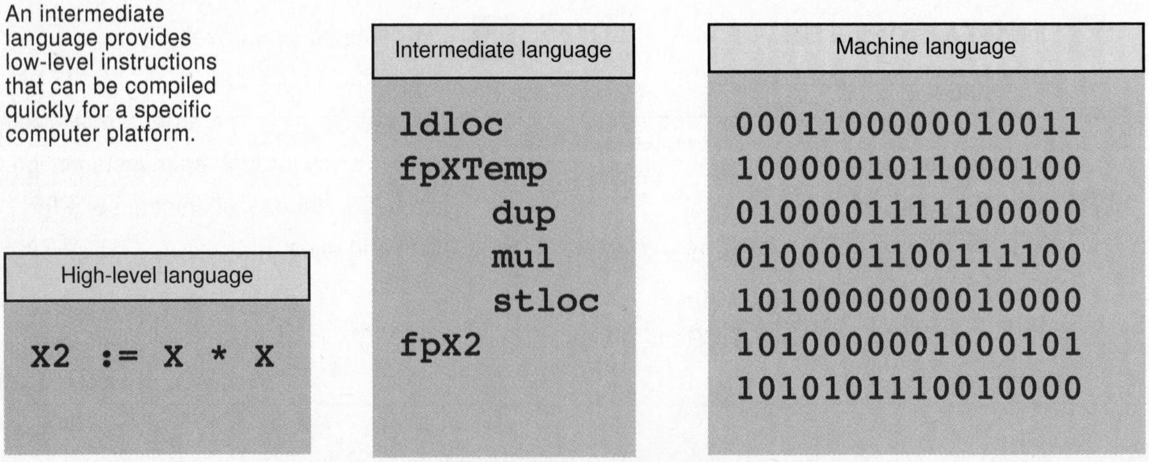

High-level language

```
X2 := X * X
```

Intermediate language

```
ldloc
fpXTemp
     dup
     mul
     stloc
fpX2
```

Machine language

```
0001100000010011
1000001011000100
0100001111100000
0100001100111100
1010000000010000
1010000001000101
1010101110010000
```

Karat agrees with Cooper's comments about programmers being unable to understand the people who use their software. She says, "The profile of the people who use systems has changed, while the system, and the culture in which they have developed, have not adjusted...The engineers and computer scientists who design hardware and software know little about the needs and frustrations of consumers."

You can read more about user-oriented software design at the **Human Factors** InfoWeb.

click

BusinessWeek columnist Stephen H. Wildstrom published Karat's Bill of Rights and asked for reader feedback. The response was overwhelming and led Wildstrom to comment in a follow-up article, "The computer industry has a lot of baffled, frustrated, and unhappy customers." Surprisingly, many readers disagreed with the tenets of the Bill of Rights. For example, Jef Raskin, a member of the Macintosh computer design team, pointed out that "the mouse was not intuitive. A person seeing one for the first time had no idea how to use it."

Until we are able to implant some kind of "instant computer genius" chip at birth, it might be that people will just have to invest some time learning how to use a computer. "It shouldn't take a Ph.D. to understand that a few hours invested in learning about the computer and its software will make subsequent products intuitively usable," wrote one *BusinessWeek* reader. Other readers questioned how much simplicity one could really expect from a computer. A computer that is as simple to use as a toaster would seem unlikely. As readers pointed out, a toaster is designed to do only one thing, whereas a computer can perform many different tasks, depending on the software that it uses.

Who is right? Can technology be simplified, yet remain powerful enough to accomplish complex tasks? A branch of ergonomics called Human Factors, or Human-Computer Interaction (HCI), focuses on the factors that make computers easy or difficult to use. The Human Factors InfoWeb link provides more information about HCI, and offers some additional food for thought on the usability controversy.

WHAT DO YOU THINK?

1. Can you identify with the frustration depicted in the Badday video? ○Yes ○No ○Not sure

2. Is it possible to make computer software significantly easier to use? ○Yes ○No ○Not sure

3. Would you agree that programmers do not understand the viewpoint of a typical computer user, and consequently produce bad software? ○Yes ○No ○Not sure

click to save your responses

INTERACTIVE SUMMARY

The Interactive Summary helps you to review important concepts from this chapter. Fill in the blanks to best complete each sentence. When using the NP6 BookOnCD, you can click the Check Answers buttons to automatically score your answers. Place your Tracking Disk in the floppy disk drive if you want to save your scores.

The instructions that make up a computer program are sometimes referred to as ________. Computer programmers focus on ________ computer programs, but also may plan, test, and document computer programs. In contrast, software ________ tend to focus on planning and ________ activities.

A programming language is a set of ________ and grammar rules, designed to be used for creating instructions that can ultimately be processed by a computer. The first programming languages were low-level ________ languages. Second-generation programming languages, called ________ languages, allowed programmers to write programs consisting of abbreviated op codes instead of 1s and 0s. Third-generation languages provided programmers with easy-to-remember command words, such as PRINT and INPUT. Fourth-generation languages eliminated many of the strict punctuation and ________ rules that complicated third-generation languages. Experts believe that ________ languages, such as Prolog, constitute a fifth generation of computer languages. Other experts define fifth-generation languages as those that allow programmers to use graphical or visual tools to construct programs.

Before program code can be written, a programmer needs a clear problem ________, which includes a list of assumptions, a description of known information, and a specification for what constitutes a solution. With a clear plan, a programmer can begin coding using a generic text editor, a program editor, or a ________ development environment. A program is not complete until it has been tested to assure that it contains no ________ errors or runtime errors. All computer programs should include internal documentation in the form of ________, which are explanatory comments inserted into a computer program along with lines of code.

check answers

Programming ________ affect the way that programmers conceptualize and approach a computer program. Every computer language supports one or more programming approaches. Languages such as COBOL and FORTRAN support a traditional approach to programming called the ________ paradigm, which is based on a step-by-step ________. Various planning tools, such as structured English, ________, and flowcharts, help programmers plan the steps for a procedural program. Procedural languages provide a variety of ________ structures that allow programmers to specify the order of program execution. A ________ control structure directs the computer to execute one or more instructions, not coded as a simple succession of steps. A ________ control provides a choice of paths, based on whether a condition is true or false. A ________ control, or "loop," repeats one or more instructions until a certain condition is met. The procedural paradigm provides a solid approach to problems that can be solved by following a set of steps. Procedural languages tend to produce programs that run quickly and use ________ resources efficiently.

check answers

The object-oriented paradigm is based on the idea that the solution to a problem can be visualized in terms of objects that ________ with each other. An object is a single instance of an entity. Programmers can use a ________ as a template for a group of objects with similar characteristics. Classes can be derived from other classes through a process called ________. The set of superclasses and subclasses that are related to each other is referred to as a class ________. OO programmers often use ________ modeling language diagrams to plan the classes for a program.

Objects interact to solve problems by exchanging ________, which initiate an action, process, or procedure. Programmers create ________ to define what happens once an action is initiated. Methods provide good flexibility because a concept called ________, or "overloading," allows programmers to create a single, generic name for a procedure that behaves in unique ways for different classes. The OO paradigm allows programmers to hide the internal details of objects and their methods. This process, called ________, allows objects to be easily reused, modified, and repurposed.

Computer historians believe that ________ was the first computer language to work with objects, classes, inheritance, and methods. It is a language called ________, however, that is regarded as the classic object-oriented programming language. The object-oriented paradigm has become so popular that many procedural languages have been given OO capabilities. ________, which originated at the Department of Defense, was originally a procedural language, but now provides OO features. The C language was modified into a language called ________, and again modified into C#, which allows programmers to work with objects. Recent versions of ________ Basic also provide programmers with the option of working within the object-oriented paradigm.

check answers

11

Programming languages such as Prolog support the ________ programming paradigm because they encourage programmers to describe a ________ rather than its solution. Prolog programs are typically built from a collection of facts and rules. A fact is expressed as a ________, such as shapeof, followed by series of ________ within parentheses, such as (pizza,round). A rule has a ________, which defines an outcome or fact, followed by the notation :-, which means "if." The body of the rule consists of one or more clauses that define conditions that must be satisfied to validate the head of the rule. Prolog uses a process called ________ to evaluate facts and rules in order to determine if they are true. A programmer can test a program and follow the sequence of instantiation and the state of each variable using a handy ________ feature.

Declarative languages, such as Prolog, can be used for problems that require calculations, but those problems are typically better suited to ________ languages. As a rule of thumb, declarative languages are best suited for problems that pertain to words and concepts rather than numbers. They are a good choice for applications such as ________ that contain complex relationships among records, decision support systems that handle semi-structured problems, and expert systems that require analysis of multiple, interrelated factors.

check answers 

INTERACTIVE KEY TERMS

Make sure that you understand all of the boldfaced key terms presented in this chapter. If you're using the NP6 BookOnCD, you can use this list of terms as an interactive study activity. First, try to define a term in your own words, then click the term to compare your definition with the definition that is presented in the chapter.

INTERACTIVE SITUATION QUESTIONS

Apply what you've learned to some typical computing situations. When using the NP6 BookOnCD, you can type your answers, then use the Check Answers button to automatically score your responses. Place your Tracking Disk in the floppy disk drive if you want to save your scores.

1 A friend asks you to help write a computer program to calculate the square yards of carpet needed for a dorm room. The statement "the living room floor is rectangular" would be an example of an ______. The length and width of the room would be examples of ______ information, which you would probably obtain as ______ from the user.

2 Continuing with the carpet example, you devise a set of steps, or an ______, to solve the problem. You then use a computer language to write the ______ shown below, which expresses the algorithm.

```
Input "Enter the width of the room
  in feet: "; width
Input "Enter the length of the
  room in feet: "; length
Print "Carpet needed:"
Print length*width & " square
  feet"
Print (length*width)/9 & "square
  yards"
```

3 Examine the code shown below. This program prints ______ lines of text.

```
For n = 1 To 5
    Print "Loop number " & n
Next n
```

4 You've just joined a programming team that is developing a Java program for an earth-moving equipment vendor. The lead programmer shows you a UML with labels such as Cranes, Trucks, and Front-end Loaders. With your background in object-oriented programming, you can tell immediately that these are ______, which will be coded as a series of attributes, such as `private string manufacturer`.

5 While browsing through several programs posted online, you come across the following code and realize that it is written using the ______ programming language.

```
male(frodo).
male(mungo).
male(largo).
male(balbo).
female(berylla).
female(belladonna).
female(primula).
female(sella).
parents(mungo,berylla,balbo).
parents(frodo,primula,drogo).
parents(largo,berylla,balbo).
parents(sella,berylla,balbo).
brother_of(X,Y):-
   male(Y),
   parents(X,Mother,Father),
   parents(Y,Mother,Father).
```

11

check answers

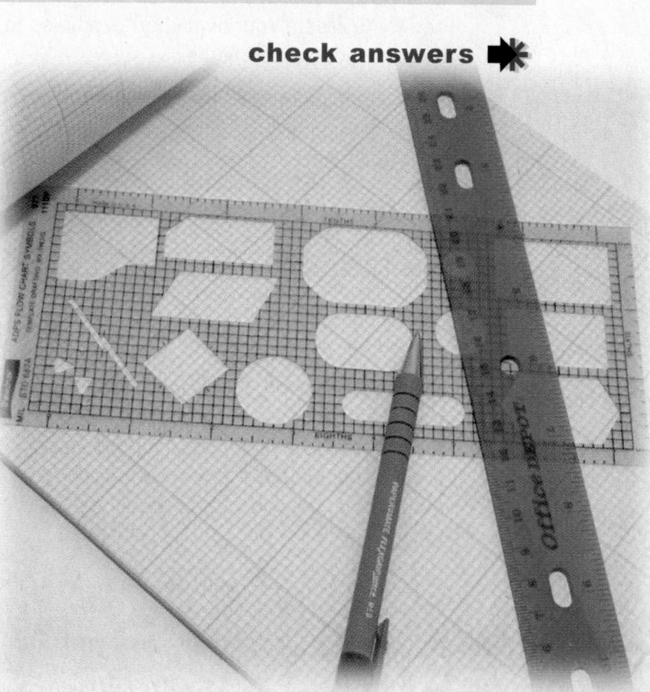

INTERACTIVE PRACTICE TESTS

When you use the NP6 BookOnCD, you can take Practice Tests that consist of 10 multiple-choice, true/false, and fill-in-the-blank questions. The questions are selected at random from a large test bank, so each time you take a test, you'll receive a different set of questions. Your tests are scored immediately, and you can print study guides that help you find the correct answers for any questions that you missed. If you are using a Tracking Disk, insert it in the floppy disk drive to save your test scores.

click to start

STUDY TIPS

Study Tips help you to organize and consolidate the information in a chapter by making lists, outlines, charts, and sketches. You can use paper and pencil or word processing software to complete most of the Study Tips activities.

1 Make sure that you can use your own words to correctly answer each of the green focus questions that appear throughout the chapter.

2 Describe how the job of a systems analyst differs from the job of a software engineer.

3 Create a diagram that shows how low-level and high-level languages relate to the five generations of computer languages.

4 Describe the three elements of a problem statement, and provide examples within the context of the pizza problem.

5 Explain the differences between an algorithm and a computer program.

6 Describe three ways to express an algorithm, and try to create your own short examples to illustrate your descriptions.

7 Give an example of a sequence control structure, a selection control structure, and a repetition control structure.

8 Using the pizza program as the basis for an example, describe how to test a program to make sure that it works correctly.

9 Explain the differences between a syntax error and a logic error.

10 Make sure that you can define each of these terms associated with object-oriented programming: object, class, superclass, subclass, attribute, message, method, inheritance, polymorphism, and encapsulation.

11 Describe the differences between event-driven, procedural, object-oriented, and declarative paradigms, and provide at least one example of a language that supports each paradigm.

12 Sketch out a UML that a programmer might use to design a program that manipulates the following objects: skateboards, scooters, electric scooters, and motorcycles.

13 Make sure that you can use your own words to define the following terms associated with the declarative paradigm: fact, rule, predicate, arguments, goal, instantiation, and backtracking.

14 Write a few Prolog facts that describe your relationships to members of your family.

15 Describe two ways in which a Prolog program can be set up to accept user input.

16 Describe the differences between machine language and assembly language.

17 Use your own words to explain how the process of compiling differs from the process of interpreting a program.

18 Explain how an intermediate language relates to the compilation process.

Making waybill and tracking information available to customers, drivers, sorting centers, and various FedEx departments is not simple because the data must be accessed from a variety of computers and communications equipment, which requires data in several different formats. An enterprise computing system is able to unite these disparate hardware platforms and software applications by creating what appears to be one large information system, accessible to a variety of customers and company employees. Without its enterprise computing system, FedEx would not have the technology to handle the shipping volume required to remain the world's leading overnight courier.

What's the difference between an enterprise system and an information system? The difference between an enterprise system and an information system is one of scope. Whereas an information system, such as a transaction processing system, decision support system, or expert system (discussed in Chapter 9), is dedicated to one set of related tasks, an enterprise computing system encompasses the tasks associated with multiple information systems, as well as the task of integrating these systems to work together and share data.

FedEx's office automation system handles word processing, e-mail, and other office functions. A transaction processing system handles payroll and accounting. A decision support system allows the Marketing Department to analyze data and make marketing decisions. A Web server provides online access to shipping rates, package tracking information, and transit times. An enterprise computing system integrates these diverse information systems so that they can share data and computing resources. For example, FedEx's enterprise system allows the Web site to automatically display a package's delivery status, using data collected by a FedEx driver, when a package is delivered to its destination.

What is the scale of an enterprise system? Enterprise computing systems are classified as "large-scale" systems because they contain from a few dozen to several thousand computers. The size of a specific system depends on several factors—the size of the organization, the number of transactions processed each day, the number of users accessing data, and the geographical area in which computers and users are located.

To get some idea of the scale of enterprise computing systems, consider that Sabre's ticketing system provides airline, hotel, tour, and car rental information to over 60,000 travel agencies worldwide. The computer systems that run online games may be required to handle as many as 80,000 simultaneous players during peak times. The enterprise computing system used by UPS (United Parcel Service) boasts 15 mainframes, 208 terabytes of storage space, 911 mid-range computers, 226,000 personal computers, 4,500 servers, and 96,000 wireless DIADs—the "delivery information acquisition devices" carried by UPS drivers. These are remarkable numbers, but they become even more impressive when you realize that these companies are growing, and their computer systems are expanding every year.

Can an enterprise computing system expand to meet the demands of a growing business? A well-designed computer system must change to meet demand. Standard information systems, however, often have limited capacity for expansion. For example, imagine a health insurance company with a processing center in Denver, Colorado. When the number of claims outstrips the processing center's capacity, the company opens a new office in St. Louis, Missouri. The offices have similar, but separate, information systems. Claims from the eastern U.S. are routed to the St. Louis office, while claims from western states are routed to the Denver office. These separate information systems prove to be less than optimal, however, because they cannot share data for clients who move or receive medical care in more than one region.

An enterprise computing system would provide a better solution for the health insurance company because it is designed for scalability. **Scalability** refers to the ability of a computer system to shrink or grow as requirements change. "Scaling up" and "scaling out" are two methods for increasing the capacity of computer systems. **Scaling up** means increasing individual machine performance by adding processors, memory, and storage capacity. **Scaling out** means adding more computers to increase the overall size of a system.

The most effective enterprise systems are those that provide cost-effective and time-sensitive scalability. Cost-effective scalability means that the system can grow without a large financial outlay. Time-sensitive scalability means that the system can be scaled without disabling it for a long period of time.

Enterprise computing systems may provide several scalability options. For example, enterprise-level claims processing application software may allow both the Denver and St. Louis offices to share one database in which all claims are stored. Another enterprise solution would be to set up a distributed database server with one node in Denver and another in St. Louis. Yet a third option would be to set up two database servers and synchronize them at given intervals. These options are illustrated in Figure 12-2.

FIGURE 12-2

An enterprise computing system may provide several scalability options, such as sharing a database, distributing the database, or synchronizing databases at specified time intervals.

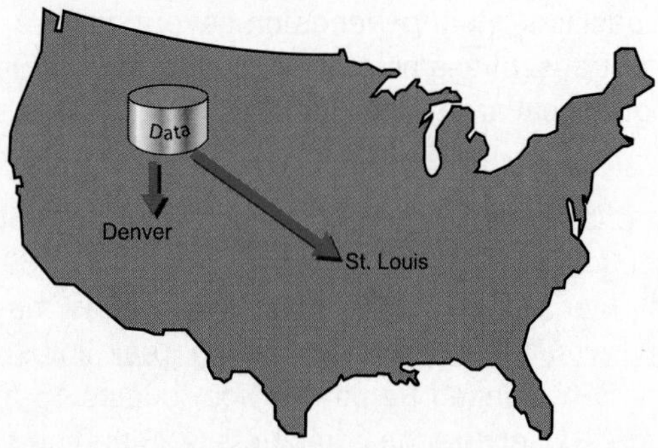

Option: Sharing a single database

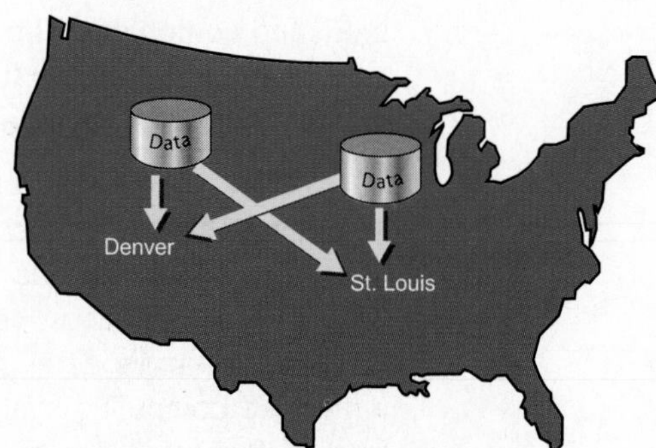

Option: Distributing the database

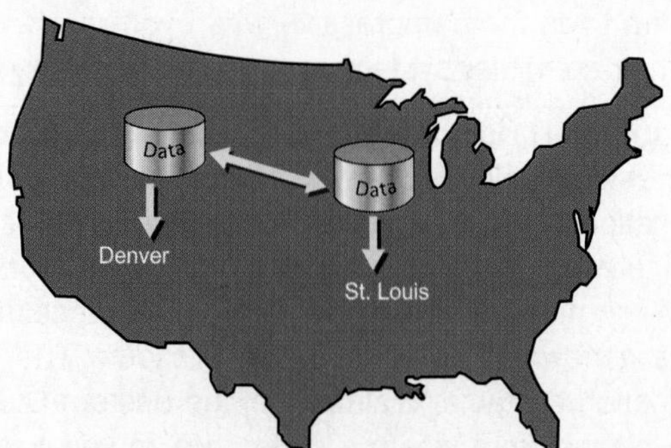

Option: Periodically synchronizing two databases

What is enterprise system integration? The process of connecting two or more information systems in a way that allows scalability and data sharing is referred to as **enterprise system integration**. This process encompasses both enterprise hardware integration and enterprise application integration.

Enterprise hardware integration refers to the process of connecting different types of hardware. Connections are made possible through the use of specialized hardware or software that allows different types of devices to interoperate. For example, suppose that the reporters and editors who work for a newspaper publisher use Windows computers on a LAN for word processing and research. The publisher's graphic design and layout experts use Macintosh computers connected to an AppleTalk network. Each of the LANs also includes printers, scanners, and other devices such as tape backup units. To allow a reporter using a Windows computer to print documents on a printer connected to the AppleTalk network, at least two links must be established. First, there must be a physical link that allows the reporter's computer to communicate with the printer on the AppleTalk LAN. Typically this link is established by connecting the AppleTalk and the Windows LANs so that computers on either network can access the printer. There also must be a link that allows the two devices to understand each other's commands and data. This link is accomplished through software or hardware drivers. Once these two links are established, the hardware is integrated and a reporter can print directly to the printer on the Macintosh network. This example only takes into account two separate LANs. In a typical large-scale computing system, hardware integration may involve hundreds or even thousands of diverse devices and LANs. Figure 12-3 shows how an enterprise system integrates many different hardware devices.

FIGURE 12-3

Enterprise-level hardware integration links diverse types of processing, input, output, and storage equipment.

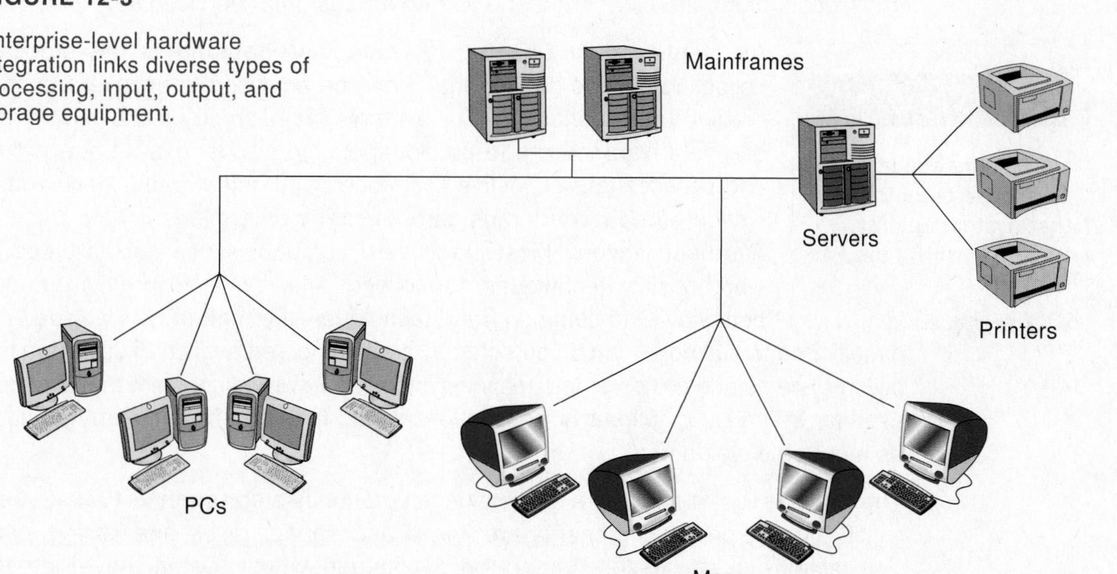

12

Enterprise application integration (EAI) is the process of configuring software applications so that they can exchange data. Applications that exchange data can streamline processing by allowing quick and easy access to all information pertaining to a query, procedure, or transaction. For example, the company that provides you with cellular telephone service may integrate its billing, transaction, and subscription software so that you can go to one Web site to pay your bill, view recent telephone call data, or change your calling plan.

How can an enterprise integrate applications? Enterprise application integration can be achieved using four techniques: database linking, application linking, data warehousing, and common virtual systems.

Database linking is a process that allows databases to share or replicate information, as required. For example, the company that issues your credit card uses a computer system to process credit card charges. Information about cardholder transactions is stored using a database server. Because hundreds of thousands of transactions may be processed every day, one database server is not sufficient; multiple database servers are required. These servers must be linked in order to share information, so that, for example, you are not allowed to exceed your credit limit. Often, database management software automates this linking and makes EAI possible.

Application linking is a process that allows computer systems to share information at the application level. Linked applications work together to provide services and display information that was previously available only by accessing each of the multiple applications individually. For example, a credit card company has customer service representatives who answer customer questions about credit balances, late payments, and lost cards. Customer service representatives use a software application that allows them to keep track of customer questions and requests for information. However, the customer service representatives require access to transaction records as well. One way to provide this information would be to allow customer service representatives to link directly to the transaction processing database. However, this scheme would force customer service representatives to access two separate applications for every customer query, slowing down service and introducing potential errors. A better solution would be to link the two applications, so that the customer service application automatically accesses the transaction database and displays transaction information formatted and filtered for customer service use.

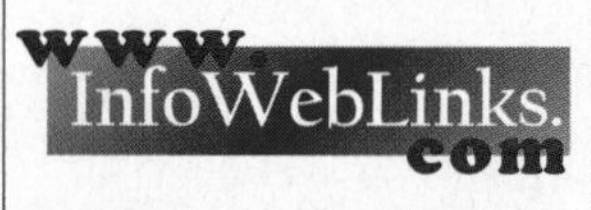

Learn more about enterprise techniques that protect against fraud by visiting the EAI InfoWeb.

click

As mentioned in Chapter 10, **data warehousing** is the process of collecting historic data so that it can be analyzed to uncover trends and predict future behaviors. For example, your credit card company might use data warehousing to predict spending trends, market new products and services to prospective customers, and detect fraud. Have you ever wondered how your credit card company determines if your credit card has been stolen? Most credit card companies use sophisticated data warehousing techniques to collect, analyze, and predict fraudulent behavior. One common fraud technique—the theft of newly issued cards directly from a mailbox—can be detected by combining and analyzing data from transaction systems and customer information systems. A newly issued card that is suddenly used for an unusual number of transactions would fit the theft profile and be flagged as a possible stolen card.

The cutting edge of enterprise application integration is a **common virtual system**, in which all enterprise components are linked and appear to be one unified system. Transactions or processes running on a common virtual system have immediate access to any data stored on the enterprise system, regardless of where the data exists. In the case of a credit card company, a common virtual system would allow a person with the appropriate security access to locate a particular credit card transaction, and then quickly access information about the cardholder who performed the transaction, information about marketing trends for that particular marketing segment, sales data from the store where the transaction took place, and any other relevant information stored in the credit card company's enterprise computing system.

HIGH-PERFORMANCE COMPUTING

What is high-performance computing? In 1996, thousands of people watched as chess champion Garry Kasparov nearly met his match playing chess against a computer nicknamed Deep Blue. He barely won the six-game series, but immediately challenged the computer to a rematch. IBM designers went to work upgrading and improving Deep Blue. The following year, Kasparov resigned the match only 19 moves into the sixth game. Deep Blue had won (Figure 12-4).

FIGURE 12-4

Kasparov played Deep Blue on a conventional chess board. Moves were relayed to the computer by a technician stationed at a keyboard.

The team that developed Deep Blue is working on an even more sophisticated chess-playing computer. You'll find more information about interesting HPC projects at the HPC Applications InfoWeb.

Deep Blue is probably the best known example of high-performance computing. The term **high-performance computing** (HPC) refers to a branch of computer science that focuses on ways to optimize the processing capabilities of computers. High-performance computing systems are designed to handle computationally complex tasks, extremely large data sets, and operations that require lightning fast response. For example, Deep Blue was optimized for playing chess and had the capacity to evaluate 200 million chess moves every second.

High-performance computing systems are not limited to simply playing chess. They are used for a wide range of tasks, including car design, weather forecasting, and genetic research. Many HPC applications involve scientific research, such as simulating the aerodynamics of space vehicles, or modeling the folding action of a protein. HPC is uniquely suited for such research, which typically requires massive numbers of computations based on complex numerical models and huge data sets. Conventional computing systems are far too slow to complete such computations in a reasonable period of time. For example, an HPC computer called ASCI Q performs calculations for the U.S. Department of Energy at a rate of 30 teraFLOPS. To put that processing speed into perspective, in one hour a supercomputer running at 30 teraFLOPS can complete the calculations that would require 60 years for a standard personal computer to complete.

Whereas the processing speed of a typical personal computer is measured in megahertz, the speed of HPC systems is typically measured in FLOPS or MIPS. **FLOPS**, is an acronym for "floating-point operations per second." Floating-point numbers, such as 5.0, .333, and 3.142, can include fractional parts and are typically displayed with decimal places. In contrast, integers are whole numbers. Floating-point operations take much longer to compute than integer operations, and occur frequently in HPC applications. **MIPS** is the acronym for "millions of instructions per second," and indicates the speed at which a computer executes instructions of any kind. The chart in Figure 12-5 highlights the difference in processing speed for personal computers and high-performance computers.

FIGURE 12-5 Processing Speed

Measurement	Abbreviation	Instructions per Second
MegaFLOPS	MFLOPS	1 million
GigaFLOPS	GFLOPS	1 billion
TeraFLOPS	TFLOPS	1 trillion
PetaFLOPS	PFLOPS	1,000 trillion

Typical personal computer
2.2 GHz (about 537 megaFLOPS)

High-performance computer
(12 teraFLOPS)

For additional examples of compute-intensive problems that affect research related to many aspects of your daily life, connect to the Compute-intensive Problems InfoWeb.

click

What is "compute intensive"? A **compute-intensive** problem is one that requires massive amounts of data to be processed using complex mathematical calculations. Molecular calculations, atmospheric models, and cosmological research are all examples of projects that require massive numbers of data points to be manipulated, processed, and analyzed.

Scientists at the Department of Energy had a compute-intensive problem on their hands when they studied the atomic behaviors of materials used for magnetic storage devices, such as hard disks and magnetic tapes. The study required a series of 30 trillion calculations for every atom in a cube of iron two millionths of a centimeter across. Because a cube this size contains 1,458 atoms, that worked out to an astounding 45 quadrillion calculations! What's even more astounding is that the scientists involved in this project admitted that the size of the project wasn't big enough to completely understand the behavior of magnetic materials. To do that, an iron cube containing 27,000 atoms would be needed—about 20 times more atoms than in the original project.

The complexity of the calculations required for much of today's critical research in medicine, engineering, and space exploration is what drives computer scientists to continue to develop newer and faster HPC systems. Even with the massive computing power now available, researchers and scientists often find that certain compute-intensive calculations are not practical to run on today's systems.

Luckily, there are specialized storage systems designed to store large amounts of data. An organization implements these storage systems for the same reasons it may have a central library or repository for physical resources, such as books or printed reports. Rather than storing data in individual departments or computers, it is easier to organize, maintain, and retrieve information stored in a central location.

One high-capacity storage system, called a **storage area network** (SAN), is a network of storage devices and data servers designed to function as a node on a wider network. A SAN storage device, such as a hard disk or tape, simply stores data. A SAN data server manages the storage devices and works in conjunction with additional SAN data servers to provide an interface to the SAN. When computers connected on a network containing a SAN access or store data, they interact with the SAN in the same way they might interact with a standard storage device. A request for file access is captured by the SAN data server, and all of the SAN storage devices work together as an integrated whole in order to retrieve data, as shown in Figure 12-9.

FIGURE 12-9

A storage area network consists of storage devices and a SAN data server. The SAN can be accessed from any of the enterprise network's servers, such as the NT, UNIX, and Linux servers shown here.

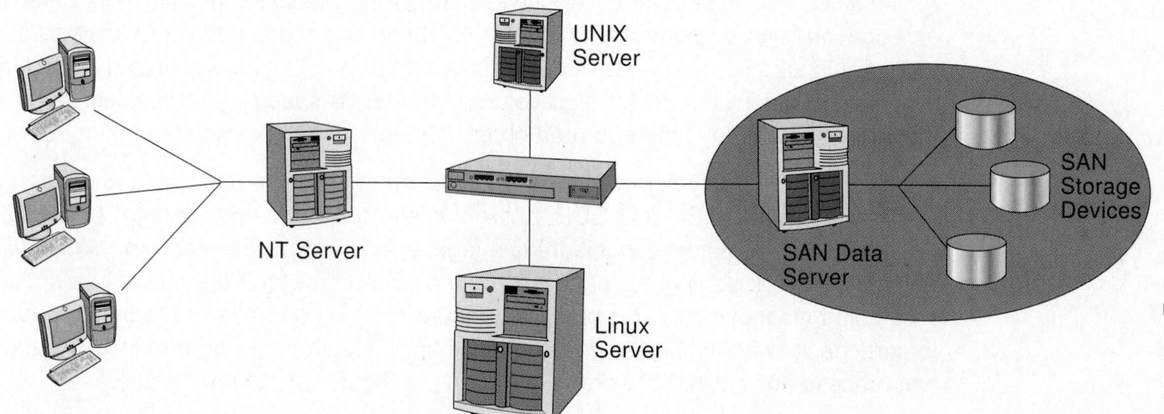

12

SANs are typically found in the corporate data centers of large supermarket chains, financial institutions, and other nationwide companies. SANs are also used to store the data that populates Web pages. For example, BN.com, the Web-based bookseller owned by Barnes & Noble, uses a Compaq SAN to store up to 7 terabytes of order and inventory data. Other advantages of SANs include scalability and storage management. SANs are easily scalable because storage devices or servers can be added at any time. SANs also typically provide **storage management services**, such as the ability to automatically store multiple copies of every file, or provide exact copies of storage media via mirroring.

Mirroring is the process of creating a real-time "mirror copy" of a storage medium, such as a hard disk or CD. Mirroring a hard disk, for example, requires two hard disks—a master and a mirror. Whenever a file is created, changed, or deleted on the master disk, that file is also created, changed, or deleted on the mirror disk. Mirroring differs from simply copying because it happens in real time. If the master disk fails, the mirror disk can immediately take over the duties of the master disk. SANs make mirroring easy because they contain multiple storage devices, but mirroring can be accomplished with any storage system that contains at least two distinct storage mediums.

A typical enterprise system also includes network attached storage devices. **Network attached storage**, or NAS, refers to storage devices designed to be attached directly to a network without requiring a server for management. A NAS device typically contains a built-in network interface card. Each NAS device is assigned an IP address by the network administrator and can be connected directly to any network, as shown in Figure 12-10.

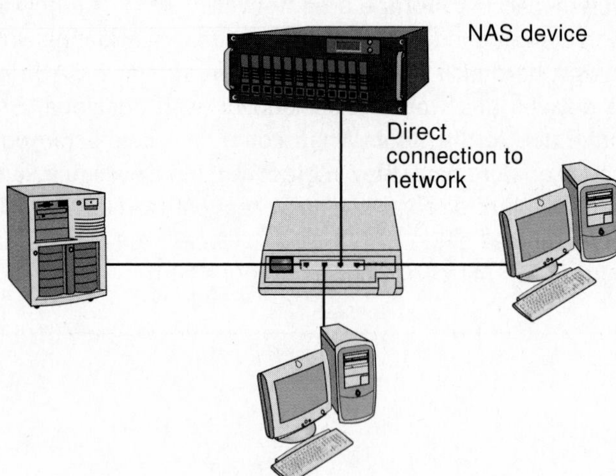

FIGURE 12-10

Network attached storage contains a built-in network card for direct connection to a network.

Do enterprise systems require special input devices? Adding data to an enterprise computing system can be accomplished in a variety of ways. Much of the data stored by enterprise computing systems has been entered from a keyboard. Enterprise systems also collect data using a wide variety of other input devices, such as optical scanners and digital cameras.

As the amount of input to an enterprise system grows, the speed at which it is collected and converted to computer-readable format becomes more and more important. A variety of input devices can provide enterprise systems with high speed and automated input capabilities required for high-volume data. High-speed input devices, such as the scanners used by banks to read checks, handle large volumes of input.

Banks deal with a very high volume of checks that must be read, sorted, and cleared. Two technologies, MICR and OCR, allow banks to automate check processing. **MICR** (magnetic ink character recognition) is a legacy technology developed in 1958. MICR automates check sorting by reading a routing code printed on the check in a special font, using magnetic ink. This specially printed routing code allows magnetic readers to sort checks with almost 100% accuracy. MICR is also fast—modern MICR readers can process up to 2,400 checks (like the one in Figure 12-11) per minute.

FIGURE 12-11

Printed checks contain MICR or OCR printing that can be read quickly by a high-volume input device.

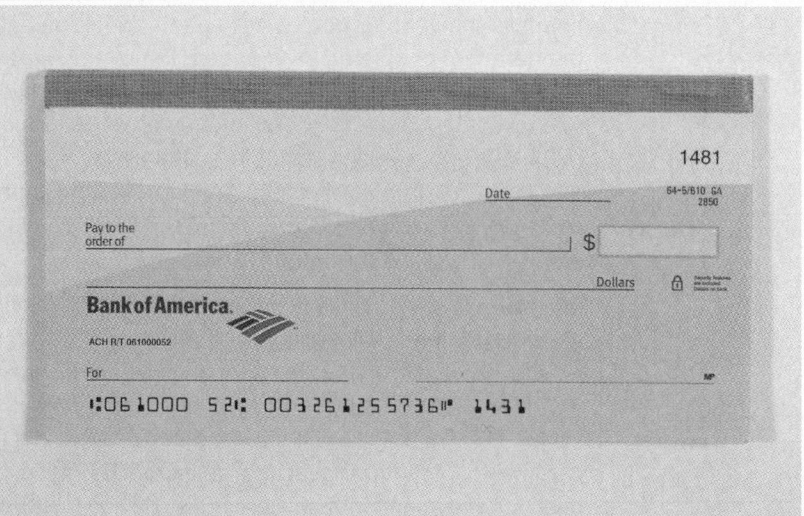

Middleware is a key technology for today's enterprise systems. Learn more at the Middleware InfoWeb.

click

Middleware can be written using standard programming languages such as C++ and Java, or it can be written using languages and protocols specifically designed for communicating among diverse systems. One such protocol, called **SOAP** (Simple Object Access Protocol), allows a program running on one operating system, such as Windows, to communicate with a program running on a different operating system, such as Linux, using Web-based communications protocols such as HTTP and XML. SOAP defines exactly how to encode an HTTP or XML file in order to call a program from another operating system, send parameters, and receive a response. Other tools for creating middleware include SNMP and Java 2 Platform Enterprise Edition.

HPC SOFTWARE

Does high-performance computing require special software? Unlike enterprise systems, high-performance computing systems rarely run commercial software. Custom software provides two important advantages for high-performance computing: speed and specialized applications.

Organizations use custom software to increase computational speed. Commercial software applications are usually written to run on a variety of computers and hardware devices and, as such, are written primarily with compatibility and interoperability in mind. In contrast, custom software routines are tightly coupled with the hardware that runs them. Custom software is almost always faster than commercial software because it can be optimized to take full advantage of hardware capabilities. For example, high-performance software can be customized to use all available processors and virtually eliminate processor idle time. In the same way, software can be designed to use specialized high-speed input and output devices at their maximum capacities.

Speed is not the only benefit of custom software. Organizations develop custom software for high-performance systems because these systems often perform tasks for which commercial software is not available. Most HPC projects involve very specialized research, and there is no off-the-shelf application that provides the sophistication, speed, or specialized content required. Also, the complexity of HPC hardware often makes it impossible to run off-the-shelf applications.

IBM's Blue Gene Supercomputer requires custom software both for speed and because the necessary application software is not available commercially. In 1999, IBM announced Blue Gene—a supercomputer that runs at 1 petaFLOPS, that is, 1,000 trillion operations per second. Blue Gene is designed to model protein folding, a biological phenomenon thought to be at least partially responsible for diseases such as Alzheimer's, cystic fibrosis, and mad cow.

Modeling proteins is a big job, even for a supercomputer. Scientists estimate that it would require three years to model 100 milliseconds of a protein-folding scenario at 1 petaFLOPS speeds. However, they believe that the use of sophisticated software techniques, such as streamlined algorithms, threading, and the ability for simulations to migrate from one thread to another, can considerably speed up the modeling process.

Designing, writing, and testing sophisticated HPC software requires time, expertise, and financial resources. An ongoing effort of the National HPCC Software Exchange (NHSE) makes a selection of HPC software available on the Web. The NHSE Web site (Figure 12-17) provides links to download sites, software reviews, and tutorials about HPC algorithms.

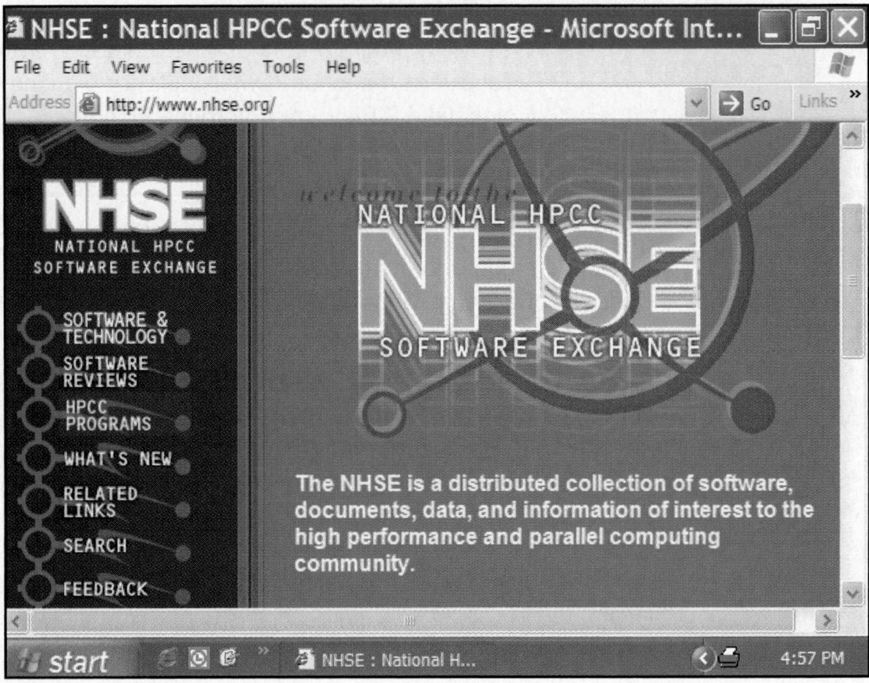

FIGURE 12-17

The NHSE Web site provides links to HPC software.

QUICKCheck Section B

1. A(n) ________ computer system has become outdated due to technology advances or changing organizational requirements.

2. One type of hardware that is typically found on an enterprise system is a(n) ________ server, which is a modular electronic board designed to be inserted into a rack.

3. A storage ________ network is a network of storage devices and data servers.

4. One way to increase the speed at which a program runs is to use ________ processing, the practice of simultaneously using two or more processors to process a request.

5. Three characteristics of enterprise-level software applications are that they are scalable, ________, and available on a variety of platforms.

6. ________ is a type of software that allows diverse software applications to share data.

7. High-performance computing systems typically use ________ software instead of commercial software applications.

check answers

Section C ENTERPRISE AND HIGH-PERFORMANCE ARCHITECTURE

Today's mega roller coasters provide a heart-stopping ride, and yet their architecture makes them much safer than the rickety wooden structures that populated carnivals in the days of poodle skirts and saddle shoes. The architecture of a structure specifies its components and the way in which those components are assembled. The architecture for a well-built structure is effective, efficient, and reliable.

The architecture of a computer system specifies the devices it includes and how those devices are connected. The "right" architecture for a specific enterprise or high-performance computer system depends on a variety of factors, such as geographical coverage, number of users, desired response time, required processing time, and security. In this section, you'll learn more about the design, organization, and configuration of enterprise and high-performance computer systems.

CENTRALIZED ARCHITECTURE

What is the simplest architecture for enterprise and high-performance systems? The earliest computer systems that provided services for enterprises were based on centralized architecture. A **centralized computing system** consists of one central computer surrounded by terminals, as shown in Figure 12-18.

12

FIGURE 12-18

A centralized computing system typically consists of a mainframe computer that processes data for a collection of terminals.

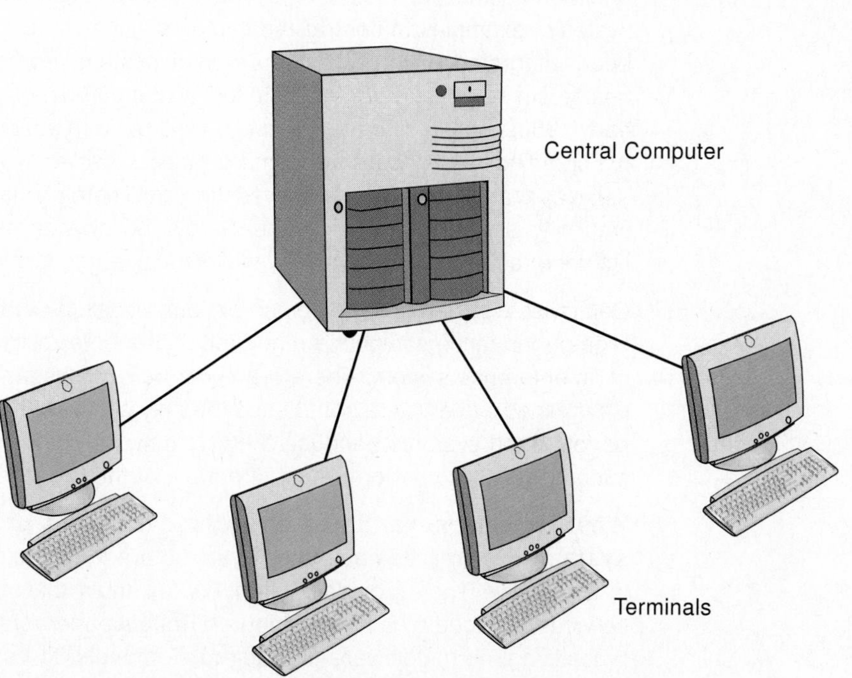

In a centralized computing system, the primary processing device is typically a mainframe computer, referred to as a **host computer**, which performs most or all of the processing for the entire system. Users communicate processing requests to the host computer using terminals. A **terminal** is an input/output device that features a keyboard and screen, but has no storage capacity and very limited processing capability. Popular terminals for centralized legacy systems include the IBM 3270 and DEC's VT-100. Personal computers can also be connected to mainframe hosts. These PCs, however, must run **terminal emulation software**, which makes them appear to the host computer as "dumb terminals" that cannot store or process any data. Figure 12-19 explains more about the differences between terminals and personal computers.

FIGURE 12-19

A terminal resembles a personal computer, but a close look usually reveals that a terminal has no storage device. A typical terminal features a display unit and a keyboard unit, but rarely a separate system unit.

Although centralized computing systems are not popular choices for today's enterprise systems, examples of centralized systems still exist. Some centralized systems have been integrated into a larger enterprise system. For example, it's likely that your hometown or college library installed a computerized card catalog in the 1970s or early 1980s. These centralized systems still perform adequately today, and replacement or upgrading is not necessary. Some libraries, however, want to offer expanded computer services that allow patrons to access the card catalog via the Web, and provide library staff with a variety of management tools. To provide such services, a library might incorporate the centralized legacy system in a larger, less centralized enterprise system.

Centralized systems are popular options for high-performance computer systems. High-performance computing rarely requires the flexibility, availability, and compatibility of an enterprise system. Therefore, a centralized system may be an adequate choice. Centralized systems are sometimes the only choice available for the very fastest high-performance systems because they typically rely upon one very fast, high-powered supercomputer to perform most, if not all, of the processing required.

What are the advantages and disadvantages of a centralized computing system? Centralized computing systems are the simplest of the many architectures in use today. They provide straightforward tools that allow many people to access services provided by a host computer. Because the host computer performs all of the processing, no middleware is required. Terminals do not store data or programs that are required by other components of the system, so terminal malfunctions have little effect on the functionality of the entire system.

Administering a centralized system is also very easy. Because the host computer is the only device on the network that processes data or stores files, administering the system is almost as simple as administering a single computer. No client software exists on the terminals, so upgrading or installing new software involves only the host system. Monitoring user access and processing speed, adding new users, and other administration tasks are similarly easy.

Centralized computer systems have disadvantages as well. Because all of the processing takes place on a single host computer, if that computer fails, the entire system fails. Centralized systems often have scalability limits based on the storage, memory, processing, and connectivity capacity of the host computer. For example, the addition of 100 more terminals might not be possible without purchasing, installing, and configuring a more powerful host computer.

DISTRIBUTED ARCHITECTURE

What is a distributed computer system? A **distributed computer system** is a collection of connected computers in which processing, data, and application software are dispersed among more than one physical computer. Distributed computer systems are commonly used for both standard information systems and enterprise systems. A simple distributed system might consist of only two computers connected in a client/server configuration—for example, a database server with a client computer connected to it. More complex distributed systems consist of multiple servers, storage devices, and client computers. The largest distributed system is the Internet itself, with millions of servers connected to millions of clients. Figure 12-20 illustrates an example of a distributed computer network designed for a medium-sized business.

FIGURE 12-20

A distributed computer system includes a variety of servers and clients, all with the capability to process and store data.

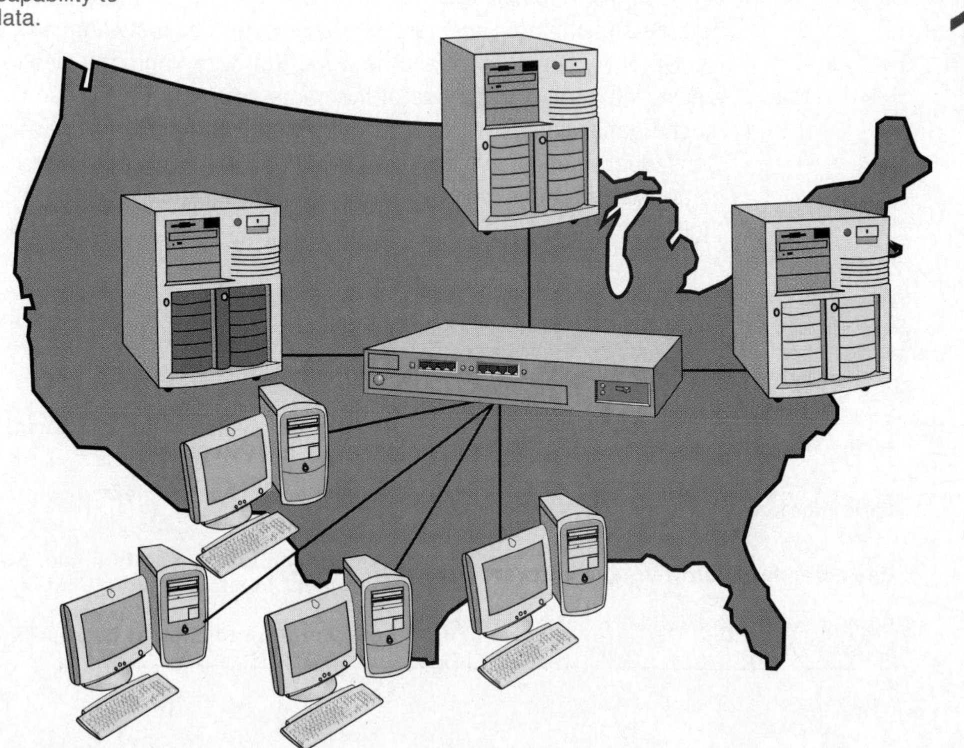

What are the advantages and disadvantages of distributed computer systems? Distributed computer systems are popular due to their scalability, reasonable cost, and performance. In contrast to centralized systems, whose scalability is limited to the processing capability of the single host computer, distributed systems can be scaled up or down by adding or removing devices. A small organization may require only one server connected to five or ten workstations. As the organization grows, a distributed system makes it possible to add more workstations, connect additional servers, and group computers into an efficient structure. Distributed systems may also be scaled to encompass a large geographical area. An organization might be small, but it may need to share data among sites located in different cities or states. A distributed system can span cities and connect users located just about anywhere around the world.

Distributed architecture is cost-effective because specialized hardware or software is typically not required. Most modern operating systems allow computers to be connected simply by installing a standard network card and connecting a few cables. Because standard hardware and software are used, the system can be upgraded as newer components appear on the market. Also, distributed systems allow organizations to put expensive, fast computers to work doing the most difficult and complex functions, while using low-end, slower, less expensive machines for those tasks that don't have such high requirements. For example, a university's distributed system might use an expensive mainframe server to run its student record software and a moderately priced blade server for accounting, but use inexpensive desktop PCs as employee workstations and student registration terminals.

The main disadvantage of distributed systems is the level of complexity involved in management. Problems in the system can be difficult to track down because every computer on a distributed network processes data and interacts with other computers. For example, if a distributed system becomes infected with a virus, it is often very difficult to find the infected computers and clean them before they infect other computers on the network.

Upgrading and installing new software and hardware on a distributed system can also be time-consuming. Hardware upgrades, such as installing faster network cards, may involve every computer on the network. Software upgrades also must be coordinated to ensure that multiple versions of the same software are not running on the system. For most organizations, the advantages of distributed systems outweigh the disadvantages. Consequently, most enterprise systems and an increasing number of high-performance computing systems are based on distributed computing architecture. The table in Figure 12-21 summarizes the advantages and disadvantages of distributed systems.

FIGURE 12-21 Advantages and Disadvantages of Distributed Systems

Advantages	Disadvantages
Easily scalable	System management is more complex than centralized systems
Expandable over a large geographical area	Viruses and other problems have the potential to affect many users
Uses standard hardware and software	Repairs and upgrades often take place on equipment located at remote sites
Simple tasks are handled by inexpensive computers	Software upgrades must be coordinated

Is the Internet a grid system? Certainly some parts of the Internet provide resources for grid computing systems. The Internet and all of the computers it connects, however, are better described as a distributed system that includes both tiered and grid systems. In fact, just about any computer on the Internet could be part of a grid system and part of an enterprise system at the same time. The computer located on a desk in an office could easily be part of an enterprise system, a distributed system, and a grid system. The different types of architectures are not mutually exclusive.

CLUSTERING

What is clustering? In a computing system, a **cluster** is a group of two or more devices connected together to distribute processing, input, output, or storage workloads, and adapt to equipment failure. Processing clusters, like the one in Figure 12–25, can be thought of as "super servers." They provide the same functions as a normal server, but because a cluster consists of more than one computer, it is not as susceptible to equipment failure and also provides speed benefits. Clusters are often used as servers for business-critical functions, such as e-mail, storage, the Web, and e-commerce.

FIGURE 12-25

A cluster is a group of computers that takes the place of a single server on a network.

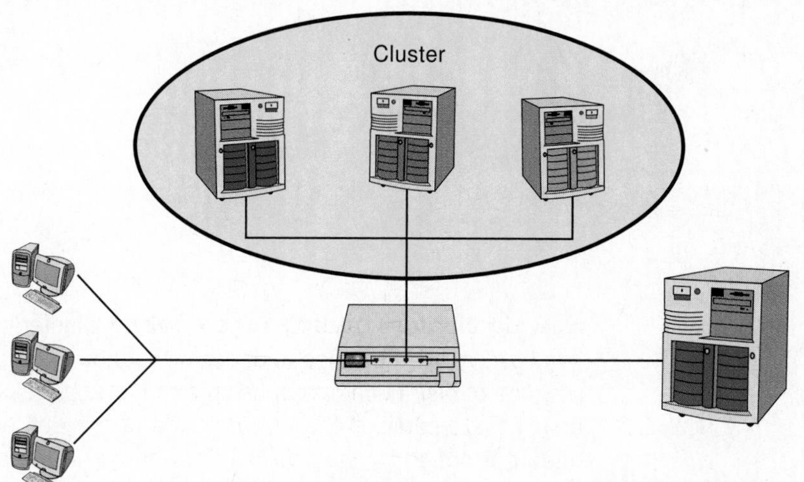

12

Each computer in a cluster is called a **cluster node**. A cluster requires special cluster management software on each node. In addition to cluster management software, the application software that runs on the cluster must be "cluster-aware," meaning that it supports the distribution of work among several servers. Cluster management software is available from third-party software publishers. Some operating systems, such as Windows 2000 Advanced Server, offer built-in clustering support. Clusters provide an important configuration option for computer systems because they can improve reliability, provide parallel processing, and handle variable workloads.

Clusters can be incorporated into both enterprise and high-performance computing systems. Enterprise systems use clusters primarily to support services that must be available continuously. It is also very common for HPC systems to use clusters for their parallel processing abilities. For example, in the summer of 2002, the NSF (National Science Foundation) installed a series of HPC systems at four sites in the U.S. These systems are available to scientists and researchers for use in a variety of compute-intensive projects. Each site consists of a cluster of Intel-based computers running the Linux operating system, and processing data at a speed of at least 1 teraFLOPS. Clustering was chosen for its ability to support parallel processing, and because the NSF requires around-the-clock availability.

What is fault tolerance? Fault tolerance refers to a computer system's ability to react gracefully to unexpected software or hardware failures. A cluster provides fault tolerance by detecting node failure and transferring workloads, as required. This process of transferring service from a failed node to a working node is referred to as **cluster failover**. The ability to handle failures without a break in service makes clustering ideal for situations that require 24/7 operation—jargon for "up and running 24 hours a day, 7 days a week." As shown in Figure 12-26, the availability of more than one server in a cluster makes it possible to failover to a secondary server if the main server fails.

FIGURE 12-26

When one computer in a cluster fails, a process called cluster failover transfers service to a working computer.

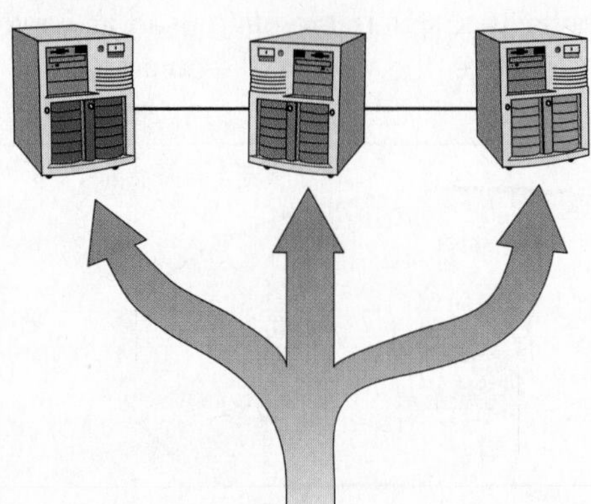

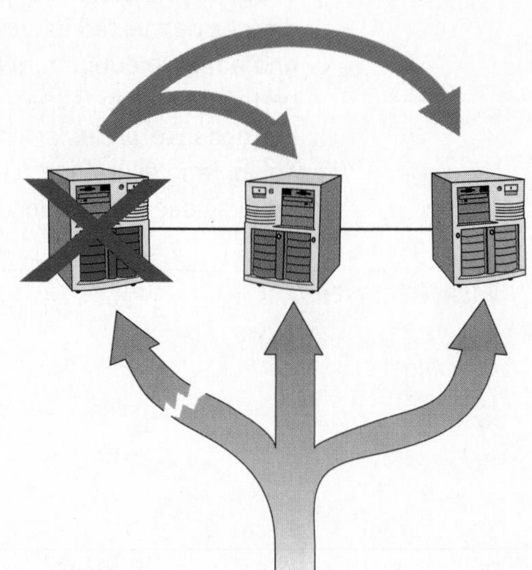

How do clusters optimize resources? Clustering optimizes computing resources by allowing cluster nodes to share workloads and data. **Load balancing** refers to the practice of distributing processing and storage tasks among the nodes of a cluster in a way that optimizes the performance of the entire system. Load balancing is most often performed by the application running on the cluster, as opposed to the cluster management software or operating system.

To understand how load balancing works, consider a cluster of two servers and one storage device that are configured to handle e-mail for an ISP. All incoming mail is held on the shared storage device until the recipient is ready to receive it. How does this cluster handle many simultaneous requests for e-mail from ISP subscribers? It would be possible to configure the cluster so that one computer—let's call it Server A—handles as many e-mail requests as it can until it is overwhelmed. When Server A is operating at full capacity, Server B might begin to process e-mail requests too. This scheme, although logical, does not make effective use of a cluster's load balancing capabilities because as a computer reaches maximum capacity, its efficiency tends to decrease.

A better scheme for load balancing distributes the workload before Server A becomes overwhelmed. When Server A reaches a specified level of performance—say 60% of capacity—Server B is configured to "kick in" and help with the workload.

Is every node in a cluster active at all times? A cluster can be configured as an **active-active cluster** so that all nodes are active at the same time. The application software that runs on an active-active cluster must perform the load balancing activities to allow each node to participate in the application processing functions. Designing a software application to run on an active-active cluster is a difficult and time-consuming process and, as a result, very few applications available today are truly active-active. For true parallel computing, however, active-active clustering is required.

A more common configuration is an **active-passive cluster**, which contains one node that is active at all times, and additional nodes that are ready in case of failover. As with an active-active cluster, applications that run on an active-passive cluster must be cluster-aware and designed in a way that allows failover.

What is a Beowulf cluster? A **Beowulf cluster** is a collection of off-the-shelf computers that is interconnected and configured as a cluster to handle high-performance computing tasks. The original Beowulf (pronounced BAY oh wolf) system was developed in 1994 at the Goddard Space Flight Center by Thomas Sterling and Donald Becker. They theorized that a high-performance computer system running in the gigaFLOPS range could be created using standard, off-the-shelf hardware and software. Their theory turned out to be correct, and they were able to create the first Beowulf system out of 16 Intel DX4 computers connected by 10 Mbps Ethernet. Clustering provided high-performance parallel processing without the costs and specialized equipment normally associated with high-performance systems.

Although a Beowulf cluster might seem similar to grid computing, there are differences between the two. The computers on a Beowulf cluster are dedicated to the cluster and run cluster applications. In contrast, nodes on a grid system are typically personal desktop systems that run desktop applications in addition to grid applications. Cluster nodes are also under the administrative jurisdiction of the cluster, whereas grid nodes are administered by individual PC owners. Today, Beowulf clusters are popular with organizations such as educational research facilities, which require fast systems, but are unable to pay the high costs associated with high-performance computers. In addition to being cost-effective to build, Beowulf clusters can be upgraded easily and inexpensively as new technology appears on the market.

QUICKCheck Section C

1. A(n) ______ computing system uses a simple architecture in which terminals communicate with a single mainframe computer.
2. A collection of connected computers in which data and application software are dispersed to more than one server is a(n) ______ computing system.
3. An enterprise system is often arranged in multiple ______ or layers of computers, each dedicated to performing a particular task.
4. A(n) ______ computing system is a network of computers in which each computer is treated as a generic and equal resource.
5. A(n) ______ is a sort of "super server"—a group of computers that provides the same functions as a standard server, but also protects against computer failure and provides speed benefits.

check answers

LAB 12-C GRID COMPUTING

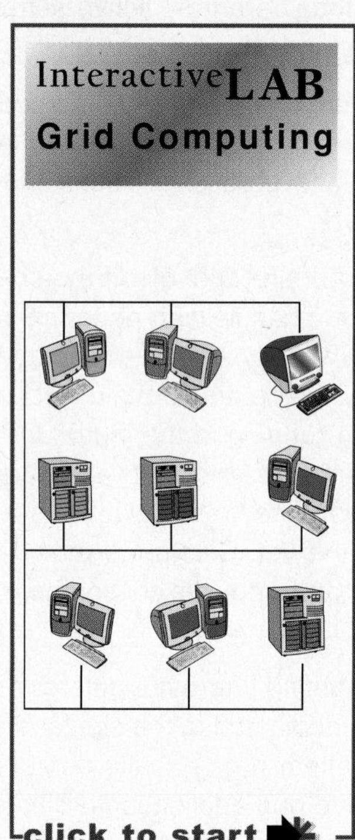

In this lab, you'll learn:

- The basic elements of a grid computing system, such as SETI@home
- The purpose of grid client software
- How to download and install grid client software
- The methods used by grid client software to become active during idle CPU cycles
- What happens on a client computer during a typical processing session
- How to view the results produced by the SETI@home screensaver
- The role of server-side computers for managing a grid
- The configuration of SETI@home servers
- How server-side computers integrate the results uploaded by grid clients
- To recognize the security threats to grid clients, and take steps to safeguard your computer
- About the security threats to grid servers, and how to determine whether security measures seem like appropriate protection for grid clients
- How to determine whether or not a grid project is legitimate

LAB Assignments

1. Start the interactive part of the lab. Insert your Tracking Disk if you want to save your QuickCheck results. Perform each of the lab steps as directed, and answer all of the lab QuickCheck questions. When you exit the lab, your answers are automatically graded and your results are displayed.

2. Connect to the SETI@home Web site: *setiathome.ssl.berkeley.edu/* and locate as much information as you can about security. After reading this information, do you feel confident that all necessary steps have been taken to protect grid participants? Why or why not?

3. Enter the search term "donate CPU cycles" in a Web search engine, then follow any one of the links to a site (other than SETI@home) that requests your idle CPU cycles for a charitable cause. Describe the purpose of the project. Determine the approximate size of the grid client software and what sort of data it processes.

4. Browse through the site for the previous exercise to determine whether or not you think it is legitimate. Write a one-page report that describes the site, includes its URL, and provides specific details about how you evaluated the site's legitimacy.

Disasters and viruses have caused billions of dollars worth of damage over the past few decades. You can learn more about disasters and disaster recovery by connecting to the Disaster Recovery InfoWeb.

click 

Acts of war once affected only computer systems that were located on battle fronts. With a recent increase in terrorist incidents, however, civilian areas have become targets. Acts of war, such as bombing, can cause physical damage to computer systems. Cyberterrorism can also cause damage, using viruses and worms to destroy data and otherwise disrupt computer-based operations, which now include critical national infrastructures such as power grids and telecommunications systems.

Viruses can cause damage to just about any computer system. You might have experienced the nuisance of rooting out a virus from your personal computer. That inconvenience pales when compared to the potential effect of a virus on an enterprise computing system. The Nimbda virus, a worm spread via e-mail and infected Web sites, is estimated to have caused more than $590 million in damage when it infected more than 8.3 million computers worldwide in 2001.

How are large-scale computer systems protected from threats? No computer system can be completely risk-free, but there are some proactive measures that administrators of large-scale computer systems can take to protect systems from threats. These countermeasures can be grouped into four categories: deterrents, preventative measures, corrective procedures, and detection activities.

Deterrents reduce the likelihood of deliberate attack. Common deterrents include security features such as multi-level authentication and password protection. Monitoring software that tracks users, file updates, and changes to critical systems also acts as a deterrent. Physical deterrents, such as providing only limited access to critical servers, also fall under this category. See Figure 12-30.

FIGURE 12-30

Physical deterrents provide one line of defense against disasters.

Preventative measures shield vulnerabilities to render an attack unsuccessful or reduce its impact. Firewalls that prevent unauthorized access to a system are one example of a preventative measure.

Corrective procedures reduce the effect of an attack. Data backups, disaster recovery plans, and the availability of redundant hardware devices all are examples of corrective procedures.

Detection activities discover attacks and trigger preventative or corrective measures. For example, antivirus software detects viruses entering a system, and can be configured to automatically clean the system or quarantine infected files. Theft or vandalism can be detected by periodic hardware inventories.

DATA CENTERS

Does data center design help to minimize risks? The hardware and software that run most enterprise and many high-performance computing systems are housed in a data center. A **data center** is a specialized facility designed to house and protect computer systems and data. A data center typically includes special features that enhance security, such as fireproof and earthquakeproof buildings, sprinkler systems, power generators, physical security such as secure doors and windows, and anti-static floor coverings.

Data centers are designed to proactively reduce the risk of data loss that might occur as a result of a disaster. The best way to protect against risk is to avoid it altogether, and data centers can reduce or negate the effects of specific types of disasters. One company that actively uses data centers is NTT/Verio, an ISP that provides Web hosting services in more than 170 countries. NTT/Verio currently has more than 20 different data centers located in the U.S., Europe, Australia, and Asia. The company stores data for thousands of organizations, and loss of information in even one data center would be a disaster. NTT/Verio managers designed a series of data centers with risk prevention in mind. Each data center incorporates special risk management features for dealing with fires, power outages, security, and environmental concerns.

A typical data center may be located in the basement of a building, or even underground (Figure 12-31). One commercial data center, USDCO, is housed 85 feet below ground in an abandoned gypsum mine near Grand Rapids, Michigan. Underground data centers provide some level of protection against natural disasters, such as storms and fires, and are not susceptible to extreme changes in surface temperature. In general, data centers are not located in earthquake, flood, or tornado prone areas.

FIGURE 12-31

Many critical data centers are located in underground bunkers.

Data centers typically include equipment to keep computers functioning during power outages. Most areas experience occasional power failures or blackouts. These failures can be costly to organizations whose goal is to offer 24/7 coverage. As a result, one of the most basic requirements for a data center is a supply of uninterrupted power from high-capacity, battery-operated UPSs (uninterruptible power supplies) and backup power generators. A data center must also protect and maintain its own power grid. For example, fuel tanks must be protected against explosions or fire, and batteries must be kept at room temperature for proper functioning.

Physical security is critical to data centers. Most data centers limit physical access via fingerprint identification systems, badges, or security guards. Steel doors divide the centers into secure areas. Motion detectors and automated alarm systems prevent unauthorized movement through the building. In addition, many data centers are located close to police and fire departments.

Conditions in a data center must be monitored at all times. Computerized detection systems monitor sensing devices that track temperature, humidity, water, smoke, fire, air flow, power levels, security systems, and many other metrics. Cameras may be placed in air ducts, under raised floors, and in computer chassis to detect intruders, pests such as mice or rats, or chemical leaks. Figure 12-32 shows the features of a typical data center.

FIGURE 12-32

A data center is designed to protect equipment and data from a variety of disasters.

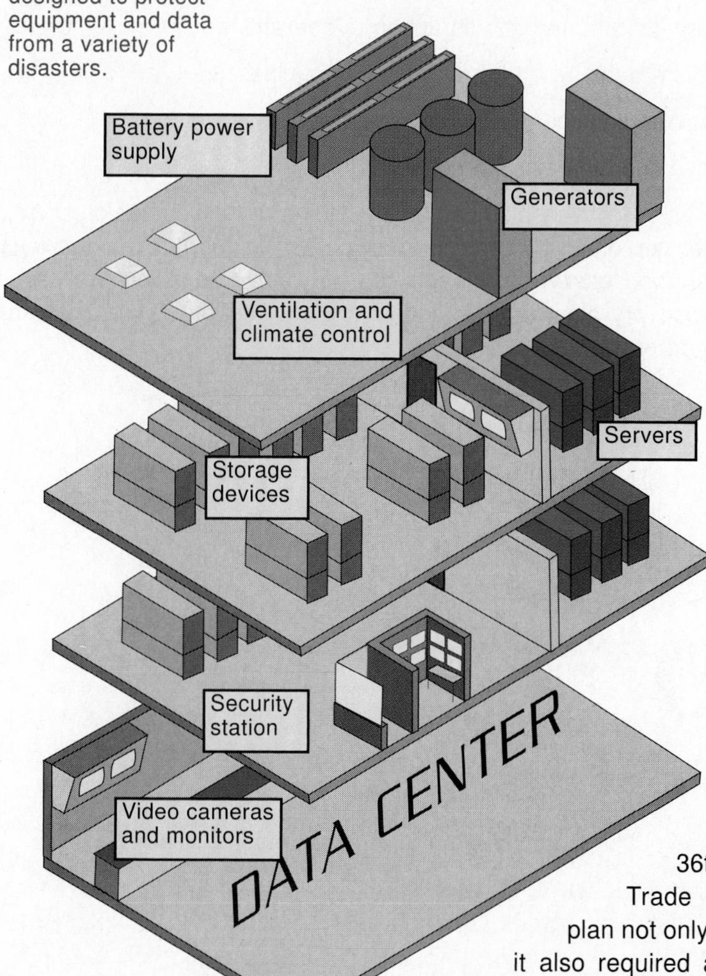

DISASTER RECOVERY PLANS

What if disaster strikes? Despite the best risk prevention measures, disasters that destroy data can and do occur. One of the most destructive disasters in history was the World Trade Center collapse on September 11, 2001. Surprisingly, very few companies affected by the disaster experienced critical data loss. Most companies were able to reconstitute their computer systems because the World Trade Center bombing eight years earlier prompted many companies in the towers to design disaster recovery plans. A **disaster recovery plan** is a step-by-step plan that describes the methods used to secure data against disaster, and explains how an organization will recover lost data if and when a disaster occurs.

12

One company that designed a disaster recovery plan after the 1993 bombing was Kemper Insurance, located on the 35th and 36th floors of the north tower of the World Trade Center. Kemper's disaster recovery plan not only detailed what to do in case of disaster, it also required a mock disaster recovery exercise at least once a year. In these yearly exercises, IT employees went through the process of reconstructing the company's computer system from scratch at an off-site location. They configured new hardware, installed the required software, and restored data from backup tapes. In response to the 9/11 catastrophe, Kemper Insurance IT employees followed the disaster recovery plan and recreated the computer system at another Kemper Insurance site. Kemper Insurance was up and running by 4:00 a.m. on September 12th—less than 24 hours after one of the largest disasters in history.

Disaster recovery plans must deal not only with calamities such as the World Trade Center collapse; they also must take into account the day-to-day events that could potentially cause data loss. Backup tapes can become corrupted, an employee might spill coffee onto the most critical storage device in the building, or a virus can slow down the network to the point that it's unusable. A well-formulated disaster recovery plan should account for all kinds of trouble, from the most minor "glitch" to the most destructive disaster. Specifically, an enterprise-wide disaster recovery plan should:

- Ensure the safety of people on the premises at the time of a disaster
- Continue critical business operations
- Minimize the duration of a serious disruption to operations
- Minimize immediate damage and prevent additional losses
- Establish management succession and emergency powers
- Facilitate effective coordination of recovery tasks

The existence of a disaster recovery plan can be the difference between an organization rebounding after a disaster, or simply ceasing to exist. The Kemper Insurance example illustrates how quickly and easily information can be recovered, even from severe disasters. Disaster recovery plans are as critical to data security as data backups, firewalls, and password protection.

QUICKCheck Section D

1. Three concepts that assure good quality of service are reliability, ________, and serviceability.
2. Response time is an example of a quality-of-service ________.
3. The process of identifying potential threats to computer systems, implementing plans to avoid threats, and developing steps to recover from disasters is referred to as ________ management.
4. Human error, natural disasters, and security breaches are all examples of common ________ that can affect a computer system.
5. A(n) ________ center is a facility specifically designed to house and protect computer systems and data.
6. Guidelines that describe the way an organization will rebuild and restore its computer system after a disaster is called a disaster ________ plan.

check answers

TECHTALK

HIERARCHICAL STORAGE MANAGEMENT

Have you ever wondered how big businesses, governments, and other large organizations store all of the information they collect and generate? The IRS alone processes more than 232 million tax returns every year, and that data must be stored for at least seven years. A 2000 study conducted at the University of California estimated that people will generate more information between 2000 and 2003 than was created in all the years prior to 2000. In 1999 alone, the equivalent of 250 megabytes of information were generated for every adult and child—a total of 1.5 billion gigabytes! This number is expected to double every year for the foreseeable future. The process of organizing and storing all this information is a challenge, even with fast computers and large storage devices. As a result, most large organizations collect old data and organize it in storage archives. One way that organizations archive data is through the use of hierarchical storage management.

What is hierarchical storage management? Hierarchical storage management (HSM) refers to the practice of moving infrequently accessed data to a succession of increasingly inexpensive storage devices. The process of moving data from one storage device to another can be automated using HSM software. A major advantage of HSM systems is cost savings. As data ages, it can be moved from expensive hard disk storage to less expensive storage media, such as optical disks and digital tapes.

An HSM system uses a variety of tiered storage devices, referred to as a "storage hierarchy," to store managed data. A **storage hierarchy** is a collection of several types of storage devices, typically organized from high-cost, fast media at the top of the hierarchy, to slower, low-cost media at the bottom. An HSM system typically has between one and three tiers, depending on the requirements of the organization. As data ages, it is moved from the top tier of the hierarchy toward the lowest tier. For example, a file may be moved from the first storage tier to the second storage tier when it hasn't been accessed in 30 days. Typically, the first storage tier is a hard disk or other fast-access storage medium. If the file has not been accessed for another 30 days—making it 60 days since the last access—it is then moved to the second tier. The second tier might be an optical disk drive or a tape drive. The process of moving data as it ages from one storage tier to another is referred to as **migration** or "relocation" (Figure 12-33). 12

FIGURE 12-33

Data in an HSM system migrates to lower levels of the storage hierarchy.

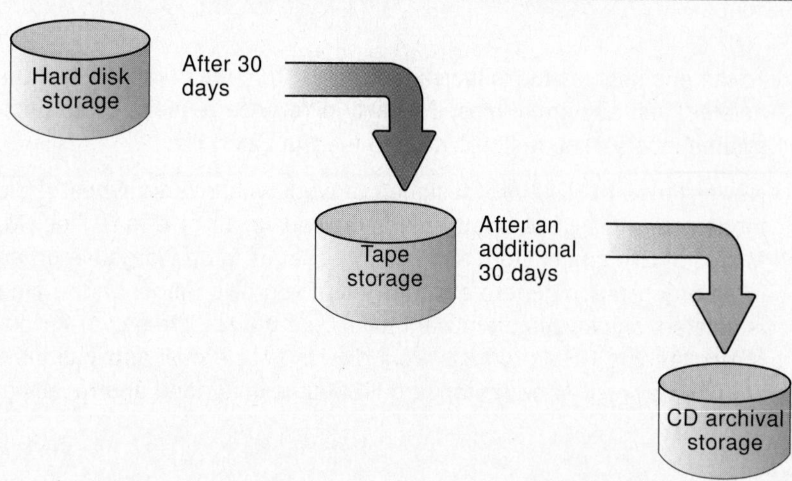

What happens when someone needs to access migrated data? Data is retrieved from long-term storage by recalling it. In the context of HSM, the term **recall** refers to the process of locating and retrieving data from the storage hierarchy. Recall is sometimes referred to as "restoration." When a file is recalled, it is removed from long-term storage, and placed in its original location. Once a file is recalled, it remains in its original location and is subject to its original migration criteria.

How do HSM systems work? An HSM system allows administrators to set migration criteria to determine when and to which location a file is relocated. The first decision an administrator is required to make is which files will migrate. Certain files, like executable files and system files, should never migrate. Other files, such as old data files, very large files, and any file that must be stored for future use, like tax documents, should migrate. Migration criteria might include file creation date, date of last access, file size, filename, and file type.

After the system administrator determines which files are to migrate, he or she must decide how the files will progress through the storage hierarchy. A file does not necessarily move through each successive level of the storage hierarchy. It might move from the top level of the hierarchy directly to the bottom level. For example, an administrator might know that certain files, such as outdated inventory reports, will be accessed rarely and can be moved directly to the bottom tier of the storage hierarchy.

When moving a file to a different level of the hierarchy, the software that controls an HSM system does not eradicate all traces of the file from its original location. Instead, it truncates the file, leaving behind the filename, size, and attributes. The data contained in the file is moved to long-term storage, and a pointer is left in its place. The pointer, called a **stub** or "placeholder," allows an HSM system to locate the data at a later date, just as the call number on a library book allows you to find a particular book on a library shelf. Figure 12-34 shows how HSM applications truncate files.

FIGURE 12-34

The migration process leaves behind a stub that can be used to access migrated data.

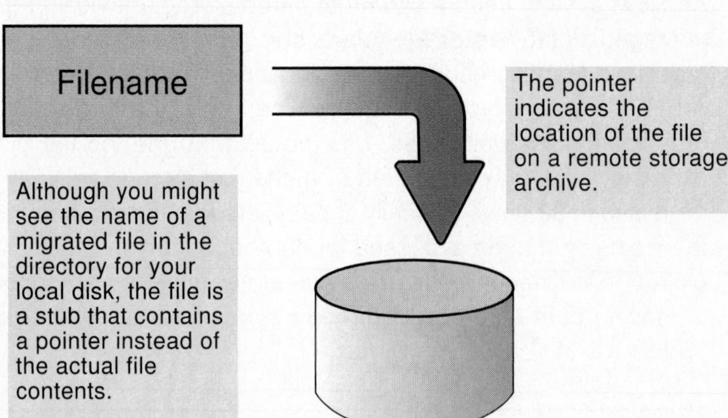

Filename
The pointer indicates the location of the file on a remote storage archive.
Although you might see the name of a migrated file in the directory for your local disk, the file is a stub that contains a pointer instead of the actual file contents.

To the end user, a stub is indistinguishable from the original file. Stubs can be opened, copied, or even deleted, just as normal files. The only difference a user might notice is a short pause while the HSM system locates and restores data to the truncated file.

Newer forms of HSM are designed to work with diverse types of digitally formatted information. One modern use for HSM is the migration and recall of e-mail files. Many e-mail applications, such as Microsoft Exchange, store all e-mail messages in one large file on an e-mail server. As the employees in an organization generate e-mail, this file grows. Although the file shrinks when an e-mail message is deleted, employees often want to leave e-mail on the server for both business and legal reasons. As a result, some HSM products work directly with e-mail applications to move old e-mail to hierarchical storage devices. As with standard HSM files, migrating and recalling e-mail is seamless to the user.

PROJECTS

An NP6 Project is an open-ended activity that will help you apply the concepts you have learned. Many projects require resources in addition to your textbook, such as current magazines, library materials, or Web access. When you tackle a project, be prepared to use your critical thinking skills, logical analysis, and your creativity.

1 **Issue Research: Donating CPU Cycles** The Issue section of this chapter focused on nonprofit grid computing efforts, such as SETI@home. For this project, write a two-five page paper describing one aspect of this technology. You might explore grid computing success stories and failures. You might want to delve into the technology that powers grid computing, or you might want to focus on the potential risks to consumers who volunteer for grid computing projects. To begin this project, consult the Idle CPUs InfoWeb (see page 657) and link to the recommended Web pages to get an in-depth overview of grid computing. As you write your paper, make sure that you can back up your statements with facts and references to authoritative articles and Web pages. You can place citations to these pages (including the author's name, article title, date of publication, and URL) at the end of your paper as endnotes, on each page as footnotes, or along with the appropriate paragraphs using parentheses. Follow your professor's instructions for submitting your paper via e-mail or as a printed document.

2 **High-performance Computing** For this open-ended project, research an aspect of high-performance computing that interests you. When your research is complete, incorporate it into a two-three page article for a consumer-level technology magazine, such as *Wired*. Some topics you might select include:

- The history of HPC systems
- Today's fastest HPC system
- The evolution of chess-playing computers
- How to obtain processing time on an HPC system
- HPC use in movies
- The future of high-performance computing

3 **Become a Disaster Expert** Suppose that you are a manager of an IS department, and you must write a disaster recovery plan. First, describe the computer systems you oversee, including descriptions of hardware, software, and important data. Then, create a disaster recovery plan that protects your installation against the following scenarios:

- The building that houses the IS Department catches fire, and the entire building is destroyed.
- You find that the room that holds backup tapes has become infested with tape-eating mice. All backup tapes in the room were destroyed.
- You discover that a disgruntled former employee stole an administrator's password to your system, and has been illegally accessing the system for over a year. You don't know if the former employee has stolen information, introduced viruses, or destroyed files.

ADDITIONAL PROJECTS

TIP

Click  to access the Web for additional projects.

QUICK CHECK ANSWERS

CHAPTER 1

QuickCheck A
1. central
2. stored
3. system
4. False
5. False
6. operating

QuickCheck B
1. backbone
2. TCP, Transmission Control Protocol
3. servers
4. voice
5. False
6. False
7. national, dial-up
8. False
9. logging in, logging on
10. False

QuickCheck C
1. URL, Uniform Resource Locator
2. case
3. HTML, Hypertext Markup Language
4. home
5. True
6. False
7. query
8. directory, index

QuickCheck D
1. header
2. MIME, Multipurpose Internet Mail Extension
3. True
4. server
5. POP, Post Office Protocol; SMTP, Simple Mail Transfer Protocol
6. inbox; outbox

QuickCheck TechTalk
1. operating system
2. POST, power-on self-test
3. safe
4. True

CHAPTER 2

QuickCheck A
1. digital; analog
2. binary, base 2
3. True
4. extended ASCII
5. ASCII; binary
6. True
7. integrated circuit, IC, microprocessor

QuickCheck B
1. ALU, Arithmetic Logic Unit
2. control unit
3. True
4. clock, system clock
5. megabytes, MB
6. capacitors
7. ROM, read-only memory
8. CMOS, complementary metal oxide semiconductor

QuickCheck C
1. pits
2. access
3. random; sequential
4. density
5. False
6. controller
7. False
8. DVD, DVD-ROM

QuickCheck D
1. expansion
2. slots
3. driver
4. resolution
5. depth
6. False
7. ink jet, ink jet printers

QuickCheck TechTalk
1. machine
2. op, operation
3. pointer
4. register

CHAPTER 3

QuickCheck A
1. executable
2. properties
3. high; machine
4. compiler
5. system

QuickCheck B
1. resource
2. memory, RAM
3. interface
4. kernel
5. multiuser
6. network, server
7. server; desktop

QuickCheck C
1. production
2. spreadsheet
3. file; database
4. graphics
5. digital
6. vertical

QuickCheck D
1. setup
2. zipped, compressed
3. uninstall
4. copyright
5. shareware
6. source
7. domain

QuickCheck TechTalk
1. True
2. system
3. user
4. editor

CHAPTER 4

QuickCheck A
1. conventions
2. reserved
3. format
4. root
5. specification, path
6. date

QuickCheck B
1. save as
2. logical
3. tracks;
   sectors
4. file
5. allocation

QuickCheck C
1. .exe
2. sector
3. worm
4. False
5. True
6. checksum
7. stealth
8. hoax

QuickCheck D
1. backup
2. Registry
3. boot
4. copy disk, disk copy
5. My Documents

QuickCheck TechTalk
1. header
2. support
3. native
4. conversion

CHAPTER 5

QuickCheck A
1. waveform
2. bandwidth
3. physical;
   logical
4. circuit;
   packet
5. Ethernet

QuickCheck B
1. ARPANET
2. routers
3. latency
4. TCP, Transmission Control
   Protocol;
   IP, Internet Protocol
5. dynamic
6. domain

QuickCheck C
1. modulation;
   demodulation
2. baud
3. downstream;
   upstream
4. always-on
5. ISDN, Integrated Services Digital
   Network
6. latency, delays
7. True

QuickCheck D
1. False
2. site
3. drive mapping, mapping
4. router, hub/router
5. translation

QuickCheck TechTalk
1. seven, 7
2. physical;
   application
3. stack
4. True

CHAPTER 6

QuickCheck A
1. hypertext
2. tags
3. browser
4. HTTP, hypertext transfer protocol
5. port
6. cookie

QuickCheck B
1. editor
2. head
3. external
4. graphic
5. PNG, Portable Network Graphics
6. mailto
7. map
8. Web page tables, tables
9. frame, HTML frame, Hypertext
   Markup Language frame

QuickCheck C
1. DHTML, Dynamic HTML
2. XML, eXtensible Markup
   Language
3. XHTML, HTML 5
4. client
5. bytecode
6. ActiveX

QuickCheck D
1. digital
2. cookies
3. sniffer
4. False
5. True

QuickCheck TechTalk
1. plain text;
   ciphertext
2. symmetric
3. public
4. PGP, Pretty Good Privacy

API (Application Program(ing) Interface) A set of application programs or operating system functions that can be utilized by a program. 600

APL The acronym for A Programming Language, a high-level scientific programming language used to manipulate tables of numbers. 553

Animated GIF A type of GIF image that displays a sequence of frames to create the appearance of continuous motion. 294

Antivirus software A computer program used to scan a computer's memory and disks to identify, isolate, and eliminate viruses. 189

Apple I An unassembled computer kit released in 1977 by Apple Computer Corp. for computer hobbyists. 395

Apple II A complete microcomputer system developed by Apple Computer Corp. introduced in 1978 that helped broaden the personal computer market beyond hobbyists. 395

Apple Lisa A personal computer system developed and manufactured by Apple Computer Corp. that featured one of the first graphical user interfaces. 396

Apple Macintosh First released in 1984, it was one of the first commercially successful personal computers sold with graphical user interface software. 396

Application development tool Software, such as 4GLs, expert system shells, and component objects that can be assembled into applications software for an information system. 466

Application linking A process that allows one or more software applications to exchange data. 616

Application software Computer programs that help you perform a specific task such as word processing. Also called application programs, applications, or programs. 12, 117

Application specifications A detailed description of the way that the software for an information system should interface with the user, store data, process data, and format reports. 469

Application testing The process of testing newly developed application software by running unit tests, integration tests, and system tests. 472

Archiving The process of moving infrequently used data from a primary storage device to a storage medium such as a CD-ROM. 86

Argument In the context of Prolog programming, an argument describes a predicate and is enclosed in parentheses in a Prolog fact. 587

ASCII (American Standard Code for Information Interchange) A code that represents characters as a series of 1s and 0s. Most computers use ASCII code to represent text, making it possible to transfer data between computers. 60

ASF (Advanced Streaming Format) Microsoft's video format for streaming video on the Web. 354

ASP (Active Server Page) An HTML document which includes scripts that are processed by a Microsoft Web server before sending a response back to the user. 314

Assembly language A low-level computer programming language that uses simple commands and is translated into machine language by an assembler. 551

Assumption In the context of programming, a condition that you accept to be true, which often places limits on the scope of the programming problem. 554

Asynchronous protocol A data transmission method in which the sender and receiver are not synchronized by a clock signal, and must use start and stop bits to control the beginning and ending of transmissions. 227

ATM (Asynchronous Transfer Mode) A network technology that transmits all packets in a message over the same channel. 230

Atanasoff-Berry Computer (ABC) An early electronic computer prototype that incorporated the use of vacuum tubes for data processing instead of mechanical switches. 389

Attribute In a database, the columns in a table that are equivalent to fields. In object-oriented databases it is a data element that is stored as part of an object. 500

Audio editing software A program that enables users to create and edit digital voice and music recordings. 143

Audio Interchange Format (.aif) An audio file format developed by Apple that is a popular cross-platform audio format. 366

Automatic recalculation A feature found in spreadsheet software that automatically recalculates every formula after a user makes a change to any cell. 135

AVI (Audio Video Interleave) A video file format, developed by Microsoft, that is the most common format for desktop video on the PC. 354

B2B (Business-To-Business) An e-commerce exchange of products, services, or information between businesses. 310

B2C (Business-To-Consumer) An e-commerce exchange of products, services, or information between businesses and consumers. 309

B2G (Business-To-Government) An e-commerce exchange of products, services, or information between businesses and governments. 310

Backtracking In the context of Prolog programming, backtracking is the process of evaluating all combinations of facts and rules. 591

Backup A duplicate copy of a file, disk, or tape. Also refers to a Windows utility that allows you to create and restore backups. 193

Backup software A set of utility programs that performs a variety of backup related tasks, such as helping users select files for backup. 200

Bandwidth The data transmission capacity of a communications channel. Digital signals are measured in bits per second, analog signals in Hertz. 222

BASIC (Beginners All-purpose Symbolic Instruction Code) A simple high-level programming language that was popularized by Microsoft in the 1970s. 553

Batch processing A processing system that involves holding a group of transactions for processing until the end of a specified period of time. 449

Baud rate The number of times per second that a signal in a communications channel varies. 242

Beep code A series of audible beeps used to announce diagnostic test results during the boot process. 45

Benchmarks A set of tests used to measure computer hardware or software performance. 68

Beowulf cluster Several off-the-shelf computers that are interconnected and configured as a cluster to perform high-performance computing tasks. 643

Beta test A testing phase near the end of the software development process in which a software product is tested in real-world computer environments, often by end-users. 404

Binary digits Series of 1s and 0s representing data. 58

Binary number system A method for representing numbers using only two digits, 0 and 1. Contrast to the decimal number system, which uses ten digits: 0, 1, 2, 3, 4, 5, 6, 7, 8, and 9. 59

Biological computing The use of DNA molecules to perform computing tasks. 431

Bit The smallest unit of information handled by a computer. A bit is one of two values, either a 0 or a 1. Eight bits comprise a byte, which can represent a letter or number. 11

Bitmap graphic An image, such as a digital photo, that is stored as a gridwork of colored dots. 332

Blade server A modular circuit board in a pizza-box sized housing that contains one or more processors and may include storage. Often mounted in a rack with other similar devices and used as servers. 621

BLOB (Binary Large OBject) A collection of binary data that is stored in a single field of a database. 515

Bluetooth A wireless technology used in conjunction with standard Ethernet networks that allows data transfer rates between 200 and 700 Kbps, up to a maximum range of 35 feet. 256

BMP The native bitmap graphic file format of the Microsoft Windows OS. 341

Body section A part of a Web page that begins with the <BODY> tag and contains the text, graphics, and links. 291

Boolean operators A set of search operators such as AND, OR, and NOT that help form complex queries. 529

Boot disk A floppy disk or CD that contains the files needed for the boot process. 197

Boot process The sequence of events that occurs within a computer system between the time the user starts the computer and the time it is ready to process commands. 44

Boot sector virus A computer virus that infects the sectors on a disk that contain the data a computer uses during the boot process. The virus spreads every time the infected disk is in the computer when it boots. 186

Bootstrap program A program stored in ROM that loads and initializes the operating system on a computer. 121

BPR (Business Process Redesign) A technique for improving a business by making radical changes to existing business procedures or organizational structure. 448

Broadband A term used to refer to communications channels that have high bandwidth. 222

Broken link A non-functioning Web link. 296

Browser A program that communicates with a Web server and displays Web pages. 28

Brute force method A method of breaking encryption code by trying all possible encryption keys, usually employing supercomputers. 319

Business An organization that seeks profit by providing goods and services. 444

Byte An 8-bit unit of information that represents a single character. 11

Bytecode A compiled Java applet that is executed by Java Virtual Machine. 303, 598

C A compiled procedural language that provides both high-level commands and low-level access to hardware. 553

C# A derivative of C++ programming language developed by Microsoft. 553

C++ An object-oriented version of the C programming language. 553

C2C (Consumer-To-Consumer) An e-commerce exchange of products, services, or information between consumers. 309

Cable modem A communications device that can be used to connect a computer to the Internet via the cable TV infrastructure. 19, 244

Decision support worksheet A tool used by a project team to evaluate the criteria for each solution by assigning a score and a weight to each criteria which are then compared in a table. 467

Decision table A tabular method for listing rules and specifying the outcomes for various combinations of rules. 587

Declarative paradigm An approach to the programming process in which a programmer writes a program by specifying a set of statements and rules that define the conditions for solving a problem. 586

deColmar's Arithmometer The first commercially successful, mass-produced mechanical calculator. 387

Decryption The process of converting ciphertext into plaintext. 318

Defragmentation utility A software tool used to rearrange the files on a disk so that they are stored in contiguous clusters. 183

DELETE An SQL keyword that removes a record from a table. 527

Demodulation The process of changing a received signal back to its original state (for example, when a modem changes an audio signal back to a digital pulse). 241

Denial of Service attacks An attack that is designed to overwhelm a network's processing capabilities, shutting it down. 187

DES (Data Encryption Standard) An encryption method based on an algorithm developed by IBM and the National Security Agency that uses 56-bit symmetric key encryption. 320

Design phase The process a project team uses for figuring out how to implement a new system. This phase is undertaken after the analysis phase is complete. 464

Desktop computers Computers small enough to fit on a desk and built around a single microprocessor chip. 6

Desktop operating system An operating system such as Windows Me or Mac OSX that is specifically designed for personal computers. 122

Desktop publishing software Software used to create high-quality output suitable for commercial printing. DTP software provides precise control over layout. 128

Desktop video Videos stored in digital format on a PC's hard disk or CD. 353

Detail reports Organized lists generated by a management information system (for example, an inventory list). 450

Device driver The software that provides the computer with the means to control a peripheral device. 92

DHTML (dynamic HTML) A variation of the HTML format that allows elements of Web pages to be changed while they are being viewed. 300

Dial-up connection A connection that uses a phone line to establish a temporary Internet connection. 18

Dictionary-based compression A data compression scheme that uses a code word to represent common sequences of characters. 372

Difference Engine A mechanical calculator design created by Charles Babbage that used steam power for fully automatic operation. It was never built. 388

Differential backup A copy of all the files that changed since the last full backup of a disk. 196

Digital Any system that works with discrete data, such as 0s and 1s, in contrast to analog. 11

Digital camera A camera that takes and stores a digital image instead of recording onto film. 333

Digital certificate A security method that identifies the author of an ActiveX control. A computer programmer can "sign" a digital certificate after being approved. 306

Digital device A device that works with discrete (distinct or separate) numbers or digits. 58

Digital electronics Circuitry that's designed to work with digital signals. 58

Digital signal processor Circuitry that is used to process, record, and playback audio files. 366

Digital video camera A device used to collect, store and process video in a digital format. 355

Digitize To convert non-digital information or media to a digital format through the use of a scanner, sampler, or other input device. 61

Digitizing tablet A device that provides a flat surface for a paper-based drawing, and a "pen" used to create hand-drawn vector drawings. 346

DIMM Short for dual in-line memory module, a DIMM is a small circuit board that holds RAM chips. A DIMM has a 64-bit path to the memory chips. 63

DIP (dual in-line package) A chip configuration characterized by a rectangular body with numerous plugs along its edge. 63

Direct conversion The simultaneous deactivation of an old computer system and activation of a new one. 474

Direct satellite service (DSS) A service that uses a geosynchronous or low-earth orbit satellite to send television, voice, or computer data directly to satellite dishes owned by individuals. 249

Directory A list of files contained on a computer storage device. 172

Disaster recovery plan A step-by-step plan that describes the methods used to secure equipment and data against disasters, and how to recover from disasters. 651

Disk density The closeness of the particles on a disk surface. As density increases, the particles are packed more tightly together and are usually smaller. 80

Distributed computer system A collection of connected computers in which processing, data, and application software are dispersed among more than one physical computer. 635

Distributed database A database that is stored on different computers, on different networks, or in different locations. 506

Distributed processing An information system design in which data is processed on multiple workstations or servers. 465

Distribution disks One or more floppy disks or CDs that contain programs and data, which can be installed to a hard disk. 148

Dithering A means of reducing the size of a graphics file by reducing the number of colors. Dithering uses patterns composed of two or more colors to produce the illusion of additional colors and shading. 340

DMA Short for direct memory access, DMA refers to specialized circuitry that transfers data between drives and RAM, bypassing the CPU. 82

DOCSIS (Data Over Cable Services Interface Specification) A security technology used for filtering packets to certain ports. 245

Document production software Computer programs that assist the user in composing, editing, designing, and printing documents. 128

Documentation A permanent record that explains how a computer program works. 560

Domain name Short for "fully qualified domain name;" an identifying name by which host computers on the Internet are familiarly known (for example, "cocacola.com"). 235

Domain name servers Computers that host the domain name system database. 236

Domain name system A large database of unique IP addresses that correspond with domain names. 236

DOS (disk operating system) The operating system software shipped with the first IBM PCs, and used on millions of computers until the introduction of Microsoft Windows. 126

Dot matrix printer A printer that creates characters and graphics by striking an inked ribbon with small wires called "pins," generating a fine pattern of dots. 96

Dot pitch The diagonal distance between colored dots on a display screen. Measured in millimeters, dot pitch helps to determine the quality of an image displayed on a monitor. 93

Downloading The process of transferring a copy of a file from a remote computer to a local computer's disk drive. 17

Downstream In direct satellite service terminology, the direction in which DirecPC satellites transmit, from the satellite to the user. 242

Drawing software Programs that are used to create images with lines, shapes, and colors, such as logos or diagrams. 141, 346

Drive bays Areas within a computer system unit that can accommodate additional storage devices. 78

Drive mapping In network terminology, assigning a drive letter to a network server disk drive. 258

DSL (Digital Subscriber Line) A high-speed Internet connection that uses existing telephone lines, requiring close proximity to a switching station. 20, 247

DSL modem A device that sends and receives digital data to and from computers over telephone lines. 248

DSLAM (DSL Access Multiplexor) Special equipment used to interpret, separate, and route digital data in telephone lines for DSL providers. 247

DSS (Digital Satellite System) A type of Internet connection that uses a network of satellites to transmit data. 20

DTD files (Document Type Definition files) A type of file that defines how markup tags are interpreted by a browser. 301

DVD (Digital Video Disc) An optical storage medium similar in appearance and technology to a CD-ROM but with higher storage capacity. The acronym stands for "digital video disc" or "digital versatile disc." 86

DVD drive An optical storage device that reads data from CD-ROM and DVD disks. 10

DVD-RAM A technology that allows users to record data on a DVD disk. 87

DVD-ROM A DVD disk that contains data that has been permanently stamped on the disk surface. 86

DVD-RW A technology that allows users to record data on a DVD disk. 87

DVD+RW A DVD technology that allows users to record and change data on DVD disks. 87

DVD-Video DVD disks that contain digital movies. 86

Dye sublimation printer An expensive, color-precise printer that heats ribbons containing color to produce consistent, photograph-quality images. 95

Dynamic IP address A temporarily assigned IP address usually provided by an ISP. 235

Dynamic Web publishing A way of displaying data in a database as customized Web pages as needed. 508

EAI (Enterprise Application Integration) The use of networked software and databases for providing unrestricted sharing of data in an organization. 448

Ear training software Software used by musicians to develop tuning skills, recognize keys, and develop musical skills. 143

EBCDIC (Extended Binary-Coded Decimal Interchange Code) A method by which digital computers, usually mainframes, represent character data. 60

E-commerce Short for electronic commerce, it is the business of buying and selling products online. 16, 309

EDI (Electronic Data Interchange) The ability to transfer data between different companies using networks which enable companies to buy, sell, and trade information. 448

Educational software Software used to develop and practice skills. 144

EIDE Short for enhanced integrated drive (or device) electronics, EIDE is a disk drive technology formally known as ATA. 82

Eiffel An object-oriented programming language with syntax similar to C. 553

Electronic mail (E-mail) A single electronic message or the entire system of computers and software that handles electronic messages. 36

Electronic wallet Software that stores and processes customer information needed for an e-commerce transaction. 315

E-mail Messages that are transmitted between computers over a communications network. Short for electronic mail. 16

E-mail account A service that provides an e-mail address, and mailbox. 36

E-mail attachment A separate file that is transmitted along with an e-mail message. 37

E-mail client software Software that is installed on a client computer and has access to e-mail servers on a network. This software is used to compose, send, and read e-mail messages. 41

E-mail message A computer file containing a letter or memo that is transmitted electronically via a communications network. 36

E-mail servers A computer that uses special software to store, and send, e-mail messages over the Internet. 40

E-mail system The collection of computers and software that works together to provide e-mail services. 40

Employment agency A placement service that works on the behalf of employees to help find employers for people who are seeking work. 427

Encapsulation An object-oriented technique in which the internal details of an object are "hidden" in order to simplify their use and reuse. 585

Encryption The process of scrambling or hiding information so that it cannot be understood without the key necessary to change it back into its original form. 318

ENIAC (Electronic Numerical Integrator and Computer) An early electronic computer prototype that was designed for the U.S. Army for calculating trajectories and was completed in 1945. 390

ENIGMA A German cipher machine used during WWII to send encoded military messages. The encrypted data was eventually cracked by COLOSSUS. 390

Enterprise application integration (EAI) The process of configuring software applications so that they can exchange data. 615

Enterprise computing The use of one or more information systems that share data and typically provide information to hundreds or thousands of users who may be located in diverse locations. 612

Enterprise hardware integration The process of using specialized hardware and software to connect diverse types of hardware enabling them to exchange data. 615

Enterprise system integration The process of connecting two or more information systems in a way that allows scalability and data sharing. 615

Entity-relationship diagram (ERD) A diagram that graphically depicts relationships between record types. 498

Equipment manufacturers Companies that design and manufacture computer hardware and communication products. 398

Ergonomics The science of designing safe, comfortable, efficient machines and tools for human use. 414

ERP (Enterprise Resource Planning) A system of business management that integrates all resources of a business, including planning, manufacturing, sales, and marketing. 448

Ethernet A type of network on which network nodes are connected by coaxial cable or twisted-pair wire; the most popular network architecture, it typically transmits data at 10 or 100 megabits per second. 229

Even parity protocol In a parity bit error-checking system, the requirement that there be an even number of bits in a data block. 227

Event In the context of programming, an action or change in state that requires a response from the computer. 558

Event-driven paradigm An approach to programming in which a programmer creates programs that continually check for, and respond to, program events, such as mouse clicks. 559

Event-handling code The program segment that instructs the computer how to react to events, such as mouse clicks. 558

Exa- Prefix for a quintillion. 61

Exception report A report generated by a management information system, listing information that is outside normal or acceptable ranges, such as a reorder report showing low-stock inventory items. 451

Executable file A file, usually with an .exe extension, containing instructions that tell a computer how to perform a specific task. 11

Executive information system (EIS) A special type of a decision support system that is designed to provide senior managers with information relevant to strategic management activities. 452

Expansion bus The segment of the data bus that transports data between RAM and peripheral devices. 88

Expansion card A circuit board that is plugged into a slot on a PC motherboard to add extra functions, devices, or ports. 88

Expansion port A socket into which the user plugs a cable from a peripheral device, allowing data to pass between the computer and the peripheral device. 90

Expansion slot A socket or "slot" on a PC motherboard designed to hold a circuit board called an expansion card. 88

Expert system A computer system incorporating knowledge from human experts, and designed to analyze data and produce a recommendation or decision (also called knowledge-based system). 453

Expert system shell A software tool used for developing expert system applications. 454

Export routine A program that copies data out of a software package such a spreadsheet software, and into a database. 524

Extended ASCII Similar to ASCII but with 8-bit character representation instead of 7-bit, allowing for an additional 128 characters. 60

External entity A person, organization, or device that exists outside an information system, but provides it with input or receives output. On a DFD, usually represented by a square. 478

External information Information obtained by organizations from outside sources. 446

External link A hyperlink that links to a location outside the Web site. 295

External style sheet A template that contains formatting specifications for a group of Web pages. 292

External video A video on the Web that, when the link to it is clicked, downloads and opens in a media player window. 361

Extranet A network similar to a private internet that also allows outside users access. 228

Fact In the context of Prolog programming, a fact is a statement incorporated into a program that provides basic information for solving a problem. 586

Fault tolerance Refers to a computer system's ability to react gracefully to unexpected software or hardware failures. 642

FDDI (Fiber Distributed Data Interconnect) A high-speed network that uses fiber-optic cables to link workstations. 230

Fiber-optic cable A bundle of thin tubes of glass used to transmit data as pulses of light. 221

Field The smallest meaningful unit of information contained in a data file. 137, 494

Field format A specification for the way that data is displayed on the screen and printouts, usually using a series of Xs to indicate characters and 9s to indicate numbers. 516

Field name A name that identifies the contents of a field. 494

Field validation rule A specification that a database designer sets up to filter the data entered into a particular field. 516

Fifth-generation languages Either declarative languages, such as Prolog, or programming languages that allow programmers to use graphical or visual tools to construct programs. 552

File A named collection of data (such as a computer program, document, or graphic) that exists on a storage medium, such as a hard disk, floppy disk, or CD-ROM. 11

File allocation table (FAT) A special file that is used by some operating systems to store the physical location of all the files on a storage medium, such as a hard disk or floppy disk. 181

File compression utility A type of data compression software that shrinks one or more files into a single file that occupies less storage space than the separate files. 374

File date The date that a file was created or last modified. 173

File format The method of organization used to encode and store data in a computer. Text formats include DOC and TXT. Graphics formats include BMP, TIFF, GIF, and PCX. 171

File header Hidden information inserted at the beginning of a file to identify its properties, such as the software that can open it. 61

File management Any procedure that is used to organize computer-based file systems. 174

ISA (Industry Standard Architecture) A standard for moving data on the expansion bus. Can refer to a type of slot, a bus, or a peripheral device. An older technology, it is rapidly being replaced by PCI architecture. 89

ISDN (Integrated Services Digital Network) A telephone company service that transports data digitally over dial-up or dedicated lines. 20, 248

ISDN terminal adapter A device that connects a computer to a telephone jack, and translates the data into a signal that can travel over an ISDN connection. 248

ISP (Internet Service Provider) A company that provides Internet access to businesses, organizations, and individuals. 20

Iterative SDLC A series of phases that outlines the development process of an information system where each phase is allowed to repeat as needed in the development process. 459

Java A platform-independent, object-oriented, high-level programming language based on C++, typically used to produce interactive Web applications. 303, 553

Java applets Small programs that add processing and interactive capabilities to Web pages. 303

Java Virtual Machine (JVM) A component found in most browsers that executes Java applets. 303, 598

JavaScript A scripting language, based on Java, that is used to design interactive Web sites. 302

JIT (Just In Time) A manufacturing system in which the parts needed to construct a product are received at the assembly site only as needed. 448

Job search agent An automated program that searches one or more databases and notifies you when it finds a lead on a specific job type. 426

JOIN An SQL command that allows the temporary joining and simultaneous accessing of data from more than one table. 532

Joining tables In SQL terminology, the act of creating a relationship between tables. 532

Joint application design (JAD) A widely accepted design technique that is based on the idea that the best information systems are designed when end-users and systems analysts work together on a project as equal partners. 457

JPEG (Joint Photographic Experts Group) A format that uses lossy compression to store bitmap images. JPEG files have a .jpg extension. 293, 342

Kernel The core module of an operating system that typically manages memory, processes, tasks, and disks. 121

Key frame Frames at equal intervals in a digital video clip that contain all data for that frame. The rest of the frames in the video contain only the information that is different from the preceding key frame. 374

Keyword 1) A word or term used as the basis for a database or Web-page search. 2) A command word supplied by a programming language. 32, 550

Kilobit (Kbit or Kb) 1,024 bits. 61

Kilobyte (KB) Approximately 1,000 bytes; exactly 1,024 bytes. 61

Knowledge base The collection of facts and rules obtained from experts that forms the information base of an expert system. 454

Knowledge engineering The process of designing, entering rules into, and testing rules in an expert system. 472

Known information In a problem statement, information supplied to the computer to help it solve a problem. 555

Label In the context of spreadsheets, any text used to describe data. 133

LAN (local area network) An interconnected group of computers and peripherals located within a relatively limited area, such as a building or campus. 7, 228

Lands Non-pitted surface areas on a CD that represent digital data. (See also Pits.) 78

Laser light A focused beam of light that, with a clear line of sight, can transmit data over long distances. 222

Laser printer A printer that uses laser-based technology, similar to that used by photocopiers, to produce text and graphics. 95

Latency The elapsed time it takes for a packet of data to arrive at its destination. 233

LCD (liquid crystal display) A type of flat panel computer screen, typically found on notebook computers. 9, 92

LCD screen (See LCD.)

Leading Also called line spacing, the vertical spacing between lines of text. 131

Legacy system A computer system that has become outdated due to technology advances or changing organizational requirements. 621

Leibniz Calculator A mechanical calculator capable of performing the four arithmetic functions and helped develop the technology for the first commercially successful calculator. 387

Level 1 cache (L1 cache) Cache memory built into a microprocessor chip. L1 cache typically can be read in one clock cycle. 68

Level 2 cache (L2 cache) Cache memory that is located in a chip separate from the microprocessor chip. 68

Line printer A printer which produces an entire line of text (as opposed to a single character) in one operation. 625

Line spacing (See Leading.)

Linear editing A video editing technique that records segments of video from one tape to another. 358

Link tags HTML code that is used to designate text as a hyperlink in a document. 279

Links Underlined text that allow users to jump between Web pages. 26

Linux A server operating system that is a derivative of UNIX and available as freeware. 125

LISP (LISt Processor) A declarative programming language that excels at handling complex data structures, artificial intelligence research, and very complex programs. 553

List price The price set on a product by the manufacturer. 403

Load balancing The process of distributing processing and storage tasks among the nodes of a cluster in a way that optimizes the performance of the entire system. 642

Logic error A run-time error in the logic or design of a computer program. 559

Logical address A network address that is assigned to a network device when the physical address is in an incorrect format. 223

Logical data type A data type specifying that a field in a data file is used to store true/false or yes/no data. 514

Logical port A non-physical connection point between network nodes. 283

Logical storage models Also referred to as metaphors, any visual aid that helps a computer user visualize a file system. 177

Logical topology Network topology that corresponds with the way messages flow across the network, not necessarily identical to the network's physical topology. 225

Lookup routine A validation process used by database designers to prevent data entry errors by searching for the entry in a file or database table. 517

Loop The section of program code that is repeated because of a repetition control structure. 571

Lossless compression A compression technique that provides the means to reconstitute all of the data in the original file, hence "lossless" means that this compression technique does not lose data. 373

Lossy compression Any data compression technique in which some of the data is sacrificed to obtain more compression. 373

Low-level language A computer language that requires a programmer to write instructions for specific hardware elements such as the computer processor, registers, and RAM locations. 550

MAC address (Media Access Control address) A unique address given to an NIC. 257

Mac OS The operating system software designed for use on Apple Macintosh and iMac computers. 124

Machine code Program instructions written in binary code that the computer can execute directly. 98

Machine language A low-level language written in binary code that the computer can execute directly. 115, 551

Macro A small set of instructions that automates a task. Typically, a macro is created by performing the task once and recording the steps. Whenever the macro is played back, the steps are repeated. 186

Macro virus A computer virus that infects the macros that are attached to documents and spreadsheets. (See Macro.) 186

Macs (Macintosh computers) A personal computer platform designed and manufactured by Apple Computer. 13

Magnetic storage The recording of data onto disks or tape by magnetizing particles of an oxide-based surface coating. 77

Mail merge A feature of document production software that automates the process of producing customized documents, such as form letters and advertising flyers. 132

Mail order A type of retailing where a merchant takes orders by telephone or from an Internet site, then ships orders by mail or other courier service. 407

Mailing list server Any computer and software that maintains a list of people who are interested in a topic, and facilitates message exchanges among all members of the list. 16

Mailto link A link on a Web page that automatically opens a pre-addressed e-mail form. 295

Mainframe computer A large, fast, and expensive computer generally used by businesses or government agencies to provide centralized storage processing and management for large amounts of data. 8

Maintenance phase The day-to-day operation of an information system, including making modifications and correcting problems to insure correct operation. 475

MAN (Metropolitan Area Network) A public, high-speed network that can transmit voice and data within a range of 50 miles. 228

Management information system (MIS) A type of information system that manipulates the data collected by a transaction processing system to generate reports that managers can use to make business decisions. 450

Managers People who make decisions about how an organization carries out its activities. 445

Manual calculator A device that helps solve mathematical calculations and does not contain any algorithms. 386

Manufacturer direct The selling of products by hardware manufacturers directly to consumers, by means of a sales force or mail order. 407

Manufacturing technician A computer professional who participates in the fabrication of computer chips, systems, and devices. 412

Many-to-many relationship A relationship in which one record in a particular record type can be related to more than one record in another record type, and vice versa. 497

Mark-8 A microprocessor based computer system developed by Jonathan A. Titus in 1974 that helped lead to the development of personal computers. 394

Market share A company's share, or percentage, of the total market. 404

Market tiers Categories of computer companies that separate these companies by size, longevity, and market share. 405

Marketing channels Marketing outlets such as retail stores or mail order for computer-related products. 406

Markup language A language that provides text and graphics formatting through the use of tags. Examples of markup languages include HTML, XML, SGML. 276

Massively parallel processing (MPP) The process of linking multiple processors, each with its own bus, memory, and operating system. 628

Mathematical modeling software Software for visualizing and solving a wide range of math, science, and engineering problems. 136

Mathematical operators Symbols such as + / * -, that represent specific mathematical functions in a formula. 134

Mean time between failures (MTBF) A statistic that indicates the average length of time that a device is expected to operate without malfunctioning. 648

Mechanical calculator A machine capable of implementing algorithms used to solve mathematical calculations. 387

Media tags HTML code that specifies how to display media elements in a document. 279

Megabit (Mb or Mbit) 1,048,576 bits. 61

Megabyte (MB) Approximately 1 million bytes; exactly 1,048,576 bytes. 61

Megahertz (MHz) A measure of frequency equivalent to 1 million cycles per second. 67

Megapixels Millions of pixels, expresses the resolution and quality of an image. 335

Member In a network database model, a record type related to another record type higher up in the network model. 499

Memo data type A data type that specifies that a field in a data file can contain variable-length text comments (also called memo field). 514

Memory The computer circuitry that holds data waiting to be processed. 5

Memory card reader A device that connects to a PC via a USB or Serial cable that reads data from a flash memory module. 334

Message In the context of object-oriented programming, input that is collected and sent to an object. 579

Message header The section of an e-mail document that contains the address, subject, and file attachment information. 36

Metafiles Graphics files that contain both vector and bitmap data. 348

Metasearch tool A program that performs broad-based Web searches, such as searching more than one job database at a time. 426

Method The actions that an object can perform. 578

MICR (Magnetic Ink Character Recognition) The use of specialized inks and fonts (such as check routing numbers) to allow printed material to be read by machines. 624

Microcomputer A category of computer that is built around a single microprocessor chip. 6

Microprocessor An integrated circuit that contains the circuitry for processing data. It is a single-chip version of the central processing unit (CPU) found in all computers. 6, 66

Microprocessor clock A device on the motherboard of a computer responsible for setting the pace of executing instructions. 67

Microsoft Windows An operating system, developed by Microsoft Corporation, that provides a graphical interface. Versions include Windows 3.1, Windows 95, Windows 98, Windows Me, Windows XP, Windows NT, and Windows 2000. 122

Microwaves Electromagnetic waves with a frequency of at least 1 gigahertz. 222

Middleware A type of software that acts as an intermediary between two other software packages. 630

MIDI (Musical Instrument Digital Interface) A standardized way in which sound and music are encoded and transmitted between devices that play music. 368

MIDI sequence Digitally encoded music stored on a computer. Usually is a file with a .mid, .cmf, or .rol file extension. 368

MIDI sequencing software Software that uses a standardized way of transmitting encoded music or sounds for controlling musical devices, such as a keyboard or sound card. 143

Migration In the context of hierarchical storage management (HSM), the process of moving data from one storage tier to another. Also called relocation. 653

MIME (Multipurpose Internet Mail Extension) A conversion process used for formatting non-ASCII messages so that they can be sent over the Internet. 37

Minicomputer A mid-range computer, somewhat larger than a microcomputer, that can carry out processing tasks for many simultaneous users. 6

MIPS (Millions of Instructions Per Second) A measure of the speed at which a computer executes instructions of any kind. (As opposed to FLOPS, which measures floating point execution speed.) 618

Mirroring A technique for creating a real-time "mirror image" of a storage medium, such as a hard disk. 623

Mission An organization's goal or plan, and reflected by the organization's activities. 444

Mission statement The written expression of an organization's goals and how those goals will be accomplished. 444

MITS Altair The first commercial microcomputer. It was based on the Intel 8080 processor and sold primarily to computer hobbyists. 394

Modem A device that sends and receives data to and from computers. (See voice band modem, cable modem.) 10, 241

Modified waterfall SDLC A series of phases that outlines the development process of an information system where each phase can overlap and be repeated as necessary in the development process. 459

Modulation The process of changing the characteristics of a signal (for example, when a modem changes a digital pulse into an analog signal). 241

Molecular computing The use of individual molecules to build components that perform functions similar to transistors and other components of microchips. 430

Monitor A display device that forms an image by converting electrical signals from the computer into points of colored light on the screen. 9

Monochrome bitmap A bitmap image that contains only the colors black and white. 338

Motherboard The main circuit board in a computer that houses chips and other electronic components. 63

Mouse An input device, located on the surface of a desk, that allows the user to manipulate objects on the screen by clicking, dragging, and dropping. 9

MP3 A file format that provides highly compressed audio files with very little loss of sound quality. 143, 366

MP3 encoding software Software that compresses a WAV file into an MP3 file. 143, 366

MP3 encoder Software that compresses a WAV file into an MP3 file. 367

MP3 player Software that plays MP3 music files. 143

MPEG (Moving Pictures Expert Group) A highly compressed file format for digital videos. Files in this format have a .mpg extension. 354

MRP (Manufacturing Resource Planning) A system of business management where an optimum manufacturing plan is generated based on a wide variety of data. 448

MSIL (Microsoft Intermediate Language) An intermediate language that is the result of compiling code from the .NET framework. MSIL must be further compiled at runtime. 599

Multidimensional database A database that provides built-in methods to display and store data in a multidimensional structure. 537

Multiparadigm language A programming language that supports more than one paradigm, such as object-oriented and procedural paradigms. 553

Multiple-user license Legal permission for more than one person to use a particular software package. 257

Multiprocessor architecture A type of computer design that incorporates more than one microprocessor to increase processing capacity. 627

Multi-partite viruses A computer virus that is able to infect many types of targets by hiding itself in numerous locations on a computer. 190

Multitasking operating system An operating system that runs two or more programs at the same time. 122

Multiuser operating system An operating system that allows a single computer to deal simultaneously with processing requests from multiple users. 122

Nanometer A unit of length that is one billionth of a meter. (A meter is about 39 inches.) 66

Nanosecond A unit of time representing 1 billionth of a second. 72

Napier's Bones A manual calculator created by John Napier that could be used to perform mathematical calculations by manipulating numbered rods. 387

Narrowband A term that refers to communications channels that have low bandwidth. 222

Native file format A file format that is unique to a program or group of programs and has a unique file extension. 171

Natural language query A query using language spoken by human beings, as opposed to an artificially constructed language such as machine language. 140

NetBIOS/NetBEUI A networking protocol developed by Microsoft and typically used for Microsoft networks. 256

Netiquette Internet etiquette or a set of guidelines for posting messages and e-mails in a civil, concise way. 39

Network address translation (NAT) An Internet standard that allows a LAN to use one type of IP address for LAN data, and another type of address for data to and from the Internet. 260

Network attached storage (NAS) Storage devices that are designed to be attached directly to a network, rather than to a workstation or server. 624

Network card An expansion board mounted inside a computer to allow access to a local area network. Also called a network interface card (NIC). 19

Network database A collection of physically linked records, in a one-to-many relationship, in which a member (child) can have more than one owner (parent). 499

Network interface card (NIC) A small circuit board that sends data from a workstation out over a network, and collects incoming data for the workstation. 223

Network operating system Programs designed to control the flow of data, maintain security, and keep track of accounts on a network. 122

Network service providers (NSP) Companies that maintain a series of nationwide Internet links. 233

Network set Related record types containing an owner and members. 499

Network specialist/administrator A computer professional who plans, installs, and maintains one or more local area networks. 411

Neural network A type of expert system that uses computer circuitry to simulate the way in which the brain processes information, learns, and remembers. 455

Newsgroup An online discussion group that centers around a specific topic. 16

Node In a network, a connection point; in a hierarchical database, a segment or record type. 223

Non-linear editing A digital video editing technique that requires a PC and video editing software. 358

Nonprofit organizations Organizations with political, social, or charitable goals that are not intended to generate a profit. 444

Normalization The process of analyzing data to create the most efficient database structure. 517

Notation software Software used to help musicians compose, edit, and print their compositions. 143

Notebook computers Small, lightweight, portable computers that usually run on batteries. Sometimes called laptops. 6

Novell network A local area network that uses Novell NetWare as its operating system. 228

N-tier systems A distributed computing system that is divided into some number (n) of tiers. 637

Numeric data Numbers that represent quantities and can be used in arithmetic operations. 59

Numeric data type A data type assigned to fields in a data file containing numbers that can be manipulated mathematically. 514

Object In an object-oriented database or programming language, a discrete piece of code describing a person, place, thing, event, or type of information. 575

Object attribute In a database, is equivalent to a field and contains the smallest unit of data. 501

Object code The low-level instructions that result from compiling source code. 115, 598

Object-oriented database A database model that organizes data into classes of objects that can be manipulated by programmer-defined methods. 138, 501

Object-oriented methodology A method of developing an information system that treats an information system as a collection of objects that interact with each other to accomplish tasks. 459

Object-oriented paradigm An approach to programming that focuses on the manipulation of objects rather than on the generation of procedure-based code. 575

OCR (Optical Character Recognition) A technique for converting printed documents into digital data, usually through the use of a scanning device and character-recognition software. 625

Office automation system A system that automates or computerizes routine office tasks, such as producing documents, tracking schedules, making calculations, and facilitating interoffice communications. 448

OLAP (Online analytical processing) A system that consists of computer hardware, database software, and analytical tools that are optimized for analyzing and manipulating data. 535

OLTP systems (Online Transaction Processing Systems) Interactive online transaction processing methods that use a "commit or rollback" strategy to ensure accurate transaction processing. 449

One-time-use credit card A number or code distributed by credit card companies that allows consumers to make purchases while keeping their actual credit card number hidden. 315

One-to-many relationship A relationship in which one record in a particular type may be related to more than one record of another record type. 497

One-to-one relationship An association between database entities in which one record type is related to one record of another type. 498

Online job bank An online database of job opening announcements that spans many industries or just one specific industry. 425

Online processing An interactive method in which each transaction is processed as it is entered. 449

Online shopping cart An e-commerce cookie that stores information about items selected and collected for purchase. 311

OODBMS (Object oriented database management system) Database management software used to construct an object-oriented database. 505

Op code Short for operation code, an op code is an assembly language command word that designates an operation, such as add (ADD), compare (CMP), or jump (JMP). 98

Open source software Software, such as Linux, that includes its uncompiled source code, which can be modified and distributed by programmers. 155

Operand The part of an instruction that specifies the data, or the address of the data, on which the operation is to be performed. 98

Operating system (OS) The software that controls the computer's use of its hardware resources, such as memory and disk storage space. 12, 118

Operational planning The scheduling and monitoring of workers and processes. 445

Operational tags HTML code used to specify the basic setup and database integration for Web pages. 279

Optical storage A means of recording data as light and dark spots on a CD, DVD, or other optical media. 78

Organization A group of people working together to accomplish a goal. 444

Organizational chart An organizational structure used to coordinate the activities of the people in the organization such as a hierarchy of employees. 445

OSI model (Open System Interconnection model) A network model that specifies that a communications network will use seven layers of protocols. 261

Output The results produced by a computer (for example, reports, graphs, and music). 5

Owner In a network database model, a record type that has relationships with other record types at lower levels of the network. 499

P3P (Platform for Privacy Preferences Project) A specification that allows Web browsers to automatically detect a Web site's privacy policies. 286

Packet A small unit of data transmitted over a network or the Internet. 16, 225

Packet sniffer A program that monitors data as it travels over networks. 313

Packet switching A technology used by data communications networks, such as the Internet, where a message is divided into smaller units called "packets" for transmission. 226

Page layout The physical positions of elements on a document page, such as headers, footers, page numbers, and graphics. 131

Paint software The software required to create and manipulate bitmap graphics. 141, 332

Paragraph alignment The horizontal position (left, right, justified, centered, for example) of the text in a document. 131

Paragraph style A specification for the format of a paragraph, which includes the alignment of text within margins and line spacing. 131

Parallel conversion A type of system conversion in which the old computer system remains in service while some or all of the new system is activated. 474

Parallel processing A technique by which two or more processors in a computer perform processing tasks simultaneously. 68, 627

Parameter A delimiting variable used to modify a command, i.e., /ON modifies the DIR command so it displays files in order by name. 528, 550

Parent node In a hierarchical database, a record type that has paths to other record types lower in the hierarchy. 499

Parity bit A bit added to the end of a data block to allow for error checking during data transmission. (See Even parity and Odd parity.) 227

Pascal A high-level, procedural programming language developed to help computer programming students learn the structured approach to programming. 553

Pascaline An early mechanical calculator capable of performing addition, subtraction, division, and multiplication. 387

Passive matrix screen A display found on older notebook computers that relies on timing to ensure that the liquid crystal cells are illuminated. 94

Password A special set of symbols used to restrict access to a user's computer or network. 22

Path A file's location in a file structure. (See File specification.) 172

Payroll software A type of horizontal market software used to maintain payroll records. 147

PC card (PCMCIA card) A credit card-sized circuit board used to connect a modem, memory, network card, or storage device to a notebook computer. 90

PCI (Peripheral Component Interconnect) A method for transporting data on the expansion bus. Can refer to type of data bus, expansion slot, or transport method used by a peripheral device. 89

PCMCIA slot A PCMCIA (Personal Computer Memory Card International Association) slot is an external expansion slot typically found on notebook computers. 90

PCs Microcomputers that use Windows software and contain Intel-compatible microprocessors. 13

PCX The PC Paintbrush file format that incorporates a compression algorithm. 341

PDA (personal digital assistant) A computer that is smaller and more portable than a notebook computer (also called a palm-top computer). 7

Peer-to-peer The process by which one workstation/server shares resources with another workstation/server. Refers to the capability of a network computer to act as both a file server and workstation. 18

Peer-to-peer network A network where workstations act as both a file server and a client. 230

Peripheral device A component or equipment, such as a printer or scanner, that expands a computer's input, output, or storage capabilities. 11

Personal computer A microcomputer designed for use by an individual user for applications such as Internet browsing and word processing. 6

Personal finance software Software geared toward individual finances that helps track bank account balances, credit card payments, investments, and bills. 136

Personal firewall software Software that is designed to analyze and control incoming and outgoing packets. 246

Personal information manager Software that specializes in keeping track of personal data, such as appointments or addresses. 137

Person-to-person payment An e-commerce method of payment that bypasses credit cards and instead, uses an automatic electronic payment service. 317

PGAs (pin-grid arrays) A common chip design used for microprocessors. 63

PGP (Pretty Good Privacy) A popular program used to encrypt and decrypt e-mail messages. 321

Phase change technology A writable CD and DVD technology that uses disks with a modifiable crystal structure, and allows users to add, modify, and delete data. 86

Phased conversion A type of information system conversion in which one module of a new information system is activated at a time. 474

Phonemes Units of sound that are basic components of words, and are produced by speech synthesizers. 369

Photo editing software The software used to edit, enhance, retouch, and manipulate digital photographs. 141

Physical address An address built into the circuitry of a network device at the time of its manufacture. 223

Physical storage model A representation of data as it is physically stored. 180

Physical topology The actual layout of network devices, wires, and cables. 224

PIECES framework A concept developed by James Wetherbe, to help identify problems in an information system. Each letter of PIECES stands for a potential problem (Performance, Information, Economics, Control, Efficiency, and Service). 458

Pilot conversion A type of system conversion in which a new information system is first activated at one branch of a multi-branch company. 474

Ping (Packet Internet GropeR) A command on a TCP/IP network that sends a test packet to a specified IP address and waits for a reply. 233

Pipelining A technology that allows a processor to begin executing an instruction before completing the previous instruction. 68

Pits Spots on a CD that are "burned," representing part of a data unit. 78

Pixels Short for picture element, a pixel is the smallest unit in a graphic image. Computer display devices use a matrix of pixels to display text and graphics. 93

Pixel interpolation A process that is used by graphics software that averages the color of adjacent pixels in an image. 337

Pixelated Describes the effect of increasing the size and thus decreasing the quality of an image. 337

PL/1 (Programming Language 1) A business and scientific programming language developed by IBM in 1964. 553

Plaintext An original, un-encrypted message. 318

Planning phase The first phase of an information system project with the goal of creating a Project Development Plan. 456

Platform A "family" or category of computers based on the same underlying software and hardware. 13

Plug and Play The ability of a computer to automatically recognize and adjust the system configuration for a newly added device. 92

Plug-in A software module that adds a specific feature to a system. For example, in the context of Web browsers, a plug-in adds the ability to play files referenced from the <EMBED> tag. 281

PNG (Portable Network Graphics) A type of graphics file format similar to but newer than GIF or JPEG. 293, 342

Point size A unit of measure (1/72 of an inch) used to describe the height of characters. 130

Polymorphic viruses Viruses that can escape detection from antivirus software by changing their signatures. 190

Polymorphism In the context of object-oriented programming, the ability to redefine a method for a subclass. Also called overloading. 580

POP (Post Office Protocol) A protocol that is used to retrieve e-mail messages from an e-mail server. 40

POP server A computer that receives and stores e-mail data until retrieved by the e-mail account holder. 41

PostScript A printer language, developed by Adobe Systems, which uses a special set of commands to control page layout, fonts, and graphics. 96

POTS An acronym for "plain old telephone service." 240

Power-on self-test (POST) A diagnostic process that runs during startup to check components of the computer, such as the graphics card, RAM, keyboard, and disk drives. 44

Predicate In a Prolog fact, the predicate, such as likes, describes the relationship between the arguments in parentheses, such as (john, mary). 587

Presentation software Software that provides tools to combine text, graphics, graphs, animation, and sound into a series of electronic "slides" that can be output on a projector, or as overhead transparencies, paper copies, or 35-millimeter slides. 142

Primary key A field in a database that contains data that is unique to a record, such as a social security number. 514

Printer Control Language (PCL) A standard language used to send page formatting instructions from a computer to a laser or ink jet printer. 96

Printer server A device that controls a cluster of printers by distributing jobs that arrive in its print queue—a list of documents that require printing. 625

Private attribute An attribute for an object, class, or record that can be accessed only from the program routine in which is defined. 576

Private IP addresses IP addresses that cannot be routed over the Internet. 260

Problem statement In an organization, a one-sentence statement that identifies what needs to be improved or fixed; in software engineering, a definition of elements that must be manipulated in order to achieve a result or goal. 554

Procedural language Computer languages used to create programs composed of a series of statements that tell the computer how to perform a specific task. 562

Procedural paradigm An approach to programming in which a programmer defines the steps for solving a problem. 562

Procedure Step-by-step instructions for performing a specific job or task. 569

Procedure handbook A section of code that performs activities but is not included in the main sequential execution path of a program. 473

Process A systematic series of actions that a computer performs to manipulate data; typically represented on a DFD by a rounded rectangle. 478

Process specifications Written explanations of what happens to data within a process. 480

Processing The manipulation of data using a systematic series of actions. 4

Program editor A programming tool, similar to a word processor, but that provides specialized editing and formatting features to streamline the programming process. 556

Program specification A description of the elements to be included in a computer program. 557

Programming language A set of keywords and grammar rules (syntax) that allows a programmer to write instructions that a computer can execute. 115, 550

Programming paradigm Refers to a programming methodology or approach, as in the term object-oriented paradigm. 553

Project development plan A planning document that is the final result of a planning phase, which is reviewed and approved by management. 456

Project management software Software specifically designed as a tool for planning, scheduling, and tracking projects and their costs. 147

Prolog A declarative programming language used to develop expert systems modeled after human thinking. 553

Properties The characteristics of an object in programs. 114, 557

Proprietary services Services specific to or offered by one company. 22

Protocol stack A group of protocols that work together and are used by a specific network technology. 263

Prototype An experimental or trial version of a device or system. 389

Pseudocode A notational system for algorithms that combines English and a programming language. 565

Public attribute An attribute for an object, class, or record that can be accessed from any routine in a program. 576

Public domain software Software that is available for use by the public without restriction except that it cannot be copyrighted. 155

Speech synthesis The process by which computers produce sound that resembles spoken words. 369

Spelling checker A feature of document production software that checks each word in a document against an electronic dictionary of correctly spelled words, then presents a list of alternatives for possible misspellings. 129

Spelling dictionary A data module that is used by a spelling checker as a list of correctly spelled words. 129

Sports games A type of entertainment software that simulates playing in sporting events. 146

Spreadsheet A numerical model or representation of a real situation, presented in the form of a table. 133

Spreadsheet software Software for creating electronic worksheets that hold data in cells and perform calculations based on that data. 133

SQL (Structured Query Language) A popular query language used by mainframes and microcomputers. 140, 526

SQL keywords A collection of special command words that issue instructions to an SQL database. 527

SQL query A query created by SQL database client software that collects user input which can operate directly on a database to carry out a user's instructions. 526

SSL (Secure Sockets Layer) A security protocol that uses encryption to establish a secure connection between a computer and a Web server. 313

Stateless protocol A protocol that allows one request and response per session, such as HTTP. 283

Static IP address A permanently assigned and unique IP address, used by hosts or servers. 235

Static Web publishing A simple way to display the data in a database by converting a database report into an HTML document. 507

Statistical compression A data compression scheme that uses an algorithm that recodes frequently used data as short bit patterns. 372

Statistical software Software for analyzing large sets of data to discover patterns and relationships within them. 136

Stealth viruses Viruses that can escape detection from antivirus software by removing their signatures and hiding in memory. 190

Storage The area in a computer where data is retained on a permanent basis. 5

Storage area network (SAN) A network of storage devices and data servers configured to function as a single node on a wider network. 623

Storage device A mechanical apparatus that records data to and retrieves data from a storage medium. 76

Storage hierarchy The collection of storage devices in a hierarchical storage system, typically arranged from high-cost, fast media at the top, to low-cost, slower media at the bottom. 653

Storage management services A collection of software- and hardware-based data storage services, such as the ability to automatically store multiple copies of a file. 623

Storage medium The physical material used to store computer data, such as a floppy disk, a hard disk, or a CD-ROM. 76

Storage metaphor A likeness or analogy that helps people visualize the way that computers store files. 177

Store-and-forward technology A technology used by communications networks in which an e-mail message is temporarily held in storage on a server until it is requested by a client computer. 40

Stored program A set of instructions that resides on a storage device, such as a hard drive, and can be loaded into memory and executed. 5

STP (Shielded Twisted Pair) A type of cable consisting of two wires that are twisted together and encased in a protective layer to reduce signal noise. 221

Strategic planning The process of developing long-range goals and plans for an organization. 445

Strategy games A type of entertainment software that allows one or more players to participate in a strategy-oriented game. 146

Streaming video An Internet video technology that sends a small segment of a video file to a user's computer, and begins to play it while the next segment is sent. 361

Street price The average discounted price of a product. 403

Strong encryption Encryption that is difficult to decrypt without the encryption key. 319

Structured English Vocabulary and syntax used by systems analysts to concisely and unambiguously explain the logic of a process. It is limited to words defined in a data dictionary and to specific logical terms such as "if...then,". 565

Structured file A file that consists of a collection of records, each with the same set of fields. 137, 494

Structured methodology A method of developing an information system that focuses on the processes that take place within the information system. 459

Structured problem A problem for which there exists a well-established procedure for obtaining the best solution. 446

Stub A type of placeholder. In the context of hierarchical storage management, a stub holds the place for a file that has migrated to archival storage. 654

Style A feature in many desktop publishing and word processing programs that allows the user to apply numerous format settings in a single command. 131

Subclass In object-oriented programming, a subclass is derived from a superclass and inherits its attributes and methods. 577

Subdirectories Directories found under the root directory. 172

Subroutine A section of code that performs activities or manipulates data but is not included in the main sequential execution path of a program. 569

Success factors System requirements that also serve as an evaluation checklist at the end of a development project. 461

Summary report A report generated by a management information system that combines or groups data and usually provides totals, such as a report of total annual sales for the past five years. 451

Superclass In object-oriented programming, a superclass can provide attributes and methods for subclasses. 577

Supercomputer The fastest and most expensive type of computer, capable of processing more than 1 trillion instructions per second. 8

SVG (Scalable Vector Graphics) A graphics format designed specifically for Web display that automatically resizes when displayed on different screens. 349

SVGA (Super Video Graphics Array) SVGA typically refers to 800 x 600 resolution. 93

SXGA (Super eXtended Graphics Array) A screen resolution of 1280 x 1024. 93

Symmetric key encryption An encryption key that is used for both encryption and decryption of messages. 320

Symmetric multiprocessing (SMP) A type of parallel processing in which a single operating system controls multiple processors sharing a common bus and memory. 627

Synchronous protocol A method of serial communication in which the transmission of data occurs at regular intervals synchronized by the computer's internal clock (for example, used for the communication that takes place on the main circuit board of a computer). 226

Syntax In the context of programming languages, syntax refers to the grammar rules that create valid program statements. 550

Syntax error An error that results when an instruction does not follow the syntax rules, or grammar, of the programming language. 559

Synthesized sound Artificially created sound, usually found in MIDI music or synthesized speech. 368

System conversion The process of deactivating an old information system and activating a new one. 474

System development life cycle (SDLC) The series of phases that outlines the development process of an information system. 458

System documentation Descriptions of the features, hardware architecture, and programming of an information system written for programmers, designers, and analysts who maintain the system. 473

System operator The person responsible for the day-to-day operation of a computer—usually a mainframe or supercomputer. 476

System palette A selection of colors that are used by an operating system to display graphic elements. 340

System requirements (1) Specifications for the operating system and hardware configuration necessary for a software product to work correctly. (2) The criteria that must be met for a new computer system or software product to be a success. 148, 461

System Requirements Report A report generated at the conclusion of the analysis phase by a project team that has studied a system and determined the system requirements. 462

System software Computer programs that help the computer carry out essential operating tasks. 12, 117

System testing The process of testing an information system to ensure that all the hardware and software components work together. 472

System unit The case or box that contains the computer's power supply, storage devices, main circuit board, processor, and memory. 9

Systems analysis and design The process of planning and building an information system. 456

Systems analyst A computer professional responsible for analyzing information requirements, designing new information systems, and supervising the implementation of new information systems. 411, 457

Systems programmer The person responsible for installing, modifying, and troubleshooting the operating system of a mainframe or supercomputer. 476

T1 A high-bandwidth telephone line that can also transmit text and images. T1 service is often used by organizations to connect to the Internet. 249

T3 A type of ISDN service that uses fiber-optic cable to provide dedicated service with a capacity of 45 megabits per second. 249

Table An arrangement of data in a grid of rows and columns. In a relational database, a collection of record types with their data. 132, 500

Tactical planning Short- or near-term decisions and goals that deploy the human, financial, and natural resources necessary to meet strategic goals. 445

Tape backup A copy of data from a computer's hard disk, stored on magnetic tape and used to restore lost data. 83

Tax preparation software Personal finance software that is specifically designed to assist with tax preparation. 136

TCP (Transmission Control Protocol) One of the main protocols of TCP/IP that is responsible for establishing a data connection between two hosts and breaking data into packets. 234

TCP/IP (Transmission Control Protocol/Internet Protocol) A standard set of communication rules used by every computer that connects to the Internet. 15

Technical support specialist A computer professional who provides phone or online help to customers of computer companies and software publishers. 411

Technical writer A person who specializes in writing explanations of technical concepts and procedures. 412

Telecommuting The act of using available technology to work from home or another off-site location. 414

Telenet A common way to remotely control another computer or server on a network or the Internet. 18

Temporal compression A data compression scheme that, when applied to video or audio data, eliminates unnecessary data between video frames or audio samples. 374

Tera- Prefix for a trillion. 61

Terabyte Approximately 1 trillion bytes. 233

Terminal An input/output device that features a keyboard and screen, but has no storage capacity and very limited processing capability. 634

Terminal emulation software A type of utility software that allows a personal computer to emulate a terminal. 634

Test area A portion of a computer system where software testing can occur without disrupting an organization's regular information system. 472

Text editor A program similar to a word processor that is used to create plain, unformatted ASCII text. 289

Text-to-speech software Software that generates speech, based on written text, that is played back through a computer's sound card. 369

Thermal transfer printer An expensive, color-precise printer that uses wax containing color to produce numerous dots of color on plain paper. 95

Thesaurus A feature of documentation software that provides synonyms. 130

Third-generation computers Computers characterized by using integrated circuits instead of transistors or vacuum tubes for data processing 393

Third-generation languages Programming languages, such as FORTRAN, BASIC, and COBOL, that followed assembly languages and provided English-like keywords. 551

Tier In the context of distributed computing system, a group or layer of computers that performs a specific task. 637

Tiered computer system A computer system that is configured into layers, with each layer assigned a specific task. 637

TIFF (Tag Image File Format) A file format (.tif extension) for bitmap images that automatically compresses the file data. 341

Token Ring network A type of network on which the nodes are sequentially connected in the form of a ring; the second most popular network architecture. 229

Top-level domain The major domain categories into which groups of computers on the Internet are divided: com, edu, gov, int, mil, net, and org. 236

Topic directory A list of topics and subtopics arranged in a hierarchy from general to specific. 33

TQM (Total Quality Management) The process by which an organization analyzes and implements ways to improve the quality of its products and/or services. 448

Traceroute A network utility that records a packet's path, number of hops, and the time it takes for the packet to make each hop. 233

Trace feature In the context of Prolog programming, a tool that allows programmers to follow the execution path through the rules contained in a program. 596

Tracing software Software that locates the edges of objects in a bitmap graphic, and converts the resulting shape into a vector graphic. 348

Tracks A series of concentric or spiral storage areas created on a storage medium during the formatting process. 180

Transaction An exchange between two parties that can be recorded and stored in a computer system. 449

Transaction processing system (TPS) A system that keeps track of transactions for an organization by providing ways to collect, display, modify, and cancel transactions. 449

Transceiver A combination of a transmitter and a receiver used to send and receive data in the form of radio frequencies. 222

Transistors A computer processing technology created by Bell Laboratories in 1947, characterizing second generation computers, which replaced vacuum tubes for data processing. 392

Transponder A device on a telecommunications satellite that receives a signal on one frequency, amplifies the signal, and then retransmits the signal on a different frequency. 222

Trigger event An event that activates a task often associated with a computer virus. 185

Trojan horse A computer program that appears to perform one function while actually doing something else, such as inserting a virus into a computer system, or stealing a password. 186

True Color bitmap A color image with a color depth of 24 bits or 32 bits. Each pixel in a True Color image can be displayed using any of 16.7 million different colors. 339

Tuple In a relational database, a row in a table, which is equivalent to a record. 500

Turnkey system A complete information system that consists of both hardware and commercial software. 466

Twisted-pair cable A type of cable, with RJ-45 connectors on both ends, where two separate strands of wire are twisted together. Used to connect nodes on a network. 221

UDMA (Ultra DMA) A faster version of DMA technology. 82

Ultra ATA A disk drive technology that is an enhanced version of EIDE. Also referred to as Ultra DMA or Ultra IDE. 82

UML (Unified Modeling Language) The current standard for object-oriented documentation. 481, 576

Unicode A 16-bit character representation code that can represent more than 65,000 characters. 60

Uninstall routine A program that removes software files, references, and Registry entries from a computer's hard disk. 152

Unit testing The process of testing a completed application module, to make sure that it operates reliably and correctly. 472

UNIVAC The first commercially successful digital computer. 391

UNIX A multiuser, multitasking server operating system developed by AT&T's Bell Laboratories in 1969. 125

Unstructured problem A problem for which there is no established procedure for arriving at a solution. 446

Unzipped Refers to files that have been uncompressed. 151

UPDATE An SQL keyword used to alter the values in a database record. 531

Uplink port A connection port on a router to which additional hubs can be attached. 255

Uploading The process of sending a copy of a file from a local computer to a remote computer. 17

Upstream The process of transmitting data from your home computer to the Internet. 242

URL (Uniform Resource Locator) The address of a Web page. 27

Use case Tasks performed by an actor in an information system. 481

Use case diagram Documentation of the users and their functions of an information system. 481

Usenet A worldwide Internet bulletin board system of newsgroups that share common topics. 16

User documentation Descriptions of how to interact with an information system or program, including instructions on use, features, and troubleshooting. 473

User ID A combination of letters and numbers that serves as a user's "call sign" or identification. Also referred to as a user name. 22

User interface The software and hardware that enable people to interact with computers. 120

Utilities A subcategory of system software designed to augment the operating system by providing ways for a computer user to control the allocation and use of hardware resources. 121

UTP (Unshielded Twisted Pair) A type of cable consisting of two unshielded wires twisted together. It is less expensive and has more signal noise than a shielded twisted pair. 221

UXGA (Ultra eXtended Graphics Array) A screen resolution of 1600 x 1200. 93

V.44 A voice-band modem standard introduced in 2001 that implements a compression protocol that increases the speed at which data is transmitted. 242

V.90 A standard used by all modems since 1998 that provides a maximum speed of 56Kbps. 242

V.92 A voice band modem standard that has the potential to provide uplink speeds of 48 Kbps (in contrast to V.90 speeds of 32 Kbps). 242

Vacuum tube An electronic device that controls the flow of electrons in a vacuum and represents binary data. 391

Value A number used in a calculation. 133

Vaporware Software that is announced but not produced. 403

VAR (Value-Added Reseller) A company that combines one product with additional hardware, software, and/or services to create a system designed to meet the needs of specific customers or industries. 408

Variable A named storage location that is capable of holding data, which can be modified during program execution. 589

Variable-length field A field in a data file that can accept any number of characters up to a maximum limit. 495

VBScript A scripting language, based on Visual Basic, that is used to design interactive Web sites. 302

VDE (Visual Development Environment) Programming tools that allow programmers to build substantial parts of computer programs by pointing and clicking, rather than entering code. 557

Vector graphic Images generated from descriptions that determine the position, length, and direction in which lines and shapes are drawn. 344

Vertical market software Computer programs designed to meet the needs of a specific market segment or industry, such as medical record-keeping software for use in hospitals. 147

VGA (Video Graphics Array) A screen resolution of 640 x 480. 93

Video capture device A device that is used to convert analog video signals into digital data stored on a hard drive. 357

Video capture software Software used to control the capture process of digital and analog video data. 357

Video editing software Software that provides tools for capturing and editing video from a camcorder. 144, 358

Videoconferencing camera (Also called a Web camera.) An inexpensive digital camera that attaches directly to a computer and creates a video by capturing a series of still images. 355

Videogame console A computer specifically designed for playing games using a television screen and game controllers. 7

Viewable image size (vis) A measurement of the maximum image size that can be displayed on a monitor screen. 93

Virtual memory A computer's use of hard disk storage to simulate RAM. 71

Virus hoax A message, usually e-mail, that makes claims about a virus problem that doesn't actually exist. 191

Virus signature The unique computer code contained in a virus that helps with its identification. Antivirus software searches for known virus signatures to identify a virus. 189

VisiCalc First released for the Apple II, VisiCalc was the first electronic spreadsheet. 395

Visual Basic An event-driven programming environment where the programmer designs forms graphically and codes procedures in BASIC which responds to all form options. 553

Voice band modem The type of modem that would typically be used to connect a computer to a telephone line. (See Modem.) 18

Voice over IP (VoIP) A technology that allows computer users with Internet access to send and receive both data and voice simultaneously. 242

Volatile A term that describes data (usually in RAM), which can exist only with a constant supply of power. 71

Voluntary turnover rate An indicator of job satisfaction based on the frequency employees choose to leave a job. 413

Walkthrough In the context of programming, a method of verifying that an algorithm functions properly when using realistic test data. 567

WAN (wide area network) An interconnected group of computers and peripherals that cover a large geographical area, such as multiple branches of a corporation. 228

Waterfall SDLC A series of phases that outlines the development process of an information system where each phase is a discrete step in the development process. 459

Wave (.wav) An audio file format created as Windows "native" sound format. 366

Waveform audio A digital representation of sound, in which a sound wave is represented by a series of samples taken of the wave height. 364

Wavetable A set of pre-recorded musical instrument sounds in MIDI format. 368

Weak encryption Encryption that is relatively easy or simple to decrypt without the encryption key. 319

Web Short for World Wide Web. An Internet service that links documents and information from computers distributed all over the world, using the HTTP protocol. 26

Web authoring software Computer programs for designing and developing customized Web pages that can be published electronically on the Internet. 128, 290

Web page header Also called "header," a subtitle that appears at the beginning of a Web page. 291

Web page table A grid of cells that are used as layout tools, for elements such as text and graphics placement on a Web page. 296

Web pages Documents on the World Wide Web that consist of a specially coded HTML file with associated text, audio, video, and graphics files. A Web page often contains links to other Web pages. 26

Web palette A standard selection of colors that all Internet browsers can display. 340

Web portfolio A hypertext version of a resume containing links to Web sites of former employers or schools. 423

Web servers Computers that use special software to transmit Web pages over the Internet. 27

Web site Usually a group of Web pages identified by a similar domain name, such as www.cnn.com. 16, 27

Web site designer A computer professional who creates, tests, posts, and modifies Web pages. 412

Web-based e-mail An e-mail account that stores, sends, and receives e-mail on a Web site rather than a user's computer. 40

What-if analysis The process of setting up a model in a spreadsheet and experimenting to see what happens when different values are entered. 133

Wi Fi A nickname for wireless networks that use 802.11b protocol. 256

Windows Explorer A file management utility included with most Windows operating systems that helps users manage their files. 178

Windows Registry A crucial set of data files maintained by the operating system that contains the settings needed by a computer to correctly use any hardware and software that has been installed on the system. 157

Windows Startup Disk A disk that is created by the user to load the operating system and the CD-ROM drivers, allowing for system restoration. 197

Wireframe A representation of a 3-D object using separate lines, which resemble wire, to create a model. 350

Wireless network Networks that use radio or infrared signals (instead of cables) to transmit data from one network device to another. 228

Word processing software Computer programs that assist the user in producing documents, such as reports, letters, papers, and manuscripts. 128

Word size The number of bits a CPU can manipulate at one time, which is dependent on the size of the registers in the CPU, and the number of data lines in the bus. 67

Workers People who perform the tasks necessary to carry out an organization's mission. 445

Worksheet A computerized, or electronic, spreadsheet. 133

Workstation (1) A computer connected to a local area network. (2) A powerful desktop computer designed for specific tasks. 7, 223

Workstation installation Installation of software on a network server to be accessed from workstations. The process copies some of the program files to a workstation's local hard drive, and updates the workstation's Windows Registry and Start menu. 257

World Wide Web Consortium (W3C) An international consortium of companies involved with the Internet and developing open standards. 276

Worm A software program designed to enter a computer system, usually a network, through security "holes" and then replicate itself. 186

Write-protect window A small hole and sliding cover on a floppy disk that restricts writing to the disk. 81

Xerox Alto An early personal computer prototype developed by Xerox Corp. that featured, among other things, a graphical user interface that became influential in the development of the Apple Macintosh. 396

XForms A database technology that provides an alternative to HTML forms by providing more flexibility and an interface to XML documents. 509

XGA (Extended Graphics Array) XGA usually refers to 1,024 x 768 resolution. 93

XHTML The follow-up version to HTML 4. 301

XML (eXtensible Markup Language) A document format similar to HTML, but that allows the Web page developer to define customized tags, generally for the purpose of creating more interactivity. 301

XML DBMS A database management system that provides authoring and query tools for designing and managing collections of XML documents. 505

XML parser A tool in most browsers used for reading XML documents. 301

XSL (eXtensible Stylesheet Language) A technology that is similar to XML, used to create customized tags for displaying data in an XML document. 301

Z3 An early electronic computer prototype designed by Konrad Zuse that was the first to incorporate the use of binary numbers for data representation. 389

Zipped Refers to one or more files that have been compressed. 151